# WRITING FOR LAW PRACTICE
## SECOND EDITION

Elizabeth Fajans, Ph.D.
Associate Professor of Legal Writing
Brooklyn Law School

Mary R. Falk
Associate Professor of Legal Writing
Brooklyn Law School

Helene S. Shapo
Professor of Law
Northwestern University School of Law

New York, New York
Foundation Press
2010

© 2010 By THOMSON REUTERS/FOUNDATION PRESS

195 Broadway, 9th Floor
New York, NY 10007
Phone Toll Free 1–877–888–1330
Fax (212) 367–6799
foundation–press.com

Printed in the United States of America

**ISBN** 978–1–59941–630–4

Mat #40807315

## Acknowledgments

Writing is both a solitary and communal activity. Though we sit alone at our computers, our heads teem with the insights and suggestions of others. We would like to thank those colleagues who gave us help with this book: Debra Bechtel, Rosemary Campagna, Kathleen Darvil, Caitlin Cameron Denker, Susan Irion, Claire Kelly, Joseph Kimble, Tom Morsch, Howard Nagelberg, Dana Brakman Reiser, Sara Robbins, and Sue Susman. David Lee and Amanda MacDonald, and Margaret Cahoon, three of Helene Shapo's students, also gave us valuable assistance.

And, as always, Elizabeth and Mary acknowledge their debt to their assistant, Rose Patti, who gave this manuscript the same tough love she has given all our others. We owe her (big time). Helene thanks her assistant, Derek Gundersen, for his efficiency and patience on the first edition and Michael P. Sobczack for his work on the second edition.

Finally, Elizabeth Fajans and Mary Falk want to thank Dean Joan G. Wexler, of Brooklyn Law School, who generously supported this project.

*This book is dedicated by*

*Elizabeth Fajans to the memory of her father, Irv Fajans;*

*Mary R. Falk to her father, William A. Falk, and her husband, Omar K. Lerman, with love and admiration; and*

*Helene S. Shapo to Marshall, Ben, and Nat.*

# Contents

## Appendices

# INTRODUCTION

---

This book aims to send you out into practice as able and confident crafters of legal documents by teaching 1) the nuts-and-bolts construction of common practice documents and 2) sophisticated writing skills that cut across documents. Together, these two kinds of knowledge create competence and confidence.

In addition to helping you to create contracts, pleadings, regulations, and other new documents, this book aims to consolidate and enhance the writing skills you learned starting out in law school—objective issue analysis and persuasive writing. Now that you are no longer a "novice," but rather, an "expert" student of the law, those basic skills need to become sophisticated skills appropriate to the varied and complex situations you will encounter in practice. Accordingly, we take another look at office memos and appellate briefs.

This book is divided into three parts that correspond to the three major modes of written communication in the law: litigating, informing and persuading, and rule-making. Each part begins with fundamental skills that all legal writers need and then moves on to chapters covering documents for which those skills are especially crucial. For each document, there are sections providing relevant background and detailing its basic components, the composition process, and any special concerns particular to that document. In addition, there is a sample for each document, in-class exercises, and out-of class assignments. Some assignments are based on several hypotheticals that run throughout the text to provide more sustained and realistic practice and to enable you to produce a writing portfolio that displays a variety of skills in a single context.

The first of the three parts of this text focuses on litigation documents. It covers complaints, which initiate a civil action; answers, in which the defendant responds to the allegations of the complaint with denials and admissions and sometimes raises defenses; and motions, written requests to the court during the pendency of the litigation. The skills chapter for this part focuses on conceptualizing.

No document that lawyers write can succeed without strategizing and conceptualizing, so this skill cuts across all parts of this book. But we discuss it in this part of the book because the most important skill a lawyer brings to bear in litigation documents is thinking the legal problem through. In complaints and motions, concept is primary and expression is secondary: combining facts with law, the lawyer shapes the litigation by formulating the theory of the case, strategizing allegations or defenses, deciding what relief to request, and asking the court for rulings—on the admission or suppression of evidence, for example—that may determine the outcome of the case. If you litigate, you must become an educated consumer of the many "boilerplate" forms of litigation documents. These are useful and time-saving practice aids, although you must think each case through carefully and know when to use the boilerplate mold and when to break it.

For example, imagine that a prospective client tells you that he has developed the same genetically transmissible disease that killed his mother—but his mother's physician never told him that he risked developing the disease, which is easily curable when detected early. You know that the negligence law of your jurisdiction, embodied in a simple form complaint, requires that the defendant have a duty of care to the plaintiff and breach that duty and that the plaintiff suffer injury as a result of the breach. Matching up the facts with the law, it appears that the element of duty is missing, because the physician's duty was to his patient, not to her son, your prospective client. You might conclude that—however sad your prospective client's plight and however morally criticizable the physician's omission—the wrong is not justiciable. On the other hand, you might reach a different conclusion by thinking outside the boilerplate. Since the physician undoubtedly had a duty to warn his patient that her disease was genetically transmissible, you might conclude that that duty was for the benefit of the patient's family, and therefore that the duty "ran" to her children. Despite the lack of precedent in your jurisdiction, you might decide to take the case, raising your novel, but reasonable and equitable, theory of a physician's duty to third parties at risk from genetically transmissible diseases.[1] And you might just get a day in court for your client and make good law.

Conceptualizing involves more than painting the big picture, however. It means being sure that the parts of your document add up to a whole without gaps or overlaps—for example, that you have not omitted any element of a cause of action alleged in a complaint. It also means broadening or narrowing your language to suit your purpose. For example, in a negligence complaint against a landlord, you might allege broadly that the defendant "failed to ensure that security equipment was adequately maintained in working order" or narrowly that the defendant "failed to repair the front-door lock." This decision could be consequential, because the first may be easier to deny than the second; on the other hand, the more general allegation broadens the scope of discovery.

The second part of this book focuses on documents that seek to inform, to persuade, or both. It begins where your first-year legal writing left off. To the office memoranda and trial or appellate briefs you have already studied, it adds letters to clients, adversaries, office colleagues, and third parties, and judicial opinions. The focus of the first skills chapter in Part Two is clarity—the skill of getting across to the reader. This skill is also relevant to all legal documents, but it is especially important when a reader is trying to grasp a sustained and perhaps complicated legal analysis or argument, and thus it is a signature skill of the documents in this part. A few straightforward principles underlie the composition of lucid, readable sentences and paragraphs that "flow" because they have coherence and cohesion. For example, look at the first and second drafts of a sentence from a letter to a client who wishes to move out-of-state with her child against the wishes of the child's father.

First Draft: A request for removal of a child from the state that is made in good faith by a custodial parent and that is not for the purpose of the frustration of the exercise of visitation rights of another parent will be considered by the

---

[1] *See Safer v. Pack,* 291 N.J. Super. 619, 677 A.2d 1188 (1996); *Pate v. Threlkel,* 661 So. 2d 278 (Fla.1995).

court based on the test of whether it is in the best interests of the child.

Second Draft: When a custodial parent asks to move out-of-state with her child, the court will give permission if it determines that the move is in the best interests of the child and that the request is made in good faith and is not an attempt to frustrate the other parent's visitation rights.

Although the second draft is not much shorter, it is far easier to read than the first because the second sentence follows several basic clarity principles. For example, it uses simple, human subjects ("custodial parent" in the dependent clause and "court" in the main clause) in contrast to the abstract, 39-word subject of the first sentence ("A request...another parent"). The second sentence also uses verbs to express actions ("asks to move," "frustrate") rather than putting the actions in nouns, as the first does ("request for removal," "frustration"). If you follow these and the other prescriptions in the first fundamental skills chapter of Part Two, you may never see the unhelpful directives "wordy" or "awkward" in the margins of your draft again.

The second skills chapter in Part Two focuses on persuasion. Persuasive documents succeed best when your narration of the facts, characterization of the parties, and arguments are responsive to the emotional or doctrinal core of the case—to its theme. In the fact section, you want to reveal your "take" on the facts through the parties' words and actions. For example, if you are raising the novel theory that a physician has a duty to warn third parties at risk from a genetically transmissible disease, describe the progression of the disease when it goes undiagnosed and undetected. This underscores the need for recognizing the duty more effectively than direct proselytizing. Or, if you are advancing the theory that a physician's duty is to the patient only, focus on the warnings the physician gave the patient to discuss with his or her children the importance of medical testing.

If facts can be written to incline readers to find in your favor, legal analysis provides them with the justification for doing so. To be persuasive, your analysis must be clear and thorough. Too many briefs leave this job to the court—often to the detriment of the client. As one court said, it is insufficient to "toss a bunch of concepts into the air with the hope that either the trial court or the opposing party will arrange them into viable and fact-supported legal theories."[2] Thus this chapter provides a summary of the types of legal argument and counter-argument that may help you to find and develop arguments. It also reviews framing authority persuasively.

Part Three of *Writing for Law Practice* looks at rule-making, drafting the high-stakes prose of legislation, contracts, and wills. This is the most exacting challenge faced by a legal writer—using language to create legal relationships—entitlement, duty, agreement, prohibition, permission. Because rule-making documents must stand the tests of time and unwillingness to be bound, they require not just clarity, but precision as well, the subject of the first skills chapter in this section. Rule-making documents must reflect the client's intention as closely as possible, with flexibility where appropriate, but with no unintended wiggle-room. The enemies here are syntactic (word-order) ambiguity and semantic (word-choice) ambiguity. For example, imagine that as counsel to the Acme Corporation you have drafted and negotiated an employment contract between the Corporation and Joan Smith. The clause concerning severance pay is as follows.

> Employee will receive six months severance pay upon termination of her employment by the Acme Corporation.

Joan Smith leaves Acme Corporation to go back to school. She demands six months severance pay, citing the contractual language above, and sues when the company refused to pay. Smith's attorney argues that she was entitled to severance pay because she was no longer employed "by the Acme Corporation." You argue that the severance pay clause applies only to "termination by the Acme Corporation of Smith's employment." Both are correct readings of the language of the clause, which is a classic example of syntactic ambiguity—"by the Acme Corporation" can modify either "termination" or "employment."[3] You also

---

[2] *State v. Jackson*, 600 N.W.2d 39 (Wis. Ct. App. 1999). Our thanks to Chris Wren for drawing our attention to this case.

[3] Peter Siviglia discusses this example in *Writing Contracts: A Distinct Discipline* 12 (Carolina Academic Press 1996).

argue that common sense, context, and practice in the industry support your reading of the clause. But even if the judge agrees with you, careless drafting will have cost needless expense, time, and anxiety. Thus, precision is the signature skill of rule-making documents.

The second skills chapter is on document design. Psychologists have found that visual presentation has an effect on readers' understanding and retention of material. Readers can grasp complicated arguments and detailed information more easily when the writer uses appropriate fonts, hierarchical headings, white space, and other graphic design principles. This is particularly true when lay persons need to read unfamiliar documents like consumer insurance policies, contracts, or wills. That is why we have placed document design in Part Three, the rule-making section. Nonetheless, good design principles can also make lawyers' letters and court briefs more readable, and although lawyers must always heed statutory or court rules on formatting, they should apply graphic design advice whenever possible.

Finally, a note on "drafting" and "writing." Lawyers talk about "drafting" rule-making documents. The composition of some litigation documents, like complaints and answers is also frequently described as "drafting." But it is customary to speak of "writing" memos and briefs. Curiously—in a profession that prides itself on using language precisely—there is no precise, universally agreed-upon definition of "drafting." We think that the better usage is that of the late Professor Reed Dickerson, who reserved "drafting" for the composition of rule-making documents—documents that require drafting-table precision. Yet Professor Dickerson's understanding of the term is less pervasive than the competing usage of "drafting" to encompass the writing of *all* documents that are based on, but contain no explicit legal analysis or argument. This usage expands "drafted" documents to include the litigation documents in Part One as well as the rule-making documents in Part Three. In addition to the absence of explicit legal analysis, these documents also share an impersonal voice—unlike the letters, appellate briefs, judicial opinions, and office and trial memoranda of Part Two. Although legal writers "do drafts" of the more personal and analytical documents in Part Two, in the lexically distinct sense of writing successive revised versions, they rarely talk of "drafting" a brief or memo.

Professor Dickerson's distinction between "drafted" rule-making documents and all the rest is more meaningful for student and teacher than the distinction between impersonal, non-analytical documents and persuasive, analytical documents: statutes and complaints have little in common except what they lack. Yet the use of "drafting" to describe the composition of litigation documents, especially pleadings, has taken root so firmly in the legal community that we decided that resistance was fussy and futile. Nonetheless, we think that the distinction made in this book between three types of legal documents is both meaningful and useful—whether we speak of "writing" or of "drafting" them.

# Part One

# Chapter 1

# *BASIC SKILLS: CONCEPTUALIZING*

---

## A. THINKING IT THROUGH

The basic process of creating legal documents is that of any serious non-fiction writing. There are four steps or phases—gathering information, conceptualizing, writing a complete working draft, and revising. We focus this first skills chapter on conceptualizing, not only because it is the first stage in which the writer's creativity is brought to bear, but also because it is the one skill that is crucial to all the documents a lawyer writes. In the three documents chapters that follow, we discuss complaints, answers, and motions, litigation documents for which conceptualization is not just one essential skill, but rather, the defining skill.

Instead of saying that we focus here on the skills required for the conceptualization phase, we might more accurately say, however, that we focus here on the skills required for the conceptualization *phases*, because the composition process is so rarely linear. Even experienced writers go back and forth between the steps. It often happens, for example, that as we put our ideas on paper, we generate new ideas that send us back to the first stage for more information.

## 1. Gathering Information

A description of some of the concerns appropriate to the information-gathering stage is a necessary introduction to our discussion of conceptualization. Information-gathering has two aspects: getting the relevant facts and understanding the law. Both require great care—even a small error can be disastrous. Consider the cautionary tale of an attorney who was retained to handle a straightforward commercial debt-collection suit. The client-creditor told the attorney that the debtor was William Jones, Inc. The attorney drew up and filed a complaint against William Jones, Inc. The complaint was not answered, with the result that a default judgment was entered against William Jones, Inc. Unfortunately, the judgment was unenforceable because William Jones was not in fact incorporated, and there was thus no entity against which the judgment could be enforced. The creditor had no choice but to start over, and the attorney, having failed to discover the creditor's mistake and thus failed his duty to gather facts carefully, deservedly bore the loss of income.

Hasty and sketchy legal research can be equally disastrous. In law practice, more than in many fields, it is not enough to have *some* relevant information: you need *all* the relevant information, as a law student who was working as an intern at her dream placement, a famous public interest law center, soon learned. Her supervisor gave her an assignment to research a narrow question of Constitutional law. The student researched the topic, using Boolean searches on one of the on-line subscription services. She found a body of cases on point, though none very recent, and wrote a fluent and well-organized memo. The supervisor praised the student's memo and sent it on to the national office. The attorney who read it there discovered—fortunately before incorporating the research into her brief for the Supreme Court—that the student's research had missed an entire line of more recent cases through her reliance on just one research tool. The terms of the debate had changed, and the student's Boolean searches had therefore not found the new cases. The student's supervisor (who had done a poor job of supervising) was humiliated and blamed the student for that as much as for her incomplete research. The student kept her internship, but the rest of her tenure was uncomfortable, and it took her a long time to regain her confidence.

When you are in practice, avoiding this kind of mistake will be somewhat easier because your legal research will usually be narrowly focused within an area with which you are already familiar. Indeed, even the prior stage of fact-gathering presupposes sufficient expertise to ask the right questions. But if you are working in unfamiliar territory, it is unusual, and usually undesirable, to work unsupervised. A contract drafted by a brilliant litigator may turn out to be an invitation to litigation.

You should also bear in mind that in order to be complete, your research often needs to cover more than substantive law. Procedure can be vital, including and especially local court rules. Court rules have proliferated in recent years, particularly in the federal courts, and a misstep can be costly for your client and your reputation with the court. Equally important is that you know the basic components and local conventions of your document, whether complaint, contract, motion, or office memo. Standardized forms, or "boilerplate" can be helpful in this respect—although, as discussed below, forms can also be dangerously misleading. Checklists prepared by experts are also a good resource, though like boilerplate, they are only a starting point.

Finally, in addition to being thorough, your research needs to be efficient. The judge may want a memo in 48 hours, and your supervisor may want the research yesterday. Moreover, research can be costly, especially on-line research using subscription services. As with thoroughness, familiarity will also help efficiency.

Once you've gathered facts and researched the law, you are ready to move on to the conceptualization phase—using your information appropriately and creatively. Although we use the linear notion of "moving on" here, you should not be dismayed if the composition process doubles back on itself, alternating between research and conceptualization, as it climbs the mountain. Indeed, Professor Dickerson considered it a mistake for legal writers to attempt to finish their research before beginning to conceptualize their documents.

> The writer who tries to do all his research before he starts to write often finds out later that he has researched many irrelevant or insignificant things...while he failed to research things that came to light too late to handle adequately.... Besides, if he over-researches before starting to write, he risks snuffing out potentially valuable insights of his own.... He also risks creating a formidable psychological hazard by inundating himself with detailed materials...to the point of sapping his will to write.[1]

---

[1] Reed Dickerson, *Materials on Legal Drafting* 102 (West Pub. 1981), quoting *Legal Drafting: Writing as Thinking, or Talk-back from Your Draft and How to Exploit It*, 29 J. Leg. Educ. 373 (1978).

This is powerful advice, but it must be followed with caution—be certain that you follow up with the research necessary to ground your insights within the law. If you are the kind of writer who can't give up on an ingenious idea that doesn't work, Professor Dickerson's strategy is not for you.

The rest of this skills chapter focuses on the conceptualization stage of the writing process. The big lesson to take away here is: *Think it through for yourself.* Although cases of first impression are rare, it is equally true that no case is ever entirely like any other. If you rely blindly on boilerplate forms, you risk disserving your client and the law.

## 2. Brainstorming

Once you have gathered enough information for a provisional understanding of the problem, you need to sit down and start to brainstorm, that is to sketch out the big picture, selecting appropriate legal concepts, fitting law to fact and fact to law. Your minimum goal for this phase is a complete hierarchical outline of your document, though depending on the type of document and your own writing process, you may also generate a considerable amount of provisional text.

In the context of legal writing, a hierarchical outline is one that classifies ideas into legally cognizable categories; within each category ideas are sub-divided into their smallest meaningful components. An outline of a complaint in a civil suit would be organized by cause of action, with each cause of action broken down into its component elements. An outline of an employment contract would be organized by provision, *e.g.,* duties, compensation, termination, etc. The provisions would be sub-divided into their logical components, where appropriate—*e.g.,* compensation might be broken down into salary, bonuses, and benefits; benefits might be further sub-divided into life insurance and health insurance. A motion to suppress evidence in a criminal trial would be divided into the separate grounds advanced, *e.g.,* violations of the Fourth Amendment, of Due Process, and of the *Miranda* doctrine.

As well as dividing by legal theory—by cause of action, defense, ground, or issue—the law classifies by factual theory. For example, a suppression motion grounded in the invalidity of a search warrant could argue both that the warrant was based on information of an unreliable informant and that the information did not constitute probable cause. A negligence complaint might allege that the area was poorly lit and that the floor was slippery—two different factual theories of breach.

Outlines are easy to describe, but not always easy to create, especially when your document is complex or the situation is novel. How you begin depends in part on the nature of the document and in part on your own writing process. One good way to get started on most writing projects is to brainstorm with a knowledgeable colleague or mentor. When two people discuss a problem, they invariably come up with more good ideas than if both thought it through individually. One practitioner suggests that as well as throwing ideas back and forth with someone familiar with the issue or case at hand, you try to find "an independent brainstormer such as a law partner who specializes in mediation, or one with an expertise in a relevant area."[2] This is because one's "'team' may share common biases or a shared point of blindness."[3] A variation on communal brainstorming is described by this same practitioner:

> I learned [this technique] from a law school classmate...who...at first blush did not seem to be especially creative...[but who] was an amazingly disciplined questioner. Once he inquired about a subject I had studied in depth. When he finished his unrelenting, systematic questions, both [he] and I knew more about the subject than when he started.[4]

Of course, methodical inquiry is not the only path to understanding a complex situation.

> [I]t is often better to flirt playfully with problems than obsess upon them. And we need to learn to listen to our intuition. It is not "the force" that will enter our brains and imbue us with insight. Instead, it is our minds trying to communicate something we already dimly sense.[5]

---

[2] Tom Galbraith, *The Joy of Motion Practice*, 24 No. 2 Litig. 15, 17 (Winter 1998).

[3] *Id.*

[4] *Id.*

[5] *Id.*

Yet intuition has two necessary preconditions.

> (1) the lawyer must absorb the facts and theories her mind will work with, and (2) she must care about the case deeply enough that her subconscious mind will turn and twist these concepts until it connects them in unexpected ways—the grand moment of "ah hah."[6]

All too soon, the moment comes to stop talking and pondering, and begin putting words on paper. For routine documents like apartment leases or employment contracts, most writers without the time or inclination to reinvent the wheel will appropriately begin with boiler-plate and checklists; we give some guidelines for their effective use later in this chapter. More challenging documents require a process that suits your individual writing temperament and level of experience. Some writers—especially very experienced drafters—can sit down, review their notes, and develop an effective outline. Other writers use variations of two brainstorming techniques—"dump lists"[7] and "zero drafts"[8]—to work toward an outline. To make a "dump list," you simply dump facts and ideas onto paper in no particular order, as they occur to you. Then, read over the list and group your facts and ideas into general categories (for litigation and rule-making documents like complaints, statutes, or contracts) or major issues (for analytical and persuasive documents like office memos or appellate briefs). Fit subcategories and subissues into those categories. Next, put your categories or issues in a provisional order. Order is often dependent on type of document–but importance and chronology are the most common ranking devices. Finally, integrate the facts into the resulting outline.

Some writers find it helpful to use large sheets of unlined paper for this process and to organize their thoughts graphically, with

---

[6] *Id.* at 16, citing Peter D. Baird, *Legal Creativity, Flashes, Blocks, and Toads*, 12 No. 4 Litig. (Summer 1986).

[7] Although Mary Ray and Barbara Cox do not use this term, they discuss this listing process in *Beyond the Basics: A Text for Advanced Legal Writing* 12 (West 2d ed. 2003).

[8] Jill N. Burkland & Bruce T. Petersen, *An Integrative Approach to Research: Theory and Practice,* in *Convergences: Transactions in Reading and Writing* 199 (Bruce T. Petersen, ed., Natl. Council of Teachers of English 1986).

circles and boxes, arrows and connecting lines. This technique allows more free-play of ideas. For example, "[c]reating timelines and diagramming complex relationships is often useful. Breaking complex transactions into simple components, such as who got how much money from whom can cut through confusing pretenses."[9]

Another way to begin is to plunge right in and write a "zero draft"—a rougher than rough draft of the text of your document written without conscious concern for organization, comprehensiveness, or style.[10] Then you can highlight the important concepts and cut-and-paste them into a hierarchical outline, noting and filling gaps. "Zero drafts" are an excellent starting place even for experienced writers with a knack for outlining. This is because the act of writing itself generates ideas. Professor Dickerson called this phenomenon "writing as learning," explaining that "in the course of writing, the author, after what might seem like trying to strike a damp match, soon finds that he is party to a two-way conversation....[T]he manuscript is talking back...."[11]

Of course, "dump lists" and "zero drafts" are not mutually exclusive or even necessarily discrete techniques. Depending on the nature of the document, the complexity of the issues, and your own best writing process, you may settle on some hybrid form, alternating text and list. The important thing is to get the ideas flowing.

For example, assume that you are a new associate in a Minneapolis law firm who has just interviewed Nancy Williams, the potential plaintiff in Casefile 1 in Appendix A. She has been through a terrible ordeal: not only was she subjected repeatedly to the unwanted sexual attentions of her supervisor, Michael Bryant, but her complaints were then ignored by her employer, the Board of Parish Life of Grace Church. Moreover when she threatened to file a sexual harassment complaint, she was summarily fired—despite an excellent work record as director of the Church's youth programs, the respect and affection of her co-workers, and an employment contract with a year to run. The Board told her she

---

[9] Galbraith, *supra* n. 2 at 16.

[10] Burkland & Petersen, *supra* n. 8 at 199.

[11] Dickerson *supra* n. 1 at 103.

was being fired because she had "inappropriate relationships" with teenagers in her program, an accusation she vehemently denies. In the wake of her firing by the Board, Williams became severely depressed, attempted suicide, and was briefly hospitalized. She has recovered substantially, and her first choice would be to return to the job she loved, especially because her former supervisor has retired.

Although litigation is not your client's strategy of choice, you need to know what legal claims she has before you attempt to engage in negotiations with her former employer. Your firm has successfully resolved sexual harassment cases for plaintiffs and potential plaintiffs before—this is why Williams has chosen your firm—and although you're a new lawyer, you know enough to get a start.

Working from your notes, you proceed to "dump" facts and ideas on paper. Then you set to work brainstorming possible claims. After a while, your paper looks like this.

P = soc. worker at church

Ds = church board (BPL) & Bryant (clergy) SUE WHICH FOR WHAT ?

*P. was hired Feb 2003–2 yr K...termination only for "cause" w/ 30 days notice... P. does good job ...Newspapers write up her successes...but...Bryant hits on her from beginning...touching hair neck, small of back, thighs (!), "embraces." CHECK—Could this be com. law BATTERY, even crim. sex offense?? She protests, he doesn't stop, wants her to go away w/him HOSTILE WORK ENVIRONMENT—NO Quid Pro Quo?—check w/client on this. P tells BPL They tell her to put up w/until he retires, have Xtian compassion for him etc. BPL does nothing. FAILURE TO REMEDY—so VICARIOUS liab. for SEX HAR by BPL. In Oct., P complains again ...says she will file sex discrim. chges v. them & Bryant. 1 wk later P. fired, they say she has inappropriate rels. w/ youths in her program (PRETEXT?).. She can show was doing good job, newspaper clippings, etc REPRISAL UNDER SEX HAR STAT, BREACH OF K... what about DEFAMATION? CHECK this...Also, what about WHISTLE-BLOWER STAT.? Or NEGLIGENT RETENTION of abusive employee B. .... Treatment of P. here is extreme...CHECK... could be INFLICTION OF EMO.*

*DISTRESS? Intent'l or neg? Elements? P. gets depressed, tries to kill self, hospital, now out-patient. could go back to work soon... REMEDIES reinstatement (?), stat. har remedies, compens (includes? back pay, suffering, past & future med. expenses), punitive dam., costs & att'y fees, maybe crim. penalties?*

Clearly, you are going to need more information—both fact and law—before you can make a definitive assessment of Williams' potential claims. You will need to investigate the possibilities of a criminal complaint alleging battery or a sex offense and a civil cause of action in battery against Bryant, as well as a cause of action for intentional or negligent infliction of emotional distress. A number of causes of action vis-a-vis the Board will also need to be explored: defamation, violation of Minnesota's whistle-blower statute, and negligent retention of its employee, Bryant. In addition, you will need to check further with Williams to see if there was *"quid pro quo"* as well as "hostile environment" harassment (the two types of legally cognizable sexual harassment). Nonetheless, you can now tentatively outline causes of action for harassment against Bryant under the Minnesota Human Rights Act, and for vicarious sexual harassment and reprisal under the Minnesota statute against the Board, as well as causes of action for breach of Williams' employment contract on two separate factual theories—lack of notice and lack of legitimate cause for the termination of her employment.

I. "Hostile Environment" Sexual Harassment (Bryant)
   A. B. was P's supervisor at all relevant times.
   B. B. touched P., made sexual remarks, sexual suggestions, repeatedly.
   C. P. always made clear that touching, sexual remarks & suggestions unwelcome.
   D. P. was damaged professionally, emotionally, financially by B's conduct.
II. Vicarious "Hostile Environment" Sexual Harassment (BPL)
   A. Harassment by B. as alleged in "I" above.
   B. BPL knew of harassment; told by P.
   C. BPL did nothing to investigate or remedy

III. Reprisal (BPL)
    A. P. threatened to file sex discrimination charges against BPL
    B. BPL immediately fired P.
    C. BPL said P "had inappropriate relationships with teenagers in her program."
    D. This was pretext; in fact P's performance demonstrably excellent.
    E. P. was damaged professionally, emotionally, & financially by BPL's conduct.
IV. Breach of Contract (BPL)
    A. P & BPL had 2-year contract entered into in February, 2003, providing termination for cause after 30 days written notice to P.
    B. In November, 2003, P. fired by BPL without notice.
    C. As a result of failure to give notice, BPL breached contract.
V. Breach of Contract (BPL)
    A. P. & BPL had 2-year contract entered into in February, 2003, providing termination for cause after 30 days written notice to P.
    B. In November, 2003, P. fired despite excellent performance, thus without cause.
    C. By terminating employment without cause, BPL breached contract.

## 3. Adapting Boilerplate

All practitioners, even the most experienced and innovative, use standard forms as a resource when they write. When a situation is indeed straightforward, this is appropriate. But expert writers know when to fill in the blanks, when to edit and adapt boiler-plate, and when to work from scratch. The great danger of boilerplate, besides its unreadable legalese, is that it creates cookie-cutter thinking—as the proverb says, "When all you have is a hammer, everything looks like a nail."

In order to be able to use boilerplate effectively, you must understand the legal significance of every word, sentence, and paragraph. Begin with a good understanding of the essential components of your document. In the *documents* chapters of this book, you will find descriptions of essential and optional components. Do not make the mistake of believing that a provision in a form contract that you do not understand is necessary or even harmless. Do not assume that a mystery provision is legal "magic dust" without which there would be no contract or will. Find out what it means. If necessary, ask a more experienced practitioner: do not be too surprised if the answer is "I don't know—we just always put it in," and do not be deterred from investigating its legal import.

Once you understand all the components of a form, you can use it advisedly, whether as a model or as a checklist. You will find that even the best forms can use some improving. The boilerplate contracts, complaints, wills, and notices of motion of even the best practitioners contain legalese; sometimes the prose is less clear and precise than it could be. Yet most attorneys find that writing the creative sections of a summary judgment motion leaves little time to rewrite the legalese of the boilerplate notice of motion. Moreover, new attorneys are afraid to correct these forms. Yet these forms would slowly improve if, whenever you have the occasion to make a judicious improvement, you do so.

A common time-saving device akin to the use of boilerplate forms also deserves a word of caution. Attorneys often use documents created for one client as word-processing templates for the next client's document. This useful practice has risks beyond the risks of cookie-cutter representation described above. All too often, hasty proof-reading and reliance on spell-checking create a document in which the particulars of client X's case surface in client Y's motion, agreement, or complaint. At worst, these gremlins can compromise the substance of the document; at best, they give client Y the impression of being represented in sloppy, assembly-line fashion. If you use real documents for word-processing templates, be sure to proofread your final document carefully, ideally in hard copy, where errors are easier to spot.

——————————— *Exercise 1.1* ———————————

*Brainstorm the problem described below.*

*Your Aunt Liz the photo-journalist has asked for your help. The news agency she works for has assigned her to its London bureau for the next two years.*

*She has decided to rent her house to her best friend's son and daughter-in-law, Jim and Jenny, who are attending law school at the university near her home. She doesn't want to make a profit—she just wants the house lived in, most of the basic expenses (property taxes, electric bills, etc.) paid, and wear-and-tear kept to a minimum. She is also happy to provide her tenants with a nicer place to live than they could otherwise afford on a student budget. The house is in the suburbs of a New England city and 150 years old. The furnishings are old, too, and have sentimental value at least. The house is on an acre of land with a lawn and garden of which Aunt Liz is very proud. (She is willing to pay for help to take care of the garden while she's gone.) She would like Jenny and Jim to continue to employ the housekeeper who comes in once a week to clean. And she would like them to look after her two cats.*

*Aunt Liz has wisely decided that fond though she is of Jim and Jenny, who are enthusiastic about the plan, an agreement in writing is advisable to clarify the rights and responsibilities of the parties. Fortunately, this is within your area of expertise. It is, however, a* sui generis *kind of situation in which boilerplate lease forms will not be much help.*

*Using a "dump list" or "zero draft" approach, conceptualize the agreement. What will it need to cover? Since this is not an arms-length transaction, but a deal between friends, be sure to consider the interests of the tenants as well as those of the owner. When you run out of things that need to be provided for, turn your jottings into an outline of the provisions that you think should be in the agreement. Be sure to classify, sub-divide, and order them in logical, lawyerly fashion. You will undoubtedly also come up with questions for Aunt Liz—make a list of them.*

---

## B. TESTING IT OUT

Whatever combination of boilerplate and inspiration you use, the moment arrives when you have on paper a substantial idea of the content and structure of your document. This may be a detailed outline or an outline and some tentative blocks of text. The next step in the conceptualization process requires you to test your document to see whether it adheres to traditional principles of lawyerly composition.

The most effective way to check your outline is to check for just one thing at a time. You should look first at the *content* of your document and then at its *structure*. At this stage, your review of *content* essentially evaluates your selection of legal concepts and your integration of facts into them. Some important questions are whether your document as outlined is

1) complete,
2) internally consistent, and
3) at the appropriate level of generality.

When you have finished a careful check for *content*, turn to a review of the *structure* of your outline, focusing on the following traditional rules regarding division and sequence:

1) division should be governed by one principle where appropriate;
2) division should be into parts that are mutually exclusive, not overlapping;
3) the whole should be the sum of its divisions; and
4) the sequence of parts should be logical.

## 1. Checking Content

### a. Completeness

First, check to see that your document is complete–in the sense that all the components that give it legal validity are there, but also in the sense that it maximally advances your client's interests or intentions within the bounds of law and ethics. A complaint is valid if it contains allegations of all elements of a cause of action and a demand for relief; however, even such a document can be incomplete if it overlooks legal or factual theories that could advance your client's cause. For example, if as Nancy Williams' attorney (see above and Casefile 1 in Appendix A), you drafted a complaint that did not allege two separate factual theories of breach of contract (failure to provide notice and failure to provide legally sufficient cause), you would not have completely served Williams' interests. A draft contract is complete in the legal sense so long as it contains an exchange of lawful promises and a place for the parties' signatures, but if it neglects provisions that are vital to protect your client's interests (for example, a warranty), it is incomplete. Similarly, a motion to suppress a client's statement to law enforcement that competently raises one ground for re-lief (for example, violation of a wiretapping statute), but omits another viable ground (for example, a violation of the Fifth Amendment's protection against compelled self-incrimination) is woefully incomplete.

Finding what we have left out is not easy. Checklists are only a beginning. To see whether we might have advanced other theories, raised other issues, alleged other causes of action or defenses, it can be helpful to scan the table of contents of a hornbook, treatise, form-book, or lawyer's desk-book in the relevant area of practice. To check for gaps in a contract, regulation, or other document that needs to stand the test of altered circumstances, changed minds, or simple ill-will, create hypotheticals. Checking your draft of a separation agreement for a couple with children, for example, ask "what if?" What if the parent with residential custody of the children wants to move far away? What if the parent providing health insurance becomes unemployed? What if a child doesn't want to go to college? The "what if?" technique is also helpful for complex statutes and regulations, which are notoriously gap-prone. By checking the draft of an academic honor code and asking "what if" faculty fail to perform the duty to report plagiarism, a drafter was able to see that she had provided no sanctions for breach of this duty, which was therefore arguably no duty at all.

### b. Consistency

Consistency is almost as important as completeness. Thorough brainstorming means we throw in everything but the kitchen sink, sometimes including mutually exclusive ideas. In some documents, this inconsistency is both acceptable and usual. Complaints may allege alternative theories of liability, and motions and appellate briefs often contain arguments in the alternative. It is permissible, for example, to argue that your client was misidentified and that, alternatively, his use of force was justified, though depending on the strength of the arguments and other considerations, argument in the alternative might not be a sound strategy.

In other documents—especially the "rule-making" documents discussed in Part Three of this book—inconsistency is a grave and consequential flaw. If an honor code distinguishes between intentional and negligent plagiarism in its definitions and prohibitions, then it is inconsistent to impose sanctions without regard to this distinction. If a contract provides for binding arbitration, a provision providing that the parties will negotiate in good faith before resorting to litigation is inconsistent. If a clause in a will devises all the testator's real property to his wife, then a clause devising the testator's home to his daughter is inconsistent. The use of boilerplate is a frequent culprit here—we insert the appropriate provision, but forget to delete the inappropriate one.

The "what if" inquiry also helps us see inconsistencies in the form of unintended consequences inconsistent with our clients' intentions or interests. Assume that Nancy Williams has decided to sue the Church governing board that fired her, and that as her attorney, you are considering including a cause of action for negligent infliction of emotional distress. If you do so, how will the defendants respond? Perhaps they will move to have Williams examined by their psychiatrist, claiming she has put her mental state in issue. In addition to being an ordeal for the client, could this bring to light facts that could jeopardize her chances of being reinstated to her beloved job as part of a settlement? Even the most innocent-sounding provisions in an agreement can have unintended consequences inconsistent with the client's intentions. A provision that requires the parties to a contract to negotiate in good faith before going to binding arbitration can lead to litigation about whether one party or the other negotiated in good faith, defeating the intention to avoid litigation.[12]

## c. Level of Generality

Thinking a document through in lawyerly fashion also requires that we pay attention to level of generality, that is, to the relative breadth or narrowness, the generality or specificity of the concepts we employ. Some documents by their nature encourage or require one or the other. In some jurisdictions, complaints may be

---

[12] Peter Siviglia, *Writing Contracts: A Distinct Discipline* 27–28 (Carolina Academic Press 1996). This is a common boiler-plate provision that nobody thinks to object to because we're all in favor of good faith. There is a lesson in the critical reading of boilerplate here.

framed very broadly (a simple claim of "negligent conduct" may suffice), but motions require great particularity (a broad claim of a "Fourth Amendment violation" would not suffice).

In most cases, however, the conceptual choice of broad or narrow is a strategic matter, often one of great consequence. The visitation provision of a separation agreement might be framed broadly to permit a non-custodial parent to return the children late to the custodial parent "for reasons beyond the non-custodial parent's control," or it might be framed narrowly to excuse only lateness "caused by emergency medical care, hazardous weather conditions, or cancelled air-flights." Generality creates flexibility, but it can also generate disputes, especially between parties who perceive themselves to have very different interests. The more generally worded provision would ease compliance between parties to an amicable separation, but bitterly divided parents would be better served by particularity—if they can agree to the particulars in the first place.

As you continue to check content, you will frequently find that new facts or close contemplation of the facts forces you to refine, reconceptualize, or rename a provision or section. Sometimes, to accommodate the facts, you need to create a more general category—or to create two or more sections or provisions out of one. For example, suppose you wrote the following definition in an academic honor code.

> "Plagiarism" means quoting or paraphrasing another's work without using quotation marks and without acknowledging the source, reading material not authorized by the instructor while preparing an assignment, or asking another person to proofread and correct your work.

This definition fails because the term "Plagiarism" is too narrow for the facts described. Asking another person to proofread your work or reading material not authorized by the instructor is not plagiarism. To accommodate all these particulars, we must choose a more general term to define. "Cheating" is more general than plagiarism, indeed plagiarism is a type of cheating. Perhaps this is the appropriate term to define, or perhaps you really need two definitions—one of which encompasses the other.

> "Cheating" means plagiarism, unauthorized collaboration, or unauthorized use of materials.
>
> "Plagiarism" means quoting or paraphrasing another's work without acknowledging the source.

Here plagiarism is defined separately, but also nests within the larger category to which it belongs.

─────────────── *Exercise 1.2* ───────────────

*A. The small ocean-side town of Sea Grove is concerned that its new marina for pleasure boats will cause the harbor to become polluted. The town commissioners have come up with a few drafts of a prohibition to be included in a new town ordinance. Seeking a lawyer's input, they have asked you to comment on their drafts. With particular attention to the generality or specificity of the provisions, describe the likely effect and viability of each version. When you go back to the commissioners with your critique of the drafts, you may want to ask some questions: list them.*

1.  No boat owner shall discharge human waste or cause human waste to be discharged into the harbor.
2.  The dumping of toxic substances into the harbor is prohibited.
3.  The release of any waste product into the harbor is prohibited.

*B. Comment on the following draft outline of the Statement of the Case portion of an appellate brief.*

  I.  Procedural History
 II.  The Evidence at Trial
    A. The Prosecution's Case
    B. The Defense Case
    C. The Summations
    D. The Jury Instructions
    E. The Verdict and Sentence

## 2. Testing Structure

Once you are satisfied that your document promises to be comprehensive, consistent, and at the appropriate level of generality, it is time to test out the structure of your outline for logical and appropriate division into parts and for appropriate sequencing of those parts.

### a. Consistent Principles of Division

One way to test structure is to ask what principle or principles of division govern—or should govern—your document. In other words, you need to think about how best to cut up the material. Unless the context requires otherwise, one single principle of division should govern. For example, a hierarchical outline divided into major sections on "extortionists," "murderers," and "robbers" is acceptable, because the division is consistently by type of crime. But the division into "extortionists," "murderers," "robbers," "schizophrenics," and "substance abusers" is technically incorrect, because it uses two different principles of division: type of crime and psychiatric label.

In a practical context, if you were outlining a memo discussing Nancy Williams' possible claims, you would use the "single-principle" rule to divide her claims by defendant (Bryant and the church board), by type of cause of action (statutory and common law), or by cause of action (sexual harassment, reprisal, breach of contract). In a letter to Ms. Williams, you might use yet a different "cutting implement," that of remedy (reinstatement, compensatory damages, punitive damages) in recognition that this, not legal theory, is her major interest. But a division that used more than one way of slicing—for example, the division of Williams' claims into "sexual harassment," "claims against the church board," and "claims seeking reinstatement"—would not be logical and would undoubtedly confuse the client.

In some documents, you may need to use more than a single principle of division, however, because in rule-making documents, large-scale division is often less a function of principle than a function of convention. Statutes, for example, are traditionally divided into preambles, definitions, substantive provisions, and administrative provisions. Within each part, however, it is usually good practice to observe the single-principle rule. In addition, in drafting as in life, concerns sometimes shift as you proceed with a task. For example, a letter to Nancy Williams may first be divided into a discussion of claims and then shift into a discussion of remedies, or the substantive provisions of a statute may be divided into prohibitions and affirmative duties, while the administrative provisions are divided into chronological procedural steps. Even in this situation, however, you want to think about principles of division and strive for as much consistency as possible.

### b. Mutual Exclusivity

The second rule of division requires all the parts of a whole to be mutually exclusive. For example, the division of "domestic felines" into "cats, kittens, and pedigreed" is incorrect, because the divisions overlap: some cats are kittens, all kittens are cats, and some kittens and cats are pedigreed. Violation of this mutual-exclusivity-no-overlap rule often coexists with a violation of the single-principle-of division rule: overlap is often the result of using more than one principle of division. Here, for example, the overlap is the result of dividing by age and by pedigree. Or, to take another example, if you were outlining a memo discussing Nancy Williams' possible claims, the division of Williams' claims into "sexual harassment claims, claims against the church board, and claims seeking reinstatement" would violate the mutual-exclusivity rule because claims against the board overlap with both sexual harassment claims and claims for which the remedy is reinstatement.

We add an important caveat here—the mutual-exclusivity rule, like the single-principle rule of division, is a "default" rule that may be violated when usefulness is better served by breach. Thus, for example, a health insurance contract might include, among others, the following sections: "Medical Coverage," "Psychiatric Coverage," "Obstetrical Coverage," and "Coverage of Experimental Procedures." These categories overlap in obvious ways: obstetrics is a branch of medicine, and so is psychiatry. Experimental procedures might be medical, obstetrical or psychiatric. Even though there are multiple overlaps, however, the insured might find that this breakdown makes it easier to get information, and therefore, appropriateness to context trumps logical division.

On the other hand, discretion to disregard the rules in this type of situation should not become license to disregard them when their application will add to the clarity and effectiveness of your document.

### c. The Sum of the Parts Should Equal the Whole

A third requirement with respect to division in a hierarchical outline is that the sum of the parts equal the whole. The classic example of division that fails this rule is the division of "humanity" into "men and women"—the obvious flaw is that the third age category, "children," is missing. This requirement restates in structural terms the substantive requirement that no essential component of a document, no element of a cause of action, no prong of a test, be omitted. Thus, allegations that the church board fired Williams shortly after she threatened to file a sexual harassment complaint would not add up to reprisal, because there is a missing element: the reason provided for the dismissal must have been pretextual.

The requirement that parts equal the whole has another application to hierarchical outlines, however. Any division must create more than one sub-division—the "no-A-without-a-B" rule. We can all see that the division of the whole "humanity" into just one sub-division, "people" is illogical and silly, but if we are not careful we create outlines that breach the same rule. For example, the following point heading for an appellate brief is incorrectly structured.

> I. WHEN THE POLICE ARREST THE DRIVER OF A VE-
>    HICLE, THEY MAY NOT SEARCH THE BELONGINGS
>    OF A PASSENGER IN THE VEHICLE UNLESS THEY
>    HAVE PROBABLE CAUSE FOR SUCH A SEARCH.
>    A. <u>The Fourth Amendment is violated by a search of the
>       belongings of a passenger in a vehicle after the driver's
>       arrest.</u>

The problem here is that sub-point "A" is just a restatement of point "I." One solution is simply to delete the sub-point. The other is to find the genuine parts of the whole and set them out. For example, here "A" might be "Supreme Court precedent suggests that a search of a vehicle passenger violates the Fourth Amendment." Sub-point "B" might be "A vehicle passenger's interest in privacy outweighs the law enforcement interest in searching her belongings."

---

*Exercise 1.3*

---

*Evaluate the division of "law books" into "casebooks, reporters, and paperbacks." Does it observe the three traditional rules of structure discussed above, which require 1) that consistent principles of division should be used, 2) that parts should be mutually exclusive, and 3) that the whole should be the sum of its parts? Might context justify at least one of the breaches of the rules here?*

---

### d. Logical Sequence

Finally, once you have tested the division of your outline, you need to pay attention to sequence. The order of the parts needs to be logical and appropriate. Chronological order and order of importance are the two most common orders, but there are others—from general to specific, from usual to unusual, from strongest to weakest, and even alphabetical order. Different principles of ordering are appropriate for different situations and even different sections. Regulations intended for the use of laypersons ordinarily follow chronological order—in an unfamiliar area, we always want to know "What is the first thing I should do?" But the "Definitions" section in that regulation would probably precede the first chronological section because it would contain information important and relevant to each section. Moreover, the definitions would be arranged alphabetically even if the parts of another section follow a different ordering scheme.

In contrast, the arguments in an appellate brief might not follow chronology, which would put a point arguing illegal arrest before one arguing erroneous jury instructions, for example, but rather, might be organized with the strongest argument first, or the argument that would afford the broadest relief first. A complaint would most likely begin with the cause of action that alleges the most egregious behavior; in the Williams case, the complaint would probably begin with the sexual harassment allegations against Bryant rather than with the breach of contract claim. In matters of sequence, as in everything concerning the composition of legal documents—except ethical practice—effectiveness is the touchstone.

At this point, you are ready to start on a full "first" draft. Before you proceed, however, you should be sure to research any new questions that have arisen during the "thinking it through" and "testing it out" processes. The other skills chapters in this book, *Clarity, Persuasion,* and *Precision* are designed to help with the writing and editing phases.

---------------------------- *Exercise 1.4* ----------------------------

*Brainstorming a separation agreement, you have come up with the following "dump list" of things that have to be included. Turn it into an outline, paying attention to principles of division and sequencing. Assume for the purposes of this exercise that nothing has been omitted.*

| | |
|---|---|
| School vacations | Certificates of deposit |
| Spousal support | Liability for current & past taxes |
| Basic child support | Health insurance |
| Child-care expenses | Weekend possession |
| School and college | Automobiles |
| Child health care expenses | Jewelry |
| Custody & visitation | "Remarriage" definition |
| House | "Emancipation" definition |
| Household effects | Life insurance |
| Checking accounts | Pension & retirement plans |
| Stocks & bonds | Covenant not to incur debt |

---------------------------- *Exercise 1.5* ----------------------------

*You've come up with a tentative outline for the substantive provisions of the rental agreement between Aunt Liz and Jim and Jenny that you started working on in Exercise 1.1. Now check your outline, for substance and structure, following the guidelines in Testing It Out. Is the outline complete, or are there important contingencies left uncovered? Are the provisions internally consistent? Are they sufficiently general/specific? Does one principle of division govern? Do provisions overlap? Are larger provisions the sum of their sub-divisions? Are the provisions in a consistent and useful sequence? Has*

*your review generated more questions for Aunt Liz? Re-organize, adding any*
*necessary information.*

    I. Taxes
       A. Property
   II. Utilities
       A. Electricity
       B. Telephone
  III. Heat
  IV. Maintenance of Home
       A. Indoors
       B. Outdoors
       C. Major Repairs
       D. Minor Repairs
   V. Security Deposit
  VI. Responsibilities of Owner
       A. Lawn and Garden
       B. Pet Care
       C. Damages not Occasioned by Tenants' Negligence
 VII. Insurance
       A. Fire
       B. Theft
       C. Liability
VIII. Return of Security Deposit

---

### *Exercise 1.6*

*Testing for consequences is a vital part of the conceptualization process. Assume that you work for State of Pacifica legislator Bill Patterson, whose concern about the problem of strategic lawsuits against public participation—known as "SLAPP" suits—is the subject of Casefile 4 in Appendix A.*

*SLAPP suits are civil lawsuits filed against non-governmental individuals and groups, usually for having communicated with a government body, official, or the electorate, on an issue of some public interest or concern. SLAPP suits seek to retaliate against political opposition, attempt to prevent future opposition and intimidate political opponents, and are employed as a strategy to win an underlying economic battle, political fight, or both. The SLAPP plaintiff's goal is not necessarily to "win" the lawsuit, but rather to deter public participation. This goal is realized by instituting or threatening multimillion-dollar lawsuits to intimidate citizens into silence. SLAPP suits have a chilling effect on the exercise of two core democratic freedoms: the First Amendment rights of free speech and "to petition the government for a redress of grievances."*

*In response to an increasing use of SLAPPs over the past decade, many states have passed "anti-SLAPP" legislation. Your boss believes the time has come for the state of Pacifica, too, to take action against SLAPP suits. But which one of the widely varying approaches of the other states is the appropriate model? One of the most significant aspects of anti-SLAPP legislation is the breadth of the statute as measured by its definition of "public participation." Your boss has asked you to evaluate some typical definitions of "public participation." First, read through the five definitions below. Which seems to be broadest? Which seems to be narrowest? Then read the four typical SLAPP scenarios that follow the definitions and see how many of the plaintiffs' activities fit within each of the definitions. Which definition should be included in Patterson's draft statute if he wishes it to protect the broadest spectrum of speech and participation? Which definition protects the least activity? Which fall somewhere in between?*

## Definitions

### Minnesota

"Public participation" means speech or lawful conduct that is genuinely aimed in whole or in part at procuring favorable government action.

### Delaware

"Public petition and participation" means any efforts to report on, comment on, rule on, challenge or oppose any application for a permit, zoning change, lease, license, certificate or other entitlement for use or permission to act from any government body.

### California

"Act in furtherance of a person's right of petition or free speech in connection with a public issue" includes: (1) any written or oral statement or writing made before a legislative, executive, or judicial proceeding, or any other official proceeding authorized by law; (2) any written or oral statement or writing made in connection with an issue under consideration or review by a legislative, executive, or judicial body, or any other official proceeding authorized by law; (3) any written or oral statement or writing made in a place open to the public or a public forum in connection with an issue of public interest; (4) or any other conduct in furtherance of the exercise of the constitutional right of petition or the constitutional right of free speech in connection with a public issue or an issue of public interest.

## Georgia

"Act in furtherance of the right of free speech or the right to petition government for a redress of grievances in connection with an issue of public interest or concern" includes any written or oral statement, writing, or petition made before or to a legislative, executive, or judicial proceeding, or any other official proceeding authorized by law, or any written or oral statement, writing, or petition made in connection with an issue under consideration or review by a legislative, executive, or judicial body, or any other official proceeding authorized by law.

## Massachusetts

The words "a party's exercise of its right of petition" shall mean any written or oral statement made before or submitted to a legislative, executive, or judicial body, or any other governmental proceeding; any written or oral statement made in connection with an issue under consideration or review by a legislative, executive, or judicial body, or any other governmental proceeding; any statement reasonably likely to encourage consideration or review of an issue by a legislative, executive, or judicial body or any other governmental proceeding; any statement reasonably likely to enlist public participation in an effort to effect such consideration; or any other statement falling within constitutional protection of the right to petition government.

### Fact Patterns

**1.** Aggro-business, Inc. owns and operates a farm. It had a contract with Ace Aerial, a licensed commercial aerial sprayer, for the spraying of its fields with pesticides. Jonathan Fraser owns property nearby. He believes that the spraying is improper and complains that the pesticides drift onto his and other nearby property. He has voiced his concerns about Aggro-business to numerous government officials and agencies and also founded the "Group Against Aerial Spraying of Pesticides" ("GAASP") to foster public awareness regarding the spraying of aerial pesticides. Aggro-business has sued both GAASP and Fraser, alleging that Fraser has engaged in a course of tortious behavior, including making false complaints to governmental entities, designed to interrupt Aggro-business' operations, and that as a result of Fraser's complaints to public agencies, Ace Aerial cancelled its contract with Aggro-business, and that as a result, the fields were not sprayed, and the corn crop was destroyed by insects. Aggro-business and its manager allege intentional infliction of emotional distress, tortious interference with business relationships and contracts, and related causes of action, and contend that alleged business interruptions have resulted in economic damages of three million dollars. Are Fraser's activities within any of the above definitions of public participation?

**2.** Fifteen residents of the town of Green Creek, concerned with the protection of wetlands draining into the creek, signed a petition opposing a town permit for construction of six single-family residences. The developer sued all the residents individually for tortious interference with business relationships and contracts, alleging two million dollars in damages. Are the residents' activities within any of the definitions of public participation?

**3.** Jennifer Walton sought and obtained an abuse protection order against her former boyfriend, Matthew Fabre. In response, Fabre filed a civil complaint against Walton asserting a claim of abuse of process (wrongful use of the courts) arising out of her application for the abuse protection order. He claims $5,000,000 in damages. Does Walton's application fall within any of the definitions above?

**4.** Bullish, Inc. is a financial website that organizes individual bulletin boards or "chat-rooms," each one dedicated to a single publicly traded company. The chat-rooms at Bullish are open and free to anyone who wants to read the messages; membership is also free and entitles the member to post messages about the subject company. Brite Idea, Inc. is a large publicly traded technology corporation that is the subject of a chat-room at Bullish. Linda Costello and Michael King each posted messages critical of the corporate performance and corporate governance of Brite Idea. Brite Idea sued Costello and King, alleging trade libel and defamation, and demanding five million dollars in damages. Are defendants' actions within any of the above definitions?

--------------------- *Assignment 1.1* ---------------------

*You have met with a new client, Tess Crane, about a possible lawsuit. Crane's son, Sam, was injured when he fell from an old fire tower owned by the Nevada Bird Sanctuary Society. You have interviewed the client about the incident and done some preliminary legal research. The statute and cases that seem most relevant are N.R.S. 41.510; Frasure v. United States, 256 F. Supp.2d 1180 (D. Nev. 2003); Hogle v. Hall, 916 P.2d 814, 819 (Nev. 1996); Hammersmith v. Jean Development West, 907 P.2d 975, 977 (Nev. 1995); Moody v. Manny's Auto Repair, 871 P.2d 935, 940-44 (Nev. 1994); and Kimberlin v. Lear, 500 P. 2d 1022 (Nev. 1972).*

*After reading the interview notes and sources cited above, brainstorm the problem. You'll need to make preliminary decisions about who may sue whom and on what legal and factual theories. Begin by "dumping" facts and ideas on paper. Then create an outline of possible claims, connecting facts with the elements of the claims. Note any question, factual or legal, that will need to be resolved before you can make a definitive assessment of the likely claims and their relative merit.*

## Interview Notes

The mission of the Nevada Bird Sanctuary Society ("NBSS") is to conserve and restore ecosystems, focusing on birds and their natural habitats. It owns a 200 acre sanctuary in Sparks. The sanctuary is open to dues paying members, who use it for birding, hiking, and picnicking.

Tess Crane and her family live at 1203 Rock Road, Sparks, Nevada 89521, which is several miles outside of Reno. They have a family membership at NBSS, a non-profit organization. Last summer, on August 26, 20__, she gave her twelve-year-old son,

Sam, and several friends who were visiting him permission to spend the day at the bird sanctuary, which is not far from where they live. While hiking there, the boys came upon an old wooden fire tower at the top of a hill and decided to climb it to see the view. The tower was built in 1919 and is about 60 feet high. An old wire fence circled the tower, but there were gaps where the fence had come loose from the posts. The roof of the lookout station was missing shingles, the screens were torn, and some boards had cracks and mold. There was a broken chain with a "no trespassing" sign lying on the bottom step, but some of the letters were rusty and hard to read. "Attention Members" had been painted on the top of the sign. The children began the climb, but as Sam crossed the first landing, the floorboards broke. Sam fell about fifteen feet to the ground. He was unable to walk and was in great pain.

Some of the boys stayed with Sam, while others went to get help. In the sanctuary's parking lot, they met couple who had a cell phone. The woman called both 911 and Sam's mother, who met the EMTs at the site of the accident. Sam was taken to the hospital, where he was treated for a fractured ankle and dislocated shoulder. His arm was gently maneuvered into position and put in a sling for several weeks. He needed surgery for his ankle. The doctors used staples to stabilize the pieces of bone in position. After surgery, Sam was housebound for two weeks, during which time Tess Crane took off from work and cared for him. Because the ankle was not weight-bearing, Sam used crutches for 8 weeks. He needed rehabilitation, partly paid for by health insurance, for both ankle and shoulder. Even now, Sam is suffering from limited mobility and walks with a stiff gait. The orthopedist thinks this is unlikely to change.

The NBSS is incorporated in Nevada and has its headquarters at 345 N. Virginia Street, Reno, Washoe County, Nevada 89520. NBSS purchased the 200-acre parcel, which has a parking lot on the junction of route 99 and route 6, about seven months ago from Rick Nissam, who lives at 915 Crescent Circle, Reno, Nevada 89520. Nissam owns a lumber and paper company. The woman who helped the boys, Vanessa Taylor, is on the board of the NBSS. She said that Nissam had told the NBSS that the fire tower was one of the oldest in Nevada, but needed some work.

Crane talked to several of her neighbors about the tower's dangers. One of them, Sheila Larson, worked for Nissam until five months ago. She said that when she hiked past a year ago, she noticed insects swarming around the posts and sawdust and insect wings on the soil around them. Sheila Googled these signs of insect infestation and found they matched that of termites. Crane wants to sue for Sam's injuries.[13]

---

[13] Note: this assignment is loosely based on a problem created by Deborah Schmedemann & Christina Kunz.

# Chapter 2

# *LITIGATING: COMPLAINTS*

---

## A. IN GENERAL

In this chapter and the two that follow, we discuss three of the most fundamental documents that lawyers draft in the course of litigation: complaints and answers—the basic pleadings that set the course of litigation—and motions, which are requests to the court in the course of litigation. We discuss these documents here, after the skills chapter on conceptualization, because that is where their great challenge lies. Although, like everything we draft in law practice, pleadings and motions should be clearly and carefully drafted, the quality of their prose is secondary to the acuity of theory and strategy. Because all good litigation strategy looks several moves ahead, it is a good idea to read straight through all three litigation chapters.

In addition to the primacy of conceptualization, there is another characteristic of litigation documents that sets them apart from most of the other documents in this book: the requirements for form and content are intensely local. The relevant rules vary so widely from jurisdiction to jurisdiction, from court to court, and from cause of action to cause of action that all of the advice and information below must be read with a caveat: *know your local rules.*[1] Although today most types of mistakes in pleading or motion practice are not fatal to the client's cause, a few still are fatal,

---

[1] You must know the rules at all levels—not only the basic procedural rules as promulgated by the legislature and high court, but also rules at the county level, court level, and even courtroom level. Fortunately, you will have the help of colleagues, formbooks, and office samples as well as the published rules themselves. Be sure to check pocket parts and supplements for recent changes. The on-line legal research services maintain substantial databases of practice rules and forms. Many court systems also have websites, an especially good source of up-dated information about the rules.

most are expensive, and all are destructive of the court's respect for attorney and client alike.

In our three chapters on litigation documents, we revisit ground that you covered in Civil Procedure, this time with a different, more practical, emphasis. As you learned there, the pleadings– principally, the plaintiff's complaint and the defendant's answer—contain the parties' basic contentions to the court and to each other concerning the controversy. The complaint is the basic "affirmative" pleading and the answer is the basic "responsive" pleading.[2] To a greater or lesser extent, these documents commit the parties to their version of events and the legal implications of those events. Pleadings traditionally served four functions: they gave notice of the parties' claims, they informed the parties about the factual bases of the claims, they narrowed the issues for trial, and they weeded out unmeritorious claims. Under the influence of the Federal Rules of Civil Procedure, the role of pleadings in civil litigation has diminished—in many jurisdictions, notice is the lone function left to them—and the role of discovery and motion practice has proportionately increased.

In the complaint, discussed in this chapter, the plaintiff alleges at least one legally cognizable civil wrong on the part of the defendant. In the answer, discussed in the next chapter, the defendant narrows the issues by denying, admitting, or pleading insufficient knowledge of the individual allegations in the complaint. Defendant often further focuses the issues in the answer by raising "affirmative" defenses like the statute of limitations—defenses from outside the four corners of the complaint that may doom plaintiff's claims even if plaintiff's version of events is correct.

Because pleadings, and especially, complaints, occupy such a prominent place in the litigation process, novice drafters often imagine that they are difficult to draft. In fact, it is quite easy to draft a competent complaint in most types of controversies in most jurisdictions. While thus less problematic than the new-

---

[2] Although, as noted below, there was once a bewildering variety of other affirmative and responsive pleadings, most jurisdictions today recognize just a few others—for example, a "counterclaim" by defendant against plaintiff, a "cross-claim" by one defendant against another, a "third-party" claim by defendant against a non-party, and responsive pleadings (variously called "answers" or "replies") to those affirmative pleadings. Because the skills required are essentially the same skills needed to draft complaints and answers to complaints, we discuss only complaints and answers here.

comer might think, complaints are nonetheless more demanding than many practitioners believe, and likely to become even more so if emerging trends in civil procedure continue. In order to understand this seeming paradox of pleading at the beginning of the 21$^{st}$ century, it is helpful to consider the history of pleading.

## 1. From the Forms of Action to Code Pleading

From the medieval beginnings of the common law until the middle of the 19$^{th}$ century, pleading and cause of action, form and substance, were one. Each one of dozens of cognizable grievances was its own "form of action," often with a bewildering Law French or Law Latin name—assizes of *novel disseisin* or of *mort d'ancestor;* writs of *besaiel* or *quare impedit;* or actions of covenant, *detinue, replevin,* or *assumpsit,* for example. Once the appropriate "form of action" was chosen—no easy matter in itself—lawyer's and client's travails had just begun. Each form of action had its own distinct, torturous, and mandatory procedure.[3] Once plaintiffs managed to file their grievances with the proper persons in the proper format in the proper manner, the parties began the stylized ritual of narrowing the issues to a single triable issue. Successive pleadings were volleyed back and forth, with each side providing only the information it chose to supply, framed as it chose. As one commentator put it, "complaint, answer, replication, rejoinder, surrejoinder, rebutter, surrebutter, and perhaps more. The common law seemed to run out of pleadings only when it ran out of names."[4]

In the middle of the 19$^{th}$ century, major statutory reforms rationalized the pleading process considerably, making the courts more efficient and somewhat more litigant- and lawyer-friendly. Common law and equity were merged, the forms of action were eliminated, one procedure was instituted for all cases, and the formerly numberless pleadings were reduced to complaint,

---

[3] F.W. Maitland, *The Forms of Action at Common Law: A Course of Lectures* 1–2 (A.H. Chaytar & W.J. Whittaker, eds., Cambridge U. Press 1958).

[4] David D. Siegel, *Practice Commentaries,* 7B McKinney's Consolidated Laws of New York 720–21 (West 1993).

answer, reply, and demurrer.[5] These reforms were embodied in the Field Code, named after its drafter, David Dudley Field, and first enacted in New York in 1848. By the end of the 19th century, the Field Code had been adopted by the majority of the States.[6]

"Code pleading" or "fact pleading"—as pleading under the Field code became known—requires that the plaintiff's complaint provide "[a] plain and concise statement of the facts constituting the cause of action...."[7] The apparent simplicity of this formulation proved illusory. The difficulties in code pleading came to revolve around just one word—"facts"—but they were daunting. Courts drew consequential distinctions between "evidentiary" facts, "ultimate" facts (sometimes called "material" facts), and conclusions of law; often, only those allegations held to be ultimate facts were permitted. Complaints deemed to stray into evidentiary facts or conclusions of law could subject the plaintiff to expensive repleading, at best. The distinctions among the three types of allegations are best shown by an example. In a malpractice action, the allegations that the surgeon amputated the plaintiff's left foot and that only the plaintiff's right foot was gangrenous would be allegations of *evidentiary fact*. The allegation that the surgeon amputated the wrong foot would be an allegation of *ultimate fact*. Finally, it would be a *conclusion of law* to allege that the surgeon "breached his duty to adhere to the accepted standard of professional care." Although these distinctions are reasonably clear in this example designed to make them clear, they are harder to make in practice, largely because they are distinctions in degree rather than in kind; evidentiary fact, ultimate fact, and conclusion of law are points on a spectrum with many intermediary points.[8] Fortunately, even courts that still require plaintiff to state "facts" rarely indulge in the kind of hair-splitting about the nature of facts that once tormented practitioners and obstructed the courtroom doors.

---

[5] The demurrer is the equivalent of the modern motion to dismiss for failure to state a cause of action. *See infra*, Chapter 4, *Motions*, Section A (2)(d).

[6] Stephen N. Subrin, Thomas J. Main, Mark S. Brodin, *Civil Procedure: Doctrine, Practice, and Context* 282–83 (Aspen 2000).

[7] N.Y. Laws 1851, c. 479, sec. 1.

[8] Charles Alan Wright & Arthur R. Miller, *5 Fed. Prac. & Proc. Civ. 2d* § 1202 (West 1990).

## 2. Notice Pleading

By the middle of the 20th century, a new wave of reform tackled the conundrums of fact-pleading and other restrictive pleading practices that had survived the innovations of the Field Code. The new approach to pleading was embodied in the Federal Rules of Civil Procedure, which became law in 1938. Unlike the Field Code, which for all its simplification of the pleading process still tended in common-law fashion to put procedure ahead of substance, the Federal Rules are the embodiment of an "equity-based vision"; their "predominant theme was that procedure should be subordinate to and should not interfere with substance."[9]

The Federal Rules created "notice-pleading": a complaint under the Rules need only provide the defendant with bare notice of the claimed grievance. All that is required in most instances is "a short and plain statement of the claim showing the pleader is entitled to relief."[10] The majority of states have adopted the spirit, and often the letter, of Rule 8.[11] Minnesota's Rule of Civil Procedure 8.01, for example, borrows the "short and plain statement" language, while Section 3013 of New York's Civil Practice Law and Rules requires "statements...sufficiently particular to give the court and parties notice of the transactions, occurrences, or series of transactions, intended to be proved and the material elements of each cause of action or defense."

---

[9] Subrin et al., *supra* n.6, at 291.

[10] Fed. R. Civ. Pro. 8 (2003). For practical purposes, "claim" as used in Rule 8 is synonymous with "cause of action," the more usual term in state law. We use the two interchangeably in our chapters on litigating documents; "claim" has the real advantage of being one word instead of three.

[11] A bare majority of states conform their civil procedure to the Federal Rules; under the influence of the Federal Rules, most other states have liberalized their pleading rules to greater or lesser extents. Once the rule, strict fact pleading is now the exception. Subrin et al., *supra* n. 6, at 313. Even in jurisdictions retaining the requirement that the plaintiff plead "facts" sufficient to state a claim, pleadings are characteristically construed liberally and a distinction is rarely made between evidentiary and ultimate facts, although unsupported conclusions of law may be deemed insufficient statement of a claim. *Compare, Voorhees v. Preferred Mut. Ins. Co.,* 607 A.2d. 1255, 1260 (N.J. 1992) (complaint sufficiently stated claim by alleging "negligent" conduct) *with Stredny v. Wyeth Laboratories,* 58 Pa. D. & C. 2d 665 (Pa. Com. Pl. 1965) (allegation of "negligent manufacture" of polio vaccine insufficiently particular). In any jurisdiction where the pleading rules still require "facts," it is essential to understand how that requirement is interpreted by the courts.

Whatever their wording, notice-pleading statutes tend to have one thing in common—the absence of the treacherous word "facts." For example, the New York pleading statute quoted above requires "statements." A plaintiff in a notice-pleading jurisdiction may allege evidentiary facts, ultimate facts, and even pure conclusions of law, so long as the complaint provides notice of a legally cognizable grievance. In some jurisdictions, a tort claim can be alleged by putting X's in boxes on an official form. Moreover, the plaintiff is under no obligation to name the cause of action pleaded, and may even name it incorrectly. So long as the elements of a legally cognizable claim are discernible, the complaint is legally sufficient, and at worst, plaintiff will be required to clarify it.[12] It is not surprising, then, that the received wisdom of law practice calls the complaint a "no-brainer."

As pleading practice has become simplified and pleadings less and less informative, the role of discovery and its probing deposition sessions has expanded, taking on two of the traditional roles of pleadings—informing the parties about the facts and narrowing the issues. In theory at least, discovery is a more effective and realistic way to narrow the issues than the volleying back and forth of paper pleadings in which the parties can choose how much to say and how to say it. "A pleading is like a lecture hall in which the class may not ask questions. Disclosure is the seminar in which the questions fly back and forth with gusto."[13]

### 3. Artful Pleading

It might appear from this brief history of pleading that the painstaking crafting of complaints is not only a lost art, but a well-lost one. Yet this is far from true. There are important reasons to learn artful pleading. First, despite the immense reach and influence of the Federal Rules, notice pleading is not acceptable in all jurisdictions,[14] and even notice-pleading jurisdictions require

---

[12] For example, Rule 15(a) of the Federal Rules of Civil Procedure provides that leave to amend an inartfully drafted complaint will be "freely given when justice so requires." Fed. R. Civ. P. 15(a) (2003).

[13] Siegel, *supra* n. 4, at 726.

[14] *See, e.g.,* Candyce Vana Ingwersen, 4 *Standard Pennsylvania Practice 2d* § 23:18 (West 2003) ("A complaint in tort is sufficient when the *ultimate facts* relied upon to show neg-

that some cause of action be pleaded with particularity—fraud and defamation are frequent exceptions to notice pleading.

Second, no matter how permissive the current pleading requirements are in your jurisdiction, you need to know how to do more than meet the minimal requirements of notice pleading because there are signs of a climate change in litigation philosophy, most noticeably in the federal courts.[15] A quarter-century ago, most courtroom doors were wide-open to litigants and their grievances. Since then, however, Congress has more than once shown itself hostile to the original spirit of the Federal Rules. For example, the Private Securities Litigation Reform Act of 1995 requires class-action plaintiffs alleging fraud in the securities market to do so with great particularity.[16] Moreover, some federal courts apply "heightened" pleading requirements to a variety of claims, including CERCLA actions, civil conspiracy, and even negligence.[17] The Supreme Court itself has thus far stopped short of requiring "heightened fact pleading of specifics" in Rule 8 complaints, although it does now require "enough facts to state a claim of relief that is plausible," not merely "conceivable."[18]

This climate change is more perceptible in some jurisdictions than in others, but it is the rare state legislature that has not

---

ligence…are so clearly and fully stated that they themselves would entitle the plaintiff to a favorable verdict if they were to go undisputed.") (emphasis added).

[15] *See* Subrin et al., *supra* n. 6, at 274-77; *see generally* Richard L. Marcus, *The Puzzling Persistence of Pleading Practice*, 76 Tex. L. Rev. 1749 (1998).

[16] 15 U.S.C.A. §78u-4(b)(2) (West 2003). The Act requires the complaint in a class action securities lawsuit to specify all statements alleged to be misleading and give specific reasons why each was misleading; allegations of misleading statements based on information and belief must state with particularity all facts on which belief is based; where proof of a state of mind is required by the statute, the complaint must "state with particularity facts giving rise to a strong inference that the defendant acted with the required state of mind." This seems a long way from the "short and plain statement" of Rule 8 of the Federal Rules of Civil Procedure.

[17] *See* Christopher M. Fairman, *The Myth of Notice Pleading*, 45 Ariz. L. Rev. 987, 1011-59 (2003)

[18] *Bell Atlantic Corp. v. Twombly*, 550 U.S. 544, 556-557, 563, 570 (2007); *See also Ashcroft v. Iqbal*, 129 S.Ct. 1937, 1949-1954 (2009) (applying *Twombly*, over a 4-justice dissent, in a suit for damages against federal officers alleged to have violated plaintiff's constitutional rights). In *Twombly*, the Court officially "retired" its famous statement in *Conley v. Gibson*, 355 U.S. 41, 45-46 (1957), that "a complaint should not be dismissed for failure to state a claim unless it appears beyond doubt that the plaintiff can prove no set of facts in support of his claim which would entitle him to relief."

enacted at least one litigation-hostile statute. Thus, although it would be an exaggeration to say that pleading requirements are coming full circle, it would be unwise for an attorney entering civil practice today to assume that drafting the complaint will remain the least part of the job. An experienced practitioner contemplating the Private Securities Litigation Reform Act might well agree with Frederick Maitland, who noted more than a century ago that although we have buried the forms of action, "they rule us still from their graves."[19]

Finally, however strict or liberal the pleading requirements, artful pleading is a skill worth having because complaints have rhetorical as well as instrumental force: that is, they can affect the course of litigation by persuasion as well as by legal effect. Barely ten percent of all civil actions go to trial, and of those, many are not tried before a jury. Because a jury is so unlikely to hear your client's story, the rhetorical impact of your complaint assumes real importance. Defense counsel is of course a primary audience, and the drafter's major concern here is largely on tactical and instrumental impact—focused on eliciting admissions and on narrowing the scope of discovery, for example. Yet three other audiences should not be neglected: the defendant, the court, and the plaintiff.

In modern pleading practice, the complaint is the first and the last opportunity for the plaintiff to tell his story directly to the defendant,[20] and a well-told story may well influence the defendant to seek a prompt settlement. The court is another powerful audience. Its appraisal of the merits can be crucial even as it decides purely procedural issues. Often it is vital for the court to learn more than the bare outlines of the plaintiff's story. Although this is especially true when the allegations make out a compelling, even shocking tale,[21] a skillful narrative account of plaintiff's ill-treatment at defendant's hands is always an option worth considering.

---

[19] Maitland, *supra* n. 3, at 1.

[20] The defendant's answer will contest plaintiff's allegations, but modern pleading rules ordinarily give no opportunity to rebut defendant's denials, although reply to defendant's affirmative defenses is permitted in some jurisdictions.

[21] Civil rights cases are the classic example. *See, e.g.,* Herbert Eastman, *Speaking Truth to Power: The Language of Civil Rights Litigators,* 104 Yale L.J. 763 (1955).

Always bear in mind that although the plaintiff herself may not be a primary audience for your complaint, she is a concerned reader. Simple respect for the plaintiff as a member of the human community suggests that her story should not be reduced to boilerplate.

## B. COMPONENTS

There are two essential, defining components that all complaints in civil actions must have, regardless of jurisdiction, court, or cause of action: a *statement of the claim* itself (often called the *body* of the complaint) and a *demand for judgment and relief* (often called the *ad damnum clause*). The presence (or absence) and form of all of the other components is dictated by local rule or convention. As you read the descriptions that follow, you should refer to the sample complaint. You should note that in order to provide the maximum number of features in a simple factual context, we have set our sample in a fictional notice-pleading jurisdiction.

### 1. Caption and Introductory Sentence

The *caption* identifies the court and parties. To the right of it, the document is identified as a complaint. Often, as here, provision is made for adding the index or docket number assigned by the clerk of the court when the complaint is filed. Be warned that such is the proliferation of local court rules that even the order of the parties or the precise placement of the caption on the page may be mandatory.

The ritual *introductory sentence,* often called the *commencement,* follows the caption and directly precedes the statement of the claim. The introductory sentence is still too often expressed in archaic language; some boilerplate forms enshrine relics of the forms of action, medieval formulations like "And now, to wit, comes Alice Adams by and through her attorney, Benjamin Bailey, complaining of defendant Charles Connelly and saying...." These formulations contain no legal "magic dust," and the better modern practice is a simple statement like "Plaintiff Alice Adams makes the following allegations against defendant Charles Connelly through her attorney, Benjamin Bailey."

## 2. Statement of the Claim

Depending on your jurisdiction, you may be required to begin the *statement of the claim* by alleging one or more of the following: subject matter jurisdiction, personal jurisdiction, and venue. In federal court, all three must be alleged. The rules in other jurisdictions, and within jurisdictions, vary widely. State courts of general jurisdiction may require no allegations regarding jurisdiction or venue; state courts with subject matter jurisdiction limited to cases where more (or less) than a certain monetary amount is in controversy most often require the complaint to allege the amount at stake. It is vital to know what must be pleaded in your court. It is also important to know what need not be pleaded; a complaint alleging subject matter jurisdiction in a court with no such requirement looks sloppy and amateurish—no way to impress the judge. (But you should note that statements of the claim often begin with descriptions of the parties and their residence even when rules do not require the pleading of personal jurisdiction or venue.)

The statement of the claim is divided into numbered paragraphs. (The better practice is ordinarily to put just one allegation in each paragraph; this matter and whether to frame allegations generally or specifically are discussed below in *Special Concerns*.) Allegations of matters not personally known to the plaintiff are made "on information and belief." This is always the better practice, but it is absolutely essential in a verified complaint, where plaintiff swears to the truth of his allegations. Bear in mind, however, that allegation on "information and belief" is not a license for sloppiness—"information and belief" must be based on reasonable inquiry.

Where several causes of action stem at least in part from the same transaction, it is usual to begin with a section headed "Common Allegations" or "Facts Common to All Counts," or "Background." Traditionally, the individual counts that follow begin with a paragraph on the order of "Plaintiff realleges the allegations contained in paragraphs 3–10 above." The alternative, repeating allegations verbatim from count to count might violate the proscription against unnecessary length contained in most rules of pleading.

Although notice pleading does not require causes of action to be named in the complaint, separate counts should at a minimum begin with numbered headings. Where a complaint names more than one defendant, the heading of each cause of action should specify which defendant is complained of.

When you are certain that the facts alleged in a given section make out one particular named cause of action, putting the name of the cause of action in the heading makes a more reader-friendly complaint—some practitioners do not label their causes of action for this very reason, not wishing to give opposing counsel unnecessary help. Whether to label or not is a case-by-case decision, but given that the court is a very influential secondary audience, we think such reader-friendly devices are most often appropriate. It is a mistake to believe that everything that makes opposing counsel's job harder benefits your side.

### 3. *Ad Damnum* Clause

The contents of the *ad damnum* clause are almost always prescribed by statute or rule. In some kinds of cases in some courts, specific amounts must be pleaded; in some situations, pleading a specific amount limits recovery to that amount; in yet other situations, specific amounts may not be pleaded. Be sure you know the rule for your court. Where multiple counts are alleged, the drafter often has the choice of pleading damages at the end of each individual count or collecting them in one omnibus *ad damnum* clause at the end of the statement of the claim. It is usual to end the *ad damnum* clause with a request for "interest, costs, and disbursements," although in many jurisdictions these are included in plaintiff's recovery by operation of law.

### 4. Signature and Verification

Our sample complaint is dated at the end—even where not required, this is good practice. Our sample also provides the address and telephone number of counsel for plaintiff, as well as the name of the firm. This information is most often required. Our sample is signed by counsel—the plaintiff does not ordinarily sign. In many jurisdictions counsel's signature is required, and the attorney is held to warrant by her signature that on the basis of reasonable inquiry, she believes that the allegations in the complaint are not frivolous.[22]

Do not confuse *signature* with *verification*. Our sample complaint has a verification clause in which the plaintiff swears under oath that the pleading is true to the plaintiff's knowledge, except for allegations made on information and belief, which latter allegations the plaintiff believes to be true. Some courts require verification of complaints in some or all types of controversies; some court rules make it optional. A plaintiff who swears falsely to the truth of allegations commits perjury. Where verification is required, attorneys may be permitted to verify in place of the plaintiff—if, for instance, the plaintiff is out of the jurisdiction.[23] One usual consequence of a verified complaint is that the answer must also be verified, exposing the defendant to the penalties of perjury.

---

[22] *See, e.g.,* Fed. R. Civ. P. § 11 (2003) (providing, *inter alia* that an attorney must sign her pleadings, and that by so doing, she certifies that, based on reasonable inquiry, she believes that the claims in her pleadings are warranted by existing law or a non-frivolous argument for an extension of existing law or a for a change in the law and that there is evidentiary support for the allegations of the pleading). *See also* 22 N.Y. Comp. Codes, R. & Regs. I, 130-1.1 (2002); Wis. Stat. § 802.05 (West 2003).

[23] Attorneys should verify in a client's stead only when absolutely necessary and with great care not to swear to personal knowledge of matters of which in fact they have no personal knowledge. This is perjury. Indeed, it is a bad idea even when the attorney has such personal knowledge, because it may subject her to being called as a witness by the defendant—an eventuality that would very likely put the attorney in violation of the Code of Professional Responsibility DR 5-102. *See, e.g.,* Mark Davies, *Comment, West's McKinney's Forms,* 1A, 586–87 (1992).

## C. SAMPLE COMPLAINT

Superior Court of the State of Atlantis
County of Sussex

-------------------------------------------------------

Jeffrey Hustin,
Plaintiff,

      -against-                                    COMPLAINT
                                            Index No. Civ. _____

Michele Freeman and
The Regents of the University of Atlantis,
Defendants.

-------------------------------------------------------

Plaintiff Jeffrey Hustin makes the following allegations against defendants Michele Freeman and the Regents of the University of Atlantis through his attorney, Paul Wilens.

### Background

1. This is an action for damages in excess of $50,000.[24]
2. Plaintiff is a citizen of the state of Atlantis. He resides at 320 Dune Drive, Atlantis City, Atlantis.
3. Upon information and belief, defendants are citizens of the state of Atlantis.[25]
4. At all times relevant to the allegations in this complaint, defendant Michele Freeman was a Professor of Law at Sussex University School of Law in Atlantis City and a visiting Professor of Law at the University of Atlantis School of Law ("the Law School").
5. At all times relevant to allegations in this complaint, plaintiff was an Assistant Professor of Law at the University of Atlantis School of Law.[26]

---

[24] This first paragraph alleges subject matter jurisdiction.

[25] Because this is a verified complaint, plaintiff is especially careful to allege on "information and belief" matters of which he does not have personal knowledge, but which he believes to be true based on reasonable investigation.

[26] Paragraphs 2–5 provide basic information about the parties.

## Count One: Defamation
### *(Both Defendants)*

6. In October, 20__, plaintiff applied to the Status Committee of the Law School for academic tenure and promotion to the rank of Associate Professor.
7. The Status Committee comprises the entire tenured faculty of the Law School, and its function is to evaluate and act upon applications for tenure and promotion.
8. As a visiting professor, defendant Freeman was not a member of the Status Committee.
9. On or about March 12, 20__, defendant Freeman wrote a memorandum to the thirty-two members of the Status Committee of the Law School concerning plaintiff's application.
10. This memorandum was sent to all members of the Status Committee on or about March 12, 20__.
11. On information and belief, all members of the Status Committee read the memorandum written by defendant Freeman about the plaintiff.
12. Defendant Freeman's memorandum, annexed to this complaint as Exhibit A, contained the following.

"Although superficially plausible and original, upon closer inspection, Professor Hustin's article 'Plain Language: A Cognitive Contradiction in Terms' turns out to be not only derivative, but disturbingly resonant with distinct echoes of the work of several earlier (and unacknowledged) scholars." "Professor Hustin has verbally abused and humiliated students, both in and out of class, and on at least one occasion, he threatened a student with bodily harm if the student complained to the administration about his class." "He [Professor Hustin] seemingly has no capacity to relate to his students or to his colleagues."[27]

13. All of the statements from defendant Freeman's memorandum quoted in paragraph 12 above concerning plaintiff are false.
14. All of the statements quoted in paragraph 12 above are defamatory in that they tend to expose plaintiff to contempt, aversion, ridicule, and disgrace, and to induce a bad opinion of him in the minds of right-thinking persons.

---

[27] Why are the allegations in this paragraph made with great particularity, even though Atlantis is a notice-pleading jurisdiction? Why is it not sufficient to allege, for example, that "defendant said words *to the effect that....*"?

15. On information and belief, defendant Freeman's memorandum was the only communication of its nature received by the Status Committee, and upon information and belief, all other evaluations of plaintiff's scholarship and teaching abilities were positive.
16. As a result of the publication by defendant Freeman of her memorandum, plaintiff's application for tenure and promotion was rejected by the Status Committee.
17. As a further result of the publication by defendant Freeman of her memorandum, the Status Committee declined to rehire plaintiff as an Assistant Professor.
18. As a still further result of the publication by defendant Freeman of her memorandum, plaintiff has been unable to find employment as a law teacher in any other law school.
19. As a result of the publication by defendant Freeman of her memorandum, plaintiff has suffered injury to his professional career, including loss of his job, loss of income, destruction of professional and personal relationships, and severe mental distress and anguish.
20. Defendants Regents of the University of Atlantis are vicariously liable to plaintiff for the actions of their employee, defendant Freeman.

### Count Two: Intentional Infliction of Emotional Distress
*(Both Defendants)*

21. Plaintiff realleges paragraphs 6–13 above.[28]
22. Defendant Freeman's conduct in writing the memorandum to the Status Committee detailed above in paragraph 12 is so extreme and outrageous as to be intolerable in a civilized community.
23. As a result of defendant Freeman's conduct, plaintiff suffered severe emotional distress.
24. Plaintiff's distress was intentionally, or at a minimum, recklessly, caused by defendant.[29]
25. Defendants Regents of the University of Atlantis are vicariously liable for the action of their employee, defendant Freeman.

---

[28] Here, plaintiff realleges conduct relevant to both causes of action, rather than repeat his earlier allegations. This is a useful technique, but the drafter must be sure to use the correct paragraph numbers.

[29] In contrast to the defamation allegations, plaintiff's allegations of intentional infliction of emotional distress are really conclusions of law. Is this acceptable? Is it good strategy in this complaint?

WHEREFORE, plaintiff demands judgment against defendants as follows:

(1) Compensatory damages in an amount not less than $700,000;
(2) Punitive damages in an amount not less than $2,000,000;
(3) Interest, the costs and disbursements of this action, and attorney's fees; and
(4) Such other and further relief as the court deems just.

Dated: Atlantis City, Atlantis
February 2, 20__.

_____ [30]

Paul Wilens
Hogan, Herzen, Wang & Wilens
Attorney for Plaintiff
5 Judiciary Square
Atlantis City, Atlantis
(111) 874-2901

## VERIFICATION

State of Atlantis      )
County of Sussex    )

On February 2, 20__, Jeffrey Hustin personally appeared before me, a Notary Public for the State of Atlantis and County of Sussex. Being duly sworn, Jeffrey Hustin deposed and said that he is the plaintiff in the above action and that the facts set forth in the complaint are true, except for those statements made upon information and belief, and as to those statements, he believes them to be true.[31]

_____

Sworn and subscribed before me this 2nd day of February, 20__.

_____

Notary Public
My Commission expires May 31, 20__.

_____

[30] The attorney will warrant by his signature that based on reasonable inquiry, he believes the complaint is not frivolous.

[31] Complaints alleging defamation must be verified in virtually all jurisdictions, exposing the plaintiff to the penalties of perjury. Why do you think defamation is treated differently from most other causes of action?

## D. WRITING PROCESS

The process of drafting a complaint is that described in the first chapter of this book: information gathering, conceptualizing, writing a first full draft, and revising and polishing. As with all composition, the process is unlikely to be linear. Research into possible causes of action will often send you back to your client for more facts, for example. As we describe the complaint-drafting process, we'll ask you to imagine that you are a new associate in a personal injury firm. A partner has asked you to work on the case of Janet Spence, who seems very likely to become a client of the firm based on her initial conversation with the partner. All you know so far is that Spence is a middle-aged physical therapist who sustained leg injuries when she was struck by an automobile that rolled down a ramp in a parking garage, pinning her against her own parked car.

### 1. Gathering Information: Getting the Facts

Gathering the facts by interviewing the client is a delicate and difficult business, particularly when the plaintiff's injury or loss is extensive or traumatic. Yet the costs of not getting the whole story, or the true story, can be significant for attorney and client alike. The rare client may lie or deliberately conceal information—but there is little an attorney can do about outright falsehood except refuse to represent clients when after reasonable inquiry, their allegations appear unworthy of belief.

More frequently, missing information or misinformation comes from a client who wants to tell the truth, but who is poorly inter-viewed. It is all too easy to ask questions that push the client's allegations to fill in the blanks in boilerplate complaints. It also happens that professionals whose work exposes them to human distress take refuge in formality, seeming cold and disapproving. At least three of the plaintiffs in our casefiles—Nancy Williams, who claims she was sexually harassed, and Charles and Emily Johnson, alleging the wrongful birth of a severely disabled child—have stories that were surely difficult to tell, demanding a skilled and empathic interviewer. Janet Spence's story seems less emotionally charged, but you won't know the whole story unless you interview her skillfully.

Research has identified factors that inhibit full communication between lawyer and client and factors that facilitate communication.[32] Factors that inhibit openness on the client's part include fear that the attorney will disapprove of the client if the client tells the whole story and fear that the attorney will refuse to represent him if the client reveals information that weakens his case. Clients may also hesitate to relate intimate facts that might embarrass the attorney, or withhold facts because recalling the details of a traumatic event is so painful. Clients may also fail to volunteer crucial information because they believe that their role is simply to answer the attorney's questions and they fear that what they have to add is irrelevant to their case. Conversely, some clients withhold information because they lose interest in the questions; a client might need the freedom to talk about a legally irrelevant, but compelling, part of the story before he can focus on the relevant details.

A patient and observant interviewer can mitigate these inhibitors in a number of ways. First, the interviewer can promote openness through explicit and implicit empathy. Many a client has been encouraged to tell his story in painful but necessary detail by a simple "I hear you" from his lawyer. Second, a word or two of approval—praise for the client's memory, for example, or his candor or meticulous record-keeping—can help counter the client's fear of being judged harshly by the attorney. An attorney who gives good reasons for her questions may also motivate a reluctant interviewee; the attorney might explain, for example, that she needs all the facts if the client is to be compensated for the wrong done and if the defendant is to be prevented or deterred from injuring others.[33]

Much of the secret of effective interviewing is learning how to listen. The best advice about listening that we know was given to a group of law students by a playwright who interviews people and creates plays out of their stories.

---

[32] The discussion of inhibitors and facilitators of communication that follows is adapted from David A. Binder & Susan C. Price, *Legal Interviewing and Counseling: A Client Centered Approach* (West 1977).

[33] *Id.; see* J. P. Ogilvy, Leach Wortham & Lisa G. Lerman, *Learning From Practice: A Professional Development Text for Legal Externs* 86–87 (West Wadsworth 1998) (discussing inhibiting and facilitating factors).

Listening is not just hearing what someone tells you word for word. You have to listen with a heart. I don't want that to sound touchy-feely; it is not. It is very hard work. If I do three interviews a day, I can be exhausted, because the process of hearing everyone requires that I empty myself out. While I'm listening, my own judgments and prejudices certainly come up. But I know I won't get anything unless I get those things out of the way. Whether I'm a lawyer or a doctor, I have to get myself present, and the client or the patient has to take charge. The question is, how can you be fully present and there for them?[34]

Assume that in your interview, prospective client Janet Spence discusses her injuries knowledgeably and without much apparent distress. She is very articulate about the accident itself. She describes in detail the garage's practice of permitting tenants to leave their cars at the side of the ramp leading to the lower level of the garage for subsequent parking by the garage attendant. She also tells you about the accident itself. According to Spence, a BMW sedan left at the top of the ramp by its owner, Michael Corcoran, rolled down as Spence stood near the bottom of the ramp in back of her own car. At the time of the accident, Corcoran himself had just gotten out of the car and was standing at the top of the ramp, about to leave the garage.

Corcoran's vehicle struck Spence, pinning her against her own vehicle and breaking both her legs. A garage attendant quickly freed her and summoned help. The attendant observed that the emergency brake handle in Corcoran's vehicle did not appear to be in the engaged position. (The police accident form also recorded this fact.)

When she finishes her description of the accident, you ask whether there is anything else that might be relevant, and (possibly fearing to appear stupid by raising irrelevant details) she replies that she doesn't think so. You are about to end the interview—but if you do, you will miss something that could be important. A careful listener would sense hesitation and discomfort on Spence's part and probe further, suggesting that perhaps something else upsetting had happened. In fact, if you did so,

---

[34] Karen W. Arenson, *The Fine Art of Listening*, N.Y. Times 34 (Jan. 13, 2002) (quoting Anna Deavere Smith).

Spence would tell you now that as she stood pinned between the cars, screaming for help, the owner of the vehicle verbally abused her, continuing his tirade until the ambulance arrived. An expression of dismay at such bad behavior or perhaps just a sympathetic silence elicit from Spence more details: the vehicle owner made no attempt to summon help or to help the garage attendant free her, but, rather, kept screaming at her, "Why didn't you get out of the way, you stupid old bat?" (She won't tell you this, but the reason she didn't tell you earlier is because you are a young man of about Corcoran's age.)

These new facts don't bear on Corcoran's alleged negligent parking of his vehicle, but they might suggest a claim for negligent or intentional infliction of emotional distress, and they certainly show him in a bad light.

Once you are confident that the potential plaintiff has given you a candid and detailed narrative that appears to have legal merit, you are ready to move to the next stage. Of course, you will talk to the client again—for example, when research into a novel theory or into a possible defense leads to a need for more facts. Most importantly, you will talk to the client again when you have finished researching and brainstorming. You may decide that the client has one or more very strong claims—but the decision to litigate is the client's alone, and it must be made after a full and informed consideration of all her options.

### 2. Gathering Information: Researching the Law

Begin by researching any unfamiliar cause of action or potential cause of action carefully. You will need to find out, for example, whether Corcoran's abusive treatment of Spence after the accident gives rise to a claim of negligent or intentional infliction of emotional distress. Even where you are familiar with the elements of a cause of action—*e.g.*, negligent infliction of personal injuries— be sure that there are no special pleading rules that you need to take into account. For example, complaints in jurisdictions with no-fault automobile insurance statutes must frequently include allegations that the plaintiff sustained serious injuries and that damages exceed a statutory threshold.

You must of course research defendant's potential affirmative defenses as carefully as you research plaintiff's potential claims;

even the most meritorious claim is doomed if the statute of limitations has run. Yet you should beware of a tendency of new drafters—giving up too easily when caselaw or statute seems at first reading to go against you. Remember that no case is ever precisely like another, and while we are bound to avoid frivolous claims, a subtle analogy or distinction can make a case meritorious. So don't cut short your research at the first discouraging word: further research may suggest that your case fits within an exception to the statute, or that you can make a principled argument for an extension of analogous law or even for a change in the law.

Finally, although boilerplate forms and samples from the office files are an important research tool, try to hold off consulting them until you have done some brainstorming. Forms can close your mind to other theories of the case.

## 3. Conceptualizing

Once you have gathered facts that appear, as in Spence's case, to make out at least one claim and done some preliminary research on other available causes of action, the time has come to conceptualize the plaintiff's claims, asking what, who, and where. Start with a big sheet of unlined paper–this is better for brainstorming than lined paper or a blank computer screen. What are the facts of the incident? What causes of action arise from these facts? What defenses will the defendant(s) be likely to raise? What kinds of relief should be demanded? If money damages are to be demanded, how much? Whom should the plaintiff sue? Of course, Spence should sue the owner/operator of the vehicle. But perhaps she also has a case against the garage, with its dangerous parking procedures. Where should the suit be filed? Do considerations of personal jurisdiction, subject matter jurisdiction, and venue restrict plaintiff to one court, or is there a choice of forum? If there is a choice of forum—between federal court and state court, for example—which court is likely to be the better choice? Your choice of forum will be based not only on favorable procedural and substantive law, but also on the court's perceived receptiveness to claims like your client's.

In terms of parties and claims, you should be as inclusive as ethics and good sense permit. One way to be sure you have not overlooked any viable causes of action is to browse the table of contents of a form-book, deskbook, treatise, or other practitioner's guide. Be sure to include all factual theories as well as all legal theories. For example, Spence's cause of action for personal injuries is based on one legal theory (negligence) but at least two separate factual theories (failure to set the emergency brake and failure to repair it, for example). It is usually permissible to plead in the alternative, alleging inconsistent causes of action.[35]

Boilerplate form complaints and samples from the office files are an inevitable and often helpful resource for the drafter. But as noted earlier, forms and samples must be used with care. They can lead the hurried drafter astray in at least two ways: by causing him to omit a viable theory, because they do not include it, and by causing him to include a frivolous allegation, because they include it. Beware of out-dated forms also. If you are using a form-book, be sure to check the supplement or pocket-part to be sure that the law has not changed.

Once you have sketched out the basic causes of action—separating them by both legal theory and factual theory—you face the next conceptual challenge: which facts to allege, how to combine (or separate) them in paragraphs, and how generally or specifically to frame them. Because of its importance, this part of the complaint-drafting process is discussed below in the *Special Concerns* section.

When you arrive at a tentative outline of causes of action and the facts supporting them, test it out, checking especially for comprehensiveness and for unintended consequences.

## 4. Writing the First Full Draft

When you have a basic outline of the complaint and some rough drafts of allegations, be sure to answer any new questions—legal or factual—that have come up by talking to the client again and filling any gaps in your legal research. On the basis of your best thinking and the most comprehensive information, you are ready

---

[35] For example, Rule 8(e)(2) of the Federal Rules of Civil Procedure permits "as many separate claims or defenses as the party has regardless of consistency." Fed. R. Civ. P. 8(e)(2) (2003).

to write a complete draft. If you have done enough work at the conceptualization stage, this should be quite easy.

## 5. Revising and Polishing

As you revise your draft, keep your focus on the effect your allegations will have on the course of litigation—on the defendant's answer, on motion practice, on discovery—and also on its likely effect on other audiences. Follow this good advice from an expert.

> After one has finished drafting a complaint, one should try to answer it oneself. That exercise will reveal drafting and pleading defects and will disclose whether defendant may weasel out of answering certain allegations because of loose drafting. One should never forget that statements in a pleading are admissions. One wishes to force the other side to make admissions while avoiding making them oneself.[36]

When you can reasonably conclude that your complaint is appropriate to its goals, proofread and polish carefully. Be certain that you have expressed the allegations simply: genuinely confusing allegations will give the defendant the opportunity to deny what would otherwise have to be admitted. Worse still, confusing allegations may waste your client's time and money by prompting the defendant to make a motion for a more definite statement instead of answering the complaint.[37]

Proofread carefully—be sure that paragraphs are numbered consecutively and that references to previous paragraphs are correct. Cutting and pasting and inserting and deleting are especially hazardous in a document with numbered sections. If you use a complaint in an earlier case as a template, be sure to change all the particulars throughout the complaint. The transformation in mid-complaint of Janet Spence into previous client Stanley Robinson, "she" into "he," or Corcoran's BMW into a previous

---

[36] Davies, *supra* n. 23, at 26.

[37] Under the Federal Rules, a complaint "so vague and ambiguous that a party cannot reasonably be required to frame a responsive pleading..." may entitle the defendant to a more definite statement. Fed. R. Civ. P. 12(e) (2003). Similar rules exist in state courts.

defendant's Ford Explorer will be embarrassing. Mistakes like these give the court, your client, and your adversary the impression of hasty and sloppy work. Try to proofread in hard copy, where errors are easier to see.

If you need further incentive to proofread meticulously, consider this: in the course of litigation, your complaint is likely to be quoted by your adversary, and perhaps even by the court. All quotation must be verbatim, of course—errors and all. Your adversary will point out your missing apostrophe or other error with a self-satisfied "[sic]." Counsel's typos have been known to make it all the way to opinions of the United States Supreme Court. Don't give your mistakes this opportunity for upward mobility.

If you have not filed the same type of complaint in the same court before, be sure to recheck the court rules to be certain that your format is correct—caption, paper size, ink color, font size, fasteners, cover. Be certain the court clerk does not reject your complaint on the day before the statute of limitation precludes the claim.

Be sure that your client not only sees the complaint, but actually reads it before it is filed. This is especially critical in a verified pleading, where the client swears to the truth of his allegations under penalty of perjury. Even if the facts are precisely those your client told you, you do not want to risk the following exchange during discovery, at the deposition of your client.

| | |
|---|---|
| Opposing Counsel: | Is this your complaint? |
| Your Client: | Yes. |
| Opposing Counsel: | Did you ever read it before today? |
| Your Client: | No. |
| Opposing Counsel: | Is this your signature swearing that the allegations in the complaint are true? |
| Your Client: | Yes. |
| Opposing Counsel: | Why did you sign this if you hadn't read it? |
| Your Client: | Because my attorney told me to.[38] |

Now that you have a carefully drafted complaint that has been reviewed by your client, you are ready for the last step: filing the

---

[38] Davies, *supra* n. 23, at 585.

complaint with the court and serving it on your adversary. Local rules will tell you how to do this.

## E. SPECIAL CONCERNS

A central concern of an attorney drafting a complaint is how much information to include in the body of the complaint and in how much detail. This concern is really three concerns—sufficiency, strategy, and storytelling.

### 1. Sufficiency

Even the most creatively conceived and strategized complaint risks dismissal if it does not allege every element of a cause of action. Procedural rules in all jurisdictions—notice-pleading and fact-pleading alike—authorize dismissal of a complaint for failure to state a claim. Although the Federal Rules and its many state cognates require only notice of a claim, the claim must be one entitling the pleader to relief, that is, a legally cognizable claim, and there can be no such claim that does not contain all of the elements of at least one cause of action.[39] For example, if the drafter of a complaint alleging sexual harassment forgets to allege that the harassment negatively affected plaintiff's employment, the drafter may have told a sorry tale, but she has not made out a cause of action. The defendant will certainly and with justification move to dismiss for failure to state a claim. Even though the court will probably permit the plaintiff to replead, counsel's omission will have needlessly wasted time and money.

In addition to making out every element of a claim, a complaint must display the degree of particularity required for that claim in that jurisdiction. If you rely on conclusions of law, alleging the existence of a "contract" without specifics, or accusing defendant of "negligent conduct" without specifying the precise actions complained of, a court in a fact-pleading jurisdiction may well grant defendant's motion to dismiss for failure to state a cause of action. Moreover, even in notice-pleading jurisdictions, certain

---

[39] In the federal courts, a complaint may be dismissed for "failure to state a claim upon which relief can be granted." Fed. R. Civ. P. 12(b)(6) (2003). For a discussion of motions to dismiss for failure to state a claim or cause of action, *see infra*, Chapter 4, *Motions*, Section A(5).

claims must be pleaded with particularity. If local rules require defamation to be pleaded with particularity, it is not sufficient to allege, for example, that defendant "suggested that plaintiff's article was not his original work and made other derogatory statements to similar effect." Like the omission of an element of a cause of action, failure to plead specifics will rarely doom your client's cause—amendment and repleading are widely available—but it is both embarrassing and costly.

Finally, while you must make sufficient allegations, you should confine those allegations strictly to the elements of plaintiff's claims. When you anticipate an affirmative defense, it is tempting to try to rebut it by allegations in the complaint. Many courts will support defendant's refusal to answer such allegations, however, deeming them "surplusage."[40] All you will have accomplished is to give your adversary a helpful preview of your litigation strategy. Worse, in your attempt to rebut the defense, you may inadvertently have made damaging admissions.

## 2. Strategy

Your tactical aim is to draft allegations that will focus discovery where you want it and elicit the maximum number of significant admissions from defendant. Admissions are desirable not only because they reduce your work in discovery and your proof at trial, but also because they are the last word on the subject: unlike trial evidence, which the fact-finder may believe or reject, admissions, once made, will be accepted as true for the remainder of the proceedings.

The goals of focused discovery and maximum admissions are best served by allegations as precise and narrow as your knowledge and that of plaintiff allow. Although permissible in notice-pleading, broad and conclusory allegations will certainly be denied (*e.g.*, "Negligence on the part of defendant caused the automobile to roll down-hill, striking plaintiff"). In some notice-pleading jurisdictions, defendant will merely respond to such an allegation by noting that it is a conclusion of law and therefore requires no answer. Moreover, if conclusory allegations render your complaint so vague or ambiguous that defendant cannot

---

[40] Charles Alan Wright & Arthur R. Miller, *Fed. Prac. & Proc. 2d* § 1276 (West 1990).

reasonably be expected to answer it, defendant will make, and win, a motion for a more definite statement.

Wherever possible, you should frame allegations so precisely and accurately that they cannot be denied without falsehood—although you may well include a conclusory allegation as a separate paragraph, in order to make absolutely plain the nature of your claim. If you are absolutely certain of a significant fact, *e.g.*, in our hypothetical, the cause of the accident, you should allege it. ("The defective condition of the emergency brake caused the car to roll backwards down the hill.") Bear in mind that you are permitted to plead alternative and inconsistent theories—you may also allege that defendant's failure to engage the emergency brake caused the car to roll. But you should make narrow allegations *only* where you are certain of your facts—in Spence's case, if there is no doubt that the emergency brake was disengaged. If you are wrong (*e.g.*, the transmission was at fault), defendant will simply deny the allegation and you will be no further along than if you had simply alleged "negligence" on defendant's part. If you did not know for certain that the brake was disengaged, you might allege in the alternative "defective condition of the vehicle" and "failure of the defendant to park his vehicle safely."

In addition to being stated as narrowly or broadly as good litigation strategy requires, allegations should ordinarily be made singly, one per paragraph. Each paragraph should ideally contain just one allegation stated in just one sentence so that defendant is forced to give a clear answer. Pleading rules sometimes request one allegation per paragraph, where practicable;[41] and in any event, making two allegations in one sentence is asking for trouble. For example, there are two material allegations in the sentence "The accident was caused by a faulty emergency brake, a condition whose existence was known, or should have been known, to defendant." If pleading rules permit the defendant to deny the entire paragraph because he denies part of it, the defendant's denial will leave plaintiff's counsel wondering what has been denied—both allegations, or just one. If the allegations had been separated, defendant might have admitted that the brake was defective, but denied that he knew or should have known about it. If pleading rules require the defendant to answer every

---

[41] *See* Fed. R. Civ. P. 10 (2003); N.Y. Civ. Prac. L. & R. § 3014 (McKinney 2003).

allegation individually, the plaintiff's conjoining of allegations will not be so consequential, but there is still a real chance that defendant will miss an allegation, answer mistakenly, or answer so confusingly that plaintiff will misunderstand the answer.[42]

Combining conclusions of law with specific allegations also muddies the water. Confronted with the allegation "The car rolled down-hill because of defendant's negligent failure to repair the emergency brake," defendant might deny the entire paragraph because he denied the allegation of negligence, even though he would have been compelled to admit an allegation that the faulty emergency brake caused the car to roll. Relentless conclusory accusations of wrong-doing are often counter-productive.

Finally, where you are reasonably sure of a fact but do not know it of your own knowledge, you should always allege it "on information and belief." If you are certain of the date of an occurrence, say "On May 30, 2002...." Resort to the time-worn formulation "on or about May 30, 2002...." when you are not sure, bearing in mind that a complaint in which everything is alleged "on information and belief" and everything happens "on or about..." suggests lack of inquiry (and lack of interest) on the part of plaintiff's counsel.[43] The key—ignored to their detriment and that of their clients by too many practitioners—is to know what you know and what you do not know.

## 3. Storytelling

The allegations in a competently drafted complaint are legally sufficient and responsive to the appropriate strategic concerns. Yet, as noted earlier, their effectiveness can often be enhanced by narrative skill. By using some basic storytelling devices—character, scene, detail, and point of view—you can give your complaint rhetorical as well as instrumental force. Just a few artful

---

[42] For a discussion of the requirements for defendant's answer to plaintiff's complaint, *see infra*, Chapter 3, *Answers*.

[43] Sometimes "on or about..." is good strategy, however. Since, like all allegations in the complaint, dates are admissions by the plaintiff, you will not want to allege precise dates where defendant is likely to raise a statute of limitations defense. Stating the precise date may make it possible for defendant to move immediately for dismissal of the complaint.

touches can turn boilerplate into a story that elicits in the reader belief in its truth and a desire to make plaintiff whole.[44]

For example, you can develop the characters in your complaint, plaintiff and defendant, so they feel real, not like cardboard prototypes. Character can be established directly—through a description in the identification of the parties—or indirectly through actions, or even through a single quote. For example, describing plaintiff as "a physical therapist employed at Palmetto Children's Hospital" creates a positive impression of her character. Defendant's character, in contrast, could emerge from his words after the accident ("When he saw that his car had struck plaintiff, defendant screamed at her, 'why didn't you get out of the way, you silly old bat'").

Setting the scene carefully helps the reader see events unfold. A careful description of the multilevel parking garage and its ramps would make the accident in our hypothetical frighteningly real.

Detail—whether one telling detail or numerous carefully researched details—is crucial to effective narration. Detail elicits emotion, creates mental pictures, stimulates associations, and gives credibility to narrative. There is no rule of thumb about how much detail to provide. This is most usually a function of how much reasonably certain detailed knowledge the drafter possesses and how the strategic and rhetorical goals of the complaint relate to each other. In our hypothetical, specific details of plaintiff's injuries and treatment would make her story more than just a generic car accident. Single details like the makes and models of their respective vehicles (her KIA, his BMW) would also speak volumes about the parties.

But never confuse useful detail with unnecessary, unhelpful descriptive adjectives. For instance, the drafter might be tempted to allege that "the defective condition of the emergency brake caused the defendant's vehicle to roll rapidly down the steep ramp." The defendant might (at worst) deny this allegation in totality, or (at best) make a confusing answer to it, because the vehicle rolled slowly or the ramp is not steep, even though the

---

[44] For more on the use of storytelling techniques in complaint drafting, see Elizabeth Fajans & Mary R. Falk, *Untold Stories: Restoring Narrative to Pleading Practice,* 15 J. Legal Writing Inst. 3 (2009).

cause was indeed the defective brake. Although the precise gradient of the ramp would lend credibility to the story and the storyteller, calling it "steep" seems mere rhetorical flourish. The most effective stories are often the simplest. In our case, the reader does not have to be told that the ramp was "steep" or the descent "rapid" in order to imagine the plaintiff's terror as several tons of steel rolled toward her.

Finally, like detail, point of view and voice can be used to lend credibility to plaintiff's story. In traditional complaints, the point of view and voice are unmistakably that of a lawyer, and at best, the uninflected, unemotional tone of the allegations conveys a sense of objectivity and trustworthiness, so long as the story is not smothered in legalese. Yet credibility can often be further enhanced if the allegations comprise a third-person narrative told from the plaintiff's point of view and told, if not in plaintiff's own voice, at least in a voice the plaintiff can recognize. In our hypothetical, the story could be told effectively from either point of view, though the accident begs to be told from the point of view of the startled and helpless plaintiff seeing and hearing the car roll closer and closer to her.

---

### *Exercise 2.1*

*Read the draft of the body of a complaint in an action for professional malpractice that follows. Assume that plaintiff is not required to plead jurisdiction or venue. Can you identify allegations of evidentiary fact, allegations of ultimate fact, and conclusions of law? Would these allegations pass muster in a fact-pleading jurisdiction? In a notice-pleading jurisdiction? Assuming the allegations state a cause of action, do you think defendant's likely answers will meaningfully narrow the issues?*

1. Defendant Carolyn Miller is an attorney licensed to practice law in the state of _____.
2. On June 5, 20__, plaintiff engaged defendant to represent him in an action for false imprisonment and personal injury action against Morrison's Department Store.
3. As a result of the attorney-client relationship created by the parties, defendant had a duty to represent plaintiff with the reasonable care, skill, and diligence possessed by the ordinary attorney in similar circumstances.

4. Defendant failed to represent plaintiff with such care, skill, and diligence.

5. Defendant's failure to adequately represent plaintiff was a breach of her duty to plaintiff.

6. As a result of defendant's breach of her duty to plaintiff, plaintiff sustained injury. Specifically, plaintiff's injury includes the loss of a verdict, settlement, or award, and the interest that plaintiff would have recovered but for defendant's breach of her duty.

7. The injury sustained by plaintiff was proximately caused by defendant's breach of her duty. Plaintiff committed no negligent acts or omissions that contributed to his injury.

———————————— *Exercise 2.2* ————————————

*Critique and revise the following paragraph excerpted from a complaint alleging psychotherapy malpractice, editing the allegations and breaking them into individual paragraphs to create more effective allegations.*

10. Defendants were negligent and careless in services rendered for and on behalf of plaintiff, in negligently and carelessly neglecting to heed the plaintiff's condition, in negligently departing from accepted practices in the services rendered for and on behalf of plaintiff, in failing to perform indicated procedures appropriate to plaintiff's condition and in failing to follow good practice, specifically: in or about January, 2003, defendant Adams misdiagnosed and then treated plaintiff for the condition known as multiple personality disorder; upon information and belief, after making said misdiagnosis, defendant Adams sought professional supervision from both defendants Barker and Callahan, who supported and confirmed defendant Adams in said misdiagnosis; defendants Barker and Callahan separately treated plaintiff for the condition known as multiple personality disorder; thereby, defendants failed to properly treat plaintiff.

———————————— *Exercise 2.3* ————————————

*Analyze the negligence complaint for Janet Spence below. It was drafted by filling in the blanks of an official complaint form in a notice-pleading state.*

*1) Identify legalese and propose rewrites.*

*2) Determine which allegations are evidentiary fact, which are ultimate facts, and which are conclusions of law.*

*3) Assess the strategic value of the allegations as framed here. Will they elicit meaningful admissions and denials from defendant? What will the effect on discovery be? How might the allegations be more usefully framed?*
*4) Assess the impact of this complaint on other audiences—specifically, the court and the plaintiff. How could we revise to create a draft that would be strategically sound and at the same time a narrative that does justice to plaintiff's story?*

Superior Court of the State of Pacifica
County of Ocean

_____

Janet Spence,
        Plaintiff,                                    COMPLAINT

    -against-
                                   Index No. _____
Michael Corcoran,
        Defendant.

_____

Plaintiff, by her attorney, Susan J. Fox, for her complaint against the defendant, respectfully shows to the court and alleges:

1. That at all times herein and hereinafter mentioned, plaintiff was and still is a resident of the county of Ocean, city of Palmetto, State of Pacifica.
2. Upon information and belief, that at all times herein mentioned, defendant, Michael Corcoran, owned, operated, managed, maintained, and controlled a certain automobile bearing Pacifica Registration No. 784371721 for the year 20__.
3. That at all times herein mentioned, the plaintiff was lawfully upon premises known as the E-Z Park Garage located at 356 South Shore Drive, city of Palmetto, county of Ocean, state of Pacifica.
4. That at all times herein mentioned, there was a vehicular ramp inside the said premises.
5. That on or about the third day of June, 20__ at about 6:00 P.M. thereof, the plaintiff was lawfully upon the lower portion of said ramp.
6. That at that time and place, the vehicle of the defendant, which had previously been parked at the upper portion of the ramp

by defendant, rolled down the ramp, striking plaintiff, pinning plaintiff against another vehicle, and causing plaintiff to sustain serious and severe injuries.

7. That the accident and the resulting injuries were caused by the negligence of the defendant.

8. That the defendant was negligent in operating, maintaining, and controlling his vehicle in a careless and imprudent manner; in failing to operate the emergency brake; and in so failing to operate, maintain, and control the motor vehicle so as to avoid the occurrence of the accident.

9. That by reason of the foregoing, plaintiff Janet Spence sustained serious and severe injuries to her person which have rendered her sick, sore, lame, and disabled, causing her great pain and suffering and limiting and restricting her activities; upon information and belief, the disability and suffering will be permanent.

10. That by reason of the foregoing, plaintiff Janet Spence was obliged to seek and receive medical advice, care, and treatment in an effort to alleviate her pain and suffering and be cured of her injuries; upon information and belief, this plaintiff will be obliged to seek and receive further medical advice, care, and treatment in the future as a result of her injuries.

11. That by reason of the foregoing, plaintiff Janet Spence has been damaged in the sum of one million ($1,000,000) dollars.

12. That as a result of the foregoing, plaintiff has sustained economic loss greater than basic economic loss, as defined in subsection (d) of section 7194 of the Insurance Law of the State of Pacifica. [*no-fault insurance law*].

13. That as a result of the foregoing, plaintiff has sustained serious injury, as defined in subsection (e) of Section 7194 of the Insurance Law of the State of Pacifica. [*no-fault insurance law*]

WHEREFORE, Plaintiff Janet Spence demands judgment against the defendant in the sum of one million ($1,000,000) dollars; all together with the costs and disbursements of this action.

_____

Attorney for Plaintiff
150 Court Street
Palmetto
Pacifica 90212
(678) 342-1957

---
## *Exercise 2.4*
---

*Critique the two complaints that follow. Both were filed in federal court. Both are straightforward "slip-and-fall" complaints alleging negligent conduct by the defendants. There, however, all similarity ends. Example A is a bare-bones notice-pleading complaint, while Example B fleshes out its allegations. Assume both would be sufficient to survive a motion to dismiss for failure to state a claim. Compare the two complaints, focusing on strategy and storytelling. What practical and strategic considerations might explain the sparseness of one and the fullness of the other? How will each focus discovery? Elicit admissions? How and how successfully are character, scene, detail, and point of view used?*

*Note that these complaints have been excerpted to focus on substantive allegations: procedural matters such as subject matter and personal jurisdiction, venue, and signatures have been omitted.*

### Example A

UNITED STATES DISTRICT COURT,
NORTHERN DISTRICT, ALABAMA

------------------------------------------------x
                        :

MARY SUE BREEDEN,        :
            Plaintiff,   :     **COMPLAINT**
                        :
      v.               :
                        :
HILTON HOTELS CORPORATION, :
a Delaware corporation; et al.   :
          Defendants.  :
------------------------------------------------x

* * * *

Plaintiff Mary Sue Breeden hereby complains of the defendants Hilton Hotels Corporation, a Delaware corporation, [and other named defendants]…. The claims, actions and causes of action described herein arise out of a March 21, 2002, injury event occurring in Alexandria, Egypt.

## JURISDICTION

\* \* \* \*

## IDENTIFICATION OF PARTIES

4. The plaintiff, Mary Sue Breeden is a resident citizen of Morgan County, Alabama, residing at 2805 Lexington Avenue, SW, Decatur, Morgan County, Alabama 35603.

5. Defendant Hilton Hotels Corporation is a Delaware corporation whose principal place of business is located in the State of California (hereinafter "Hilton Hotels"). Hilton Hotels, however, conducts business in at least two locations within the Northern District of Alabama.

\* \* \* \*

9. On March 21, 2002, the plaintiff was a business invitee on the premises of the Hilton Borg El Arab Resort, Matrouh Desert Road, Borg El Arab, Egypt, in or near Alexandria, Egypt (hereinafter, "the Premises").

10. At all times relevant hereto, … [the Defendants] were the owners of; through their agents, the possessors of; and otherwise through such agents and employees, exercised control, maintenance, supervision and/or management over the Premises.

11. On March 21, 2002, the Defendants negligently and/or wantonly caused, permitted, allowed, or created a dangerous condition to exist on the Premises in the form of water on a tiled surface over which pedestrian traffic was allowed. The Defendants had actual notice and/or had constructive notice of this condition and/or failed to exercise reasonable care with respect to their maintenance of the Premises, thereby negligently and/or wantonly failing to discover and remove this condition.

12. As a proximate consequence of the aforesaid negligence and/or wantonness, the plaintiff was caused to slip and fall, and to incur the following injuries and damages: injury, incurred hospital, doctor and medical expenses, … physical pain, permanent disability and impairment, and mental anguish.

WHEREFORE, … the plaintiff Mary Sue Breeden demands judgment against the Defendants, jointly and severally, in the amount of Five Hundred Thousand And No/100 Dollars ($5,000,000.00), plus costs.

\* \* \* \*

**Example B**

UNITED STATES DISTRICT COURT,
SOUTHERN DISTRICT OF NEW YORK
-----------------------------------------------------------x
                                     :

ROBERT H. BORK,
             Plaintiff,                :           **COMPLAINT**
                                       :
            v.                       :
                                       :

THE YALE CLUB OF NEW YORK CITY,  :
a Delaware corporation; et al.         :
                   Defendants.    :
-----------------------------------------------------------x

\* \* \* \*

## NATURE OF THE ACTION

1.  This is a personal injury action brought against Defendant Yale Club of New York City (the "Yale Club") for its negligent and grossly negligent failure to maintain reasonably safe facilities.

## PARTIES

2.  Plaintiff Robert H. Bork is a resident and citizen of Virginia. He was injured while visiting the Yale Club in New York, New York, to give a speech at an event there on June 6, 2006.

3.  Defendant Yale Club of New York City is a private club with its principal place of business at 50 Vanderbilt Avenue, New York, New York 10017. The Yale Club offers guestrooms, restaurants, athletic, banquet and meeting facilities for its members and their guests.

## VENUE AND JURISDICTION

\* \* \* \*

## FACTUAL ALLEGATIONS

6.  On the evening of June 6, 2006, the New Criterion magazine held an event (the "New Criterion event") at the Yale Club. The New

Criterion invited Mr. Bork, among other guests, to deliver remarks at the event.

7. The New Criterion hosted the event in a banquet room at the Yale Club. As the host of the event, the Yale Club provided tables and chairs where guests could sit during the reception and the evening's speeches. At the front of the room, the Yale Club provided a dais, atop which stood a lectern for speakers to address the audience.

8. Because of the height of this dais, the Yale Club's normal practice is to provide a set of stairs between the floor and the dais. At the New Criterion event, however, the Yale Club failed to provide any steps between the floor and the dais. Nor did the Yale Club provide a handrail or any other reasonable support feature to assist guests attempting to climb the dais.

9. When it was his turn to deliver remarks to the audience, Mr. Bork approached the dais. Because of the unreasonable height of the dais, without stairs or a handrail, Mr. Bork fell backwards as he attempted to mount the dais, striking his left leg on the side of the dais and striking his head on a heat register.

10. As a result of the fall, a large hematoma formed on Mr. Bork's lower left leg, which later burst. The injury required surgery, extended medical treatment, and months of physical therapy.

11. Mr. Bork suffered excruciating pain as a result of this injury and was largely immobile during the months in which he received physical therapy, preventing him from working his typical schedule before the injury. The months of relative inactivity weakened Mr. Bork's legs so that he still requires a cane for stability. In addition, Mr. Bork continues to have a limp as a result of this injury.

## FIRST CAUSE OF ACTION
### [Negligence]

12. The allegations set forth in paragraphs 1 through 11 of this Complaint are realleged and incorporated by reference as if fully set forth herein.

13. The Yale Club had a duty to provide reasonably safe facilities in its reception and meeting rooms, including providing a safe dais of reasonable height and with stairs between the floor and the dais and a supporting handrail.

14. At the New Criterion event, the Yale Club breached its duty to provide reasonably safe facilities by failing to provide a safe dais and stairs between the floor and the dais, a supporting handrail, or any

other reasonable support feature to protect its guests attempting to mount that dais.

15. It was reasonably foreseeable that, by failing to provide a safe dais and stairs between the floor and the dais, a supporting handrail, or any other reasonable support feature, a guest such as Mr. Bork attending the New Criterion event would be injured while attempting to mount the dais.

16. The Yale Club's negligent failure to provide reasonably safe facilities, and in particular, its failure to provide a safe dais and stairs between the floor and the dais, a supporting handrail, or any other reasonable support feature to protect its guests attempting to mount the dais, caused Mr. Bork to fall while attempting to mount the dais and caused his extensive and continuing injuries.

17. As a result of the Yale Club's negligence in failing to provide reasonably safe facilities, Mr. Bork has suffered actual damages. These damages include pain and suffering, a continuing leg injury, medical bills and related costs of treatment, and lost work time and income. The long-term effects of his injuries continue to manifest themselves.

\* \* \* \*

## PRAYER FOR RELIEF

**WHEREFORE**, Plaintiff demands the following relief against Defendant:

A.  Awarding actual damages resulting from Defendant's wrongdoing in excess of $1,000,000;

B.  Punitive damages in an amount to be proven at trial;

C.  Pre- and post-judgment costs, interest and attorney's fees;

D.  Such other and further relief as this Court may deem appropriate and equitable.

\* \* \* \*

―――――――――――― *Assignment 2.1* ――――――――――――

*Revise the sample complaint in Section C above,* Hustin v. Freeman and the Regents of the University of Atlantis, *as though it were to be filed in your local state court of competent jurisdiction. Once you determine what court that would be, you will need to research the rules pertaining to complaints filed in that court alleging the causes of action in our sample. You will need to know whether notice pleading is permitted, and if not, how strict the fact-pleading rules are. (If you are in a fact-pleading jurisdiction, you may take pedagogical license to invent facts as needed.) You will also need to know at a minimum whether jurisdiction and/or venue must be pleaded, whether a specific amount may (or must) be pleaded in the* ad damnum *clause, whether signature is required, and whether the plaintiff must verify the complaint.*

———————————— *Assignment 2.2* ————————————

*Based on the facts in the interview summary in Casefile 1 in Appendix A, draft a complaint for Nancy Williams to be filed in a Minnesota court against her former supervisor, Michael Bryant, and her former employer, the Board of Parish Life of Grace Church. Assume you have decided to allege sexual harassment under the Minnesota Human Rights Act ("MHRA") against both Bryant and the Board. In addition, you will include a claim of "retaliation" by the Board (also under the MHRA). Finally, you will allege breach of contract by the Board. The relevant portions of the MHRA are included in the casefile.*

———————————— *Assignment 2.3* ————————————

*Assignment 1.1 in "Conceptualizing" asked you to brainstorm and tentatively outline claims arising out of an incident described by a new client, Tess Crane. Her son was injured when he fell from an old fire tower in the Nevada Bird Sanctuary. (If you have not done Assignment 1.1, that will be your first step!) Assume no relevant facts or cases have come to light other than those mentioned in Assignment 1.1. Based on your earlier work, draft a complaint in this case, following the Nevada procedural rules that follow. Include a cover sheet that explains both the strategic decisions you made about what claims to bring against whom and by whom, and a discussion of how the defendants might respond to your complaint.*

**Rules of Practice for the Second Judicial District Court of the State of Nevada**

### Rule 10. Form of pleadings.

1. All pleadings and papers presented for filing must be flat, unfolded, firmly bound together at the top, on white paper of standard quality, not less than 16-lb. weight and 8 1/2 x 11 inches in size. All papers must be typewritten or prepared by some other duplicating process that will produce clear and permanent copies equally legible to printing. The print size shall not be more than 10 characters per inch, *e.g.*, pica. Carbon or

photocopies may not be filed, except as provided in paragraphs 4 and 6 of this rule. Only one side of the paper may be used.

All papers presented for filing, receiving or lodging with the clerk shall be pre-punched with 2 holes, centered 2 3/4" apart 1/2" to 5/8" from the top edge of the paper. All original papers shall be stamped ORIGINAL between the punched holes in red ink.

The lines on each page must be double spaced, except that descriptions of real property may be single spaced. Pages must be numbered consecutively at the bottom.

2.   No original pleading or paper may be amended by making erasures or interlineations thereon, or by attaching slips thereto, except by leave of court.

3.   The following information shall appear upon the first page of every paper presented for filing:

(a)   The document code…[the document code here is "COMP"]; the name, Nevada State Bar identification number, address and telephone number of the attorney and of any associated attorney appearing for the party filing the paper; whether such attorney appears for the plaintiff, defendant, or other party; or the name, address and telephone number of a party appearing in proper person, shall be set forth to the left of center of the page and shall be single spaced. The space to the right of center shall be reserved for the filing marks of the clerk.

(b)   The title of the court shall appear at the center of the page, below the information required by paragraph one as follows:

IN THE SECOND JUDICIAL DISTRICT COURT OF
THE STATE OF NEVADA IN AND FOR THE
COUNTY OF WASHOE

(c)   Below the title of the court shall appear in the space to the left of center, the name of the action or proceeding, *e.g.,*

JOHN DOE,
                              Plaintiff

      vs.

RICHARD ROE,
                              Defendant.

(d) In the space to the right of center at lines 11 and 12, shall appear the case number and the department number as follows.

Case No. CV99-00000

Dept No. 1

(e) The title of the pleading, motion or other document must be typed or printed on the page directly below the name of the parties at the action or proceeding. The title must be sufficient in description to apprise the respondent and clerk of the nature of the document filed, or the relief sought, *e.g.*, Defendant's Motion for Summary Judgment against Plaintiff John Doe; Plaintiff's Motion to Compel Answers to Interrogatories.

(Example)

CODE
NAME
BAR NUMBER
ADDRESS
CITY, STATE, ZIP CODE
TELEPHONE NUMBER
ATTORNEY FOR:

IN THE SECOND JUDICIAL DISTRICT COURT OF
THE STATE OF NEVADA IN AND FOR THE
COUNTY OF WASHOE

_____

JOHN DOE,

Plaintiff,

vs.

RICHARD ROE,

Defendant.

Case No. CV99-00000

Dept. No. _____

_____

COMPLAINT

**N.R.S. 13.040   Venue...**

1. ...[T]he action shall be tried in the county in which the defendants, or any one of them, may reside at the commencement of the action; or,

if none of the defendants reside in the state, or if residing in the state, the county in which they so reside be unknown to the plaintiff, the same may be tried in any county which the plaintiff may designate in his complaint....

### N.R.C.P. Rule 8    General Rules of Pleading
### (a) Claims for Relief

A pleading which sets forth a claim for relief...shall contain (1) a short plain statement of the claim showing that the pleader is entitled to relief, and (2) a demand for judgment for the relief to which he deems himself entitled. Relief in the alternative or of several different types may be demanded. Where a claimant seeks damages of more than $10,000, the demand shall be for damages "in excess of $10,000" without further specification of amount.

### N.R.S. 12.080.    Parent or guardian may maintain action for injury of minor child

The father and mother jointly, or the father or the mother, without preference to either may maintain an action for the injury of a minor child who has not been emancipated, if the injury is caused by the wrongful act or neglect of another. A guardian may maintain an action for the injury of his unemancipated ward, if the injury is caused by the wrongful act or neglect of another, the action by the guardian to be prosecuted for the benefit of the ward. Any such action may be maintained against the person causing the injury, or, if the person is employed by another person who is responsible for his conduct, also against that other person.

## Subject Matter Jurisdiction

NRS 4.370 1(b) confers jurisdiction upon Justices Courts in civil actions for damages for personal injury, if the damages claimed do not exceed $10,000. The District Courts have jurisdiction over such actions only if plaintiff claims more than $10,000 in damages.

# Chapter 3

# *LITIGATING:*
# *ANSWERS*

---

## A. IN GENERAL

The answer is first and foremost what its name suggests—a pleading in which defendant responds to the allegations in plaintiff's complaint. Defendant's response lets plaintiff and the court know which allegations defendant intends to dispute; in so doing, defendant "joins the issue" for resolution by the fact-finder. Defendant must respond in one of three ways to each allegation: he may deny it, admit it, or assert that on the basis of reasonable inquiry, his knowledge and information are insufficient to permit him to form a belief as to its truth.[1] Pleading insufficient knowledge and information has the effect of a denial.

In addition to this purely responsive function, the answer may also contain defendant's affirmative defenses.[2] By pleading an affirmative defense, defendant tells plaintiff, "Even if your allegations are true and establish every element of your claim against me, you will lose anyway, and here is the reason why." Some of the most common affirmative defenses are statute of limitations,

---

[1] Some courts, especially those in fact-pleading jurisdictions, permit defendant to answer "neither admitted nor denied..." so long as defendant provides a valid reason. The most common reasons concern the sufficiency of the complaint, for example, "because the allegation is a conclusion of law, and therefore, no answer is required."

[2] We say "may" here because defendant frequently has the option of raising some affirmative defenses by motion, *before* joining the issue by answering the complaint. However, if defendant chooses not to make a motion before answering, the defendant *must* ordinarily plead his affirmative defenses in the answer, and risks waiving defenses by not doing so. As so often in litigation, "it's all in the timing." Obviously, it is crucial to know the rules in your court regarding answers, pre-answer motions, and post-answer motions. For more on motion practice, *see* Section E, *Special Concerns*, and Chapter 4, *Motions*.

statute of frauds, lack of personal or subject matter jurisdiction, and contributory negligence.

Affirmative defenses are the modern pleading equivalent of the common law's "confession and avoidance." Although at common law, the defendant was required to admit ("confess to") plaintiff's allegations in order to avail herself of "avoidance" defenses, this is no longer the case. Just as plaintiff may plead in the alternative, so may defendant answer in the alternative: "I deny your allegations, but even if they are true, I have other defenses."

Beyond responding to allegations and pleading affirmative defenses, defendant may wish to raise claims against the plaintiff, called "counter-claims," or claims against a co-defendant, called "cross-claims." In that event, he will often raise such claims in the answer. Defendant may even be permitted to include claims against the other parties that are unrelated to the allegations of the complaint. If defendant has claims against someone other than plaintiff or a co-defendant arising out of the same transaction, they must usually be raised in a separate pleading, called a "third-party complaint."

The procedural rules regarding the raising of cross-, counter-, and third-party claims vary greatly from jurisdiction to jurisdiction—for example, whether a claim *must* be raised when answering on pain of waiver, or whether it *may* be raised; whether unrelated or third-party claims may be raised in the answer; whether claims are required to be included in the answer proper or in a separate document. These are complex rules the new civil practitioner must learn. Fortunately, the actual drafting of counter-claims, cross-claims and third-party claims is more straightforward. They are all affirmative pleadings, and thus their components, drafting process, and strategic concerns are identical in all important respects to those of complaints.

## 1. Responding to the Allegations of the Complaint

The essence of the answer is defendant's response to the allegations of the complaint. How you formulate your client's answers will depend to a great extent on local pleading rules. Although the permitted and required forms of response vary, some considerations are constant.

First and most important, plaintiff's allegations must be answered in good faith. Zealous advocacy neither requires nor justifies playing games with facts. Explicitly or implicitly, all pleading rules require fair answers to the plaintiff's allegations.[3]

Second, answers should always be drafted with care as well as with candor. In many jurisdictions, an allegation that is neither denied nor met with an assertion of "insufficient knowledge" is deemed admitted.[4] Although some attorneys in those jurisdictions deliberately and habitually make admissions by omission rather than stating them explicitly, it is hard to imagine a principled rationale for this practice, which seems to arise from a reluctance to make any admissions at all and from a desire to sow as much confusion in the plaintiff's camp as possible. When candor requires admissions, make them expressly; as one commentator points out, admissions by omission may only lead your boss and the court to wonder whether you know what you are doing.[5]

Most courts require that defendant respond individually to each and every allegation, using plaintiff's paragraph numbering for reference, stating, for example "Defendant denies the allegations in paragraph four, except that he admits to owning the property at 270 Shore Road," or "As to paragraph five, defendant has insufficient knowledge or information to form a belief as to its truth."[6] Even if plaintiff has combined multiple allegations in one paragraph—whether important facts, inconsequential details, or conclusions of law—defendant's answer should address each one specifically. Where court rules do not expressly prohibit denying an entire paragraph because the defendant denies one allegation contained in it, the defendant's duty to answer in good faith and the attorney's ethical and statutory duties would appear

---

[3] *See, e.g.,* Fed. R. Civ. P. 8(b) (2003) and N.J. R. Governing Civ. Prac. 4:5-3 (West 2003), both providing that denials "must fairly meet the substance" of the allegations denied.

[4] *See, e.g.,* N.Y. Civil Practice Law & Rules, 30189(a) (any allegation not denied directly or by alleging insufficient knowledge will be deemed admitted); Fed. R. Civ. P. 8(b) (2003) deems allegations "admitted when not denied in the responsive pleading"; the effect is to prohibit "the introduction of evidence contrary to allegations in the complaint which have not been denied." Jay E. Grenig, *2B West's Federal Forms, District Courts, Civil,* § 2020 (4th ed. West 1994).

[5] Mark Davies, 1A *West's McKinney's Forms, Civil Practice Law & Rules* § 4:381 (West 1992).

[6] *See, e.g.,* N.J. R. Governing Civ. Prac. 4:5-3 (West 2003), providing that "[a] pleader who intends in good faith to deny only a part or a qualification of an allegation specify so much of it as is true and material and deny only the remainder."

to condemn this pleading practice.[7] At best, such denials create undue confusion and the result in undue delay and expense when plaintiff moves for clarification. At worst, they can mislead plaintiff to his detriment and result in sanctions for defendant.[8]

The "general denial," in which defendant denies the complaint as a whole, is disfavored in most jurisdictions and is forbidden in many.[9] The rationale behind this disfavor is that it is hard to imagine a complaint in which there is nothing at all to admit; there is almost always something that candor compels defendant to admit—a name or date, the existence of a place or object, the fact of ownership or residence. Thus, a general denial is rarely an honest answer. Even where a general denial is permitted and can be made in good faith, a paragraph-by-paragraph denial may be preferable: it lets the court and plaintiff see that the answer has been thought through, that it is not hasty stonewalling. Indeed, the paragraph-after-paragraph repetition of "Defendant denies the allegations..." is even more likely than a general denial to give the court the desired impression that plaintiff's claims lack merit.

At the other end of the spectrum from general denials, but also disfavored in most jurisdictions, are answers in which defendant tells her side of the story. If plaintiff alleges that defendant was driving the vehicle that collided with his on the Los Angeles

---

[7] *See supra* n. 3, about defendant's duty to respond in good faith; *see also, e.g.,* Fla. Pldg. & Prac. Forms § 2:56 (West 1992) n.3, (Florida Rules of Admin. 2.060(d) require attorney to certify that there is "good ground to support" answer); *see generally* Fed. R. Civ. Pro. 11 (2003).

[8] The textbook example of a worst-case scenario is *Zielinski v. Philadelphia Piers, Inc.,* 139 F. Supp. 408 (C.D. Pa. 1956), discussed in Stephen Subrin, Thomas J. Main & Mark S. Brodin, *Civil Procedure, Doctrine, Practice, & Context* (Aspen 2000). In *Zielinski,* defendant denied an entire paragraph of allegations because it disputed the truth of one single allegation. The paragraph alleged that a vehicle under defendant's control had been negligently operated and caused injury to plaintiff. The only disputed fact was control—defendant had leased the vehicle to another company. The confusion and delay resulting from defendant's denial caused the statute of limitations to run, barring plaintiff's suit against the second company. The court subsequently deemed defendant's denial an admission, in effect punishing it for failing to respond to each specific allegation.

[9] *See, e.g.,* 2A Mich. Pldg. & Prac. § 24.1 (2d ed., West 1995) (denials required to be "explicit"); 3 Wis. Pldg. & Prac. Forms § 21.14 (3d ed. West 1998) (general denials abolished); N.J. R. Governing Civ. Prac. 4:5-3 (West 2003) (pleader may not generally deny allegations); *but see* Fed. R. Civ. Pro 8(b) (defendant may make a general denial of all the allegations).

Freeway on July 10, 2003, defendant may not respond "Defendant was in Cleveland on July 10, 2003," unless pleading rules expressly provide for this form of response; in most jurisdictions, she is limited to denying plaintiff's allegation. Jurisdictions that forbid or disfavor narrative answers typically call them "argumentative denials"; jurisdictions that encourage or require them typically call them "explanations."[10] As you might imagine, notice-pleading jurisdictions most often forbid narrative answers and fact-pleading jurisdictions often permit them.

Where defendant is permitted or required to give his version of events, he should first make an explicit denial of plaintiff's allegations. His explanation should conform to the applicable local pleading rules—usually the same rules that govern allegations in a complaint. Like the plaintiff in the complaint, defendant should take full advantage of the opportunity to tell his side of the story, while avoiding exaggeration or other inappropriate rhetorical flourishes and bearing in mind that his allegations are admissions.

A form of denial universally disfavored is the "negative pregnant"—an ambiguous denial that may or may not contain admissions. A negative pregnant is created by recasting the plaintiff's allegation as a denial, for example "Defendant denies that his vehicle collided with plaintiff's vehicle on the Los Angeles Freeway on July 10, 2003." This "denial" may also be read as an admission that defendant was involved in a collision with plaintiff, but that the date or place were different, or perhaps that he did not own the vehicle. Allegations containing the conjunctive formulations so characteristic of traditional legal prose will also create pregnant negatives when recast as denials. For example, the allegation "Defendant owned, operated, controlled, managed, and maintained said vehicle" will produce the negative pregnant "Defendant denies that he owned, operated, controlled, managed, and maintained said vehicle," which may be deemed to admit that defendant owned, operated, controlled, and managed the vehicle, but that she did not maintain it.

---

[10] *See, e.g.,* Davies, *supra* n. 5 ("argumentative denial" does not directly deny the allegation and may even be deemed an admission); *but see, e.g.,* 5 Stan. Pa. Prac. 2d § 26:37 (West 1992) (in answer, defendant should aver "what did happen...the facts constituting the denial").

It should be clear from the above examples that a negative pregnant can only be created from a sentence that contains more than one allegation. For example, if plaintiff alleges only "Defendant is a resident of California," the denial "Defendant denies that she is a resident of California" cannot be construed to contain an admission. The more allegations that plaintiff combines in one sentence, the more the ambiguities multiply if defendant makes this form of reply.

Negative pregnant denials should be avoided. Before the general liberalization of pleading rules in the last century, a negative pregnant would have been deemed an admission; although far less likely under modern pleading rules, such a dire result is still possible if the import of the denial is not clear. Moreover, even if the purported denial is not deemed an admission, defendant may be ordered to clarify the answer. At a minimum, ambiguous denials give the impression of sloppy or shady pleading, not an impression any practitioner wants to leave with the court.

The best way to avoid the negative pregnant is not to recast plaintiff's allegations as denials at all, but rather, to respond in this fashion: "Defendant denies the allegations in paragraph four, except that she admits to ownership of the vehicle at the time alleged." If you must answer by recasting plaintiff's allegations, provide clarification, for example: "Defendant denies that her vehicle, or any vehicle under her control, was involved in a collision with plaintiff's vehicle on the Los Angeles Freeway on July 10, 2003, or at any other time or any other place." The negative pregnant that arises from denial of a conjunctive ("and") list can be avoided by making the list disjunctive ("or") in the denial, for example, "Defendant denies that she owned, operated, controlled, managed, *or* maintained said vehicle."

## 2. Pleading Affirmative Defenses

The pleading rules in most jurisdictions provide lists of affirmative defenses.[11] Commonly listed defenses are lack of subject matter or personal jurisdiction, statute of limitations, statute of frauds, res judicata, incapacity to sue or be sued, contributory negligence, payment, failure of consideration, release, discharge

---

[11] *See, e.g.,* Fed. R. Civ. P. 8(c) (2003); Mich. Ct. R. 2.111 (West 2003).

in bankruptcy, waiver, mistake, fraud, laches, and duress. These lists are typically supplemented by catch-all clauses,[12] however, because the very concept of affirmative defenses to civil suits is a slippery one. The best definition—an affirmative defense is any defense arising from "new matter" not appearing in the complaint—is often hard to apply.[13] Some statutes also define an affirmative defense as matter which, if not pleaded, would be likely to take the plaintiff by surprise.[14] Given the vagueness of these definitions, the best rule is this: when in doubt, raise it. There is no penalty for mistakenly pleading a denial as an affirmative defense, so long as it is clear what allegations defendant disputes.[15] Moreover, given the risk that an affirmative defense will be waived if not raised in the answer, the best practice is to raise all plausible potential affirmative defenses.

The pleading of affirmative defenses is governed by the same basic rules that govern complaints. Thus, in notice-pleading jurisdictions, defendant need only give plaintiff fair warning of what affirmative defenses she asserts. It is sufficient, for example, to allege lack of personal jurisdiction without specifying the particular reason why jurisdiction is absent. In fact-pleading jurisdictions, more specificity will be required.[16] Even in notice-pleading jurisdictions, some affirmative defenses must be pleaded with specificity.[17]

In notice-pleading jurisdictions, defendant should usually make her allegations of affirmative defenses as general as pleading rules permit. This is because of the danger of waiver: if defendant raises her defense too specifically, she may waive an otherwise valid defense. For example, a defendant who raises an affirmative defense of lack of personal jurisdiction, specifying that "service of the complaint was improper" may preclude herself

---

[12] *Id.*

[13] *See* Charles Alan Wright & Arthur R. Miller, 5 *Fed. Prac. & Proc. Civ. 2d* § 1270 (West 1990).

[14] *See, e.g.,* N.Y. Civ. Prac. L. & R. 3018(b).

[15] *See, e.g., New York Life Ins. Co. v. Gamer,* 303 U.S. 161 (1938).

[16] For a review of the basics of notice-pleading and fact-pleading, *see supra,* Chapter 2, *Complaints,* Section A.

[17] For example, Rule 9 of the Federal Rules of Civil Procedure specifies the manner of pleading some defenses, including fraud, mistake, and denial of capacity to sue or be sued. Fed. R. Civ. Pro. 9 (2003).

from later arguing that the complaint had no jurisdictional basis. Where pleading rules permit, the wiser practice is to state the defense, but not the basis, alleging, for example, "The court lacks jurisdiction over the person of the defendant." If you are certain of your facts, and have good reason to believe that specificity will serve your client's interests, then you may plead in more detail, but be sure to add some qualifying phrase like "and other reasons," or "without limitation."[18]

The hazards of specificity in pleading affirmative defenses should not, however, lead the pleader to plead so generally that she does not provide fair notice of her defense. For example, in one notice-pleading jurisdiction, the bare allegation of "culpable conduct" on plaintiff's part was deemed insufficient to raise the affirmative defense of failure to wear a seat-belt.[19]

Where you can do so without fear of waiver, pleading strong affirmative defenses with more specificity than the rules require has one real advantage: it lets the court, plaintiff, and plaintiff's counsel know that you have a good case. This is probably the only advantage to such a practice, however. In the discussion of complaints in the previous section, we noted that precise allegations are desirable where possible, because defendant's responses in the answer will narrow the issues for discovery and trial. The same consideration does not apply to affirmative defenses pleaded in an answer, because in notice-pleading jurisdictions, the pleadings end with the answer—plaintiff does not respond to affirmative defenses unless the court orders such a response, called a "reply."[20]

In fact-pleading jurisdictions, drafting affirmative defenses is much like drafting the allegations in a complaint. The same degree of specificity is required, and specificity often also has tactical advantages. As in notice-pleading jurisdictions, it serves to alert the court and plaintiff to the strength of defendant's case. Moreover, where, as is frequently the case, plaintiff is required or permitted to respond to the defendant's allegations in a reply to the answer, plaintiff's responses to narrow allegations will narrow

---

[18] Davies, *supra* n. 5.

[19] *Id.* at 533, *citing Costanza v. City of New York,* 553 N.Y.S.2d 616 (Civil Ct. 1990).

[20] *See, e.g.,* Fed. R. Civ. P. 7 (2003); N.Y. Civ. Prac. L. & R. 3011, 3018(a).

the issues.[21] Nonetheless, the drafter must beware of waiving an affirmative defense by raising only a closely-related defense, a danger made greater by the exigencies of fact-pleading. Be sure to raise all plausible defenses.

## B. COMPONENTS

For the defendant's answer, as for all litigation documents, the required components and their precise format are prescribed by local rule. We describe the maximum number of components here: *caption, introductory sentence, body of the answer, affirmative defenses, affirmative claims, demand for judgment and relief (ad damnum clause), signature,* and *verification*.

### 1. Caption and Introductory Sentence

The *caption* is ordinarily copied verbatim from the complaint—including any mistakes that plaintiff may have made. To the right of the caption, the index or docket number is repeated and the document identified as an answer.

As with complaints, the *introductory sentences* in many form-books and office sample answers are framed in archaic language that goes back several centuries at least. There is no magic in those formulations; a simple opening is best: for example, "In response to the allegations of plaintiff Alice Adams, defendant Charles Connelly states the following through his attorney, Benjamin Bailey."

### 2. The Body of the Answer

The *body of the answer,* containing defendant's responses to plaintiff's allegations, ordinarily comes next. Where local rules permit, however, some practitioners begin with defendant's affirmative defenses, when those defenses are especially strong or sympathetic. In an appropriate situation, this can be effective advocacy, emphasizing the affirmative rather than the merely defensive, and putting the spotlight on defendant's story, especially

---

[21] *See, e.g.,* New Jersey Court Rules, 4:5-1; Louis S. Goldstein & Cindy Fluxgold, *Personal Injury Forms: Illinois,* § 3:34.50 (West 1992).

in one of the many jurisdictions that do not otherwise permit defendant to explain her side of the story in the answer.

Defendant responds to plaintiff's allegations in numbered paragraphs. There are two basic ways of organizing the responses. In the first pattern, defendant responds paragraph-by-paragraph, as follows.

> 1. Defendant admits the allegations in paragraph 1.
> 2. Defendant denies the allegations in paragraph 2, except that she admits that she is the owner of the property at 390 Beach Drive.
> 3. Defendant denies the allegations in paragraph 3.

In the second, defendant aggregates her responses by type, as follows.

> 1. Defendant denies the allegations in paragraphs 3, 4, 6, 7, 10, 12, &13.
> 2. Defendant is without sufficient knowledge or information to form a belief as to the allegations in paragraphs 2, 5, 8, 9, 11, & 14.
> 3. Defendant admits the allegations in paragraph 1.

One or the other of these patterns may be prescribed or usual in your local practice. If you have the choice, follow the first pattern, responding paragraph-by-paragraph: it is by far superior to aggregating your responses, for several reasons. First, matching paragraph to paragraph, the drafter is less likely to make mistakes. Aggregating responses, the drafter may easily (and disastrously) neglect to respond to a paragraph or may make a typographical error that has the effect of admitting an allegation the drafter meant to deny. Second, the first pattern makes both drafting and reading easier. Third, and most importantly, the aggregating, or "grouping" approach makes it difficult to respond specifically, too often leading the drafter to make less than candid responses. As one commentator puts it, "using this grouping approach, one inevitably tends to fudge responses...in order to force [them] into a particular paragraph...."[22] For these reasons, we follow the paragraph-by-paragraph pattern in our sample.

---

[22] Davies, *supra* n. 5.

Where the complaint realleges and incorporates earlier paragraphs, defendant's answer may do the same: "As to paragraph 14, incorporating the allegations of paragraphs 6–10 of the complaint, defendant realleges and incorporates the responses in paragraphs 6–10 of this answer." Finally, as in a complaint, allegations in an answer may be made upon information and belief.

## 3. Affirmative Defenses

Each *affirmative defense* is set forth separately, in numbered paragraphs. Affirmative defenses should be separated by headings— "First Affirmative Defense," "Second Affirmative Defense," and so on. If you are certain of the legal theory upon which a defense is based, including the name of the defense, *e.g.*, "Contributory Negligence," in the heading makes a more reader-friendly answer. If, however, the legal basis of your defense is not clear-cut, beware of naming it. As noted earlier, by giving your defense a name, you may commit yourself to one form of defense and waive another, perhaps even more viable, defense. If the complaint contains more than one cause of action, your headings should make plain the relationship of affirmative defense to cause of action—"First Affirmative Defense to Count One," for example. If the same defense relates to more than one count, you may either repeat it or use your heading to indicate that the defense applies to multiple counts—"Affirmative Defense to Counts One and Two."

## 4. Affirmative Claims

*Counter-claims, cross-claims,* and *third-party claims* follow the affirmative defenses. Their format is that of the complaint: allegations in separately numbered paragraphs, with separate headings for separate causes of action.

## 5. *Ad Damnum* Clause

As in a complaint, the *ad damnum* clause asks for judgment and relief against the opposing party. There are two basic ways to organize these requests. Defendant may make individual requests after each part of the answer. Alternatively, defendant may put all of his requests together, at the end, being sure to relate the requested relief to the specific part of the answer. Although there is more room for confusion in this organization, it is the more common, and has the advantage of letting the reader see all of the requested relief at a glance.

When an answer contains only responses to the allegations of the complaint and no counter-claim or other affirmative claim, the answer does not typically require an *ad damnum* clause. It is usual, nonetheless, for the defendant to request that plaintiff "take nothing by his action." In addition, it is customary to request costs, disbursements, and (if there is an affirmative claim) interest, although these matters are usually provided by statute.

## 6. Signature and Verification

It is good practice to date your answer, even if not required. The name, address, and telephone number of counsel are most often required. Most jurisdictions require counsel to sign all pleadings, including the answer. As noted earlier, counsel certifies by her *signature* that based on reasonable inquiry, she believes that the allegations in the pleading have a substantial basis in the law. In the *verification* clause, the defendant himself swears under penalty of perjury that to his knowledge the allegations in the answer are true, except for those allegations made on information and belief. An answer must be verified if the complaint was verified. In addition, certain types of affirmative defenses must be verified in some jurisdictions. Otherwise, verification is at the party's option.

# C. SAMPLE ANSWER

Superior Court of the State of Atlantis
County of Sussex

-------------------------------------------------------

Jeffrey Hustin,
          Plaintiff,

          -against-                                  ANSWER
                                                     Index No. Civ._____

Michele Freeman and
The Regents of the University of Atlantis,
          Defendants.

-------------------------------------------------------

In response to the allegations in the complaint of plaintiff Jeffrey Hustin, defendant Michele Freeman answers as follows, through her attorney, Lawrence Brenner.[23]

1. Defendant admits the allegations in paragraph 1 for purposes of jurisdiction only.[24]
2. Defendant is without sufficient knowledge or information to form a belief as to the allegations in paragraph 2.
3. As to the allegations in paragraph 3, defendant is without sufficient knowledge or information to form a belief, except that she admits that she herself is a citizen of the state of Atlantis.[25]
4. Defendant admits the allegations in paragraph 4.
5. Defendant admits the allegations in paragraph 5.
6. Defendant is without sufficient knowledge or information to form a belief as to the allegations in paragraph 6.
7. Defendant admits the allegations in paragraph 7.
8. Defendant admits the allegations in paragraph 8.
9. Defendant admits the allegations in paragraph 9.
10. Defendant admits the allegations in paragraph 10.

---

[23] This answer by defendant Michele Freeman responds to the sample complaint in Chapter 2. Compare allegations and answers as you read through. Note that defendant answers paragraph-by-paragraph, rather than aggregating her responses by type.

[24] The allegation in the complaint was that the action was "for damages in excess of $50,000," an allegation of subject matter jurisdiction. Why do you think defendant answered this allegation as she did?

[25] Defendant has no way of being certain where plaintiff and her co-defendants reside at the moment of her answer. She alleges lack of sufficient knowledge generally and makes a specific admission.

11. Defendant is without sufficient knowledge or information to form a belief as to the allegations in paragraph 11.
12. Defendant admits the allegations in paragraph 12.[26]
13. Defendant denies the allegations in paragraph 13.
14. Defendant denies the allegations in paragraph 14.[27]
15. Defendant is without sufficient knowledge or information to form a belief as to the allegations in paragraph 15.
16. Defendant is without sufficient knowledge or information to form a belief as to the allegations in paragraph 16.
17. Defendant is without sufficient knowledge or information to form a belief as to the allegations in paragraph 17.
18. Defendant is without sufficient information to form a belief as to the allegations of paragraph 18.
19. Defendant is without sufficient information to form a belief as to the allegations of paragraph 19.[28]
20. Defendant denies the allegations in paragraph 20.
21. As to paragraph 21, realleging and incorporating paragraphs 6–13, defendant realleges and incorporates her responses in paragraphs 6–13 of this answer.[29]
22. Defendant denies the allegations in paragraph 22.
23. Defendant denies the allegations in paragraph 23.
24. Defendant denies the allegations in paragraph 24.
25. Defendant denies the allegations in paragraph 25.

### Affirmative Defense to Defamation Claim
### (Privilege)[30]

26. The statements made in defendant's letter to the Status Committee of the University of Atlantis Law School attached as Exhibit A

---

[26] Defendant admits the truth of almost all of plaintiff's allegations concerning the background facts and her circulation of an allegedly defamatory memo concerning plaintiff's qualifications for academic tenure.

[27] Defendant denies the allegations that her statements were false and that they were defamatory.

[28] Paragraphs 16–19 of the complaint allege that various injuries were suffered by the plaintiff as a result of defendant's memo about him. Why might she have answered as she did?

[29] Where plaintiff realleges and incorporates in his complaint, defendant does the same in her answer.

[30] The heading names the affirmative defense, but generally. By specifying the precise privilege claimed (e.g., "qualified" privilege or "absolute" privilege), defendant could foreclose related defenses. Note that defendant specifies the claim to which her defense relates.

to plaintiff's complaint and restated in part in paragraph 12 of the complaint were made by defendant, a member of the bar of this State and of the legal academic community of this State, pursuant to her legitimate interest in the intellectual abilities and good character of potential members of that community and pursuant to her duty to communicate relevant information to persons with corresponding interests and duties.

27. The Status Committee of the University of Atlantis School of Law had a corresponding legitimate interest in the intellectual abilities and good character of plaintiff, a candidate for academic tenure in the field of law, and a duty to ensure that only persons of intellectual ability and good character are granted tenure.

28. Thus, the statements in defendant's letter to the Status Committee concerning plaintiff are privileged, and no liability for defamation may be premised upon them.

WHEREFORE: Defendant asks (1) that the relief claimed in plaintiff's complaint be denied and the complaint be dismissed and (2) that defendant be awarded the costs and disbursements of defending this action.

Dated: March 15, 20__.

Signed:_____[31]
Lawrence Brenner
Attorney for Defendant

Brenner, Perillo & Kahn, LLP
25 Judiciary Square
Atlantis City, Atlantis

---

[31] As with complaints, counsel is required to sign the pleading, and by so doing, counsel warrants his belief, based on reasonable inquiry, that the answer is not frivolous.

## VERIFICATION[32]

State of Atlantis       )
County of Sussex      ) ss.

On March 14, 20___, Michele Freeman personally appeared before me, a Notary Public for the State of Atlantis and County of Sussex. Being duly sworn, Michele Freeman deposed and said that she is a defendant in the above action and that the facts set forth in answer are true, except for those statements made upon information and belief, and as to those statements, she believes them to be true.

_____

Sworn and subscribed before me this 14th day of March, 20___.


_____

Notary Public
My Commission expires June 30, 20___.

_____

[32] Because the complaint was verified, the answer must also be verified, exposing the defendant to the penalties of perjury.

## D. WRITING PROCESS

As with all the documents in this book, the basic stages in the drafting of answers are gathering information, conceptualizing, writing a first full draft, and revising and polishing. As with other documents, too, the composition process is likely to be recursive, with new insights generating new research and research generating new insights. As with all the documents in this first part of our book, conceptualization is by far the most challenging stage. Deceptively simple, often short, answers nonetheless require you to think long, hard, and creatively. Counsel typically has a very limited amount of time in which to formulate *all* of defendant's arguments against plaintiff's claims; very few defenses can be raised once the answer is filed. The most meritorious afterthought defense is often the equivalent of no defense at all, exposing counsel to a malpractice claim.

In many important respects, the process of drafting an answer resembles that of drafting a complaint. You may want to review Section D, *Process,* in Chapter 2 on *Complaints,* before continuing. We will continue to follow the hypothethical case of *Spence v. Corcoran,* assuming that plaintiff Janet Spence has filed the complaint against Michael Corcoran set out above in *Exercise 2.3.* We will also assume that the complaint is adequate on its face—it states a claim upon which relief may be granted, and its allegations provide adequate notice of that claim.

### 1. Gathering Information: Getting the Facts

Gathering the facts from a client who has been served with a complaint is often more difficult than gathering the facts from a potential plaintiff. The defendant has been accused of wrongdoing, summoned to court, and threatened with substantial financial loss or other painful consequence. In this situation, it takes skill and patience to get all the important facts of the incident or transaction at issue. Unless the defendant trusts the interviewer, the defendant may stonewall, denying all allegations, or defendant may give the bare facts, leaving out telling details.

Moreover, in addition to interviewing in depth to elicit defendant's side of the story, counsel needs to interview on a broad range of related subjects, looking for possible affirmative defenses. It is a good idea to have a check-list of affirmative defenses at hand if you are not so experienced that you have internalized them. You should also be looking for possible affirmative claims— counter-claims, cross-claims, or third-party claims.

Assume that you have been asked to interview Michael Corc- oran, who has just very recently been served with the complaint set out in *Exercise 2.3.* You learn that the incident happened as it was described in the complaint: Corcoran's vehicle rolled down the garage ramp, pinning Spence against the back of her own vehicle, which was parked at the bottom of the ramp. Corcoran insists, however, that the vehicle had just come from the repair shop, and that he engaged the emergency brake before leaving the vehicle, just moments before the accident. He will have to feel comfortable in order to tell you that after the accident, the brake was found to be disengaged. He saw it with his own eyes, and the garage attendant saw it, too. It isn't easy for him to sup- ply facts that seem to call into question either his memory or his truthfulness, and to doom his defense.

In addition, Corcoran obviously feels very guilty about the in- cident and his bad behavior afterwards, when he verbally abused the plaintiff. This too will make fact-gathering difficult, because you need to probe for anything that might suggest contributory negligence on the plaintiff's part or that her injuries are less grave than the complaint makes out. You will get all that Corcoran knows only if you convey to him that you understand his feel- ings of discomfort and that defending himself within the law is not inconsistent with regret for plaintiff's suffering.

In addition to gathering facts that will help you represent de- fendant on the merits, you should also use the interview to gather information about procedural matters, the service of summons or complaint, for example, that may enable you to have the suit dismissed without ever reaching the merits. You must also check dates carefully to see whether defendant has a statute of limita- tions defense.

Finally, fact-gathering rarely ends with your interview of the client. Often, you need to do some fact-finding of your own, sometimes with the help of an expert. For example, in Corcoran's case, you would need to know whether the accident could have happened as he described it—whether, when a vehicle is parked on a slope, a defective emergency brake could disengage after being engaged, sending the vehicle rolling.

## 2. Gathering Information: Researching the Law

If you do not have a mentor or supervisor to help you, your first legal research port-of-call must be your local rules of procedure. First, you must know how much time defendant has to respond, and how, if necessary, the deadline may be extended; failure to respond within the statutory period will result in a default judgment. It is also crucial to understand defendant's procedural options. Defendant ordinarily has two basic courses of action: filing an answer or filing a pre-answer motion to dismiss the complaint.

Statutes prescribe the timing, permissible content, and effect of pre-answer motions and the relationship of answers and pre-answer motions. These statutes tend to be complex, confusing even to experts. Unfortunately, adherence to their tortuous precepts is enormously consequential—a misstep can result in the waiver of a defense. Whether defendant responds by answer or by motion is determined by the nature and strength of defendant's defenses and by multiple tactical and practical considerations. Unless you have mastered the minutiae of local practice concerning pre-answer motions and answers, or have a mentor, it is risky to undertake to represent a defendant in a civil suit. For the purposes of our discussion here, we will assume that defendant Corcoran's best course is to answer the complaint. Below, in *Special Concerns,* we have provided a brief discussion of the answer-versus-motion dilemma.

Once you have a good grasp on the relevant procedural law, you should continue your research by focusing on the merits, assessing the strength of plaintiff's case. For example, in defendant Corcoran's case, you would want to research the liability of a vehicle owner who did not know that his just-repaired vehicle had a serious mechanical defect.

In preparation for drafting an answer, your research will also focus on affirmative defenses and on any causes of action defendant may have against plaintiff or other parties, such as the car dealer, mechanic, or parking garage. A good way to get started on affirmative defenses is to leaf through the table of contents of a treatise, hornbook or practitioner's deskbook in the applicable area.

As you research potential defenses, resist the temptation to give up hope prematurely. Remember that defending has a built-in challenge—the complaint exists because a competent attorney believed the claim to have some merit. You will probably not find authority for the perfect slam-dunk defense. But you may well find a theory or analogy strong enough to provoke a settlement acceptable to your client.

## 3. Conceptualizing

When you brainstorm defendant's answer, it is essential to cast the net as wide as you can. As noted earlier in this chapter, there is a serious risk that any defense not raised in the answer will be deemed waived. The only defenses that may be raised at any time in the proceedings, even at trial, are lack of subject matter jurisdiction and failure to state a claim. Moreover, plaintiff will ordinarily be able to raise the issue of waiver at any time during the proceedings. So long as a defense is not frivolous and is raised in good faith, defendant will not be penalized if it turns out ultimately not to be an affirmative defense, or even to be unfounded. Remember that the definition of "affirmative defense" is quite elastic. Any defense that goes beyond the four corners of the complaint is likely to be an affirmative defense—even if it doesn't have a name.

As with all documents, begin with a big blank sheet of paper. Write down facts and legal concepts as they occur to you. Then begin connecting them, giving free-play to your imagination. Although boilerplate and office samples of affirmative defenses will be helpful, don't consult them until you have thought the issues through for yourself. Forms and samples can short-circuit creative and critical thought.

Moreover, boilerplate affirmative defenses pose an additional danger. Fearful of waiver, attorneys sometimes throw in every affirmative defense they find in boilerplate answers without thinking them through. The drafter's haste and ignorance will not be lost on opposing counsel and on the court. For example, an attorney defending in a wrongful death automobile accident case included a boilerplate statutory no-fault insurance defense in his answer. Since the statute in question bars litigation only where the plaintiff has not sustained "serious" injury, counsel unwittingly put himself in the position of making the novel argument that death is not a serious injury. Counsel could presumably have been sanctioned for raising such a totally frivolous defense, but he was not—he merely looked ridiculous in the eyes of the court and plaintiff's counsel. So be comprehensive, but relate law carefully to fact as you conceptualize affirmative defenses.

In the conceptual stage as in the research stage, do not despair if a water-tight defense does not appear. Novice drafters want to find the perfect solution, and feel they have failed if they do not. Perfect solutions are rare in the practice of law—and especially so in defense. If the suit against your client has been filed in good faith, it may well have some merit, and this is not your fault. If you only look for complete defenses, you run two risks—first, as noted above, you may give up, and second, you may overreach and exaggerate the merits of a defense. Neither of these outcomes will serve your client's interests.

When you have some rough drafts of affirmative defenses and of any claims against plaintiff, co-defendants or third parties, you are ready to move on to the next phase.

### 4. Writing the First Full Draft

Before you sit down to write your first full draft, be sure that you have done any research—legal or factual—necessitated by new theories that brainstorming has brought to light. Writing the draft will not be difficult if you've done a thorough job at the information-gathering and conceptualizing stages. It will, however, require great attention to detail.

Be certain that each and every allegation of the complaint is met with a clear and candid response. Be certain that numbers match—do not admit paragraph 5 if you mean to admit paragraph 6. Raise all your affirmative defenses—being certain to make allegations with the appropriate particularity or generality. Be certain to make all the allegations necessary to your affirmative defenses—do not omit any elements. Plead any counter-claims, cross-claims, or third-party claims as though you were drafting a complaint. Finally, make your claims for relief comprehensive, and ask for judgment against the plaintiff. If the complaint was verified, or if you are raising a defense that requires verification, be sure to include a verification clause.

## 5. Revising and Polishing

As you revise, put yourself in the place of the several audiences of the answer—plaintiff, plaintiff's counsel, the court, the defendant. Your answers must be so clear that plaintiff will not move for clarification, nor will the court deem ambiguous denials to be admissions. If your jurisdiction requires plaintiff to reply to affirmative defenses, try to anticipate those responses—be sure that your defenses are framed to elicit maximum admissions, narrowing the issues. If your answer includes affirmative claims, try to answer the allegations, putting yourself in the adverse party's place. Finally, ask yourself whether, to the extent that pleading rules, candor, and good strategy permit, you have put the defendant in a sympathetic light.

Answers must be proofread even more meticulously than complaints—be certain that there are no typographical errors in paragraph numbers in the answer or in references to paragraph numbers in the complaint.

As with complaints, have your client read (not just look at) the answer in your presence before it is filed, even if the client will not be verifying it. If your jurisdiction requires an attorney's signature, be sure to sign. Finally, follow the local rules for filing the answer with the court and serving it on plaintiff.

## E. SPECIAL CONCERNS: TIMING

The timing of defendant's answer is a matter of particular concern, and often of great perplexity, to the practitioner. As we noted above, the essence of the answer is defendant's response to plaintiff's allegations—defendant's "joining" of the issues for resolution by the factfinder. When a lawsuit has been commenced, defendant and counsel must decide whether to respond by joining the issue in an answer or by challenging the complaint by way of a motion to dismiss and filing an answer later, if the motion is denied.[33]

---

[33] We have simplified the choices somewhat here. In fact, most jurisdictions provide at least one, if not two, other motions that may be made before answering: A motion to strike irrelevant or "scandalous or prejudicial" material from the complaint, *see, e.g.*, N.Y. Civ. Prac. L. & R. § 3024(b), and a motion 'for a more definite statement," *see, e.g.*, Fed. R. Civ. P. 12(e) (2003). A motion to strike, rarely made, relieves defendant of

There are numerous grounds upon which a defendant may base a pre-answer motion to dismiss, although the grounds vary some-what from jurisdiction to jurisdiction. The Federal Rules of Civil Procedure and state procedural rules enumerate the permissible grounds of such motions.[34] Perhaps the most ubiquitous challenge is the motion to dismiss for failure to state a claim or cause of action. Lack of personal or subject matter jurisdiction typically may also be raised by motion before answering plaintiff's substantive allegations. Many jurisdictions also permit defendant to base a motion to dismiss on statute of limitations, statute of frauds, and other grounds that do not touch on the merits of the action.

Elaborate procedural rules govern the content of pre-answer motions to dismiss, and the relationship of motion to answer. When defendant chooses to make a motion instead of answer-ing, procedural rules require that certain defenses—for example, lack of personal jurisdiction or defective service of process—must be made in the motion or they will be deemed waived. Other defenses may be raised in the motion or in the answer, or even, like lack of subject matter jurisdiction and failure to state a claim, at any later point in the litigation.[35] As noted earlier, it is essen-tial that any practitioner engaged in civil litigation know these rules—the stakes are very high indeed.

The question of whether to join the issue or challenge the complaint by motion depends, of course, on the individual case. Many factors are relevant to a reasoned, principled, and effective decision. Consideration of the defendant's resources, the relative strength of the parties' cases, and the likelihood of early settle-ment is essential, but not conclusive. We propose here two rules

---

the duty to answer allegations defendant should not have to answer. The motion for a more definite statement, usually available in notice-pleading jurisdictions, lies where the complaint provides notice of a cause of action, but its allegations are so vague or ambiguous that defendant cannot reasonably be expected to answer.

[34] For example, under Rule 12(b) of the Federal Rules, a motion to dismiss may be based on lack of personal jurisdiction, lack of subject matter jurisdiction, improper venue, insufficiency of process (defect in the form of the summons), improper service of process, failure to state a claim, and failure to join an indispensable party. Fed. R. Civ. P. 12(b) (2003). In New York the list is similar but even longer, and includes as grounds for dismissal nine affirmative defenses: arbitration and award, collateral estoppel, discharge in bankruptcy, incapacity to sue or be sued, payment, release, res judicata, statute of limitations, and statute of frauds. N.Y. Civ. Prac. L. & R. §3201.

[35] *See, e.g.,* Fed. R. Civ. P. 12(h) (2003).

of thumb to consider. The first rule is that counsel should make a pre-answer motion to dismiss only if she reasonably believes she will win. Our second rule is that even if the motion is certain to succeed, it may not be worth making if it will not put an end to the litigation.

For example, if defendant has a straightforward statute of limitations defense, and procedural rules permit raising it by motion before the answer, the most efficient course would be to move to dismiss and then answer the complaint in the unlikely event that the motion is denied. This would be especially wise if defendant had less than a strong case on the merits, and therefore preferred not to answer unless absolutely necessary. Since a decision that the statute of limitations had run on plaintiff's claim would put an end to the litigation, a pre-answer motion is surely the best strategy. Conversely, a defendant with non-frivolous but marginal jurisdictional or statute of limitations arguments and a strong case on the merits would do better to answer the complaint, including the less than water-tight affirmative defenses in the answer.

Where dismissal will not prevent plaintiff from starting over, counsel should think twice about responding by motion. For example, when there is reason to believe that a motion to dismiss on the ground of failure to state a claim will be granted, and also reason to believe that plaintiff can in fact remedy the defects in the complaint, defendant may better advised to answer, including failure to state a claim as an affirmative defense. This is because in most instances, dismissal of the complaint before the issue is joined will leave plaintiff free to plead more artfully and start over. Once the issue has been joined, defendant may attack the weaknesses in the complaint by way of a summary judgment motion. If defendant is successful, the summary judgment order will ordinarily have the force of a judgment on the merits, precluding further litigation.

You should also note that you may incur meaningful losses by making a winning motion that does nothing but take time and drive up costs for the parties and the judicial system. Such practice may cost you the court's good opinion and the good will of opposing counsel, resources you may one day need.

In short, we suggest a presumption against pre-answer motions to dismiss unless they are both highly meritorious and likely to advance your client's interests in meaningful fashion. Certainly, engaging in motion practice merely in order to put plaintiff to the trouble and expense of responding is plainly forbidden by rules of procedure and ethics alike, although anecdotal evidence suggests that it happens far too often. Many experienced and ethical practitioners would no doubt disagree with our presumption against pre-answer motions; the matter is not a simple one. Nonetheless, we think it is a good starting point for discussion and for evolving your own litigation philosophy. We discuss the ethics of motion practice at greater length in the *Special Concerns* Section for *Motions,* Chapter 4.

---

### *Exercise 3.1*

---

*Your firm represents Michael Corcoran, defendant in the complaint in Exercise 2.3 in Chapter 2 on Complaints. The facts of the case from plaintiff Janet Spence's point of view are further set out in Section D (1) of that chapter. Working from your interview notes, a new associate has written a first draft of an answer. It is reproduced below, awaiting your critique and revisions. The associate was working with the following important facts gleaned from Corcoran's interview.*

*Corcoran owns the vehicle that struck Spence, and he was driving it on the day in question. He has no problem with "owned, operated, managed and controlled," but he says he didn't "maintain" the vehicle; that was done by the car dealer, Euro Motors. In fact, immediately before the accident, he had brought the car back to the parking garage from Euro after extensive repairs, including repairs to the transmission and emergency brake. He insists that he put the car in "park" gear, shut off the engine, and engaged the emergency brake before leaving the vehicle. He has no idea how the brake came to be disengaged. As he left the garage after parking near the top of the ramp, he heard a noise that caused him to turn around. He saw his car begin to move, and at the same time, he saw a woman he knew from the neighborhood (he now knows her name to be Janet Spence) standing at the bottom of the ramp at the rear of a parked car. She was engrossed in a conversation on a mobile phone and did not look up when he shouted to her to watch out. By the time she heeded his shouted warnings, it was too late. He feels very badly about the incident, but does not feel that it was his fault. He has heard through mutual acquaintances that Spence's injuries were not as bad as they could have been, and that she seems to be making a good recovery; one neighbor said he thought she had already gone back to work part-time.*

*Do not concern yourself for now with Spence's and Corcoran's possible claims against E-Z Park Garage and Euro Motors.*

*Remember that Pacifica is a notice-pleading jurisdiction in which there is no reply to an answer. Allegations not denied (or answered by an assertion of insufficient knowledge) will be deemed admitted. Pacifica court rules further provide that when a defendant "intends in good faith" to deny only part or a qualification of an allegation," the defendant must "specify so much of it as is true and deny only the remainder."*

Superior Court of the State of Pacifica
County of Ocean

------

Janet Spence,
          Plaintiff,                                              ANSWER

              –against–                                    Index No. ____

Michael J. Corcoran,
          Defendant.

------

   Defendant, by his attorney, Leslie T. Davis, answers the complaint of the plaintiff as follows.

1.  As to paragraph 1 of plaintiff's complaint, defendant answers that he lacks sufficient knowledge or information to form a belief as to its truth.
2.  Defendant denies that at all times mentioned in the complaint, he owned, operated, managed, maintained, and controlled an automobile bearing Pacifica Registration No. 784371721 for the year 20__.
3.  As to the allegation in paragraph 3, defendant neither admits nor denies, because it alleges a conclusion of law, to which no answer is required.
4.  As to the allegation in paragraph 4, defendant admits the allegation.
5.  As to the allegation in paragraph 5, defendant neither admits nor denies, because it alleges a conclusion of law, to which no answer is required.
6.  As to the allegation in paragraph 6, defendant denies that plaintiff sustained serious and severe injuries.
7.  As to the allegations in paragraph 6, defendant neither admits nor denies, because it alleges a conclusion of law, to which no answer is required.

8. As to the allegations in paragraph 8, defendant answers that contrary to plaintiff's allegation, he engaged the emergency brake with all due care before leaving his vehicle.
9. As to the allegations in paragraph 9, defendant denies them.
10. As to the allegations in paragraph 10, defendant denies them.
11. As to the allegations in paragraph 11, defendant denies them.
12. As to the allegations in paragraph 12, defendant denies them.
13. As to the allegations in paragraph 13, defendant denies them.

## First Affirmative Defense

Defendant affirmatively alleges that any injuries that may have been sustained by plaintiff, as alleged in plaintiff's complaint, occurred as a result of plaintiff's negligent failure to exercise ordinary care. Therefore, plaintiff's alleged injuries were caused in whole or in part, or were contributed to, by plaintiff's own negligence and not by any negligence of defendant.

## Second Affirmative Defense

Plaintiff's suit is barred by the Insurance Law of the State of Pacifica,, section 7194 (d) in that she has not suffered economic loss greater than basic economic loss as defined therein.

## Third Affirmative Defense

Plaintiff's suit is barred by the Insurance Law of the State of Pacifica, section 7194 (e) in that she has not suffered serious injury as defined therein.

For these reasons, defendant requests judgment against plaintiff and for defendant's costs.

Leslie T. Davis
Sherman, Kantor & Maxwell, LLP
300 Bayshore Boulevard
Palmetto
Pacifica 90212
(678) 343-0020

### *Assignment 3.1*

*Research your state's rules on answers. See if you can find answers to the following.*

- *Do the pleading rules of your state permit general denials?*
- *May a defendant refuse to answer allegations containing conclusions of law?*
- *Are argumentative/explanatory denials forbidden or encouraged?*
- *Do the rules provide for a reply by plaintiff to defendant's affirmative defenses?*

*Then evaluate the sample answer of defendant Michele Freeman in Section C above in light of those rules. Revise as necessary, taking pedagogical license to invent facts if your jurisdiction would require greater specificity.*

*Chapter 4*

# *LITIGATING: MOTIONS*

---

## A. IN GENERAL

Motions are perhaps the most easily defined of all the documents in this book: a motion is a request to the court made by a party during the course of litigation.[1] Yet of all the documents in this book, motions demand the most creativity of the drafter. Their concerted use (known as "motion practice") to advance a client's interest, especially before trial, requires the discipline to master complex factual and procedural scenarios and to work through strategic conundrums, the willingness to think outside the box, the patience to await the "aha!" moment, and the flexibility to modify or abandon a strategy that is not working. Of all the documents in this book, motions also offer the greatest satisfaction; like a winning appellate brief, a successful motion can do justice and make new law, but unlike a brief, it can also save essential resources of time, effort, money, and the human spirit by bringing litigation to an early and favorable conclusion. Even when it does not result in total victory, a successful motion can shape litigation to the client's advantage by disposing of non-meritorious claims, charges, or defenses; narrowing or expanding disclosure and discovery; admitting or suppressing evidence; joining or severing claims or parties; or preparing the ground for an advantageous settlement. Even an unsuccessful motion may benefit the moving party by educating the judge about the issues or testing the judge's reaction to them or, at a minimum,

---

[1] Motions are best and most often made in writing, although some motions may be made orally, especially at trial, when unexpected events impel counsel to seek immediate help from the court. Our focus here is, of course, on written motions.

by preserving the issue for appeal.[2] As one practitioner put it, attorneys are "a fortunate lot," because

> [w]e get to participate in a core miracle of civilization: the pen really is mightier than the sword. Nowhere is our involvement more immediate than in motion practice. Motion, response, reply, oral argument, and decision. Through this process, fortunes change hands; massive projects are built or halted; lives are enhanced or ruined. That we are allowed to play such a rare, critical game must evoke joy as well as reverence. Blessed with the gift, a seat at the table, we can spend our entire professional lives striving for mastery of...the process [of motion practice]....[3]

Yet motions have a dark as well as a bright side: of all the documents in this book, motions offer perhaps the most, and certainly the most varied, temptations to unethical practice. We have all heard of lawyers who threaten to "bury in paper" opponents who have limited financial resources, that is, threaten to file frivolous or inconsequential motions with the sole aim of exhausting those resources. For this reason, the *Special Concerns* discussion at the end of this chapter concerns the ethics of motion practice.

In our discussion of motions, we broaden our scope beyond civil practice to include motion practice in criminal prosecutions. Our discussion of motions continues with an overview of motion practice and goes on to describe basic types of motions.

## 1. Motion Practice

The simple definition of a motion is in sharp contrast to the complexity of motion practice. Indeed, such is its complexity that law firms often have teams of attorneys who do nothing but motion practice.

The complexity of motion practice is due in part to the huge number of available motions. A study of four courts of general

---

[2] On the pros and cons of using motions to "educate" and "test" judges, *see* David F. Herr, Roger S. Haydock, & Jeffrey W. Stempel, *Motion Practice* § 2, 13–15 (Aspen 2001). One obvious down-side to consider is the risk of revealing one's strategy too early.

[3] Tom Galbraith, *The Joy of Motion Practice*, 24 No. 2 Litig. 15 (1998).

civil jurisdiction counted 200 types of motions.[4] Some common motions, like motions to dismiss for failure to state a claim or cause of action and motions for summary judgment, are defined by statute, in state and federal rules of civil and criminal procedure. Many other motions are creatures of local rule and convention. Still others are *sui generis*, tailored to the needs of the individual case, as practitioners attempt to steer the course of litigation to their clients' advantage. In order to be cognizable, a motion need only be made in good faith, request relief that is within the court's power, and follow the local rules for format and filing. It is this essentially limitless subject matter that insures that motion practice is as creative as it is complex.

The immense variety of motions accounts for only a part of the challenge of motion practice, however. Motion-practice specialists are above all strategists deciding which motions to make and in what sequence and combination. In order to formulate motion-practice strategy, the practitioner needs several kinds of knowledge: an understanding of the historical and procedural facts of the case and of the substantive law, some sense of the temperament and track-record of opposing counsel and of the judge who will decide the motion, and a sure grasp of the applicable rules regarding motion practice. Of these, the last is often the most difficult to acquire. The rules of motion practice are usually even more complex than the rules regarding pleadings. Motion practice is governed by layer upon layer of rules: rules made by the legislature; rules made by court administrators at the state, county, circuit, district, and court level; and rules made by individual judges for practice in their courtrooms.[5] The new practitioner should never attempt to file even a single motion without a mentor—and possibly, a lucky charm.

Despite the intensely local nature of motion practice, some generalities hold. First, motions are ordinarily made "on notice"— that is, the opposing party is informed that on a date certain (typically a week or two from the date of the notice itself), a specified

---

[4] Susan L. Keilitz, Roger A. Hanson, & Henry W. K. Daley, *Civil Motion Practice: Lessons from Four Courts for Judges and Lawyers*, 33 No. 4 Judges' J. 2, 3 (1994).

[5] In New York, for example, a practitioner who wishes to file a motion in a civil suit may need to consult eight separate sets of rules that range from the state's primary civil practice statute down to the individual judge's unwritten rules and customs. Mark Davies, 2 *West's McKinney's Forms, Civil Practice Law and Rules*, § 5.1, 16 (West 1991).

request will come before the court. The purpose of notice is, of course, to allow opposing counsel to file papers in reply to the motion. When the request is too urgent to allow for the statutory notice period, a motion may be made by "order to show cause," which ordinarily shortens the notice period to as little as a day. In the exceptional situation where justice requires even speedier judicial action, for example, when an attorney seeks a restraining order or extension of a deadline, an "ex parte" motion may be made with no notice at all to the opposing party.

Second, motions are decided in one of three ways, most frequently at the court's option. They may be decided "on the papers," that is, on the written submissions alone, without oral argument or a hearing. They may be decided on written submissions and some form of oral argument, whether formal appellate-style argument or informal conversation. Or they may be decided on the papers and on evidence adduced at a hearing at which the testimony of witnesses is taken. When a hearing is held, oral argument is ordinarily permitted.

Finally, there is no equivalent of notice-pleading for motions; rather, the universal rule is that motions must state "with particularity" the legal ground upon which they are based.[6] For all its universality, the requirement of particularity is nonetheless ill-defined. One court's equation of particularity with "reasonable specification" does little to help.[7] An example of insufficient particularity may be of use, however. A federal district court deemed plaintiff's motion for a new trial in a negligence case insufficiently particular because the motion advanced the following very general grounds.

1. The learned trial judge erred in ruling on the evidence.
2. The learned trial judge erred in his charge to the jury.
3. The charge of the learned trial judge was prejudicial to the plaintiff.[8]

---

[6] *See, e.g.,* Fed. R. Civ. P. 7(b)(1) (2003), requiring a motion to "state with particularity the grounds therefore, and set forth the relief or order sought."

[7] *U.S. v. 64.88 Acres of Land, More or Less: Situate in Allegheny County, Pa.,* 25 F.R.D. 88, 90 (W.D. Pa. 1960).

[8] *Lynn v. Smith,* 193 F. Supp. 887, 888 (W.D. Pa. 1961), *cited* in Herr, Haydock & Stempel, *supra* n. 2, § 3.03[B], 3–8.

This sparse formulation does not provide opposing counsel with sufficient notice—the information in it is insufficient to enable counsel to decide how to reply. Stated with particularity (and without cloying false deference to "the learned trial judge"), the grounds for the motion might have been stated as follows.

1. The court made the following erroneous evidentiary rulings.
   a. The court permitted defendant to put before the jury evidence of plaintiff's sexual preference.
   b. The court permitted defendant to put plaintiff's driving record before the jury.
   c. The court excluded evidence of defendant's alcoholism.
   d. The court permitted defendant to testify that he was uninsured.
2. The court erroneously charged the jury that plaintiff had the burden of proving her lack of negligence.
3. The court's charge was prejudicial to the plaintiff
   a. because of the errors stated above, and
   b. because it erroneously gave the impression that the incident that gave rise to the lawsuit was an unavoidable accident.[9]

As a practical matter, motions are very rarely denied for lack of specificity. If the grounds for the motion can be understood from the context and supporting documents, the motion will usually be decided on the merits. Nonetheless, the good opinion and good temper of a weary judge with miles of motions to read before she sleeps is a powerful incentive to particularity. The more specific the motion, the better the judge's attitude. Another incentive to particularity is the drafter's relationship with opposing counsel. Seeking to prevail through sheer annoyance is as counter-productive as it is unethical.

## 2. Types of Motions

Since it would be impossible to cover the hundreds of commonly filed motions here, we have tried to do justice to the variety

---

[9] Adapted from Herr, Haydock & Stempel, *supra* n. 2, §3.03[B], p. 3–9.

of motion practice by describing the universe of motions generally and providing some examples of each category.[10] Then we narrow our focus to two classes of motions that every litigator in civil practice should be able to make: motions to dismiss and summary judgment motions.

## a. Pre-trial Motions

Motions can most easily be categorized by their place on the litigation time-line: pre-trial motions, trial motions, and post-trial motions. Pre-trial motions are by far the most numerous and most frequently filed. Indeed, in many practitioner's minds, motion practice is synonymous with pre-trial motion practice. Pre-trial motions may be further categorized by their effect on the litigation—dispositive or non-dispositive.[11] Dispositive pre-trial motions are those that seek dismissal of a claim or defense in civil litigation or dismissal of some or all counts of a criminal indictment or other charging instrument. Examples of dispositive motions in civil litigation are

1) motions to dismiss for failure to state a cause of action or claim upon which relief can be granted;
2) motions to dismiss for lack of subject matter or in personam jurisdiction;
3) motions to dismiss for failure to join an indispensable party;
4) motions to dismiss for insufficiency of form or service of process;
5) motions to dismiss on various other grounds apparent "on the face of the pleadings," such as statute of limitations, statute of frauds, lack of capacity to sue or be sued, or res judicata; and
6) motions for summary judgment, asserting that the undisputed material facts entitle the moving party to judgment as a matter of law.

---

[10] For a comprehensive survey of motions and motion practice, *see generally* Herr, Haydock & Stempel, *supra* n. 2, a thorough and very readable short treatise focused largely on civil practice in the federal courts.

[11] Of course, final disposition of a complaint or indictment is not necessarily the end of the story, unless the dismissal is "with prejudice" to refiling or the statute of limitations has run.

Examples of dispositive pre-trial motions in criminal law practice are motions arguing the unconstitutionality of the statute under which the defendant is charged and motions to dismiss for former jeopardy, for malicious or selective prosecution, for grand jury irregularities, and for running of the statute of limitations.

Most other pre-trial motions in civil and criminal practice are non-dispositive. Some, like the motion to strike scandalous or irrelevant material from a complaint and the motion for a more definite statement, address themselves to easily remediable defects in the pleadings. A more consequential class of non-dispositive pre-trial motions concerns the conduct of discovery and disclosure—the statutorily governed exchange of information and evidence between the parties to a civil suit and between prosecution and defense. As we noted in the chapter on complaints, these procedures have replaced the protracted and stylized pleading duels that narrowed the issues for trial at common law. Although discovery and disclosure take place outside the courtroom, the parties often ask the court to settle disputes that arise about their scope or conduct. Motions to compel discovery, motions for protective orders (that is, for example, to forbid discovery of particular matters, or discovery by particular methods), motions for sanctions (that is, to punish a party for abusive discovery practices or reward the party victimized by such practices), and motions to enforce or quash subpoenas addressed to third parties are all characteristic of this phase of litigation.

Another class of pre-trial motions addresses itself to case-management—for example, motions for precedence (that is, to bring a case on for trial quickly), or for continuance (that is, to postpone trial); motions to join claims or add parties, or for separate trials of individual claims and parties; and motions for a jury or bench trial. Severance motions are especially critical in criminal cases. Acquittal or conviction may depend on whether a defendant is tried with a co-defendant at a joint trial or tried singly; the presence of an unsympathetic co-defendant, or, worse, a co-defendant who has made statements to law enforcement can create undue and fatal prejudice.

Requests for advance rulings on the admissibility of evidence are among the most consequential pre-trial motions. They are frequently referred to as motions "in limine"—Latin for "on the threshold"—because they are traditionally made close to the time of trial. One such motion is the motion to suppress, especially frequent in the practice of criminal law, where it is used to seek suppression of evidence allegedly obtained by the government in violation of the defendant's constitutional rights. An example of this type of motion is found in Casefile 3 in Appendix A. Motions in limine are also known as motions to "preclude" the admission of matter believed to violate a rule of evidence or other limitation on admissibility. Where the contested evidence is vital to the proof of a claim, defense, or offense, a successful motion to suppress or preclude evidence may put an end to the litigation. Although more rarely, motions in limine are also used affirmatively, to seek the admission of controversial or novel evidence, for example, a new kind of expert testimony.

Still another class of pre-trial motions seeks substantive relief from the court. In order to preserve the status quo or prevent irreparable harm, a party to a civil suit may request a temporary restraining order or a preliminary injunction. In order to insure that disputed property will not be disposed of or that sufficient resources will be available to satisfy a judgment, parties sometimes petition the court to attach the defendant's property or garnish the defendant's income. Substantive relief may be requested in criminal prosecutions, as well. For example, a defendant may ask the court for bail or for a reduction in the amount of bail.

Finally, if counsel's motion practice strategy results in a settlement, a motion to enforce the settlement may be necessary.

### b. Motions at Trial

Since every foreseeable controversy concerning the conduct of trial should be, and usually is, settled through pre-trial motion practice, trial motions in writing are relatively few in number. Unforeseen events at trial—for instance, an improper question or unresponsive answer that may cause undue prejudice—may require the practitioner to make oral motions for curative instructions or, if the prejudice is extreme, for a mistrial. The proffer of unanticipated evidence may require a belated motion to preclude admission. Trial motions in writing concern such matters as requests for jury instructions or requests in a civil case for a specific form of verdict—a "general" verdict, a "special" verdict consisting of the jury's answers to interrogatories, or a combination of the two. Requests for judgment as a matter of law, also called a directed verdict in some jurisdictions, are invariably made in both civil and criminal cases—indeed, the practitioner who fails to make such a motion at trial will usually be precluded from making such a claim after trial.

### c. Motions After Trial

For the prevailing party in a civil suit, motion practice focuses largely on the recovery of costs and collection of judgments—and of course, on responding to the loser's motions. Where a defective verdict is arguable, the first concern of the losing party in a civil suit and of a criminal defendant convicted at trial[12] is to make a renewed motion for judgment as a matter of law, formerly known in civil practice as a judgment notwithstanding the verdict, or "JNOV." If trial errors by the court rather than errors by the fact-finder are alleged, the losing party or convicted defendant will move for a new trial. If these motions are denied, appeal will usually be the next step. If appeal is not "as of right," the losing party or convicted defendant will often move for permission to appeal to the appellate court. Appellate practice includes a number of specialized motions made by appellants and respondents alike, for example, motions to expand the record, to extend time limits or page limits, and motions to dismiss appeals.

### d. Motions to Dismiss and Summary Judgment Motions

You undoubtedly studied these two related motions in your Civil Procedure course, most probably in the context of the Federal Rules of Civil Procedure. Here, we hope to provide a broader context that will help you as you as you learn the specific rules of the jurisdiction in which you will practice. We have thus tried to describe motions to dismiss[13] and motions for summary judgment in terms of useful generalities.

---

[12] If the defendant in a criminal case is acquitted, the prosecution is ordinarily precluded from requesting judgment as a matter of law or a new trial and from appealing the acquittal.

[13] As noted above, in section A(2)(a) of this chapter, there are many grounds upon which a motion to dismiss may be based, of which the most familiar is "failure to state a claim upon which relief may be granted." Civil procedure statutes enumerate the available grounds, which universally include lack of personal or subject matter jurisdiction, failure to join an indispensable party, statute of frauds, statute of limitations, and res judicata.

Before the liberalization of civil procedure rules in the middle of the last century,[14] motions to dismiss—then known as "demurrers"—and summary judgment motions were totally distinct. Under the influence of the Federal Rules of Civil Procedure, the dividing line between the two has blurred somewhat, to the extent that in some jurisdictions both are at times equally available.

As noted above, motions to dismiss and summary judgment motions are both mechanisms for the accelerated disposition of non-meritorious claims and defenses. Both are available in all jurisdictions. Both are equally available to plaintiff and defendant—plaintiff may move to dismiss an affirmative defense in much the same way as defendant moves to dismiss the complaint, and either party may ask for summary judgment. Here, the unambiguous similarities end.

Motions to dismiss are typically made by defendant before pleading is complete—that is, before answering.[15] In contrast, summary judgment motions are ordinarily made after the issue is joined, that is, after all required pleadings are filed. Indeed, summary judgment motions are frequently filed after substantial discovery has taken place.

Motions to dismiss were traditionally made solely upon the allegations in the pleadings themselves, often referred to as upon "the face of the pleadings"; at common law such motions could not be supported by affidavits or other extrinsic proof. In modern practice, many jurisdictions maintain this stricture, while others permit some degree of extrinsic proof, especially when it is offered by the non-moving party.[16] Summary judgment motions, on the other hand, are always supported, often copiously, by affidavits and other proof, including depositions and other information obtained through discovery and disclosure. In some

---

[14] *See supra,* Chapter 2, *Complaints,* Section A (2).

[15] In most jurisdictions, labyrinthine rules govern which grounds of dismissal *may* be raised by motion before answering and which grounds *must* be raised by motion before answering or be deemed waived.

[16] In some jurisdictions, a motion to dismiss supported by affidavits or other proof from outside the pleadings will be converted into a summary judgment motion, whether automatically or at the court's option. In addition, if a motion to dismiss is made on the pleadings alone, and the judge concludes that justice will be served by an evidentiary hearing, the motion may also be converted to one for summary judgment.

jurisdictions, summary judgment proceedings routinely include evidentiary hearings.

Another important distinction between motions to dismiss and motions for summary judgment, noted above, is that a dismissal will not necessarily prevent re-pleading, but summary judgment will ordinarily be res judicata on the merits, precluding further litigation.

In order to use motions to dismiss and summary judgment motions effectively, the practitioner must understand the standards used to decide those motions and be able to make fluent arguments based upon them. In particular, she must grasp the difference between the standard for summary judgment and that of one commonly made motion to dismiss, the motion to dismiss for failure to state a claim upon which relief can be granted.

Confusingly for new practitioners, there are at least two different standards for a motion to dismiss for failure to state a claim— one basic standard for notice-pleading jurisdictions, another for fact-pleading jurisdictions, and local variations on each. Under the federal rules and the rules in many other notice-pleading jurisdictions, a complaint fails to state a claim upon which relief can be granted if it is clear that plaintiff "can prove no set of facts in support of his claim which will entitle him to relief."[17] This standard means that a complaint can be found wanting in one of three basic ways: if it omits one or more elements of a recognized cause of action, if it pleads a non-existent cause of action, or if it alleges facts that are plainly inconsistent with the wrong alleged. For example, if a complaint in malpractice fails to allege that the defendant owed plaintiff a duty, the complaint may appropriately be dismissed for failure to state a claim upon which relief may be granted, because no matter what proof of the other elements is adduced at trial, the malpractice claim would still fail. A complaint will also fail if it alleges all the elements of malpractice, but alleges malpractice by an aromatherapist in a jurisdiction that does not recognize such a cause of action. Finally, an otherwise sufficient malpractice complaint will fail if the facts alleged are inconsistent with plaintiff's claim, for example, if the only injury alleged is injury to her aesthetic sensibilities.

A complaint in a notice-pleading jurisdiction may also fail to state a claim if it neglects to state with particularity those very

---

[17] *Conley v. Gibson*, 355 U.S. 41 (1957).

few claims that must be so stated—for example, allegations of fraud or defamation. Although specific factual recitations are otherwise not required in notice-pleading, it is nonetheless at least theoretically possible that a claim or defense could be stated so conclusorily as to fail to provide notice. Presumably, if plaintiff alleged only that "defendant had a duty to plaintiff and negligently breached that duty, proximately causing physical harm to plaintiff," defendant's motion to dismiss for failure to state a claim might be granted, even though it cannot be said that "no set of facts" would entitle plaintiff to relief.[18]

In fact-pleading jurisdictions, where the motion to dismiss for failure to state a claim is often still known by its common-law name of "demurrer," a judge deciding whether the pleader has failed to state a claim begins by assuming the truth of the facts alleged. If the facts alleged do not state a claim—if one or more elements are alleged conclusorily—the motion may be granted. As in notice-pleading jurisdictions, the motion may also be granted 1) if an element is omitted, 2) if a non-existent claim or defense is pleaded, or 3) if the facts pleaded are themselves inconsistent with the pleader's claim or defense.

The standard for summary judgment is easier to articulate, but often more difficult to apply. Summary judgment is appropriate when there is no dispute as to any material fact and the moving party is entitled to judgment as a matter of law. At first glance, one might imagine that summary judgment is only appropriate in the rare situation where the non-moving party should not be litigating at all, since the undisputed facts prove her wrong; however, there are two other quite common situations in which summary judgment is appropriate: 1) where the non-moving party (usually the plaintiff) was not certain of the facts until some discovery had taken place, and 2) where the conflict is not over the facts at all, but over a legal issue.[19] Thus, there are two basic types of summary judgment motions: "fact-based" motions that turn on whether the facts are indeed undisputed, and "doctrinal" motions that turn on a pure question of law, that is, the parties

---

[18] Put another way, the "no set of facts" standard set out in *Conley v. Gibson, supra* n. 17 may be something of an exaggeration. *See* Fleming James, Jr., Geoffrey C. Hazard, & John Leubsdorf, *Civil Procedure* 147–148 (4th ed. Little, Brown 1992).

[19] Herr, Haydock & Stempel, *supra* n. 2, § 16.01[B], 16–12.

agree that there is no dispute on any material fact, but the legal significance of the facts is in dispute. For example, the defendant in a libel suit may argue that on the undisputed facts, judgment for the plaintiff is precluded by the First Amendment because the facts demonstrate that plaintiff is a public figure and that defendant was not motivated by "actual malice."[20]

Contrary to what one might expect, "doctrinal" summary judgment motions are more straightforward than motions that turn on whether there is any material question of fact. Where the moving party alleges that the facts are undisputed, two very slippery issues must be argued by counsel and decided by the court— whether the facts in question are indeed material and whether the dispute over them is a meaningful one. Thus, where lack of dispute is alleged, counsel must carefully analyze and parse the facts in the record. Precedent is rarely dispositive in such cases, because fact-based summary judgment issues are *sui generis.*

## B. COMPONENTS

Motion practice requires the drafter to produce not just one but a number of documents, known in the aggregate as motion papers. Just as the procedure for filing and arguing motions varies from jurisdiction to jurisdiction and from courtroom to courtroom, so do the required format and content of the papers. Practitioners frequently work from forms or use samples as templates. Nonetheless, an understanding of the fundamental building blocks will enable you to construct your motion papers more advisedly and effectively than will reliance on forms alone. For the moving party, the basic drafted components are the *notice of motion*, the *motion* proper, *affidavits* or other factual support, the trial *brief* (also called a trial *memorandum of law*), and a draft *order.* The non-moving party responds with a brief in opposition to the motion, and, where appropriate, with affidavits or other factual assertions in opposition.[21]

---

[20] *See, e.g., New York Times Co. v. Sullivan,* 376 U.S. 254 (1964).

[21] Although failure to respond to a motion does not ordinarily mean that the moving party wins by default, it is almost always the better practice to respond to a motion.

The notice of motion announces the moving party's intention of making a request to the court. The motion proper specifies the request. Depositions, hearing testimony, affidavits, or documentary proof provide factual support for the request. The trial brief provides legal argument in support of the request. Finally, the draft of an order granting the request saves judicial time and makes it more likely that if the court grants the motion, it will do so in the language preferred by the moving party.

Not all motions require all five of these components. For example, some jurisdictions combine the notice of motion and motion in one document. Moreover, some motions by their very nature require no affidavits or other factual support; motions to strike or for a more definite statement, traditional motions to dismiss for failure to state a cause of action, and other motions on the pleadings fall into this category. Finally, draft orders are not universally welcomed by judges.

In the balance of this section, we discuss in more detail all but one of the basic motion papers–the trial brief or memorandum of law, which is discussed in Chapter 9, *Trial and Appellate Briefs*. This is because the trial brief is a discursive, analytical, and persuasive document so fundamentally different from the other litigation documents in this book that it is more usefully studied with its close relation, the appellate brief.

Indeed, our separation of the trial memo from the rest of the motion papers emphasizes the better drafting practice. Unless the issue is so clear-cut that a few sentences of argument or a simple citation to authority will suffice (as in our sample motion to dismiss) or unless local practice requires an abbreviated "one-piece" motion that combines request and argument, the better practice is always to submit your legal argument in a separate, carefully crafted document that gives the appearance (as well as containing the distillation) of hard and thoughtful work. The discreteness of the trial memo is further underscored by the fact that it is often filed and served separately from the rest of the motion papers. When the motion requires an evidentiary hearing, the memo will ordinarily not be filed until after the hearing.

You should note that the sample trial memorandum in Section C of Chapter 9 on *Trial and Appellate Briefs* is a memo in support of the sample motion for summary judgment that appears in Section C of this chapter; read the brief after you read the summary judgment motion.

## 1. Notice of Motion

Like all motion papers, the notice of motion begins with a caption identifying the court and the parties. The docket, index, or indictment number is indicated to the right of the caption. Under the caption, a title identifies the document as a notice of motion and specifies the type of request being made. The amount of specificity depends on the complexity of the litigation. In a relatively simple action like the automobile-collision lawsuit in our first sample, generic identification as a motion to dismiss for failure to state a claim is sufficient. In a complex case with multiple parties, claims, and motions, it is advisable to label your motions very specifically, in order to help busy judges and clerks sort through mountains of paper—for example, "Defendant Smith's Motion for Summary Judgment on the Wrongful Death Claim." This description should appear on all of your motion papers.

The text of the notice is almost always pure boilerplate. The essential contents—the date, time, place, and subject matter of the movant's request to the court—are almost always compressed into one long sentence and too often expressed in legalese. Revise them when you can.

## 2. The Motion

The motion itself sets forth with particularity the moving party's request and the ground for it, often in numbered paragraphs. In a final, unnumbered paragraph that usually begins with a ritual "WHEREFORE," the drafter formally petitions the court for relief. This petition may include a request for an evidentiary hearing or an additional request for any other or further relief that the court deems appropriate.

Motions must be dated at the end and provide the attorney's name, address, and phone number. Often, the attorney must also sign the motion. By his signature, the attorney warrants that the motion is not undertaken for purposes of delay or harassment.[22]

---

[22] Under Rule 11 of the Federal Rules of Civil Procedure and its many state cognates, an attorney's signature on a motion certifies 1) that the motion is not made to harass the opponent or for any other improper purpose; 2) that her legal arguments are based on existing law or are plausible law-reform arguments; 3) that the factual allegations

## 3. Affidavits

Affidavits are notarized, sworn statements of fact in support of the motion. They may be made by anyone with relevant information—the parties, their witnesses, the attorney herself—but the actual drafting is almost always done by the attorney.

Below the caption, affidavits begin with an introductory paragraph indicating that the affiant is making a sworn statement. Often, this introduction specifically acknowledges that the statement is made "under penalty of perjury." If the affiant will be asserting any facts "upon information and belief," rather than upon personal knowledge, the introduction should so state. The conventional "magic dust" at the beginning of many boilerplate introductions—the archaic "s.s." ("so sworn"), for example—can safely be omitted.

After this introduction, the facts are stated in short, numbered paragraphs. Each relevant fact ordinarily has its own paragraph, and irrelevant facts are omitted except where needed to make the narrative comprehensible. Where facts are stated "upon information and belief," the drafter should so specify.

At the end of the affidavit, space is provided for notarization of the affiant's signature.

## 4. The Order

A draft order serves two purposes. It saves judicial time and energy. More important for the drafter, it allows her to frame the relief in the most favorable terms for her client, in hopes that the judge will sign the order as drafted. Like motions, orders should be framed with particularity; no judge can be expected to sign a judicial blank check.

---

have evidentiary support, or if asserted upon information and belief, are likely to have evidentiary support after a reasonable opportunity for further investigation; and 4) that denials of factual allegations likewise have (or are likely to have if on information and belief) evidentiary support. *See* Fed. R. Civ. P. 11(b) (2003); *see also Thomas v. Capital Sec. Services., Inc.*, 836 F.2d 866, 874 (5th Cir. 1988).

# C. SAMPLE MOTIONS

## *MOTION TO DISMISS FOR FAILURE TO STATE A CLAIM*

SUPERIOR COURT OF THE STATE OF PACIFICA
COUNTY OF OCEAN

```
-------------------------------------------------   No. C-03-724
Jennifer Rios,                                  )   NOTICE OF MOTION TO
                    Plaintiff                   )   DISMISS FOR FAILURE
                        -against-               )   TO STATE A CLAIM[23]
Natasha Simmons,                                )
                    Defendant                   )
-------------------------------------------------
```

You are notified that on June 27, 2003, at 10 A.M. or as soon thereafter as counsel can be heard, defendant Natasha Simmons, through her attorney Jonathan Allen, will move this court, located at 250 Oleander Drive, Room 830, in Palmetto, County of Ocean, State of Pacifica, for an order dismissing plaintiff's action against defendant on the ground that the complaint fails to state a claim upon which relief may be granted.[24]

To: Elizabeth Nesbitt
    Attorney for Plaintiff
    700 Shore Drive, Suite 13
    Palmetto, Pacifica

    Clerk
    Superior Court of the State of Pacifica
    250 Oleander Drive
    Palmetto, Pacifica

---

[23] The motion is clearly labeled.

[24] The notice of motion is a single long sentence of some 70 words, but it conveys the necessary information quite clearly.

SUPERIOR COURT OF THE STATE OF PACIFICA
COUNTY OF OCEAN

```
-------------------------------------------------  No. C-03-724
Jennifer Rios,                       )  MOTION TO DISMISS
              Plaintiff              )  FOR FAILURE TO
                   -against-         )  STATE A CLAIM
Natasha Simmons,                     )
              Defendant              )
-------------------------------------------------
```

Defendant, through counsel, moves this court for an order pursuant to P.R.C.P. §12(b) dismissing this action for failure to state a claim upon which relief can be granted.

As grounds for this motion, defendant states as follows.[25]

1. Under P.R.C.P. § 12(b), a complaint that fails to state a claim upon which relief may be granted is subject to dismissal.
2. Plaintiff's complaint states that the motor vehicle collision that is the basis of this action took place when plaintiff's vehicle collided with the rear of defendant's stopped vehicle.
3. Plaintiff's complaint further alleges that defendant's vehicle was stopped because of a third vehicle stopped in front of defendant.
4. Under established law of the state of Pacifica, a driver who strikes the rear of a stopped vehicle is presumed to be negligent. *Johnson v. Moses,* 254 P. Rep.2d 517, 519 (1957); Pacifica Jury Instructions § 17:5(b)(1).[26]
5. Under these same authorities, a motorist who is lawfully stopped when struck in the rear is not negligent.
6. From the face of plaintiff's complaint, it appears that defendant could not have been negligent, because she was lawfully stopped.
7. From the face of the complaint, plaintiff was negligent.[27]
8. Thus, plaintiff's complaint fails to state a claim upon which relief can be granted.
9. Defendant is entitled to dismissal of this action.

---

[25] The drafter goes on to state the grounds of defendant's motion with specificity.

[26] Where the law is clear and its application to the facts beyond dispute, no trial memorandum of law is necessary; indeed, it would probably just annoy a busy judge to have to read a brief arguing the obvious. Citation to authority is necessary, however.

[27] Factual support for defendant's motion comes from "the face of the complaint," that is, the motion is based on the pleadings alone. Thus, it is a true motion to dismiss or "demurrer." If defendant supported her motion with extrinsic evidence—for example, affidavits or depositions—many courts would simply deem it a motion for summary judgment. Some courts might require defendant to refile the motion, however.

WHEREFORE, defendant respectfully requests that this court dismiss the action against her and grant such other and further relief as this court deems appropriate.

Dated this 17th day of June, 20__.

By:_____

Jonathan Allen
Allen, Jensen & Fontana, LLP
Attorneys for Defendant
300 Oleander Drive, Suite 204
Palmetto, Pacifica
(222)787-3401

---

SUPERIOR COURT OF THE STATE OF PACIFICA
COUNTY OF OCEAN
------------------------------------------------No. C-03-724

| Jennifer Rios, | ) ORDER DISMISSING |
|  Plaintiff | ) COMPLAINT FOR FAILURE |
|    -against- | ) TO STATE A CLAIM |
| Natasha Simmons, | ) |
|  Defendant | ) |

------------------------------------------------

Defendant Natasha Simmons has moved by her attorney, Jonathan Allen, for a judgment pursuant to P.R.C.P. 12(b) dismissing the complaint in the above action for failure to state a claim upon which relief may be granted.

Upon reading the motion dated June 17th, 20__, the summons and complaint served in this action, and upon hearing Jonathan Allen, counsel for defendant, in support of the motion, and Elizabeth Nesbitt, counsel for the plaintiff, in opposition to the motion, and after due deliberation, it is

ORDERED that the motion to dismiss be granted and that judgment be entered dismissing the complaint in this action with prejudice to renewal and awarding defendant costs in the amount of three thousand dollars.[28]

Enter,

_____

Justice of the Superior Court

---

[28] How does the draft order here insure that defendant will get the maximum benefit from dismissal of the action?

## *MOTION FOR SUMMARY JUDGMENT*

Superior Court of the State of Atlantis
County of Sussex

\--------------------------------------------------

Jeffrey Hustin,

|                       | Plaintiff,    | Index No. Civ.\_\_\_\_ |
|                       |               | DEFENDANT FREEMAN'S |

                Plaintiff,

-against-

Michele Freeman and
The Regents of the University of
Atlantis,

                Defendants

Index No. Civ.\_\_\_\_
DEFENDANT FREEMAN'S
NOTICE OF MOTION
  -for-
PARTIAL SUMMARY
JUDGMENT
Oral argument is requested[29]

\--------------------------------------------------

PLEASE TAKE NOTICE that upon the affidavit of defendant Michele Freeman, sworn to on the 21st day of July, 20\_\_, and the complaint, answer, and transcripts of depositions in this case, a motion pursuant to Rule 56 of the Atlantis Rules of Civil Procedure will be made in the Motion Part of this Court on August 27th, 20\_\_ in room 300 of the Sussex County Superior Court, located at 1 Judiciary Square, Atlantis City, Atlantis. At 9:30 in the morning of that day, or as soon thereafter as counsel can be heard, counsel will ask this Court for an order pursuant to At. R. Civ. P. 56 dismissing the defamation count in the complaint in the above action and directing that summary judgment be entered in favor of defendant and against plaintiff on that claim on the ground that the defense of privilege is established as a matter of law, and for such other relief as this Court deems just.

The above action is for defamation and intentional infliction of emotional distress.

---

[29] Note that the motion is very specifically labeled to indicate to the judge not only the nature of the motion, but also that it is made only by defendant Freeman and that it is for "partial" summary judgment.

Pursuant to At. R. Civ. P. 87(b), answering affidavits, if any, must be served on the undersigned counsel at least seven days before the return date on this motion.[30]

Lawrence Brenner
Attorney for Defendant
Brenner, Perillo & Kahn, LLP
25 Judiciary Square
Atlantis City, Atlantis
(111) 989-0548

To: Paul Wilens
Hogan, Herzen, Wang & Wilens
Attorney for Plaintiff
5 Judiciary Square
Atlantis City, Atlantis
(111) 874-2901

Clerk
Superior Court
County of Sussex
1 Judiciary Square
Room 600
Atlantis City, Atlantis

Superior Court of the State of Atlantis
County of Sussex

----------------------------------------------------

Jeffrey Hustin,                                              Index No. Civ.____
            Plaintiff
            -against-                                         AFFIDAVIT IN SUPPORT
Michele Freeman and                              OF DEFENDANT FREEMAN'S
The Regents of the University of            MOTION FOR PARTIAL
Atlantis,                                                       SUMMARY JUDGMENT
            Defendants

----------------------------------------------------

State of Atlantis   )
County of Atlantis )[31]

---

[30] In the state of Atlantis, as in a some other jurisdictions, there is no document labeled "motion," just a very specific "notice of motion."

[31] Following the caption, affidavits always indicate the state and county in which they are sworn. Traditionally, "s.s." for "so sworn" appeared to the right of the location. It adds nothing.

Michele Freeman, being duly sworn, swears under penalty of perjury to the truth of the following statements, except for those made upon information and belief, and as to those, she believes them to be true.[32]

1. I am one of the defendants in the above action.
2. Plaintiff alleges in his complaint that I made false statements concerning him in a letter to the Status Committee of the University of Atlantis School of Law which were defamatory in that they tended to expose plaintiff to contempt, aversion, ridicule, and disgrace and to induce a bad opinion of him in the minds of right-thinking people. He also alleges that these statements caused the Status Committee to deny his application for academic tenure and to decline to rehire him. He further alleges that by making these statements, I intentionally or recklessly caused him to suffer severe emotional distress.
3. In the answer, filed on March 15, 20__, I denied, *inter alia,* making false statements concerning plaintiff and intentionally or recklessly causing him severe emotional distress. I freely admitted making the statements to the Status Committee, however.
4. In my answer, I also set out the affirmative defense of qualified privilege, alleging that as a member of the bar of this state and of its legal academic community, I had a legitimate interest in the intellectual and moral fitness of candidates for academic tenure in the law and a duty to report any relevant information to those persons with corresponding interests and duties. I further alleged that because my statements about the plaintiff concerned those interests and duties and were made to persons with the corresponding interests and duties, that is, the Status Committee, those statements were privileged, and no liability for defamation or infliction of emotional distress could be premised upon them.
5. I have attended and testified at a deposition at which I and other defendants were examined as well as attending the deposition of the plaintiff. I have discussed the pleadings and depositions in this case with my attorney, who advises me, and I believe, that the complaint is without merit and that the defense of privilege is established sufficiently to warrant this court, as a matter of law, in

---

[32] In this introductory paragraph affiant swears to the truth of her statements (except those made on information and belief) and acknowledges that falsehood will expose her to prosecution for perjury.

granting summary judgment in my favor on the claim of defamation and dismissing that count of the complaint.[33]

6. The facts with regard to the issue raised by the pleadings are the following. I am a tenured Professor of Law at the University of Sussex Law School. During the academic year 20__–20__, I was a visiting professor at the University of Atlantis School of Law, where plaintiff, an Assistant Professor of Law, was applying for tenure and promotion. During my year at Atlantis Law School, facts that I believed relevant to plaintiff's fitness for academic tenure at a law school—and indeed, his fitness to teach at all—came to my notice.

7. First, I had reason to doubt the originality of plaintiff's scholarship. Reading plaintiff's article entitled "Plain Language: A Cognitive Contradiction in Terms," in or around January of 20__, I was reminded of an article written by my mentor, the late Professor Alfred Greenall. When I compared the text of plaintiff's article with Professor Greenall's article, I found disturbing similarities in ideas and paragraphs and sentences that were not only close in structure, but occasionally identical in wording. The texts of the two articles, with the similarities underscored and noted in the margins are attached to this affidavit as Defendant's Exhibit A.

8. Second, I witnessed behavior toward students on plaintiff's part that convinced me that he was unfit to teach. My office was next door to plaintiff's, and we could not help overhearing each other's conversations. On one occasion, also in or around January of 20__, a student came to discuss a low grade with plaintiff. When she persisted in her complaints that plaintiff's grading was unfairly harsh, I heard plaintiff tell her that she might as well quit, she was "too stupid" to be in law school, if not "too stupid to live," that she had only been admitted because she was a minority student, an "affirmative action mistake," and that she should be grateful he only gave her a C minus. On another occasion, in or around February of 20__, when another student persisted in challenging his grade, plaintiff told him that if he did not like his grade, maybe the student "would like to settle it outside in the street," because plaintiff would be "happy to beat the crap out of [the student]." The affidavits of

---

[33] In the first five paragraphs, the affiant identifies herself and provides background information that brings the reader up to date on the litigation itself. Note that the drafter has resisted the temptation to use intensifiers. In this context, the only overtly "persuasive" formulation—in paragraph 3, defendant notes that she "freely" admitted making the statement about plaintiff—is indeed persuasive.

these two students in support of my motion for summary judgment have been separately filed with this Court.

9. Although, as a visiting professor, I could not vote on plaintiff's applications for tenure and promotion, I believed then, and still believe, that it was my duty as a member of the bar and as a member of the legal academic community to communicate the above information concerning plaintiff to the Status Committee, and I accordingly wrote the letter, attached to the complaint as Plaintiff's Exhibit A, detailing my doubts about plaintiff's fitness.[34]

10. I believe that the above facts demonstrate that I shared with the Status Committee an interest in the intellectual ability and good character of persons seeking tenured membership in legal academia and that the information I communicated with respect to plaintiff was relevant to our shared interests and duties.[35]

11. In view of the foregoing, I submit that my letter to the Status Committee concerning plaintiff was privileged and thus not subject to an action for defamation.

_____
Michele Freeman

State of Atlantis   )
County of Sussex ) ss.

On July 21, 20__, Michele Freeman personally appeared before me, a Notary Public for the State of Atlantis and County of Sussex. Being duly sworn, Michele Freeman deposed and said that she is a defendant in the above action and that the facts set forth in this affidavit are true, except for those statements made upon information and belief, and as to those statements, she believes them to be true.

_____
Sworn and subscribed before me this 21st day of July, 20__.

_____
Notary Public
My Commission expires September 30, 20__.

---

[34] Paragraphs 6–9 tell the story from the affiant's point of view, using telling quotes and reference to supporting documentation. The neutral tone is appropriate here, for two reasons. First, the affiant is herself a lawyer, and second, her point is precisely that she is a truth-teller who does not exaggerate.

[35] Paragraphs 10–11 sum up, bringing together facts and law.

## D. WRITING PROCESS

The process of preparing motion papers begins with the grand design of motion practice. One litigator describes it this way.

> The most enjoyable part is sorting our way to a strategy. Cases come to us in a jumble. From clients the facts pour out, colored by outrage and truncated by denial. And from our adversaries comes a calculated presentation designed to emphasize their factual and legal strengths and to obfuscate their weaknesses. We cannot be drawn in by either. Our first task is to get as near as we can to the bottom of things, and next, to establish realistic goals. We then construct a method of presentation, a conceptual framework that we hope will persuade our judge.[36]

Thus, painstaking information-gathering—"getting to the bottom of things"—and conceptualization are critical to effective motion practice. Moreover, whether your case is criminal or civil, complex or seemingly straightforward, you should begin working on motion strategy from the very first minute you become involved in the case—that is, "front-loading"[37] your research and brainstorming. Starting early means that you will not fall into either of the two deep pits that procrastinating litigators (and their clients) fall into: learning the facts too late or learning the law too late. Equally important as not falling into pits, however, is rising to great heights; starting early promotes the creativity that will let you tower over your adversary. Without adequate lead time, you will end up just "going through the motions"—filing boiler-plate shot-gun motions and reacting to your adversary's strategy rather than shaping the litigation. Even if you prevail through the sheer strength of your client's case, you will not earn the respect of the court or of the opposing counsel, and you may have caused your client unnecessary expense.

Thus, your first job is to make an "early, accurate assessment of the factual and legal eccentricities of [your] case."[38]

---

[36] Galbraith, *supra* n. 3, at 15.

[37] *Id.*

[38] *Id.*

## 1. Gathering Information: Getting the Facts

Motion practice requires a sure grasp of the procedural and historical facts of your case. You must review all of the documents filed to date. Except in the very rare instances when motion practice will focus on pure points of law, you need a comprehensive and nuanced understanding of the historical facts. In pre-trial motion practice, this is a more than usually demanding chore, because it requires that you assemble facts from many sources. In a civil suit, the pleadings, discovery and disclosure materials, affidavits, interviews, and even fair inference are among many sources. In a criminal prosecution, the indictment and other charging documents, police reports, client statements to law enforcement, scientific reports, client and witness interviews, and the transcripts of any prior hearings are just a few sources of facts. In addition to the multiplicity of sources, the legal cognizability of sources also complicates fact-gathering: the drafter must know which facts are properly part of the record to date and which are not, because you may never base argument on facts not in the record. When you find a gap in the record, fill it (if you can) with a properly filed affidavit or exhibit—not with conjecture.

## 2. Gathering Information: Researching the Law

Experienced litigators come to the research stage with a basic familiarity with the doctrinal basis of the most common motions, a knowledge base you will gradually acquire. Once brainstorming has progressed from the "macro" stage—deciding whether and how to make a specific motion—focused research becomes necessary. How much narrowly focused research you should do on a particular motion and how many potential motions should be researched in depth is a complicated question that pulls the litigator in two opposite directions. On the one hand, we want to pursue every non-frivolous issue that can be resolved to our client's advantage. We want to do thorough and creative work that moves the law in good directions. At the same time, legal research is a costly business. The decision to research a novel, long-shot issue should always take into account the drain on resources.

Knowledge of the substantive law must be complemented by knowledge of the rules of motion practice in your court. As we noted earlier, these rules can be elaborate, many-layered and of infinite variety. The timing of motions, the content and format of motion papers, and the procedure for filing and arguing are all crucial to the success of your motion strategy. In motion practice, as in all law practice, good ideas alone do not make a competent practitioner.

## 3. Conceptualizing

Once a litigator has a good basic knowledge of the law and as complete a knowledge of the facts as possible, she should let her mind roam. Then, slowly, motion strategy will begin to take tentative form, sometimes only after some necessary trips down conceptual blind alleys. Once a strategy emerges, it is time to test its appropriateness by asking some hard questions about every piece of the strategy. For every potential motion, the authors of the leading treatise on motion practice suggest that you consider the following.

- Whether there is another way to achieve the same result—will your adversary agree to an informal request, for example, resulting in a stipulation between the parties.
- Whether the motion is likely to be granted in whole or in part.
- Whether the motion is likely to advance or reduce the likelihood of settlement.
- Whether the potential benefit of the motion outweighs the time, effort, and expense of making it.
- Whether the client understands the need for the motion and is aware of potential costs as well as the potential gain and supports the motion.
- Whether the motion will positively or negatively affect the judge's view of the case and the client.
- Whether the motion will have a positive or negative effect on the judge's opinion of the drafter.
- Whether the motion will negatively affect relationships with opposing counsel.[39]

---

[39] *Herr, Haydock & Stempel, supra* n. 2, § 2.01, 2-3 – 2-4.

If the motion gets a high score on this test, it is time to finish the information-gathering and draft the papers.

## 4. Writing the First Full Draft

The most demanding part of drafting motion papers is writing a clear, concise, and persuasive trial memorandum of law, a process described in Chapter 9 on *Trial and Appellate Briefs*. None of the other components is difficult to draft; they mainly require careful adaptation of forms and attention to detail. There are, however, two concerns that merit discussion here: the sequence in which motion papers are drafted and the drafting of affidavits.

a. The sequence in which motion papers are presented and read is invariably that described above: Notice, Motion, Affidavit, and Memorandum of Law. But what is the most effective order of drafting? One expert has a clear answer: papers should be written in reverse order from the order in which they are read.[40] Thus, the legal argument section of the memo should be written first, followed by the statement of facts section of the memo, the affidavits, and finally, the motion and notice of motion. This sequence has much to recommend it. First, it puts the emphasis where it should be, on the conceptual infrastructure of the motion. Second, drafting the memo first often helps the writer to understand the issues better. When we write, we learn. Sometimes our own draft memo will lead us to revise our motion strategy. Further, drafting the argument helps us to separate relevant facts from irrelevant. Finally, drafting the memo first gives the writer a chance to set it aside while he prepares the rest of the papers, and thus, to come back to it with a fresher eye.

Yet for all its advantages, we recommend this very professional process with one serious caveat: do not let the desire for a winning argument lead you—consciously or unconsciously—to put words in your affiants' mouths or otherwise tweak or "improve" the facts. A writing process that puts legal argument before fact is only a good process if the writer is conscious of the risk and resists temptation.

b. Lawyers ordinarily draft all the affidavits in support of a motion, not just their own. This is because the attorney has a

---

[40] Davies, *supra* n. 5, § 5.5, at 25.

clearer sense of which facts are relevant and can articulate them concisely, "packaging" the facts so they can be easily read by busy judges and their clerks. When lawyers draft affidavits for others, however, they need to be aware not only of the danger noted above—distorting the facts—but also of the temptation to be conclusory or argumentative. When you draft an affidavit, it will be because there is no better way to get the facts before the court. Depositions are generally looked upon more favorably than affidavits, because the deponent is subject to cross-examinations. Since by their nature, affidavits have a somewhat suspect "self-serving" air, they should be composed with care and restraint. Straightforward and specific statement of the facts is ordinarily the best approach.

Although drafted with the care and restraint that their nature mandates, affidavits can nonetheless be recognizable personal accounts, and when the situation requires, compelling narratives. No matter what the subject matter, affidavits should always be drafted in the first person: the third-person legalese formulation "Affiant states that ..." is as senseless as it is lifeless. Moreover, as with complaints, narrative techniques such as character, scene, detail, point of view, and voice should be a permanent part of the affidavit-drafter's skill-set. Indeed, when an affidavit will support a client's petition for important substantive relief—political asylum or child custody, for example—the drafter has a duty to tell the client's story not just fully and truthfully, but artfully and credibly.[41]

## 5. Revising and Polishing

When you revise and polish any documents that you have adapted from forms or samples, be sure that you have filled in the blanks with correct information. Be sure that the parties' names are spelled correctly, that the docket or index number is correct, and that the motion is correctly titled. Be certain that the dates are correct: if you are required to give your adversary ten business days' notice, be sure to count and recount the days.

---

[41] For more on the use of narrative in affidavit drafting, see Stacy Caplow, *Putting the "I" in Wr*t*ng: Drafting an A/Effective Personal Statement to Tell a Winning Refugee Story*, 14 Legal Writing 249 (2008).

If you have drafted affidavits for others, be certain that they read their affidavits before signing. If the affidavit is short, you can ask the affiant to read it aloud to be certain that he has read it. Experienced practitioners know that most clients will sign anything their lawyer puts in front of them. Be sure your affidavit reflects the affiant's understanding of the facts.

Check to see that you provided all the documents required. For example, some courts require that summary judgment motions include a list of the uncontested facts. If your motion papers are complex, with numerous affidavits and exhibits, be sure to "package" them carefully for maximum readability and ease of reference. Sometimes visual aids like timelines or diagrams are effective additions. Index tabs are particularly helpful.

## E. SPECIAL CONCERNS: THE ETHICS OF MOTION PRACTICE

Motion practice is a blank canvas that the litigator paints to suit the individual case. The finished design may be starkly minimalist, or complex and densely detailed, or somewhere in between—but it will be unique, because there are no required motions and no limit to the number of motions that may be filed or to their subject matter.

Yet the very fluidity that makes motion practice so creative also makes it an ethical minefield. Pre-trial motion practice poses some of the worst temptations to unethical practice. The rules for ethical motion practice are clear, although their application is sometimes less than straightforward. The most frequently dishonored rules are these three.

- Never make a motion in order to delay the proceedings or annoy or impoverish your adversary.
- Never base your motion on facts not supported by the record, except when there is good reason to assert facts "on information and belief."
- Never make a motion unless there is a plausible legal ground.

These principles are embodied in the Disciplinary Rules of the ABA Code of Professional Responsibility. For example, Rule 7-102 forbids an attorney from doing anything to "assert a position, delay a trial, or take other action on behalf of his client when he knows that such action would serve merely to harass or maliciously injure another."[42]

Of the three rules, the prohibition on playing fast-and-loose with facts is the most straightforward. A fact either is or is not in the record, and carelessness or willful violation are the only explanations for a motion grounded in factual misrepresentation. The other two rules are not always so simple. It is sometimes difficult to know whether a motion was made "merely" to increase the adversary's costs or whether the strain on his finances is incidental. Moreover, although all authorities agree that motions with no plausible legal basis are frivolous and thus impermissible, it is not always clear where the line between frivolous and plausible lies.

Discussing the ethics of motion practice, many experts note that behavior that violates ethical rules rarely advances the client's or attorney's interests.[43] Indeed, such conduct can disadvantage both quite spectacularly. In one notable case, an attorney overstated facts in order to avoid summary judgment. When the real facts emerged at trial, the judge realized that but for the attorney's misrepresentations, summary judgment would have been granted. Enraged, the judge awarded the offending attorney's adversary all the fees the adversary had incurred since the denial of her summary judgment motion: some 2 million dollars.[44] In addition to material losses, attorneys who are perceived to engage in sharp and shady motion practice lose their credibility with the court and the respect and good will of their peers.

Nonetheless, we believe one can over-emphasize the counter-productivity of unethical behavior. Stressing the consequences of such conduct for the actor suggests that it is not a problem unless it is discovered. Moreover, a narrow focus on consequence suggests (wrongly, we hope) that lawyers need a practical incentive to do the right thing.

---

[42] ABA Code of Professional Responsibility, Disciplinary Rule 7-102 (1979).

[43] *See, e.g.,* Herr, Haydock & Stempel, *supra* n. 2, § 7.02[D].

[44] *See In re Brand Name Prescription Drugs Litigation,* 1999 WL 301653 (N.D. Ill 1999), cited in *Id.* §7.07, 7–20.

Finally, some ethicists would argue that conduct satisfying professional rules of conduct in itself does not necessarily satisfy overarching rules of universal ethics.[45] Imagine, for example, that you represent a defendant served with a very poorly drawn complaint by a plaintiff of limited means whom you believe to have an excellent case against your client. You believe that you have non-frivolous grounds to move for dismissal for failure to state a claim. You also believe that the plaintiff does not have the resources to defend properly against such a motion. You also believe that if the court grants your motion and grants plaintiff leave to refile his complaint, the statute of limitations will run, effectively terminating the litigation. Your motion would not be filed "merely" to frustrate justice, and would thus not violate Disciplinary Rule 7-102. The motion would serve your client's interests admirably. Yet depending on how unequally matched the adversaries and how egregious the injury on which the complaint is based, a thoughtful practitioner might have qualms about filing the motion, even though his duty to represent his client would seem not only to permit, but to require, doing so. Similarly, although frivolous motions are forbidden by traditional legal ethics, defense counsel might feel bound to raise even the most wildly improbable arguments in a death penalty case. In sum, there is much to debate about the relation of universal ethical principles to professional or "role" ethics and no easy answers—but, at a minimum, we must remain open to the questions.

---

### *Exercise 4.1*

*Critique the following draft of the body of a motion to suppress evidence in a criminal case. What problems do you see? Revise it to eliminate problems that rewriting can solve. Are there problems that re-wording alone can't solve?*

---

[45] *See, e.g.,* Richard Wasserstrom, *Roles and Morality,* in *The Good Lawyer* (David Luban, ed. Rowman & Littlefield 1984).

IN THE DISTRICT COURT IN AND FOR REGENT COUNTY
STATE OF ATLANTIS

---------------------------------------------------------

| | |
|---|---|
| State of Atlantis ) | |
| ) | |
| –vs– ) | |
| ) | Indictment No. 582/03 |
| Jonathan Parsons, ) | |
| Defendant. ) | |

---------------------------------------------------------

## MOTION

Comes now the defendant, Jonathan Parsons, by and through his attorney, and moves the court to suppress evidence and dismiss the indictment in the above-entitled matter due to the fact that defendant was unlawfully and illegally arrested and searched and that he was unlawfully and illegally questioned and that the evidence obtained incident to said unlawful and illegal arrest, search, and questioning was essential to the proof of the guilt or innocence of this defendant and that said evidence which was so illegally and unlawfully obtained incident to said illegal and unlawful arrest, search, and questioning is inadmissible and should be suppressed as violative of the constitutional rights of said defendant and the Rules of Evidence and the laws and statutes of the State of Atlantis and the Constitution of the United States.

WHEREFORE, Defendant prays this Honorable Court that the motion be sustained, that all evidence obtained by use of the illegal arrest and search and questioning of the defendant be suppressed and the indictment dismissed.

---

## *Exercise 4.2*

*Assume that a malpractice complaint containing only the allegations below was filed against attorney Carolyn Miller within the statute of limitations in a court with jurisdiction over the parties and the subject matter. The complaint has been filed in a notice-pleading jurisdiction with civil procedure rules identical to the Federal Rules.*

*Assume that defendant Miller never agreed to represent the plaintiff, Ben Abelman. Plaintiff spoke to another attorney in the firm, Daniel Carstairs, who interviewed the plaintiff and told him he had an excellent case. Carstairs said he was about to go on medical leave, but would "give the case to his colleague Carolyn Miller, who would handle it." Carstairs became acutely ill and died without mentioning the case to defendant Miller. The statute of limitations on plaintiff's false imprisonment and personal injury claims ran before the file was found in Carstairs' papers.*

*What motion(s) might defendant Miller's counsel make based on the face of the complaint itself? Draft the motion(s).*

Plaintiff alleges as follows.

1. Defendant Carolyn Miller is an attorney licensed to practice law in the state of _____.
2. On June 5, 20__, defendant was engaged to represent plaintiff in an action for false imprisonment and personal injury action against Morrison's Department Store.
3. Defendant failed to represent plaintiff with care, skill, and diligence.
4. Defendant's failure to adequately represent plaintiff was a breach of her duty to plaintiff.
5. As a result of defendant's breach of her duty to plaintiff, plaintiff sustained injury. Specifically, plaintiff's injury includes the loss of a verdict, settlement, or award, and the interest that plaintiff would have recovered but for defendant's breach of her duty.
7. The injury sustained by plaintiff was proximately caused by defendant's breach of her duty. Plaintiff committed no negligent acts or omissions that contributed to his injury.

─────────────────── *Exercise 4.3* ───────────────────

*Assume that you are a member of the firm that is representing plaintiff Jeffrey Hustin in the action against Michele Freeman and the Regents of the University of Atlantis that is the subject of the sample complaint in Chapter 2, the sample answer in Chapter 3, the sample motion for partial summary judgment in this chapter, and the sample trial memorandum of law in Chapter 9. On behalf of plaintiff Hustin, you will, of course oppose defendant Michele Freeman's motion for partial summary judgment, which is based on her claim that her allegedly defamatory statements about your client were privileged communications.*

*To that end, you have asked a new associate to draft plaintiff Hustin's affidavit in opposition to the motion. The associate's draft follows. Before reviewing it, refresh your recollection of the case by consulting the previously filed documents. Then critique the draft, making recommendations for revision. You will need to consider whether the draft affidavit contains sufficient information relevant to the issue, and whether all the information in the affidavit is in fact either relevant or necessary for the reader's comprehension.*

*You will also need to assess the style, tone, and preparation of the draft. Is the tone appropriate to its purpose and audience? Does it do a good job of telling plaintiff's story? Is the preparation careful?*

Superior Court of the State of Atlantis
County of Sussex

----------------------------------------------------------

| | |
|---|---|
| Jeffrey Hustin, | Index No. Civ.____ |
| Plaintiff, | |
| -against- | AFFIDAVIT |
| Michele Freeman and | |
| The Regents of the University of Atlantis, | |
| Defendants. | |

----------------------------------------------------------

State of Atlantis    )
County of Atlantis  )

Geoffrey Hustin, being duly sworn, says as follows.

1. I am the plaintiff in the above action, commenced by a duly filed complaint dated February 5, 20__, which was duly served upon defendants on February 10, 20__, well within the statute of limitations. The complaint is annexed to this affidavit as Plaintiff's Exhibit A. The background to plaintiff's action is as follows. In October, 20__, plaintiff applied to the Status Committee of the University of Atlantis Law School for academic tenure and promotion to the rank of Associate Professor.
2. The Status Committee comprises the entire tenured faculty of the Law School, and its function is to evaluate and act upon applications for tenure and promotion.
3. Because she was only a visiting professor, defendant Michele Freeman was not a member of the Status Committee.
4. Despite her lack of any legitimate interest in the matter, on or about March 12, 20__, defendant Freeman wrote a memorandum to the thirty-two members of the Status Committee of the Law School concerning plaintiff's application.

5. This memorandum was sent to all members of the Status Committee on or about March 12, 20__.

6. Every member of the Status Committee read the memorandum written by defendant Freeman about the plaintiff.

7. Defendant Freeman's memorandum, annexed to this affidavit as Exhibit B, contained statements about plaintiff that were defamatory, in that they tended to expose him to contempt, aversion, ridicule, and disgrace, and to induce a bad opinion of him in the minds of right thinking persons.

8. All of the statements from defendant Freeman's memorandum concerning plaintiff are false.

9. Defendant Freeman's memorandum was the only communication of its nature received by the Status Committee, and all other evaluations of plaintiff's scholarship and teaching abilities were extremely positive. They are attached to this affidavit as plaintiff's Exhibit C.

16. As a result of the publication by defendant Freeman of her memorandum, plaintiff's application for tenure and promotion was rejected by the Status Committee, the Committee declined to rehire plaintiff as an Assistant Professor of Law, he was unable to find any other suitable employment, and he has consequently suffered grievous harm, including the destruction of personal and professional relationships.

17. Defendant Freeman's conduct in writing the memorandum to the Status Committee is so extreme and outrageous as to be intolerable in a civilized community.

18. As a result of defendant Freeman's conduct, plaintiff suffered severe emotional distress.

19. Plaintiff's distress was intentionally, or at a minimum, recklessly, caused by defendant.

20. Defendants Regents of the University of Atlantis are vicariously liable for the actions of their employee, defendant Freeman.

21. On July 21, 20__, defendant filed a notice of her intent to ask for summary judgment, on the erroneous ground that her statements to the Status Committee were privileged and therefore could not render her liable for defamation. The instant affidavit is made in opposition to defendant's frivolous claim.

22. Despite defendant's argument to the contrary, her statements were in fact not privileged because, as noted above, they were utterly and totally false, and, additionally, her statements were made out of spite and with a high degree of awareness that they were false.

23. Therefore, defendant's motion for summary judgment must be denied in its entirety.

_____

Geoffrey Hustin

State of Atlantis      )
County of Sussex     ) ss.

On August 10, 20__, Geoffrey Hustin personally appeared before me, a Notary Public for the State of Atlantis and County of Sussex. Being duly sworn, Geoffrey Hustin deposed and said that she is one of the plaintiffs in the above action and that the facts set forth in this affidavit are true, except for those statements made upon information and belief, and as to those statements, she believes them to be true.

_____

Sworn and subscribed before me this 10th day of August, 20__.

_____ ***Exercise 4.4*** _____

*The affidavit excerpted below was drafted for submission in a will contest. What legal argument does it support? Does it do so effectively? Identify the storytelling techniques used by the drafter. (For more background information on this case, see Section 4(c) in Chapter 7, Letters.)*

### Affidavit of Joan Kavanaugh[46]

I, Joan Kavanaugh, being duly sworn and under oath, state that:

1. I am over 18 years of age and am otherwise competent to give testimony in this case.
2. This affidavit is made based upon my personal knowledge.
3. This affidavit is true and correct to the best of my knowledge.
4. If called to testify, I would give evidence consistent with this affidavit.
5. Timothy Morse was my uncle.
6. I visited my uncle Timothy twice in the two months prior to his death.

_____

[46] Our thanks to Margaret Cahoon for drafting the affidavit on which this example is based.

7.   On my first visit, on or about March 25, 20__, Steven Lewis answered the door, opening it only slightly and stating that I could not see my uncle without calling in advance. I did not know Mr. Lewis and had never seen him with my uncle. I later learned he had been my uncle's housekeeper for the last six months of my uncle's life.

8.   On or about March 29, 20__, I called ahead to arrange my second visit and spoke to Steven Lewis, who answered the phone. We arranged a visit on April 1, 20__.

9.   Mr. Lewis again answered the door on my second visit, but again opened the door only slightly. When I said I had made an appointment, he waited a short period before letting me in.

10.  Mr. Lewis followed me upstairs to my uncle's room, where my uncle was confined to his bed. Mr. Lewis stayed in the room for the duration of my visit.

11.  My uncle looked tired and weak and did not get up to greet me or get out of bed at any time during my visit.

12.  My uncle was not very talkative during my visit, which was different from his usual jovial and chatty manner.

13.  When I asked my uncle if his sons John and James had come to visit, he looked at Mr. Lewis. Mr. Lewis nodded, and my uncle said, "My sons haven't bothered to call me."

14.  When I asked my uncle how he was feeling, he began a sentence with "The doctors say," but Mr. Lewis coughed loudly, interrupting him. After that he said he was feeling "tired but not too bad."

15.  When I asked my uncle if there was anything he needed me to take care of, he responded, "Steven has been taking care of my affairs for me."

16.  When I got up to leave, Mr. Lewis also got up to escort me out. As I reached the door to his room, my uncle cried out my name, but when I turned back, he was silent and then said quietly, "Goodbye, Joan."

17.  That is the last time I saw my uncle before he died.

─────────────── *Assignment 4.1* ───────────────

*Assume that a complaint has been filed in County Court, Hennepin County, Minnesota, against Michael Bryant and the Board of Parish Life of Grace Church, on behalf of Nancy Williams, whose case against Bryant (her former supervisor) and the Board (her former employer) is described in Casefile 1 in*

*Appendix A. (If you wrote a complaint for Ms. Williams as requested by Assignment 2.2 in the chapter on complaints, you may use that complaint as a basis for your motion. If your class has not done that assignment, your teacher will supply you with a complaint.)*

Assume that you are an associate in the law firm representing defendant, the Board of Parish Life of Grace Church. No answer has yet been filed, because your boss believes that the Board has grounds for moving to dismiss the complaint on jurisdictional grounds. She thinks a viable argument can be made on the Board's behalf that adjudicating Williams' claims would violate the Establishment Clause of the First Amendment and the Freedom of Conscience Clause of the Minnesota Constitution. She has asked you to research the issues and then draft a motion, pursuant to Rule 12.08(c) of the Minnesota Rules of Civil Procedure, to dismiss the complaint for lack of subject matter jurisdiction. Prepare a notice of motion, motion, and draft order. (Your work on Williams v. Grace Church *will continue in Assignment 9.2 in* Trial and Appellate Briefs, *which asks you to write a memorandum of law.)*

---

### *Assignment 4.2*

Assume that in the litigation described in Assignment 4.1 and based on the facts in Casefile 1 in Appendix A, the defendant Board of Parish Life made the motion to dismiss for lack of subject matter jurisdiction, both sides submitted briefs, oral argument was held, and the court denied the motion. The Board of Parish Life answered the complaint, admitting to the existence of the employment contract with Nancy Williams described in and annexed to her complaint, but effectively denying the rest of her allegations, either by outright denials or by alleging insufficient information to form a belief. The discovery phase of the litigation has begun. The Chair of the Board of Parish Life, Walter Bishop, was the first to be deposed; an excerpt from his deposition follows.

Assume that you work for the firm that represents plaintiff Nancy Williams. Based on Bishop's deposition, make a motion for summary judgment. On which cause(s) of action will you ask summary judgment? Prepare a notice of motion, motion, and draft order. You may either include your legal argument in the motion proper or draft a short trial memorandum of law to support your argument.

### Deposition of Walter Bishop
### (Excerpt)

Q.  I understand there came a time when you were no longer satisfied with plaintiff's work performance.

A. Well, it wasn't her work so much as her behavior that we believed was inappropriate.

Q. So her work was satisfactory?

A. Yes, but we had an e-mail from a young woman, apparently someone on our women's basketball team, complaining about her morals.

Q. And what was the nature of this complaint?

A. The message said Ms. Williams had been seen touching another girl who was on the team.

Q. Is that verbatim what the message said, or were there details.

A. She said she had seen Ms. Williams with another girl on the team, after a game, touching her, and she—the writer, that is—thought we ought to know.

Q. That was it?

A. That was enough for us. We, that is the other board members and myself, thought it was morally inappropriate for Ms. Williams to relate that way to a teenager.

Q. Did you investigate the matter further, to determine what kind of touching or even whether the writer was truthful?

A. Well, the writer didn't sign the e-mail or put her real name in her address, so we couldn't follow up, but although we would have preferred to have more, we really didn't think we needed to know any more than we already knew.

Q. If you remember, when was this e-mail received?

A. We printed it out, so I know it was on October 5, 20__.

Q. And then you fired her on November 10 of that year?

A. That's correct. We felt we didn't have any choice.

Q. How was her termination effected? Did you write her a letter? Telephone her? E-mail? Call her in?

A. We thought it was better to terminate her in person, effective immediately, at our Board meeting on November 10, to avoid her making any, you know, trouble.

Q. So she had no advance warning?

A. No, we didn't think we needed to do that, and we thought it would be better for all concerned.

—————————— *Assignment 4.3* ——————————

*Three years ago, your firm represented Maureen Brown in her divorce action against David Brown. The divorce decree provided for joint custody of the couple's young son, with primary residential custody of son Kevin to Maureen. The couple have continued to reside in the New Jersey town where they lived during their marriage, but now Maureen wishes to move with Kevin to Washington State. A colleague has already drafted a petition to the Superior Court, whose permission is necessary when a custodial parent wishes to relocate with a minor child. He has now turned the case over to you. Please read the petition and the leading New Jersey case,* Holder v. Polanski, *544 A.2d 852 (N.J. 1998).*

*A.  Role- play an interview with Ms. Brown and draft an affidavit in support of her petition. The affidavit should, of course, contain facts relevant to the court's concerns under* Holder. *Ms. Brown will come in to our office for an interview next week. To prepare for that interview, read the petition and* Holder *and make a list of 10-15 important questions you would want to ask Ms. Williamson. Bring your list to class. After the interview, you will draft the affidavit. Use the form that appears at the end of this assignment.*

*Or*

*B.  Draft an affidavit based on a summary of an interview with Ms. Brown provided by your professor. Use the form that appears at the end of this assignment.*

**SUPERIOR COURT, CHANCERY DIVISION**
**MATRIMONIAL PART**
**COUNTY OF ATLANTIS**
----------------------------------------X

**PETITION FOR PERMISSION**

**MAUREEN BROWN**
            Petitioner

- against -

**TO RELOCATE**

**DAVID BROWN,**
            Respondent.

**DOCKET NO. 57/___**

----------------------------------------X

TO THE SUPERIOR COURT:

The undersigned Petitioner respectfully shows that:

1. Petitioner is the natural mother of Kevin Brown, age 7, born December 17, 20__, and resides at 310 Central Avenue, Seagrove, New

Jersey. Respondent is the natural father of Kevin Brown and resides at 67 Hughes Street, Seagrove, New Jersey.

2. Petitioner was the Plaintiff in a divorce action, entitled Brown v. Brown, Index No. 776/__, and the above-named Respondent was the Defendant in that action.

3. A decree dated two years ago, May 30, 20__, was made in the divorce action. Under this decree, the Separation Agreement of the parties dated April 15, of that same year, was incorporated but not merged into such judgment. The Separation Agreement provides for joint legal custody of Kevin, with physical custody and right of day-to-day supervision to Petitioner. There is a provision in the Separation Agreement that Petitioner may not remove the child from the state of New Jersey except upon permission of the Superior Court.

4. Since the entry of the divorce decree, there has been a change of circumstances in that Petitioner wants to accept an offer of employment from a corporation with its offices in Seattle, Washington. These and other relevant circumstances are detailed in Petitioner's Affidavit in Support of this Petition, attached to and filed with the Petition.

5. By reason of this change of circumstances, this Court should:
   a. Permit Petitioner to remove the child to the State of Washington when Petitioner moves to that state; and
   b. Modify support and visitation in such manner as to the Court seems fair and reasonable.

6. No previous application has been made to any court or judge for the relief requested here.

WHEREFORE, Petitioner respectfully asks that permission to remove be granted and that the said Order of the Superior Court, dated May 30, 20__ be modified in the respects detailed above, for such other relief as to the Court may seem just and proper, and in the alternative, for a hearing on her petition.
Dated: February __, 20__

_____
Petitioner

[Verification]

[Attorney certification]

**SUPERIOR COURT, CHANCERY DIVISION
MATRIMONIAL PART
COUNTY OF** _____

-----------------------------------------X

**[ADD TITLE OF CAUSE]**

|                                  | **AFFIDAVIT IN SUPPORT OF PETITION FOR PERMISSION TO RELOCATE**
**Docket No.** _____ |

**AFFIDAVIT IN SUPPORT OF
PETITION FOR PERMISSION
TO RELOCATE
Docket No.** _____

-----------------------------------------X

STATE OF NEW JERSEY)
COUNTY OF _____ )

_____, being duly sworn, deposes and says:

   1. I am the petitioner above-named.

   2. This affidavit is submitted in support of petitioner's request for an order permitting her to remove her minor child _____ from the state of New Jersey, modifying the divorce decree in the action entitled _____ dated _____, granting such other relief as to the Court may seem just and proper, or, in the alternative, granting a hearing on her petition.

   3. [NOW TELL THE STORY, IN AS MANY PARAGRAPHS AS YOU NEED.]

* * *

   WHEREFORE, it is respectfully requested that the Court grant the relief requested and such other relief as to the Court may seem just and proper, or, in the alternative, grant a hearing on the petition.


_____
Signature


_____
Date


*[Notarization]*

# *Part Two*

# Chapter 5

# *BASIC SKILLS:*
# *CLARITY*

---

## A. INTRODUCTION

Lawyers' sentences are like a coral reef: they keep on growing and growing. Every new idea, caveat, exception, condition, timetable, hypothetical, or modification adds a clause. The result, as the following example shows, is verbal sprawl.

> After this policy has been in effect for sixty days, it is subject to cancellation only for non-payment of premium (*oh, but also...*); if your driver's license (*hey, what about the licenses of others?*), or that of any driver who customarily uses your auto, has been suspended (*just suspended?*) or revoked; or (*wait a sec—there's more*) for discovery of fraud or material misrepresentation in obtaining the policy or presenting a claim (*oops, almost forgot that one*), but not without forty-five days' notice (*must remember due process*)—by post (*put it in writing*)—of the reason for the cancellation (*whew, made it!*).

But if these long, rambling sentences often show effective conceptualization, they fall short of effective presentation. Readers respond best to shorter sentences that they can hold in their minds,[1] to sentences that exhibit clear and logical connections between words and parts, and to sentences that tell stories about characters. Readers also need to be able to bridge the synapse between adjacent sentences almost instantaneously and to comprehend each sentence's connection to the topic of the paragraph. Clarity is important to most written documents, but it is especially crucial when we seek to convey complex analysis in a memo or

---

[1] Twenty-five words is a good, average length.

make complex arguments in persuasive documents. Thus, clarity is a signature skill of all the documents in Part Two of this book: letters, office memoranda, trial and appellate briefs, and judicial opinions. This chapter will focus in turn on the two main components of clarity: reader-friendly sentences and unified and cohesive paragraphs.

## B. CLEAR SENTENCES

The law deals with abstractions and with complex subject matter. Yet, the more abstract and complex the content of a sentence, the harder a writer has to work to make it clear. Punctuation that aids the reader in parsing the sentence (in seeing its parts) is obviously critical to this endeavor. So is careful attention to grammar, the set of rules that classifies parts of speech and that governs the ways we group those parts and move them around in a sentence. Equally important, but less obvious, are principles of construction that are conducive to reader comprehension. For example, linguists have learned that readers comprehend more quickly sentences in which the subject is immediately followed by a verb than they comprehend sentences in which the verb is deferred to the end. A writer may delay giving the verb without violating any grammatical rule, but ready understanding is too often the price.

This section will begin with principles of good sentence construction and then review some key rules of grammar and punctuation.

### 1. Good Sentence Construction

When we talk about sentence constructions that promote easy comprehension, three insights are paramount: readers understand sentences that tell stories more easily than sentences that discuss abstract concepts, readers need the subject and verb to come early in the sentence in order to anticipate and comprehend the ensuing content, and readers need the complex information that has been deferred to the end of sentences to be tightly organized. Each of these insights has syntactic—or sentence structure—ramifications.

## a. Telling the Story

Since readers have an easier time understanding and remembering narrative, as many of our sentences as possible should tell stories. The story may be short—spanning only the duration of the sentence—but the hallmark features of a narrative should be present: the sentence needs characters and a plot. As in the example that follows, the character usually appears as the grammatical subject of the sentence, and the verb tells us about the character's action, thereby creating a narrative. (For easy identification, we have put characters in bold type and their actions in italics.)

> **The appellant** *did not participate* in the responsibilities of parenthood: **he** *did not take* Cassidy to the doctor, *make* him meals, *attend* parent-teacher conferences, or *chauffeur* him to play dates and activities.

Sometimes the character is an institution or organization instead of a person, but this does not vary the basic agent/action pattern.

> **The family court** *properly denied* appellant's order of filiation because **he** *failed* to grasp his opportunity to develop a relationship with Cassidy.

Of course there are many sentences that seem to have no characters and no action. This is true of passive voice sentences that omit the agent of the action, as in "the responsibilities of parenthood were not undertaken." Such constructions should ordinarily be avoided because sentences without characters tend to distance readers from the subject matter and render them indifferent.[2] Moreover, depopulated sentences are often deceptively abstract. In fact, characters often lurk in possessive pronouns, in the objects of prepositions and verbs, and in adjectives.[3]

---

[2] Writers sometimes depopulate their sentences deliberately. In some persuasive documents, they may wish to distance the reader from the event.

[3] Joseph Williams, *Style: Ten Lessons in Clarity and Grace* 71–72 (6th ed., Longman 2000).

> The tendency **of at-risk families** to try to protect **their** children from **judicial** oversight is well known.

Here, "families" is not the subject of the sentence but is a character hidden both in the possessive pronoun "their" and the object of the preposition "of;" the court is secreted in the adjective "judicial." Concealing characters makes it harder to comprehend the story, however. The characters should be pulled from their hiding places and made to take their place as subjects.

> **Family court judges** *know* that **at-risk families** *try to protect* their children from the court's oversight.

Of course, many sentences are about concepts or things, not characters and their actions. Law talk is, after all, as often about rules and policies as about defendants and plaintiffs. Fortunately, the principles of syntax that we derived from storytelling can be put to use in abstract discussions. For example, we can treat abstract concepts as if they were actors and then make those concepts do things.[4]

> The **consequences** of driving while intoxicated *compel* us to criminalize the offense.

If the subject of the sentence is not a character, it can at least be a pseudo-actor.

When you find your actors and set them up as subjects performing actions, your word order will more closely match the syntax of the sentence to the chronology of an event. When verbs do not express a character's actions, the "plot" sequence is often hard to follow.

> The reluctance to perform a reassessment of the efficacy of the sentencing guidelines *means* the continued overcrowding of our prisons with small-time drug offenders.

---

[4] *Id.* at 75.

Although not indecipherable, this sentence is harder to understand than one with an actor/action pattern and active verbs.

> Because **legislators** *are* reluctant to reassess the efficacy of the sentencing guidelines, **small-time drug offenders** *will continue to overcrowd* the prisons.

Finally, when the subject of the sentence is an actor who performs actions, the sentence is more likely to have active verbs, not nominalizations, and will therefore be shorter, livelier, clearer, and easier to remember. Nominalizations are the noun forms of verbs. Often they appear as the subject of a sentence, bumping the character to a different position—as in this heavily nominalized sentence in which the character, the legislature, is buried in the adjective of a prepositional phrase that modifies the nominalized subject "revision."

> A revision of **legislative** sentencing guidelines will result in a *decrease* in the prison population.

You can shorten the sentence and restore logical order if you convert the nominalizations "revision" and "decrease" into active verbs and return the character to the subject.

> If the **legislature** *revises* its sentencing guidelines, the **prison population** will *decrease*.

Nominalizations also and often appear as the object of the verb:

> The defendant *had* **knowledge** of a conspiracy.

These nominalizations need to be converted too.

> The defendant *knew* about the conspiracy.

Particularly baffling are sentences that couple nominalizations and prepositional phrases, a combination that obscures and bedevils chronological sequence.

> A client's lack of legal knowledge does not mean decisions on trial strategy should be made by legal counsel without consultation.

Chronology is restored by turning the subjects into characters and converting the nominalizations into active verbs.

> Although **clients** *may not know* much law, **counsel** *should consult* them about trial strategy.

### b. Leading with Subject and Verb

It follows from what we have said that the most important relationship in a sentence is that between the subject and verb. A reader cannot begin to predict the outcome of a sentence until both are known. Thus the subject and verb need to be near each other and to appear early in a sentence. Adherence to these strictures has important ramifications on the syntax of a sentence. It means, for example, that writers should avoid both long subjects composed of nouns and modifiers and long interruptions separating subjects and verbs, because both these constructions delay the verb's entrance. This in turn means that the information that was embedded in the subject or contained in the interruption should be relocated to the end of the sentence, where it is most easily absorbed. In fact, readers understand a sentence more easily when its general point is made first. The general point provides context for the details that follow.

Writers need to avoid long subjects—subjects composed of a noun and a string of modifiers describing that noun—because they postpone the action. In the following sentence, the subject is in bold and the verb is in italics.

> **Imposing criminal liability on an unwitting food stamp recipient who purchased groceries at a store that inflated its prices to such purchasers** *struck* the court as beyond the intended reach of the statute.

Here a twenty-one word subject—consisting of a main subject ("imposing criminal liability"), a prepositional phrase ("on an unwitting food stamp recipient"), and two modifiers ("who purchased groceries at a store" and "that inflated its prices")—delay the entrance of the verb "struck." The sentence is easier to grasp if the writer begins with the ending. The reversal enables the writer to lead with a short subject and verb and to put the substantive details in the object position at the end of the sentence, the position where details are most easily absorbed.

> **The court** *said* it was beyond the intended reach of the statute to impose criminal liability on an unwitting food stamp recipient who purchased groceries at a store that inflated its prices to such purchasers.

Long phrases or clauses separating the subject and verb also strain comprehension.

> **Equitable estoppel**, which prevents the enforcement of rights that would ultimately result in fraud or injustice to the person against whom enforcement is sought, *is imposed* in the interest of fairness.

The sentence is clearer when the long interruption either leads into or ends the sentence. When complicated material is in the object position of the sentence, it can be more easily contemplated.

> **Equitable estoppel** *is imposed* in the interest of fairness to prevent the enforcement of rights that would ultimately result in fraud or injustice to the person against whom enforcement is sought.

When the subject and verb are far apart, the writer often loses track of them, a situation that often results in errors, as in the following sentence.

> A **delay** of almost five years by the EEOC in bringing a suit against an employer under Title VII *may be barred* on the basis of laches.

Here the subject "delay" does not make sense with the verb "may be barred." It is the lawsuit, not the delay, that may be barred.

The writer had obviously forgotten the subject by the time she got to the verb.

> **The EEOC lawsuit** *may be barred* on the basis of laches because the **EEOC** *delayed* filing suit for almost five years.

Keeping subject and verb together and near the beginning is especially important to effective issue statements and questions presented. In office memoranda and persuasive briefs, these are frequently the reader's first encounter with the complex subject matter of the document. Giving priority to the subject and verb helps the reader.

> **Not:** Whether **an administrative law judge who awarded treble compensatory damages in a sex discrimination action brought by a former probationary grounds keeper for a university** *improperly applied* the punitive damage standard. (Long subject)
>
> **Not:** Whether **an administrative law judge**, in awarding treble compensatory damages in a sex discrimination case brought by a former probationary groundskeeper for a university, *improperly applied* the punitive damage standard. (Long interruption)
>
> **But:** Whether **an administrative law judge** *improperly applied* the punitive damage standard when she awarded treble compensatory damages in a sex discrimination case brought by a former probationary groundskeeper for a university.

——————— *Exercise 5.1: Beginnings* ———————

*Diagnose problems. Rewrite so the subject of the sentence is short and is near the verb. Make sure characters are not hidden in adjectives, prepositional phrases, or possessives. Instead, pull them out and make them into subjects. Edit for nominalizations and passive voice.*

1. The approach that the statutes should be deemed to apply to state prisoners because the statutes are broadly worded has been rejected.

2. Generally, courts avoid interference in ecclesiastic matters because of fear of excessive entanglement based on the constitutional principle of separation of church and state.

3. While the rule invites judicial flexibility, it does not countenance reliance by the court on a single factor when others show reliability.

4. Records made in the course of regularly conducted activity will be taken as admissible.

5. The judicial creation and extension of privileges should be done cautiously.

6. That the legislature's intent was to prevent toxic dumping was emphasized by the court.

7. The first factor, requiring evidence of plaintiff's intent to serve process before he issued a fraudulent invitation to the defendant to enter the jurisdiction, cannot be met.

8. The Act contains an underlying recognition that disclosure of bureaucracy can be a benefit to the public.

9. The belief that he had to choose between two evils rendered defendant's request to proceed *pro se* involuntary.

10. Some people, especially those receiving services covered by insurance with only a nominal copayment, exploit the services available to them.

11. The agreement whereby she would support him while he wrote a textbook, in return for which he would support her once it was finished, was held enforceable.

12. Comment on the efficiency of industry regulated labeling programs was solicited.

13. Since the building was not owned but was leased by our client, permanent occupancy could not be assumed.

14. A complaint that alleges that a plaintiff, a dentist, delivered to defendants for repair an anesthetic machine that he had purchased from them, that defendants were negligent in replacing the color-coded decal on the machine with the result that, intending to administer oxygen to a patient, plaintiff in fact administered nitrous oxide, causing the death of the patient, that, as a result, plaintiff's mental condition was such that he was unable to carry on his professional work and because of the damage to his reputation was obliged to withdraw from practice state a valid cause of action permitting recovery by plaintiff for such pecuniary loss as may be proved but not permitting recovery for the emotional injury he claimed to have resulted.

## c. Ending Effectively

When the end of the sentence carries the substance of the sentence, writers must work to make those ends comprehensible. Two techniques to control this part of the sentence are putting related ideas in parallel constructions and using sentences with resumptive and summative modifiers, that is, modifiers that extend sentences by elaborating on a key word (resumptive) or key idea (summative) in the sentence.

### i. Parallelism

Parallelism is a good way of coordinating related ideas. When your sentence includes a series of ideas, those ideas should be syntactically parallel, that is, the grammatical pattern should be repeated to highlight where each new idea in the series begins. The coordination usually begins after the subject or after the verb and requires that nouns be paired with nouns, clauses with clauses, present tense verbs with present tense verbs, etc. In the following sentence, the beginning of each parallel item is in italics.

> A psychiatrist's examination for mental capacity to write a will should include *a medical diagnosis* based on a thorough history and clinical examination, *details* of the mental status examination that document testamentary capacity with particular reference to ideation and cognition, and *an opinion* regarding the probability that a psychiatric or neurological disorder has affected testamentary capacity.

Faulty parallelism occurs when one element in the series breaks the anticipated pattern and undermines the cadence and continuity.

> A psychiatrist's examination for mental capacity to write a will should include *a medical diagnosis* based on a thorough history and clinical examination, *details* of the mental status examination on testamentary capacity with particular reference to ideation and cognition, and *whether it is* prob-

able that a psychiatric or neurological disorder has affected testamentary capacity.

Faulty parallelism can also obscure the relation between the parts of a sentence.

The company violated the Robinson-Patman Act when the chairman of the board *sent* letters to end users *promoting* a particular dealer and *furnishing* a technician to that dealer in order to offer repair services to its end users.

The wrong verbs are made parallel here. The chairman violated the Act twice: once by sending letters that promoted a dealer and once by furnishing a technician to the dealer. "Furnishing" should match "sent," not "promoting." The faulty parallelism makes it look like the letters were the only violation of the Robinson-Patman Act. Correct parallelism clears up that confusion.

The company violated the Robinson-Patman Act when the chairman of the board not only *sent* letters to end users promoting a particular dealer, but also *furnished* a technician to that dealer in order to offer repair services to its end users.

ii. Resumptive and Summative Modifiers

You can also put new information, or information in a long subject or interruption, in a resumptive modifier or summative modifier, both of which are modifiers that are attached to the end of the sentence.[5] A resumptive modifier repeats a key word in the sentence and then proceeds to elaborate on that key word.

The appellant did not participate in the *responsibilities* of parenthood, *responsibilities like taking Cassidy to the doctor, making him meals, attending parent-teacher conferences, or chauffeuring him to play dates and activities.*

---

[5] *See id.* at 176–177.

A summative modifier "sums up" in a noun the central idea of the sentence and then elaborates on that idea.

> The legislature has delayed reassessing the efficacy of its sentencing guidelines, *a postponement that causes the continued overcrowding of prisons with small-time drug offenders.*

To keep the main idea of the sentence intact, it is often helpful to turn material in interruptions into a resumptive modifier, as the resumptive modifier in the second sentence below illustrates.

> Many schools do not have the physical facilities, *including a sufficient level of sophisticated technology,* to host this conference.
>
> Many schools do not have the physical facilities to host this conference, *facilities that must include a sufficient level of sophisticated technology.*

Resumptive and summative modifiers also promote clarity by preventing the ambiguous reference of "which" clauses.

> Many schools do not have the physical facilities to host this conference, *which must include a sufficient level of sophisticated technology.*

It is unclear whether "which" refers to facilities or conference. A resumptive modifier would eliminate this confusion.

> Many schools do not have the physical facilities to host this conference, *facilities that must include a sufficient level of sophisticated technology.*

In the next sentence, it is not clear whether "which" refers to the twisting of rules or the mistaken belief:

> Some attorneys twist the rules of discovery in the mistaken belief that the adversary system permits them to do so, *which arouses the anger of judges.*

A summative modifier clarifies the meaning.

> Some attorneys twist the rules of discovery in the mistaken belief that the adversary system permits them to do so, *a practice that arouses the anger of judges.*

One collateral benefit of organizing the most complex information in your sentence into coordinated clauses or resumptive or summative modifiers at the end of your sentence is that it is an ideal way of ensuring the early appearance of the subject and verb.

─────────────── *Exercise 5.2: Endings* ───────────────

*A. Correct the faulty parallelism in the following sentences.*

1.  There are three tests under DR5-105 for representing conflicting interests: full disclosure of the nature of the conflict; obtaining the consent of the client; and whether the lawyer can adequately represent the interests of both clients.
2.  In determining whether the bookcases could be removed from the rental property, the court applies the four-prong fixture test:
    1.  alterations made to the property to facilitate installations of equipment;
    2.  who bore the cost of expense;
    3.  removal without damage to the premises;
    4.  whether the item is particularly adapted to the particular present use—in that it would not be equally useful elsewhere.
3.  Courts consider three factors: (1) whether the defendant's threats were "true threats" and not protected under First Amendment; (2) the willfulness of the threat under the reasonable person standard; and (3) if the threat was knowing.
4.  The suspect had a scar on the right side of his face, a birthmark on his forehead, and was sporting a new beard.
5.  The judge threw the gavel, yelled at the lawyer, and was overruling the objection for the twelfth time that day.
6.  Upon vacating, the Tenant agrees to pay for all utility services due and have same discontinued, to see that the property is swept out and all trash or other refuse is removed from the premises, that the doors and windows are properly locked or fastened, and that the key is returned to the Landlord or Agent.

7. Koby's interaction with the Human Rights commission included doing inventory of past issues and assistance with current European cases.

8. *This exercise includes a review of the principles of division and sequence discussed in Chapter 1, Section C(2). Put the items in this list into parallel form. Then group into categories with headings. Finally, put in an appropriate sequence.*

FACTORS IN PERSUASIVENESS
1. Style—be reasonable and sincere
2. Practiced delivery increases persuasiveness
3. Listen carefully to others
4. Appear to listen carefully to others
5. Research all aspects of an issue thoroughly
6. Brevity is generally desirable
7. Audio/visual presentations increase persuasiveness
8. Eye contact is critical—intro, ending and everywhere
9. Introduction is critical
10. Simple, clear structure is best
11. Professional language
12. Suggest desired result
13. Remain pleasant and professional

B. *Add a summative modifier to the following sentences.*

1. He could not guarantee the defendant would appear in court because the defendant had not called him in several days.
2. The court held that, under the Fourth Amendment, an anonymous tip of reckless driving was insufficient to justify an investigative stop.

*Add a resumptive modifier to the following sentences.*

3. The trend is toward recognizing the right to privacy and punishing unwarranted intrusion.
4. Although the statute of limitations will normally begin to run at the time of injury, cases have established a discovery rule exception in medical malpractice cases, which move that time forward to when the patient is aware or should be aware that medical treatment caused the injury.

## 2. Concision

As important as the syntactic principles just discussed is concision. Roundabout, repetitive, and wordy sentences are difficult to understand; they tire readers and sap their attention. Memory and patience are strained by throat-clearing introductions; circumlocutions; and unnecessary adjectives, adverbs, or synonyms. In contrast, comprehension and retention improve when a point is expressed concisely. The chart below summarizes techniques for avoiding wordiness.

### AVOIDING WORDINESS

| | |
|---|---|
| **Reduce Metadiscourse to the Essential:** Metadiscourse is writing that directs the reader to topic, structure, point-of-view, or logical connection rather than writing directed to substance. Some metadiscourse is helpful. Too much is soporific. | **Not:** *Next it is important to examine in some detail what are unanimously held to be* the leading three cases on establishment clause doctrine. **But:** Three cases form the bedrock of establishment clause doctrine. |
| **Use a Word for a Phrase** | **Not:** Due to the fact that **But:** Because |
| | **Not:** In the event that **But:** If |
| | **Not:** Regardless of the fact that **But:** Although |
| **Eliminate Unnecessary Explanation & Detail:** Assess your audience. Novices need more information than experts. | **Not:** This paper was shredded into small pieces. **But:** This paper was shredded. |
| | **Not:** In order to evaluate this appeal, we must look to Section 3702, which is the controlling authority, and then to the precedents. **But:** Section 3702 governs this appeal. |

| | |
|---|---|
| **Eliminate Redundancy** | **Unnecessary Synonyms:** last will and testament, each and every, terms and conditions |
| | **Redundant Adjectives:** very unique, unexpected surprise, free gift |
| | **Redundant Categories:** *in the area* of tort law (in tort law), *during the period of* his incarceration (during his incarceration), old tenement *buildings* (old tenements) |
| **Eliminate Unnecessary Adjectives and Adverbs, Especially Intensifiers** | **Not:** The prosecution *clearly* failed to meet its burden of proof. **But:** The prosecution failed to meet its burden of proof. |
| | **Not:** This was a *clear* breach of the duty of care. **But:** This was a breach of the duty of care. |
| **Avoid Unnecessary Use of "Of"; Use Possessives Instead** | **Not:** The injuries of the plaintiff were serious. **But:** The plaintiff's injuries were serious. |
| **Avoid Unnecessary Negatives** | **Not:** We ask you to admit defendant's confession not because we do not believe he will not otherwise be convicted, but because the confession was voluntary and therefore admissible as a matter of law. **But:** Although we believe defendant will be convicted even without his confession, it should be admitted as a matter of law because he confessed voluntarily. |

The following example demonstrates how ignoring the guidelines in this chart above can make a sentence painful to read. Note that the whole problem here is wordiness, not syntax.

> It is accurate to say that [*excessive metadiscourse*] the concept [*redundant category*] of whistleblowing refers to situations [*another redundant category*] in the course of which [*phrase for a word*] employees in good faith report and recount [*redundant pair*] activities conducted by their employers in the course of the employers' business [*many words where a few will do*] that do not comport with [*unnecessary negative*] existing [*unnecessary adjective*] law.

The rewrite below cuts the sentence to readable dimensions, expressing the same idea with 32 fewer words.

> Whistleblowing means employees' good-faith reporting of their employers' illegal business practices.

Although concision generally promotes comprehension, be aware that this is not always the case. Sometimes a few extra words are just what is needed to make an idea come clear or to establish a cordial tone.

––––––––––––––––––––––– *Exercise 5.3* –––––––––––––––––––––––

*Edit for wordiness—excessive detail and explanation, metadiscourse, phrases instead of words, unnecessary pairs, nominalizations, etc.*

1.  It is necessary to understand that in previous times, the principle of the existence of a reasonable expectation of privacy with respect to trash or garbage that was shredded into small pieces prior to its being disposed of by the defendant seemed to be a legal assumption on the part of federal courts of appeal.
2.  The statute here–in requiring the discharge of a juror who is unavailable for continued service "by reason of illness or other incapacity, or for any other reason"–invests a trial court with latitude to make a balanced determination affecting the administration of justice based on the facts required to be adduced, recognizing that criminal proceedings should not be unnecessarily

or unfairly delayed against the interests of either the defense or the prosecution, especially when the trial is under way and so many other participants are involved.

3. Although settlement will probably not result in the compensation of your damages to the same extent as that which would occur if you prevail at a formal hearing, it is a much quicker and more flexible process.

4. One argument that is deserving of the utmost attention is that consumers should continue to benefit from lower clothing prices that result from extensive price competition among apparel producers who do business with discount operations.

5. The issue of whether a document is a judicial record is clearly and completely separable from the issue of whether protective orders should be modified.

6. A will shall not be valid unless it is signed by two witnesses.

7. Any and all persons operating motor vehicles of any type and kind whatsoever in the District of Columbia shall obtain liability insurance.

8. The findings and determinations hereinafter set forth are supplementary and in addition to the findings and determinations previously made in connection with the issuance of the aforesaid order; and all of the said previous findings and determinations as well as the supplementary findings and determinations are hereby ratified and affirmed.

9. During the representation of a criminal defendant, an attorney must demonstrate an adherence at all times to the rules of professional conduct.

10. Courts consistently grant immunity to websites that merely provide a forum for posts. One important case to grant immunity to this type of website is *Global Royal.* In that case, the plaintiff filed a defamation claim against a website based on a posting about the plaintiff's business that a user placed in the "con artist" category. The court held that a website that is only a forum for user posts is not liable.

---

## 3. Syntactical Problems

We are not concerned in this chapter with an exhaustive review of the rules of grammar. Rather, our focus here is on syntactical mistakes that defeat clarity. Faulty parallelism (discussed above in Section B (1)(c)), the ambiguous placement of modifiers, and unclear pronoun reference are the three sources of greatest confusion.

## a. Misplaced Modifiers

Modifiers are words or clusters of words that describe another word in the sentence. If modifiers are not close to the words they modify, then the parts of a sentence are mis-connected. Misplaced modifiers are modifiers that have strayed and, as a result, describe the wrong word.

> *By driving while intoxicated,* **the court** said the defendant was morally and legally culpable.

The modifier (in italics) wrongly suggests the court was the intoxicated driver. The modifier must be moved closer to the noun it is intended to modify.

> The court said **the defendant**, *in driving while intoxicated,* was morally and legally culpable.

## b. Dangling Modifiers

Dangling modifiers also create confusion. A modifier dangles when the word being described is omitted from the sentence.

> *Citing drunken driving as the leading cause of highway accidents,* liability on social hosts was imposed.

In this sentence, the entity doing the citing—the court—never makes it into the sentence at all. The speaker needs to be inserted.

> *Citing drunken driving as the leading cause of highway accidents,* **the court** imposed liability on social hosts.

## c. Squinting Modifiers

A squinting modifier is confusing because it is placed so as to modify both what precedes it and the word that follows it.

> The witness's testimony **exonerating** the defendant *substantially* **damaged** the prosecution's case.

It is unclear whether the testimony "substantially exonerated" the defendant or whether the prosecution's case was "substantially damaged." The modifier must be moved so as to modify only one word:

> The witness's testimony *substantially* **exonerating** the defendant damaged the prosecution's case.
>
> or
>
> The witness's testimony exonerating the defendant **damaged** the prosecution's case *substantially*.

## d. Pronouns

Personal pronouns can be another cause of bewilderment. Although context usually makes the reference of pronouns clear (*e.g.* "Mr. Donne said he would break the bad news"), it does not always, as the following examples show.

> The officer told the complainant that she had to file a report.
>
> Officer Jill Nelson told Lois Vargas that she had to file a report.

Lack of context makes the antecedent of the pronoun "she" unclear in the first sentence. We do not know which of the two parties is female, so we do not know which party must file the report. Characters of the same gender render the antecedent unclear in the second. To fix the ambiguous pronoun reference, the writer must either repeat the noun or restructure the sentence.

Officer Jill Nelson told Lois Vargas to file a report.

For a discussion of the ambiguous reference of "which" clauses and how to use resumptive and summative modifiers to avoid this problem, see Part B(1)(c).

―――――――――――― *Exercise 5.4* ――――――――――――

*Diagnose and correct the modifier and pronoun mistakes in the sentences below.*

1. She complained about the Rev. Bryant's persistent sexual advances to the Board of Trustees.
2. After determining that a memo is a business record, the memo must be made or transmitted by a person with knowledge at or near the time of the transaction and be made in the ordinary course of business.
3. The court discharged the jury because it was biased.
4. By firing you, I believe the Board violated your contract.
5. Defining the contract terms clearly prevents misunderstanding.
6. By firing you, your contract was violated.
7. Jane called Mrs. Smith after her hospitalization.
8. To be found grossly unqualified, the court must determine that the juror is unfit to serve because of bias or misconduct.
9. That violent crime had declined partially eased community unrest.
10. The plaintiff's handbook for employees expressly forbids the sharing of trade secrets, of which defendant received a copy when she began work.
11. By granting a preliminary injunction, the defendant will undoubtedly suffer losses.
12. Gagged and trussed up in a canvas bag, Cleveland teacher Linda Smith told police investigators how she was kidnapped to Florida.
13. Damaged by fire and flood, Ann Jones renovated a Civil War period cottage in Boston and rents it to visitors.

## 4. Punctuation

Because a few rules of punctuation are simply arbitrary (for example, the requirement that periods and commas be put inside quotation marks, but semicolons and colons outside), many people think punctuation is arbitrary. Believing the myth that commas belong where one would pause in speech, other people mistakenly believe punctuation is largely subjective. What most fail to realize is that punctuation is one of the greatest tools of clarity available to a writer. Like a system of case citation—which enables a reader to figure out the volume, reporter, series, page number, jurisdiction and date of a case—uniform use of punctuation marks assists a reader in figuring out the relationship of words in a sentence: what modifies what, whether a word is plural or possessive, and how many elements are in a series. Thus correct punctuation is not only a mark of literacy, but a way to crystallize meaning.

*a. Commas*

i. Setting off Clauses or Phrases

One use of the comma is to set off clauses or phrases that lead into, interrupt, or close a sentence. These commas are visual signals that help readers to separate the main sentence from its subordinate parts. Thus, you put a comma after an introductory clause, phrase, or transition word.

> *Although the deposition was scheduled for Tuesday,* the witness did not return from a trip until Wednesday.
>
> *After receiving a summons,* John called his lawyer.
>
> *Moreover,* a suspect class must exhibit immutable characteristics.

The introductory comma is especially important for clarity when its absence might create a misreading.

> After the court decides the motion will be moot.

Without a comma it is initially unclear whether "motion" is the object of "decides" or the subject of "will be moot." Although a second reading of the sentence makes plain that "motion" is the subject—because otherwise the sentence would be a fragment—any unnecessary confusion slows the reader. A comma after "decides" eliminates confusion by showing the reader where the main clause begins.

> *After the court decides*, the motion will be moot.

You also put a comma before a phrase or clause tacked on to your sentence like an afterthought.

> We settled the terms, *although the parties were not entirely satisfied.*

Finally, be sure to use commas to set off nonrestrictive modifiers. A nonrestrictive modifier adds information about a primary word in a sentence, but the information is not strictly essential to the sentence. You could delete the modifier, in other words, without changing the meaning of the statement. This is not true with a restrictive modifier, which narrows the word it is modifying; the omission of such a modifier changes the meaning of the sentence. Thus, clarity depends on understanding and respecting the difference between restrictive and non-restrictive modifiers because each has a different impact on meaning. Consider the sentences below.

> **Nonrestrictive:** The circuit court, *sitting en banc*, reversed its earlier decision.
>
> **Nonrestrictive:** The police seized the crates, *which contained cocaine.*
>
> **Restrictive:** The police seized the crates *that contained cocaine.*

In the first sentence, the author could omit the nonrestrictive modifier, "sitting en banc," without altering the meaning of the sentence: the decision is reversed in either case. Similarly, in the second sentence, deleting the nonrestrictive modifier, "which contained cocaine," would not alter the meaning of the sentence. With or without the nonrestrictive modifier, it is clear that the police seized all the crates, although adding the nonrestrictive modifier also supplies the reason for that seizure. In contrast, the third sentence suggests that the police seized only some of the crates—only those that held cocaine. The restrictive modifier limits the scope of "crates" to those with contraband. Deleting the modifier would alter the meaning of the sentence.

In addition to using commas to identify a modifier as nonrestrictive, you need to use "that" and "which" advisedly. "That" always introduces a restrictive modifier. "Which" can be restrictive or nonrestrictive—but careful writers reserve it for nonrestrictive modifiers. In rule-making documents, the better practice is to use "that," never "which," in restrictive clauses. The use of restrictive and non-restrictive clauses is discussed further in Chapter 11, *Precision*, Section B(4).

## ii. Separating Items in a Series

Another device that helps a reader to parse a sentence correctly is the use of serial commas to separate the items in a series of three or more. Although informal and journalistic practices permit a writer to omit the comma that precedes the conjunction before the last element in the series, the better practice is to use it–the last serial comma can clarify the number of items in the series and their proper division. In the following sentence, the last comma is omitted, and the divisions are murky as a result.

> The magazine company listed jobs in accounting, subscriptions and advertising and public relations.

Without the comma, it is unclear whether there are three jobs or four. With the comma, the divisions are immediately clear.

> The magazine company listed jobs in accounting, subscriptions, and advertising and public relations.

## iii. Before Conjunctions Connecting Independent Clauses

Finally, a comma is used before a coordinating conjunction (*and, but, or, nor, for, so, yet*) that connects two sentences. This comma promotes clarity by letting the reader know that another complete thought follows.

> The legislative history of the statute evolved over a period of years, *and* for that reason, it speaks somewhat indistinctly to the question of whether criminal liability depends upon the defendant knowing that the weapon could be fired automatically.

### b. Semicolons

There are only two proper uses of the semicolon. First, a semicolon is used to connect two sentences not joined by a coordinating conjunction or separated by a period.

> The mandatory life sentence does not constitute cruel and unusual punishment; the trial court's sentence is thus affirmed.

If a transition leads into the second sentence, a semicolon goes before the transition word and a comma goes after it.

> The mandatory life sentence does not constitute cruel and unusual punishment; *therefore*, the trial court's sentence is affirmed.

Most writers use a semicolon to connect two sentences when the content is closely related or when a sharp contrast is being drawn. The semicolon thus comments on and clarifies the relationship of the sentences. Nonetheless, it would be equally correct to separate them with a period or connect them with a coordinating conjunction preceded by a comma.

> The mandatory life sentence does not constitute cruel and unusual punishment. *Therefore*, the trial court's sentence is affirmed.

> The mandatory life sentence does not constitute cruel and unusual punishment, *and therefore*, the trial court's sentence is affirmed.

The second use of semicolons has a greater bearing on clarity. Semicolons are used to separate elements in a series when one or more of the items has internal commas. In this situation, the semicolons demarcate the elements more clearly.

> Defendant has been convicted of fraudulent use of a credit card, for which he was sentenced to three years in a state penitentiary; of passing a forged check, for which he served four years; and of obtaining money by false pretenses, for which he received, under the recidivist statute, a life sentence.

Lawyers often use semicolons to separate elements in a series when the elements themselves are long, even when no element has internal commas. This use of semicolons in place of commas is not confusing, but it is the punctuation equivalent of legalese, and thus best avoided.

### c. Em-dashes and Parentheses

Just as writers use both commas and semicolons to keep the items in a series clearly separated, so parentheses and em-dashes (long hyphens) are often used to set off an interrupting or afterthought phrase that contains internal punctuation. In the following example, the reader is initially uncertain whether the sentence opens with a list or whether the first noun—"qualifications"—is followed by a modifier.

> His qualifications, education, employment history, character references, were put forward.

The uncertainty disappears if em-dashes or parentheses are used.

> His qualifications—education, employment history, character references—were put forward.

> or

> His qualifications (education, employment history, character references) were put forward.

You can think of em-dashes and parentheses as punctuation "synonyms" of commas. They should be substituted for commas when substitution promotes clarity.

> **Not:** We need to research legislative intent, committee reports, predecessor statutes, and amendments.
>
> **But:** We need to research legislative intent—committee reports, predecessor statutes, and amendments.
>
> **Or:** We need to research legislative intent (committee reports, predecessor statutes, and amendments).

*d. Colons*

Colons are used to introduce a list when the words preceding the list form a complete statement.

> For the rule to apply, the following three elements must be present: (1) the conduct must be intentional, (2) the conduct must be outrageous, and (3) the conduct must cause injury.

A colon is also used to introduce a quotation, formal question, amplification, or example.

> Social host liability is both consistent with and supportive of a social goal: the reduction of drunken driving.

Like semicolons, colons are overused by lawyers. Much of the colon use in boilerplate is archaic and incorrect by modern standards. "Legalese" colons very frequently follow sentence fragments, as in the following.

> Coverage does not include loss caused by:
> A. theft committed by any insured, or any person renting the premises, or
> B. theft in or to a dwelling under construction.

*e. Apostrophes*

Apostrophes distinguish possessives from plurals. Without the apostrophe in the following example, we have a plural, not a possessive. Moreover, it is impossible to know how many defendants there are—a situation that interferes with clarity.

> The court said the *defendants* argument had no foundation in law.

For a singular possessive, add *'s* to the noun (if the noun ends in *s* you may add either an apostrophe alone or *'s*, though *'s* is perhaps clearer); for a plural possessive, use an apostrophe alone.

> **Singular possessive:** The court said the *defendant's* argument had no foundation in law.
>
> **Singular possessive:** The *witness'* testimony was brief. Or: The *witness's* testimony was brief. (Whichever usage you adopt, be consistent.)
>
> **Plural possessive:** The court said the *defendants'* argument had no foundation in law.
>
> **Plural possessive:** The *witnesses'* testimony was brief.

An exception to the rule requiring apostrophes to indicate possession is possessive pronouns. "Its" is the possessive of "it." "It's" is the contraction of "it is." "Your" is the possessive of you. "You're" is the contraction of you are. With possessive pronouns, the lack of an apostrophe indicates possession.

Finally, be careful not to follow a possessive noun with an appositive—a noun that identifies or explains the noun beside which it is set. Do not write:

> The court rejected the defendant's, Board of Parish Life, free exercise argument.

You cannot make a noun the equivalent of a possessive noun or pronoun. Say instead:

The court rejected the defendant Board of Parish Life's free exercise argument.

or

The court reject the free exercise argument of the defendant, Board of Parish Life.

---

## *Exercise 5.5*

**A.** *Diagnose and correct the punctuation errors.*

1. You signed an initial two year employment contract with the Board of Parish Life believing you had found the perfect position.
2. When Ms. Williams sought to end the harassment her attempts were shunned. First by Reverend Bryant, then by the Personnel Sub-Committee, and finally by yourselves.
3. Church's are free to enter into contracts.
4. A student, who knows another student has engaged in academic dishonesty, shall notify a faculty member.
5. At the academic hearing, the student may:
   a. present evidence on her or his behalf;
   b. call witnesses; and
   c. cross-examine witnesses.
6. A student upon receiving a judgment may appeal the decision.
7. Each student may have an advisor although he or she need not be a lawyer.
8. Plagiarism is an offense against the profession, therefore law schools must penalize students who plagiarize.
9. Thompson is an innovative businessman, a successful salesman and executive and owner of a dot.com company.
10. Plagiarism, the intentional, knowing, or reckless use of another person's words, phrases, or ideas without attribution, is prohibited.
11. Such participation, he claims was fundamentally unfair.
12. The court has jurisdiction over minor children, who are natives of New York.

13. To be granted judicial relief for misappropriation of a trade secret the plaintiff must prove by a preponderance of the evidence the following elements.

14. Defendant's punishment, harassment, retaliation, and eventually dismissal, of plaintiff for her resistance to censorship states a cause of action.

15. One category of testimonial statements is limited to extrajudicial statements contained in formalized testimonial materials, affidavits, depositions, and confessions.

16. Plaintiffs appeal the grant of summary judgment, arguing that the plaintiff's fraud action was not time-barred.

17. Under Minnesota Human Rights Law, sexual harassment means unwelcome sexual advances, requests for sexual favors, sexually motivated physical contact or other verbal or physical conduct or communication of a sexual nature.

18. The manager disregarded Ms. Williams complaints.

19. The law allows for recovery of damages for attorneys fees.

20. Confidential business information is information that would injure a companies competitive standing.

21. Joan was severely injured, lacerated, bruised, and bloodied, when she learned her boyfriend had been killed.

22. The court issued it's findings after which the appellate court reversed the judgment.

23. To reiterate the court's decision is final.

24. The Supreme Court held that the Age Discrimination and Employment Act, which covered employees of a state or political subdivision of a state, 29. U.S.C. § 630(b)(2), a provision that would seem unambiguously to cover state judges, did not apply to state judges because the provision did not unambiguously reveal that Congress intended such a result.

25. If the legislature concludes that refusal to yield to a party line in an emergency is no longer a problem it may repeal the statute prohibiting this conduct.

26. The prosecutor and the defense lawyer while on trial in Buffalo discovered a mutual interest in billiards.

27. One court, which does not permit oral argument on excessive sentence motions, is the Appellate Division Second Department.

28. This court which is located in the business district requires three separate security checks.

29. The attorney handles a variety of cases, criminal, medical malpractice, real estate and mergers and acquisitions.

30. Its not an easy case to win.

31. The defendants' fingerprints were all over the weapon, however, he decided to go to trial anyway.

32. The student had a heavy course load: criminal law, taught by Professor Card, legal writing, taught by Professor Tide, civil procedure, taught by Professor Rosario, contracts with Professor Habib, and legal process, which is taught by Professor Doe and his teaching assistant.

33. She works at the Womens Rights Project.

34. Brooks restraint was praised by the court yet it yielded nothing in the end.

35. Defendant was one of the few vineyard's employees, who knew the procedures for making off-dry chardonnay.

36. The major influences on wine quality are: soil, moisture, and temperature.

37. West was employed by the plaintiff; and she was not free to disclose the procedure.

**B.** *Diagnose and correct the errors in the following passage.*

The Appellate Division moved our decisional law one step further, a significant step, when it ruled that a social host, who serves liquor to a visibly intoxicated minor, may be held liable for the injuries inflicted on a third party as a result of the subsequent drunken driving of the minor. Practically all of the considerations urged against liability were present there. The court noted: it was a social setting at someone's home, not at a tavern, the one who provided the liquor to the intoxicated minor was a host (not a licensee) and all of the notions of fault and causation pinning sole responsibility on the drinker were present. The only difference was that the guest was a minor but whether he was obviously so, or whether the host knew is not disclosed in the opinion.

In expanding liability, Linn followed the courts rational in Rappaport that the duty involved is a common law duty, it does not arise from the statute and regulation prohibiting sales of liquor to a minor; neither of which applies to a social host.

## C. CLEAR PARAGRAPHS

There are two principles of effective paragraphing. First, clear paragraphs have unity and cohesion. Paragraph unity is achieved when every sentence in the paragraph bears on a single topic. Paragraph cohesion is achieved when readers are able to bridge the synapse between adjacent sentences effortlessly because the connection between sentences is unmistakable. A cohesive, unified paragraph is not, therefore, the sum of its individual sentences. It is not enough for sentences to be intrinsically clean and illuminating. Rather, a cohesive, unified paragraph is one in which the reader can easily reconstruct the writer's point because the writer has accurately assessed and appropriately responded to the reader's level of familiarity with the subject matter and need for transitions. Second, clear paragraphs indicate their place in the larger document through the use of transition sentences that bridge steps within an analysis or connect topics within a discussion.

### 1. Paragraph Unity

A unified paragraph announces the discrete topic that is its particular province and then sticks resolutely to that topic. Topic sentences and paragraph headings promote unity by focusing a discussion and providing context. Context is essential to the communication process because it enables a reader to infer missing details and to make connections that are not explicit in the text itself. Without a sentence or heading establishing context, a topic may be difficult to infer and points difficult to connect, as in the following passage used in an experiment on the importance of context to comprehension and recall.

> The procedure is actually quite simple. First you arrange things into different groups. Of course, one pile may be sufficient depending on how much there is to do. If you have to go somewhere else due to lack of facilities that is the next step, otherwise you are pretty well set. It is important not to overdo things. That is, it is better to do too few things at once than too many. In the short run this may not seem

> important but complications can easily arise. A mistake can be expensive as well....[6]

Only those readers who were told that the title of the passage was "Washing Clothes" could recall the tasks and order of steps mentioned. The experiment thus illustrates an important point about communication. Titles, headings, and topic sentences establish the context that glues sentences together to render the meaning of a paragraph clear.

> *Given that memoranda are admissible under Rule 803(6), the fact that they happen to be in computerized form should have no legal significance.* Indeed, the focus of Rule 803 (6) is on the admission of reliable business documents, and therefore, the critical factor in determining whether a document satisfies the business purpose rule is the reason the message was prepared and sent, not the means by which it was transmitted. Accordingly, it is of no consequence that a business document was created on and transmitted by a computer.

Not only do topic sentences orient the reader, but they have a collateral benefit for the writer: they help the writer to articulate and stay on point—to weed out digressions and to separate issues.

## 2. Paragraph Cohesion

Section B of this chapter centered on writing clear individual sentences—by creating, for example, sentences that tell stories and that lead with the subject and the verb. In a series of sentences, however, any one of those principles of sentence structure may need to be sacrificed to paragraph cohesion. The best sentence structure in a paragraph is that structure which facilitates easy comprehension. Cohesion between sentences has higher priority than the structure of any particular sentence. This section describes some of the key techniques used to promote cohesion.

---

[6] J. D. Bransford & M. K. Johnson, *Contextual Prerequisites for Understanding: Some Investigations of Comprehension and Recall*, 11 J. Verbal Learning And Verbal Behavior 717, 724 (1972).

## a. Topic Strings

One way to achieve cohesion is to focus the grammatical subjects of the sentences within a paragraph on the topic of the paragraph, creating a consistent *topic string*.[7] This does not mean that every sentence must have the same grammatical subject, but it does mean using words that evoke that topic, as in the following example.

> *The use of extra-sensory, non-intrusive equipment* to investigate people and objects is not a search for purposes of the Fourth Amendment. *A thermal imager* that detects from outside a home the heat that is emitted from the grow lights used in indoor marijuana cultivation is just such a non-intrusive extra-sensory device. *An imager, which is an infra-red camera,* involves no embarrassing search of a person. *It* is even less intrusive than a drug detection dog sniffing people and their luggage at an airport because the *infra-red camera* measures heat that is outside the home. Thus, *its use* is not a search within the meaning of the Fourth Amendment.

## b. Cohesive Patterns

Cohesion is often achieved when a new sentence repeats information given in the prior sentence (the *given information*) before providing *new information*.[8] This pattern is effective because readers tend to relate what they are reading to what they already know about the subject. A dovetailing, interlocking pattern of *given information/new information* mirrors that reading process. The interlocking pattern we have been describing here is also known as an AB:BC pattern because it looks like this:

A_____B

  B_____C

    C_____D

---

[7] Williams, *supra* n. 3, at 103–108.

[8] *See id.,* which discusses these techniques in detail.

> When a custodial parent requests permission to relocate, the courts *presume her good faith. This presumption* rests on the premise that the custodial parent's decision to move took into consideration *the child's best interest. That interest* is served here because the move would improve the child's school district and provide greater extracurricular opportunities.

Syntactical structures can be manipulated to achieve this *given information/new information* organization. For example, one legitimate use of passive voice is to shift the object of a sentence into the initial subject position in order to express old information that links the sentences.

> Students' first amendment rights can be abridged if their conduct creates *a substantial disruption. No substantial disruption* was caused by Kimberly Brossard, however, when she wore a tee-shirt that said "Drugs Suck" to school.

The repetition of "substantial disruption," made possible by the passive construction, bridges the sentences.

The AB:BC pattern is not the only pattern helpful to paragraph cohesion. Parallel sentence structures can also promote cohesiveness, especially in a series of sentences beginning with similar introductory phrases.

> *In Minnesota's Human Rights Law*, the drafters broadly characterized the types of places considered public. *In New York's law*, the drafters more specifically listed places considered public.

The parallel AB:AC structure suggests the text will review several state human rights laws.

Of course, if the paragraph is not focused on a central concept, no amount of interlocking or parallelism will result in meaningful cohesion.

> The murder suspect was apprehended carrying a *gun. Guns* are used in many *crimes.* Indeed, most *robberies* involve *guns. Guns* are very *dangerous.* Of course, *danger* is common, caused even by extreme weather.

Although these sentences are cohesive—in that they follow a given information/new information pattern—they violate the principle of paragraph unity. Without a central topic, no technique of cohesion is sufficient.

### c. Transitional Expressions and Complex Sentences

Transitional expressions are a good way of bridging sentences because they explicitly establish one of the four connections between sentences—additive, temporal, adversative, and causal. The additives (*in addition, and, moreover*) expand ideas in the text by simple accretion. Temporal conjunctions (*then, finally, in conclusion*) clarify the relationships among textual components by establishing sequence. Adversatives (*yet, however*) enable a writer to qualify, refute, or question a previous idea. Causals (*thus, because, as a result*) provide explanations and support for other statements. Properly used, transitional expressions and conjunctions are helpful signposts—especially if they appear near the beginning of the sentence so the relationship is immediately apparent.

> E-mail *also* has particular guarantees of trustworthiness not shared by paper memoranda. Hard copies of records can be lost, destroyed, or manipulated. *However,* e-mail transactions are embedded both onto the hard drives of stand-alone computers and onto the archiving systems of the Internet servers. *Thus, even when* the transmitter thinks he or she has deleted or changed the text, it is relatively easy to verify and even recover "deleted" or "manipulated" e-mails. *In addition,* e-mail systems track the sender and receiver, and one can ascertain the date of receipt, as well as the time that the e-mail was opened. In the context of litigation, such precision should be highly valued.

Some researchers have noticed that the relationships established by transitional expressions often exist even in their absence, that is, the reader can sometimes infer the relationship because other ties carry the reader across the sentence boundaries.

> The officers were not trespassing on defendant's property. Their surveillance of his property took place during an over-

> head helicopter flight in public air space and from a public sidewalk.

We can infer the second sentence is support for the first through the use of pronouns. Indeed, in persuasive writing, the very lack of a transition is sometimes the most effective transition.

> The victim's mother waited all that day and the next. He did not come home.

If the point is not obvious, however, cohesion is threatened.

> The rules of appellate procedure are designed to compel an appellant to focus an appellate court's attention on the issues of fact and law that the appellant contends were mistakenly decided by the trial court. The court sometimes makes allowances for a pro se litigant's inability to write by the rules. There are limits to the shortcomings in a brief that can be overlooked.

We need transitional expressions to bridge these sentences.

> The rules of appellate procedure are designed to compel an appellant to focus an appellate court's attention on the issues of fact and law that the appellant contends were mistakenly decided by the trial court. The court sometimes makes allowances, *however*, for a pro se litigant's inability to write by the rules. *Nonetheless*, there are limits to the shortcomings in a brief that can be overlooked.

Complex sentences are another, and equally effective, way of connecting ideas. A complex sentence is a sentence with a dependent and an independent clause. A dependent clause is a clause beginning with a subordinating conjunction, a word that establishes the clause's temporal or logical relation to the independent clause. These subordinating conjunctions (*although, since, because, when, while, if*—to name just a few) often do the same work as transitional expressions: they clarify the relationship between ideas in separate clauses.

> **Complex sentence:** *Although* defendants argue that Title II of the Americans with Disabilities Act and § 504 of the Rehabilitation Act do not apply to state prisons, the defendants have not refuted plaintiff's demonstration that numerous Department of Justice regulations make explicit the statutes' applicability to prison.

> **Transition word:** Defendants argue that Title II of the Americans with Disabilities Act and § 504 of the Rehabilitation Act do not apply to state prisons. *However,* the defendants have not refuted plaintiff's demonstration that numerous Department of Justice regulations make explicit the statutes' applicability to prison.

All these techniques enable writers to focus on a topic and to provide bridges between sentence boundaries—to achieve, in short, unified and cohesive paragraphs like that below.

> To be guilty of menacing, a defendant must place a person in fear of imminent *serious physical injury*. *Serious physical injury* is that which presents a substantial risk of death or causes a serious disfigurement or protracted impairment of health. *Because* the defendant in *Jackson* covered the victim's mouth with duct tape and threatened to rape her, the court concluded there that the defendant's conduct put the victim in fear of protracted impairment of health. Here, *however,* the prosecution cannot establish analogous conduct putting complainant in fear of serious physical injury.

The topic sentence adequately establishes the context–one element of the crime of menacing—and the next three sentences bear on that requirement. Dovetailing, transitional expressions, and complex sentences all promote paragraph cohesion.

### 3. Paragraph Transitions

Transition sentences contribute to cohesion at the document level by summarizing what has gone before as well as announcing the next step in the larger analysis or narrative.

> *Not only do courts regularly admit interoffice memoranda, but they have already admitted as a business record under Rule 803 (6) the technological predecessor to e-mail, the telex message.* In *United States v. Gregg*, the Eighth Circuit held that telex messages between an exporter and his clients were clearly admissible as business records because they were kept in the course of regularly conducted business activity. Similarly, the Third Circuit held that telex messages to a cargo ship qualified as an admissible record.

Transition sentences usually appear at the beginning of a paragraph and sometimes summarize what has been said as well as introduce what is to come, but they can also be effective at the end of a paragraph.

———————————————— *Exercise 5.6* ————————————————

*Add transition words, complex sentences, and dovetailing to make these paragraphs cohesive. Restructure sentences to create a consistent string of topics if necessary.*

1. Compensatory damages can be sought in both claims. These damages are to compensate you for wages lost when you were dismissed and for your current and future medical needs. A recent case allowed a person to recover for future emotional distress. We would need your psychiatrist to testify. Keep in mind that a court case can be lengthy and unpredictable. Based on the facts of our case, we stand a strong chance of prevailing.

2. The Church entered into a two-year contract with Ms. Williams in January 2002. She introduced several innovative programs as Youth Minister of Grace Church, which dramatically increased attendance. The Church terminated her employment on November 10, 2002.

3. An employer may discipline an employee for engaging in speech, even on an issue of public concern, if that speech causes such a disruption in the office's function as to outweigh the interests of the speaker and the community. The position of the employer here is that it did not dismiss plaintiff for her speech. The claim is it dismissed plaintiff for alleged deficiencies in her job performance. The balancing test invoked has no application to this case.

# Chapter 6

# BASIC SKILLS: PERSUASION

---

## A. INTRODUCTION

This chapter is devoted to the specialized rhetorical skills that characterize the persuasive documents discussed in Part Two of this book: briefs, which seek to convince a court of the rightness of their arguments; judicial opinions, which endeavor to convince readers of the rightness of a decision; letters, when they seek to persuade the recipient to a particular course of action or point-of-view; and office memoranda, to the extent the writer wants the analysis to convince the reader of its rightness.

We do not focus here on persuasive techniques that rest on the surface of the text, such as calling the opposing party "plaintiff" or "defendant" rather than by name, or putting unfavorable facts or arguments into dependent rather than independent clauses. There may often be good reason to employ these techniques, but truly persuasive documents succeed on a deeper level. They find the "core theme" of the case and then support it in the presentation of the facts and in the analysis and application of relevant law and policy.

## 1. Audience

Persuasiveness begins with an awareness of audience. For example, when you write a letter, it helps to know something about the recipient's values, age, interests, employment, past experiences, physical condition, emotional stability, and level and quality of education. This background enables you to make informed decisions about formality of language and level of analysis. When you write an opposing attorney, it is useful to know about the adversary's negotiating techniques. With a trial judge or a panel of judges, your briefs might be stronger if you knew, for example, the judge's or the court's respective sentencing practices or jurisprudence. Or, finally, if you were writing an opinion, it might be useful to think about which of an opinion's multiple audiences is the primary one for that decision—the parties, the bar, the appellate court, or even posterity. Whether gleaned from personal interaction, colleagues, or print and electronic sources, information about audience will enable you to tailor your persuasive document more effectively.

Other than reminding you of the importance of audience here, however, we leave this topic to the document chapters. Because the audience differs for each type of persuasive document, general discussion is of limited use.

## 2. Finding the Core Theme

Articulating the core theme of the case is the persuasive writer's first and often most consequential task. This means developing a "take" on the facts and the law that makes the reader want you to prevail. Your core theme may be predominantly narrative or predominantly doctrinal. Once envisioned, this theme should inform your fact statement and legal analysis, as discussed in more detail in the next sections of this chapter.

To find the theme of a case, you must first become familiar with the facts and the controlling law. Then, you need to come up with an approach that is likely to persuade because it weaves favorable facts into an argument that comports with law and equity and that minimizes or neutralizes unfavorable facts.

Whether your core theme is predominantly narrative or doctrinal is an important choice. Take the case of Nancy Williams, the client in Casefile 1 in Appendix A, who was summarily dismissed by her employer, Grace Church, after she threatened to file a sexual harassment complaint. In respectively pressing and resisting Williams' claims of harassment, reprisal, and breach of contract, her attorneys and the attorneys for Grace Church would inform their arguments with very different themes. Williams' counsel would focus on narrative—on her egregious treatment, on the unrelenting perils of a talented and long-suffering employee whose pleas for help went unanswered and whose employers not only piled insult on injury, but now try to hide behind the

Establishment Clause of the First Amendment and the freedom of conscience clause of the Minnesota Constitution. Counsel for Grace Church, on the other hand, would down-play the human drama, insisting at every turn that this is a case about freedom of religion and the constitutionally mandated separation of Church and State. In the Church's arguments, Williams' "victim" theme would become a minor background story about an unstable young woman and a former employee with a regrettable weakness. Thus, a narrative theme can effectively counter a doctrinal theory, and vice-versa. At the extremes, however, the technique can backfire. For example, it is more callous than convincing to begin an argument in a death sentence case by asserting, "This is a case about federalism."

Admittedly, the underlying facts and law of a case do not always seem to have a central theme, nor do they always suggest a tidy theory. Instead, a case may seem to present a series of apparently disparate facts and issues that cannot immediately be unified or framed. Nonetheless, discrete events can often be grouped under an umbrella. Imagine, for example, that you are an appellate practitioner whose client was convicted of a drug sale. His defense at trial was entrapment. Your client testified that he obtained drugs for "Tiffany" (an undercover government agent) because she told him that her boyfriend would beat her if she came home without drugs for him. Reading the transcript of the trial you conclude that evidence of your client's drug-dealing is irrefutable. And the jury clearly chose to believe the undercover agent, who denied emotionally coercing your client. But you notice a number of details—a remark by the prosecutor in his summation bolstering the credibility of the agent, an improper question posed to your client on cross-examination concerning his fraudulent use of a credit card ten years ago, a confusing jury instruction on defendants as interested witnesses, and a request by the jury for a re-reading of "all testimony concerning the conversations between the defendant and the agent" and for a re-reading of the court's charge on credibility. Pulling all this together, you find a viable core, the theme of your brief: your client was the victim of relentless, unfair attacks on his credibility. Now that you have your theme, you can use the techniques discussed in the balance of this chapter to craft a statement of the facts and arguments that embody that theme. Note that even if you found numerous disparate errors that did not cohere, you might still have a theme: "the case where nothing went right."

─────────────── *Exercise 6.1* ───────────────

*Find and analyze the opposing core themes in the following excerpts from the introductions to the briefs filed in* Rumsfeld v. Forum for Academic and Institutional Rights, Inc. ("FAIR"), *547 U.S. 47 (2006). [Note that citations have been omitted.] At issue was the constitutionality of legislation providing that educational institutions would lose federal funds if they denied military recruiters access to their campuses equal to that accorded to other recruiters. Summarize the narrative at the heart of each party's argument. How does each party characterize the legislation at issue? What fundamental American values do both parties invoke to justify their respective positions?*

**Petitioner Rumsfeld:**

Article 1 of the Constitution vests Congress with the power to "raise and support" military forces for the defense of the United States. Enlisting qualified men and women in the military is essential in fulfilling that task. Except when military exigency has required resort to conscription, Congress has relied on voluntary enlistment as the most effective means of meeting its staffing needs. As a result, the defense of the United States depends on the ability of the armed forces to attract men and women who have the skills needed for the Nation's defense.

To meet that challenge, Congress has long required the armed forces to "conduct intensive recruiting campaigns" to encourage military enlistments. As the demands of military service have grown more complex, the military has placed increasing emphasis on recruiting students from colleges and universities. At times, however, institutions of higher education have sought to restrict campus recruiting by the military.

Drawing not only on its authority to raise and support the armed forces, but also on its authority to "provide for the common Defense and general Welfare of the United States" and its authority to enact all laws necessary and proper to effectuate its Spending Power, Congress has enacted measures to encourage institutions of higher education to open up their campuses to military recruiters. In 1972, Congress enacted a law directing the Department of Defense to withhold funds from educational institutions that barred military recruiters from their campuses.

**Respondent Forum for Academic Institutional Rights:**

Law schools have long expressed the view that discrimination is morally wrong and fundamentally incompatible with the values of the legal profession. They have consistently expressed that view by word and by deed. If an employer intends to discriminate against a school's students on the basis of race, gender, or any other characteristic that is unrelated to merit, the school will not offer the employer affirmative assistance in recruiting.

By extending their antidiscrimination policies to sexual orientation, law faculties have taken a stand on one of the most divisive moral issues of our time. Through these policies, law schools protest sexual-orientation discrimination directed at their students and teach the leaders of tomorrow that it is wrong to abet invidious discrimination of any sort.

When law schools' antidiscrimination policies clashed with the military's discrimination on the basis of sexual orientation, Congress passed the Solomon Amendment, which punishes the entire university with the loss of virtually all federal funds if any department adheres to such a policy. In its current form the Solomon Amendment requires law schools to provide not merely "access to campuses" and "access to students on campuses," but much more. Law schools must furnish affirmative assistance "in a manner that is at least equal in quality and scope to the access that is provided to any other employer." That means the school must disseminate the military's recruiting brochures, post its bulletins, make appointments with students, and reserve spots for the military in its private forums for exchange of information, on pain of losing virtually all federal contracts or grants. In some schools hundreds of millions of dollars are at stake, for projects as diverse (and unrelated to military recruiting) as cancer research, particle accelerators, and investigations into the promise of school voucher programs.

As much as the government tries to portray its position as a plea for equal treatment, it is nothing of the sort. It is a demand for exceptional treatment—a demand to be the only discriminatory employer that a law school will assist. It is, moreover, not just a demand that law schools stay neutral with regard to the government policy they protest, and just suffer military recruiters in their own forums. Nor is it just a demand that they lend military recruiters some assistance. It is a demand that a law school accord the military "most-favored-recruiter" status, even as the recruiters discriminate against the school's own students.

Congress could not directly command that private institutions disseminate or host the military's message. . . . Congress cannot achieve the same ends by couching the penalty as a denial of the "benefit" of millions of dollars in unrelated funding.

──────────────────── *Exercise 6.2* ────────────────────

*Peter Scorn was apprehended recently by the F.B.I. after Scorn failed to appear last November for sentencing on his conviction for possessing and selling cocaine. Scorn almost got away after his friend, Meryl Jackson, apparently tipped him off that the agents were looking for him. The government is considering bringing a federal charge against Jackson for hiding Scorn's whereabouts from the federal agents.*

*Read the following interviews and case summaries. Then, decide the following.*

A. *Assume you are defense counsel.*
  1. *What is your core theme for your defense of Meryl Jackson?*
  2. *What law would you rely upon?*
  3. *What facts would you emphasize?*
  4. *What facts are unfavorable and how might you neutralize or mitigate them?*
B. *Assume you are the U.S. Attorney.*
  1. *What is your core theme for the prosecution of Meryl Jackson?*
  2. *What law would you rely upon?*
  3. *What facts would you emphasize?*
  4. *What facts are unfavorable and how might you neutralize or mitigate them?*

### Excerpt from Interview of Federal Agent Straight

Q. Why did you go to Wilton, Vermont on October 1, 20__?
A. We had received a tip that Peter Scorn was hiding there.
Q. Who is Peter Scorn?
A. Peter Scorn is wanted by the F.B.I. In October of last year Scorn was convicted of possessing and selling cocaine. He was supposed

to be sentenced in November, but he never showed up. A federal warrant was issued for his arrest.

Q. What happened when you got to Wilton?

A. I visited the restaurants and stores in the town, showing the store owners Scorn's picture and asking whether they had seen him.

Q. Did there come a time when you questioned workers at the Cup n' Saucer?

A. Yes. I asked the owner and the waiters and waitresses whether they recognized the photograph of Peter Scorn and whether they had seen him.

Q. What was their response?

A. They all denied knowing or having seen Peter Scorn.

Q. Did there come a time that day when you located Peter Scorn?

A. Yes. One of the village residents recognized the photograph and told us where Scorn was living. It was a basement room in a ski house in a secluded area north of town. Apparently Scorn supported himself as a ski instructor in the winter and worked as a tour guide for an excursion boat on Lake Whitham in the summer.

Q. What happened when you arrived at Scorn's address?

A. Scorn was gone. When we replayed Scorn's answering machine we heard a message that had been left earlier that day saying, "This is Meryl. Some people from out-of-town asked for you in the restaurant a little while ago. I thought you would want to know."

Q. Did you find Scorn that day?

A. Yes. We arrested him a few hours later in Benton, Vermont, twenty miles from Wilton, with his suitcases in the trunk of his car.

### Excerpt from Interview of Joe Savan

Q. What is your occupation?

A: I own and manage the Cup 'n Saucer in Wilton, Vermont.

Q. Were you present at the restaurant on October 1, 20__?

A. Yes.

Q. Do you recall who was working that day?

A. Yes. Tony Tile and Meryl Jackson.

Q. Did anything unusual happen that day?

A. Yes. An F.B.I. agent came in. He identified himself as an agent and then showed us a picture of some guy and asked if we had seen him.

Q. Did you recognize the photograph?

A. No.

Q. Did Meryl Jackson say she recognized the photograph?

A. No. I remember that she said she didn't know him and hadn't seen him.

Q. Do you recall what happened after that?

A. The agent left the café. Meryl had a couple of customers and she brought them their orders. Then she asked me if she could make a phone call. I said sure. She went in the back and made a call. She was speaking softly so I couldn't hear what she was saying.

### Excerpt from Interview of Tanya Nickle

Q. Do you recall when Scorn first came to Wilton?

A. Yes. It was last fall. I remember distinctly because I went to a small get-together Meryl had to welcome him.

Q. Can you recall being introduced to Peter Scorn at that gathering?

A. Yes.

Q. Was he introduced to you by the name of Peter Scorn?

A. Oh, no. Meryl introduced him to me as Thomas Percy.

Q. How did you learn that his name really was Peter Scorn?

A. Later on that evening I was chatting with Meryl. I guess she had had a little too much wine to drink. She confided that Thomas's name really was Peter Scorn but that he had asked his friends to call him by a different name in public because he had never shown up for sentencing on some federal drug charge because he just couldn't face going to prison.

Q. Did Meryl tell you anything else during this conversation?

A. Yes. She told me that she couldn't blame him for taking off. Meryl said that from everything she had heard from another friend who had done time for a felony, life in the penitentiary was miserable.

Q. Are you aware of any further contact between Peter Scorn and Meryl Jackson?

A. Yes. I know that he was often short on cash. A few times this year Meryl said she gave him a few hundred dollars to help him get by. She and some of their other friends also gave him some extra clothes during the winter and I remember a number of occasions when they picked up his tab for dinner.

### § 1071: Concealing A Person from Arrest

Whoever harbors or conceals any person for whose arrest a warrant or process has been issued...so as to prevent his discovery and arrest, after notice or knowledge of the fact that a warrant or process has been issued for the apprehension of such person, should be fined under this title or imprisoned.

## United States v. Silver

Defendant's character and circumstances can be considered when deciding if the jury can infer defendant had knowledge of the warrant. Here, defendant watched a news report on the fugitive's escape from prison. The court said it was logical to infer that defendant, an ex-con, knew warrants are issued for this. Defendant rented a motel room under an assumed name, purchased disguises and a gun, and then phoned the fugitive telling him to come to the motel with all his possessions. This was the kind of active conduct which indicates concealment. The disguise was meant to aid the fugitive in avoiding detection.

## United States v. Fulbite

Defendant knew fugitive was wanted by police, but there was no evidence that defendant knew of the warrant. Knowledge that a fugitive is evading the police in general is insufficient to establish knowledge of a warrant.

## United States v. Magna

Harbor means to lodge or to care for after secreting the offender. Conceal means to hide, secrete, or keep out of sight. The terms are construed narrowly and require affirmative physical action to establish the acts are calculated to obstruct the efforts of authorities to effect arrest. Physical transportation of a fugitive, sheltering a fugitive on one's property, or obstructing arrest are affirmative acts. Here, the defendant had rented a hotel room for the fugitive, visited the room, lent the fugitive a few hundred dollars, used an alias when introducing him, and lied to the FBI when an agent asked if the fugitive had been in contact. These acts do not constitute the active conduct of hiding or secreting

## United States v. Lockhard

Defendant harbored and concealed a fugitive. He convinced a business partner to sign his interest in the partnership over to the fugitive under his alias. He arranged for a driver's license with an alias for the fugitive. He decoyed the FBI away from the house when he thought the fugitive was there. There is no other explanation for his consistent behavior than that defendant intended to shield the fugitive from arrest.

### United States v. Giambi

Defendant acted to prevent apprehension when he brought groceries to the fugitive's home several times a week so the fugitive could stay out of sight and when he yelled "Run, Nick, it's the Feds" when agents knocked on the door.

### United States v. Staci

Locking the door to block authorities from searching, discovering and apprehending the fugitive, who was inside the house, was an affirmative act violating the statute.

---

## B. PERSUASIVE FACTS

Whether recounted in a brief, memorandum, letter, or opinion, fact statements are an opportunity to mold the audience's perception of the event. The importance of this cannot be overestimated: the audience's "take" on the facts not only motivates the audience to regard the case in a particular light, but in some cases, it even influences the issue to be decided and therefore the law that controls it. For example, how you describe the facts from Casefile 1 in Appendix A leading up to Nancy Williams' dismissal from Grace Church might determine whether it was unlawful reprisal for threatening to file a sexual harassment complaint, or a matter of church governance constitutionally insulated from judicial oversight under the first amendment.

Legal storytelling is of course subject to many constraints—for example, the rules of evidence, the demands of legal relevance, and the "four corners" of the record. Trial briefs and opinions must distill and condense the record while including the material facts. Appellate briefs and opinions must accept the factual findings of the lower courts, but mold them to the issues on appeal and the standard of review. Yet candor is the most important constraint of all: fact statements must comport with the norms, ethical aspirations, and disciplinary rules of the profession. Rule 3.3 of the Model Rules of Professional Conduct prohibits nondisclosure or misstatements of facts, including statements of purported facts that are not supported by the record.

Thus legal storytelling is a creative endeavor that operates under particular constraints. It is especially hard to make the facts compelling in the appellate context, where the judicial process by its very nature has rendered the original event remote. At the trial stage, court and counsel tailored the human event into an incident for judgment; each successive decision transformed it further, distancing the reader from the original event and making it abstract and impersonal.

Nonetheless, there are techniques that will help you to make your statement of facts compelling. First, let the theme of the case inform your narration of the events and your characterization of the parties. Second, unfold your narrative and feed in the facts along a time line that makes the parties' actions and reactions plausible and understandable. Third, though you must narrate the story without editorializing, arguing, or ascribing emotions or intent to the parties, you can effectively reveal your characters through their words and actions: show rather than tell the reader what kind of people the parties are. Finally, use other traditional storytelling techniques—scene-setting, detail, and diction—to make your facts credible.

## 1. The Theme of the Case Should Inform Your Narrative

It is a good idea to begin your narrative with an introductory paragraph that reflects your theory of the case and provides a spin on events that influences the rest of the narrative.

Two introductory paragraphs from statements of facts in appellate briefs follow, one from defendant-appellant's brief and one from respondent-prosecutor's brief.

### Defense

On the morning of September 19, 20__, the complainant, Paula L., was confronted by a man wearing a tweed jacket, a hat, and white sneakers as she was sitting in a car of a subway train in Manhattan. The man lacerated her arms and wrists with a knife, grabbed her pocketbook, and then fled from the train seconds later when it stopped at a station. Ten to fifteen minutes later, appellant, who was wearing blue jeans and was shirtless, was apprehended in the vicinity of the station. The police brought appellant back to the subway station, and the complainant identified him as the perpetrator.

### Prosecution

On September 19, 20__, at 8:30 a.m., defendant approached seventy-nine-year-old Paula L. on an IRT subway train and tried to grab her purse. As she vigorously clung to it, he slashed both her arms and wrists with a large knife, and broke her thumb as he wrenched the purse away from her grasp.

In statement one, mistaken identification is defense counsel's theme. The statement of facts therefore opens with a focus on the complainant's description of the perpetrator's attire, a description that does not tally with the defendant's appearance when he was apprehended; the seeds of doubt are thus planted. In contrast, the prosecutor, in statement two, views this case as a straightforward assault and robbery, playing on the reader's sympathy for the elderly victim. Thus he opens with a graphic description of the assault and robbery itself—the violence of which is vividly evoked through verbs.

You can also use headings to keep your core theory of persuasion in the forefront throughout the statement of facts. If your theory on appeal is that your client's credibility was unfairly attacked throughout the trial, you can focus the narrative with headings like "The Prosecution's Comments on Credibility," "The Court's Interested Witness Charge," "The Jury's Question on Credibility."

### 2. Organization and Chronology Should Make the Narrative Plausible and Clear

Whether in briefs, letters, or opinions, fact statements tend to be organized in one of two ways. Some open with a compelling event that captures attention and shades a reader's impression of the rest of the narrative. After this critical moment has been highlighted, the writer then backtracks, filling in background and providing details while unfolding the complete story. Other statements open with more classic introductory paragraphs. These are useful when context and background are needed to ground the issues on appeal. In addition, where a case involves two or more very different legal questions, you may want to use an introductory paragraph that sets out the context for all the issues and then a topical organization in which you raise the facts relevant to each question. Thus, for example, you might have an introduction giving the background on a defendant's larceny trial and follow with a section on the pre-trial suppression hearing, a section on the trial proper, and a section on the motion for a new trial. You might also need to begin with a summary when the facts are long and complicated and an overview is helpful, as in the following passage.

> Defendants, Dr. Perkel and his associate Dr. Venin, are pediatricians certified by the American Board of Pediatrics and licensed to practice medicine in this state. They treated infant plaintiff, Ann Schroeder, from May 1970 until September 1974. During that time, they failed to diagnose Ann's illness as cystic fibrosis, a genetically transferred disease. Because Mr. and Mrs. Schroeder, Ann's parents, were not told that they were carriers of cystic fibrosis, they claim that they were deprived of an informed choice of whether to assume the risk of a second child. Before they learned that Ann suffered from cystic fibrosis, Mrs. Schroeder became pregnant. One month after learning of Ann's affliction, Mrs. Schroeder gave birth to a second child, Thomas, who also suffers from cystic fibrosis.[1]

After this introductory summary, you can proceed to relate the facts in detail.

When your case involves a dramatic event, you might want to start with that event, using a plot formula one well-known novelist recommends: ABDCE or Action, Background, Development, Climax and Ending.[2]

---

[1] *Schroeder v. Perkel*, 432 A.2d 834, 836 (N.J. 1981).

[2] Anne Lamott, *Bird by Bird: Some Instructions On Writing and Life* 62 (Anchor Books 1995), quoting Alice Adams.

You begin with action that is compelling enough to draw us in, make us want to know more. Background is where you let us see and know these people, so that we learn what they care most about. The plot—the drama, the actions, the tension—will grow out of that. You move them along until everything comes together in the climax, after which things are different for the main characters, different in some real way. And then there is the ending: what is our sense of who these people are now, what are they left with, what happened, and what did it mean?[3]

Using this formula, a fact statement for Nancy Williams based on the facts in Casefile 1 in Appendix A—whether in a brief or opinion, or even in a letter opening settlement negotiations—might look like that below.

## *Action*

On February 10, 20__, Nancy Williams, a 30-year-old woman with Master's degrees in social work and divinity, was hired as Director of Youth Social Services by Grace Church, a large and prominent inter-denominational Protestant church in Minneapolis. Soon after Ms. Williams' arrival, it became apparent that the Rev. Bryant, married and 65-years old, was attracted to her. He began to make sexual advances that were unwelcome to Ms. Williams, whose fiancé had remained in the East temporarily. According to Ms. Williams, the Rev. Bryant, who referred to himself jokingly as "the tactile preacher," frequently "came up behind me and ran his fingers through my hair and down my back, letting his hand come to rest on the small of my back," from which position she invariably removed it. On many occasions, he put his hands on Ms. Williams' waist and pulled her tight against his body, admonishing her for being "an uptight WASP" when she struggled out of his embrace. The Rev. Bryant also invited Ms. Williams to spend weekends with him at a remote wilderness lodge that the Church maintained as a retreat center. He constantly referred to the two of them

---

[3] *Id.*

as "lovers," and insisted on Ms. Williams' companionship outside the workplace.

## Background

Ms. Williams had moved to Minneapolis from New York City after she was hired by the Board of Parish Life ("the BPL"), which is responsible for all personnel decisions. The BPL is composed of the members of the Board of Deacons and the Board of Trustees, who are elected by the congregation. Ms. Williams and the BPL signed an initial two-year employment contract, and she took up her work enthusiastically, and apparently with great success. Her innovative programming dramatically increased attendance at the Church's sports and tutoring programs, and her counseling services for truants and other troubled young people—she combined traditional psychotherapy with spiritual counseling—were the subject of several positive articles in the Minneapolis press. Ms. Williams was well-liked at the Church by both clergy and congregation. In addition to Ms. Williams, the professional staff consisted of an Administrative Minister, a Social Justice Associate, a Pastoral Services Minister, a Music Director, and a Senior Minister, the Rev. Bryant, whose responsibilities included preaching and supervising the rest of the professional staff.

## Development

When the Rev. Bryant first began his advances to Ms. Williams, she tried admonishing him. When it became clear that her reproofs would have no deterring effect no matter how often repeated, Ms. Williams complained to the Personnel Sub-Committee of the BPL. When that body failed to investigate or take any action, she complained to the BPL itself. The BPL declined to take any action other than advising Ms. Williams to "exercise some Christian compassion and forbearance" toward the Rev. Bryant, and not expect him "to be a women's libber at his age." The most sympathetic members urged her to "try and put up with it until he retires," because although "he is a hopeless old lady-killer, he doesn't mean any harm."

### *Climax*

In the meantime, the Rev. Bryant's interest in Ms. Williams continued unabated. Finally, Ms. Williams told the BPL that she was going to file sex discrimination charges against him and against the BPL with the Minnesota Department of Human Rights. On November 10 of last year, one week after this conversation, the BPL summarily fired her. The reason stated for her discharge was that she "had inappropriate relationships" with teenagers in her youth groups. Ms. Williams denied this allegation, but to no avail.

Ms. Williams was devastated by the BPL's action. On Thanksgiving Day, she took an overdose of Valium, but was fortunately rescued when her fiancé asked her neighbors to look in on her. She spent several weeks in the psychiatric facility at Lakeland-University Hospital, and is currently undergoing intensive outpatient treatment for "severe reactive depression." Nonetheless, her psychiatrist believes that she will probably recover completely in time and that she will be able to return to her career.

### *Ending*

Ms. Williams is entitled to damages for pain and suffering, medical expenses, and lost wages. Moreover, given that the Rev. Bryant retired on January 1 of this year, Ms. Williams would like to return to her position at Grace Church—which, but for Rev. Bryant, was otherwise "the job of her dreams."

Sometimes, however, straightforward chronology is the most compelling way to tell a story. Traditional narrative structure organizes events into a familiar progression that moves from background to disruption to efforts at resolution to conclusion. This structure has the effect of highlighting background facts and of meeting reader expectation that a story will indeed begin at the beginning. Thus, a writer who wishes to emphasize Nancy Williams' exemplary performance of her "dream job" might choose this way to tell the story.

Finally, in organizing your facts, you will want to remember one strategy stressed in most first-year legal writing texts: emphasize favorable facts and de-emphasize unfavorable ones. In terms of organization, this means that you begin and end with facts advantageous to your client because readers remember openings and endings more than material in the middle. It is important to create a good first impression and to exit on a positive note. It follows that unfavorable facts generally appear in the middle of the narration, perhaps even in the middle of a paragraph that opens and closes more affirmatively.

Remember, however, that the location of an unpropitious fact may make the fact less memorable, but does not necessarily make it less damaging. It is far more effective to minimize or neutralize a fact by developing a core theme that can account for it than merely to bury it.

### 3. The Parties Should Come Alive

More interesting than action is the impact action has on lives. Nothing is more consequential, therefore, than bringing the parties to life. To do that effectively, you need to find out as much as possible about them and then think about how to present your insights so as to render your client more sympathetic than your adversary.

Probably the best way to reveal character is to let an external aspect of a character speak for itself. Let appearance, statements, and conduct mirror a party's interior essence. Thus, for example, comments made by a member of the BPL to Nancy Williams— "you can't expect him to be a women's libber at his age," or "he's a hopeless old lady-killer but doesn't mean any harm"—are revealing enough for a reader to infer old-school chauvinism without any gloss provided. This technique—the show, don't tell technique[4]—is one of the most effective in a writer's arsenal.

It is, of course, harder to make some clients sympathetic than it is others, in particular the criminal defendant, the government, and the corporate client. One frequently employed helpful tactic is to make the criminal defendant "a proxy for an ideal" so that, for example, "holding against the client is a holding against the

---

[4] *See also* Steven D. Stark's discussion of this technique in *Writing to Win: The Legal Writer* 106–107 (Main Street 1999).

Fourth Amendment."[5] Analogously, you could make the libel defendant a proxy for the First Amendment. Other helpful strategies include presenting the criminal defendant as a man who is less of a threat to society than a threat to himself, like a drug addict who is his own worst enemy. Audiences tend to hope the defendant's better nature will prevail.[6] But beware of trying too hard to make a client sympathetic. Sometimes you best humanize your client by being realistic: "She may be a drug-dealer, but she's not a murderer."

Corporate clients and government agencies also need to be humanized. Some corporations can be portrayed as a "little guy" up against a "big guy": even Microsoft is a "little guy" when up against the United States Government.[7] The balance would shift, however, if it were "Mom and Pop's Software" against Microsoft. Audiences are naturally inclined to side with the less powerful party. This technique can work with government agencies also. Although it might seem difficult to generate support for a police department's dubious sting operation, you might achieve it if the police are seen as engaged in a battle against an infamous drug cartel.

Some corporations are known for their philanthropy or their willingness to give employees shares in the company. If this information can be included in the fact statement, it might soften the corporate image. In addition, it is sometimes possible to showcase an individual in a corporation whose behavior is particularly benevolent (or malevolent),[8] and thereby imbue the institution with some of the characteristics of one of its leaders. But beware: when this technique becomes obvious, you risk alienating the reader.

### 4. The Tale Should Be Well Told

In addition to a well-developed story line and skillfully drawn characters, there are other narrative techniques that can enhance

---

[5] Brian J. Foley & Ruth Anne Robbins, *Fiction 101: A Primer for Lawyers on How to Use Fiction Writing Techniques to Write a Persuasive Facts Section*, 32 Rutgers L. J. 459, 473 (2001).

[6] *Id.* at 470.

[7] *Id.*

[8] *Id.* at 475.

the effectiveness of persuasive fact statements. Setting a vivid scene, focusing point of view carefully, and making good use of detail and diction are all worth considering.

Elaborate descriptions are not necessary in order to set a scene that furthers your core theme. For example, in the Williams fact statement, the "remote wilderness lodge" where the plaintiff's supervisor expected her to spend time with him is sufficient to suggest plaintiff's helpless isolation and her supervisor's dishonorable intentions.

Writers of persuasive fact statements also do well to consider point of view since it provides depth, interest, and credibility. Storytellers choose omniscient narrators, single or multiple points of view, reliable or unreliable narrators. Experienced appellate practitioners have learned from them how to use point of view skillfully, employing both omniscient and individual points of view. The fact statement as a whole should impress the reader as the account of an objective, all-knowing, reliable observer of the proceedings in the court or courts below. This means that the writer should not crudely slant facts or characterize the court's rulings—lest the record reveal the writer as an unreliable narrator. Within this larger narrative, however, individual points of view can surface in ways that further the writer's theme. Recounting trial evidence, the writer can focus on the client's or client's witnesses' point of view, quoting from the record to let individual voices speak. For example, in the Williams' fact statement, one quote from the plaintiff lets the reader into plaintiff's experience with uncomfortable immediacy when she alleges that her supervisor "came up behind me and ran his fingers through my hair and down my back."

Detail and diction are also effective ways of molding a reader's perception. You should describe favorable facts in detail and unfavorable facts generally, using the connotations of words for maximum effect. Thus, to return to our earlier robbery example, defense counsel summarizes the perpetrator's assault and uses an abstract, medical term ("the man lacerated her arms and wrists") while the prosecutor describes the assault in more detail and with more graphic verbs ("he slashed her arms and wrists with a large knife, and broke her thumb as he wrenched the purse away from her grasp"). Another very different example of effective use of detail is found in the Williams fact statement, where the writer specifies that plaintiff attempted suicide "on Thanksgiving Day." The mere mention of this family holiday conveys her feelings of desolation more effectively than if her feelings were actually described.

──────────────── *Exercise 6.3* ────────────────

*Good examples of molding the reader's perception of events can be found in the fact statements of* Shuttlesworth v. City of Birmingham, *394 U.S. 147 (1969) and* Walker v. City of Birmingham, *388 U.S. 308 (1967), decisions that evolved out of the same civil rights protest and were written by the same judge, Justice Stewart.[9] In* Shuttlesworth, *the Court held that the city's parade ordinance was unconstitutional and the petitioner's criminal conviction for violating that ordinance could not stand. In* Walker, *the Court held that petitioners who deliberately violated an injunction were not entitled to have the constitutional issue of the generality of the language in the city parade ordinance considered at a contempt hearing. What persuasive strategies are used in each?*

### *Shuttlesworth v. City of Birmingham*
### *394 U.S. 147 (1969)*

On the afternoon of April 12, Good Friday, 1963, 52 people, all Negroes, were led out of a Birmingham church by three Negro ministers, one of whom was the petitioner, Fred L. Shuttlesworth. They walked in orderly fashion, two abreast for the most part, for four blocks. The purpose of their march was to protest the alleged denial of civil rights to Negroes in the city of Birmingham. The marchers stayed on the sidewalks except at street intersections, and they did not interfere with other pedestrians. No automobiles were obstructed, nor were traffic signals disobeyed. The petitioner was with the group for at least part of this time, walking alongside the others, and once moving from the front to the rear. As the marchers moved along, a crowd of spectators fell in behind them at a distance. The spectators at some points spilled out into the street, but the street was not blocked and vehicles were not obstructed.

───────────────

[9] Ken Swift drew our attention to these cases in his article, *Teaching Students to Utilize the Facts Section*, in 16 The Second Draft 11 (Dec. 2001).

At the end of four blocks the marchers were stopped by the Birmingham police, and were arrested for violating § 1159 of the General Code of Birmingham. That ordinance reads as follows:

> It shall be unlawful to organize or hold, or to assist in organizing or holding, or to take part or participate in, any parade or procession or other public demonstration on the streets or other public ways of the city, unless a permit therefor has been secured from the commission.

The petitioner was convicted for violation of § 1159 and was sentenced to 90 days' imprisonment at hard labor and an additional 48 days at hard labor in default of payment of a $75 fine and $24 costs. The Alabama Court of Appeals reversed the judgment of conviction, holding the evidence was insufficient "to show a procession which would require, under the terms of § 1159, the getting of a permit," that the ordinance had been applied in a discriminatory fashion, and that it was unconstitutional in imposing an "invidious prior restraint" without ascertainable standards for the granting of permits. The Supreme Court of Alabama, however, giving the language of § 1159 an extraordinarily narrow construction, reversed the judgment of the Court of Appeals and reinstated the conviction. We granted certiorari to consider the petitioner's constitutional claims.

### *Walker v. City of Birmingham*
### *388 U.S. 307 (1967)*

On Wednesday, April 10, 1963, officials of Birmingham, Alabama, filed a bill of complaint in a state circuit court asking for injunctive relief against 139 individuals and two organizations. The bill and accompanying affidavits stated that during the preceding seven days:

> "Respondents [had] sponsored and/or participated in...'sit-in' demonstrations, 'kneel-in' demonstrations, mass street parades, trespasses on private property...."

The bill stated that these infractions of the law were expected to continue and would "lead to further imminent danger to the lives, safety, peace, tranquility and general welfare of the people of the City of Birmingham," and that the "remedy by law [was] inadequate." The circuit judge granted a temporary injunction as prayed in the bill, enjoining the petitioners from, among other things, participating in or encouraging mass street parades or mass processions without a permit as required by a Birmingham ordinance.

Five of the eight petitioners were served with copies of the writ early the next morning. Several hours later four of them held a press conference. There a statement was distributed, declaring their intention to disobey the injunction because it was "raw tyranny under the guise of maintaining law and order." At this press conference one of the petitioners stated: "That they had respect for the Federal Courts, or Federal Injunctions, but in the past the State Courts had favored local law enforcement, and if the police couldn't handle it, the mob would."

That night a meeting took place at which one of the petitioners announced that "[i]njunction or no injunction we are going to march tomorrow." The next afternoon, Good Friday, a large crowd gathered in the vicinity of Sixteenth Street and Sixth Avenue North in Birmingham. A group of about 50 or 60 proceeded to parade along the sidewalk while a crowd of 1,000 or 1,500 stood by "clapping, and hollering, and [w]hooping." Some of the crowd followed the marchers and spilled out into the street. At least three of the petitioners participated in this march.

Meetings sponsored by some of the petitioners were held that night and the following night, where calls were made. On Easter Sunday, April 14, a crowd of between 1,500 and 2,000 people congregated in the midafternoon in the vicinity of Seventh Avenue and Eleventh Street North in Birmingham. One of the petitioners was seen organizing members of the crowd in formation. A group of about 50, headed by three other petitioners started down the sidewalk two abreast. At least one other petitioner was among the marchers. Some 300 or 400 people from among the onlookers followed in a crowd that occupied the entire width of the street and overflowed onto the sidewalks. Violence occurred. Members of the crowd threw rocks that injured a newspaperman and damaged a police motorcycle.

---

## C. PERSUASIVE ANALYSIS

If facts make your readers want to respond as you request, persuasive legal analysis enables them to do so. Persuasive analysis requires more than persuasive rhetoric, however. In fact, recent empirical studies confirm that neither judges nor laypersons are easily swayed by persuasive rhetoric alone.[10] Instead, decision-makers rely predominantly on the quality of the evidence and the content and strength of the argument. A 1999 survey of 355 federal judges reveals, perhaps not too surprisingly, that sound legal analysis is the most important attribute of a persuasive brief. It also documents that only 23 percent of those judges surveyed are satisfied with the legal analysis they are given. Although they say lawyers usually adequately identify issues and present controlling authority, advocates' analogic thinking was thought to be deficient: factual and legal comparisons were superficial, and policy and issue distinctions were not probed.[11] In addition, advocates neither pursued the implications of a decision or a rule, nor thoughtfully addressed contrary readings of law and counter-arguments. The same study reveals organization as the second most valued characteristic of persuasive writing. Seventy-six percent of all judges polled want advocates to provide readers with a roadmap.[12]

One important conclusion to draw from this survey is that conceptualization and clarity are not skills separable from persuasion but are in fact skills at its heart. Giving good reasons is the main weapon of the advocate and the primary means of justification for a decision-maker. Clear and discriminating analysis and reasoning promote credibility and therefore persuasiveness. Thus,

---

[10] Kristen K. Robbins, *The Inside Scoop: What Federal Judges Really Think about the Way Lawyers Write*, 8 J. Leg. Writing Inst. (2002); Christy A. Visher, *Juror Decision Making: The Importance of Evidence*, 11 Law & Human Behavior 1 (1987); Michael J. Saks, *What Do Jury Experiments Tell Us About How Juries (Should) Make Decisions*, 6 S. Cal. Interdisciplinary L. J. 1 (1997).

[11] Robbins, *supra* n. 10. Chris Wren has compiled a list of opinions making the same point, of which the following are only a small sampling: *Sanchez v. Miller*, 792 F.2d 694, 703 (7th Cir. 1986), *cert. denied*, 479 U.S. 1056 (1987) ("It is not the obligation of this court to research and construct the legal arguments open to parties...."); *U. S. v. Berkowitz*, 927 F.2d 1376,1384 (7th Cir.), *cert. denied*, 506 U.S. 1083 (1993) (perfunctory arguments, undeveloped arguments, and arguments unsupported by citation to pertinent record and legal authority may be deemed waived); *State v. O'Connell*, 508 N.W.2d 23 (Wis. Ct.App. 1993) ("We do not consider undeveloped arguments"); *Williamson v. Opsahl*, 416 N.E.2d 783, 784 (Ill. App. 1981) ("[A] reviewing court is entitled to have the issues defined with pertinent authority cited and is not simply a depository in which the appealing party may dump the burden of argument and research").

[12] Robbins, *supra* n. 10.

persuasion requires that we work harder on making discerning factual, legal, and policy arguments. Our focus in this part of our chapter on persuasion is, therefore, on developing the kinds of reasons that are convincing because they are sound, and on writing about them clearly and authoritatively.

## 1. Draw from All Types of Legal Argument

Conclusions alone are not persuasive. They must be backed up with persuasive arguments, as many and varied as possible. Thus, whether writing a brief, memo, letter, or opinion, your familiarity with a typology of legal argument is fundamental to the persuasive enterprise. Moreover, if you can identify the types of arguments present in an opposing brief, it becomes easier not only to conceptualize, but also to identify missing arguments and counter-arguments. This in turn helps you to generate new arguments and to test the comprehensiveness and validity of both your adversary's conclusions and your own. Similarly, if you can identify the missing steps in the reasoning of a lower court's opinion, you may generate grounds for an appeal or reversal.

Legal argument can be variously classified, but one useful division is into four basic categories: argument from precedent, interpretive argument (based on interpreting language in enacted law), normative argument (grounded in morality and social policy), and institutional argument (a broad category including, e.g., federal preemption, legislative prerogative, and judicial efficiency arguments). Argument from precedent and interpretive argument are "rule-based" arguments. Normative and institutional arguments are more policy-based and frequently made in conjunction with rule-based arguments. They explain why existing common law should or should not extend to a new factual situation, why a novel application of a constitutional provision is or is not appropriate, or why a particular statutory interpretation has desirable or undesirable consequences. Within each category of argument, traditional arguments are met by traditional counter-arguments—although, when an argument cannot be easily countered within its own category, it can often be minimized by emphasizing an entirely different line of argument.

## a. Arguments from Precedent

The paradigmatic argument from precedent is, of course, that a prior binding decision compels the result in the case at bar because the two cases are alike in all meaningful respects or are distinguishable in significant ways. Essential to this line of analysis are the reasons why the cases are alike or are distinguishable.

Analysis becomes more complicated when reaching the desired result requires you to frame the holding of precedent broadly or narrowly. Assume, for example, that precedent allows a defendant to raise an entrapment defense if the police mount a "sting" operation and instruct their agent to target the defendant. In your case, the police did not name your client as a target, but described him in a way that led the agent to him. As defense counsel, you will interpret precedent broadly, arguing that describing without naming is the same as targeting a named individual for the purposes of entrapment, and that the description of your client was in any case so specific as to be tantamount to naming. The state will interpret precedent narrowly, arguing that descriptions are often too general to be the equivalent of naming, as the description was in this case. In other words, arguing from precedent requires you to scrutinize the facts and law to find a way of interpreting them that is plausible and beneficial to your case, and that anticipates your adversary's rebuttal. However, you should be aware that whenever you urge broadening or narrowing a rule, you usually support your argument from precedent with normative or institutional arguments like those described later in this section, giving reasons why your interpretation of the rule is a good one.

## b. Interpretive Argument

Interpretive arguments begin with the fixed language of constitutions, statutes, and regulations. The traditional rule is that, if the text has a plain meaning, a court will enforce that meaning without looking at other evidence. If the language is unclear—if, for example, it exhibits syntactic or semantic ambiguity[13]—interpreters need to examine extrinsic evidence to determine what the legislature intended by that language. For instance, a

---

[13] *See* Section B of Chapter 11, *Precision.*

court may examine the statute's preamble or related provisions within the same statute. Comparisons to parallel statutes might reveal interesting similarities or differences, as might interpretations of the statute's language by lower courts, by administrative agencies charged with enforcement, by scholars, or by courts of other jurisdictions. Especially for federal statutes, the statute's legislative history will be memorialized in documents and records, and might reveal what the legislators intended by the language or articulate some of the social policies and historical events or trends that prompted the statute's enactment.[14]

If extrinsic evidence is not conclusive as to legislative intent behind ambiguous language, interpretive argument may rely on the many traditional "canons," rules of interpretation or construction. The canons are rarely decisive, however. Indeed, they have been famously likened to the "parry" and "thrust" of a fencing match.[15] For each canon, there is a "counter-canon." For example, although one canon commands respect for plain meaning, another holds that plain meaning may be disregarded if it is contrary to legislative intent.[16]

Assume, for example, that you must determine whether pleasure boats fall under the Limitation of Liability Act, 46 U.S.C., app. §183(a) (1996), which permits an owner of "any vessel" to limit his liability for personal injuries and property damage caused by collisions at sea to the value of the owner's boat and its cargo after the collision, provided that the owner is without "privity or knowledge" regarding the accident. Consider first the plain language of the statute. An argument for including pleasure boats is that the plain meaning of "any vessel" is "any and all vessels": it does not distinguish between pleasure and com-

---

[14] You need to be aware that different records have different weight. The best indicator of legislative intent is the final committee report. *See Monterey Coal Co. v. Federal Mine Safety & Health Review Comm.*, 743 F.2d 589, 598 (7th Cir. 1984); *Sierra Club v. Clark*, 755 F.2d 608, 615 (8th Cir. 1985). The statements by the statute's sponsor in a floor debates are accorded substantial weight, *Federal Energy Administration v. Algonquin SNG, Inc.*, 426 U.S. 548, 564 (1976), although the remarks of individual legislators are given little weight, *Ernst & Ernst v. Hochfelder*, 425 U.S. 185, 203 n. 24 (1976), unless they are consistent with the statute's language. *Brock v. Pierce County*, 476 U.S. 253, 263 (1986). We are grateful to Darby Dickerson, who did this research.

[15] Karl Llewellyn, *Remarks on the Theory of Appellate Decisions and the Rules or Canons About How Statutes Are To Be Construed*, 3 Vand. L. Rev. 395 (1950).

[16] *Id.* at 403.

mercial vehicles. Furthermore, Section 188 of the Act states that "except as otherwise specifically provided," Section 183 applies to "all seagoing vessels and also to all vessels used on lakes or rivers...." Although a variety of vessels, including pleasure craft are specifically excluded from Sections 183(b)–(e), no vessel is specifically excluded from Section 183(a). Moreover, the statute has been amended a number of times and Congress has never excluded pleasure boats. Thus it appears that, by its plain meaning and in its statutory context, §183(a) includes pleasure boats.

Yet there is an equally strong counter to this convincing plain-meaning argument. The legislative history of §183(a) makes it clear that the statute was intended to encourage international shipping by limiting the liability of the commercial owner. There is absolutely no reference in the legislative history to pleasure craft, and it is clear that the legislature was not even considering pleasure boats when it passed the act a century ago. Thus, many district courts have concluded that the act does not apply to owners of pleasure boats because such application, though supported by plain language and statutory context, is contrary to legislative intent.[17]

In order to persuade, a proponent of either of these plausible interpretations—plain language or plain language trumped by legislative intent—would be well-advised to provide the support of normative and institutional arguments.

### c. Normative Arguments

Normative arguments assert that a rule or result is a good one (or bad), under accepted norms of morality, social policy, economics, or corrective justice. An example of normative argument, grounded both in morality and in social policy, comes from a United States Supreme Court decision overturning the Court's own precedent to hold that in capital cases, fact-finding regarding aggravating or mitigating circumstances must always be made by a jury and may not be entrusted to the judge.[18] In support of the Court's change of direction, Justice Scalia argued that permitting a

---

[17] *See, e.g., In the Matter of Myers,* 721 F. Supp. 39 (W.D.N.Y. 1989). We take this example from a problem devised by Ann McGinley.

[18] *Ring v. Arizona,* 536 U.S. 584 (2002).

court to make such findings would threaten one of our core values as a nation, our belief in the jury as guarantor of the rights of a criminal defendant; indeed, permitting judges to determine the ultimate penalty would render society "callous to the need for [the jury's] protection by regularly imposing the death penalty without it."[19] Indeed, normative arguments frequently arise in discussions about constitutional rights, which are often defined as those "deeply rooted in this nation's history and language."[20] When issues touch on core values—like abortion, assisted suicide, sodomy, gay or inter-racial marriage—courts often look to the traditions and customs of society to guide them.

Normative arguments can also be grounded in simple justice between the parties. For example, arguing that "any vessel" should not include pleasure craft for the purposes of a drastic limitation of the boat owner's liability under 46 U.S.C. 183(a), counsel for plaintiff who suffered serious injuries in a boating accident could also make a normative argument. She might argue that justice between the parties would not be served by limiting defendant's liability to the $1,000 that defendant paid for his used jet-ski.

### d. Institutional Arguments

Institutional arguments assert the appropriateness or practicality of a rule or result in the context of the various institutions of our government. Two common types of institutional argument concern the roles of judiciary, legislature, and executive, and the relationship between state and federal law. Other institutional arguments consider the practical effect of a rule or result on the administration of justice.

Like normative arguments, institutional arguments can provide decisive support when there are conflicting lines of authority, or competing interpretations of statutory language, or when the writer wishes to justify a departure from precedent or criticize a contrary position. For example, in the death-penalty case holding that the Constitution permits only juries, not judges, to

---

[19] *Id.* at 612 (Scalia, J., concurring).

[20] *Moore v. City of East Cleveland*, 431 U.S. 494, 503 (1977).

weigh mitigating and aggravating factors, Justice O'Connor's dissent advanced an institutional argument: the decision would open the floodgates, unleashing a flood of petitions challenging defendants' sentences and burdening the courts.[21]

Another kind of institutional argument might be advanced by counsel for the defendant jet-ski owner in the limitation-of-liability case discussed above. He might argue that it is for Congress, not the courts, to decide whether pleasure boats should be excluded from the reach of §183(a). He might also add a "slippery slope" argument to this separation of powers argument, noting that anarchy would result if courts ignored the law every time they believed that "fairness" required such a result.[22]

Convincing policy arguments require a two-step analysis.[23] First, the writer spells out the consequences of following one interpretation or approach rather than another. Second, the writer explains why one approach is preferable to the other. For example, a night curfew on teenagers could reduce crime because statistically most juvenile crime–illegal drinking, drunk driving, sexual and racial assaults–occur at night. At the same time, a night curfew impinges on parental rights and curtails legitimate teenage activities like babysitting and movies. In evaluating the consequences of such an ordinance, an advocate could argue that a blanket curfew is an overly broad response to a slight rise in crime rates and exceptions would be needed to protect the rights of parents and children.

The chart below shows some of the most common arguments and counter-arguments. Of course, not all types of arguments are available in every context, nor are all arguments equally persuasive in every context. Effective persuasive writers evaluate the strength of their arguments, checking for logical fallacies and other flaws, in order to avoid exaggeration and overreaching.

---

[21] *Ring v. Arizona*, 536 U.S. at 620.

[22] These arguments convinced the court in *Moeller v. Mulvey*, 959 F. Supp. 1102 (D. Minn. 1996).

[23] For a more developed discussion of this, see Wilson Huhn, *Five Types of Legal Analysis*, 45-50 (2d ed. Carolina Academic Press 2008).

# The Varieties of Legal Argument[24]

| *Argument* | *Counter-Argument* |
|---|---|

## A. Argument from Precedent

| | |
|---|---|
| 1. Precedent must be followed; the facts are meaningfully similar. | 1.a) The facts are meaningfully different. |
| | 1.b) Precedent should be overruled. |
| 2. Precedent should be extended from an analogous situation. (*E.g.,* "Describing a person is analogous to naming.") | 2. The situation is not sufficiently analogous. (*E.g.,* "Describing is too general to be the equivalent of naming.") |
| 3. There are 2 competing lines of persuasive precedent: line A is better because.... | 3. Line B is better because.... |

## B. Interpretive Argument

| | |
|---|---|
| 1. The plain meaning of the statute should be applied. (*E.g.,* "Any vessel means all vessels.") | 1.a) The statute is ambiguous. |
| | 1.b) The plain meaning conflicts with legislative intent, creates an absurd result, etc. (*E.g.,* "The Congressional record makes it clear that the statute was intended to limit the liability of owners of commercial vessels.") |
| | 1.c) The language must be read in context. |

## C. Normative Argument

| | |
|---|---|
| 1. Morality requires this result. (*E.g.,* "Innocent victims must be compensated.") | 1. The result is not moral (*E.g.,* "It is wrong to impose liability on an owner without privity or knowledge of the boating accident.") |
| 2. Good social policy requires this result. (*E.g.,* "Limitations on liability promote maritime commerce.") | 2.a) Society will not benefit. (*E.g.,* "A shipowner should ensure that those operating his vessel are competent.") |
| | 2.b) There may be some benefit, but the harm outweighs the benefits. |
| 3. Economic concerns support this result. (*E.g.,* "The loss will be shifted from the victim to the negligent shipowner.") | 3. Economic concerns do not support this result. (*E.g.,* "There will be an unduly negative impact on the recreational boating industry." |

---

[24] This chart is adapted from Elizabeth Fajans & Mary R. Falk, *Scholarly Writing for Law Students: Seminar Papers, Law Review Articles, and Law Review Competition Papers* (2d ed. West 2000).

4. Justice between the parties justifies the result. (*E.g.,* "Defendant's egregious conduct warrants tolling the statute of limitations.")

4. Justice between the parties requires the opposite result. (*E.g.,* "Plaintiff should not be rewarded for 'sleeping on her rights.'")

### D. Institutional Argument

1. This is the kind of decision courts are best-equipped to make.
2. This is an area where the state is free to make law.
3. This rule would "open the floodgates."

1. This is the kind of decision best made by the legislature.
2. Federal law preempts state law.

3.a) Few litigants would/could invoke this rule.
3.b) The gates are already open
3.c) There can't be too much justice.

4. Courts/Juries would have difficulty with this vague standard.
5. This is a bright-line rule, easy to apply.
6. This rule creates a "slippery slope."

4. Courts/Juries use standards like this all the time.

5.a) The rule is inflexible.
5.b) Draw the line somewhere else.
6. The rule is narrow and precise.

———————————— *Exercise 6.4* ————————————

*Read the following edited and excerpted version of the opinion of the New Jersey Supreme Court in* Kelly v. Gwinnell, *476 A.2d 1219 (N.J. 1984). Citations are omitted.*

**A.** *Identify the types of arguments the court makes, remembering that there are four basic categories of legal argument: arguments from precedent, interpretive arguments, normative arguments (moral, social policy, and justice arguments), and institutional arguments.*

**B.** *Assume you are representing a social host defendant in another state and need to counter the plaintiff's arguments based on* Kelly *below. What arguments could you make? What types of arguments are they?*

### *Kelly v. Gwinnell*

This case raises the issue of whether a social host who enables an adult guest at his home to become drunk is liable to the victim of an automobile accident caused by the drunken driving of the guest. Here the host served liquor to the guest beyond the point at which the guest was visibly intoxicated. We hold the host may be liable under the circumstances of this case.

\* \* \* \*

The Appellate Division's determination [to the contrary] was based on the apparent absence of decisions in this country imposing such liability (except for those that were promptly overruled by the Legislature). The absence of such determinations is said to reflect a broad consensus that the imposition of liability arising from these social relations is unwise. Certainly this immunization of hosts is not the inevitable result of the law of negligence, for conventional negligence analysis points strongly in exactly the opposite direction. "Negligence is tested by whether the reasonably prudent person at the time and place should recognize and foresee an unreasonable risk or likelihood of harm or danger to others." *Rappaport v. Nichols.* When negligent conduct creates such a risk, setting off foreseeable consequences that lead to plaintiff's injury, the conduct is deemed the proximate cause of the injury. "[A] tortfeasor is generally held answerable for the injuries which result in the ordinary course of events from his negligence and it is generally sufficient if his negligent conduct was a substantial factor in bringing about the injuries." *Rappaport.*

\* \* \* \*

When the court determines that a duty exists and liability will be extended, it draws judicial lines based on fairness and policy. In a society where thousands of deaths are caused each year by drunken drivers, where the damage caused by such deaths is regarded increasingly as intolerable, where liquor licensees are prohibited from serving intoxicated adults, and where long-standing criminal sanctions against drunken driving have recently been significantly strengthened to the point where the Governor notes that they are regarded as the toughest in the nation, the imposition of such a duty by the judiciary seems both fair and fully in accord with the State's policy. Unlike those cases in which the definition of desirable policy is the subject of intense controversy, here the imposition of a duty is both consistent with and supportive of a social goal—the reduction of drunken driving—that is practically unanimously accepted by society.

While the imposition of a duty here would go beyond our prior decisions, those decisions not only point clearly in that direction but do so despite the presence of social considerations similar to those involved in this case—considerations that are claimed to invest the host with immunity. In our first case on the subject, *Rappaport,* we held a licensee liable for the consequences of a customer's negligent operation of his automobile. The customer was a minor who had become intoxicated as a result of the consumption of liquor at various premises including the licensee's.

\* \* \* \*

The Appellate Division moved our decisional law one step further, a significant step, when it ruled in *Linn v. Rand* that a social host who serves liquor to a visibly intoxicated minor, knowing the minor will thereafter drive, may be held liable for the injuries inflicted on a third party as a result of the subsequent drunken driving of the minor. There, practically all of the considerations urged here against liability were present: it was a social setting at someone's home, not at a tavern; the one who provided the liquor to the intoxicated minor was a host, not a licensee; and all of the notions of fault and causation pinning sole responsibility on the drinker were present. The only difference was that the guest was a minor—but whether obviously so or whether known to the host is not disclosed in the opinion.

In *Rappaport,* we explicitly noted that the matter did not involve any claim against "persons not engaged in the liquor business." We now approve *Linn* with its extension of this liability to social hosts.

\* \* \* \*

We impose this duty on the host to the third party because we believe that the policy considerations served by its imposition far outweigh those asserted in opposition. While we recognize the concern that our ruling will interfere with accepted standards of social behavior; will intrude on and somewhat diminish the enjoyment, relaxation, and camaraderie that accompany social gatherings at which alcohol is served; and that such gatherings and social relationships are not simply tangential benefits of a civilized society but are regarded by many as important, we believe that the added assurance of just compensation to the victims of drunken driving as well as the added deterrent effect of the rule on such driving outweigh the importance of those other values. Indeed, we believe that given society's extreme concern about drunken driving, any change in social behavior resulting from the rule will be regarded ultimately as neutral at the very least, and not as a change for the worse; but that in any event if there be a loss, it is well worth the gain.

\* \* \* \*

Some fear has been expressed that the extent of the potential liability may be disproportionate to the fault of the host. A social judgment is therein implied to the effect that society does not regard as particularly serious the host's actions in causing his guest to become drunk, even though he knows they will thereafter be driving their cars. We seriously question that value judgment; indeed, we do not believe that the liability is disproportionate when the host's actions, so relatively easily corrected, may result in serious injury or death. The other aspect of this argument is that the host's insurance protection will be insufficient. While acknowledging that homeowners' insurance will cover such liability, this argument notes the risk that both the host and spouse will be jointly liable. The point made is not that the level of insurance will be lower in relation to the injuries than in the case of other torts, but rather that the joint liability of the spouses may result in the loss of their home and other property to the extent that the policy limits are inadequate.

It may be that some special form of insurance could be designed to protect the spouses' equity in their homes in cases such as this one. In any event, it is not clear that the loss of a home by spouses who, by definition, have negligently caused the injury, is disproportionate to the loss of life of one who is totally innocent of any wrongdoing.

\* \* \* \*

We do not agree that the issue addressed in this case is appropriate only for legislative resolution. Determinations of the scope of duty in negligence cases has traditionally been a function of the judiciary. The history of the cases cited above evidences a continuing judicial involvement in these matters. Without the benefit of any Dram Shop Act imposing liability on licensees, legislation that is quite common in other states, this Court determined that such liability nevertheless existed. We did so in 1959 and have continued to expand that concept since then.... The subject matter is not abstruse, and it can safely be assumed that the Legislature is in fact aware of our decisions in this area. Absent adverse reaction, we assume that our decisions are found to be consonant with the strong legislative policy against drunken driving.

\* \* \* \*

Given the facts before us, we decide only that where the social host directly serves the guest and continues to do so even after the guest is visibly intoxicated, knowing that the guest will soon be driving home, the social host may be liable for the consequences of the resulting drunken driving. We are not faced with a party where many guests congregate, nor with guests serving each other, nor with a host busily occupied with other responsibilities and therefore unable to attend to the matter of serving liquor, nor with a drunken host. We will face those situations when and if they come before us, we hope with sufficient reason and perception so as to balance, if necessary and if legitimate, the societal interests alleged to be inconsistent with the public policy considerations that are at the heart of today's decision.

\* \* \* \*

The financial impact of an insurance premium increase on the home-owner or the tenant should be measured against the monumental financial losses suffered by society as a result of drunken driving. By our decision we not only spread some of that loss so that it need not be borne completely by the victims of this widespread affliction, but, to some extent, reduce the likelihood that the loss will occur in the first place. Even if the dissent's view of the scope of our decision were correct, the adjustments in social behavior at parties, the burden put on the host to reasonably oversee the serving of liquor, the burden on the guests to make sure if one is drinking that another is driving, and the burden on all to take those reasonable steps even if, on some occasion, some guest may become belligerent: those social dislocations, their importance, must be measured against the misery, death, and destruction caused by the drunken driver. Does our society morally approve of the decision to continue to allow the charm of unrestrained social drinking when the cost is the lives of others, sometimes of the guests themselves?

---

## 2. Frame Authority Persuasively

Although we readily accept the notion that the facts of the case have to be "found" and fashioned into a narrative informed by the legal issue, the idea that governing law also needs to be "found" is counter-intuitive. The law is the law. It exists in legislation. It is articulated in judicial opinions. Yet because the law is not always clear, because it is sometimes in conflict, because its scope may not be clearly delineated, and because it may be differently articulated by different courts, law does sometimes need to be "found." This means lawyers and judges can with justification describe it in different ways to reach different results. Effective persuasive writing requires attention to framing and reframing the law, and introducing that synthesis clearly.

Even where the law is clear about which standard of review applies in a given situation, the standard may be described differently depending on whether affirmance or reversal is contemplated. Thus, in *United Steelworkers v. NLRB,* the D.C. Circuit stated that the National Labor Relations Board's finding must be upheld unless it

> "has no rational basis" or is "unsupported by substantial evidence." It is not necessary that we agree that the Board reached the best outcome in order to sustain its decisions. The Board's findings of fact are "conclusive" when supported by substantial evidence on the record considered as a whole. The Supreme Court has recently instructed that a decision of an agency such as the Board is to be reversed *only* when the record is *"so compelling* that *no reasonable factfinder* could *fail* to find" to the contrary.[25]

Affirming the Board's findings in that case, the Court emphasized that reversal is a narrow exception. To make its point, the court uses language that admits of no qualification ("only," "so compelling," etc.). Yet, the same court described the standard somewhat differently in a case that rejected a finding by the Board.

> The court will not disturb an order of the NLRB unless, reviewing the record as a whole, it appears that the Board's factual findings are not supported by substantial evidence or that the Board acted arbitrarily or otherwise erred in applying established law to the facts at issue.... However, our review "must take into account whatever in the record fairly detracts from [the] weight of the evidence cited by the Board to support its conclusions." We will not "merely rubber stamp" NLRB decisions.[26]

---

[25] *United Steelworkers of America, AFL-CIO-CLC, Local Union 14534 v. N.L.R.B.,* 983 F.2d 240, 244 (D.C. Cir. 1993), cited in Patricia M. Wald, *The Rhetoric of Results and the Results of Rhetoric: Judicial Writing,* 62 U. Chi. L. Rev. 1371, 1392 (1995). (Emphasis added.)

[26] *Synergy Gas Corp v. N.L.R.B.,* 19 F.3d 649, 651 (D.C. Cir. 1994), cited in Patricia M. Wald, *The Rhetoric of Results and the Results of Rhetoric: Judicial Writing,* 62 V. Chi. L. Rev. 1371, 1392 (1995).

While paying lip service to its policy of deference, the court pointedly reminds the reader of its power to reverse.

In addition to characterizing rules favorably, persuasive analysis will often require you to synthesize a whole group of cases in ways that clearly, fairly, but favorably support your core theme. Assume you are working on an environmental case. John McGhee had purchased property on which there was a pond already contaminated. After the Environmental Protection Agency (EPA) notified him of the contamination, McGhee put up signs around the pond warning of the contamination and began sealing off access to the pond. The EPA decided, however, that McGhee has not exercised due care or taken precautions required by The Comprehensive Environmental Response, Compensation, and Liability Act ("CERCLA"), 42 U.S.C. §9601 et seq., because he has done nothing to remediate the condition of the pond. You have found and must synthesize the following three cases in order to explain the law to the court, to your adversary, or in a decision.

### Case 1

The defendant Witt owned the contaminated site at the time hazardous materials were dumped there. When the EPA informed him the site was contaminated, he did nothing except to put up several berms, which were later knocked down by trucks. The defendant then stopped paying property taxes on the site, hoping the county would foreclose. The court held the defendant had not exercised due care because he took no affirmative steps to protect the environment and did nothing to clean up the property.

### Case 2

The defendant Lofton Co. purchased land contaminated with creosote and continued activities that increased the contamination. The court said that because defendant did nothing to remove the contaminating product or to clean up the site, it had not exercised due care.

*Case 3*

The defendant Offner purchased property that had been a dry cleaning plant. When he learned of the contamination by chemical pollutants, he installed a water filtration system and amended the leases to require tenants to avoid discharging wastes into the septic systems. The court decided Offner had exercised due care.

To frame the law from the perspective of McGhee, your introduction to the precedents would distinguish the duties of a person who owned the property at the time of contamination from those of an owner who purchased already contaminated property.

> CERCLA requires a landowner to exercise due care in regard to contaminated property. Due care requires that a defendant take some affirmative steps to protect the public. However, the steps need not include clean-up of the site. A defendant must clean up the site only when the defendant owned the property at the time the contamination occurred or had contributed to the contamination.

To frame the law from the EPA's perspective, you would stress the protections required.

> CERCLA requires a landowner to exercise due care and to take precautions against further harm. Due care and precautions require affirmative steps to prevent additional contamination and ensure against harm to the public. Thus the defendant was required to begin remediating the contaminated conditions of the pond on his property.

After these introductions, you would go on to explain the cases.

## 3. Provide Substantial Reasoning

To be convinced by legal reasoning, readers need more than repeated contention. They need reasoning that thoughtfully and creatively probes the analogies and implications of a rule or an argument.

Assume you are handling a case that involves the question of when the statute of limitations begins to run for the purposes of a suit alleging defamatory statements posted on the Internet. The plaintiff, who waited fifteen months from the first posting of the alleged defamation to bring suit on a twelve-month statute, argues that each hit on the site is a re-publication and that the statute has not yet run.[27] The defendant argues that the "single publication rule" for the publication of defamatory material in magazines or newspapers controls. Under that rule, the statute begins to run on the date of first publication, not the date of the last sale, so the twelve-month period has run.

To support his contention persuasively, the defendant must first explain the policies behind the single publication rule and the consequences of its abolition, and then show why those policies pertain to electronic publication. A creative use of legal analogy might look as follows.

> The single publication rule, adopted in *Gregoire v. G.P. Putnam's Sons*, 83 N.E.2d 152 (N.Y. 1948), prevented the statute of limitations from being reset each time a copy of a publication was sold. That situation would thwart the legislature's intent to bar actions after a prescribed limitations period in order to encourage open dissemination of information and ideas, promote prompt filing of claims, and limit the scope of liability.
>
> These policy considerations apply to Internet publications and may be even more significant in the electronic world than in the print world. Given the instantaneous and worldwide ability to communicate on the Internet, the failure to apply the single publication rule would seriously inhibit the dissemination of ideas and vastly increase the scope of liability.

It is important to address opposing arguments thoughtfully. One way is to show that there is a flaw in one element of the opponent's legal argument—a misinterpretation of language, precedent, intent, or tradition. The text is not clear but ambiguous;

---

[27] This example is based on *Firth v. State*, 775 N.E.2d 463 (N.Y. 2002).

the framers did not anticipate current events; there are conflicting lines of authority; there are distinguishable facts or different policy concerns; there are competing traditions or new traditions; the policy consequences are undesirable or not served by the law. Assume, for example, that the plaintiff in our defamation case argued that modifications of the Web page on which the allegedly defamatory statements were made fell under a re-publication exception, which resets the statute of limitations when the release of defamatory material in a separately published edition of a book or newspaper is intended to reach a new audience. The defendant can make an argument based on factual distinctions, for example, explaining perhaps that the addition of information unrelated to the defamatory matter is not a re-publication of defamatory matter on a web page intended to reach a new audience and therefore does not invoke the policy considerations for the re-publication exception.

Another way to rebut legal argument is to assert one type of argument is less valid than another type.[28] Thus, Justice Scalia scorns arguments based on legislative intent, arguing legislators' intent is rarely uniform and often impossible to ascertain. The best way to interpret a statute is to infer intent from the text itself. Thus, an argument based on textual analysis is more legitimate than argument based on legislative history.

Arguments can also be made more substantial by contextualizing law and dramatizing its impact on human life. In support of his contention that prisoners retain a constitutionally protected privacy interest in their cells, Justice Stevens powerfully dramatized the practical consequences of a contrary rule as follows.

> Measured by the conditions that prevail in a free society, neither the possessions nor the slight residuum of privacy that a prison inmate can retain in his cell can have more than the most minimal value. From the standpoint of the prisoner, however, that trivial residuum may mark the difference between slavery and humanity.
>
> ...
>
> Personal letters, snapshots of family members, a souvenir, a deck of cards, a hobby kit, perhaps a diary or training manual

---

[28] Huhn, *supra* n. 23, at 45-50.

for an apprentice in a new trade, or even a Bible—a variety of inexpensive items may enable a prisoner to maintain contact with some part of his past and an eye to the possibility of a better future. Are all of these items subject to unrestrained perusal, confiscation, or mutilation at the hands of a possibly hostile guard?[29]

Argument can also be enhanced by creative juxtapositions. For example, Judge Posner effectively characterized General Motors' lackluster response to sexual harassment by contrasting it to the government's successful efforts in a far more difficult context: "The U.S. Navy has been able to integrate women into the crews of warships; General Motors should have been able to integrate one woman into a tinsmith shop."[30]

Finally, because law students spend so much time and effort learning to make legal arguments, as new practitioners, they sometimes neglect to make critical non-legal arguments. Writing persuasive letters often requires you to supply practical, non-legal reasons motivating the reader to comply with the writer's requests. For example, an attorney who represents David, who was disinherited under his father's will, may write to the client's cousin Beth asking for information about her deceased uncle's mental condition, stressing the closeness of the cousins' family ties in order to convince Beth to comply with the attorney's request.

───────────────── *Exercise 6.5* ─────────────────

*Consider the following explanations of the law, excerpted from different drafts of the thesis paragraph of an argument in which the writer contends that the decision of the court below is not a "collateral order" and is therefore unreviewable. Analyze the shortcomings of the first draft and virtues of the second draft.*

---

[29] *Hudson v. Palmer*, 468 U.S. 517, 542 (1984) (Stevens, J., dissenting). The case was brought to our attention by an article by Martha C. Nussbaum, *Poets as Judges: Judicial Rhetoric and the Literary Imagination*, 62 U. Chi. L. Rev. 1477, 1497–98 (1995).

[30] *Carr v. Allison Gas Turbine Div., General Motor Corp.*, 32 F.3d 1007, 1012–13 (7th Cir. 1994).

## Draft 1

The strict rule that only final judgments on the merits are appealable in federal court has been somewhat mitigated in recent years by the judicially created "collateral order" doctrine, which permits interlocutory appeals. An order will be deemed collateral when it conclusively determines the disputed question, resolves an important issue separate from the merits of the action, and would be effectively unreviewable on appeal from a final judgment.

## Draft 2

A decision that is not final and not on the merits is expressly unreviewable under 28 U.S.C. §1292. The "collateral order" doctrine permits rare exceptions to this rule, but only where the decision in question 1) conclusively determines the disputed question, 2) resolves an important issue that is entirely independent of the merits, and 3) could not be effectively reviewed on appeal from a final judgment.

--- *Exercise 6.6* ---

***A.*** *Our client is Paul Vine, who is a resident of Oregon. Last April, he was served with a notice that the Secretary of State of Illinois had been served with process as agent for him (as Illinois statute permits) by Plaintiff Able, who was suing him for injuries that Able received in an automobile accident in Illinois in which Vine was involved. Vine then contacted his attorney.*

*Last October, Vine received a call from his friend Ralph in Chicago, who told Vine that he had tickets for the sixth and seventh games of the World Series to be played in Wrigley Field on November 1st and 2nd and had a ticket for Vine if he wanted to go. Vine agreed to go. The next day, Vine's attorney told him that his trial was scheduled in Chicago for October 31st. Vine said he would be there.*

*Vine arrived in Chicago the morning of October 31st; the trial began at 2:00 p.m. Vine testified that afternoon and the next morning. The afternoon of the 31st, the Cubs won the series in the fifth game. The trial ended at 11:00 a.m. Nov. 1st and Vine had a ticket home for 2:00 p.m. The flight was delayed, and Vine toured the area around the airport and had lunch at an expensive restaurant. When he returned to O'Hare, he was paged and served with process in a contract case brought by Butin. We have moved to quash this service of process. Read the case summaries below and then write the introductions requested below.*

– *Write an introduction (of no more than a few sentences) to the case prec-edents from the perspective of your client, Paul Vine.*
– *Do the same for Butin.*

### Case 1

The defendant, a Michigan resident, went to Illinois as a co-defendant in a contract case. He arrived the day before the trial and testified. During a three-day break for Memorial Day, he was asked to and attended a meeting of officers of the foundation for which he worked. He did not know about the meeting before he came to Illinois. After the trial resumed, defendant was served with process in another litigation.

Service is quashed. The general rule is that a person from another state cannot be served with process in a civil action while temporarily within the state where service is had while in attendance at a trial as party, witness, or counsel and while present solely for that purpose.

The defendant's attendance at the meeting of officers was not contemplated in the purpose that brought him to the state, it was unforeseen, and it occurred before the trial was completed. He did not delay his departure from the jurisdiction to attend.

### Case 2

Mark Bell a California resident, was notified on March 16, 1948, that litigation in which he was defendant was set for trial on January 19th, 1949 in Chicago. Defendant was in the business of manufacturing pottery. On December 8, 1948, Bell learned that a series of kiln-drying lectures was to be given in Chicago at the time of the trial, and he wanted to attend the lectures whenever he was not required in connection with the trial. He arrived in Chicago the evening of January 16th, called his attorney and was told that the attorney would see him on the next two afternoons because he was busy in the mornings. Bell called the kiln-drying lectures and was told he could enroll and attend those two mornings, which he did. The trial began January 19th and Bell was served with process in another litigation that afternoon.

Service of process is quashed. Although Bell arrived two days before the trial and attended lectures for his business, he is allowed a reasonable time going to, attending, and returning. Two days to consult with the attorney is reasonable, and although he knew about the lectures before he arrived, his main and controlling reason to come to Illinois was for the trial.

*Case 3*

Defendant Cox, a resident of Ohio, testified as a witness in tort litigation in Chicago. She was served with process at the courthouse during the time of this trial. During the time Cox was in Chicago, Cox attended many social activities with friends, including theater events for which her friends purchased tickets for Cox after Cox arrived in Chicago, although they had purchased their own tickets before Cox arrived.

Service of process is quashed. There is no evidence that Cox entered the jurisdiction for any purpose other than testifying. She was not required to refrain from visiting her friends while here and participating in normal social activities, especially since it appears that activities were planned after she arrived.

**B.** *Our client is Elaine Lord. Ms. Lord's grandfather, George, promised to give her $250,000 if she quit her job and stayed home. He later repeated that promise in front of other people. Relying on the promise, Ms. Lord quit her job. The grandfather died six months later, and the executor of his estate refused to pay the $250,000. (The gift was not in the will). Read the case summaries below and then write the introduction requested.*

- *Write an introduction to the precedents from the perspective of Elaine Lord.*
- *Do the same for the grandfather's executor.*

*Case 1*

West, an elderly woman with heart trouble, quit her job after her employer promised to her, in writing and in front of a group of business people, that he would provide her with a pension. The employer died suddenly soon after and his successors refused to pay the pension. West sued. The court enforced the promise because West had relied on it.

*Case 2*

Shortly after her husband died, a young woman, Yates, received a letter from her brother-in-law (her husband's brother) telling her that if she moved to his farm he would give her and her children a place to stay. Relying on that promise, the woman boarded up her home and moved to her brother-in-law's. Two years later, he changed his mind and evicted her and her children from his farm. The court did not enforce the promise.

*Case 3*

An elderly wealthy woman, Tess Green, signed a pledge to a charity, a private library, to give $10,000, and her collection of rare books. The library, in reliance on Green's pledge, remodeled a room in the library to accommodate the books, spending close to $10,000. Green died, but her will did not include the gifts to the library. The court enforced the promise.

**C.** *A child, Bart was born in 1994 in California to Carole D. who was married and lived with her husband, Gerald D. Gerald is listed as the father on the child's birth certificate. Carole and Michael H. had had an affair for some two years before Bart was born and blood tests show to 98.5% probability that Michael is the father.*

*When Bart was four months old, Gerald moved to New York from California for business; Carole remained in California and lived with Michael for five months, although she and Bart visited with Gerald a few times. Michael held Bart out as his child. Carole then returned to her own home, but when Bart was two she lived with Michael again for eight months. Carole has now reconciled with Gerald and they are living together again and have a child of their own. Michael has filed a filiation action to be declared Bart's father and for visitation. California law imposes a presumption rebuttable only by the husband that a child born to a married woman is the child of the marriage. Michael claims that the presumption infringes his due process rights to establish paternity. Read the summaries below and then write the introductions requested below.*

- *Write an introduction to the precedents from the perspective of Gerald D.*
- *Do the same for Michael.*

*Case 1*

The state of Illinois brought a dependency proceeding on behalf of two minor children living with their father, William Stanley. The mother and father had never married but had lived together with their two children for ten years. The mother died. The state declared the children wards of the state under an Illinois statute that provided that children of unmarried fathers, upon the death of the mother, are declared dependents without a hearing as to the father's fitness as a parent.

The court held that Stanley was entitled under due process to a hearing as to his parental fitness before his biological children could be taken from him.

### Case 2

Ardell Thomas had a nonmarital child that she raised in her own home. Ms. Thomas never married the biological father Leon Quentin and never lived with him. The father visited the child from time to time and brought gifts. Ms. Thomas married and when the child was eleven her husband petitioned to adopt. Quentin opposed the adoption. The state statute provides that only the mother's consent is required for adoption of a nonmarital child who has not been legitimated. Under the statute, the father has no standing to object.

The court held that Quentin's rights under the due process clause had not been violated.

### Case 3

The unmarried mother and biological father, Jim Cass, of two children lived together for five years, representing themselves as husband and wife. Cass was named on the children's birth certificates as their father. He and the mother supported the children. The mother moved out with the children to live with another man, not telling Cass where they were. The mother married one year later, and after two years her husband petitioned to adopt the children. Cass learned of their whereabouts only one year after their marriage and visited them several times. State law permits an unwed mother, but not an unwed father, to block an adoption by withholding consent.

The court held that Cass was entitled to a hearing to determine parental unfitness before his rights as a parent could be terminated.

---

## *Assignment 6.1*

---

**A.** Write a persuasive statement of fact for the Johnsons, the plaintiffs in Casefile 2 in Appendix A.

**B.** Write a persuasive statement of fact for defendant Wagner in Casefile 2.

# *Chapter 7*

# *INFORMING AND PERSUADING: LETTERS*

---

## A. IN GENERAL

Letters are the most frequent type of writing that lawyers do. By "letters," we mean e-mail and other electronic communication as well as communication by mail, and our suggestions apply to both. Lawyers often write several letters a day, and they should probably write even more than that. One of the most common complaints from clients to local bar associations is that their lawyers do not communicate with them enough.[1] Rule 1.4(a) of the Model Rules of Professional Conduct requires an attorney to "keep a client reasonably informed about the status of the matter and promptly comply with reasonable requests for information." Moreover, the ABA's Ethics 2000 Commission amendments to the Model Rules of Professional Conduct require that lawyers communicate in writing with their clients on a variety of matters.[2] "Writing" is defined as "a tangible or electronic record of a communication or representation," including e-mail and video and audio recordings.[3] Thus, in many matters, communicating in writing now appears to be a lawyer's ethical obligation.[4]

---

[1] Nancy J. Moore, *Revisions Not Revolution*, 88 ABA J. 48 (Dec. 2002). In Illinois, the Attorney Disciplinary Commission reported that complaints about lack of communication accounted for 34 per cent of the investigated charges against attorneys in 2002, leading to two disbarments, 33 suspensions, and three censures.

[2] *Id.* at 48–49. These include a client's informed consent and agreement to the lawyer's fee referral, and a lawyer's advice to a client with whom the lawyer enters into a business arrangement to seek independent counsel. *Id.*

[3] *Id.*

[4] *See* Owen G. Fiore, *Communication—Or Be Held Liable*, 141 Trusts & Estates 23 (Nov. 2002).

## 1. Purpose and Audience

Lawyers' letter writing covers a range from simple cover letters or transmittal letters to opinion letters, which are in effect formal documents in which the writer provides a legal opinion. In between on the spectrum of formality are demand letters, in which an attorney demands that the recipient take or cease taking a certain action; letters to opposing counsel, which can be similar to persuasive documents; letters to business clients, which may be informal memoranda for clients who have special needs for information; and letters to other parties requesting or giving information.

Thus letters are written for several purposes, one of which is to leave a paper trail of the lawyer's work—for example, of advice given to a client, of responses correcting wrong information, and of deadlines to be met. Even a relatively simple transmittal letter will document that you sent the enumerated papers, explained their purpose, and informed the recipient of the deadline for their return.

Letters often have multiple audiences as well as multiple purposes. When you write an office memorandum, or a memorandum in support of or in opposition to a motion, or an appellate brief, you have a good idea of your target audience: the attorney who assigned the memo, the judge who is hearing the motion, or the judges who will hear the appeal. You may even be able to assess the individual characteristics of the readers of these documents. For example, the judge may be a specialist in the issues raised by the litigation. Although with letters you are writing for a targeted audience, your letters often will have an audience beyond the recipient. Letters sent by e-mail are easily forwarded to other readers. A letter to a corporate executive will likely go to the corporate legal department; a letter to an opposing party will go to that party's attorney.[5] You need to write for your primary audience, but with an eye to the others who may read the letter. If necessary, you may have to write a different letter for different audiences.

---

[5] A lawyer who knows that the other party is represented by a lawyer may not communicate with that party about the subject of the representation without the other lawyer's consent. ABA Model R. Prof. Conduct 4.2.

Once you have a sense of your purpose and audience, you will be better able to make important decisions. These decisions include

- how much to explain, especially about the law;
- how much factual detail to supply;
- whether to use legal terms, with or without definitions and examples;
- whether to discuss case authority, and if so, how much detail to include;
- whether to provide citations;
- how much of your research to reveal to opposing counsel in an adversary setting; and
- how strongly to recommend to a client one or more of the available options.

## 2. Organization

Some of your most important decisions concern the organization of your letter. First and foremost, think about what information the recipient needs from your letter. A business client wants solutions, recommendations, and summaries of risks and benefits, not abstract legal theory. A lay client wants to know what to do with all the documents you enclosed. All clients want the information they need to make an informed decision. Make it clear from the outset that you are writing to transmit that information.

Second, as with any good writing, letters should be organized to conform to the way people process information. For each new segment of a letter, or each new topic within a segment, begin with a summary of what you will say, not with the details. Start with the general point to provide your reader with the context and then move on to the details.

Third, impose a structure on the internal organization, especially on the analysis and factual development of longer letters, such as advisory letters. Organize by topics and categories of information, and use topic headings where they will help clarify your structure for the reader. For example, if you are writing to a client about her divorce, you could divide the discussion into property settlement, child custody, and child support. A fourth topic might be the client's need for a new will.

## 3. Tone

The tone of your letter helps to establish how the reader perceives you, especially if the letter is your first contact. Once formed, that opinion is hard to change. Thus, it is important to establish an appropriate tone for your audience and your purpose. Then, do not shift tone during the course of the letter. For example, do not start a letter with great formality and then shift to informal language, or do the opposite. And, even if your letter is informal, it should not be casual. Even an attorney's e-mail correspondence should be appropriate as to tone and not lapse into inappropriate informality to clients and other lawyers.

The salutation, or greeting to the recipient, begins to set the tone of your letter as one that is relatively formal or informal. The salutation can set the tone of your letter simply by addressing the recipient formally by title and last name, or informally by first name. Your choice depends on the custom of where you are working, and on how well you know the recipient. Under the more traditional guidelines, address a person by the last name unless you are writing to someone you know personally or have worked with before. In the latter cases, use the person's first name or you may sound insulting. On the other hand, you may put off a person whom you address by first name if do not know her or know her well, especially if that person is older than you, or is in a position of greater authority. And you do not want to address a woman by her first name and a man by his title and last name in a communication to both unless you know the woman very well and do not know the man.

Some law firms and businesses now encourage informality and ask that you address your clients by first name, unless there are reasons not to, such as the client's age or nationality. Many countries' traditions require greater formality than is usual in this country, especially in their form of business address. If there is no custom to follow, however, one way to decide which name to use is by how you will sign your own name. If you sign just with your first name, then you should address the recipient by first name unless that person is much older than you.

Besides the form of address, other factors influence the tone of the letter. Contractions make your language informal. Slang and colloquialisms, like "for starters," or "the flip side," will make your letter too casual. However, despite a common misconception among lawyers, personal pronouns do not make a letter too informal. Lawyers often use passive voice to avoid using personal pronouns. So instead of simply writing "I filed this motion last week," they will say, "The motion was filed last week." Generally, there is nothing wrong with putting people, in the form of pronouns, into your letters.[6] Indeed, you can establish rapport and avoid dry and abstract letters by talking to your client, using the pronoun "you." If you think of and address your client as "you," you will more likely couch your letter in terms your client understands. If you refer to yourself as "I," you become an individual. If you want to establish a joint enterprise, then use "we" ("we should review the rewritten contract for errors"). But do not use the editorial "we" when you really mean "I" or "you."

If you correspond by e-mail, be especially careful to address the recipient correctly, and to maintain the right tone. Because people write e-mail quickly, they often write more informally and briskly than they would if they were writing a letter. If your law firm's custom is to address clients by their title and last name, you should use that form of address for your e-mail also, at least initially. Write full sentences, using correct English, so that your e-mail messages are not sloppy or so concise as to sound rude. And re-read your message to ensure that your tone is business-like and polite.

For any type of correspondence, avoid pomposity, insult, phoniness, sarcasm, and paternalism. These strategies are self-defeating and will earn you a reputation not as a tough lawyer, but as one to avoid doing business with. Remember that you often will be working with the recipients of your letters, perhaps over a long period of time, and that some of the recipients, for example, the opposing attorney, may prove to be repeat performers. Even in demand letters, polite but firm language is more effective than insults, exclamation points, abrasive rhetorical questions, frequent underlining, and constant imperative sentences. You may want to emphasize one or two important points with underlining or italics, but keep that type of emphasis to a minimum.

There are techniques to soften the tone of correspondence, such as that of indirection. Too much clarity or concision can sometimes

---

[6] *See* Section B(1)(a) of Chapter 5, *Clarity.*

be counter-productive,[7] especially if the writer and recipient will be working together. Tense demands and responses create a hostile atmosphere between the parties. Instead, you can soften your tone by using passive voice. Although passive voice is not usually recommended as a technique of writing style, it can be a useful technique of indirection to soften a demand. For example, a sign on a New York City church door says "Food is not to be eaten on church steps," instead of the more concise imperative sentence "Do not eat on church steps."

You may also use interrogative sentences to avoid the direct confrontations of imperatives. Instead of "give us the full financial data by this Friday," you could ask, "Can you provide us with the full financial data by this Friday so that we can review them before we meet?" You could also use polite and explanatory declarative sentences like, "We would appreciate receiving the fall financial data by this Friday so that we can review them before we meet."[8] The writer could also use the word "please" to soften an imperative.

Even a letter refusing a demand or request often can be written politely. Instead of an abrupt refusal, give reasons for the refusal, explaining for example, that the materials do not yet exist ("we have not yet completed the draft of the licensing agreement"); or that they are already available ("the terms of the agreement are all in the draft we mailed last week"); or that the requester may not want the recipient to comply ("the contract terms are confidential and it may not be in your interest to share them at the meeting"); or that the recipient cannot comply with the request ("our computer system will be down for the next two weeks"). The important point is to look for the tactful and polite response rather than the abrupt and rude one.

Finally, your tone will also be established by your proofreading. If you do not correct spelling and grammatical errors, you may be seen as someone who does not get anything right.

---

[7] And, of course, insults can be more than counterproductive. *See* Michael Higgins, *Insulting Letters May Get Lawyer Suspended*, Chi. Trib. (Aug. 13, 2002) for the tale of an attorney who was suspended for 30 days for writing letters so insulting to the recipient that they "tend[ed] . . . to bring . . . the legal profession in disrepute."

[8] These examples are taken from Elizabeth Fajans & Mary R. Falk, *Linguistics and the Composition of Legal Documents: Border Crossings*, 22 Legal Stud. F. 697 (1998).

## B. TYPES OF LETTERS

### 1. Letters to Clients

For those matters that do not come within the Model Rules requirement of a writing,[9] a lawyer must first decide whether to communicate to a client by letter or e-mail, by telephone, or in person. If the matter is one that involves or will involve litigation, and thus discovery, then you may not want to commit your thoughts to paper. Although documents between attorney and client are often privileged, the privilege may be waived, sometimes inadvertently.[10] For example, if you e-mail privileged information to a client, the client may inadvertently forward it to another person. Moreover, if the client is distressed, a face-to-face conference might be appropriate, so that you can immediately address those concerns. Another consideration is cost. If your client has requested that you keep costs down, you may not want to run up your time composing a letter, at least not a lengthy one.[11]

If the subject matter of your communication is complicated and lengthy, however, and you have gone to the trouble of doing research and thinking it through, or if it comes within the requirements of the new ABA amendments, you should reduce the results to writing. Then you and your client will have a document that retains the results of your work.[12]

#### a. Cover Letters

#### i. In General

Letters to clients are as varied as your clients and the reasons for writing. One common type of letter is simply a cover letter, that is, a transmittal letter for documents or other enclosures. The letter should enumerate the enclosed materials, and then explain

---

[9] *See* Section A of this chapter.

[10] James C. Freund, *Lawyering, A Realistic Approach to Legal Practice* 66 (Law. J. Seminars Press 1979).

[11] *Id.*

[12] *Id.* at 65–66.

the enclosures if necessary. In addition, tell the client what things she needs to do in the order she needs to do them. For example, "Please sign both copies of the lease and return one copy to the rental agent in the enclosed envelope."

Your transmittal, or cover, letter may also be sent as an e-mail message. If you are sending attachments or posting documents to the message, you need a short message explaining the documents and how the recipient should respond. Of course, if the client must sign or keep the originals, you must send these documents by mail. Because international correspondence is frequently done by e-mail, your instructions should be explicit about time zones. For example, instead of telling the client to review the attachment and "get back to me by Friday at noon," explain "by Friday at noon New York time." "Friday at noon" for a recipient in Tokyo is far different from that day on the east coast of the United States.

You do not need to use legalese such as "Enclosed herein, please find. . . ." Instead, use plain language like "I am enclosing the lease for the 200 Lakeview Towers building . . . ."

### ii. Components

The components of a cover letter vary depending on how many purposes the letter is to serve. The contents of a simple cover letter can often be expressed in a single sentence; however, although a one-sentence letter might seem admirably concise to the writer, a reader may perceive such a short letter as rude. So it is a good idea to begin with a polite or personal short paragraph, such as "It was a pleasure to meet with you and your husband yesterday. I am glad I could help you work out the details for your new office space."

You would then describe the enclosures and actions the client needs to take, before closing with another short, courteous paragraph reiterating your willingness to be of service.

### iii. Sample Cover Letter

The following is a sample of a somewhat longer transmittal letter.

Dear Reverend Johnson:

I have spoken to the Internal Revenue Service about your exemption from self-employment tax. I am enclosing the forms that you need in order to proceed with the exemption.

- IRS Form 4361, Application for Exemption from Self-Employment Tax for Use by Ministers and Members of Religious Orders
- Declaration of Intent
- Social Security Form 1000, disclaiming social security benefits.

I have already filled out IRS Form 4361; however, you must sign and date the form at the end.

The Declaration of Intent confirms that you understand the consequences of this exemption and that you wish to proceed. If you do, please sign and date the signature line <u>at mid page</u> where I have placed a "Sign Here" sticker. Do not sign the line at the end of the page, because that would withdraw your application.

Finally, please sign and date the Social Security Form 1000 where I have placed a "Sign Here" sticker, at the bottom of the page.

I suggest that you photocopy each completed form and keep the copy for your records.

You must mail the three forms to the Internal Revenue Service Center within ninety days from the date of this letter in order for your exemption to take effect for your past years of ministerial service. If you do not mail these forms within ninety days from the date of this letter, your exemption will not take effect until this tax year.

I have enclosed a stamped addressed envelope for you to return the forms to the IRS.

It has been a pleasure working with you. I hope to be able to help you again.

Your truly,

Hiram Jackson

---

### Exercise 7.1

*Your client John Lopez has been involved in a car accident with Kristina Tang. He sustained damages to his car and personal injuries, and you acted for him to settle his claim with Tang's insurance company. However, before he can get his settlement check, the insurance company needs him to fill out a release form and provide other documentation—a physician's report, photographs that Lopez took at the accident scene, information about his own insurance policy, and Lopez's statement of the facts of the accident. Write your client a cover letter 1) to instruct him about the insurance company's request, 2) to enclose the release form, 3) to advise Lopez to get a complete physical examination at Tang's insurer's expense and report the results to you before signing the release, 4) to arrange a meeting with him to go over the settlement agreement, and 5) to ask him to bring the release form to the meeting. Assume that you have been dealing directly with the insurance company. Include your own explanations where you wish.*

---

### b. Advice Letters

### i. In General

Lawyers frequently write advice letters, in which they analyze a client's legal problem and advise the client on a course of action. A traditional full advice letter may be like a shortened legal memorandum and include many of the components of a legal memorandum:[13] an introductory paragraph, if needed; a summary of the facts or background of the issue you are analyzing for the client; an analysis of that issue; a conclusion that advises the client of the options available; and your recommendations and suggested next steps. A difficult task for lawyers (and law students) is to write about the law and give advice in language that the client will understand and to do so without talking down to the client. To do this, you must evaluate your client's ability to understand the abstract and technical language of the law, then translate that legal language into one that the particular client can understand. Use examples generously to illustrate your explanations.

### ii. Components

**Opening paragraph**: Lawyers traditionally begin their letters by stating the issue that the letter addresses and providing back-

---

[13] Some law firms now follow a practice of sending business clients a short cover letter and a legal memorandum analyzing the client's problem instead of an advice letter.

ground of dates of prior meetings and other communications. For example, a letter to a client may begin,

> Dear Ms. Hoyt:
>
> This will confirm our telephone conversation today regarding your obligation to charge sales tax on the sales of your products over the Internet.

In this or the next paragraph, many lawyers also summarize their conclusions or advice, perhaps saying that they will explain in more detail below. A good summary will also tell the recipient what she should do next. For example, the letter might continue,

> You must charge taxes on sales to Illinois residents because you are in Illinois, the customer is in Illinois, and you are shipping the products from Illinois. I am enclosing the forms that the Illinois Department of Revenue requires you to fill out and return. I will explain below how to fill them out.
>
> Your liability for out-of-state taxes is not as clear. As I explain below. . . .

Although lawyers are trained to begin legal documents by restating the issue, and other lawyers usually expect this sequence of information, restating the issue may not be a necessary or desirable opening for correspondence to non-lawyers, especially if they have been working with you on the issue and are familiar with it. A letter to a business client, for example, could begin with your recommendation and a concise summary of your reason for that recommendation. For example, you could begin the letter to a business client like this:

> Re: Sales Tax on Internet Sales
>
> Dear Ms. Hoyt:
> You will have to charge sales taxes on sales to Illinois residents; however, I suggest that you do not yet collect and pay out-of-state taxes because the law regarding your liability is not as clear.

Lawyers disagree over how directive they should be in advising their clients. Some lawyers prefer to analyze the available alternatives, but emphasize that their clients must decide which options to choose. Then the lawyer could add a sentence to the introduction, such as "If you conclude that you should begin paying out-of-state taxes immediately, I have outlined the steps that you should follow."

If you are writing to a client with whom you have a long standing relationship, or one who appreciates a personalized correspondence, then begin your letter on a more personal note, hoping that she enjoyed her vacation, for example, or that her workload has eased now that she has hired an assistant.

**Summary of facts**: Many, but not all, letters should include background information about the issue. For most advice letters or letters to business clients, for example, you need to include facts about the transactions involved. Letters discussing pending litigation should include facts about the case. Your analysis and advice depend upon getting the facts accurately. Many lawyers ask the client to review the facts in the letter and tell them of any corrections and additions that are necessary.

**Analysis**: A lawyer traditionally begins her analysis with the applicable law and then applies that law to the client's particular issue. Then the analysis includes alternatives available under the law. This format, however, may not be helpful to a reader who is not a lawyer, who more likely first wants to know what consequences the law has for him. Thus, you have to shape this part of your letter and the vocabulary you use to the needs of the particular recipient. When you write to a layman, you have to translate abstract legal terms into a vocabulary the recipient understands.

**Closing**: Close with your conclusions and advice. Give enough information to help the client make the necessary decisions.[14] Then suggest the next steps. For example, you may ask the client to make an appointment so that you can review the alternatives with him. A closing could be as follows:

---

[14] ABA Model R. Prof. Conduct 1.4(b) (1999) requires a lawyer to "explain a matter to the extent reasonably necessary to permit the client to make informed decisions regarding the representation."

I suggest that you ask your accountant to set up a separate account for out-of-state taxes. If you wish to talk about this and other alternatives, please call me at your convenience.

End your letter with your signature preceded by a phrase such as "Yours truly." Your full name should be typed under your signature.

## iii. Sample Advice Letters

The following is a sample of an advice letter in traditional form. Note that the writer did not include statutory citations, case authority, etc.[15] Ms. Hoyt wants to know about her tax liability. She is not a lawyer and will not be reading the tax statutes or any cases interpreting them.

CONFIDENTIAL

January 11, 20__

Ms. Maryanne Hoyt
American National Co., Inc.
2232 Near North Avenue
Chicago, IL 60611

Re: Sales and Use Taxes

Dear Ms. Hoyt:

You asked whether American National Co., Inc. must pay or collect retail occupation ("sales") or use taxes on sales made over the Internet in states where purchasers of your products live.

As the laws now stand, you are obligated to do so only with respect to sales to customers who live in Illinois, where the company is located. However, this is an extremely controversial subject and it is quite likely that we will see new developments in the law as well as aggressive enforcement efforts in some jurisdictions. I explain in more detail below my analysis of the situation.

As I understand it, you intend to offer persons who visit your Internet web site an opportunity to purchase the same products as those offered

---

[15] We are indebted to Tom Morsch, the Director of the Northwestern University School of Law Small Business Opportunity Clinic, for providing the letters on which these samples are based.

in your retail outlet. These products may be purchased in the conventional manner by sending an order by mail to your store in Chicago or by placing an order online through the web site. Since your offer will be made through use of the Internet, it will, theoretically at least, attract buyers in each of the fifty states as well as in foreign countries.

Substantially all states have sales and use taxes. There is a large body of law regarding the interpretation and application of these taxes, including the tax statutes themselves, administrative regulations and rulings, cases in the state courts, and cases in federal courts on the constitutionality and applicability of such laws to interstate transactions. It would be an enormous undertaking and very costly for me to review and advise you with respect to the laws in each of the fifty states. Accordingly, as we agreed, I have limited my analysis to Illinois, New York, and California, namely your home state and two additional states that have large populations, well-developed case law, and strong enforcement policies. If you would like me to do so, I can expand the analysis. However, it is quite likely that the advice I am giving you in this letter can be generally relied upon in the majority of other states.

Illinois. Illinois has a sales tax, technically called the Retailers Occupation Tax. As the name suggests, this is a tax that a retailer must pay based on its sale of tangible personal property at retail (i.e., a sale to a person who uses or consumes the item as opposed to a wholesaler or distributor that re-sells the item to a third party). Illinois also has a so-called use tax. This is a tax that buyers of tangible personal property must pay on retail purchases that, for one reason or another, have not been subjected to the Retailers Occupation Tax, and which sellers must "collect" from the buyer and pay over to the State.

It is quite clear from the regulations and rulings of the Illinois Department of Revenue that the sales tax applies to each sale where both the seller and the buyer are located within Illinois and where the property is delivered within the state, regardless of whether the transaction is consummated in a face-to-face setting, through the mail, over the telephone, or by means of the Internet.

The applicable tax rate in Illinois is 5% of the retail-selling price plus an additional 1.5% surcharge for transactions within Chicago. Other municipalities have different surcharges, but it is unlikely that your volume of sales in any municipality will be very large. Accordingly, you may want to use the Chicago rate as a guide for all sales to buyers located within Illinois. If you need further information on the reporting and payment of the Illinois sales tax, you can contact the Illinois Department of Revenue directly at 1-800-[telephone number], or by visiting the Department's web site at [web site].

<u>California and New York</u>. Your obligations to these two states are quite different from your situation in Illinois. These states have sales and use taxes similar to the Illinois taxes described above, but it is doubtful whether either state will impose its payment or collection obligations on a company that has its sole place of business and maintains its stock of goods in another state, i.e., in Illinois. I believe that this holds true even though the buyer may be located within the boundaries of the other state and may order the goods through an electronic medium by means of which the seller's offer to sell is transmitted into the state where the buyer is located.

As indicated above, the applicability of sales and use taxes to out-of-state sellers who take orders over the Internet is a highly controversial subject. Congress and state legislatures are currently considering amending the laws on sales taxes and use taxes because so much revenue is being lost to Internet sales.

Any changes in the sales and use tax laws will undoubtedly be accompanied by considerable coverage in the press and will permit American National to make whatever changes in its billing practices are necessary in order to comply with new requirements. Moreover, it is likely that the local taxing authorities will single out the large Internet retailers long before they take steps to enforce their laws against smaller firms like yours. Under the circumstances, you may decide to rely on the existing law rather than take action now in anticipation of changes in the tax laws or state enforcement policies.

I hope that I have answered your questions. If you have questions or if you would like to discuss any aspect of the matter in more detail, please call me at the number set forth above.

Sincerely,

Hiram Jackson

As we suggested above, a lawyer's advice letter need not always follow the traditional full format. This is particularly so in the case of a business client with whom the lawyer has been in a working relationship. The following is a version of the letter to Ms. Hoyt that begins immediately with the answer to her question, and explains the reason for that answer without specific analysis of the law. Note that the writer knows Ms. Hoyt and has worked with her previously (the salutation is to "Maryanne," and the language is somewhat less formal than in the previous letter).

The last sentence of the letter is an example of a less directive approach to the client's decision.

January 11, 20__

Ms. Maryanne Hoyt
American National Co., Inc.
2232 North North Avenue
Chicago, IL 60611

Dear Maryanne:

This will confirm our telephone conversation regarding your obligation to charge sales and use taxes on the sale of the products over the Internet.

You definitely have to charge taxes on sales to Illinois residents. This is because you are located in Illinois, the customer is located in Illinois, and the products are shipped from a location in Illinois. I have enclosed rate information and the required forms from the Illinois Department of Revenue.

Your liability for out-of-state taxes is not nearly as clear because you have no physical presence in the other states and because customers submit their orders and you ship your products across state lines. Furthermore, the question of which rules should be applied to Internet sales is a matter of considerable controversy. Companies like the large catalog sellers line up on the side that they have no tax liability, and traditional retailers and tax authorities line up on the side that they do. I have enclosed a recent article on the subject. My suggestion is that you wait to see what kind of enforcement activity develops in this area over the next year or so before beginning to pay any out-of-state taxes.

There is always a risk that some state will come after you looking for back taxes, penalties, and interest on sales to residents of that state. However, this is a relatively small risk and you may wish to assume it. I suggest that you consult your accountant to create a reserve on your books to cover the contingent liability.

I can research the matter more fully. If you want me to pursue this matter, please call at your convenience. In the last analysis, however, this is essentially a judgment call that you will have to make, and we should discuss the options more fully.

Sincerely,

Hiram Jackson

enclosures

———————————————— *Exercise 7.2* ————————————————

*Your client Maryanne Hoyt owns an eight-unit apartment house in Lake City, Pacifica. Ms. Hoyt does not live in the building. The tenants in one of the units want to renew their lease, which expires next month. Ms. Hoyt has decided not to renew that lease, but first asks your advice.*

*The tenants are two sisters who are hearing disabled. They have recently begun keeping a German Shepherd "hearing dog," Pierre. Pierre barks whenever the telephone or the doorbell rings, or the smoke alarm goes off. Ms. Hoyt's form lease does not permit her tenants to keep pets. The other residents of the building have complained about the noise of the dog barking, and about the fact that the sisters have kept a pet in their apartment. They also complain that the dog is not well trained and the carpets in the hall and lobby smell from the dog's urine. The dog was trained by the tenants' brothers and is not an official hearing dog certified by any training facility. Moreover, the sisters lived on their own without a dog before getting Pierre.*

*The sisters have told Ms. Hoyt that if she does not renew the lease they will bring charges under the Fair Housing Act, 42 U.S.C. §§ 3601 et. seq., the Pacifica Fair Housing Act, and the city anti-discrimination ordinance.*

*These are the relevant parts of the applicable legislation. Write a letter advising Ms. Hoyt if she must renew the lease.*

### 1. Fair Housing Act 42 U.S.C. § 3603

(b) *Exemptions*

Nothing in section 3604 of this title . . . shall apply to . . . rooms or units in dwellings containing living quarters occupied or intended to be occupied by no more than four families living independently of each other . . . if the owner actually maintains and occupies one of such living quarters as his residence . . . .

§ 3604 . . . It shall be unlawful . . .

(1) To discriminate in the sale or rental . . . of a dwelling to any buyer or renter because of a handicap[16] of—

(A) that buyer or renter . . . .

---

[16] Hearing impairment is a handicap under the Fair Housing Act.

(3) For purposes of this subsection, discrimination includes . . .

(B) A refusal to make reasonable accommodations in rules, policies, practices or services, when such accommodations may be necessary to afford such person equal opportunity to use and enjoy a dwelling . . . .

## 2. Pacifica Fair Housing Act §101

If an individual's vision, hearing or mobility is impaired, it is discrimination for a person to refuse to rent or sell housing to the individual . . . because he or she keeps an animal that is specially trained to lead or assist the individual with impaired vision, hearing or mobility . . . .

## 3. Lake City Equal Opportunity Ordinance § 3

A landlord may not deny or withhold from any eyesight impaired, hearing impaired, or mobility impaired person housing because that person owns a guide animal. Provided that:

1. The tenant may be charged for damages caused by the animal . . .

2. The landlord is not required to modify the premises . . .

3. The animal's owner may be required to provide current proof that the animal has successfully passed a course of training at a school of training for such animals.

---

### c. Opinion Letters

The opinion letter conveys the attorney's formal answer to the client's legal question, typically asking whether a course of action is legal. For example, the attorney may have been asked by a bank to determine whether a customer of the bank has good title to his home or business property in order for the bank to grant a loan, and whether that loan will have priority over other indebtedness. The opinion letter may follow the same format as the advice letter; however, law firms often follow their own standard format. Law firms also often designate the attorneys who may issue these letters on behalf of the firm. Because a new associate will not typically be asked to write a formal opinion letter, we do not discuss it in any further detail.

## 2. Demand Letters

### *a. In General*

As its name suggests, a demand letter is a letter written on behalf of a client in which the attorney demands that the recipient take or cease taking a certain action. For example, an attorney may write to demand that the recipient stop infringing her client's copyright, or that he pay the landlord the two months' overdue rent plus penalty, or that he stop pouring untreated sewage into the town lake. The letter is written to the party whose conduct is at issue, but if the party has an attorney, it must be written directly to that party's attorney.[17] The letter's tone is firm and formal; a rude, strident letter will not advance your cause.

Some demand letters try to mitigate their harshness by proposing different ways the recipient might comply with the demand, operating on the assumption that a show of good will and flexibility might more readily secure the recipient's cooperation than an overt threat. This conciliatory gesture is often followed by a reminder of the consequences that will result from an uncooperative response.

### *b. Components*

If the attorney has not communicated with the recipient before, then she begins the letter by introducing herself as the attorney for her client. She then should identify the dispute, providing the background of the dispute and the legal reasons for the client's demands. The attorney then firmly identifies the client's demands and the consequences of non-compliance. A demand letter should be specific about the client's demands and the consequences if the recipient fails to meet them. This means that, as the attorney, you must consult with your client to ensure that you know the client's goals and the deadline by which the demand should be met.

---

[17] ABA Model R. Prof. Conduct 4.2 (1999) requires an attorney to communicate with an opposing party through that party's attorney.

## c. Sample Demand Letters

The following correspondence begins with a demand letter, is met by the recipient's own responsive demand letter, and ends with a response from the initial writer ultimately suggesting settlement.[18]

Two points should be made about these letters on behalf of Tri-Max Pods, Inc., specifically, and a caution made about demand letters generally. The letters demonstrate the importance of garnering as many facts as possible, prior to making the demand. These parties' demands each depended on their own version of the facts, and their fact-finding was incomplete. The exchange also demonstrates the importance of maintaining a civil tone throughout. Hiram Jackson wisely suggested a "businesslike solution" to settle the dispute. His offer of settlement would have been difficult to suggest, and would be less likely to meet with a favorable response, if he had originally written an aggressive, belligerent letter.

As to demand letters generally, many lawyers caution that some demand letters may provoke a declaratory judgment action if the letters are very specific as to threatened consequences. This is especially so if the recipient is eager to file first in order to pick the jurisdiction of the litigation.

**CERTIFIED MAIL**
**RETURN RECEIPT REQUESTED**

February 7, 20__

Griffin Richmond, Inc.
123 Green Street
Lakeview, IL 62456

Dear Mr. Richmond:

We represent Tri-Max Pods, Inc., an Illinois corporation of Shorehaven, Illinois.

It has come to our attention that you have applied by serial number 2/000000 to register the trademark "Tri-Max" for camera tripods, and

---

[18] Our thanks again to Tom Morsch who supplied the letters on which these examples are based.

that the date of your first use of the trademark in commerce is claimed to be January 1, 2008. We are writing to inform you that our client has been offering camera tripods under the trademark "Tri-Max" since 2007. Although we do not know if this prior use was known to you when you selected your trademark, your sale of camera tripods under this name or licensing of the name to third parties would constitute a clear act of unfair competition and an infringement of our client's exclusive legal rights.

Under the circumstances, we demand your immediate written assurance that you will withdraw your application for registration of the trademark "Tri-Max." We also demand that you discontinue efforts to sell tripods and similar equipment and attachments under the trademark "Tri-Max," and that you destroy all price lists, product literature, and other items bearing this trademark.

Tri-Max Pods, Inc. hereby reserves all of its legal rights including the right to oppose your pending application, Serial Number 2/000000, and to seek injunctive relief, damages and attorney fees.

> Very truly yours,
>
> Hiram Jackson
> Attorney for Tri-Max Pods, Inc.

---

**VIA CERTIFIED MAIL**                              February 19, 20__

Mr. Hiram Jackson
Law Firm

> Subject:  Infringement of Tri-Max mark
> by Tri-Max Pods, Inc.

Dear Mr. Jackson:

We represent Griffin Richmond, Inc.

In summary, the allegations contained in your letter dated February 7, 20__, are unfounded and unsupported. Based on our investigation, we have noted that your client filed for Articles of Incorporation on December 15, 2007. As you are no doubt aware, the mere filing for Articles of Incorporation establishes no trademark rights.

Further, upon extensive review of its website, we found no indication whatsoever that your client has publicly asserted rights to Tri-Max or any variation thereof. In fact, the only clear assertion of any trademark rights has been with regard to the term "Pods."

Your client should be aware that our client can establish a public use date well prior to your client's filing for Articles of Incorporation.

Additionally, our client has filed for a federal trademark registration for the mark Tri-Max, U.S. Trademark Application Serial No. 2/000000. Prior to filing for a federal trademark registration, a full Thomson & Thomson search was conducted which did not identify any use by your client. Based on our client's good faith in adopting the mark, the application for federal trademark registration, and the extensive nationwide advertising and promotion of the Tri-Max mark, our client has established nationwide exclusive trademark rights to that mark.

Based on the foregoing, we view the acts of your client as constituting trademark infringement and unfair competition, among other potential causes. We, therefore, demand your written assurances that your client will immediately cease and desist all use of the term Tri-Max and amend its Articles of Incorporation to eliminate the Tri-Max portion from its name. If we do not receive the requested written assurances within ten (10) days of your receipt of this letter, we will recommend to our clients that they seek complete and effective judicial relief.

> Very truly yours,
> Samuel L. Waters
> Attorney for Griffin Richmond, Inc.

---

March 1, 20___

Samuel Waters
Law Firm

Dear Mr. Waters:

We have received your certified letter dated February 19, 20___, and have discussed it with our client.

In your letter you state that a Thomson & Thomson search conducted prior to the filing of Application Serial No. 2/000000 for the trademark Tri-Max did not disclose the use of the trademark by our client and that your client acted in good faith in adopting the mark. We have no reason at this time to question the good faith of Richmond. What we appear to have here is two companies, both apparently acting in good faith, that adopted exactly the same trademark for very similar products at about the same time. That is unfortunate for all concerned.

To the extent that the resolution of this matter turns on the parties' respective dates of first use, we can tell you that our client's first Tri Max unit was sold prior to January 1, 2008, the date of first use claimed by your client in its application, that our client was incorporated under that name on December 15, 2007, and that our client has been actively and continuously selling and offering this item for sale since it was first introduced (see enclosed mailing piece). We do not know anything about the use of the mark by your client other than Richmond's <u>claimed</u> date of first use and very recent indication that it is <u>introducing</u> such a product. We would appreciate any further information you are able to give us in support of the assertion that your "client can establish a public use date well prior to" the filing of Articles of Incorporation by Tri-Max Pods, Inc.

It appears (on the basis of very limited knowledge about the use of the mark by Richmond) that the legal rights of our respective clients are going to turn on exactly what each party was doing with respect to the trademark during the last several months of the year 2007. We can follow the traditional approach and resolve the matter through a contested proceeding in the PTO or in the courts. Eventually, one side will win and the other will lose. Alternatively, we can look for a businesslike solution in which all parties are winners. In that connection, let us advise you that our client has a pending patent application on his product as well as rights in the trademark Tri-Max. This further complicates the situation.

We have no specific proposal to make at this time, but would like to know if you see any possibility of resolving both the trademark dispute and a potential patent infringement claim, and making an innovative design available to Richmond, through an assignment of rights or a license agreement of some kind. If so, we would be pleased to discuss either such arrangement with you.

We look forward to receiving evidence in support of the claimed date of first use by Richmond or a response to the suggestions made in the immediately preceding paragraph, or both. If these are matters that you would prefer to discuss by telephone or in person, you can reach me at the number set forth above.

Very truly yours,

Hiram Jackson
Attorney for Tri-Max Pods, Inc.

Enclosure

―――――――― *Exercise 7.3* ――――――――

*Rewrite this letter written by counsel for Refrigerated Storage Corp. to the attorney for Energy Systems Inc.*

Mr. John Green
Brown and Maple, P.C.
100 State Street
City

Re: Energy Systems Inc. v. Refrigerated Storage Corp.

Dear John:

This letter is written to follow-up on my discussions with you yesterday concerning your client's ("Energy Systems Inc.") request for the administrative law judge (hereafter ALJ) to establish a schedule and procedures enabling ESI to conduct additional discovery against my client Refrigerated Storage Corp. following the filing of RSC's rebuttal testimony this past Monday and prior to the commencing of the hearing on the merits on November 9th. By the way, I do appreciate your having delineated a series of proposed deadlines for such discovery, so that RSC would have some better idea of what we might be facing in terms of the additional discovery burden during the five remaining weeks as we prepare for hearing.

However, it cannot be agreed by my client at this late point in these proceedings, to change the discovery procedures and schedule agreed to last April, or to spend additional funds, <u>not</u> to <u>mention</u> the last month of trial preparation, answering additional requests for information (RFIs) and tendering RSC's rebuttal witnesses for deposition by ESI. Our reasons for taking this position will be detailed in a formal response to your pleading due on October 6th. Certainly, the fact that ESI has already had open discovery against RSC for <u>seven months</u> following the filing of RSC's direct case last January 30th weighs heavily in our calculus. So also does the fact that RSC's position on that case has, in our view, remained essentially unchanged since our case was put on the table at that point in time. Finally, we have a hard time seeing how ESI has room to complain, especially when one compares the discovery opportunities ESI has been accorded in this case to the much more limited discovery available to litigants in some of ESI's own cases! I am sure that ESI must have some appreciation for RSC's position in this regard.

Quite honestly, both RSC, and I personally, believe that the effort, energy, money, and time that ESI would now have the parties invest in a final salvo of discovery (on top of the <u>25</u> RFIs already processed!) could be better spent if the parties were to instead devote those resources to exploring possibilities for settlement, and focus on some kind of true "middle ground" settlement that would (1) protect any legitimate concerns ESI may have over the specter of catastrophic liability, while still (2) providing RSC and other customers access to the courts in most instances where they have suffered damages as a result of difficulties caused by negligence on the part of ESI. Indeed, a more balanced limitation of liability clause, we believe, would better serve <u>ESI</u>'s interests as well, since it would have a much better chance of surviving challenge and being upheld in the highly unlikely event a negligently caused systemwide damage were to occur on the ESI system!

RSC stands ready to explore such settlement possibilities at this point in time. However, its incentives to do so are reduced with each passing day, as RSC is forced to expend more and more monies as the trial date approaches. We will not be railroaded into putting off trial any longer.

> Yours truly,
>
> Hiram Jackson
>
> Attorney for Refrigerated Storage Corp

---
### *Assignment 7.1*
---

*Based on the information in Casefile 1 in Appendix A, write a demand letter to the attorney for the Board of Parish Life, Grace Church, for your client Nancy Williams asking for her reinstatement with the church and to arrange a settlement conference.*

---

## 3. Internal Correspondence

### a. In General

Internal correspondence—for example, correspondence within a corporation, an agency, or a law firm—is often styled as an interoffice memo rather than as a letter. Unless such a document or e-mail message is used to analyze a legal question and is organized as a formal legal memorandum, however, (see Chapter 8, *Office Memoranda*), the document or e-mail is more similar to a letter than to a formal memorandum. These letters usually omit the salutation and traditional closing such as "Yours truly." Instead, an in-house memo often begins with "To," "From," and "Topic"—or "Re"—subject lines. Very short, informal memos sometimes omit these subject lines.

Lawyers may tend to be more casual when communicating within their firm or organization, but like more formal letters, these documents leave a paper trail that may be read by others. Even deleted e-mail messages may be retrieved and entered into evidence in litigation. Thus, the writer should carefully consider their content.

In-house memos, like other correspondence, are usually addressed to a person who is busy and flooded with paperwork. That person wants to understand your point and the details of your correspondence quickly. This means that you should re-read, edit for coherence and concision, use an introductory sentence or short paragraph to give an overview, and proofread even short e-mail messages before you click on "send."

Because these in-house communications are addressed to people you will be working with regularly, including supervisors and subordinates, you want to be careful about your tone. Although you should be as brief and clear as possible, you also want to be polite. Thus use indirection where necessary, instead of writing a string of abrupt orders. Be generous with your use of "please" and "thanks" or "thank you."

### b. Components

For long in-house memos, consider using an introductory summary, often called an Executive Summary, and then a longer discussion or analysis of the problem. Also use topic headings to help the reader follow along.

———————————— *Exercise 7.4* ————————————

*The following in-house memo was e-mailed by an attorney in a corporate legal department to a member of the corporation's sales staff. The attorney is expressing his displeasure with an agreement already signed by the sales staff and only then sent to the legal department. Rewrite it to edit its opening, its parallel form, its sentence structure, vocabulary, and tone.*

This raises a point worth noting: enter non-disclosure agreements very reluctantly and when we must we should have them reviewed prior to signing (yes, by lawyers) to see if we can minimize our exposure. For instance, in connection with this agreement I would have sought to clarify and narrow the meaning of "this relationship" (para. 7), would have tried to make termination of the agreement the sole remedy for improper disclosure, would have deleted "at a minimum" from the first sentence of paragraph 4, and tried to delete the second sentence of paragraph 4. Additionally, paragraph 6 should include "state or federal agencies." I don't like paragraph 8, and we would prefer the governing law to be New York (paragraph 9). It may be that each of these points were addressed, negotiated, and a determination made that capitulation was necessary to make the deal and that the deal was more important than the risk undertaken. If so, so be it. If not, so it should have been. Next time, make sure you come to the legal department before signing.

---

## 4. Letters to Third Parties

### a. In General

Lawyers sometimes write to people other than their clients, their adversaries' lawyers, or their work associates. Some of those letters are adversarial in nature, such as a letter to a witness informing him that he will be subpoenaed if necessary; some are polite requests, for example, a request to send certain business records; and some are personal, such as an application for a job and request for an interview. Some are written on behalf of your law firm or business, such as a response to these kinds of requests.

As in all other writing, the audience and purpose dictate the tone, content, and length of your letter. If you are asking the recipient to do something for you—especially if the recipient has no personal interest in the matter—then be polite and offer incentives, or appeal to her good will, if that is possible. Communication specialists advise that to persuade a reader or listener, you should appeal to your common goals.[19] If your requests have been ignored, or you must issue a warning of future consequences (for example, a subpoena), be polite, but formal and firm.[20] Letters of this kind require that you make your request or convey information quickly and clearly, and that, especially where conveying bad news, you use tact.

### b. Components

In your opening paragraph, introduce yourself and make the purpose of the letter clear. The body of the letter then provides necessary background and clarifies the action the writer wishes the recipient to take. If appropriate, you may want to close by suggesting mutually beneficial reasons or incentives for cooperating. If there are neither, however, conclude with a short paragraph thanking the recipient for her time.

### c. Sample Letter

The following is a sample of a letter requesting a relative to help in a will contest by providing information. The letter emphasizes the parties' family relationship and the recipient's relationship to the deceased testator. It invokes their common goal and ends by offering an incentive for the recipient's aid.

Ms. Joan Kavanaugh
1 West Street
Lake City

Dear Ms. Kavanaugh:

I am the attorney for your cousins John and James Morse. As you know, your cousins are preparing to file a will contest to invalidate the will of their deceased father, your uncle Timothy Morse. They will be arguing that their father lacked capacity to write the will and was under the influence of his housekeeper, Steven Lewis, at the time he executed

---

[19] *See, e.g.,* Stephen V. Armstrong & Timothy Terrell, *Thinking Like a Writer: A Lawyer's Guide to Effective Writing and Editing* 10–23 (Clark Boardman Callaghan 1992).

[20] *See* Helene S. Shapo, Marilyn R. Walter, & Elizabeth Fajans, *Writing and Analysis in the Law* 350-51 (5th ed. 2008).

the will. They know that you were fond of your uncle and that you share their commitment for their father's property to be distributed fairly.

As the will stands now, Steven Lewis will receive the lion's share of your uncle's considerable property and will be executor of the estate. Your cousins will receive only a small share. Yet Mr. Lewis worked for your uncle only the last six months of his life, at a time when your uncle was elderly and ill.

Your cousins hope that you will be able to help them prove their case. They know that you visited their father three times in the last six months when you came here to visit your parents. I would like to telephone you next week to get your impressions of your uncle's physical and mental condition and his relationship with Mr. Lewis. I would like to use that information to prepare an affidavit for you to sign that we will present to the court, along with other people's affidavits.

Your cousins are aware that your uncle left you $500 in his will. If their contest is successful and the will is declared invalid, your cousins will be your uncle's heirs, as they should be. You can be assured that they will more than make good this gift to you.

I look forward to talking with you.

> Yours truly,
>
> Hiram Jackson
> Attorney for John and James Morse

---

### *Exercise 7.5*

*Evaluate this letter from a second-year law student. Rewrite, especially to provide better introductions to the paragraphs.*

Dear <Law Firm>:

This is in response to the firm resume you sent to Northern University School of Law's Placement Office. I would like to apply for a summer associate position with <Firm>.

Answering constituent mail on trade and taxes for Senator Condor sharpened my ability to work with care and efficiency. Constituents relied on me for answers to their questions on the changes that took place in the Internal Revenue Code as a result of the Tax Reform Act of 1986. The reputation of Senator Condor also depended upon my accuracy. This experience would be helpful in work at <Firm> because your firm and its clients need people who can hit the ground running at the outset.

Studying commercial real estate development also gave me a strong background in real estate title and transactions. This included title searches and real estate closings. These skills, coupled with knowledge of contract and tort theory, will enable me to work on a large variety of legal problems that your clients may have.

I look forward to meeting with you to discuss a summer associate position. Please contact me to arrange an interview at your convenience.

Thank you for your consideration.

Yours truly,

_____

Law Student

─────────────────────── *Exercise 7.6* ───────────────────────

*You are a lawyer who is the secretary for a condominium Board of Directors. The Board has recently put into place a 5 per cent increase in the monthly assessment for each condo unit. A group of condo owners has written to protest the increase and question its need. They understood that the condo's reserves were already sufficient to meet the requirements of the bank that recently granted the condo a construction loan for major work on the elevators. The Board has asked you to prepare a draft response and circulate it to other Board members. One member who was not at the last Board meeting has returned the draft to you, saying she is not sure she understands the point of this letter. Rather than tell her that you hope she will read through the entire letter carefully, prepare another draft to make the point clear and edit the draft generally.*

To the Lakeview Condominium Owners:

The increased assessment has been approved by the Condominium Board of Directors and our accountant concurs.

The Board has authority to raise assessments pursuant to Article 4 of Lakeview's Conditions, Covenants and Declarations.

Our construction mortgage lender, ABC, requires that we have a reserve in the amount of three months' assessments. As of May 20__ our monthly assessment income amounts to $152,250—multiplied by three is $456,750. That is the amount we have to have on reserve for ABC for the loan for the elevator work.

As of June 1, 20__, our resources are as listed:

| Checking accounts | $125,250 |
| Money Market | 175,500 |
| CD's | 250,000 |
| | $550,750 |

In addition, our separate operating account as of that date, which also earns interest, amounts to $100,122.02. So our reserve and our other accounts come to $650,872.02.

Why do we have so much in the accounts over ABC's requirement? We have bills to pay over the summer, for example, the masonry work that we are now beginning.

And also, attached is a copy of p.10 of our last Financial Statement. It lists estimated costs of our common property component replacements that were detailed in the Reserve Study we did in 20__. For example, replacing some parts of the electrical system. This is a safety item. Also attached is a copy of p. 25 of that study, recommending a reserve contribution this year of $250,000. This was not realistic.

The 5% assessment increase now will allow us to contribute that much more to the reserve account.

We know these increases are painful. We also own units and we share your pain. As Directors, we have two choices. We could have done nothing as we've done over the past years and let the directors in office three years down the road bear the brunt of our inaction.

We will continue to supply you with information.

Yours truly,

_____, for the Board

---

## C. SPECIAL CONCERNS: ELECTRONIC COMMUNICATION

Like law students, lawyers use e-mail all the time in their practice. Indeed, lawyers say that e-mail (and FAX) has changed the nature of their practice in that their clients and others expect an immediate–or, at least, a very quick–response. Where a lawyer sends a quick response to an inter-office e-mail ("I plan to be at the meeting this afternoon), answers a simple question from a client ("you must sign both copies"), or arranges a meeting with opposing counsel (This Friday the 13th at 2:00 P.M. is a good time), then e-mail is easily used as a substitute for a telephone call. But where that response involves legal advice, the lawyer must be very careful not to answer too hastily before she fully considers her answer.

E-mail has changed the quantity and quality of correspondence within a firm or business organization. Communication by e-mail is simple, cost effective, and fast. Because typing and sending an e-mail message is easy, however, people send many more messages, especially in-house messages, than they would send by paper or by telephone. Lawyers complain that the number of internal messages they receive drains their time and interrupts their other work. Thus think twice before you send an e-mail with a message or question you would not have asked a partner or corporate officer in person or by telephone or interoffice memo.

Like law students also, lawyers are generally aware of the risks of e-mail, but nevertheless, they often ignore them. We consider here two particular risks in using e-mail: the inappropriate tone and poor written quality of much of the correspondence and the unintended receipt by others than the intended recipient. We also add suggestions about formatting.

In addition to the quantity of messages, lawyers complain about the quality of the e-mail they receive. People tend to write very informally, even to recipients with whom they should not be informal. For any work-related e-mail, avoid emoticons, all caps, informal language and inappropriate abbreviations ("4u" instead of "for you").

Pay particular attention to tone, which can be misinterpreted as sarcasm or impatience without voice or face-to-face communication. Like a business letter, your e-mail should sound business-like and be drafted as carefully as you would draft a business letter. Even an e-mail that is essentially a cover letter for an attachment or a short response to a message should be reviewed so that it does not come across as brusque and impolite to its recipient. For example, assume an attorney e-mails her associate asking him to delete a particular paragraph in a memo draft. Wanting to explain to the summer associate who wrote the memo the reason for the deletion, the associate e-mails back, "why?" The first attorney takes this response as a challenge to the request, and responds, "Because I don't think it's very good. Maybe you should read the paragraph for yourself." Had the associate explained the reason for asking for an explanation, he probably would have gotten a more tactful reply and avoided the inevitable bad feelings.

In addition to reviewing any e-mail message for its tone, check also for spelling (don't rely on spell-check), typographical errors, grammatical errors, and citation errors, if you include citations.

One reason to be especially careful to review your messages before you send them is that your e-mail message may not remain private or confidential. Don't send a message that should not be read by someone other than the intended recipient. If you are replying to a message that has gone out to recipients other than you, you may hit "Reply All" instead of just "Reply," and a response that is personal, or critical, or confidential will go to the whole list. Or an intended recipient may forward your message to someone else without checking with you first, or your message may be buried in a long chain of messages that gets forwarded to others. Even if your message does not get forwarded to others, it lives on in an archive that may be retrieved years later and is available for discovery in litigation. Use the telephone or face-to-face conversation for communications that should be kept private.

Formatting: Whether you are attaching a memo to your e-mail or typing the memo as the e-mail message itself, think about formatting for maximum readability. Use headings and subheadings and other devices for readability, such as bullet points. And for a long memo, provide an introductory summary.

Another aid to your reader–and to you–is to use the subject line wisely. Your recipient, such as a law firm partner, or a business executive, may be flooded with e-mail messages and may not read those with vague subject lines. So, make sure that the subject line conveys the substance of the e-mail message. Instead of the subject "X v. Y.," use "X v. Y deadline for filing the answer is tomorrow." Then in the body, make the point of the e-mail clear. Explain if a particular response is needed or if you are simply providing a status update. You also want to make sure that the recipient is able to pull up the attachment on her computer. If not, paste it in the e-mail message.

Finally, and always, reread your message before you hit send.

---
## Assignment 7.2
---

*Based on the information in Assignment 4.3, write a letter to David Brown's attorney for your client Maureen Brown, Mr. Brown's ex-wife. Ms. Brown wants to relocate from New Jersey to Washington State with the couple's young son, a move Mr. Brown opposes. The purpose of your letter is to explain Ms. Brown's desire to relocate and to try to convince David and his attorney that settlement is a good idea and a conference should be arranged. You are writing this letter before filing a petition for relocation with the court. You have never met Mr. Brown's attorney, Jennifer Dwyer. Although you interviewed Maureen Brown, the attached facts will refresh your memory.*

*Please attach a cover sheet to your letter describing the purpose/s, the audience/s, and the writing techniques you used to achieve your purpose with your audience.*

*There is no required page length, but an effective letter would probably require at least two, double spaced pages.*

### Facts

Maureen and David Brown have been divorced since 2005. They have joint legal custody of their child, Kevin (age 7). Maureen has primary residential/physical custody of Kevin. Under the agreement between the parents, Kevin lives with his mother and visits his father three days and one night a week. They split school vacations. However, David has not always been able to spend all the time with Kevin that the schedule allows because he is a private-duty registered nurse whose work schedule varies, but the parents have been able to work out changes in the visitation schedule as needed. Both parents live in Seagrove, New Jersey, a small town on the Jersey Shore. Maureen and David have thus far successfully co-parented Kevin, who is happy and well-adjusted.

Maureen has worked for ten years as a computer programmer for a large bank in Philadelphia. She has recently been recruited by Ultra-Soft, a new soft-ware company that will be setting up operations in Seattle, to design software programs. Ultra-Soft is offering Maureen a starting salary of $65 thousand/year plus stock options. (Her salary at the bank is $75 thousand.) The company has assured her that she could have flex time. She describes the job as "the chance of a lifetime" and wishes to move to Seattle with Kevin. Kevin is not sure what he thinks about this idea. Sometimes he thinks it's great, other times he says he wants to stay in Seagrove.

Maureen met the founder of Ultra-Soft on a visit to a man she had been dating for a year before her planned move to Seattle. The relationship has been getting more serious and Maureen and her friend

James Lord, a school teacher, are considering sharing a house in Seattle. Since James' work day finishes at 3 p.m., he would arrive home at about the same time as Kevin. Kevin has met James and seems to like him. Ultra-Soft would pay for Kevin's tuition at any private school in Seattle. Maureen thinks Seattle will provide Kevin with a diversity of cultural and recreational activities unavailable in Seagrove, although she admits Seagrove is a pleasant, if small town. It has no crime, very little traffic, clear air, and a healthy out-door lifestyle focused on its beautiful clean beaches.

David recently broke up with a woman he was seeing and is not currently seeing anyone else. David's mother suffers from late-stage Alzheimer's disease. She is in a nursing home ten miles from Seagrove. David's retired father and married brother also live in Seagrove. As a private-duty nurse, David earns about $400 per shift. He works mainly at the local hospital. Maureen has no close living relatives.

When Maureen told David about the Ultra-Soft offer and her desire to take Kevin with her to Seattle, David was devastated. Maureen said she thought that between them they should be able to afford the airfare required to maintain the relationship between Kevin and his father. She is willing to accept almost any visitation schedule David proposes, in particular long visits over school vacations. Her flexibility has done little to convince David, who remains opposed to Kevin's move to Seattle.

# Chapter 8

# INFORMING AND PERSUADING: OFFICE MEMORANDA

## A. IN GENERAL

A frequent type of writing that lawyers do within law firms is the office memorandum ("memo").[1] New associates and summer associates, especially in large law firms, often spend a good deal of their time researching and writing memos for more senior associates and partners. The partner assigns the associate an issue that the partner needs answered in order to advise the client, argue a motion, or write a brief. The memo is written to provide information, evaluation, and criticism about the law that controls the particular issue. The memo should identify all the issues involved in the assignment and analyze all the arguments that can plausibly be made by each party.

Although these memos are often described as "objective" writing, as opposed to "persuasive" writing, meaning that the writer is not arguing a client's case to a decision-maker, memos are nevertheless persuasive documents in that the associate wants her analysis to be convincing and to be accepted by the partner. To do so, she must give convincing and thorough reasons for her conclusions and recommendations. Moreover, the partner wants the associate to make the best case for the client, within the bounds of what can be argued fairly. If the associate gives up too easily on arguments that plausibly can be made for the client, the client's cause will not be well served. On the other hand, if the associate advocates using arguments that are in fact very weak, the partner will be at a disadvantage when advising the client, negotiating with other attorneys, or arguing in court. Instead, the

---

[1] Memoranda are also used in corporate legal departments, government agencies, etc. But our focus here is on law office memos.

associate needs to explore and evaluate—to raise all plausible arguments available to each party, evaluate their strengths and weaknesses, and determine whether weaknesses in the client's case can be overcome.

The primary audience for a memo is the assigning partner, a person who is most likely very busy and quite critical, and who will be relying on your work in order to advise a client or to go to court. The memo may also have other audiences, most of whom are also legal audiences. For example, if you are a summer associate in a law firm, the memos you write that summer probably will be placed in your file and will be read by the firm's hiring committee when the committee is deciding whether to ask you to return. Or the memo may be attached to the partner's correspondence to the client, in order to give background to the partner's advice. Thus the client is also a possible audience, as is a court. Segments of the memo may be incorporated in a brief that is submitted to a court.

## B. COMPONENTS

Because the standard complete memo can be time-consuming to prepare, and thus expensive, some law firms cut back on their use, or they use a shorter format. We have nevertheless included first the format of a typical full memo.

Most law school writing courses and law firms have a standard format for their memos; many law firms program their template into their computer software. Most standard formats include the following components, which are described below in Section 1:

1. Statement of Facts
2. Question Presented (or Issue)
3. Conclusion (or Summary or Short Answer)
4. Discussion

Section 2 below describes an alternative, a more abbreviated format that may be more appropriate for memos that analyze only a question of law or are used for a less formal memo assignment. You may want to design your own format, however, if it better suits the particular assignment you have been given.

The components of a memo are interrelated. The relevance of the facts that you include depends on the issue you are analyzing.

Facts are relevant if they help prove or disprove the particular claim you are analyzing. So you must know the issue to decide which facts are relevant. The facts that you include in the Discussion section should all be included in the Facts section. The contents of the Summary or Conclusion section depend on the outcome of your discussion. Your Summary or Conclusion section should summarize only the conclusions you reached when you analyzed the issues in the Discussion. Because the content of the memo components are all interrelated, they should be consistent. Thus, you will be writing and revising the contents of each component as you write the rest of the memo.

## 1. Format for a Memo that Applies Law to Facts

### a. Statement of Facts (or just Facts)

Often a memorandum begins with the Statement of Facts.[2] An accurate Statement of Facts is crucial for a successful analysis of the case. The partner will not be able to assess your analysis unless she knows the facts on which your analysis is based. Confine the facts to those that are relevant to the issues you will analyze and to those background facts that help the reader understand the issues. Unless you are told otherwise, write the facts for someone who does not already know them. Although the partner who assigned the memo probably also told you the facts of the case, and so knows them, your memo may be read by other people who are not familiar with the case. If the case is already in litigation, include any litigation history such as motions and jury verdicts. And describe the facts neutrally and specifically rather than adversarily and generally. For example, rather than saying that a collection agency hounded the plaintiff, you would say that the store called the plaintiff five times over a period of one month, always at dinnertime.

Include the source of the facts, such as interviews, depositions, and transcripts. For example, explain that your information about X was obtained in an interview of Y. If the case is already in litigation, make sure you cite accurately to the record or to the parties'

---

[2] Another typical organization is to begin with the issues. We describe issues in Section (b) below.

depositions. You should also make clear where you are assuming facts and where there are gaps in the facts that need to be filled.

Organize the facts so that your reader can understand them and can follow them easily. In order to do so, first, begin with the context, not with details. People process information best when they have a structure into which to place the details; so tell the partner what the case is about. For example, suppose your case involves a client that made a loan to a company for the purpose of the company acquiring a target company. Your client took a security interest in the target's assets. The firm resulting from this buyout then declared bankruptcy. The client's security interest, however, was a fraudulent transfer under bankruptcy law. The client wants to know if its claim is now subordinated to the unsecured creditors' claims.

Do not simply begin with the first event, as in this example.

> On June 1, 2008, our client Mammon Co. (Mammon) made a loan to Acquiring Corp.
>
> On June 10, Acquiring Corp. merged with Target Inc. in a leveraged buyout. Mammon took a security interest in Target's assets.
>
> On July 30, the merged firm became insolvent and filed for bankruptcy. The bankruptcy court, in an order dated August 30, 2008, held that the security interest was a fraudulent conveyance under the bankruptcy laws.

Instead, provide an overview first.

> Our client Mammon Co. made a loan to a corporation that bought out Target, Inc. Target later declared bankruptcy. The bankruptcy court has held that Target's grant of a security interest in its assets to Mammon is a fraudulent conveyance. As a result, the unsecured creditors claim that Mammon's loan is now subordinated to theirs.[3]

---

[3] If you organize your memo by placing the issue and the conclusion before the facts, you may have already supplied the context and can begin the facts with the more specific details.

Then develop the facts either chronologically or, especially for complex cases, by topics or parties involved. Chronological order, however, sometimes can include unnecessary or distracting detail, as in the first example of the Mammon Co. case. If the case requires a long and involved recitation of facts, the more you categorize the facts into topics and use simple headings, the easier it will be for your reader to understand. For example, a case involving a disabled employee's claim of job discrimination may require descriptions of the employee's job history, his absences from work, doctors' reports, administrative hearings, etc. Instead of providing an unbroken recitation of these events in chronological order, you can categorize them into topics such as "employment history in Peoria facility," "employment history in Rockford facility," "doctors' reports prior to January 2000," "state EEOC hearings."

It is a good idea at the end of the facts to include constraints that were given to you in the assignment, if any. For example, you may end with a sentence such as, "You asked me to analyze only the client's defamation claim under California law, and not her privacy claim." This type of statement is helpful because other attorneys besides the assigning partner may read your memo, and may not know why you omitted an obvious privacy claim.

Finally, a favorite practice of many lawyers is to give short-form names to the parties. Sometimes, however, this practice gets out of hand, and the fact section becomes laden with confusing parenthetical short forms, many of them unnecessary. For example, the first short form is not necessary in this sentence, "Our client entered into a lease ("The Lease") with Brooks Associates ("Brooks")" where this lease is the only one involved. Moreover, many readers would say that the second short form is not necessary either. There should be no disagreement that the short form is not necessary in this sentence, "On January 3d, our client Lee released an offering circular ("The offering circular") in his effort to issue securities." A better use is the following because the short form creates a new name: "Defendant CLR Management Services, Inc ("CMSI") moved to dismiss the complaint." Keep a critical eye on your short-form name designations. Use them if you will be referring to the subject several times. If not, prune them considerably.

————————————— *Exercise 8.1* —————————————

*Rewrite and reorganize these facts. Will you organize by grantee? In chronological order by conveyance and recording? Would an introduction to the claims help its readability? Your client is the defendant L.A. Hughes. The facts are not in controversy and are as follows.*

On May 16, 1906, Carrie B. Hoerger, a resident of Faribault, owned the lot in question, 20 Faribault Drive, which was vacant and subject to unpaid delinquent taxes. Defendant L.A. Hughes offered to pay $25 for this lot. His offer was accepted, and he sent his check for the purchase price of this and two other lots bought at the same time to Ed Hoerger, husband of the owner, together with a deed to be executed and returned. The name of the grantee in the deed was not inserted; the space for the same being left blank. It was executed and acknowledged by Carrie B. Hoerger and her husband on May 17, 1906, and delivered to defendant Hughes by mail. The check was retained and cashed. Hughes filled in the name of the grantee, but not until shortly prior to the date when the deed was recorded, which was December 16, 1910. On April 27, 1909, Duryea & Wilson, real estate dealers, paid Mrs. Hoerger $25 for a quitclaim deed to the lot, which was executed and delivered to them, but which was not recorded until December 21, 1910. On November 19, 1909, Duryea & Wilson executed and delivered to plaintiff Echo Corp. a warranty deed to the lot, which deed was filed for record January 27, 1910. It thus appears that the deed to Hughes was recorded before the deed to Duryea & Wilson, though the deed from them to plaintiff was recorded before the deed to defendant. The question is who now owns the lot.

————————————— *Exercise 8.2* —————————————

*You are the attorney for Fleet Mortgage's legal department. Fleet was served with a subpoena duces tecum, and moved to quash the subpoena. You have written a memo to analyze the issues involved in Fleet's motion. The memo will be the basis for the memo that accompanies Fleet's motion. Your first draft of the facts is below. Rewrite the facts to add a better first paragraph and transition to the rest of the memo. Add other information that you need.*

Facts

Fleet Mortgage Corporation ("Fleet") is in the mortgage banking business. It is incorporated under the laws of the State of Rhode Island

and maintains its principal offices in Milwaukee, Wisconsin. In Illinois, Fleet originates conventional home loans, Federal Housing Association ("FHA"), and Veteran's Administration ("VA") guaranteed loans through eleven branch offices. Eight of those offices are located in the Chicago area. Fleet is not a party to this litigation, which involves the issue of predatory pricing.

When Fleet originates a loan, it opens a file and processes that loan at the local branch office where the mortgagors apply for the loan. These files contain all the documents necessary to process the loan, including the financial information of the mortgagors, closing documents, and a title insurance policy. Fleet orders title insurance policies from several title insurers, including the Plaintiff and Defendant in this action.

After a loan is closed, the branch office closes its files and sends the original to Fleet's office in Milwaukee. The branch office maintains a copy of the file for approximately one year after the closing, then the copy of the file is disposed of. In Milwaukee, Fleet's Record Department places the documents from the original file on microfiche and files the microfiche according to the loan number. Once the mortgagors pay off the loan or go through foreclosure, the microfiche is placed in a separate area and filed according to the mortgagor's last name.

On or about September 6, 2008, the manager at Fleet's branch office located at 000 North Cicero Avenue was served by Plaintiff with a subpoena duces tecum in the above-captioned matter. Plaintiff has requested that the branch manager produce the following documents:

[listing documents]

These documents are not in the custody or control of the branch office served. They are maintained on microfiche in the custody and control of Fleet's Record Department in Milwaukee.

Presently before the court is Fleet's Motion to Quash the Subpoena Duces Tecum.

---

### b. Question Presented (or Issue)

The Issue, sometimes called the Question Presented, is the specific legal question, or questions, raised by the inquiry or dispute. When you are assigned a memo topic, make sure that you know what question the partner wants analyzed and answered. The Issue should be written as the question to be answered, not as a conclusion. If you write that a party has fulfilled what is a requirement of the claim, you are not posing the issue; you are answering it. So for example, if you write, "Can the state of Atlantis exercise personal jurisdiction over the out-of-state defendant if the defendant availed herself of the protections of Atlantis law?" you have concluded as to the jurisdiction point; under prevailing law, one way for the plaintiff to obtain jurisdiction over an out-of-state defendant is if the defendant "availed" herself of the protection of the law of the forum state.

Instead, you should use the facts of the case that are relevant to the question, as in "Can the state of Atlantis exercise personal jurisdiction over the out-of-state defendant where she initiated ten telephone calls to the plaintiff from her Atlantis office, took the plaintiff to lunch in Atlantis to discuss their agreement, and signed the disputed contract in Atlantis?"

### i. Readability

The issue statement is traditionally written as one interrogative sentence or as a sentence fragment that begins with the word "whether." Although many attorneys use the "whether" form, a complete interrogative sentence is a more natural wording than is a sentence fragment and is easier to understand. The best issue statements are those questions that are concisely written and can be understood in one reading. Unfortunately, many lawyers, anxious to put everything into the one sentence, include too many facts and pile clause upon clause. By doing so they create lengthy and unreadable questions. A better practice is to include only the determinative facts and to place them at the end of the sentence.

The following are some suggestions for writing readable issues:

- Begin with the claim and then move to the factual details: that is, move from the general to the specific. An example is, "Is a libel plaintiff a limited purpose public figure under the law of the District of Columbia if the plaintiff was the lead witness in a publicized corruption of justice trial, gave interviews to the press, and appeared on talk shows on national television?"
- Write your sentence in active voice rather than passive voice.

- Keep the subject and verb close together rather than separating them with many clauses and phrases.
- Use concrete nouns rather than abstract ones, especially for the subject of the sentence. Avoid gerunds as the sentence's subject.[4]

Suppose your memo involves a Statute of Frauds issue. Your client entered into an employment agreement with a law firm for five years. The firm could terminate the agreement for cause after six months, and your client could terminate for any reason after six months. The parties did not sign a written agreement, and the law firm terminated your client fourteen months after he began work. He now sues the firm, claiming that he was not terminated for cause. The law firm argues that the contract is unenforceable under the Statute of Frauds because it is a contract not to be performed within a year. A poor framing of the issue would be as follows:

> Does agreeing to work for five years but permitting the parties to terminate the agreement after six months constitute a contract not to be performed within a year and thus within the Hawaii Statute of Frauds?

In this question, the general claim, the Statute of Frauds, is not identified until the end of the sentence instead of at the beginning. Moreover, the grammatical subject of the sentence is seventeen words, beginning with the gerund "agreeing." Instead, a better subject would name a concrete thing such as "employment agreement." Finally, the subject and verb ("agreeing" and "constitute") are separated by so many words that the reader loses track of what this sentence is about. This issue could better be written as follows:

> Does an employment agreement for five years come within the Hawaii Statute of Frauds if either the employer or the employee may terminate the agreement after six months?

---

[4] A gerund is a noun created from a verb by adding "ing" to the end, as in "agreeing." For principles of good sentence structure see Section B of Chapter 5, *Clarity*.

> or

> Under the Hawaii Statute of Frauds, is an employment agreement for five years a contract "not to be performed within one year of the making thereof" if either the employer or the employee may terminate after six months?

ii. Sequence of Issues

If the memo you were assigned includes more than one issue, each should be set out separately and numbered. Then, follow the sequence in which you have organized the questions throughout the rest of the memo. Some traditional rules of legal organization will often determine the sequence.

First, put threshold questions involving whether the court can hear this case, such as whether the statute of limitations has run or the court has jurisdiction.

Then put issues in logical order for a legal dispute. Logical order typically requires you to first analyze the issue on which the next issue depends, that is, if the case goes to litigation, the court's decision on the first issue will determine whether the court must decide the next one. Some examples of logical order are, in a contract dispute, the first issue would be whether the contract for sale was valid, then, did the seller breach one of the terms. Or, in an employment dispute, first you would analyze the issue of whether the employment agreement comes within the Statute of Frauds, then the issue of whether the parties' letters constituted a writing that satisfies the Statute. In a statutory issue the sequence could be, first, the statutory issue of whether the defendant violated the breach of the peace statute, then the constitutional issue of whether the statute is unconstitutional under the first amendment. Where the second issue depends on the resolution of the first one, introduce it with a transition word that shows the logical relationship, such as "if so."

If none of the above organizing principles apply, you may decide to organize based on the issue's importance or difficulty. If one issue is a simple one and you can analyze it easily, you may want to analyze it first and dispose of it quickly. Alternatively, you may want to analyze the most important or difficult issue first while you have the reader's full attention, and then organize the other issues in descending order of importance or difficulty.

Another consideration in organizing more than one issue is to group related issues together. If you are evaluating the issues in a divorce case, for example, you may consider the laws relating to the issues of property settlement, spousal maintenance, child custody, and child support. You could group the two spousal issues concerning property matters and then the two issues involving the children. On the other hand, you could group the three issues regarding property matters and then the custody issue.

### iii. Party References

Some memo formats place the issues first, before the facts. If you use that sequence, it is a good idea to use general terms instead of specific names to describe the parties and the other facts included in the issue. The reader may not know yet who the parties are or to what facts you refer. For example, use "lender" and "borrower" rather than naming the specific parties, Mammon Corp. and Target Co. If your format places the statement of the issue after the facts, then, unless your instructions are otherwise, you can use specific names to describe people and events because the reader knows who they are.

─────────────── *Exercise 8.3* ───────────────

*The following questions were written for a memo analyzing a Fourth Amendment issue. The police, acting without search warrant, placed an electronic tracking device (informally known as a bumper beeper) on the underside of a drug suspect's car, while the car was parked on a private driveway abutting a public road. The police then followed the car by monitoring the tracking device and arrested the suspect when he removed drugs from the car to bring them into his home.*

*Evaluate these questions as if they were written by an associate of the defendant's lawyer in a memo analyzing the case for purposes of a brief prepared for a hearing to exclude the evidence.*

*Write your own question.*

**1.** Whether the installation and monitoring of an electronic tracking device, attached to the defendant's car by the police without a warrant, were a violation of the defendant's Fourth Amendment right to freedom from unreasonable searches and seizures so that evidence derived from such a search should be excluded at trial.

**2.** Do police officers invade a citizen's right of privacy and perform an illegal search under the Fourth Amendment when they place, surreptitiously and without either a warrant or the citizen's consent, an electronic tracking device on a citizen's car while that car is parked on the citizen's own driveway, and then monitor the citizen's travel on public streets?

**3.** Whether police officers' warrantless installation of an electronic tracking device on an automobile parked on private property abutting a public road and the subsequent monitoring of this device violates the Fourth Amendment's prohibitions against unreasonable searches and seizures.

**4.** Was the use of a bumper beeper by police to follow the defendant's car limited by a warrant requirement?

---

### *Exercise 8.4*

*Suppose that your memo involved a minor's consent to a medical procedure. Your client is an emergency room doctor who set the broken leg of a fourteen-year old girl and put her leg in a cast. The emergency room did not obtain her parent's consent; only the patient consented. Under standard tort law, unless a doctor acts in an emergency, a doctor commits a battery if she treats a patient without the patient's consent or treats a minor without parental consent. Tort law recognizes, however, that a mature minor can give consent to procedures that are not complex, if the procedures and their consequences are ones that the minor is able to understand.*

*Write the two issue statements for this memo.*

---

### c. Conclusion

This section, also called a Summary or Short Answer, typically follows the issue statement even in a memo format in which the issue precedes the facts. The Conclusion is a more important part of a memo than most students realize. The attorney reading your memo often will look initially to this section to get an immediate answer to the issues, and then return later to the memo to read the full analysis. In the Conclusion, you should answer each of the questions posed in the Questions Presented, in the order in which they were posed.

The Conclusion can be done in two different ways. When the section is called a Short Answer, you would provide just an answer to the question, with perhaps a one or two sentence explanation. Other memo formats require an answer to the question, followed by a longer summary of reasons for that answer. This longer section is often called a Conclusion or a Summary. Under either format, you should be sure to answer the question directly, that is, come to a conclusion and state it clearly. If your conclusion requires the reader to know the law, for example, the elements of the claim or the factors that must be balanced, then include that information.

For example, if your memo analyzes whether a plaintiff in a defamation suit is a limited purpose public figure (and therefore must prove that the defendant acted with malice), your conclusion would include the test used in that jurisdiction to determine whether an individual is a limited purpose public figure, as well as your conclusion as to the outcome of applying that test. The Conclusion below does not explain clearly the three-part test required to prove that a person is a limited public figure or answer whether that person is a limited public figure.

> Whether Ms. Goble was a limited public figure depends on whether she satisfies the three-prong *Waldbaum* test. If the trial at which Ms. Goble testified was a public controversy and Ms. Goble played a prominent role, then she was a public figure. *Waldbaum* suggests that a person's access to the media is important in determining whether a person becomes a public figure.
>
> Because a public figure must prove that the defendant acted with malice, that is, with knowledge or reckless disregard of the truth of the statements, if Ms. Goble is a limited public figure, she will be unsuccessful proving her claim.

The Conclusion below answers whether the plaintiff is a limited public figure and tells why.

> Ms. Goble was a limited purpose public figure under the law of the District of Columbia Circuit. A plaintiff is a limited

purpose public figure if she was involved in a public controversy, if she injected herself into the controversy in order to influence its resolution, and if the defendant's defamatory statements are germane to her role in the controversy.

Ms. Goble was involved in a publicized and important trial involving public officials accused of obstruction of justice, which was a public controversy. Moreover, she injected herself into the controversy by volunteering evidence to the U.S. Attorney and testifying for three days, by appearing on a morning talk show, and by holding a press conference. Finally, the defendant's defamatory statement was germane because he wrote that Ms. Goble was convicted of perjury in that trial. Thus Ms. Goble will have to prove that the defendant acted with malice.

Sometimes, however, you cannot provide a definitive answer because the law is unclear, or the question has not been answered in that jurisdiction, or not enough facts are available. If so, then qualify the answer and explain the reasons for that qualification. For example, if your memo is about the Mammon Co. and Target Inc. case described above in Section B(1)(a) and the question is the consequences of Mammon's security interest as a fraudulent conveyance, the following Conclusion tells the attorney the bad news that there is no clear answer to the question, but does not help the attorney beyond that stage.

Conclusion
There has been no definitive answer to the question of whether, after a lender's security interest has been avoided as a fraudulent transfer in bankruptcy, the lender's claim must be subordinated to unsecured creditors' claims, or whether the lender may share its claims with unsecured creditors in bankruptcy. Current fraudulent conveyance statutes, case law, and commentary do not specify which remedy is required in this situation.

This Conclusion would have been more helpful and accurate, however, if it had then included some of the writer's analysis from the Discussion section.

Most authorities characterize fraudulent conveyance law as a debt-collection device, the sole purpose of which is to prevent the unjust diminution of the debtor's estate. Consistent with this purpose, Mammon would be allowed to share with the unsecured creditors. A remedy that subordinates Mammon's claim or avoids it goes beyond the purpose of fraudulent conveyance law.

A Conclusion that includes a summary of reasons should be specific to the facts and should be self-contained, that is, the reader should be able to understand it without skipping over to other parts of the memo. So the writer should not refer to unexplained abstract doctrines, or rules, or "prongs" that can be understood only after reading the full discussion. Nor should the writer refer simply to a "majority rule" and a "minority rule" when the reader does not know what they are. Finally, the Conclusion should be a summary of the discussion and analysis that is to come. It should not include new material and analysis that is not in the memo's full Discussion section.

### d. Discussion

In the Discussion section, sometimes called Analysis or Discussion and Analysis, you explain, analyze, and evaluate the issues that the memo assignment involves. The partner will want an informative, substantive discussion and analysis that is useful for the partner's purpose, is well organized, and is concise, clear, and carefully written. This type of perfection requires a good deal of editing through more than one draft, and careful proofreading. We take up this topic in Section D below, *Writing Process*.

Begin the Discussion with a paragraph, sometimes called a thesis paragraph, that introduces your memo discussion, and supplies the context for your analysis and a roadmap of your organization. If the memo involves more than one issue, explain how they relate to each other. Many, but not all, lawyers include their conclusions in this paragraph. You should not go into the details of your analysis here, however. If you do, the reader may think that you are starting the full analysis of the issues and will be surprised when you seem to stop and then start again in the next paragraphs.

The introductory paragraphs to the discussion of the Statute of Frauds case set out in Section B(1)(b) could look like this:

> An employment agreement comes within the Statute of Frauds if it is a contract not to be performed within one year. There is no Hawaii case law deciding whether a multi-year contract that includes a defeasance clause exercisable within one year comes within the statute. Other states have reached contradictory conclusions on this issue. The majority of states hold that the contract comes within the statute because full performance requires five years; termination is not performance. However, a sizable minority hold that the contract is not within the statute because it sets out alternate means of performance. Related Hawaii precedents suggest, however, that the contract would not come within the statute and need not be evidenced by a writing.
>
> If the contract is within the statute, the two letters will not satisfy the statute's requirement that the terms be in a writing signed by the party to be charged. Only the plaintiff's letter contained the terms. Moreover, because the law firm's letter does not refer to the plaintiff's letter, the court will not incorporate the two documents by reference.
>
> However, Mr. Astor may raise an additional claim based on promissory estoppel, for which there is a basis in Hawaii law. I will supplement this memo to include that claim if you instruct me to do so.

For the rest of the discussion, where the memo involves more than one issue, maintain the sequence of issues that you have followed in the Issues and Conclusion sections, and analyze them one at a time.

Remember the importance of using introductions throughout your discussion in order to provide context for the detailed analysis that follows. For example, use an introduction when you change topic and when you analyze a line of cases. Your reader needs to know what your point is before she makes her way through the details. These introductions need be only one or two sentences. So, for example, if you are analyzing whether a plaintiff in a defamation case is a limited purpose public figure, do not begin the topic of the plaintiff's participation in a criminal trial by stringing quotations together in this way.

> Although the plaintiff was involved in litigation, she is not a limited purpose public figure. In *Time, Inc. v. Firestone*, 424 U.S. 448 (1976), the Supreme Court said [quote about litigation]. Moreover, in *Wolston v. Readers Digest*, 443 U.S. 157 (1979), the Court said, [quote about litigation].

Instead, you might begin this topic and its introduction to a line of cases by making your point, as follows.

> Although the plaintiff was involved in publicized litigation, that litigation alone does not transform her from a private citizen into a limited purpose public figure. In every Supreme Court case involving a plaintiff in litigation, the Court held that the plaintiffs, who were private figures, did not become public figures by virtue of participating in the litigation. [cite cases].

If you represent the defendant and your analysis is that the cases are distinguishable, put that point right up front.

> In those cases, however, the plaintiffs had been thrust unwillingly into the litigated controversy or were required to litigate to resolve a controversy, such as a divorce. Ms. Goble, however, initiated the visit to the U.S. Attorney, offered information against the criminal defendants, and willingly testified at their trial.

Alternatively, if your point is to distinguish the cases in two ways, put that point up front also.

> These cases may be distinguished from Ms. Goble's litigation in two ways. First the plaintiffs had been thrust unwillingly into the litigated controversy or were required to litigate the issue, for example, a divorce. [cite cases]. Ms. Goble, however, initiated the events that led to her participation in the trial. Second, none of the litigation in these precedents involved

issues of public importance, whereas Ms. Goble was involved in a trial with important consequences to the public. [Then analyze the cases].

If the discussion is a long one or if it involves more than one issue, use headings and subheadings to clarify your organization and signal a change of topic. These headings should be neutral statements rather than the conclusory point headings you would use in a brief. For example, a heading could be "Requirements for a limited purpose public figure," or, "Whether plaintiff remained a public figure after seven years." Your headings and subheadings may also be complete sentences rather than phrases, such as, "Limited purpose public figures must be involved in public controversies." Complete sentences will give more information to your reader.

Your discussion must be informative. So make sure that you include all relevant text of contracts, statutes, agency regulations, etc. The partner cannot follow your analysis of a document's language without knowing what that language is; don't force her to find the document and consult it herself. Also, supply enough information about the cases you discuss so that the partner does not have to read the case herself in order to understand it and its relevance. Unless the case is factually irrelevant (and you use it only for a point of law or a quotation), provide enough facts so that the partner understands the analogies and distinctions you draw. Explain how the cases relate to your issue; don't just string quotes together. Quote only particularly useful language, for example, language that the partner may want to use in a brief.

Remember that you are writing the memo for a lawyer and lawyers are accustomed to a particular organization of information within each issue. That information begins with the general rules and definitions that govern the particular topic. For example, in the defamation case, the issue was whether the plaintiff was a limited purpose public figure. The controlling law in that jurisdiction set out three criteria for a limited purpose public figure, the first of which is whether the plaintiff was involved in a public controversy. The court defined "public controversy" as one that was "debated publicly and . . . had foreseeable and substantial ramifications for non-participants." To begin an analysis of "public controversy," the writer would define it early in the discussion and then go on to analyze, first, whether the issue involved was debated publicly, discussing and comparing all the relevant cases and policies, and then analyze the ramifications for non-participants. A warning here, however, is not to overdo the preliminary definitions. Your reader is not going to want to go through paragraphs of definitions before she gets to any substance. Consider instead breaking up the topics into smaller chunks.

Because a strong and accurate analysis is crucial to the success of a memorandum, we return to this topic below in Section D(3), *Writing as Thinking*.

## 2. Format for a Question of Law Memo

If the memo involves just a question of law, or you are asked to use a more abbreviated format you may not need a full memo format. Instead, an alternative format to consider is one that begins with an Introduction in which you include the facts that give rise to the question and you set out the issue statement at the end of the Introduction. Follow the Introduction with a Conclusion or Short Answer and then with a Discussion.

The first issue in the Statute of Frauds case discussed earlier is a question of law: whether a multi-year contract that includes a defeasance clause comes within the Statute. If your memo assignment was confined to that one issue, you could use this abbreviated format. The Introduction would include the facts of the parties' negotiation and the terms of their agreement. The section would end with the issue as set out above in Section B(1) (b)(i). The Conclusion would be a paragraph summarizing the Discussion, or a one or two sentence Short Answer, and the Discussion would analyze the two conflicting interpretations and explain the writer's prediction based on related Hawaii Statute of Frauds cases.

———————————————— *Exercise 8.5* ————————————————

*You are a senior associate with a law firm. A new associate has given you this draft of the opening paragraphs of the first part of a Discussion section of a memo analyzing the validity of a contract for the sale of a house. You want to explain to the associate how to change this part of the Discussion. Identify*

*the changes that the new associate must make. Then rewrite the paragraphs,*
*adding material if you wish.*

## Discussion

The elements necessary to prove fraud are well outlined in the body of Michigan case law. In order to constitute actionable fraud: (1) Orosco must prove that the Smiths made material misrepresentations that were false; (2) the Smiths knew that their statements were false when they made it or made it recklessly without knowledge of its truth and as a positive statement; (3) the Smiths made a misrepresentation with intention that it should be acted upon by Orosco; (4) and Orosco acted upon it; and (5) that Orosco suffered injury due to it. These requirements are clearly set forth in both *Price v. Long Realty, Inc.*, 199 Mich. App. 461 (1993) and *State-William v. Gale*, 169 Mich. App. 170 (1988).

It is necessary that all elements be proven by Orosco or else a claim of fraud will not stand. So, the Smiths must have known at the time of making their Seller Disclosure Statements that the statements they were making were false. However, if there is knowledge on Orosco's part that he knows any of the Smiths' representations were false or that he had reason to believe beforehand that the representation of the property could have been other than true then Orosco cannot claim fraud: "Nevertheless, there can be no fraud where the means of knowledge regarding the truthfulness of the representation are available to the plaintiff and the degree of their utilization has not been prohibited." *Webb v. First Michigan Corporation*, 195 Mich. App. 470, 472, 491 N.W.2d 851, 853 (1992). *See also Schuler v. American Motors Sales Corp.*, 39 Mich. App. 276, 279-280, 197 N.W.2d 493 (1972).

## C. SAMPLE MEMO

TO:     Partner
FROM:  Summer Associate
RE:     Mr. Donald Sinclair
DATE:   August 1, 2008

FACTS: Our client, Donald Sinclair, is the defendant in a defamation lawsuit brought by Ms. Samantha Goble. Ms. Goble claims to have been defamed by Donald Sinclair because of his erroneous statement in a book that he published. Sinclair stated that Ms. Goble was convicted of perjury in connection with a well-known criminal trial that took place eight years ago. Mr. Sinclair authored a book in 2007, *Families in Court*, in which he wrote about the impact on family members of various well-known lawsuits. One chapter was about the Tess Byerman case. In 2000, Tess Byerman was tried for obstruction of justice along with Byerman's lover, Jack Prizzi, and Ms. Goble's mother, Judge Hortense Goble. Ms. Goble served as a witness in that trial. Sinclair misstated that Ms. Goble had been convicted of perjury after her participation in the Byerman trial. Contrary to this statement, Ms. Goble had neither been charged with nor convicted of perjury. If Ms. Goble is a limited purpose public figure for purposes of this litigation, she must prove that Sinclair acted with malice.[5]

The events leading up to the trial began in 1997, when Judge Goble advised her daughter to apply for a job with the District of Columbia Department of Consumer Affairs.[6] Ms. Goble, who had been unemployed, took her mother's advice and applied for a job as the Assistant to the Personnel Coordinator. The Director of the Department of Consumer Affairs at that time was Ms. Tess Byerman, a former Miss America and a well known political figure. Ms. Byerman hired Ms. Goble after a telephone interview. Around this time, Byerman's lover, Jack Prizzi, was in divorce proceedings presided over by Judge Goble. Mr. Prizzi had asked the Judge to significantly reduce his alimony payments, and the Judge granted his request shortly after her daughter secured a job with Ms. Byerman. Prizzi was a construction contractor who had several important contracts with the city.

After working as a records clerk at the Department of Consumer Affairs for two years, Ms. Goble began to suspect that Ms. Byerman had hired her in an attempt to influence the outcome of Mr. Prizzi's divorce proceedings. She approached the U.S. Attorney, Mr. Tony Valiant, and

---

[5] Paragraph providing a brief overview of the defamation issue.

[6] Paragraphs explaining facts in chronological order begins here.

agreed to aid him in investigating and prosecuting her mother, Ms. Byerman, and Mr. Prizzi for obstruction of justice. Formal charges were filed against each of the three, alleging that Ms. Byerman had sought a reduction in Mr. Prizzi's alimony payments by hiring Judge Goble's daughter, and that Judge Goble did in fact reduce the alimony payments.

The Byerman trial received significant public attention, stemming largely from extensive media coverage around the country. During the trial, Ms. Goble served as the prosecution's main witness, and as a result, she became a central focus of the media coverage. After the defendants were acquitted of the charges, Ms. Goble appeared in a press conference to discuss the trial, and later appeared on a television talk show where she received a professional makeover and made some minimal comments about the trial.

This case has been brought in federal district court in the District of Columbia. The Court of Appeals for the District of Columbia has constructed a three-part test for determining a defamation plaintiff's status as a limited purpose public figure, and as requested, this memo will discuss only the first factor, which is whether the issue involved is a public controversy.[7]

QUESTION PRESENTED:[8] Is a criminal trial for obstruction of justice a "public controversy," as required by the law of defamation in this circuit, if the trial involved obstruction of justice by three defendants, and the trial received substantial publicity and raised issues about the integrity of the judicial system?

CONCLUSION:[9] Although it is a close question, Ms. Goble's participation in the Byerman trial is a "public controversy" under the law in this circuit. The D.C. Court of Appeals defines a public controversy as one that is "debated publicly" and has "substantial ramifications for non-participants." The Byerman trial was debated publicly in the local and national media at the time. Further, the outcome of the trial had substantial ramifications for non-participants because of the issues of government corruption and official misbehavior that were at the base

---

[7] Explanation of limitation of the assignment.

[8] The question is written with the law first, then the facts. This question involves only the public controversy issue. A question about Ms. Goble as a public figure could be written as "Is a witness in a criminal trial for obstruction of justice a limited purpose public figure for purposes of her defamation claim, and the trial a public controversy, if the trial involved. . . ."

[9] The conclusion begins with an answer to the question, then provides the law (the rule in that jurisdiction), a brief analysis, and the consequence of that analysis (Ms. Goble must prove malice).

of the charges against the defendants. Ms. Goble is a limited purpose public figure, and she will have to prove that Mr. Sinclair acted with malice.

DISCUSSION:[10] Ms. Goble's suit for defamation against Donald Sinclair hinges on whether she sues as a private citizen or as a limited purpose public figure. A limited purpose public figure must prove that the defendant acted with malice, that is, acted with knowledge or with reckless disregard as to the truth of the defamatory statement. *Gertz v. Robert Welch, Inc.*, 418 U.S. 323 (1974). A private figure need prove only negligence. Ms. Goble is a limited purpose public figure. She will not be able to prove that Sinclair acted with malice, however.

The District of Columbia uses a three-part test to determine whether a plaintiff is a limited purpose public figure: (i) was there a public controversy, (ii) did the plaintiff thrust herself to the forefront of that controversy, and (iii) was the alleged defamation germane to the public controversy? *Waldbaum v. Fairchild Publications, Inc.*, 627 F.2d 1287, 1296-97 (D.C. Cir. 1980). This memo analyzes only the first part of that definition.[11]

The D.C. Court of Appeals defines a public controversy as one that is "debated publicly" and has "substantial ramifications for non-participants." *Id.* at 1297. To determine whether an issue is a public controversy, however, several Supreme Court decisions must first be considered. The Supreme Court has never held that a plaintiff was a limited purpose public figure. *See Hutchinson v. Proxmire*, 443 U.S. 111 (1979); *Wolston v. Reader's Digest Assn.*, 443 U.S. 157 (1979); *Time, Inc. v. Firestone*, 424 U.S. 448 (1976); *Gertz*, 418 U.S. 323.

The first element of a "public controversy" is that the issue must be "debated publicly." There are several Supreme Court decisions that specify the types of public attention that can give rise to the level of public debate necessary for a public controversy. First, the Supreme Court has held that there is no public controversy if everyone agrees that something is undesirable, and therefore the issue is not "debatable." In *Hutchinson v. Proxmire*, the Court held that the question of profligate government spending was not a public controversy because the public generally agrees that such spending is bad. 443 U.S. at 135. In *Wolston v. Reader's Digest Assn.*, the Court held that Soviet espionage in the United States could not be a public controversy because the entire nation was opposed to it. 443 U.S. at 167 n. 8. Similarly, there is no dispute that judges should not be bribed. Thus, the Byerman trial would not be

---

[10] The first paragraph gives an overview of the defamation topic.

[11] This paragraph and the next set out the rules in the jurisdiction.

a public controversy merely because a judge's integrity was at stake since official misbehavior is universally condemned in society.[12]

The Supreme Court has established some further limits on what types of public attention may create a public controversy. The Court has noted that newsworthiness and public interest do not automatically transform an issue into a public controversy. *See Firestone*, 424 U.S. at 458. Most notably for Ms. Goble, the Supreme Court has specifically held that private litigation does not become a public controversy merely because the public takes an interest in its outcome. *Id. See also Hutchinson*, 443 U.S. 111; *Wolston*, 443 U.S. 157. In *Firestone*, the Court held that the well-publicized divorce trial of a woman and her socially prominent husband was not a public controversy despite extensive newspaper coverage and public awareness and interest in the case. The Court noted that the plaintiff in *Firestone* "assumed no special prominence in the resolution of public questions," and therefore her private divorce proceedings were not a public controversy. 424 U.S. at 454–55. None of the litigation involved in these precedents, however, involved issues with the public impact of the obstruction of justice trial involved here. Although the Byerson litigation also provided lurid details of the defendants' private lives, unlike the plaintiff in *Firestone*, Ms. Goble assumed a special prominence in resolving a question of public importance—bribery of public officials.

Unlike the Supreme Court, the D.C. Court of Appeals has held that several seemingly private issues were public controversies.[13] The D.C. Court of Appeals has consistently linked these issues with a viable public interest. *See Tavoulareas v. Piro*, 817 F.2d 762 (D.C. Cir. 1987) (report of nepotism in oil industry); *Dameron v. Washington Magazine*, 779 F.2d 736 (D.C. Cir. 1985) (report blaming air controller for accident).

The court has steadily held that disputes that can be linked to the government are public controversies because of the need for the public and the press to monitor government officials. *See Clyburn v. News World Communications*, 903 F.2d 29, 32 (D.C. Cir. 1990). *Clyburn* involved a narcotics case where the plaintiff had business and personal ties to D.C. government officials. The case was a public controversy because it involved corruption of officials. In *Tavoulareas*, 817 F.2d at 773, the plaintiff was president of Mobil Corporation accused of nepotism toward his son. The issue was a public controversy because it involved government policy toward the oil industry. In *Dameron*, 779 F.2d 736, the dispute caused by a plane crash was a public controversy because

---

[12] This paragraph and the next analyze the Supreme Court precedents because of the weight of their authority.

[13] This paragraph introduces the cases from the D.C. Court of Appeals.

it involved the management of a program administered by the F.A.A. Underlying each of these decisions is an issue or debate that involved some area of the government. Based on these cases, the D.C. Court of Appeals shows a clear willingness to label a trial a public controversy if it can make even a tenuous connection between the subject of the trial and the government. The connection between the subject of the trial and government here is more than tenuous. The trial involved a sitting judge, a head of a city department with close connections to the mayor, and a contractor who had worked for the city. Thus, the court will likely hold that the Byerman trial involved a public controversy.

The second element of a public controversy under the law of this circuit is that it must have "substantial ramifications for non-participants." *Waldbaum*, 627 F.2d at 1297.[14] Whether an issue has substantial ramifications for non-participants depends upon the framing of the issue in the case. The Supreme Court has established a pattern of framing the issue narrowly, so that very few instances of private litigation had substantial effects on the public. In *Gertz*, 418 U.S. at 352–53, the Court defined the controversy as the plaintiff's representation of a private client in litigation, not as public debate over a police officer's conviction for murder. In *Hutchinson*, 443 U.S. at 134, the Court defined the controversy as the defendant's defamatory statement, not the use of government funding. And in *Firestone*, 424 U.S. at 454, the Court defined the controversy as the legal resolution of the Firestones' divorce proceedings, not marital difficulties of extremely wealthy individuals generally.[15]

Based on these decisions, the issue presented in Ms. Goble's case could be narrowed to focus only on her testimony in the Byerman trial about the circumstances of her hiring and the nature of her job, instead of the entire trial with its implications of official corruption. Her testimony could be characterized as having little to do with any broad issues of public concern, and therefore having had no substantial effects on the public. If the issue in Ms. Goble's case is narrowly framed, her participation does not rise to the level of a public controversy.

However, under D.C. precedents, because the Byerman trial had a strong link to the government, it may have had "substantial ramifications for non-participants."[16] Under D.C. law, the ramifications must be felt by persons who are not direct participants, *Waldbaum*, 627 F.2d at 1296, and the controversy must be a "real dispute, the outcome of which effects the general public or some segment of it in an appreciable way." *Id.* Like the *Clyburn* case, where the plaintiff had some business and

---

[14] Topic sentence introduces second element of the public controversy rule.

[15] The paragraph again analyzes Supreme Court cases.

[16] Topic sentence transition to D.C. cases.

personal ties to the government, the Byerman trial involved officials within the city government, including a sitting judge and the Director of Consumer Affairs. Although Ms. Goble was only a minor employee in the Department of Consumer Affairs, the decisions in *Tavoulareas* and *Dameron* clearly demonstrate that the D.C. Court of Appeals has a tendency to frame controversies broadly. The plaintiff in *Dameron* was just an air traffic controller but he was involved in a well-publicized and tragic airplane crash involving the F.A.A. Because of the involvement of high ranking officials, the Byerman trial raised fundamental questions about the integrity of the judicial system and the qualifications of its officers. With issues like these at stake, the D.C. Court of Appeals will likely rule that the Byerman trial had substantial ramifications for the public.

In conclusion, a court in this circuit will likely categorize the Byerman trial as one raising issues about judicial integrity and government corruption. Combined with the fact that the Byerman trial received extensive public attention during and after its time in court, the court will most likely rule that it was a public controversy.[17]

---

[17] Concluding paragraph on this issue.

## D. WRITING PROCESS

### 1. Gathering Information: Understanding the Assignment

A partner assigns a memo to get an answer to a specific question or to get specific information that the partner needs. To write a good memo, the associate should answer that question or provide that information. So the associate must be sure to understand the assignment. When the partner assigns the memo, the associate should ask questions and write down the answers, being sure to do the following.

- Get all the relevant facts, including procedural facts. Make sure you know who the parties are.
- Get all the relevant documents to review, for example, pleadings and motions if the case involves ongoing litigation; the client's prior wills and intervivos estate planning documents if the issue involves estate planning; divorce decrees and property settlement agreements if the issue involves post-divorce litigation; corporate by-laws; leases, etc.
- Determine whether the issue is limited to a particular jurisdiction or involves a broader survey of law.
- Determine how widely your research should range: should you include legislative history or just interpretative case law? Should you investigate analogous areas of the law or confine the subject matter to the exact issue?
- Determine how the memorandum will be used: are you to write adversarily so that your memo can be inserted into an appellate brief or into a memorandum supporting or opposing a motion? Or should you write more "objectively," analyzing both sides of the issue?
- If you are new to the firm and do not know its policy, find out whether there are restrictions on the use of online research time.
- Determine how soon the memo is needed and if the partner wants oral updates if this assignment involves a pressing issue.

Unless you are working on a very short deadline, check back periodically with the partner to make sure that you are on the right track, especially if your initial research raises more questions. If you have questions about an assignment, always ask.

## 2. Gathering Information: Researching the Issues

This book is not the place to teach you how to do legal research. You most likely learned the basics of legal research in your first-year writing or research course, and from the many texts available about legal research. But a few points are in order here when you do research for a memo.

- Put together a comprehensive research plan of the sources you will use, so that, if the assigning partner asks, "did you check X?" "did you check Y?" you can answer "yes."
- If your research involves an area of law with which you are not familiar, go first to secondary sources such as treatises or encyclopedias. These sources will give you background information and suggest search terms to use for indexes and online research. Do not use Boolean searches as your only tool for research in primary sources.
- Make sure you read all important cases yourself and do not just read the case headnotes. Do not be satisfied with descriptions in treatises, law reviews, and other materials.
- Be accurate when you describe cases and identify relevant constitutional, statutory, and regulatory language.
- Update your research. If a case you rely on has been overruled or a statute amended, your memo will probably be worthless.
- To avoid plagiarism, be careful to put quotations in quotation marks in your written notes, your downloaded documents, and your final memo, and to attribute ideas to their sources. When you download text to your computer, initiate a system to show when you are downloading quotations. For example, change the font or format of the text, or highlight or change the color of the font. By doing so, you will remember to quote and attribute the language.

- When you take notes from your research, cite accurately and fully so that you are not left scurrying to find the correct volume or page at the last minute and so that you provide your reader with accurate information.

## 3. Writing as Thinking

Creativity and insights in analogizing and distinguishing cases, in interpreting text, and in relating your interpretations to the policies or goals underlying the law may enable you to take on a case that at first seemed unpromising and will set you off as an able lawyer. Thus, don't spend all your time doing research and fail to leave enough time to think and write. Start to write when you have enough to think about and expect to do more research on questions that arise during the writing process. A writer's best ideas often come after she has begun writing.

Moreover, a strong analysis requires that you be creative and thoughtful. You rarely will find a case that is perfectly on point. Instead you may need to use some imagination, using analogies and distinctions not only from caselaw on the exact issues involved, but also from other closely related areas of law, if you can make plausible arguments.

One of your first tasks as you do your research is to identify the controlling statutes and relevant cases and to determine what they mean. One of the first questions your Discussion should answer is "what is the law in this particular jurisdiction?" So you must know the controlling law in that state, or the law in a particular federal circuit for federal cases, and know where that law comes from. Beyond those binding precedents, go on to bring in persuasive precedents only if they are factually or otherwise relevant, and be sure to make their relevance clear. Many issues, especially federal statutory ones, generate an impressive volume of caselaw. You have to decide which ones you will rely on and include in your Discussion. Your reader should not be left wondering, for example, why, for a case involving defamation law of the District of Columbia Circuit, you rely on cases from district courts in other circuits if the facts of those cases do not seem particularly relevant.

Carefully explain what the law means, that is, how the courts have applied it, and how those interpretations of the law will apply to your case. Explain and evaluate the arguments for your client and those that the opposing party will likely raise. In order to be persuasive, the reasons that you put forward should be legally significant; they should answer the questions that lawyers expect you to answer. A discussion is not adequate if it merely describes cases, quotes from them, and then supplies a concluding sentence like "therefore, in our case . . . , " without explaining the analogies and differences.

Moreover, do not forget the importance of using policy to strengthen your analysis. For example, if you were the attorney for Ms. Goble in the sample memo in Section C, you might add a paragraph like the one that follows to your analysis of the Supreme Court cases.

> A strong policy argument also stems from the Supreme Court's ruling that private litigation should not necessarily become a public controversy. Although the Byerman trial raised public issues, this should not be sufficient to determine that trials are public controversies. All trials, after all, can be said to raise important public issues. The trial of a recidivist criminal could be said to raise important public issues about our prison system. A divorce proceeding could be said to raise important public issues about the continuing viability of the institution of marriage. Every trial could be considered a public controversy and every active participant in those trials a public figure. This would create a virtual "open season" for defamation, an unwelcome consequence foreseen by the *Wolston* court. 443 U.S. at 169. If participating in a trial makes them more vulnerable to defamation, citizens will think twice before becoming involved in a lawsuit, or even worse, before voluntarily coming forward with information that would lead to testimony in a trial.

Different issues require different approaches. For example, a memo analyzing the case for a school board that involves student prayer at graduation will mainly emphasize distinctions from the facts of two or three Supreme Court precedents holding unconstitutional prayer at school events. On the other hand, if a memo analyzes whether a five-year employment contract comes within the Statute of Frauds if it includes a defeasance clause, and it is written for a case in a jurisdiction in which there are no relevant precedents, the writer will have to choose from a large number of cases decided in several state courts.

In Section C of Chapter 6, *Persuasion*, we discuss types of legally significant arguments: arguments from precedent, from interpreting texts, from public policy, and from institutional competence. These form the repertoire of your analysis section.

## 4. Writing Recursively

Because writing is thinking memorialized on paper, as you write, you are continuing to map out what you want to say. Often, these new ideas require you to fill in with more research, and to continue to edit your work. Thus, although you assemble your memo in a sequence of facts, issues, conclusion, discussion, you will rarely ever write in that sequence. Instead you will find that you write recursively—writing drafts of some sections, then going back and rewriting what you have already done.

One sequence that may be helpful is to begin with a rough statement of the issue or issues to keep you focused, and then outline or list the most relevant facts. Then write the Discussion, going through enough drafts to complete that section. After you write the Discussion, write the facts, making sure to include all the facts that you relied on in the Discussion. Rewrite the issue or issues into readable interrogative sentences. You can then summarize your discussion and write the Conclusion section. Many attorneys finish a final draft of the Discussion before they complete the other sections, and they write the Conclusion last.

Put the memo aside for as long as possible. Then read through the entire document to edit. Editing is not the same as proofreading. To proofread, you read through to correct typing errors, spelling errors, citation errors, etc. To edit your memo, you read through to make substantive, organizational, and sentence structure changes. Many people edit in stages. This process takes time, so you must have your first draft completed with some time left before the memo is due. Some editing stages to consider are to edit for substance, that is, whether you have analyzed the issues adequately, supported your conclusions, and not omitted logical steps. Then edit for organization and logical sequence. The information should be in a sequence that responds to your reader's needs: your paragraphs should be coherent, and your text should clearly show relationships among information, for example, by using introductions and transitions. Next edit for clarity, by checking your sentence structure and your grammar.

Most writers know their writing weaknesses and pay careful attention to correct them in the editing process. For example, if you use passive voice inappropriately, make sure you edit at the sentence level to rewrite into active voice sentences wherever possible. If you organize carefully and use clear sentence structure, you will become sought-after for your writing ability.

Finally, proofread for typos and spelling and citation errors.

---

### *Assignment 8.1*

*Darlene Romero married Ed Day in the State of Pacifica in 1990. Ed had two daughters, ages 7 and 9, from a previous marriage. The daughters lived with their father and stepmother (Ed and Darlene) for the next seven years, when they moved out voluntarily to live with their mother Jane and her new husband. Jane then successfully petitioned the family court to become the children's legal custodial parent. Jane also petitioned to set a child support obligation on Darlene Romero, who has filed an objection. The court ruled against Darlene and she has appealed to the Court of Appeals.*

*The legal issue involves the state of Pacifica family support statute that requires stepparents to contribute to their stepchildren's support. The statute reads:*

> The expenses of the family, including stepchildren, are chargeable upon the property of both husband and wife or either of them. When a petition for divorce or for legal separation is filed upon motion of the stepparent, the court may terminate the stepparent's obligation to support the stepchildren. The obligation to support the stepchildren ceases upon the entry of a decree of divorce or legal separation or upon death.

*Consider the following legal history:*

1. At common law, a custodial stepparent incurs a duty to support a stepchild by establishing a parental relationship with the child. The obligation ends when the child voluntarily leaves the stepparent's home.

2. In 1980, the state legislature enacted the family support statute in its form above, to include stepparents and stepchildren.

3. In 1990, in *Sanders v. Ella*, the Court of Appeals of an appellate district different from the one to which Romero appealed held that a stepparent's duty to support may be terminated by an event not specifically included in the statute. In *Sanders*, that event was the voluntary departure of the stepchild from the home.

4. In 1982, the state supreme court decided *Van v. Thomas* in which the court stated that the legislature must use clear and unambiguous language to depart from the common law. In *Van*, the lower court had held that a stepparent had become obligated to contribute to a stepchild's support although the stepchild had never lived with the stepparent and the stepparent had never established a parental relationship. The supreme court reversed on the ground that the statute had not changed the common law rule of when the duty to support arises.

5. In 1982, the state supreme court decided *State v. Gill*, a criminal action to enforce the state's criminal nonsupport statute, which was originally enacted at the same time as the family support statute. The criminal nonsupport statute imposes on stepparents a duty to support their stepchildren and provides that "with regard to stepchildren the obligation shall cease upon termination of the relationship of husband and wife." Violation is a misdemeanor.

In *Gill*, the court held that a stepfather who had separated from his wife continued to owe support to her children because the statutorily required event had not occurred.

*What kinds of arguments can you make as Jane's attorney? As Darlene Romero's attorney? Consider the following types of arguments, and explain how they apply to this case. Evaluate their strength.*

a. statutes in derogation of the common law are strictly construed
b. the plain meaning rule
c. expressio unius est exclusio alterius
d. statutes in pari materia should be construed together
e. if the legislature is dissatisfied with judicial enforcement of a statute, the legislature can amend the statute or return to the common law
f. legislative intent: the policy behind the family support statute regarding stepparents is to protect creditors by increasing the number of potential parties liable for the family's debts
g. legislative intent: the policy behind the criminal support statute is to preserve public funds by ensuring private support for minor children

h. the court must follow its own precedents
i. the lower court's decision is unfair
j. the result of enforcing the statute's literal language
k. judicial efficiency of enforcing the statutory bright line rule

*Now write the Discussion for a memo as the attorney for either Darlene Romero or Jane.*

---

## E. SPECIAL CONCERNS: OBJECTIVITY AND PERSUASION

There is a special tension that arises from a memo's dual purpose. The assigning attorney wants a full and accurate analysis of the issues; so memos are often called "objective" writing. But the attorney also wants to know all the arguments that can be made for the client and how you evaluate their persuasive force. The attorney does not want to give up the client's case easily, and usually wants to know, "do I have a viable claim here?" No lawyer wants to send the client out the door saying, "there's no case here," when, in fact, there may be a case there, and it very well may be one that is worth pursuing.

One difference between an office memo to a colleague and an advocacy document to a judicial decision-maker is that, in a memo, you would acknowledge the strengths of the opposing arguments and the extent to which they weaken your case. In a document to a decision-maker, you concede only those arguments that do not significantly hurt your case. For example, you may concede that the facts of a case on which you rely are distinguishable from your case, but make the point that the court's reasoning is still relevant to your facts. In a memo, however, you would acknowledge that because of the difference in the facts, the court's reasoning in the case on which you rely is not as relevant.

Only when you are asked for a memo to analyze a pure question of law, such as how an amendment changes a particular statute, may the attorney be satisfied with a purely "objective" analysis. Even in this circumstance, however, the attorney may be looking for you to give reasons to interpret the amendment in a way that will favor the client's needs.

Thus, the value of a memorandum lies in the strength of its analysis. The attorney for whom you write the memo is looking for you to evaluate the issues by analyzing all the arguments that can fairly be made. When those arguments are thoroughly supported and thoughtfully evaluated, an "objective" memorandum becomes a persuasive one as well.

———————————————— *Exercise 8.6* ————————————————

*Evaluate the weaknesses in the following memorandum, explaining your reasons. Rewrite the Facts, the Question, and Part D of the Discussion.*

Facts

A third party (the "Drawer") drew a check in the amount of $68,000.00 (the "Funds") payable to the order of John Moore (the "Payee"). Subsequently, Warren Kay Securities, Inc., (the "Customer"), a customer of Bank of Lakewood (the "Depository Bank") deposited the check ostensibly bearing the endorsement of the Payee into its business account at the Depository Bank. The Depository Bank processed the check (presumably in its usual fashion, although the facts are not clear on this point) and sent it along the "collection stream" to Mammon Bank, the Drawer's bank (the "Drawee Bank"). The check was paid by the Drawee Bank and the Funds credited to the Customer's business account at the Depository Bank.

At least three months later, the Depository Bank was contacted by the Customer who alleged that the endorsement of the Payee on the check was a forgery.

Question Presented

What is the potential liability of the Depository Bank to the following parties under Illinois law:

A. The Drawer
B. The Payee
C. The Drawee Bank.

Short Answer

Under the Uniform Commercial Code (the "UCC") and the case law, the Depository Bank may be held liable to the Drawer, the Payee or the Drawee Bank. However, the Depository Bank will be able to recover from the Customer.

Discussion

For the purposes of this discussion, it is assumed that the check was taken by a thief ("the Thief") who forged the endorsement on the check and transferred it to the Customer.

A. <u>The Drawer</u>. The Payee may sue the Depository Bank directly for conversion under UCC § 3-419. UCC § 3-419(1)(c) provides that an instrument is converted when it is paid on a forged endorsement. UCC § 3-419, on its face, deals only with actions by "true owners." Thus, by the bare terms of this provision, only the Payee, the "owner" of the check, may use § 3-419 to recover against the Depository Bank. However, the weight of authority supports the existence of a cause of action by the Drawer against the Depository Bank. *Justus Company, Inc. v. Gary Wheaton Bank,* 509 F. Supp. 103, 106 (N.D. Ill. 1981). *See also Greishaber v. Michigan National Bank,* 18 UCC 1248 (Mich. C.P. 1976); *Jones v. Commonwealth Bank & Trust Co.,* 19 UCC 1194 (Pa. D. 1976). The Court in *Justus* relied primarily on pre-UCC law to justify its finding. Pre-Code cases specifically permitted an action by a drawer against a depository bank. *Justus* at 106. Therefore, the Drawer may proceed directly against the Depository Bank under UCC §3-419 for conversion. Note that this cause of action is valid even against a depository bank who acted in good faith and in accordance with reasonable commercial standards. UCC §3-419 (3); *Justus* at 105.

B. <u>The Payee</u>. As discussed above, the Payee has a cause of action for conversion against the Depository Bank under UCC § 3-419. *Justus. Accord, Burks Drywall, Inc. v. Washington Bank and Trust Company,* 110 Ill. App.3d 569 (2d Dist. 1982).

C. <u>The Drawee Bank</u>. If the Drawee Bank is forced to recredit the Drawer's account under UCC § 4-401 because the Drawee Bank paid on a forged endorsement on a check, the Drawee Bank will seek to sue "upstream" against the parties who passed the check onto the Drawee Bank and warranted title under UCC § 4-207 (1) (a). UCC § 4-207 (1) (a) provides that each customer or collecting bank who obtains payment or acceptance of an item warrants to the payor bank that he has good title to the item. In this case, the Customer warranted its good title to the check to the Depository Bank and the Depository Bank warranted its good title to the Drawee Bank. Thus, the Drawee Bank may proceed against the Depository Bank or the Customer, and the Depository Bank has a cause of action against the Customer. In *Michigan National Bank v. American National Bank & Trust Company,* 34 Ill. App.3d 30 (1st Dist. 1975), the Court affirmed the Circuit Court's grant of summary judgment in favor of the drawee bank against the collecting bank which had warranted its title to a check with a forged endorsement and in favor of the collecting bank against the depository bank for the same reason.

D. <u>Reasonable Time</u>. UCC § 4-207 (4) provides that, unless a claim for a breach of warranty (under 4-207 (1)) is made within a reasonable time after the person claiming learns of the breach, the person liable is discharged to the extent of any loss caused by the delay in making the claim. There are few Code cases determining what constitutes a "reasonable time." Moreover, what notification would be deemed "reasonable" in a specific case depends upon the activities reviewed and the surrounding circumstances. *Home Indemnity Co. v. First National Bank of Waukegan,* 659 F.2d 796, 799 (7th Cir. 1981). In some cases, lengthy delays in reporting forgeries will not defeat a warranty claim if no damages resulted from the delays. *Id.* at 799. In *Home,* a series of errors and delays prevented the plaintiff from notifying the defendant of a forged endorsement for more than six weeks after the plaintiff had notice. The Court held that, in light of modern methods of communication with the availability of immediate electronic transmission of information, the delay in this case was unreasonable as a matter of law. *Id.* at 799. Cases from other jurisdictions provide a range of "reasonable time" from five days, in *Twellman v. Lindell Trust Co.,* 534 S.W.2d 83 (Mo. App. 1976), to sixteen months, in *Continental Bank & Trust Co. v. American Bank & Trust Co.,* 217 Pa. Super. 371 (1970).

In the case at hand, it is unknown at present how much time had passed before the Depository Bank was notified of the forged endorsement. However, the following points should be noted. UCC § 4-207 (4) only governs what is a reasonable time to assert a breach of warranty of title under § 4-207(1) (a). Thus, a delay in giving notice of a forged endorsement can only be a defense against a party receiving such a warranty—a collecting bank or the drawee bank. *Home* at 798. Therefore, unless the Drawee Bank itself had notice of the forgery, the issue of "reasonable time" under § 4-207 (4) does not arise in this case.

E. <u>Negligence</u>. There are several parties in the case at hand whose negligence, if it can be proven, would operate as an affirmative defense to the Depository Bank's liability as to that party. Thus, if the Drawer was negligent in not reporting in a timely fashion a forged endorsement of which he was aware, the Drawer would not be successful in an action against the Depository Bank for conversion. Or, if the Drawer was negligent in permitting the check to fall into the hands of the Thief, such negligence would operate to defeat his claim. Similarly, if the Payee had been expecting the check from the Drawer, and did not notify the Drawer that he had not received such check three months later, his negligence may be sufficient to relieve the Depository Bank of liability to the Payee.

Likewise, it seems clear that the Customer was negligent in accepting the check from the Thief with a forged endorsement. In fact, the Customer, the "first solvent party after the Thief," is likely to bear the ultimate liability for the loss.

## Conclusion

In the case of a forged endorsement, the Drawer, the Payee and the Drawee Bank may all proceed against the Depository Bank and will likely be successful. However, the loss will ultimately rest on the Customer.

─────────────── *Assignment 8.2* ───────────────

*Write a sentence outline of a Discussion section for the second issue in the Statute of Frauds problem, set out below, under Hawaii law. Then write the Discussion, analyzing the issue of whether the statute's requirement of a writing signed by the party to be charged had been satisfied by the two letters.*

You are a clerk for Judge William Bradley of the General Trial Court of Bear County in the state of Hawaii. An action was recently filed in Judge Bradley's court in which Barry Astor sued Geoff Hall and the firm of Hall & Hall. The offices of Hall & Hall are in Honolulu, Hawaii.

The pleadings and documents filed with the court reveal the following facts. The plaintiff, Astor, is a May 2008 graduate of the University of Atlantis, a prestigious law school. During his third year in law school, Astor interviewed with several firms but Hall & Hall was clearly his first choice. Astor had a romantic relationship with a law student who was in his class and was from Hawaii. During January of 2008, Astor had several meetings with different attorneys employed by Hall & Hall. On January 30, 2008, Astor received a call from Geoff Hall who said that his firm was ready to offer Astor employment and that he wanted to meet for a final time to discuss the details of a possible agreement.

On January 31, Astor flew to Honolulu to look around and to accept the firm's offer so long as the terms were reasonable. During his meeting with Hall on February 1, Astor was told that he would start work on June 1, 2008, at a beginning salary of $70,000 per year, to be increased to $82,000 at the end of June 2009. This agreement was to last for five years at which time a new contract would be offered, which, if everything went well, would make Astor a partner in the firm.

During the same meeting, Hall also informed Astor that the firm could terminate Astor's employment without liability within the first eighteen months if Astor's performance as an attorney did not comply with the traditional standards of Hall & Hall. In order to ease the impact of such a provision, Hall quickly told Astor that, if during that same eighteen months he became unhappy or dissatisfied working for Hall & Hall, he could also terminate the agreement without liability.

These latter provisions did not bother Astor as he was confident after an excellent performance in law school that he could meet the firm's standards. In addition, he was pleased with the option to terminate given to him because he was not sure he would like the climate in Hawaii or that he would be comfortable so far away from his family and friends. Also, his romantic relationship was getting a little shaky. After being treated to a magnificent lunch, Astor informed Hall that he would accept the firm's offer.

After this meeting Astor received the following letter from Hall & Hall signed by Geoff Hall.

February 14, 2008

Dear Mr. Astor:

On behalf of the entire firm of Hall & Hall I would like to congratulate you on your decision to join our firm. I was very pleased with the outcome of our last meeting and I am looking forward to your arrival in Hawaii.

Please write to me and let me know when you will be moving to Hawaii so that we may assist you in finding an apartment and in getting settled in general.

Sincerely,

Geoff Hall

After receiving the above letter, Astor replied in the following letter.

February 27, 2008

Dear Mr. Hall:

Thank you for your recent letter. I was also very pleased with our last meeting and I am thrilled to have accepted your offer which I understand to be the following: Employment to begin on June 1, 2008, at a starting salary of $70,000 per year, to be increased to $82,000 at the end of June 2009. I am also clear on the fact that this agreement is to last for five years, but that it may be terminated by the firm without liability and within 18 months if I do not comply with the traditional standards of performance at Hall & Hall. Similarly, I have the option to terminate without liability if I am unhappy or dissatisfied during the first eighteen months.

I will be arriving in Honolulu on May 15. I will call after that date, and thank you for your offer in your letter to help me get settled. I am looking forward to seeing you then.

Sincerely,

Barry Astor

Astor moved to Honolulu in May 2008. He commenced work on June 1 as planned. He soon made several new friends, planned to get married, and decided that it would be easy to get used to his new climate. However, on March 10, 2009, Astor was given notice that his employment was terminated. In disbelief Astor questioned Hall who said that Astor had not performed up to expectations.

After his discharge by Hall & Hall, Astor was unable to find employment as an attorney for several months. Another Honolulu firm finally hired him in July 2009, but his salary was only $60,000 per year. Astor has sued for breach of contract, alleging that Astor was fired for reasons other than his performance as an attorney and that up until he was fired his performance had been acceptable. But Hall & Hall has moved for summary judgment on the ground that the contract is barred by the Statute of Frauds because it is a contract not to be performed within a year from the making thereof, and the contract is not in a writing signed by him for the firm.

---

### *Assignment 8.3*

---

*Write a memorandum for the medical consent problem in Casefile 5 in Appendix A. The jurisdiction is the state of Kansas. Your research reveals two defenses for the doctor: he acted in an emergency and the plaintiff was a mature minor who could give her own valid consent. Write a memo that analyzes only the second question.*

---

### *Assignment 8.4*

---

*You are an aide to State of Pacifica legislator Bill Patterson, whose concern about the problem posed by strategic litigation against public participation ("SLAPP" suits) is detailed in Casefile 4 in Appendix A. Patterson would like you to write him a memo evaluating the widely contrasting "anti-SLAPP" statutes of other states. You will find those statutes in the Casefile, along with a description of the major issues posed by SLAPP suits and anti-SLAPP statutes. Two groups with opposing interests have been lobbying Pacifica legislators on the SLAPP issue. A consortium of grass-roots organizations—including environmental, historic preservation, and "anti-sprawl" groups—calling itself "Save Pacifica" would like to see a statute that provides broad protection for speech and petitioning rights, that provides mechanisms for accelerated resolution of SLAPP claims and award of costs and damages to SLAPP targets, and that places the heaviest possible burden on SLAPP filers. An association of real estate developers, builders, and property owners calling itself "Grow Pacifica," although resigned to some anti-SLAPP legislation, would like to see a statute that burdens the ordinary civil litigation process the least, allowing its members to take legal action against activists who needlessly raise the cost of doing business in Pacifica.*

*In your memo, explain to Patterson which features of which statute(s) would be most acceptable to "Save Pacifica" and which would be most acceptable to "Grow Pacifica," and why. Which statute(s) might be acceptable compromises for both sides? You do not need to do any research for this problem, but you do need to read the statutes carefully, think about the real-life impact of their provisions, and organize your memo so that a busy reader can grasp its analysis and recommendations in one reading.*

# Chapter 9

# *INFORMING AND PERSUADING: TRIAL AND APPELLATE BRIEFS*

---

## A. IN GENERAL

Lawyers write appellate briefs and trial briefs—the latter often called "trial memoranda of law"—in order to convince a court to rule in their favor. Because they thus share a general audience (judges) and a general purpose (persuasion), the two documents have much in common. Much of their similarity derives from the opposing pulls of audience and purpose—between the respectful, candid analysis the court demands and the committed partisanship that persuasion requires. Whether in a trial brief or appellate brief, the best persuasive writing for the court keeps candor and commitment in equilibrium. The basic formats and components of trial and appellate briefs are similar: questions presented, persuasive fact statements, and legal argument divided into sections by point headings. Effective trial and appellate briefs also employ the same rhetorical and conceptual strategies—the writing techniques described earlier, in the chapter on *Persuasion*.

Yet there are also differences between the two documents, differences arising out of their specific audiences and purposes. Most trial briefs are addressed during the pre-trial stages of litigation to busy judges who especially value concision and clarity. Such judges also look for arguments that will help them put the swiftest and fairest end to the litigation before them. Moreover, the audience for a trial brief is often a known quantity—a judge before whom the attorney or her colleagues has already appeared, whose temperament and views can be usefully taken into account.

The purpose of a trial brief in the pre-trial context is frequently complex. The primary purpose is of course to convince the judge to rule favorably on the motion before him. Nonetheless, the litigator often has secondary purposes—to educate the judge about a novel issue, to gain insight into the judge's reaction to the case, to make the case stand out from the mass of litigation in front of the judge, or to put the client in a sympathetic light. To suit their specific audiences and purposes, then, effective trial briefs tend to be short and sharply focused. They also tend to rely on practical, equitable, fact-based arguments rather than on lengthy consideration of precedent—unless, of course, analysis of the individual audience and purpose suggests otherwise.

Unlike trial judges, who are often known quantities, the audience for appellate briefs is most often generic and faceless. Appellate practitioners file their briefs in courts with many judges. Although the court as a whole may have a general jurisprudential leaning, fine-tuning for the specific idiosyncracies of audience is not a significant part of the appellate practitioner's strategy. Appellate court judges—especially high court judges—see themselves as guardians of the law, and although not blind to the equities of the case, they are ordinarily more concerned with the jurisprudential and institutional effects of their decisions than with the human drama.

The purpose of an appellate brief is also less complex than that of the trial brief. Appellant (sometimes called "petitioner") seeks reversal of the decision below; respondent (also called appellee)[1] seeks affirmance. Given audience and purpose, effective appellate briefs rely on sustained and sophisticated legal argument grounded in policy as well as precedent. Since appellant is usually the party seeking a change in the status quo, and reversal is a product no court really wants to buy, appellant occasionally with justification turns up the emotional level a bit, making a passionate (but dignified) appeal to justice. Respondent's purpose ordinarily dictates a different tone, one of calm reassurance that the right result was reached in the court below.

If appellate briefs require less fine-tuning for audience and purpose than do trial briefs, they pose a universe of procedural and doctrinal conundrums particular to the appellate context. Even assuming a compelling case on the merits, many obstacles loom between the writer and victory. Among the concepts ap-

---

[1] We call the parties to an appeal appellant and respondent throughout this chapter because "appellant" and "appellee" are so easily confused, both in reading and in writing.

pellate counsel must understand are finality, certiorari, preservation, standard of review, and harmless error. These concepts are rightfully the subject of entire texts.[2] The description of them that follows cannot begin to do justice to their subtlety. The brief writer must not only understand the rules that govern the appellate process, but also base complex and creative arguments on them, because they often determine the outcome of an appeal. Although in this respect counsel for appellant has both the hardest job and the greatest opportunities to "think outside the box," counsel for respondent must also know how to use the rules to benefit the client. For example, by convincing the court to apply a standard of review that is highly deferential to the decision of the trial court, counsel for respondent may prevail against counsel for appellant's stronger argument on the merits.

In most jurisdictions, only judgments or orders deemed "final" may be appealed. In a civil suit, "final" means there is nothing left to do but collect the judgment. Judgment in a criminal case is "final" when sentence is imposed. Decisions on pre-trial motions in civil suits are ordinarily not appealable unless, like an order granting summary judgment or dismissing a complaint, the court's decision puts an end to the litigation. Where a strict final judgment rule exists, as it does in the federal courts,[3] several narrow statutory and common-law exceptions permit appeals from non-final orders, which are known as "interlocutory" ("interrupting") appeals. A few jurisdictions, for example New York, permit most appeals from non-final orders in civil actions.[4] Litigators must know when appeal is permitted and when appellate review of an issue must wait.

Appellate counsel must also know when an appealable order or judgment is automatically appealable (appealable "as of right") and when, on the contrary, the court's permission ("leave to appeal" or "certiorari") is required. In different jurisdictions, permission to appeal is variously sought by motion, by letter, or by writ. No matter how or where sought, permission is rarely granted, and requests thus require skilled advocacy and careful

---

[2] *See, e.g.,* Ursula Bentele & Eve Cary, *Appellate Advocacy: Principles and Practice* (3d ed., Anderson Pub. 1998).

[3] *See* 28 U.S.C § 1291(2000); Fed. R. Civ. P. 58 (2003).

[4] N.Y. Civ. Prac. L. & R. § 5701 (McKinney 2003).

attention to court rules. Even where appeal is as of right, counsel does not have a free ride. The client's right to appeal will be lost unless counsel "takes" the appeal by filing a notice of appeal within the requisite time period, which is often quite short.

In addition, counsel must be familiar with the preservation doctrine. As a general rule, appellate courts will not consider issues that were not raised and resolved in the trial court. If the issue was not "preserved" by counsel below, the appellate practitioner will find himself with the uphill struggle of convincing the court that the issue concerns "plain error" that should be reviewed even though unpreserved. Moreover, the subject matter jurisdiction of high courts ordinarily does not permit them to review findings of fact, and intermediate courts, which ordinarily have the power to review such findings, are always reluctant to do so.

Assuming a final judgment, permission to appeal, and meritorious preserved issues within the court's subject matter jurisdiction, appellant still has a long and difficult road to reversal, and respondent still has opportunities to prevail. For example, the standard of review applied by the appellate court can determine the outcome. Where the issue is doctrinal, the appellate court will review it *"de novo"*—anew—giving no deference to the decision of the court below. In contrast to its rulings on the law, a trial court's findings of fact will be treated with great deference and will be reversed only if the appellate court deems them "clearly erroneous." Most trial rulings concerning the conduct of litigation are reviewed still more deferentially, subject to reversal only for the trial judge's "abuse of discretion." Appellate courts also treat verdicts in criminal cases with great deference, reversing only if "no reasonable juror" could have convicted the defendant. Although the distinctions among these standards of review sound clear-cut, sometimes it is not clear which standard should be applied,[5] and the brief-writer needs to argue for the application

---

[5] For example, although it is clear that *de novo* review applies to rulings on the law and the "clearly erroneous" standard applies to findings of fact made by a federal judge, questions of fact and questions of law are in reality the two ends of a spectrum. Between the two is a "no man's land" of "mixed questions of law and fact," some of which are closer to issues of law and some closer to issues of fact. Litigators regularly debate and courts consider the appropriateness of *de novo* review or review under the "clearly erroneous" standard or yet a third intermediary standard of review. Approaches to mixed questions vary from court to court, and the caselaw provides no easy answers for the appellate practitioner. *See* Bentele & Cary, *supra* n. 2.

of the standard of review that favors her client. *De novo* review favors appellants, because no deference is given to the decision of the trial court, and at the other end of the spectrum, review for abuse of discretion favors respondent.

Finally, where counsel for appellant argues that her client deserves a new trial because of an error on the part of the trial judge, if the error is deemed "harmless," the judgment will be affirmed. The error itself may have been a serious one, but unless appellant can demonstrate that it did serious damage to her case at trial, she will not be vindicated on appeal. Often, arguing the "merits" of an issue is the easy part—the real test of a brief-writer's skills is making a persuasive "harmless-error" argument. This requires an understanding of harmless-error doctrine and careful attention to the facts of the case. Like the rules regarding finality of judgments, preservation, and standard of review, harmless-error doctrine is an intellectual challenge in itself.

## B. COMPONENTS

The same menu of components serves both trial and appellate briefs, though trial briefs are ordinarily simpler, shorter, and more likely to vary their format to suit their content. Court rules tell the practitioner which components are required and frequently also specify the order of the components and impose a firm page limit. The basic brief components are *title page, question presented, table of contents (including point headings), table of authorities, jurisdictional statement, procedural history, statement of facts, summary of argument, argument with point headings,* and *conclusion.* These components are discussed below in the order in which they are ordinarily read; as discussed below in Section D, *Writing Process,* this is not the order in which they are ordinarily written.

With the exception of the title page, jurisdictional statement, procedural history, and conclusion, every component forwards the process of persuasion. It is helpful to think of the persuasive components as a progressive unfolding of your arguments—beginning with previews provided by the question presented, point headings, table of authorities, and fact statement; moving on to the summary of argument; and culminating in the closely argued points of argument themselves.

## 1. Front Matter

### a. Title page

The format and content of the title page is often specified in court rules. As with all boilerplate, pay careful attention to detail—the typo you overlook will jump out at the reader.

### b. Question Presented

In many brief formats, the question presented immediately follows the title page. In form, a question presented may be either a grammatical question (*e.g.,* "Did...?" or "Was...?") or a clause beginning with "whether." Because it is the reader's first contact with the case, the question presented must 1) make perfect sense out of context and 2) begin the process of persuasion by balancing candor and conviction, using the particulars of the case appropriately and effectively. In addition, your question must be a real question answerable by yes or no, not a conclusion of law framed as question. Finally, although this is not a universal practice, questions presented are traditionally framed so that a "yes" answer is the advocate's desired result.

Consider the following three drafts of a question presented for an appellant challenging his conviction of the offense of intentional assault with a dangerous instrument on the sole ground that he did not use a dangerous instrument. The evidence at trial showed only that appellant, a patron at a crowded bar, threw a small, thick "on-the-rocks" glass at a bartender, lacerating the bartender's cheek and eye when the glass struck her face and broke; no altercation or interaction of any sort between appellant and the complainant preceded this incident. Intentional assault with a dangerous instrument is committed when a person intends to cause physical injury (not death or serious physical injury) and causes such injury by means of a dangerous instrument. The law defines "dangerous instrument" as "any object which, under the circumstances in which it is used, is readily capable of causing death or serious physical injury." With this background in mind, assess the drafts.

> (1) Whether appellant's conviction of assault should be reversed because he did not use a dangerous instrument.

> (2) Did appellant commit assault when he merely tossed the object in the bartender's direction to get her attention?
>
> (3) Whether appellant's conviction of assault with a dangerous instrument should be reversed, where the glass he threw at the complainant bartender was small and thick and, under the circumstances, unlikely to break.

The first draft question is not a question at all, because the only possible answer is "yes," since by definition the crime cannot be committed if a dangerous instrument is not used. Put another way, this draft answers the very question it purports to ask.

The second draft question also has several problems. First, the answer that the drafter wants here is "no." The question should be reframed for a "yes"—perhaps, "Whether appellant's conviction of assault with a dangerous instrument should be reversed..." or "Did the prosecution fail to prove...." This draft has more fundamental problems, however. First, the question is not understandable out of context. The writer mistakenly assumes that the reader knows the type of assault involved, knows what the "object" was, and knows how the bartender fits into the story. In addition, and more critically, the drafter exaggerates, as shown by the words "merely," "tossed," and "in the direction of." Where the facts show that appellant did indeed throw the glass at the complainant, this mischaracterization can only hurt appellant. Moreover, because the evidence was silent as to motivation, the assertion that appellant was just trying to get attention is not supported by the record, and the writer is on shaky ethical ground.[6]

The third question is competent professional work. It assumes no knowledge of law or fact and raises a fair-minded doubt about appellant's culpability. Some writers might prefer the following more plain-English version that is a grammatical question, not a "whether" fragment, and that avoids the idiomatic use of "where."

---

[6] The ethics of brief writing are discussed below in Section E of this chapter.

> Should appellant's conviction of intentional assault with a dangerous instrument be reversed on the ground that the glass he threw at the complainant bartender was small and thick and, under the circumstances, unlikely to break?

Questions presented are difficult to write well—they must pack a lot of information and persuasive heft into one grammatical question or "whether" clause. Your question presented will be more effective if it follows the stylistic principles discussed in Chapter 5 on *Clarity;* for example, readability will be enhanced if you keep subject and verb close to the beginning and close to each other, if you use parallel construction and avoid the bad habits that create wordiness, and if you place modifiers and commas carefully. In addition, it is good practice to put law before facts, so that the reader has a context for the facts. For example, in the third draft above, the reader easily relates the facts at the end of the sentence to the concept of "dangerous instrument" that precedes them. However, if we reframe the question to put facts before law, it becomes more difficult to read and to retain because until the end of the question, there is nothing to which the reader can attach the facts at the beginning.

> Whether, where the glass he threw at the complainant bartender was small and thick and, under the circumstances, unlikely to break, appellant's conviction of assault with a dangerous instrument should be reversed.

While the difference between this version and the third draft above may seem negligible, you should bear in mind that whenever comprehension is impeded, so too is persuasion.

---------------------------------- *Exercise 9.1* ----------------------------------

*Write a question presented for the respondent prosecution in the assault with a dangerous instrument hypothetical used in the examples in the preceding section, assuming appellant's only argument is that he did not use a "dangerous instrument."*

## c. Table of Contents/Point Headings

The table of contents lists each component of the brief and the page on which it begins. The listing for argument includes all the point headings in the argument. Thus, the table of contents takes the process of persuasion one step beyond the question presented by providing an outline of the advocate's contentions.

Like questions presented, point headings should be clear to a reader with no prior knowledge of the facts or the issues. Unlike questions presented, point headings *should* be conclusory. However, they should not be mere statements of established rules of law. Finally, as in a question presented, where the issue involves the application of law to fact, a point heading will be more effective if it uses facts persuasively but not recklessly. Consider the following drafts of a point heading for the example used above in the discussion of questions presented.

> (1) An instrument is dangerous if, under the circumstances in which it is used, it is readily capable of causing death or serious physical injury.
> (2) Appellant's assault conviction should be reversed, because he merely tossed the object in the bartender's direction.
> (3) Appellant's conviction of assault should be reversed because he did not use a dangerous instrument.
> (4) Appellant did not commit assault with a dangerous instrument because the glass he threw at the complainant was small and thick and, under the circumstances, unlikely to break and cause death or serious physical injury.

The first draft is not a point heading at all, since it merely states an established rule of law. Draft (2) is properly a contention about the case, but like the second draft question presented above, it both assumes knowledge of the facts and issue and overstates the argument. Draft (3) states a clear contention about the case, but lacking any allusion to the facts, it does little to forward the process of persuasion. (Nonetheless, if the facts are too complex or too unattractive to lend themselves to a persuasive point heading, this type of bare legal conclusion may be the best choice.)

Draft (4) is the best—clear out of context and making a persuasive but reasonable contention about the case.

Where there are multiple issues or where an issue breaks down into sub-issues, your point headings should form a logical "Roman-numeral" outline of the arguments. The guidelines for such outlines are discussed in Section C of the skills chapter *Conceptualizing*. Remember that the sum of your sub-issues should be no less and no more than the issue itself, that is, that you should have no gaps and no overlaps. In particular, remember that it is logically impossible to have just one sub-issue: thus, there can be no "A" without a "B" and no "1" without a "2" in your point headings. The example below illustrates a clear violation of this rule. Since whether appellant used a dangerous instrument was the only issue in the hypothetical case used for our examples, the supposed sub-issue is really just another, more specific, way of expressing the issue itself—it is not, as a sub-issue must be, a component of the issue.

> I. Appellant was wrongly convicted of intentional assault with a dangerous instrument.
>
> A. The glass that appellant threw at the complainant was not dangerous, in that it was not readily capable of causing death or serious physical injury under the circumstances of its use.

Thus, the point heading here is better rewritten as follows.

> I. Appellant was wrongly convicted of intentional assault with a dangerous instrument, in that the glass that appellant threw at the complainant was not readily capable of causing death or serious physical injury under the circumstances of its use.

If, however, appellant had raised another issue as to his assault conviction, perhaps arguing that the evidence of intent to injure was insufficient, then he would need not one, but two sub-issues—an "A" and a "B," as in the following example.

> I. Appellant was wrongly convicted of intentional assault with a dangerous instrument.

> A. The glass that appellant threw at the complainant was not dangerous in that it was not readily capable of causing death or serious physical injury under the circumstances of its use.
>
> B. The record is devoid of any evidence of intent to cause injury.

Finally, where, as in the above example, an issue is broken into sub-issues, the major point heading may be a quite general conclusion, so long as the relevant specifics are used in the sub-point headings.

---

*Exercise 9.2*

---

*Write a point heading for the respondent prosecution in the assault hypothetical used in the preceding section. Assume appellant's only argument is that he did not use a "dangerous instrument."*

---

### d. Table of Authorities

The table of authorities is essentially an index to the authorities cited in your brief. It shows the reader the quantity and quality of authority with which you support your contentions. Short briefs rarely need a table of authorities, but the rules of some appellate courts require one. Authority is grouped in the table of authorities by type in descending order of strength–constitutions, statutes, caselaw, secondary authority. Caselaw is ordinarily grouped by jurisdiction, in descending hierarchical order, with cases from the United States Supreme Court first. When you rely on an authority many times within a brief, you may substitute *"passim"* ("throughout") for a list of all the page numbers.

### e. Jurisdictional Statement

Where required of appellant, a jurisdictional statement explains how the case comes before the court, whether by permission or pursuant to statute. It is ordinarily simple boilerplate.

## 2. Facts

### a. Procedural History

The procedural history sometimes stands alone; at other times, it and the statement of facts are subsumed under the larger heading "statement of the case." Even where it is not required by court rules, the procedural history is an essential part of any brief. It provides the court with a framework without which the historical facts have no legal significance. The procedural history is a straightforward, neutral account of the progress of the controversy through the legal system. No attempt should be made to frame it persuasively; indeed, it is positively unprofessional to do so.

### b. Statement of Facts

The statement of facts is a persuasive account of those facts contained in the official court record—and only those facts. In an appellate brief, the "four corners of the record" (to use the appellate court term) are clearly delineated: the record on appeal ordinarily consists of the official transcripts of any pre-trial hearings and of the trial and any subsequent proceedings, as well as any evidence admitted by the court, whether documentary or "real" evidence. For trial briefs, especially those supporting pre-trial motions, the record is often composed of many disparate documents—for example, pleadings, motion papers, affidavits, and documentary evidence, as well as depositions or other discovery or disclosure products. The drafter should make certain that all "facts" stated are part of the record. In addition, the contents of the record for a trial brief must conform to the requirements of the proceeding—for example, the record for a motion to dismiss for failure to state a claim consists only of the pleadings.

A persuasive statement of facts is most often a story-within-a-story—the "framing" story of the litigation and the "framed" story of the historical facts as they emerge from the record. For example, the statement of facts in an appeal from a judgment in a criminal prosecution might have an elaborate framing story—pre-trial hearings, jury selection, opening statements, prosecution's case, defense case, summations, jury instructions, verdict, and sentencing—with the historical facts of offense, investigation, arrest, etc. nested within that frame. Sometimes the frame is minimal, a simple introductory paragraph explaining where the facts come from—for example, "The following facts are summarized from the hearing on appellant's motion to suppress her statement to the police, held on July 23, 2003."

Some brief-writers begin their statement of facts with an introductory paragraph that focuses the reader on their core persuasive theme. One particularly effective way to achieve this focus is to begin with a dramatic introduction to the historical facts. This is a technique best reserved for facts that are indeed compelling, however; exaggeration only damages your credibility.

Knowing when to quote from the record and when to paraphrase is an important advocacy skill. Quotation emphasizes, while paraphrase de-emphasizes. Quotations must always be checked and double-checked for accuracy, of course, and paraphrase must never mischaracterize. Moreover, when language in the record is ambiguous, candor requires the writer to quote verbatim, not paraphrase favorably for the client. Interpretation should always be saved for argument.

Unlike your procedural history, your statement of facts need not tell the whole story of the litigation to date, but rather, should focus on the part of the story that is the basis of your argument— although you must provide enough of the whole story to make your issue understandable. For example, if you are seeking summary judgment on a wrongful death claim, you need not recount facts relevant only to other claims in the same complaint, although you must explain that there are other claims. If you are appealing a criminal conviction on the sole ground that the defendant's credibility was unfairly attacked by the prosecutor on summation, you need not recount the testimony at a pre-trial hearing seeking suppression of evidence, though you must of course summarize the evidence at trial.

All facts relevant to your legal arguments must be included, even those that "go against you." Always remind yourself that you bear no responsibility for the facts themselves; they are what they are. Your responsibility is to recount them fairly and accurately.

That said, there is still considerable room for persuasion. Indeed, your responsibility to your client requires you to put the facts in the best light that candor permits. The techniques noted in Section B of Chapter 6, *Persuasion,* will help you to use narrative structure, description, characterization, sentence structure, and word choice to maximum advantage. In addition, the use of headings to "signpost" the statement of facts can both enhance clarity and keep your argument in the forefront of your reader's mind. For example, using headings for the various stages of the proceedings ("The Prosecution's Case," "The Defense Case," "The Jury Charge," etc.) helps to orient the reader. More specific headings, for example, "Cross-examination of Defendant," "The Prosecutor's Comments on Credibility," and "The Judge's Charge on Credibility," can be used to prefigure your argument.

Statements of fact should always contain "record citations" that tell the reader where in the record to find the facts stated. Bear in mind that you must cite to the record for all facts stated—whether paraphrased or quoted directly. Record cites are ordinarily placed in parentheses at the end of each sentence. A "record footnote" explains the abbreviations used in the record cites.

When summarizing testimony, depositions, or affidavits, the drafter may summarize the testimony of each witness or affiant individually or combine their accounts into one seamless narrative, with helpful record cites explaining the location of the testimony of each witness (e.g., "Smith, T. 13; Jones, T. 47; Green, T. 162"). Recounting the testimony of witnesses to the same event sequentially usually makes for a bumpy, repetitive narrative— yet it can be a very effective way to show that the witnesses told quite different stories.

---

### *Exercise 9.3*

*John James Malone has been convicted of robbery in the third degree in a New York court. He has appealed his conviction on the ground that the prosecution failed to prove that the money he obtained from the complainant, Timothy Miller, was taken by force or threat of immediate force. Below you will find the trial transcript, the relevant statute, and a summary of the relevant caselaw.*

*A. Assume you are representing appellant Malone on appeal; write a statement of the facts for his brief.*

*B. Assume you are the assistant district attorney assigned to write the prosecution's brief; write a statement of facts.*

## Trial Testimony of Complainant, Timothy Miller

Q. Good morning, Mr. Miller.

A. Good morning.

Q. May I enquire how old you are, Mr. Miller?

A. I am twenty-seven-years old.

Q. And where do you reside?

A. Pierrepont Street in Brooklyn. In a studio apartment.

Q. What is your occupation, sir?

A. Well, I'm an actor, but I tend bar for a living. I work at the Cafe Luxembourg in Manhattan.

Q. And were you so employed on or about January 21, 20__?

A. Yes.

Q. Thinking back to January 21, 20__ did there come a time when you left your apartment?

A. Yes.

Q. At about what time, if you remember?

A. About 3:00 in the afternoon.

Q. And where were you going at that time, sir?

A. To work, on the subway.

Q. And did you board a train at that time?

A. Yes, I got on a Number Three train at Clark Street.

Q. Did you notice if there were any other persons on that train?

A. Well, the whole train, I don't know, but in my car there was just one other person down the other end, a woman, I think she was reading a bunch of papers and writing on them.

Q. And did there come a time when another person entered the car?

A. Yes, a man came through the door from the next car, at my end of the car.

Q. What did he look like?

A. He was taller than me, about six feet, his hair and clothes were dirty, and he had glary eyes.

Q. Do you see him in this room?

A. Yes, he's over there, the man wearing the blue jacket and white shirt and tie.

Q. For the record, the witness has indicated the defendant, John James Malone. Now, Mr. Miller, did anything happen after the defendant entered the car?

A. He started talking.

Q. What did he say?

A. He said, "Good afternoon, ladies and gentlemen. My name is John. I am a homeless disabled Gulf War veteran. I do not rob or steal or do drugs. I am trying to get enough money to get someplace to stay."

Q. Did you take any action at this point?

A. Well, every time I get on the train people like him come on, so I kept looking at my magazine, ignoring him.

Q. And did a time come when the defendant approached you?

A. Well, all of a sudden he's standing right over me, breathing on top of me. He goes, "You got to give me some money, you got to." "Like hell I do," I go, and I like slide over and stand up to get away from him. He's still going, "You got to give me money. I never mugged anybody, but I don't know what I could do if this goes on much longer."

Q. What happened then?

A. The train stopped short in the tunnel and he fell up against me, I was pinned to the pole. Then he puts his arm all the way around my shoulders and like holds on to me, and he goes "Look buddy, I said you got to give me money."

Q. Please tell the jury what occurred next, if anything.

A. Well, I had a ten dollar bill in my pocket, so I took it out and I gave it to him.

Q. Can you describe your feelings during this incident?

A. I was pretty nervous. He was a funny looking guy and I didn't want to take chances.

Q. After you gave the money to the defendant, what, if anything, happened next?

A. Well, then the train started moving and he sort of lurched off down the other end of the car in a hurry and into the next car.

Q. Did you see him again that afternoon?

A. Yes. When the train got to Wall Street, the next stop, I saw a police officer on the platform. I told him I was just robbed and he arrested the guy right in the next car.

## Statutes

### Robbery in the Third Degree

A person is guilty of robbery in the third degree when he forcibly steals property.

## Robbery Defined

Robbery is forcible stealing. A person forcibly steals property and commits robbery when, in the course of committing a larceny, he uses or threatens the immediate use of physical force upon another person....

## Case Law

The New York courts have interpreted the Penal Law's requirement of use of force or threat of the immediate use of force as follows:

- Force is more than "mere touching."
- Force must be used intentionally, not accidentally.
- Explicitly threatening words are not required to prove a threat of force.
- Threat may be proven by verbal conduct, physical conduct, the complainant's reasonable apprehension, or a combination of all three.
- Any threat must be of immediate force—the possibility of future physical force is not sufficient.

---

## 3. Summary of Argument

The summary of argument is more characteristic of appellate briefs than of trial briefs. Indeed, some appellate courts require a summary of argument. Whenever your argument is lengthy or complex, however, a summary of argument is a good idea even when not required. Depending on the complexity of your arguments, the summary should be from one to two pages. A summary must make sense out of context and it must be short enough and clear enough so that the reader can comprehend and retain it on one reading.

## 4. Argument

The argument proper is the final stage in the process of persuasion that began with your question presented. The point headings in the table of contents summarized your contentions, the table of authorities indicated legal support, the statement of facts provided evidentiary support, and the summary of argument has begun to expand and explain your contentions. Your task in the argument proper is to support your position with principled, detailed, and sophisticated legal reasoning—not to make vague, exaggerated, or unsubstantiated claims or otherwise engage in rhetorical dirty tricks. Although more concise argument may be appropriate in a trial brief, the need for concision does not justify assertion unsupported by reasoning or authority. Many courts will decline to consider an argument that is purely conclusory or unsupported,[7] and no court will find such argument persuasive or entertain a high opinion of the advocate who makes it. Chapter 6, *Persuasion,* can point you in the direction of more effective legal argument, helping you to exploit the full range of available arguments and to make them both more creative and more substantive.

In addition to being creative and substantive, your argument should be responsive to its context. For example, arguments in briefs in support of or in opposition to a motion should be narrowly tailored to the requirements of the motion. Thus, a writer drafting a brief in support of a motion for summary judgment should argue that no material facts are in dispute and that the moving party is entitled to judgment as a matter of law. Arguing in support of defendant's motion to dismiss for failure to state a claim requires counsel in a federal case to argue that under no set of facts would the plaintiff be entitled to relief. The appellate context requires counsel to be mindful of the many narrow gates that stand between a meritorious issue and victory on appeal—finality, jurisdiction, preservation, standard of review, and harmless error analysis.

Finally, clear organization is essential to a persuasive argument. The less a reader has to work to understand how the pieces of your argument fit together, the more likely the reader is to be persuaded. It is always a good idea to foster understanding by beginning each point and sub-point with a thesis paragraph that

---

[7] For example, the Seventh Circuit refused to consider one litigant's contention, stating, "This argument is raised in a short conclusory paragraph which contains no substantive argument, legal citations, or references to the record. This court has no duty to research and construct legal arguments available to a party." *Head Start Family Education Program v. Cooperative Educational Service Agency 11,* 46 F.3d 629, 635 (7th Cir. 1995).

introduces and summarizes the argument to follow in the familiar rule-application-conclusion pattern or some variation of it. Occasionally, some more unusual and striking way of introducing an argument is appropriate—especially in an unusual and striking case. For example, an experienced appellate practitioner was briefing the appeal of a man who was convicted of drug-dealing, even though the record showed that he had been arrested by mistake during a major drug "bust." Varying from her usual practice of introducing her argument with a traditional thesis paragraph, the attorney began her argument with a one-sentence paragraph: "Philip Hall's only crime was being in the wrong place at the wrong time." The circumstances of the case justified this unorthodox introduction, which was all the more effective because the court could not have failed to notice the departure from the attorney's usual, more measured, brief-writing style.

## 5. Conclusion

The conclusion is a purely ritual part of persuasive briefs, a sentence in which counsel formally requests relief from the court.

## C. SAMPLE BRIEFS

### 1. Trial Brief: *Hustin v. Freeman*[8]

Superior Court of the State of Atlantis
County of Sussex

---

| | |
|---|---|
| Jeffrey Hustin, | Index No. Civ.\_\_\_\_ |
| Plaintiff, | |
| -against- | MEMORANDUM IN SUPPORT OF DEFENDANT FREEMAN'S |
| Michele Freeman and The Regents of the University of Atlantis, | MOTION FOR SUMMARY JUDGMENT ON |
| Defendants. | DEFAMATION |

---

### QUESTION PRESENTED

In this defamation case, were defendant's statements about plaintiff privileged when defendant, a law professor and member of the bar, made them to a law school committee considering plaintiff for academic tenure, and for the purpose of helping the committee determine plaintiff's fitness for the status of tenured law professor?[9]

### FACTS

Plaintiff Jeffrey Hustin has filed suit against defendant Michele Freeman, alleging defamation and intentional infliction of emotional distress. Defendant Freeman is a Professor of Law at Sussex University School of Law in Atlantis City who was a visiting professor at the University of Atlantis School of Law ("the Law School") during the academic year 20\_\_–20\_\_. Plaintiff was at that time an Assistant Professor of Law at the Law School and had applied for academic tenure and promotion. His tenure application was being considered by the Law School's

---

[8] This trial brief supports the sample summary judgment motion in Chapter 4, *Motions,* and continues the hypothetical case of *Hustin v. Freeman* that provided the samples in the chapters on *Complaints* and *Answers.*

[9] Counsel states the substantive question here, without reference to summary judgment. The busy court already knows *what* the defendant wants; it needs to know *why.*

Status Committee, of which Professor Freeman was concededly not a member. (C. 4-8; D.Aff.6)*

According to her sworn statements, during her year at the Law School, Professor Freeman learned of facts that she believed relevant to plaintiff's fitness for academic tenure at a law school—and indeed, his fitness to teach at all. (D.Aff. 6)

First, Professor Freeman began to doubt the originality of plaintiff's scholarship. After reading an article that plaintiff wrote and comparing it to an earlier article by a different author, Professor Freeman "found disturbing similarities in ideas and paragraphs and sentences that were not only close in structure, but occasionally identical in wording." (D.Aff. 7) (The texts of the two articles, with the similarities underscored and noted in the margins are attached to Defendant's Affidavit in Support of her Motion as Defendant's Exhibit A.)

Second, Professor Freeman witnessed behavior toward students on plaintiff's part that convinced her that he was "unfit to teach" in a law school. On one occasion, a student came to discuss a low grade with plaintiff. When the student persisted in her complaints that plaintiff's grading was unfairly harsh, Professor Freeman heard plaintiff tell the student that she might as well quit, she was "too stupid" to be in law school, if not "too stupid to live," that she had only been admitted because she was a minority student, an "affirmative action mistake," and that she should be "grateful" he only gave her a C minus. On another occasion, when another student persisted in challenging his grade, plaintiff told him that if he did not like his grade, maybe the student "would like to settle it outside in the street," because plaintiff would be "happy to beat the crap out of [the student]." (D.Aff.8; Affidavits of these two students in support of Professor Freeman's motion for summary judgment have also been filed with this Court.)

Although as a visiting professor, Professor Freeman could not vote on plaintiff's applications for tenure and promotion, she believed that it was her "duty as a member of the bar and as a member of the legal academic community" to communicate the information concerning plaintiff to the Status Committee, and she accordingly wrote a memorandum detailing her doubts about plaintiff's fitness. (D.Aff. 9) Plaintiff

---

* Numbers in parentheses preceded by "C." refer to paragraphs of the verified Complaint by plaintiff against defendant Freeman and the Regents of the University of Atlantis, dated February 5, 20__; numbers preceded by "A." refer to defendant Freeman's verified Answer, dated March 15, 20__, and those preceded by "D.Aff." and "P.Aff." refer, respectively, to defendant Freeman's Affidavit in Support of the Motion for Summary Judgment and plaintiff's Affidavit in Opposition to the same motion.

was subsequently denied tenure and the Status Committee declined to re-hire him as an assistant professor.

Shortly thereafter, plaintiff filed suit, alleging in his complaint that Professor Freeman's memorandum to the Status Committee contained false statements about him. He claimed that the statements were defamatory in that they "tended to expose him to contempt, aversion, ridicule, and disgrace and to induce a bad opinion of him in the minds of right-thinking people." (C. 13-14) Plaintiff also alleged that these statements caused the Status Committee to deny his application for academic tenure and to decline to rehire him. He further alleged conclusorily in his complaint that by making these statements, Professor Freeman engaged in conduct "so extreme and outrageous as to be intolerable in a civilized community" and that her actions "intentionally or, at a minimum, recklessly" caused him to suffer "severe emotional distress." (C.22-24)

Defendant Freeman's memorandum, annexed to the complaint as Plaintiff's Exhibit A, contained the following language specifically complained of by plaintiff. "Although superficially plausible and original, upon closer inspection, Professor Hustin's article 'Plain Language: A Cognitive Contradiction in Terms' turns out to be not only derivative, but disturbingly resonant with distinct echoes of the work of several earlier (and unacknowledged) scholars." "Professor Hustin has verbally abused and humiliated students, both in and out of class, and on at least one occasion, he threatened a student with bodily harm if the student complained to the administration about his class." "He [Professor Hustin] seemingly has no capacity to relate to his students or to his colleagues."[10]

In her answer, Professor Freeman freely admitted to writing the memorandum to the Status Committee concerning plaintiff's fitness for tenure, but denied, inter alia, that the statements were false and that they were made with intent to cause him severe emotional distress or with reckless disregard for the likelihood of causing him such distress.

In her answer, Professor Freeman also set out the affirmative defense of qualified privilege, alleging that "as a member of the bar of this state and of its legal academic community, she had a legitimate interest in the intellectual and moral fitness of candidates for academic tenure in the law and a duty to report any relevant information to those persons with corresponding interests and duties." She further alleged that because

---

[10] The precise language used by the defendant is not vital here, because the issue is not whether the language is defamatory, but whether the statement was privileged. Nonetheless, counsel quotes verbatim because defendant's rather measured comments put her in a good light.

her "statements about the plaintiff concerned those interests and duties and were made to persons with the corresponding interests and
duties, that is, the Status Committee, those statements were privileged,
and no liability for defamation or infliction of emotional distress could
be premised upon them."

On July 21, 20__, Professor Freeman moved for summary judgment
of the defamation claim on the ground that her statements were privileged. In his Affidavit in Opposition to the summary judgment motion,
plaintiff realleged almost verbatim the allegations in his complaint.
(P.Aff. 2-15) With respect to Professor Freeman's claim of privilege, he
responded, *in toto,* that her statements were not privileged because
they were "false" and because they were made "out of spite and with a
high degree of awareness that they were false." (P.Aff. 16)[11]

<u>ARGUMENT</u>

<u>I.  DEFENDANT FREEMAN IS ENTITLED TO SUMMARY JUDGMENT
ON PLAINTIFF'S DEFAMATION CLAIM BECAUSE THE UNDISPUT-
ED FACTS DEMONSTRATE THAT DEFENDANT'S STATEMENTS
CONCERNING PLAINTIFF'S APPLICATION FOR LAW SCHOOL
TENURE WERE PRIVILEGED BECAUSE MADE IN GOOD FAITH
TO THE MEMBERS OF THE STATUS COMMITTEE WITH WHOM
SHE SHARED A LEGITIMATE INTEREST IN THE FITNESS OF
TENURED LAW PROFESSORS.</u>

Because she shared with the Status Committee of the University of
Atlantis School of Law a common interest in ensuring that academic
tenure was granted only to candidates who met the most exacting
intellectual and ethical standards, Professor Michele Freeman's statements to the Committee concerning plaintiff were privileged and her
motion for summary judgment should be granted. A "conditional" privilege attaches to a communication made by a person with a "legitimate
interest" in making it, when the communication is made to a person
with a corresponding interest, even though, without the privilege, the
communication would subject the maker to liability for defamation.
*Frazier v. Dougherty.* Once a defendant establishes entitlement to
this "common interest" privilege, the privilege constitutes a complete
defense to defamation unless plaintiff proves 1) that the communication is false and 2) that the defendant acted either out of "pure spite"

---

[11] Note that the facts are stated at considerable length in order to make it unnecessary for the court to wade through the pleadings, affidavits, etc. to piece together the
details. As much to gain the court's confidence as for its convenience, counsel has
provided careful citations to the record.

("common-law" malice) or with a "high degree of awareness" that the communication was "probably false" ("constitutional" malice). *Id.* Here, summary judgment should be granted on plaintiff's defamation claim because the undisputed facts show that the privilege "conditionally" attached to defendant Professor Freeman's actions, and plaintiff Hustin has alleged no evidentiary facts whatsoever in support of his purely conclusory allegation that defendant's actions were malicious. Thus, no triable issue of fact remains and Professor Freeman is entitled to judgment in her favor as a matter of law.[12]

The "common-interest" privilege is "broadly" applied by the courts of this State; the maker and receiver of the allegedly defamatory communication need only "have such a relationship to each other as would support reasonable grounds for supposing an innocent motive for imparting the information."[13] *Sowers v. Cathedral Veterinary Hospital.* Here, the undisputed facts bear witness to a relationship between Professor Freeman and the Status Committee of the University of Atlantis School of Law that not only meets this requirement, but far surpasses it. First, as members of the academic community, Professor Freeman and the Status Committee shared an interest in the intellectual qualifications of prospective holders of permanent membership in that community. *See Nevins v. Atlantis City Comm. Col.* (Members of an academic department have a common interest in the skills of its members).[14] Further, as attorneys, Freeman and the committee had a common interest in ensuring that tenured law teachers are persons who conduct themselves according to the ethical standards of their profession. *See Hughes v. Johnson Psychoanalytical Institute* (Head of psychiatric unit shared common interest in ethical practice of psychiatry with other prospective employers of plaintiff psychiatrist). Moreover, despite plaintiff Hustin's

---

[12] For clarity, counsel introduces the argument with a conclusion-rule-application-practical conclusion thesis paragraph. Note that although the writer applies basic summary judgment criteria, these criteria are not stated or expounded. The trial judge is undoubtedly thoroughly familiar with summary judgment doctrine and does not want to read about it—although this same judge may later spend time explaining that very doctrine in her opinion.

[13] Note that the writer states the law affirmatively for defendant. It is important to read caselaw with a eye to identifying formulations of the rule that favor your argument. The writer is careful to quote the word "broadly," thus showing that this is the court's characterization, not counsel's.

[14] Note that caselaw is described briefly and in parentheticals that provide only the most narrowly relevant facts. The judge does not want to read long summaries of cases applying settled law in garden-variety cases, and the obvious strength of defendant's argument makes dwelling on precedent unnecessary. If the issue were a novel one and counsel was aiming to "educate" the court or preview a trial strategy, it might make sense to discuss precedent at greater length.

argument to the contrary before this court,[15] it is of no legal import that Professor Freeman is not a member of the faculty of the University of Atlantis School of Law; the "common interest" doctrine does not apply only to members or employees of the same institution, corporation, or other entity. *See id.* (Psychiatrists at different hospitals and clinics shared a common interest); *Knowles v. McGarrity* (Plaintiff's employer shared a common interest with admissions officers at schools to which plaintiff was applying); *Wilson v. Palladian Partners, LP* (Common interest between defendant architectural firm and local housing authority concerning competence of plaintiff building contractor.)

In response to Professor Freeman's amply established privilege, plaintiff offers only the conclusory allegations that her statements were not privileged because they were "false" and because they were made "out of spite and with a high degree of awareness that they were false." (P.Aff. 16) Because plaintiff alleges no evidentiary facts whatsoever on this issue, there is no triable issue as to whether Professor Freeman acted with malice, common-law or constitutional. Thus, the "conditional" privilege attached to Professor Freeman's statements is rendered a complete defense to the claim of defamation, and she is entitled to judgment in her favor as a matter of law.[16]

---

[15] Trial briefs sometimes follow oral argument; on novel or difficult issues, judges often ask the parties to submit written argument.

[16] Note that counsel's argument is only three paragraphs long. Where the facts largely speak for themselves, as they do here, there is no need to try the court's patience with an elaborate argument, although of course, the writer should provide support for all assertions and leave no gaps in the argument.

## 2. APPELLATE BRIEF: *Wilson v. State*[17]

### QUESTION PRESENTED

Whether the State failed to prove beyond a reasonable doubt that appellant Donald Wilson was guilty of felony murder, although he freely admitted to participating in the underlying robbery as a lookout, where there was evidence that the deceased was assassinated by one of the principals in the robbery to carry out a private design of revenge unconnected with the robbery itself.

### PROCEDURAL HISTORY

Appellant Donald Wilson was charged with felony murder (Pen. L. §125.25) in indictment Number 652/04. He was convicted as charged after a non-jury trial held March 20–22 and 25, 20__ in Atlantis Superior Court, Snowden County and sentenced on April 30, 20__ to a term of twenty-five years to life in prison (Clarkson, J. at trial and sentence).

Notice of appeal was timely filed, and on July 12, 20__ this Court granted appellant permission to appeal *in forma pauperis* and assigned William E. Heller as counsel on appeal.[18]

### STATEMENT OF FACTS

Introduction

On February 3, 20__, an elderly Roman Catholic priest was shot to death during a robbery at St Michael's Friary in Snowden County.[19] Three and one-half years later, appellant Donald Wilson was implicated as look-out in the robbery by his eventual co-defendant, Isaac Fenton, when Fenton walked into a police station and confessed in order to "clear his conscience." Fenton told the police that another of the rob-

---

[17] This sample was adapted from a brief in a real case and set in a fictional jurisdiction. For reasons of space, it has been significantly abridged and adapted. All of the names and a few minor facts have been changed. The title page, table of contents, and table of cases have been omitted.

[18] Note that the Procedural History is a neutral statement; any attempt at persuasion here is inappropriate and would alienate the court.

[19] Note that counsel makes no effort to minimize the dreadfulness of the crime here. Appellant's interests would not be served by any attempt to omit or abridge the details. He was not accused of killing or condoning the killing, and his argument is that the horrible crime was committed in cold blood for reasons unrelated to the robbery. More importantly, however, the perceived callousness of any attempt to "sanitize" the story would detract from the credibility of appellant's argument—and of appellant's counsel.

bers, Bernard Brown, had shot the priest during the robbery, and that he did so to "punish the Caucasian race."

An employed family man with no criminal record at the time of his arrest, appellant confessed to his part in the robbery. Jointly indicted for felony murder and for lesser offenses, appellant and Fenton moved to suppress their statements to the police. When their suppression motions were denied,[20] appellant and Fenton waived their right to a jury, and a bench trial took place.

At trial, two eye-witnesses to the friary robbery recalled vividly that just as the robbers were about to flee, one of them ran upstairs to the priests' quarters, fired several shots, and then ran down again, announcing, in effect, that one of them had to die. Despite this testimony and Fenton's statement that Brown had, in fact, assassinated his victim out of a private design of revenge—evidence that the killing had not been done in furtherance of the common robbery scheme—the court convicted appellant and Fenton of felony murder. The court sentenced appellant to the maximum sentence permitted by law—twenty-five years to life in prison.[21]

### The Evidence at Trial

The State's witnesses were Fathers Peter Flynn, Francis LoBiondo, and Philip Nolan of St. Michael's Friary, Sergeant Robert Connelly and Detective Ronald Slater of the Center City Police Department, and Snowden County Medical Examiner Jennifer Lim.

On February 3, 20__, at about three o'clock in the afternoon, two men entered St. Michael's Friary and told Father Flynn, who greeted them, that they wanted to arrange a baptism. (T. 73)* Father Flynn summoned Father LoBiondo, who was in charge of such matters. While they waited for Father Lo Biondo, the two men let in two other men, one of whom remained just inside the door to the Friary. (T.75).

When Father LoBiondo came downstairs and led the men into his office, one man took out a gun and told the priests to "shut up if they didn't want to get hurt." (Flynn T.76, Lo Biondo T.127) The intruders demanded that the priests turn over the receipts from the prior night's

---

\* Numbers in parentheses preceded by "T." refer to pages of the trial transcript. Numbers preceded by "S." refer to the sentencing transcript.

---

[20] Note that, having decided that the denial of the suppression motion provided no viable issues for appeal, counsel will omit the hearing testimony from the Statement of Facts.

[21] Appellate counsel used this dramatic summary of the evidentiary facts to preview the core persuasive theory here.

Bingo game. (Flynn T.77, Lo Biondo T. 128) Father LoBiondo took the money out of a desk drawer and gave it to the men. One of the men took Father Flynn's watch. (T.78) When they heard footsteps overhead, the three robbers left the office. (Flynn T.79, Lo Biondo T.130) Two of them seemed to be heading for the Friary door, but suddenly, after some rustling noises from the floor above, the man with the gun said "uh-huh," and ran upstairs to the priests' quarters, where wheelchair-bound eighty-three year-old Father Simon-Peter Johnson resided. (Flynn T. 80, Lo Biondo T.131-33) In his room next-door to Father Johnson's, Father Philip Nolan heard running footsteps on the stairs. (Nolan T.213) Fathers Flynn, LoBiondo, and Nolan then heard gunshots from the direction of Father Johnson's room and footsteps running down the stairs and out the hall to the front door. (Flynn T. 81, Lo Biondo T.132, Nolan T.214)

Father Flynn testified that along with the retreating footsteps, he heard a man's voice say "One of them had to fall." (T. 82) Father LoBiondo testified to hearing "Somebody had to fall," (T. 134) and Father Nolan remembered hearing "One of them had to go." (T. 216)[22]

Father Nolan rushed to Father Johnson's room, where he found the old priest slumped in his wheel-chair. (T. 219) Medical Examiner Jennifer Lim testified that she conducted an autopsy on the deceased, Simon-Peter Johnson, and determined that the cause of death was a gunshot wound to the head. (T. 275).

Father Flynn identified Fenton as one of the two men let in by the other intruders; he identified appellant as the second of the two, the one who remained by the door throughout the incident. (T. 90-92). Fathers LoBiondo and Nolan were unable to make any identifications. (Lo Biondo T. 150, Nolan T. 230).

Sergeant Robert Connelly testified that on July 9, 20__, some four years after the Friary robbery, Isaac Fenton walked into the Twenty-fourth Precinct station house and told the Sergeant that he had fallen in love and wanted to "clear his conscience and turn himself around" for the woman he loved. (T. 14) To that end, he offered to provide information about an "outrageous" crime that occurred some years earlier, the "murder" of an elderly priest during a robbery. (T. 16) Fenton further told the police that there were several people involved in the robbery, and that the name of the actual shooter was Bernard Brown. (T. 17) Fenton insisted that "it wasn't necessary to shoot the priest..." but Brown did it

---

[22] In order to emphasize this testimony, crucial to appellant's argument, counsel put it in a short paragraph by itself. The testimony of each witness is described separately. Note that counsel quotes the words each witness recalls hearing. Candor requires that the reader know that each witness recalls hearing something different and that all the recalled statements are somewhat ambiguous.

because he was "into a crazy cult that the members of it thought they were gods...and their job was to punish the Caucasian race." (T. 19)

After speaking to Fenton, Sergeant Connelly notified Detective Slater, who questioned Fenton further and conducted the subsequent investigation. (Connelly T. 20, Slater T. 50) Slater concluded that Fenton knew details about the Friary robbery that only a participant would be likely to know—e.g., the precise amount of money stolen. Slater therefore began to press Fenton for more information about the perpetrators. (Slater T. 53) Fenton eventually confessed to participating in the robbery and implicated appellant, his brother-in-law, as the look-out. (Slater T. 55-58) Fenton also implicated one Michael Day as the fourth participant. (Slater T. 59)

Appellant appeared at the station house when he heard that he was being sought for questioning. (Slater T. 63) He confessed, telling Slater that he took part in the robbery because he was then unemployed, although, at the time of his arrest, appellant was employed as a nurse's aide at the Center City Nursing Home. (Slater T. 67-71) He told Detective Slater that he had stood at the door of the Friary during the robbery, and that his share of the proceeds of the robbery—the Friary Bingo receipts—was about $200. (Slater T. 69-70)

Bernard Brown was arrested, but unlike Fenton and appellant, he did not confess. (Slater T. 71) Since the statements of Fenton and appellant was the only evidence linking Brown to the crime, he could not be convicted, and thus, the alleged killer was released from custody, (Slater T. 72) and only the non-killing accomplices stood trial for murder.[23]

## Verdict and Sentence

At the end of the evidence, the court's verdict was immediate: guilty as charged for both Fenton and appellant. (T. 298)

Before sentence was pronounced on March 10, 20__, both appellant's and Fenton's counsel moved unsuccessfully to set aside the verdict of the court on the felony murder counts as contrary to the weight of the evidence.[24] (S. 6-15) Despite the facts that his role in the robbery

---

[23] The arrest and release of Brown is not relevant to the issues on appeal, but the contrast between his fate and appellant's makes appellant a more sympathetic character.

[24] In the actual case on which this sample is based, trial counsel made no such attempt to challenge the soundness of the verdict. Indeed, it appeared never to have occurred to trial counsel that there was insufficient proof that the killing occurred "in furtherance" of the robbery scheme. For that and other reasons, the other major issue in the real appeal was ineffective assistance of counsel. We note this here, because it is an example of how much damage can be done by a practitioner who stints on the conceptualization phase of lawyering, failing to think through the issues.

was a minor one, that he had a job and a stable family life, that at age 30 he had no prior criminal record whatsoever, and that he expressed great remorse for his involvement, appellant was sentenced to the maximum sentence of twenty-five years to life in prison on his felony murder conviction. (S. 20)[25]

## ARGUMENT

### I.   THE STATE FAILED TO PROVE APPELLANT GUILTY OF FELONY MURDER WHERE THE EVIDENCE SHOWED THAT THE KILLING WAS COMMITTED BY ANOTHER PARTICIPANT IN THE ROBBERY IN ORDER TO CARRY OUT A PRIVATE DESIGN OF REVENGE AND NOT IN FURTHERANCE OF THE ROBBERY SCHEME.

Without proof that the victim's death was caused in the course and in furtherance of the underlying felony, an accused may not be convicted of felony murder.[26] Pen. L. §25.25; *State v. Wood; State v. Elling.* Here, the clear inference from the prosecution's proof is that Father Simon-Peter Johnson was shot by one of the principals in the robbery in furtherance not of a common scheme to steal the Friary Bingo receipts, but rather of some monstrous private design of revenge. No rational fact-finder could have concluded beyond a reasonable doubt that appellant Donald Wilson, the unarmed lookout, was guilty of felony murder. *See Wood.* Accordingly, his murder conviction should be reversed, and the charge dismissed.

Considered, as it must be here, in the light most favorable to the prosecution, *see State v. Bingham,* the relevant evidence at trial tells a terrible story. On February 3, 2000, appellant and his co-defendant, Isaac Fenton, joined Michael Day and Bernard Brown in a plot to steal the Bingo receipts from St. Michael's Friary. The four gained entry to St.

---

[25] In the actual case, appellate counsel argued that appellant's sentence was excessive. Arguments in the alternative, of which this is an example, are of course permissible in appellate practice, although it is a good idea to think twice before making equally supportable but contradictory arguments. Nonetheless, if, for example, in a murder case, there is strong evidence of mistaken identification and of self-defense, counsel would be well advised to raise both issues.

[26] The first paragraph of argument is a simple Rule-Application-Conclusion thesis paragraph. Counsel also acknowledges in this paragraph that the standard of review is whether, when the facts are viewed "in the light most favorable to the prosecution," the court concludes that "no rational fact-finder could have found guilt beyond a reasonable doubt." Rather than state this standard of review—a very difficult standard for appellant to meet—separately, counsel weaves it into the thesis paragraph.

Michael's through a ruse and demanded that the two priests working there hand over the receipts from the prior night's Bingo game. Brown pulled out a hand-gun.

While appellant Wilson, who had no weapon of any sort,[27] stood lookout just inside the Friary door, the other three participants searched for money and valuables, threatening the priests into submission.

According to the priests, the robbers seemed on the point of leaving, when, apparently in response to a sound from an upper floor, one of them said "uh-huh" and ran upstairs. Seconds later, shots rang out, the man ran downstairs, and all of the intruders fled. Father Johnson, an infirm eighty-three year old priest, had been shot dead with a .32 handgun.

Fathers Peter Flynn, Francis Lo Biondo, and Philip Nolan all testified that as the man ran downstairs, he announced, in effect, that someone had to die.[28]

Several years after the crime, supplying information to the police because his conscience troubled him, Isaac Fenton told the police that Brown was a member of a "crazy cult" who believed themselves to be "gods" charged with exterminating the Caucasian race. Fenton also recalled Brown shouting "one of them had to fall" as he ran downstairs.

The courts of this state have consistently reversed the felony murder convictions of non-killer accomplices where, as here, the prosecution has failed to prove that the killing was done in furtherance of the common felonious design. *See State v. Elling; State v. Ryan.* A trial court's failure to instruct the jury that it must acquit in the absence of such proof will likewise result in reversal on appeal. *See State v. Blake; State v. Sobieskoda.*

In *State v. Elling,* for example, our Supreme Court reversed the conviction of the non-killer partner in an armed robbery and kidnapping scheme, where the killer's articulated motive for shooting the victim in the head was "to hear [the gun] go off."

In *State v. Sobieskoda,* reversal followed where the trial judge erroneously charged the jury that it need only find that a common felonious scheme was *in existence* at the time of the killing—omitting any men-

---

[27] Here the writer deliberately put the non-restrictive modifier "who had no weapon of any sort" between the subject ("Wilson") and verb ("stood"). Although default principles of clear prose discourage such interruption, it can sometimes be an effective tool for emphasis, especially when—as here—the interruption is short.

[28] In the Statement of Facts, counsel quoted verbatim the testimony of the three witnesses about what they heard the killer say. Here, counsel interprets that testimony favorably for appellant, but without mischaracterization.

tion of the necessity that the victim's death be caused *in furtherance* of that scheme.

Finally, in *State v. Blake,* the court reaffirmed the vitality of the reasoning behind the older cases. There, the defendant was convicted of felony murder as an accomplice. By his own account, he and his co-defendant had decided to rob an elderly woman on the street. The co-defendant dragged her into an alleyway while Blake remained on the street as lookout. Investigating minutes later, Blake found that the woman had been beaten over the head with a rock and sexually assaulted. He fled. At Blake's trial, the jury was properly charged that it must acquit if it found that the actual killing was done in furtherance of the co-defendant's own private purpose. However, when the jury requested further instructions, the court refused to reiterate this "in furtherance" charge—thereby committing reversible error. Stating that the jury would have been entitled to acquit Blake if it believed his statement, the reviewing court reversed Blake's conviction.[29]

Here, as in *Ryan* and *Sobieskoda,* the prosecution has failed to prove that the killing was done in furtherance of a common felonious scheme. Moreover, as in *Blake* and *Elling,* there is evidence of a private evil purpose. When the killer—undoubtedly Brown—came downstairs after shooting Father Johnson, he announced, "one had to die," seeing himself as a self-appointed avenger and executioner. Such a cruel purpose was plainly outside the common plan to steal the friary Bingo receipts,[30] and appellant's felony murder conviction should therefore not stand.

As the Supreme Court concluded in *Ryan* and *Sobieskoda:*

Defendant's moral guilt, as confessed by him, is clearly established. His guilty design...was the remote if not the proximate cause of the killing. Yet, however bad his moral predicament, his legal guilt may be defined only in terms of law.

---

[29] Appellate counsel has described precedent in detail—four cases described in separate paragraphs, ordinarily a technique to be avoided in persuasive writing. Yet here, the caselaw strongly favors appellant, and the details of *Elling* and *Blake* make clear that under the state Supreme Court's felony murder jurisprudence, a non-killer cannot be convicted of even the most horrendous killing unless the killing was plainly in furtherance of the underlying felony.

[30] Appellate counsel contrasts the petty and pathetic plot to steal the Bingo receipts, of which appellant was admittedly a part, to the heinous killing, for which, according to counsel's argument, appellant is not responsible.

The prosecution having failed to meet its constitutionally mandated burden of proof beyond a reasonable doubt, *see Bingham,* this Court should now reverse appellant's conviction and dismiss the felony murder charge.

## CONCLUSION

For the foregoing reasons, appellant respectfully asks this court to reverse the judgment against him and to dismiss the charge of felony murder.

## D. WRITING PROCESS

### 1. Gathering Information: Getting the Facts

The challenge for the brief-writer at this stage is not so much gathering the facts as it is assimilating and parsing them. For the appellate practitioner, the facts come ready gathered, processed, and packaged in the record on appeal. He has only to be certain that all the relevant proceedings have been transcribed by the court stenographer, who also certifies their authenticity. The trial litigator may have a slightly more difficult task, however, since she must often assemble the record from disparate sources. She may also need to supplement gaps in the record with affidavits or documentary evidence.

### 2. Gathering Information: Researching the Law

The early stages of brief-writing move back and forth between brainstorming and legal research. This is especially true of appellant's briefs. Since most appeals are from final judgments, the record on appeal is often huge and the potential issues many. Thus, appellant's counsel has a canvas on which the dots can be connected in different ways to make many quite different pictures. In addition, appellant's counsel must research much more than just substantive issues; finality, preservation, standard of review, and harmless error doctrines must often be researched. Counsel for respondent has an easier job, since the issues will have largely been defined by appellant. Whether supporting or opposing a motion, trial counsel also have a more straight-forward research task, since the issue is circumscribed by the motion. Counsel for the moving party will have done most of the research before filing the motion—it should need only fine-tuning at this stage.

For both trial and appellate briefs, research must be thorough and focused. Never rely on just one research tool; even the most carefully framed Boolean searches miss relevant documents. Even when your search produces *only* relevant cases, it has not necessarily produced *all* the relevant cases. If you miss the one case that presents the most telling analogy, you might just as well not have written the brief at all.

Unless you are an expert on a particular issue, always look at secondary sources first. They give you an overview—the forest instead of the trees. Even more important to brief-writing, some secondary sources, like law reviews, provide new perspectives and help the practitioner to "think outside the box."

## 3. Conceptualizing

The practitioner who sets out to draft a trial brief in support of a motion ordinarily has done the bulk of his brainstorming at an earlier stage, when he conceptualized the motion itself as part of his litigation strategy.[31] Counsel for the party opposing a motion and counsel for respondent in an appeal also have somewhat limited scope at the conceptualizing stage. Yet, despite facing issues framed for them by their adversaries, these practitioners can still exercise their creative powers to their clients' benefit. The challenge of responding is that of subtly altering the shape of the debate—broadening or narrowing it, putting it in a new light. If counsel for appellant has written a competent brief, respondent's brief must do more than simply answer each of appellant's contentions with the equivalent of "is not!" For example, when appellant indignantly and with some justification claims that the trial was riddled with error, respondent's best strategy is often to begin with an argument emphasizing the quality and quantity of the evidence before responding to the individual claims of error. In short, if appellant yells "The sky is falling!" respondent's best strategy is often to argue "It's just a passing shower on a sunny day."

The brief-writer's greatest conceptual challenge, however, is that faced by counsel for appellant. The issues "preserved" on the record by trial counsel are a beginning, but counsel on appeal must do more than harvest these from the record. Appellate counsel must also assess the soundness of the fact-finder's conclusions and look for unpreserved error. Despite the difficulty of prevailing on unpreserved error, many such errors or one huge error may convince an appellate court to reverse. At a minimum, they may help a court decide to reverse on the basis of preserved error.

---

[31] *See supra,* Chapter 4, *Motions,* Section D(3).

Only by attending to every detail of the record can counsel find these kinds of errors. Any lapse of attention may let a viable issue slip by, so never try to finish a transcript in one sitting or keep reading when you are tired. One appellate practitioner was reading a transcript of the trial of a client convicted of robbery. The client's trial attorney had put on two alibi witnesses and asked them about the client's whereabouts from 12 a.m. to 2 a.m. on the 23rd of March. Although much of the trial testimony concerned incidents that took place on the *night* of March 23rd, the robbery itself took place just after midnight, and thus in the early hours of March 24th. Blundering, defense counsel had asked the alibi witnesses about *the wrong day.* The appellate court agreed with counsel that appellant had received ineffective assistance of trial counsel and ordered a new trial. Had appellate counsel not been paying attention, she would not have caught the error.

Of course, it is not enough to notice details. Counsel must also pull back the zoom lens and look at the big picture. As discussed above in Chapter 6 on *Persuasion*, meaningful advocacy is only possible when we find the "core" of the case, its emotional or intellectual "hook." You know you've found it when you can imagine beginning oral argument "Your honors, this is a case about...."

As with any document that contains legal analysis or argument, writing is an invaluable part of the conceptualization phase. By experimental writing, we come to see our arguments more clearly and even find others. By writing the free or "zero" drafts described in Section B of the chapter on *Conceptualizing,* you may even end up with chunks of usable text.

After brainstorming an appeal, you may have not just one, but many non-frivolous issues. At that point, you must decide which issues to brief. Of course, if the issues cluster around a core persuasive theory, you would almost certainly brief all of the issues, so long as you do not exceed the court's page limit. If the issues do not cohere in this fashion, you have a difficult decision to make. Some experienced practitioners would advise you to brief only the very strongest issues; others would be more inclusive. Some arguments for limiting your arguments to the few strongest are that by so doing, you avoid dilution and that busy judges prefer shorter briefs. On the other hand, it is not always easy to predict how courts will react to issues; the issue that seems strong to you may seem marginal to the court, and vice-versa.

Once you have settled on the issues, you need to decide their sequence. Again, experienced practitioners differ. Some would always put the strongest issue first. Some would put issues in chronological order—that is, if there is an issue arising out of a pre-trial motion or proceeding, that issue should precede a trial issue. Likewise, under this sequence, an issue concerning counsel's opening statement would precede an issue concerning jury instructions. Some practitioners would conform their sequence to the court's decisional practice. For example, if one issue concerns the constitutionality of a statute and another concerns its applicability to appellant, some practitioners would put the latter issue first (even if it is not the stronger issue) because courts prefer to avoid deciding constitutional issues if the matter can be resolved otherwise. Finally, some practitioners always sequence their issues hierarchically, that is, they always put constitutional issues first, then statutory issues, and finally, any issues based on lesser authority. Perhaps the best way is to consider all these sequencing philosophies and decide which is most appropriate to your particular case.

### 4. Writing the First Full Draft

The first question that arises as you start your first full draft is where to begin. Once you have a thorough knowledge of the facts, know what your major arguments are, and have a firm grasp on the supporting authorities, you may start wherever you feel comfortable. By now, you should have a tentative outline of your arguments and ideally, some "zero" drafts of the argument.

From here, there are two basic ways to proceed. Some experienced brief-writers begin by turning their outlines and rougher-than-rough drafts into a good first draft of the argument. The advantage of this starting point is that when you finish your draft of the argument you will understand your issues far better than when you began. You may well have altered the outline you began with. With this clear understanding, you can write clear and effective point headings and questions presented. Moreover, you know which facts should be highlighted and which facts should be downplayed in your statement of facts.

Other writers go from their tentative outline and zero drafts to the less demanding job of writing the statement of facts. In addition to providing a break from the intellectual intensity of argument, working with the facts can crystalize your understanding of the issues.

Whether you draft the argument first or last, be sure to include citations to authority as you work. If you quote, be sure at this stage that your quotations are accurate. Putting quotes and citations in your draft is vastly preferable to plugging them in later. First, putting in cites during revision is not an efficient use of time, because it usually means re-familiarizing yourself with the authorities. Second, as time gets short, the temptation to plug a gap with a citation to an authority not quite on point may become irresistible.

## 5. Revising and Polishing

Once you have a full "good" draft of the entire brief, you are ready to revise and polish. For many practitioners, this begins with submission of the draft to a colleague. Even where there is no formal supervisory process, however, most appellate practitioners and many trial litigators prefer to have a trusted colleague critique their drafts. A reader coming fresh to the case can always offer helpful suggestions; more importantly, even the most experienced practitioner sometimes misses an issue or argument that a second reader can spot.

The writer's first task on revision is to look at the big picture—the conceptualization and organization. This should ideally be done in hard copy, because the small screen of the computer cannot tell you whether your basic design works or whether your organization has a logical (and thus persuasive) flow. After any necessary re-organization is done, text added and deleted, and necessary transitions added, polishing of grammar and style can be done on the computer, though some writers prefer to print out their new draft and polish in hard copy. As with all documents, however, proofreading is always best done in hard copy.

## E. SPECIAL CONCERNS: THE ETHICS OF PERSUASION

The Special Concerns section of Chapter 4, *Motions,* touched on the ethics of doing; here we think about the ethics of saying.

Required to be zealous advocates, but constrained as officers of the court, brief-writers walk an ethical highwire: they must vigorously assert their client's cause, but must do so within the constraints of the Model Rules of Professional Conduct and the Code of Professional Responsibility. The Code consists of canons, ethical considerations, and disciplinary rules. The canons describe norms of professional conduct, the ethical considerations articulate aspirational objectives, and the disciplinary rules establish a standard of conduct below which a lawyer is subject to censure.

These rules and codes essentially forbid making frivolous claims[32] and false statements of material fact or law.[33] In addition, Model Rule 3.3(a)(3) requires attorneys to disclose controlling legal authority directly adverse to the position of the client when the opposing counsel fails to disclose it.

Yet these professional standards forbid only the most egregious misconduct, and seemingly countenance a variety of dubious and abrasive rhetorical practices that neither convince the reader nor enhance the writer's reputation. These practices include making misleading (but not false) statements, usually by exaggerating facts, law, or opposing arguments or by giving an overly selective account of them. *Ad hominem* argument—insulting comments directed at opposing parties, opposing counsel, the court below, or anyone else advancing an argument contrary to the writer's—is another undesirable practice that does not violate professional ethics. Finally, *ad populem* argument, which seeks to convince by arousing negative emotions like hatred, fear, or revulsion is not in itself outside the norms of the profession.[34] Brief writers engage in these practices because they confuse assertiveness with aggression, wrongly believing that the latter persuades a reasonable audience.

The best approach to persuading the court is an approach that maintains the attorney's credibility. That may set the bar higher than the Code of Professional Responsibility, but it gains the audience's respect, serves truth, and promotes the integrity of the judicial system. Moreover, constant exposure to dual perspectives

---

[32] ABA Compendium of Professional Responsibility Rules and Standards, DR7-102(a), DR2-109(A) (ABA 2002); ABA Model R. Prof. Conduct 3.1 (1999).

[33] ABA Compendium, *id.*, DR7-102(A)(5); ABA Model R. Prof. Conduct 3.3 (1999).

[34] It has been argued that these rhetorical practices, although within the norms of legal ethics, violate basic notions of respect and truthfulness central to universalist ethics. *See generally*, Robert Audi, *The Ethics of Advocacy*, 1 Leg. Theory 251 (1995).

renders judges wary of over-stated arguments that distort and over-simplify. In short, the best policy is to put your case in a clear light without putting it in a false light.

─────────────────── *Exercise 9.4* ───────────────────

*Reread the sample appellate brief,* Wilson v. State, *in Section C. Imagine that you are the Assistant State's Attorney who has been assigned to write the respondent's brief.*

**A.** *Conceptualize: What would your core theory of persuasion be? What facts support your theory?*

**B.** *Draft: Write a question presented and point heading for your side. Rewrite the statement of facts from the State's perspective. Write a thesis paragraph to begin the state's argument.*

─────────────────── *Assignment 9.1* ───────────────────

*Assume that Nancy Williams, whose claims against Grace Church are the subject of Casefile 1 in Appendix A, has filed a complaint accusing the church's Board of Parish Life of sexual harassment and retaliation under the Minnesota Human Rights Act, and two counts of breach of her employment contract (firing without notice and firing without cause). If you drafted a complaint for Ms. Williams as requested by Assignment 2.2 in Chapter 2 on* Complaints, *use your complaint; if your class did not do that assignment, your teacher will supply you with a copy of Ms. Williams' complaint.*

*Assume the church board has responded to the complaint by filing a motion to dismiss the complaint for lack of subject matter jurisdiction. The church alleges that the Establishment Clause of the First Amendment and the Freedom of Conscience Clause of the Minnesota Constitution forbid adjudication of plaintiff Williams' claims. If you drafted a notice of motion, motion, and draft order for the church board as requested by Assignment 4.1 in Chapter 4 on* Motions, *use your motion for this assignment. If not, your teacher will supply a copy of the motion papers.*

**A.** *Assume that you are counsel for defendant Board of Parish Life of Grace Church. Write a trial brief (memorandum of law) in support of the motion to dismiss. Be sure that your arguments are based only on facts in the record. (The record consists only of the complaint, the employment contract incorporated into the complaint as Exhibit A, and the notice of motion, motion, and draft order.)*

–OR–

**B.** Assume that you are counsel for plaintiff Nancy Williams. Write a brief in opposition to the Board's motion to dismiss. Here, too, be sure that you do not go beyond the record.

─────────────── *Assignment 9.2* ───────────────

In Casefile 2 in Appendix A, the New Jersey trial court granted summary judgment of the Johnsons' wrongful birth suit against Dr. Joshua Wagner on the ground that the statute of limitations had run. A transcript of the hearing testimony appears in the casefile, as does the court's decision.

**A.** Assume that your firm represents the Johnsons, who are appealing the decision of the trial court, and you have been assigned to write the brief. You may assume that all of the facts in the file were elicited at the hearing held by the Superior Court on defendant's motion to dismiss on statute of limitations grounds. Draft a brief consisting of question presented, statement of the case, point heading, and argument.

–OR–

**B.** Assume that your firm represents defendant Wagner; write a brief responding to the Johnsons' argument that the trial court's decision was erroneous.

─────────────── *Assignment 9.3* ───────────────

Assume that after holding a hearing, the New York trial court denied defendant Timothy Burke's motion to suppress tangible evidence. The court wrote no opinion. The motion and the testimony at the suppression hearing are included in Casefile 3 in Appendix A. Defendant could not appeal the decision on the motion, because it was not a final judgment, and so he proceeded to trial. He was convicted as charged after a jury trial and is now appealing his conviction on the sole ground that the evidence should have been suppressed because his consent to the search of his apartment was coerced.

**A.** Assume that you are counsel for appellant Burke. Write an appellate brief consisting of question presented, statement of the case, point heading, argument, and conclusion.

–OR–

**B.** Assume that you are counsel for respondent People of the State of New York. Write a brief arguing that the trial court correctly denied appellant's motion to suppress.

## *Assignment 9.4*

*Casefile 6 in Appendix A contains plaintiff Adam Massey's complaint against his ex-wife, Stephanie Massey, alleging fraud and intentional infliction of extreme emotional distress. Defendant has filed a motion to dismiss, also reproduced in the Casefile.*

*A. Assume that you are counsel for plaintiff Adam Massey. Write a trial brief (memorandum of law) in opposition to defendant's motion to dismiss. Be sure to address only the grounds raised in the motion.*

*–OR–*

*B. Assume that you are counsel for defendant Stephanie Massey. Write a brief in support of her motion to dismiss. Be sure to address only the grounds raised in the motion.*

# Chapter 10

# INFORMING AND PERSUADING: JUDICIAL OPINIONS

---

## A. IN GENERAL

Drafting judicial opinions should be easy. After all, as law students we spend several years reading little else. Yet this very familiarity can be an obstacle. Classroom analysis focuses on the opinion's content, not on its structure or rhetorical strategies. Yet, all the while, we are internalizing many of the traditional stylistic practices of judges, and when as law clerks or decision-makers we come to write our own opinions, we tend to mimic those practices—sometimes without examining their appropriateness to the case. Thus we consider the opinion here as writers and as future law clerks and adjudicators, not as consumers. This chapter will therefore look at the audience and purpose of a judicial opinion and at its nuts-and-bolts structure. It will also discuss some of the persuasive techniques vital to an opinion's success.

It may seem incongruous to stress persuasion, given that adjudicators are, of course, sworn to neutrality, not advocacy. Indeed, their legitimacy stems from their disinterested labor within the judiciary: they may neither favor nor disfavor groups or individuals and must bring to every case an open mind. Yet when the decision has been made and the opinion is to be penned, judges often use the same rhetorical conventions as the lawyers who argue before them. However objective and rational the decision-making process, the opinion endeavors to convince its readers that the matter was properly decided. Thus judicial opinions have many of the characteristics of a persuasive document.

## 1. The Rhetorical Situation

Like most other documents, a good judicial opinion is responsive to its rhetorical situation–to its audience and purpose. The audience for an opinion is multiple. First, there are the parties involved in the dispute, as well as their respective counsel. This group needs to know what was decided and why. Second, there are the courts both above and below: the appellate court may be required to review the correctness of the lower court's decision, and the trial court or administrative agency must understand why it was affirmed or reversed in order to comply. Third, the legal community—its practitioners, students, scholars, and legislators—look to opinions as precedent, as grounds for commentary and critique, and as the basis of legislation. Finally, there is the general public, which may have an interest in the outcome of a decision because of its impact on business or general life.[1]

To differing degrees, these audiences are all interested in the three primary functions of judicial writing: dispute resolution, predictive guidance, and law-making. For the litigants, dispute resolution is a decision's most fundamental purpose. The parties want to know what the court has decided and what impact it will have on them. It is no trivial matter to serve a prison sentence, forfeit a farm, or lose parental rights, and the result is therefore the parties' primary concern. The reasons for the court's decision are also of interest to litigants and their counsel, especially if they contemplate an appeal.

Reasons and results also matter to practitioners, courts, scholars, and observers. Under stare decisis, opinions not only decide cases, but provide binding authority and guidance, in the form of explanation and justification, that enables these audiences to understand how this decision will affect other parties.

Finally, some opinions make law, whether by establishing a new rule, extending existing law, recognizing new policy considerations, or resolving a conflict of authority or interpretation. These law-making opinions require the most explanation, since, in Judge Patricia Wald's words, only thorough explanation can "reinforce our oft-challenged and arguably shaky authority to

---

[1] In addition, if you are a law clerk writing the first draft, your audience is the judge for whom you write.

tell others—including our duly elected political leaders—what to do.... One of the few ways we have to justify our power to decide matters important to our fellow citizens is to explain why we decide as we do."[2] Any decision that involves new law or policy addresses an audience that includes judges, the bar, law students, and the parties who may fall under it. In addition, legal scholars, historians, and commentators will scrutinize these opinions, trying to determine whether the court's approach or rule works well or ill in the development of doctrine. Lastly, members of the legislature will also read it and may react with bills that codify, modify, or supersede the court's ruling.

These purposes and audiences affect an opinion's rhetoric. All opinions reside somewhere on a continuum that moves from simple dispute resolution to law-making and also on a rhetorical line that moves from informing to persuading. In routine cases, where announcing the result is an opinion's fundamental function, explaining the result is the judge's primary rhetorical concern. But on those occasions when courts make law, persuasion becomes paramount. In order to assure acceptance, in order to forestall reversal, critique, doubt, and misgiving, the opinion must convince its readers of its rightness. Thus, when judges and their law clerks draft opinions in most non-routine cases, they write persuasive documents.

## 2. Decisions and Opinions

All matters before a court—whether civil action, criminal prosecution, motion or petition—terminate in a judicial writing. In trial courts, this may be only a short, boilerplate document, commonly known as an "order" or "judgment." A document of this kind is sufficient when a controversy has no precedential or institutional value.[3] Thus, given the routine nature of many legal controversies, it is not surprising that the vast majority of judicial opinions we read are written not by trial judges, but by appellate judges and their clerks. Yet trial judges also have occasion to explain the results they reach, deciding motions or sitting

---

[2] Patricia M. Wald, *The Rhetoric of Results and the Results of Rhetoric: Judicial Writing*, 62 U. Chi. L. Rev. 1371, 1372 (1995).

[3] *See* Ruggiero J. Aldisert, *Opinion Writing* 13–21 (West 1990).

as fact-finder in non-jury trials. These documents are sometimes called "decisions" rather than "opinions."[4]

In format, most trial decisions are similar to appellate opinions in that they have an introduction that identifies the parties, the nature of the case, and the issues; a fact statement; an analysis; and a disposition.[5] In function, of course, they differ. Whereas a trial court decision disposes of a motion or case before it, an appellate opinion expresses an appellate court's review of the proceedings in the court or courts below. The court looks first at whether it has jurisdiction over the appeal, including whether the matter was preserved for review in the record. If the court is satisfied on these and other matters, it considers, under the appropriate standard of review, whether the decision was correct. Appellate courts rarely disturb findings of fact, whether by judge or jury, in part because they are unwilling to second-guess the fact-finder's determination of credibility. Appellate courts will review doctrinal issues *de novo*, however, and also grant relief for legal errors below, although in most cases, they must be convinced that the error was not "harmless," but rather that it caused undue prejudice.[6]

In addition to seeing that justice is done in a particular case, appellate courts have an institutional function—they contribute to the cohesive development of the law. Finally, appellate courts have a uniformity function—they assure the consistent administration of justice in their jurisdictions.[7] All of a court's functions are reflected in an effective appellate opinion.

Where a case presents no novel issue of law or fact, an appellate court may issue a memorandum or "per curiam" opinion, which are not attributed to a particular judge and are usually brief. Where a case has presented issues of precedential, institutional, jurisprudential, or social significance, however, the court writes a full opinion. Although authored by a single judge, this opinion reflects the decision of the majority of the court as to the result and

---

[4] Joyce J. George, *Judicial Opinion Writing Handbook* 20 (4th ed., W. S. Hein 2000).

[5] You should note that in non-jury civil trials, judges sometimes write Findings of Facts and Conclusions of Law. These differ from decisions in format, if not function, in that they put Findings of Facts and Conclusions of Law in discrete sections, and number individual facts and conclusions. We do not focus on Findings of Facts and Conclusions of Law in this chapter.

[6] For further discussion, *see supra* Chapter 9, Section A in *Trial and Appellate Briefs.*

[7] Aldisert, *supra* n. 3, at 21.

the reasoning behind it. Indeed, the opinion usually incorporates points and suggestions made by those judges joining the decision. Because unanimity in an opinion signifies confidence in the decision, thereby promoting the stability of the law, judges often sign on to an opinion even if they are not in complete agreement with it. Nonetheless, when judges disagree, the majority opinion may be accompanied by separate concurrences or dissents.

Concurring opinions tend to be written when a judge believes the majority came to a correct decision, but not for the correct reasons: it either went too far or did not go far enough; it omitted important arguments or took a misguided approach. The concurrence adds reasoning in order to strengthen the holding by expanding or adjusting its rationale. Nonetheless, Judge Aldisert warns that "a separate concurring opinion is justified only when the majority is unwilling to accept the suggestion for incorporation into the main opinion,"[8] and when the concurrer's views are strongly held. Otherwise the reader may be puzzled as to why there is a separate declaration about a decision the writer has joined.

Some judges see the dissenting opinion as "the *enfant terrible* of appellate practice."[9] It "can weaken the court's authority" and "turn both opinions into high school debating exercises full of 'thrust and parry' footnotes."[10] Sometimes written out of outrage or dismay, and meant to set the record straight for posterity, a dissent expresses a judge's bottom-line disagreement with the result or the reasoning of the majority. For that very reason, other judges see dissents as a sure sign of judicial independence and vitality. "A dissenting opinion has more legitimacy than a concurring opinion because it is a statement of reasons calling for a result *different* from that of the majority."[11] Moreover, "dissents serve an important purpose because they are sometimes a predictor of future 'course corrections.' The dissenter often stakes out a position that the court may later reach,"[12] or that may be adopted by a reviewing court.

---

[8] *Id.* at 167.

[9] Roger J. Traynor, *Some Open Questions on the Work of State Appellate Courts,* 24 U. Chi L. Rev. 211, 218 (1957).

[10] Wald, *supra* n. 2, at 1413.

[11] Aldisert, *supra* n. 3, at 170.

[12] Kathy Barrett Carter, *A Passionate Dissenter: Eloquent Voice of the Court, Justice Stein Steps Down,* The Star-Ledger 9 (Sept. 3, 2002) (citing Justice Gary S. Stein, quoting U.S. Supreme Court Justice William Brennan).

## 3. Constraints

The wisdom of Solomon and a silver tongue are not the only useful characteristics of an opinion-writer. She also needs the ability to deal with institutional constraints. These constraints often make quality hard to achieve. First among difficulties is the pressure of time and volume. Overcrowded dockets mean judges need to produce opinions in quantity and with alacrity. They cannot afford writer's block, nor can they savor process. When composition must share space with other judicial tasks, it takes great skill and effort to render quality decisions in lively, clear, and thoughtful prose. Time pressures also mean that law clerks often draft opinions for their judges, and as Judge Patricia Wald reminds us, "he who wields the pen on the first draft...controls the last draft."[13] Although judges edit, rewrite, and occasionally even order a new draft, their clerks' workload and deadlines also pressure judges into accepting drafts that are acceptable in essence, if not in detail. Thus, it is not unusual for only the most significant cases to receive careful and extensive revision.

Time and workload are not the only constraints upon an appellate judge; colleagues are another. In an appellate tribunal, the author of the majority opinion writes for the court. That means obtaining a consensus, a situation that may require compromise. Negotiating the grounds for a decision, the precedents to be relied upon, and the language to be used means that the opinion finally issued is not necessarily the opinion the author most wanted to write.

Not all constraints are negative, however. An appellate judge's need to compromise is a check on unbridled exercises of power, as is a judge's obligation to write an opinion persuasively explaining the outcome. There are, moreover, other beneficial constraints that stem from legal conventions and practices. For example, judges and clerks must be sensitive to the types of arguments likely to be persuasive to the legal community, to the nature of the particular audiences addressed (counsel and reviewing judges), and to the particular interpretive requirements of legal decision-making.

---

[13] Wald, *supra* n. 2, at 1384.

Thus, an opinion writer must always weigh ends against means and write the best opinion possible, given both negative and positive constraints.

## 4. Candor and Reasoning

Candor is a troublesome issue for judges. As Judge Richard Posner says,

> Judges are not comfortable writing opinions to the effect that "we have very little sense of what is going on in this case. The record is poorly developed and the lawyers are lousy. We have no confidence that we have got it right. We know we're groping in the dark. But we're here to decide cases and here goes." Nevertheless, this is the actual character of many appellate cases that are decided in published opinions.[14]

Judges sometimes write with certitude they do not actually possess in order to promote the stability and authority of law. One law professor comments, "The court's mission is not to open debate, as might a professor's classroom questions, but rather to establish governing case law that can be understood quickly and decisively by a legion of future users."[15] Yet other judges and other legal scholars think that judges must candidly explain their reasoning for the opinions to be really useful. This candor means not only acknowledging difficult and troubling cases, but also, and even more importantly, explaining the actual reasons behind the result. As Judge Robert A. Leflar says, "Often, neither formal logic nor interpretation of prior precedent constitute real reasons either for moving the law in new directions or for refusing to move it."[16] Admitting this is important, he says, because

> [l]awyers and other judges can be misled by pretense.... [R]easons that truly supported a rule a half-century ago may no longer

---

[14] Richard A. Posner, *Judges' Writing Styles and Do They Matter?*, 62 U. Chi. L. Rev. 1421, 1441 (1995).

[15] Richard Cappalli, *Improving Appellate Opinions*, Judicature 286, 319 (May/June 2000).

[16] Robert A. Leflar, *Quality in Judicial Opinions*, 3 Pace L. Rev. 579, 581 (1983).

support it, though other relevant reasons do. In such a case, it is not enough to cite the precedent; the currently good reason must also be given. Nor is it ever enough to say simply that "public policy" justifies the result. There are a thousand different public policies.... The specific policy must be identified and its relevancy made clear. Simply stated, neither precedent nor policy genuinely justifies a result except as its own basis affords the justification.[17]

Leflar says that there are three basic kinds of reasons upon which a decision rests and that judges should be honest about which one or ones motivate their decisions: authority reasons, rightness (corrective justice) reasons, and goal (social consequences) reasons.[18]

Authority reasons are appropriate, Leflar says, when cases are squarely controlled by statutes or binding precedents. A case is controlled by precedent when the two are alike in important ways and the differences are not material. These are the easy cases. Harder cases may require an examination of underlying substantive reasons. Rightness reasons deal with matters like culpability, malice, good faith, and other socio-moral norms and are often invoked when judges are seeking to do corrective justice in the matter before them. Goal reasons are those that militate for justice in the future by promoting social policies like public health, judicial efficiency, or fair labor practices.[19] Opinions that are honest about the grounds they rest upon furnish "better guidance to one who seeks to discover from them what the next case will hold."[20] When judges do not give real reasons, predictability suffers.

## B. COMPONENTS

Except when an individual controversy suggests some modification, judicial opinions typically have a five-part format:

---

[17] Robert A. Leflar, *Honest Judicial Opinions*, 74 Nw. U. L. Rev. 721, 723 (1979). *See also* William D. Popkin, *The Dynamic Judicial Opinion*, Issues in Legal Scholarship, Dynamic Statutory Interpretation< http://www.bepress.com/ils/iss3/art7 >(2002).

[18] Leflar, *Honest Judicial Opinions*, *supra* n. 17, at 737.

[19] *Id.*

[20] *Id.*

1. Introduction
2. Statement of the Issue/s (as a separate section or in the introduction or at the start of the analysis)
3. Statement of Facts
4. Analysis, including a background explanation of the law and an analysis in which the law is applied to the facts of the case
5. Disposition

## 1. Introduction

The introduction to a decision or opinion orients the reader to the nature of the action. In a trial court decision, the writer will identify the parties, the type of action, and the issues. The writer will then explain how the matter came before the court, for example, on a motion to dismiss or a motion for summary judgment, and the relief sought. In an appellate opinion, enough background must be given for the decision to be easily under-standable. Thus, the introduction ought to identify the parties, including their roles in the proceedings; indicate the nature of the controversy (such as breach of contract) and the result in the court(s) below; and explain the nature of the issues on appeal and how the case reached the appellate court.

Some judges like to preview "the issue and the outcomes"[21] in the introduction so that anxious parties are not held in suspense and interested parties can more readily follow the analysis. Other judges object to this because "it gives the impression that the opinion is just the rationalization of a preordained decision, rather than an exploration."[22] Since judges do indeed reach their decisions before they begin drafting, however, and since opinions are not mystery stories but dispositions of consequential disputes, we favor giving the conclusion from the start.

## 2. Statement of the Issues

If not included in the introduction, the questions to be decided by the court are set out in the next section. It is a well-known

---

[21] Patricia M. Wald, *How I Write*, 4 Scribes J. Leg. Writing 55, 61 (1993).

[22] Richard Posner, *supra* n. 14, at 1437.

axiom of appellate practice that the power to frame the issue is the power to compel decision in your favor. Thus, attorneys struggle to get judges to accept their formulation of the issues because it is judges who enjoy that ultimate power to ask the question that mandates the answer they have in mind.

Whether issue statements in an opinion should be neutral is a matter of some disagreement. Judge Aldisert thinks the phrasing should be as neutral as possible—or should even favor the losing party—to underscore the impartiality of the tribunal.[23] Other judges are more willing to admit the persuasive element. As Justice Frankfurter said, "Tell me the answer you want and I will phrase the question." The difference in phrasing is very apparent in the majority opinion and dissent in *Lehr v. Robertson*.[24]

> The question presented is whether New York has sufficiently protected an unmarried father's inchoate relationship with a child whom he has never supported and rarely seen in the two years since her birth.
>
> Justice Stevens, writing for the majority
>
> The question in this case is whether the State may, consistent with the Due Process Clause, deny notice and an opportunity to be heard in an adoption proceeding to a putative father when the State has actual notice of his existence, whereabouts, and interest in the child.
>
> Justice White, dissenting[25]

Wherever you come down on the neutrality-vs-persuasion debate, the issue statement should be clear and concise. As in an advocate's question presented, the first half of the sentence should set out the legal question so as to provide the context for the second half, which provides the factual details upon which a determination depends.

---

[23] Aldisert, *supra* n. 3, at 90–92.

[24] 463 U.S. 248 (1983).

[25] *Id*. at 268.

## 3. Statement of Facts

Fact statements often begin by stating the burden of proof or standard of review. These make a difference in how the audience reads the facts: if it knows that it must look at the facts in the light most favorable to the non-moving party, for example, it is better able both to measure the success with which the moving party has met that burden and to anticipate the legal analysis that follows.

After this comes a narrative statement of facts. If the facts are long and complex, it may be useful to begin with a summary that provides a roadmap and to use topical headings to categorize the facts that raise different legal issues. The statement is usually written in the past tense and follows a chronological order, although in an appropriate case, the ABDCE structure described in Section B of Chapter 6, *Persuasion*, may also be used.

The statement should include only the facts that are necessary for an understanding of the case or the appeal and may not, of course, include any facts that are not in the record. Thus, the rendition is selective. If the writer finds she is omitting a lot of facts, however, or including a lot that are not strictly relevant, it may be because the writer has made the wrong decision. If, for example, much background is needed to evoke emotions that justify the decision, or if relevant facts must be omitted, then perhaps the statement has been tailored a bit too closely for ethical decision-making. Thus, selectivity and objectivity must be balanced. Nonetheless, fact statements can be very potent support for the opinion's analysis since they contextualize law and dramatize its impact on human life. For more on their persuasive crafting, we refer you again to Section B of Chapter 6.

## 4. Analysis

The heart of an opinion is the analysis of the issues. When the analysis is complicated, a well-written decision begins with a summarizing roadmap. After this, it proceeds as would a memo or brief, issue by issue, sub-issue by sub-issue. If the law on an issue is well established, and the only question is its application, the writer should set out the law. If the issue is one of first impression, the writer should set out the legal background and the holdings and reasoning of any decisions on analogous issues in that jurisdiction and then examine decisions on the issue by courts in other jurisdictions. If the issue is a legal, doctrinal one, however, the writer must decide what is the right rule.

Once the law is explained sufficiently, it is applied to the facts—where the issue is fact-based. The decision should not just be announced; the writer should instead explain fully and candidly why she reached that conclusion, being careful to provide a conclusion for each issue raised in the case. These conclusions culminate in the disposition of the case.

## 5. Disposition

The last section of an opinion is the disposition of the case. In a trial opinion, it should describe the decision reached and the relief granted or penalty imposed. In an appellate opinion, a single sentence will usually suffice when the judgment or order is affirmed. But when the judgment is reversed and remanded in whole or in part, more detailed instructions are needed to inform the trial tribunal exactly what consideration is expected of it and to let the parties know where they stand.

## C. SAMPLE OPINION

We have chosen an opinion, *Schroeder v. Perkel,* 432 A.2d 834 (N.J. 1981), that does an admirable job of explaining a difficult issue clearly and candidly. In the interest of space, we have edited out references to some collateral issues and we have edited string and parallel cites down to one citation.

### SCHROEDER v. PERKEL

Pollock, J.

| | |
|---|---|
| Issue/Posture<br><br>Who's Who | The sole issue on this appeal is the propriety of a grant of partial summary judgment to defendant physicians in a "wrongful conception" or "wrongful birth" action brought by the parents of a child with cystic fibrosis. |
| Introduction | The parents allege that the negligent failure of defendants to diagnose cystic fibrosis, a hereditary disease, in their first child deprived the parents of an informed choice whether to have a second child. Consequently, the parents seek to recover the incremental medical costs associated with raising the second child, who also suffers from cystic fibrosis. They claim that these costs are attributable directly to the negligence of the defendants. |
| Decision<br>Announced | The trial court denied defendants' motion for summary judgment, but the Appellate Division reversed. We granted certification.... We reverse the judgment of the Appellate Division and remand the matter for trial. |

### I. FACTS

| | |
|---|---|
| Standard of<br>Review | Because this appeal presents for review an order of partial summary judgment for defendants, we must accept as true all the allegations in plaintiffs' complaint, affidavits and depositions and accord to them the benefit of all reasonable inferences. *Portee v. Jaffee,* 84 N.J. 88, 90 (1980). |
| | Defendants, Dr. Perkel and his associate Dr. Venin, are pediatricians certified by the American Board of Pediatrics and licensed to practice medicine in this state. They treated infant plaintiff, Ann |

**Summary of Facts—An Overview**

Schroeder, from May 1970 until September 1974. During that time, they failed to diagnose Ann's illness as cystic fibrosis, a genetically transferred disease. Because Mr. and Mrs. Schroeder, Ann's parents, were not told that they were carriers of cystic fibrosis, they claim that they were deprived of an informed choice of whether to assume the risk of a second child. Before they learned that Ann suffered from cystic fibrosis, Mrs. Schroeder became pregnant. One month after learning of Ann's affliction, Mrs. Schroeder gave birth to a second child, Thomas, who also suffers from cystic fibrosis.

**The Disease**

Cystic fibrosis is one of the most common fatal genetic diseases in the United States and affects approximately one out of every 1,800 babies. An insidious and incurable disease, cystic fibrosis is carried by some parents as a recessive gene.... Cystic fibrosis cannot be detected in a fetus. A safe, simple and highly reliable test, however, can be performed shortly after birth. Known as the "sweat test," it involves an analysis of perspiration, which contains an abnormally high concentration of salt in someone suffering from cystic fibrosis. A positive test indicates not only that both parents are carriers, but also the probabilities that future children of those parents will be afflicted with cystic fibrosis.

**Detailed Facts**

As an infant, Ann suffered from a digestive disorder diagnosed by Dr. Swiney, a general practitioner, as colic. When the symptoms persisted through her second year, Dr. Swiney referred Ann to the defendant physicians.

.... Dr. Venin did not perform a sweat test. Instead, he relied on a stool test performed by Dr. Swiney, and he assured Mr. and Mrs. Schroeder that the stool test ruled out cystic fibrosis. Nonetheless, Dr. Venin admits that the stool test is not the correct or preferred test to use in diagnosing cystic fibrosis....

In June 1974, Mr. and Mrs. Schroeder read a newspaper article describing the symptoms of cystic fibrosis. Feeling that the article described Ann's condition, they asked Dr. Venin about the possibility of cystic fibrosis. According to Mrs. Schroeder, Dr.

Venin told her in July 1974 that Ann "couldn't possibly have cystic fibrosis," an assertion disputed by Dr. Venin. Mrs. Schroeder stated that Dr. Venin informed her that the stool test performed by Dr. Swiney had eliminated the possibility of cystic fibrosis and that Ann definitely was not suffering from this disease.

When Ann's condition worsened in September 1974, Dr. Venin referred her to Dr. Grotsky, a specialist in digestive disorders. Dr. Grotsky performed the sweat test. The test established that Ann suffered from cystic fibrosis. Unfortunately, by that date Mrs. Schroeder was in the eighth month of her pregnancy with Thomas. The delay in the diagnosis had precluded Mr. and Mrs. Schroeder from making an informed choice as to whether or not to assume the risk of conceiving a second child with cystic fibrosis. The delay also had prevented them from making an informed choice whether Mrs. Schroeder should have an abortion.... A sweat test performed on Thomas two weeks after his birth revealed that he, like his sister, was afflicted with cystic fibrosis.

**The Case So Far**

Mr. and Mrs. Schroeder instituted this action on behalf of themselves and Ann and Thomas. In an amended complaint, they asserted four causes of action.... In Count Three, Mr. and Mrs. Schroeder sought damages in a "wrongful birth" action for the failure of defendants to advise them that Ann suffered from cystic fibrosis, thereby depriving Mr. and Mrs. Schroeder of the alternative of preventing the conception of Thomas. They sought damages not only for the incremental medical costs, but also for the mental anguish involved in caring for Thomas....

Defendants moved for summary judgment on all four counts....

...

**Procedural History**

With respect to Count Three, the trial court granted defendants' motion for summary judgment as to the claim of Mr. and Mrs. Schroeder for mental anguish, but denied the motion on the Schroeders' claim for incremental medical expenses from the alleged wrongful birth of Thomas. The Appellate Division reversed the order granting summary judgment for defendants on the claim of Mr. and Mrs. Schroeder for mental anguish, but also reversed and entered judgment for defendants on the claim for incremental medical expenses.

[T]he only issue before us is the propriety of the judgment for defendants entered by the Appellate Division on the claim of Mr. and Mrs. Schroeder for incremental medical costs for their second child, Thomas, who suffers from cystic fibrosis.

## II Analysis

In determining the rights and duties of the parties, we must consider initially whether the defendant physicians owed a duty to Mr. and Mrs. Schroeder to diagnose Ann's affliction and to inform them that she suffered from cystic fibrosis. If that duty exists, we must then consider whether Mr. and Mrs. Schroeder have asserted facts establishing a breach of the duty. Finally, we shall consider

Roadmap

whether Mr. and Mrs. Schroeder have asserted sufficient facts to establish that the breach of duty proximately caused the extraordinary medical expenses that they claim they will sustain in caring for Thomas.

Defendants contend that Ann was their patient and that their duty was to her, not her parents. In effect, they contend that they had no duty to Mr. and Mrs. Schroeder to advise them that their infant child was suffering from cystic fibrosis. The implication is that, if defendants had no duty to Mr. and Mrs. Schroeder, then defendants cannot be liable for depriving them of the decision not to have another child. Consequently, the defendants argue they cannot be liable for the expenses Mr. and Mrs. Schroeder will sustain in caring for Thomas. We disagree....

The scope of duty in negligence, except as limited by policy considerations, is coextensive with the reasonable foreseeability of the consequences of a negligent act. *Portee v. Jaffee, supra,* 84 N.J. at 94–96....

Issue: Duty

The foreseeability of injury to members of a family other than one immediately injured by the wrongdoing of another must be viewed in light of the legal relationships among family members. A family is woven of the fibers of life; if one strand is damaged, the whole structure may suffer. The filaments of family life, although individually spun, create a web of interconnected legal interests. This Court has recognized that a wrongdoer who causes a direct injury to one member of the family

**Authority Argument**

may indirectly damage another. Consequently, husbands and wives have causes of action for loss of consortium when the other spouse is injured. *Ekalo v. Constructive Serv. Corp.,* 46 N.J. 82, 95 (1965) (recognition of claim by wife for loss of husband's consortium).... Parents can recover for loss of companionship and advice in an action for the wrongful death of a minor child, *Green v. Bittner,* 85 N.J. 1, 4 (1980); an infant can recover against a tortfeasor for prenatal injuries suffered as a result of injuries to the mother in an automobile accident, *Smith v. Brennan,* 31 N.J. 353, 361 (1960). A parent has a cause of action for mental anguish resulting from viewing the suffering and death of a child caused by the negligence of a tortfeasor. *Portee v. Jaffee, supra,* 84 N.J. at 101. As a corollary to their duty to provide medical care for their children, parents can maintain an independent action to recover from a tortfeasor for medical expenses incurred for a child. *Friedrichsen v. Niemotka,* 71 N.J. Super. 398, 402 (Law Div.1962)....

Foreseeability of harm to parents from an injury to a child flows not only from the bonds between parent and child, but also from the responsibility of parents to provide medical care for their children.... Indeed, the willful failure of parents to provide "proper and sufficient" medical care for their child is a crime. *N.J.S.A. 9:6-1; N.J.S.A. 2C:24-4.* In this case, we were informed at oral argument that Mr. and Mrs. Schroeder have borne and will continue to bear the expense of medical treatment of Thomas.

**Corrective Justice Argument**

It would be unreasonable to compel parents to bear the expense of medical treatment required by a child and to allow the wrongdoer to go scot-free.... In this context, a wrong should not go unrequited and an entire family left to suffer because of the dry technicality that Thomas has the primary obligation to pay for his own medical expenses. In addition, exoneration of the defendants would provide no deterrent to professional irresponsibility and would be contrary to the direction of our decisions in family torts. *Id.*

**Public Policy Argument**

A physician's duty thus may extend beyond the interests of a patient to members of the immediate family of the patient who may be adversely affected by a breach of that duty. Here, the physicians had not only a duty to Ann, but an independent duty to the Schroeders to disclose to them that Ann suffered from cystic fibrosis. The wrong allegedly committed by defendants was the failure to disclose material information. The defendants should have foreseen that parents of childbearing years, such as Mr. and Mrs. Schroeder, would, in the absence of knowledge that Ann suffered cystic fibrosis, conceive another child. They should have foreseen also that a second child could suffer from cystic fibrosis and that, if so afflicted, would sustain certain medical expenses. *See generally* Note, 87 *Yale L.J., supra,* at 1506–1508.

**Public Policy Argument**

. . .

Assuming the truth of the facts set forth in opposition to the motion for summary judgment, defendants thus owed a duty of care to Mr. and Mrs. Schroeder. Ann's history and symptoms supported the conclusion that Ann probably suffered from cystic fibrosis. Dr. Venin's notes indicated he should have ruled out cystic fibrosis, and Mr. and Mrs. Schroeder asked him whether Ann suffered from the disease. They also asked him about administering a sweat test, but he assured them it was not necessary. If performed, the sweat test would have disclosed that Ann suffered from cystic fibrosis. His failure to diagnose Ann's cystic fibrosis and to advise Mr. and Mrs. Schroeder that Ann suffered from the disease was a breach of his duty to them.

**Issues: Causation & Damages**

The normal measure of damages for the commission of a tort is all damages proximately caused by the injury. *Berman, supra,* 80 N.J. at 432. The application of that standard has perplexed courts where the tort results in the birth of an afflicted child.... In *Berman*, in part because of the constitutional right of a woman to abort a pregnancy, the Court recognized that the parents had a cause of action for deprivation of the right to decide whether to bear a child with Down's Syndrome. Nonetheless, the Court found "[t]roublesome" the measure of damages and denied recovery for the expenses in raising and supervising a child with Down's Syndrome. *80 N.J. at 432.*

. . .

Divergent results of different courts or of different members of the same court reflect the complexity of the problem. Inherent in all the cases are sensitive issues concerning procreation and the right to prevent it by contraception or abortion. Those issues may affect judicial nerves differently with correspondingly different reactions. Another consideration that may affect courts in different ways is that the cause of action involves injury arising out of the conception and birth of a person not yet born. Also, courts may vary in their perception of the relationships and responsibilities of one family member to another. In brief, the problems of wrongful conception and wrongful birth involve an evaluation not only of law, but also of morals, medicine and society. Thus, it is not surprising that the same issue may elicit divergent judicial responses.

While we recognized the claim for wrongful birth in *Berman*, we declined to allow recovery for the normal expenses of raising a child. A critical factor distinguishes the claim of Mr. and Mrs. Schroeder for the extraordinary medical expenses of raising a child with cystic fibrosis from the claim of Mr. and Mrs. Berman. Mr. and Mrs. Schroeder seek damages more proportionate to the wrong of defendants than those sought by Mr. and Mrs. Berman, who sought recovery for the ordinary cost of raising and educating their child. The damages sought by Mr. and Mrs. Schroeder are the medical, hospital and pharmaceutical expenses needed for Thomas' survival. That kind of expense, regularly

*Margin notes:*
Candor

Corrective
Justice
Argument

measured by the courts, includes the prescription of enzymes and antibiotics, checkups every one or two months and hospitalization, which typically occurs only in emergencies or towards the end of the life of the victim. Mr. and Mrs. Schroeder also intend to seek recovery for the cost of daily therapy to Thomas. Until now that therapy has been provided by them without any outside assistance. At trial they must prove the probability not only of the need and cost of the therapy, but that it will be rendered by someone other than themselves. They cannot recover for services that they have rendered or will render personally to their own child without incurring financial expense.

**Corrective Justice Argument**

By limiting damages to those expenses that are actually attributable to the affliction, we are not conferring a windfall on Mr. and Mrs. Schroeder. Although they may derive pleasure from Thomas, that pleasure will be derived in spite of, rather than because of, his affliction. Mr. and Mrs. Schroeder will receive no compensating pleasure from incurring extraordinary medical expenses on behalf of Thomas. There is no joy in watching a child suffer and die from cystic fibrosis.

**Authority Argument**

In other settings, New Jersey law has allowed for the recovery for the reasonable value of past and future medical services necessitated by a defendant's tortious conduct. *Coll v. Sherry,* 29 N.J. 166, 174 (1959) (allowance for recovery of damages for past and future medical care and treatment necessitated by tortious injury); *Work v. Philadelphia Supply Co.,* 95 N.J.L. 193, 196 (E. & A. 1920) (plaintiff may recover "such reasonable outlay in the future as may be necessary to heal herself and her injuries"). And in settings similar to those before us, courts in other states have awarded to parents recoveries for medical treatment for afflicted children. *Becker v. Schwartz, supra,* 386 N.E.2d at 813, (recovery for care and treatment of children with Down's Syndrome born as consequence of physicians' tortious conduct); *Gildner v. Thomas Jefferson Univ. Hosp.,* 451 F.Supp. 692, 695 (E.D.Pa.1978) (parents may recover damages for medical expenses and emotional pain caused by child born with Tay-Sachs disease not properly diagnosed by physician's amniocentesis report)....

**Public Policy Argument**

Those cases are consistent with New Jersey public policy that a physician should be liable for losses proximately caused by his negligent deprivation of a woman's right to decide whether or not to bear a child. *Berman, supra,* 80 N.J. at 431–432. The medical expenses attributable to the cystic fibrosis of their son are part of Mr. and Mrs. Schroeder's loss caused by the deprivation of their right to choose whether to conceive a second child. If it is proved at trial that the defendant physicians deprived Mr. and Mrs. Schroeder of their right to choose whether or not to give birth to a child afflicted with cystic fibrosis, defendants should be liable for the incremental medical costs of a child born with that affliction. In the changing landscape of family torts our decision in this case merely advances the frontier a little farther.

**Disposition stated with Specificity**

We reverse the partial summary judgment for defendants on the third count of the complaint and remand the matter for trial.

## D. WRITING PROCESS

The writing process for judicial opinions is not quite like any other. For a trial judge, the process may begin with notes taken during the proceedings on testimony and arguments on the motions relevant to the outcome. For the appellate judge, it may begin with a law clerk's bench memo. These memos give the judge a brief preview of the case's factual and procedural history and of the arguments raised in the briefs. Often the clerk recommends a disposition. The bench memo may be as short as a page or two, or significantly longer if the case is complex. Law clerks will also research the case for the judge, reading all the cases upon which counsel relies to check that they stand for the proposition for which they are cited, as well as other relevant cases. Thus from the outset, there is a lot of collaboration between judge and clerks.

Collaboration also characterizes the bench conference. Not only must the outcome and basic rationale for the decision be agreed upon, but the judges often debate the precedents to be relied upon, a well as the articles, treatises, and commentaries to be cited. After the bench conference, the judge assigned to the opinion will often discuss the approach to be taken with her clerk and then direct her clerk to write the initial draft. Many law clerks study the decisions of their judges as a guide to style and organization. When the draft is done, the judge takes over, rewriting as appropriate to ensure the opinion reflects her analysis of the case. The collaboration may not end there, however, but may extend to line editing and stylistic criticism.

Whether the first draft is written by clerk or judge, the author may decide not to write the opinion in the order it must be ultimately assembled. For example, some writers may want to delay writing the facts until the analysis is finished because it may become easier to select and arrange facts after they have worked through the issues and know the gravamen of the reasoning. Moreover, although it is likely the writer came to a conclusion about the case before beginning the opinion, writing is an exploration, and it is quite possible that the grounds for the decision may change focus or direction as she tries to explain and justify it, even requiring some further research. Thus some write the introduction after the analysis, while others are prepared to rewrite the introduction so that it more accurately reflects the issues and conclusions that were crystallized while composing the discussion itself.

Despite the pressures of time and volume, thorough explanation is essential. This often means refuting the arguments that were rejected as well as expounding those that were convincing. As one veteran state supreme court justice put it:

> Any opinion of the court has got to be understandable not only to lawyers and judges, but hopefully, any members of the press or public who care to read it.... We try very hard, in the court's opinions, to expound on our thinking, explain the alternatives, discuss the arguments for the other result and explain why they are not persuasive.[26]

Only thus can the opinion achieve the ideal of being "clear, comprehensive, logical, and persuasive."[27]

When revising, it is especially important to check and double-check that cited authority accurately supports the points made.

## E. SPECIAL CONCERNS

Judicial writing is driven by two conflicting and competing impulses. There is the institutional mandate requiring objective decision-making, but also an institutional need for those decisions to be met with communal acceptance. The latter impulse pushes the judge toward a rhetoric of persuasion—a rhetoric that can be compelling and thoughtful, but also lacking in candor if overdone. The best opinions use rhetorical devices only to bolster clear explanations of the grounds of their results.

In order to write a judicial opinion that convinces the reader of the rightness of its result, experienced drafters rely on the basics of persuasive writing described in our chapter on *Persuasion*. In addition, they employ rhetorical devices particular to the judicial opinion. Understanding these techniques will help the novice opinion-writer. Here we discuss two of the most characteristic rhetorical traits of judicial opinions: the judicial persona and the judicial voice.

---

[26] Carter, *supra* n. 12, quoting former Justice Gary S. Stein of the New Jersey Supreme Court.

[27] *Id.*

## 1. The Judicial Persona

The writer of an opinion is, inevitably, a character in that opinion. Character is revealed in the tone of voice the author adopts, in the attitudes the author assumes the reader will have toward the parties and the content of the text, and in the way the author treats sources and materials. In the context of opinions, one well-known law and literature professor describes judicial personae as resembling one of two types, the authoritarian "boss" judge or the "teacher" judge.[28] And, although it is rare to encounter either of these types in their pure form in contemporary opinions, few opinions are without their traces.

In the world of the authoritarian "boss" judge, the "ultimate boss" is the law—the constitution, statute, ordinance, or precedent that is "simply authoritative, composed in plain English—therefore plainly readable and simple—and to be read literally."[29] The judge is thus an "intermediate boss," a middle-management executive whose role is to state and apply the law rather than to make, interpret, justify, or explain it. The "boss" judge tends therefore to be conclusory in his characterization of law and treatment of precedent and to write abstractly. An extreme example of this persona is found in the terse adherence-to-precedent rationale of *Osterlind v. Hill,* where the heirs of a man who drowned lost a suit against the man who had rented the decedent a canoe and who failed to rescue him when the canoe overturned. The sentences have no individual human subjects.

> In view of the absence of any duty to refrain from renting a canoe to a person in the condition of the intestate, the allegations of involuntary intoxication relating as they do to the issues of contributory negligence become immaterial. The allegations of willful, wanton or reckless conduct also add nothing to the plaintiff's case. The failure of the defendant to respond to the intestate's outcries is immaterial. No legal right of the intestate was infringed. [Case dismissed].[30]

---

[28] James Boyd White, *Judicial Criticism*, 20 Ga. L. Rev. 835, 855 (1986).

[29] *Id.*

[30] *Osterlind v. Hill,* 160 N.E. 303 (N.Y. 1928). We thank Jethro Lieberman for bringing this case to our attention.

In contrast, the democratic judge speaks with the voice of a teacher who believes legal texts require explanation and translation. For example, a "teacher" judge deciding *Osterlind* might dispose of the case the same way as the "boss" persona, but he would justify the decision differently, delving into the policies that militate against a duty to rescue, for example, instead of simply relying on precedent. The teacher judge, therefore, explains the law for both the legal community and the general public. In so doing, the judge recognizes that the law being applied is, at least in part, of his or her own creation, as illustrated in *Schroeder:*

> [C]ourts may vary in their perception of the relationships and responsibilities of one family member to another. In brief, the problems of wrongful conception and wrongful birth involve an evaluation not only of law, but of morals, medicine, and society. Thus, it is not surprising that the same issue may elicit divergent judicial responses.[31]

There are correlations between the two kinds of judicial personae just discussed and the three kinds of justifications discussed earlier in this chapter—authority reasons, social goal reasons, and corrective justice or "rightness" reasons. "Boss" judges generally rely on authority reasons rather than social goal and rightness reasons.[32] If, however, a case does not easily fall under established authority, "boss" judges prefer corrective justice reasons to goal reasons. In contrast, "teacher" judges are more willing to discuss policy and equity, offering both goal and rightness justifications.

For cases that present few disputed facts and no new issue of law, judges and clerks can comfortably don a "boss" persona and rest on authority reasons. But for cases requiring the opinion writer to interpret, create, choose between, or strike down rules, "teacher" personae are more appropriate and substantive reasons more helpful. In these situations, a judge who carefully explains the grounds of the decision furnishes the best guidance as to its meaning and scope.

---

[31] *Schroeder v. Perkel*, 432 A.2d 834, 841 (N.J. 1981).

[32] Leflar, *Honest Judicial Opinions, supra* n. 17, at 736.

## 2. The Judicial Voice

The two personae described above have been associated with two rhetorical styles. There is the magisterial style—which, as one commentator says, "we tend to associate with authoritative judging. All magisterial/authoritative opinions have in common their reliance on 'given' first principles—often associated with 'formalistic' legal reasoning."[33] The magisterial voice conveys a sense of inevitability, unanimity and objectivity.[34] It relies on rhetorical devices that promote certainty—often intensifying or simplifying, rarely hedging or qualifying. The majority opinion in *United States v. Dickerson* is written in this voice.

> In response to the Supreme Court's decision in *Miranda v. Arizona,* 384 U.S. 436 (1966), the Congress of the United States enacted 18 U.S.C.A. § 3501 with the *clear* intent of restoring voluntariness as the test for admitting confessions in federal court. Although *duly* enacted by the United States Congress and signed into law by the President of the United States, the United States Department of Justice has *steadfastly* refused to enforce the provision. In fact, after initially "taking the Fifth" on the statute's constitutionality, the Department of Justice has now asserted, without explanation, that the provision is unconstitutional. With the issue *squarely* presented, we hold that Congress, pursuant to its power to establish the rules of evidence and procedure in the federal courts, acted *well within* its authority in enacting § 3501. As a consequence, § 3501, rather than *Miranda,* governs the admissibility of confessions in federal court. Accordingly, the district court erred in suppressing Dickerson's voluntary confession on the grounds that it was obtained in *technical* violation of *Miranda.*[35]

---

[33] Popkin, *supra* note 17, at 12.

[34] For an interesting discussion of the magisterial, or "monologic," voice, *see* Robert Ferguson, *The Judicial Opinion as Literary Genre*, 2 Yale J.L. & Humanities, 201, 204–208 (1990).

[35] *United States v. Dickerson*, 166 F.3d 667, 671 (4th Cir.) (emphasis supplied), *rev'd*, *Dickerson v. United States*, 530 U.S. 428 (2000).

The unwavering confidence expressed in this opening paragraph creates a sense of infallibility and inevitability. Congress has not just the "intent" of restoring pre-*Miranda* law, it has the "clear intent." The statute was not only "enacted," it was "duly" enacted. The Department of Justice has "steadfastly" refused to apply § 3501. The issue is "squarely" presented. Congress acted "well" within its authority. In contrast to all this magnification, the *Miranda* violation found by the District Court is reduced in scale to a mere "technical" violation.

In contrast to the magisterial voice is the exploratory, rational, temperate, and sometimes more personal tone often associated with a teacher judge expounding the law. In trial opinions and appellate concurrences and dissents, this voice is characterized by the first person singular. More importantly, the judge acknowledges disagreements, for example, among panel members, and admits questions and doubts, as in the following concurrence and dissent.

### [Concurrence]

I join with the majority of the Court...in recognizing and extending relief available to the aggrieved parents in this type of medical malpractice case. However, I disagree with the majority...first, for failing to appreciate fully the nature of the cause of action and the character and extent of the injuries of such parents; and second, for failing to recognize, independently, the injuries and right of redress of the infant plaintiff.[36]

### [Dissent]

The majority holds that § 3501 governs the admissibility of confessions in federal court because *Miranda* is not a constitutional rule. I don't know whether it is or not, but before I had to decide, I would want thoughtful lawyers on both sides to answer one question for me. If *Miranda* is not a constitutional rule, why does the Supreme Court continue to apply it in prosecutions arising in state courts?... This question illustrates that the § 3501 issue is so sweeping we

---

[36] *Schroeder,* 432 A.2d at 843 (Handler J., concurring).

> should not be delving into it on our own. In this case, we should follow our usual practice of deciding only the issues raised by the parties.[37]

The magisterial voice that characterizes many majority opinions often reflects the reassuring fact that the decision-makers have achieved an authentic consensus. The more personal, exploratory voice that draws the reader into the deliberative process offers another kind of reassurance—it reflects a kind of contemporary, democratic sensibility.[38]

——————————————— *Exercise 10.1* ———————————————

*A. Describe the judicial persona and voice in each of these two excerpts. Explain how these are manifested in the language of the court.*

### 1. Palmer v. Board of Ed. of City of Chicago, 603 F.2d 1271 (7th Cir. 1979)

Plaintiff states the issue to be whether or not a public school teacher in her classes has the right to refuse to participate in the Pledge of Allegiance, the singing of patriotic songs, and the celebration of certain national holidays when to do so is claimed to violate her religious principles. The issue is more correctly stated to be whether or not a public school teacher is free to disregard the prescribed curriculum concerning patriotic matters when to conform to the curriculum she claims would conflict with her religious principles. Plaintiff also claims her ultimate discharge denied her due process of law.

Plaintiff, a member of the Jehovah's Witnesses religion, was a probationary kindergarten teacher in the Chicago public schools. After her appointment, but prior to the commencement of classes, plaintiff informed her principal that because of her religion she would be unable to teach any subjects having to do with love of country, the flag or other patriotic matters in the prescribed curriculum. Extraordinary efforts were made to accommodate plaintiff's religious beliefs at her

---

[37] *Dickerson*, 166 F.3d at 697 (4th Cir. 1999), (Michael J., dissenting) *rev'd*, *Dickerson v. United States*, 530 U.S. 428 (2000).

[38] As Popkin remarks, "the magisterial voice establishes a judicial distance that is incompatible with the democratic demand for public accountability," *supra* n. 17, at 13.

particular school and elsewhere in the system, but it could not reasonably be accomplished.

* * * *

Plaintiff in seeking to conduct herself in accordance with her religious beliefs neglects to consider the impact on her students who are not members of her faith. Because of her religious beliefs, plaintiff would deprive her students of an elementary knowledge and appreciation of our national heritage. She considers it to be promoting idolatry, it was explained during oral argument, to teach, for instance, about President Lincoln and why we observe his birthday. However, it would apparently not offend her religious views to teach about some of our past leaders less proudly regarded. There would only be provided a distorted and unbalanced view of our country's history. Parents have a vital interest in what their children are taught. Their representatives have in general prescribed a curriculum. There is a compelling state interest in the choice and adherence to a suitable curriculum for the benefit of our young citizens and safety. It cannot be left to individual teachers to teach what they please. Plaintiff's right to her own religious views and practices remains unfettered, but she has no constitutional right to require others to submit to her views and to forego a portion of their education they would otherwise be entitled to enjoy. In this unsettled world, although we hope it will not come to pass, some of the students may be called upon in some way to defend and protect our democratic system and Constitutional rights, including plaintiff's religious freedom. That will demand a bit of patriotism.

### 2. *Russo v. Central Sch. Dist. No. 1,* 460 F.2d 469 (2d Cir. 1972)

Events that occur in small towns sometimes have a way of raising large constitutional questions. Henrietta, New York, a town of approximately 6,500 residents, is the geographic setting of this important case, in which we are asked to decide whether the dismissal of Mrs. Susan Russo, a high school art teacher, for what in the end amounts to a silent refusal to participate in her school's daily flag salute ceremonies, violated her constitutional rights under the First Amendment. As in *James v. Board of Education,* 461 F.2d 566 (2d Cir. 1972), decided by the Court just a few months ago, we must ascertain, and ultimately assess, the sometimes conflicting interests of the state on the one hand, in maintaining and promoting the discipline necessary to the proper functioning of schools, and the interest of a teacher, on the other, freely to exercise fundamental rights of expression and belief guaranteed by the Bill of Rights. There is, however, more to this case than even that difficult balancing test requires, for we are mindful of the fact that the problems associated with the short-hand phrase, "flag salute," bare a complex of deep emotions, calling into question the meaning of patriotism and loyalty, and the different significance those words have for different people. This case, therefore, is made more difficult for us, "not because the principles of decision are obscure but because the flag involved is our own." *West Virginia State Board of Education v. Barnette,* 319 U.S. 624, 641 (1942).

\* \* \* \*

It is our conclusion that the right to remain silent in the face of an illegitimate demand for speech is as much a part of First Amendment protections as the right to speak out in the face of an illegitimate demand for silence, *see Sweezy v. New Hampshire,* 354 U.S. 234 (1957); *West Virginia State Board of Education v. Barnette, supra.* Beliefs, particularly when they touch on sensitive questions of faith, when they involve not easily articulated intuitions concerning religion, nation, flag, liberty and justice, are most at home in a realm of privacy, and are happiest in that safe and secluded harbour of the mind that protects our innermost thoughts. To compel a person to speak what is not in his mind offends the very principles of tolerance and understanding which for so long have been the foundation of our great land. "If there is any fixed star in our constitutional constellation," Mr. Justice Jackson said in *Barnette,* "it is that no official, high or petty, can prescribe what shall be orthodox in politics, nationalism, religion, or other matters of opinion or force citizens to confess by word or act their faith therein. If there are any circumstances which permit an exception, they do not now occur to us." *West Virginia State Board of Education v. Barnette, supra,* 319 U.S. at 642. We believe that to be an accurate and thoughtful statement of the underlying spirit of the First Amendment and we abide by it here.

Accordingly, the judgment is reversed, and the case is remanded to the district court for proceedings not inconsistent with this opinion.

**B.** *Now read the following excerpts from* Russo *and* Palmer *in which the courts discuss and apply precedent. Evaluate and compare the use of caselaw, looking at how the two courts use Supreme Court rulings and how they analogize and distinguish the facts of precedent, in particular, how* Palmer *distinguishes* Russo.

### 1. *Russo v. Central Sch. Dist. No. 1*, 469 F.2d 623 (2d Cir. 1972)

If the central character in this drama were one of Mrs. Russo's students, rather than the teacher herself, we might dispose of this case with a simple reference to the Supreme Court's decision in *West Virginia State Board of Education v. Barnette*, 319 U.S. 624 (1943). There the Court was of the view that "in connection with the pledge, the flag salute is a form of utterance." 319 U.S. at 632. "To sustain the compulsory flag salute," the Court said, "we are required to say that a Bill of Rights which guards the individual's right to speak his own mind, left it open to public authorities to compel him to utter what is not in his mind." *Id.* at 634. The Court declined to do so, and invalidated a West Virginia statute and a Board of Education resolution.

\* \* \* \*

It has been stated that children, in many instances, have more limited First Amendment rights than do adults. *See, e.g., Ginsberg v. New York*, 390 U.S. 629 (1968) (obscenity); Emerson, Toward A General Theory of the First Amendment, 72 Yale L. J. 877, 938, 939 (1963); *see also, Tinker v. Des Moines Independent School Dist.*, 393 U.S. 503, 512 (1969), (Stewart concurrence). But here, the school board, as it did in *James v. Board of Education*, 461 F.2d 566 (2d Cir. 1972), would have us decide that the rights enjoyed by school children are broader than the First Amendment rights of their teachers. In *James*, we declined that invitation. The *James* case, which called into question the right of a teacher to silently protest America's involvement in the Vietnam war by wearing a black armband in school, was decided after the Supreme Court's decision in *Tinker* which expressly granted that right to children, where no substantial disruption resulted from the protest. We held that Mr. James could not be dismissed from his employment as a teacher for engaging in protected expression. Similarly, in this instance, the Supreme Court's *Barnette* decision teaches that school children may not be compelled to utter the pledge of allegiance when it offends their conscientiously held beliefs to do so. There is little room in what Mr. Justice Jackson once called the "majestic generalities of the Bill of Rights," *West Virginia State Board of Education v. Barnette*, 319 U.S. at 639, for an interpretation of the First Amendment that would be more restrictive with respect to teachers than it is with respect to their students, where there has been no interference with the requirements of appropriate discipline in the operation of the school, *Tinker v. Des Moines Independent School Dist.*, *supra*, 393 U.S. at 509. We add, however, as we did in *James*, that nothing in the First Amendment requires a school administration to wait until disruption has actually occurred before it may take protective action. Conduct which leads, or is likely to lead, to violence in the schools is not to be tolerated. *James v. Board of Education, supra*, 461 F.2d at 572. But such conduct is not involved in this case. We take guidance, instead, from the Supreme Court's instruction in *Tinker*, whose lesson is that neither students nor teachers "shed their constitutional rights to freedom of speech or expression at the schoolhouse gate." 393 U.S. at 506.

\* \* \* \*

By our holding today we do not mean to limit the traditionally broad discretion that has always rested with local school authorities to prescribe curriculum, set classroom standards, and evaluate conduct of teachers and students "in light of the special characteristics of the school environment," *James v. Board of Education*. But where in fact, as in this case, a dismissal is directed because a teacher has engaged in constitutionally protected activity, that dismissal may not stand.

### 2. *Palmer v. Board of Ed. of City of Chicago*, 603 F.2d 1271 (7th Cir. 1979)

In *Epperson v. Arkansas*, 393 U.S. 97, 107 (1968), the Court held invalid as offending the First Amendment an Arkansas statute prohibiting the teaching of a particular doctrine of evolution considered contrary to the religious views of most citizens. The Court recognized, however, that the states possess an undoubted right so long as not restrictive of constitutional guarantees to prescribe the curriculum for their public schools. Plaintiff would have us fashion for her an exception to that general curriculum rule. The issue is narrow.

Our decision in *Clark v. Holmes*, 474 F.2d 928 (7th Cir. 1972), *cert. denied*, 411 U.S. 972 (1973), is of some guidance. In that case the complaint about a university teacher was that he ignored the prescribed course content and engaged in unauthorized student counseling. We held that the First Amendment was not a teacher's license for uncontrolled expression at variance with established curricular content. The individual teacher was found to have no constitutional prerogative to override the judgment of superiors as to the proper content for the course to be taught. In *Ahern v. Board of Education*, 456 F.2d 399 (8th Cir. 1972), the court upheld a teacher dismissal for insubordination on the basis that the Constitution bestowed no right on the teacher to disregard the valid dictates of her superiors by teaching politics in a course on economics. In *Adams v. Campbell County School District*, 511 F.2d 1242 (10th Cir. 1975), the court stated that the Board and the principal had a right to insist that a more orthodox teaching approach be used by a teacher who was found to have no unlimited authority as to the structure and content of courses.

Plaintiff relies on a cross-section of First Amendment cases, but they are of little assistance with the specific issue in this case. Plaintiff argues that the defendants are trying to determine and limit the extent of her religious freedoms. The facts do not justify that legal perspective. The issue in this case is not analogous to a case:

(a)  where plaintiff is forced by statute to display on his automobile license plate a patriotic ideological motto repugnant to a follower of the Jehovah's Witnesses faith, *Wooley v. Maynard*, 430 U.S. 705 (1977); or,

(b)  where the state attempts to prohibit the issuance of a professional license because of the applicant's beliefs, *Baird v. State Bar of Arizona*, 401 U.S. 1 (1971); or,

(c)  where First Amendment rights may be chilled by a governmental investigative and data gathering activity causing actual or threatened injury, *Laird v. Tatum*, 408 U.S. 1 (1972); or,

(d)  where a person's right to the free exercise of his religion is conditioned on the surrender of his right to office, *McDaniel v. Paty*, 435 U.S. 618 (1978); or,

(e)  where a religious sect is forced to send its children to a public school contrary to the sect's religious beliefs, *Wisconsin v. Yoder*, 406 U.S. 205 (1972); or,

(f)  where students are being required to participate in a patriotic pledge contrary to their beliefs, *West Virginia State Board of Education v. Barnette*, 319 U.S. 624 (1943); or,

(g)  where the wearing of armbands by students in a Vietnam protest could not be prohibited where it did not interfere with school activities or impinge upon the rights of others, *Tinker v. Des Moines Independent Community School District*, 393 U.S. 503 (1969).

Plaintiff also cites *Russo v. Central School District No. 1*, 469 F.2d 623 (2d Cir. 1972), *cert. denied*, 411 U.S. 932 (1973), as squarely considering the present issue, but it does not. The court held that a high school art teacher could not be dismissed for her silent refusal to participate in her school's daily flag ceremonies. She would only stand silently and respectfully at attention while the senior instructor led the program. Her job was not to teach patriotic matters to children, but to teach art. The court carefully indicated that through its holding it did not mean to limit the traditionally broad discretion that has always rested with local school authorities to prescribe curriculum.

———————————— *Exercise 10.2* ————————————

*Revise the judicial opinion that follows, to make it easier to read and understand. It needs a more helpful introduction and clearer organization, at a minimum. Headings would also make the reader's job easier. You should also evaluate the court's analysis, especially its explanation of the law and the reasons provided for its decision. What kind of reasons does the court give? How well does the court support its conclusions?*

### *Carter v. Malone*, 545 N.E. 2d 5 (Ind. Ct. App. 1989)

Appellants Mr. and Mrs. J. C. Carter appeal an adverse possession judgment in favor of Edward and Dadine Malone. The court awarded the Malones a seven-foot wide strip of property on Lot 164 in Wolf's Second Addition to the City of Elkhart. In 1970, the Malone family purchased Lot 163 and the one-story frame house on it. In 1971, the Malones built a garage which protruded onto Lot 164 by 1.2 feet. In 1981, the Carters purchased vacant Lot 164. In 1984, before measuring the lot, the Carters offered to purchase a four-foot strip of land from the Malones. The Malones refused the offer to purchase.

After measuring the property, the Carters discovered that the Malones' garage protruded onto their lot and the Malones' house was less than four feet from the property. In 1984, the Carters constructed a duplex rental property on Lot 164.

In 1987, the Malones filed a complaint for adverse possession. Following a hearing, the trial court ruled in favor of the Malones and stated in part:

> The court finds that the plaintiffs herein had established sufficient adverse possession of said subject real estate from 1970, and that from 1970 to date had evinced the statutorily required adverse, visible, notorious and exclusive claim of ownership over the real estate. This evidence is substantiated by the defendants' offer to purchase a portion of that real estate from the plaintiffs upon the

impending construction of his duplex on the adjoining property. Further substantiating the plaintiffs' position in this case is the fact that for a substantial number of years a garage erected by the plaintiff was on a portion of the disputed real estate. The court having totally reviewed the evidence in this case now finds that the law is with the plaintiff and against the defendant and that more than adequate and sufficient evidence exists of the required adverse possession and that plaintiff is entitled to a judgment of a portion of the real estate between the property to and including the mid-line of the tree and hedgeline contained therein; and a judgment should be and hereby is awarded to the plaintiff subject to legal definition being included for the award herein.

Appellants question the sufficiency of the evidence supporting adverse possession. Record title is the highest evidence of ownership, and is not easily defeated and while title may be defeated by adverse possession, mere possession is the lowest evidence of ownership. In order for possession of real estate to ripen into title, it must be adverse, actual, open, notorious, exclusive, continuous and under a claim of right for the prescribed statutory period. *McCarty v. Sheets*, 423 N.E.2d 297, 298 (Ind. 1981). Successive periods may be tacked together to attain the prescribed statutory period. *Ford v. Eckert*, 406 N.E.2d 1209, 1210 (Ind. Ct. App. 1980).

The evidence showed that a row of trees and bushes existed on Lot 164. The trial court awarded the Malones a strip of land to the mid-line of tree and hedge-line. The Malones trimmed the trees and hedges and mowed the lawn around the row of trees since 1970. Periodic or sporadic acts of ownership such as maintenance activities, standing alone, are not sufficient to constitute adverse possession. *McCarty*, 423 N.E. 2d at 300–301.

The trial court relied on evidence that the Carters made an offer to purchase a four-foot strip of the Malones' Lot 163. The Malones' house was less than four feet from the Carters' Lot 164.

The adverse possessor's claim must be limited to that portion over which he exercises palpable and continuing acts of ownership, as being the quantity which he claims as his own, there being no other evidence, in such case, to enable us to determine the quantity. Where the quantity of land involved is small, the rule as to the location of the line is exacting possession to the line during all the statutory period must be definitely shown. *Id.* at 300.

The Carters' offer to purchase was made before the lot was measured and on the mistaken assumption that the Malones' house was more than four feet from the property line. In refusing the Carters' offer to purchase, Edward Malone stated, "No, because we own out to the hedges and we have been taking care of 'em." The Malones' claim to the strip of land was based on sporadic acts of maintenance and a verbal response to the Carters' mistaken offer to purchase. Periodic acts of yardwork and a verbal claim in response to a mistaken offer to purchase do not establish palpable, continuing or exacting acts of ownership sufficient to constitute adverse possession.

The Malones argue that the row of trees and bushes establish a possession or use line which supports open and conspicuous possession of the strip of property. The existence of a possession or use line was a factor noted in affirming an adverse possession award in *Oswald v. Paston,* 509 N.E.2d 217, 220 (Ind. Ct.App. 1987). In that case, a surveyor for the adverse possessor testified that he noticed a possession or use line. Additional evidence showed that the adverse possessor mowed, fertilized and planted flowers and a tree in the disputed area. The adverse possessor had trucks drive onto the disputed area to deliver fill dirt. The adverse possessor maintained a seawall in the disputed area and ordered a worker for the record titleholder off the disputed land.

In contrast, the Malones did not have a surveyor testify that a use or possession line existed. The row of trees and bushes grew wild, were noncontinuous and had gaps where people could walk back and forth. When the Carters cut down trees, planted grass, trimmed bushes, built a partial fence and cement stoop in the disputed area, the Malones did not protest. The evidence was insufficient to support the trial court's award of adverse possession to the mid-line of trees and bushes.

The garage built 1.2 feet over the property line established sufficient evidence for adverse possession of the area occupied by the garage. The trial court erred in awarding the Malones more land than actually occupied by the garage.

Reversed and remanded with instructions to enter judgment consistent with this opinion.

——————— *Assignment 10.1: Trial Opinion* ———————

*Read Casefile 3, which contains Timothy Burke's motion to suppress evidence (marijuana) and a summary of relevant portions of the hearing on the motion. Then write an opinion granting or denying the motion to suppress evidence.*

*In writing your opinion, focus on the decision-making as well as the opinion-writing process. How did you reach your decision? What kinds of considerations entered into your thinking—binding or persuasive authority, sympathy, social policy, personal values, economics, effect on future cases, etc.? Which were paramount? Did you change your mind along the way? Reflection on the decision-making process will help both your reasoning and persuasiveness.*

---

### Assignment 10.2: Appellate Opinion

*Charles and Emily Johnson brought an action in wrongful birth in Superior Court in Newark against Joshua Wagner, M.D. As guardian* ad litem *of their daughter, Dora Johnson, Ms. Johnson also brought an action for wrongful life. (See Casefile 2 in Appendix A.) The defendant moved for dismissal of the wrongful birth count on statute of limitations grounds. Assume that the trial court granted the defendant's motion and dismissed the Johnsons' claim. It wrote a short opinion, included in the casefile. The Johnsons have appealed. You are clerking for Judge Fitch of the appellate division of the New Jersey Superior Court. Judge Fitch is on the panel assigned to decide the appeal. Briefs have been filed and oral argument held. Critique the trial court opinion. Then choose one of the alternatives below and write a well-reasoned judicial opinion deciding the issues raised. (Your professor will either give you the relevant cases or ask you to research the issues presented.)*

**A.** *At the bench conference, the majority decided to reverse the order of the court below and reinstate the Johnsons' claim. Judge Fitch has been assigned to write the majority opinion, and she in turn has asked you to draft it.*

–OR–

**B.** *At the bench conference, the majority decided to affirm the order of the court below, dismissing the Johnsons' claim on statute of limitations grounds. Judge Fitch has been assigned to write the majority opinion, and she in turn has asked you to draft it.*

*In writing your opinion, focus on the decision-making as well as the opinion-writing process. How did you reach your decision? What kinds of considerations entered into your thinking—binding or persuasive authority, sympathy, justice to the parties, social policy, personal values, economics, effect on future cases, etc.? Which were paramount? Did you change your mind along the way? Reflection on the decision-making process will help both your reasoning and persuasiveness.*

———————————— *Assignment 10.3* ————————————

*You are a judge in a New Jersey court specializing in claims that involve the family. Every county in New Jersey has such a court—but your county, Seagrove, is mythical. The case of* **Massey v. Massey,** *Docket Number 12-3-456 is before you.*

*Plaintiff Adam Massey has sued defendants Stephanie Massey and Daniel Costello, alleging intentional infliction of extreme emotional distress (both defendants), fraud (Stephanie Massey), and unjust enrichment and reimbursement of child support (Daniel Costello). Stephanie Massey has moved to dismiss the complaint against her for failure to state a claim on which relief can be granted, alleging two separate grounds.*

*Draft a judicial opinion deciding Stephanie Massey's motion. The Complaint and Defendant's Notice of Motion are in Appendix A, Casefile #6.*

*In writing your opinion, focus on the decision-making as well as the opinion-writing process. How did you reach your decision? What kinds of considerations entered into your thinking—binding or persuasive authority, sympathy, social policy, personal values, economics, effect on future cases, etc.? Which were paramount? Did you change your mind along the way? Reflection on the decision-making process will help both your reasoning and persuasiveness.*

# Part Three

# Chapter 11

# *BASIC SKILLS:*
# *PRECISION*

---

## A. INTRODUCTION

Uncertainty of meaning often creates rich and complex layering in fiction, but it produces costly and time-consuming litigation in legal documents, especially rule-making documents. Whether public or private—whether statute, regulation, contract, or will—the prose of rule-making, called normative prose, tells those within its reach what to do or not do. It creates the "norm" to which we must adhere, establishing legal rights, privileges, prohibitions, duties, and status. Drafting normative prose is the most exacting kind of writing that lawyers do.

The challenge of this kind of writing arises because rules

1. must stand the test of time,
2. must successfully bind those who want to wiggle in and those who want to wiggle out,
3. must provide fair notice of what is required or forbidden, and
4. must often harmonize the differing views and interests of multiple parties.

While the goal of normative prose is easy to state, it is difficult to achieve. Law students are more than familiar with cases involving disputes over ambiguous provisions. Indeed, the failure of drafters to produce air-tight legal instruments is the very stuff of courtroom and classroom.

Successful normative prose requires a kind of ultimate clarity we call precision. Precision is achieved only when we exercise maximum control—within our limited human capability—over word choice (semantic control) and over sentence structure (syntactic control). Put another way, effective normative prose displays a degree of specificity and certainty that is commensurate with the instrument's objectives.[1] You neither want to circumscribe needlessly, nor do you want to generate unnecessary uncertainty. The trick of precision lies in finding the appropriate place on a spectrum that goes from absolute specificity through increasing degrees of generality, ending in vagueness. Balance is all.

Uncertain meaning in normative prose can be ascribed to one of five causes: incompleteness (confusion that results from faulty conceptualization); semantic ambiguity (confusion that results when a word has more than one accepted lexical meaning); vagueness (confusion that results from terms whose definitional boundaries are uncertain) and its close relation, generality (confusion that results from uncertainty about what particulars fall within the general term); syntactic ambiguity (confusion that occurs whenever more than one role can be assigned to a part of a sentence);[2] and contextual ambiguity (confusion that arises because of a document's inconsistencies and contradictions). In this text, we use the term "ambiguity" in a narrow sense, to mean "uncertainty between relatively few (usually two) distinct alternatives."[3]

Whether semantic, syntactic, or contextual, ambiguity is always to be avoided; it is an open invitation to litigation and inevitably compromises the effectiveness of our documents. Vagueness and generality can be appropriate or at least acceptable compromises, but both must be used advisedly, with an understanding of the possible consequences.

Our aim in Section B of this chapter on precision is to help you recognize and avoid the enemies of clear and precise prose that are briefly described above. Then, in Section C, we discuss three techniques that promote precision and fight uncertainty: the careful and consistent use of words of authority, the use of definitions, which can cure some semantic problems, and the use of tabulation, which uses layout to resolve some syntactic ambiguities. Although instances of syntactic and semantic ambiguity will undoubtably survive the recommendations in this chapter,

---

[1] F. Reed Dickerson, *The Fundamentals of Legal Drafting* 29 (Little, Brown, & Co. 1965).

[2] Our taxonomy of imprecision is adapted from Layman E. Allen & C. Rudy Engholm, *Normalized Legal Drafting and the Query Method*, 29 J. Legal Educ. 380, 381 (1978).

[3] *Id.* at 383.

if you adhere to the suggested practices, you will reduce the occasions upon which you are forced to let others determine the meanings of your documents.

The documents discussed in the three succeeding chapters are those that require the most precision—legislation and regulations, contracts, and wills.

## B. THE ENEMIES OF PRECISION

### 1. Incompleteness

As discussed in the chapter on conceptualization, incompleteness can create confusion when the drafter omits information essential to the interpretation or implementation of a provision. Thus, the "unwritten" (appearing as omissions, gaps, and loopholes) is a notable source of confusion in drafting since a legal instrument cannot be smoothly and fairly administered if it is not complete. But for that to happen, the lawyer must anticipate as many eventualities as possible, as well as their legal and practical consequences and then provide for those contingencies.

Incompleteness can exist on the sentence level because of missing information. For example, passive voice construction can produce ambiguity because the agent of the action is omitted. Incompleteness does not result from placing the subject of the sentence in the object position, but it can result when, as is often the case with passive constructions, the writer omits the agent of the action altogether: "Complaints of harassment must be directed to the Committee on Working Conditions"—but by whom? Who must make them? Must it be the alleged victim, or may a witness or supervisor complain?

Incompleteness can also stem from loopholes and missing provisions. A provision that says "Any employee who believes that he or she has been harassed by another employee must direct a complaint to the Committee on Work Conditions within ten days of the alleged incident" fails to inform us whether the complaint may be oral as well as written and whether it must specify the date, time, place, parties, and nature of the alleged infraction.

Sometimes, omissions and gaps create loopholes or other inequities. For example, a group of law professors noticed a consequential gap in proposed federal bankruptcy legislation concerning the homestead exemption,[4] a provision exempting specified property from creditor attachment and levy under 11 U.S.C. §522. The pending provisions limited homestead protection for those who violate securities laws, commit fraud while in a fiduciary capacity, or commit one of a few specific intentional torts. But the law professors believed that the list was under-inclusive. Although it would include corporate executives who falsify financial records (those uppermost in the minds of the legislators at the time this bill was drafted), convicted felons who had no securities fraud on their criminal record would be free to claim the full homestead exemption.

## 2. Semantic Ambiguity

Written language can be as confounding as omissions. Semantic ambiguity arises when a word in a sentence has more than one lexical (dictionary) meaning. For example, in the prohibition, "No drinking near a school," "drinking" is ambiguous because it has at least two distinct lexical meanings: "swallowing liquid" and "consuming alcohol." It is thus impossible to know for certain whether sipping spring water in the schoolyard is forbidden. Or, to take another example, the meaning of "all doctors have parking privileges" is ambiguous because we cannot determine whether "doctor" means "physician," "chiropractor," "holder of a doctorate," "veterinarian," or all of the above. If physicians alone are intended to have parking privileges, that narrower term ought to be used.

Semantic ambiguity frequently results when we try to express numerical limits. For example, it is difficult to make clear the beginning and end of a time period when setting a schedule. "Clerkship applications will be accepted *from* February 1 *to* February 15" can mean February 1 and 15 are included, but it also can be read to exclude those dates. "*Between* February 1 *and* February 15" or "*to, until,* or *by* February 15" pose the same problem. Better is "Clerkship applications will be accepted *on* February 1,

---

[4] E-mail from Elizabeth Warren, Prof., Harvard L. Sch., to Ted Janger, Ass't Prof., Brooklyn L. Sch., Pending Bankruptcy Bill (April 29, 2002) (Copy on file with the authors).

*through and including* February 15." "*After* January 31 and *before* February 16" seems equally clear.

Age limits are another tricky area. "More than" is ambiguous in the age context. If you write, "Admission free for persons more than 65 years old," there is a question whether persons a nanosecond past their sixty-fifth anniversaries are included or only those 66 years old. Try "65 or older" or "those who have passed their sixty-fifth birthday" or "those at least 65 years of age."

The problem of semantic ambiguity is even more pervasive than the above examples suggest, however, because many ordinary everyday words with seemingly unambiguous lexical definitions are indeterminate at their margins and subject to interpretive dispute. Thus, in *Smith v. United States*,[5] the Supreme Court justices disagreed about the meaning of "use" in 18 U.S.C. § 924 (c)(1), which provides additional punishment for anyone who "during and in relation to any crime of violence or drug trafficking crime... uses or carries a firearm...." One justice argued that the ordinary, prototypical meaning of "use" suggests the statute be applied only if a firearm is used as a weapon.[6] Another argued that trading a firearm for drugs is "use" of a firearm and is, therefore, "'use' within the everyday meaning of that term."[7]

The lesson of *Smith* is that our control over semantic ambiguity exists only in the drafting stage—in choosing words deliberately and carefully. Thus, Congress should have defined its term and written "uses a firearm as a weapon" directly into the provision itself if it intended "use" to have a prototypical meaning. On the other hand, if Congress wanted debate about the meaning of "use" or was unable to reach agreement on the term, it appropriately left it undefined.

### 3. Vague and General Language

Vagueness arises when it is unclear what a term does and does not include. Thus, in the prohibition "No drinking near a school," the term "near" is vague because it is impossible to know what

---

[5] 508 U.S. 223 (1993).

[6] *Id.* at 242 (Scalia, J., dissenting).

[7] *Id.* at 228.

distance from a school is included and what excluded: is 100 feet included in or excluded from "near"?

Generality is closely related to vagueness, but it nonetheless can be usefully distinguished. Terms are general when they include numbers of particulars, yet it is clear which terms are included in the general term and which are excluded. In our example, "school" is a general term because it includes many particular kinds of teaching institutions—elementary schools, universities, high schools, driving schools, vocational schools, for example. But "school" is not vague, because we cannot think of anything that might be outside as well as inside its boundary.[8] Put another way, vague terms have movable, porous boundaries, and general terms have solid, fixed boundaries.

In many cases, drafters are less concerned with finding *le mot juste* than with wording a provision so that it will secure passage of a bill or signatures on the dotted line. Vague and general terms help parties to reach consensus; the parties may not be able to agree on precise terms but they are able to compromise by agreeing to more flexible terms. In addition, a lawyer may fear omitting an example if she attempts too much precision. Thus, precision sometimes yields to efficacy. For example, to save a contract, parties may agree to give a supplier a "reasonable" time to supply the contracted-for goods rather than "twenty-four hours." A lease may provide that a landlord may not "unreasonably" withhold consent for the tenant to assign the lease rather than provide that the landlord may withhold consent "only if the proposed assignee earns less than $50,000 a year or is a convicted felon." A statute may provide that a business entity may not engage in "unfair" competition rather than provide that the entity may not "collude with one or more other business entities to control the price of their goods." And the U.C.C. may provide that disclaimers of warranties must be "conspicuous" rather than require "fourteen-point type and red ink." The terms "reasonable," "unfair," and "conspicuous" are vague words, purposely chosen in the above contexts because specificity was undesirable.

Finally, a lawyer also may use vague or general terms because the document must survive into the future. The Constitution, for

---

[8] Or perhaps you can think of something. At the margins, the distinction between vagueness and generality is elusive.

example, has endured over the centuries in part because of vague and general terms like "due process." Thus, unlike the ambiguous use of terms with more than one meaning, which is almost always unintended, the use of vague and general terms rather than precise or specific ones is sometimes a deliberate choice by an experienced drafter.

With general terms, the greatest challenge is in achieving the appropriate level of generality. Should condominium rules ban all "household pets" in order to maintain quiet and clean common areas when only "dogs" bark and need to be taken out? Should a law school honor code punish "academic dishonesty" when it intended to punish "plagiarism" only? Do you want to leave all your "personal property" to your spouse, or only your "household effects"? Do you want your "descendants" to inherit or only your "children"?

One disadvantage of vague or general terms, however, is that, if the document is disputed, the drafter cedes power to the judiciary or other third-party decision maker to interpret the terms—and the third parties may not interpret the terms as the drafter would have done. For example, a court interpreted the term "family" very broadly in an ordinance providing that "the landlord may not evict the family of a deceased tenant of record." The court held that "family" included a deceased tenant's domestic partner, who was then protected from eviction, a result probably not contemplated by the drafter.

Documents with vague terms face another danger. If a drafter uses terms that are vague, the document may not be enforceable because a court deems it void for vagueness. This doctrine especially applies to criminal statutes because the severity of criminal sanctions requires clear notice of forbidden conduct. The doctrine also applies to other drafted documents, however. A lease renewal option, for example, may be void and unenforceable if it does not supply renewal terms. Lease terms to renew at a rent "comparable to that of similar facilities"[9] or a rent that does not "exceed the cost-of-living index"[10] have been held unenforceable.

One way to limit potential problems with general terms especially is to stipulate their meaning in a definition section. (See

---

[9] *Phipps v. Storey*, 601 S.W.2d 249 (Ark. App. 1980).

[10] *Heral v. Smith*, 803 S.W.2d 938, 940 (Ark. App. 1991).

Section C(2) on *Definitions.*) Assume the drafters of the eviction ordinance mentioned above want to keep control over the meaning of "family" and thought about the problem the term would pose. They could have defined the term, for example, to include "coinhabitants who have a long and close relation with the tenant of record, such as by emotional and financial commitment and interdependence." The definition is broad enough to protect some domestic partners and foster children but narrow enough to exclude roommates. Of course, this definition is not litigation-proof because of the vague terms "emotional and financial commitment," "interdependence," and "long and close relationship." More precise terms would be "at least two years, maintain joint savings and checking accounts," and "named as beneficiary in life insurance and pension plans." The decision to be specific, vague, or general depends therefore on the different interests and concerns of multiple parties and drafters.

### 4. Syntactic Ambiguity

Beyond semantic uncertainty looms the more complicated problem of sentences that are intrinsically ambiguous because conflicting rules govern their interpretation. Syntactic ambiguity occurs when a sentence has more than one distinct meaning because its parts can be fitted together in more than one way: it is unclear which words a conjunction is connecting, which pronoun refers to which noun, which adjectives or adverbs modify which nouns or verbs. Does "To be eligible, you must be an American law professor" mean that law professors who are American are eligible or that professors of American law are eligible? In other words, is "American law" a compound adjective modifying the noun "professor" or does "American" modify the compound noun "law professor"? Because there are two competing but equally valid ways to view the syntax, grammar cannot clear up the confusion.

One of the most common syntactic problems is generated by the scope of modifiers in a series. It is not always clear whether modifiers positioned at the beginning and end of a series describe the nearest element only, or the entire series: "Places of public accommodation are *wholesale or retail* stores and establishments *dealing with goods and services of any kind.*" In this sentence, it is questionable whether the restrictive modifier "dealing with goods and services of any kind" modifies only the last noun "establishments," or whether it also modifies "stores." The doctrine of the last antecedent holds that a modifier describes the noun at the end of the series only. Under this rule, "dealing with goods and services" modifies "establishments" alone. Militating against the last-antecedent rule, however, is a grammatical principle called the across-the-board rule. Under this rule, the restrictive modifier applies to the entire series, that is, to both stores and establishments.[11] Similarly, although an adjective placed before a series generally modifies only the first element in a series,[12] the across-the-board rule could be applied to interpret "wholesale or retail" as modifying "establishments" as well as "stores."

There is no simple way to resolve these disputes because one rule does not simply trump the other. What is instead involved are two conflicting interpretive strategies that can be used for deriving meaning. In this regard, grammatical rules are as helpful or unhelpful—as determinate or indeterminate—as the canons of statutory construction, which similarly and often conflict.[13] In these situations—when canons, rules, or interpretative strategies conflict—context can sometimes clarify the more appropriate interpretation. For example, one could reason that "wholesale or retail stores" do not offer services, just goods, and that "dealing with goods and services" therefore modifies only establishments. If context does not clarify scope, however, the sentence can be rewritten to avoid this type of ambiguity. Often the most effective way to clarify the scope of modifiers is to use tabulated sentence structure. See Section C(3) of this chapter.

The placement of prepositional phrases can also create ambiguity. Take the following example: "A key aspect *of the line-up* that his lawyers overlooked was the lighting conditions." In this sentence,

---

[11] *See* Lawrence Solan, *The Language of Judges* 29–34 (U. Chi. Press 1993). This can be referred to as "coordinate structure constraints" or the "across-the-board rule." *Id.* at 34.

[12] *Id.* at 58–59.

[13] For example, the canon "if the language is plain and unambiguous, it must given full effect" conflicts with the canon "not when literal interpretation would lead to an absurd result." See Karl Llewellyn, *Remarks on the Theory of Appellate Decisions and the Rules or Canons about How Statutes are to be Construed*, 3 Vand. L. Rev. 395 (1950); Solan, *supra* n.11, at 38.

it is unclear whether the phrase "that his lawyers overlooked" modifies "line-up" in the prepositional phrase or the noun "key aspect." Thus, it is unclear whether the line-up was entirely overlooked or only the key aspect of it. Moreover, no syntactic rule helps us to parse the sentence. The only way to avoid the ambiguity presented by this kind of sentence is to construct it differently at the outset: when a prepositional phrase separates a noun from its modifier ("that his lawyers overlooked"), the prepositional phrase should be eliminated or relocated: "A key aspect that his lawyers overlooked *in the line-up* was the lighting conditions." (See Section 5(B)(3) of Chapter 5, *Clarity*, for a discussion of how misplaced, dangling, and squinting modifiers create confusion.)

Confusion also arises when a reader cannot figure out if a modifier is restrictive or non-restrictive, a situation that results from misuse of the relative pronouns "that" and "which" and from careless punctuation. A restrictive modifier defines and limits the word it modifies and is often introduced by the pronoun "that," as in: "The car *that hit her* was a black sedan." The writer is restricting the world of cars to that one involved in an accident. A restrictive modifier follows the word it describes with no intervening punctuation. A non-restrictive modifier is introduced by the pronoun "which" and contributes additional, non-essential information about the word it modifies. Non-restrictive modifiers are surrounded by commas when they appear in the middle of a sentence or are preceded by a comma if they appear at the end of a sentence: "My car, *which was recently repaired,* is running well now," or "He finally got a car, *which means my chauffeuring days are over.*"

Problems of meaning arise, however, when "which" is used restrictively or "that" is punctuated non-restrictively. Take the following sentence: "I leave to my son all my certificates of deposit which are less than $10,000." It is unclear here whether the modifier is restrictive or non-restrictive—it uses "which," but omits the comma that signals non-restrictive meaning. The confusion is consequential, as illustrated by the two alternatives.

> I leave to my son all my certificates of deposit, which are less than $10,000.
>
> *Versus*

> I leave to my son all my certificates of deposit that are less than $10,000.

The first sentence gives all the testator's certificates of deposits to the son and explains that they come to less than $10,000. The second sentence gives only those certificates that are less than $10,000.

An historic example comes from a draft of the 1974 Republican Party Platform's policy statement against "any attempts to increase taxes which would harm the recovery." In this statement, the platform opposed only those taxes that could be considered harmful to economic recovery. The sentence was corrected to "any attempts to increase taxes, which would harm the recovery"[14] in order to imply any increase is harmful.

Pronouns are yet another source of syntactic ambiguity and are discussed in Section 5(B)(3) of Chapter 5, *Clarity*.

## 5. The Ambiguity of "And" and "Or"

"And" and "or" are difficult to use because the terms can create both syntactic ambiguity and semantic ambiguity. Syntactic ambiguity can occur when "and" is used because English allows writers to avoid repetition by grafting one part of the sentence onto another "base" part of the sentence. This grafting sometimes makes it unclear what "and" is connecting. Consider this sentence:

> Persons who are physically disabled and mentally ill are eligible for reduced transportation rates.

One correct interpretation of this sentence is that "persons" is a base for two separate modifiers: "persons who are physically disabled" and "persons who are mentally ill." The sentence means that two types of persons are eligible for reduced transportation rates. Another correct interpretation is that the "and" does not connect the two modifiers to the base word "person," but instead connects "physically disabled" and "mentally ill," the two objects

---

[14] *Quoted in* Claire Kehrwald Cook, *Line by Line: How to Edit you Own Writing*, 199 (Houghton Mifflin Co. 1986).

in the modifier "who are physically disabled and mentally ill." This reading suggests eligibility for reduced rates requires both characteristics. Since each reading is a correct interpretation, you must alter the sentence structure to avoid ambiguity. It may help to use correlative conjunctions, that is, paired conjunctions like "either...or," ""both...and," or " neither...nor."

> Persons who are *either* physically disabled *or* mentally ill are eligible.
>
> or
>
> Persons who are *both* physically disabled *and* mentally ill are eligible.

As well as being syntactically ambiguous, "and" and "or" are semantically ambiguous. Usually "and" is considered conjunctive (additive) and "or" is considered disjunctive (alternative). But it is not always clear whether a drafter is using "or" inclusively (A or B, or both) or exclusively (A or B, but not both).[15] In addition, it is sometimes unclear whether "and" is intended conjunctively (A and B considered together) or disjunctively (A and B considered separately).[16] Consider the following sentence:

> Holders of beer and liquor licenses may sell cigarettes.

"And" could have a joint meaning—you must hold two licenses before you sell cigarettes—or it could be interpreted severally— you need one or the other. This uncertainty has led to the use of the expression "and/or" in drafting, but expert drafters prefer using correlative conjunctives, as demonstrated above, or other alternatives like "either or both of the following" or "A or B, or both,"[17] as in, "Holders of beer or liquor licenses, or both, may sell cigarettes."

---

[15] *See* Dickerson, *supra* n. 1, at 76–78.

[16] *Id.*

[17] *Id.*

## 6. Contextual Ambiguity

Contextual ambiguity stems from internal contradiction or inconsistency. If one part of the document calls for all disputes to be submitted first to mediation, another cannot provide for arbitration as the first step. If one party is referred to as the complainant, that complainant should not suddenly be called the aggrieved party. Terminology should be used consistently.

Contradiction and inconsistency usually arise because the instrument is long and complicated and the offending clauses are far apart. It is helpful to comb through documents checking that related clauses—for example, clauses on dispute resolution—are consistent with each other. These across-the-board checks should be done systematically. While checking consistent use of definitions, for example, do each definition individually, and to stay focused, check nothing else.

One related cause of contextual ambiguity is the practice of incorporation by reference.[18] Although incorporation of outside material prevents repetition and guards against conflicts between a legal instrument and the legal context in which it fits, outside materials need to be read carefully to determine their suitability for incorporation. The materials might not fit the situation perfectly. They might have needed revising, but were never screened carefully enough for the need to be noticed.

The world of uncertainty described above is summarized in the chart that follows.

---

[18] For a lengthier discussion, *see id.* at 96–97.

# UNCERTAINTY

| Incompleteness | Semantic Ambiguity | Semantic Uncertainty | Syntactic Ambiguity | Contextual Ambiguity |
|---|---|---|---|---|
| Missing Provisions or Information | Words Have Two or More Meanings | Words Unclear | Parts of Sentence Not Related Clearly | Internal Inconsistency |
| "Notice of violation must be given": to whom, by whom, in what form? | "Residence": Legal domicile or second home? | Vagueness: "Near a hydrant"—how close is near? | 1. And/or Ambiguity: "Persons who are physically disabled and mentally ill are eligible"—either or both? | 1. Contradiction: Conflicting Provisions—Mediator or Arbitrator? |
| | | Generality: "Family"—child, spouse, cousin, domestic partner? | 2. Scope of Modifiers: "retail stores and establishments"—does retail apply to establishments or just stores? | 2. Inconsistency: Do Complainant and Aggrieved Party refer to the same person? |
| | | | 3. Restrictive or Non-restrictive: "my account which is in Citibank." vs. "my account, which is in Citibank." | 3. Inconsistency with materials incorporated by reference. |

## C. TECHNIQUES FOR PRECISION

### 1. Words of Authority

It is particularly important to use words of authority consistently. Words of authority are verbs that create rights, duties, and discretion, and although documents would be infinitely clearer if these verbs were used consistently and uniformly, they frequently are not—creating another source of ambiguity.[19] Most problematic are the terms "shall," "may," and "must."

A good deal of litigation occurs because "shall" and "may" are used imprecisely. The better usage is to use "may" to give discretion, as in "vehicle owners *may* apply for vanity license plates" or "the court *may* award attorney fees to the prevailing party." Use "shall" to impose a duty, as in "the Department of Motor Vehicles *shall* promulgate vehicle registration regulations" or "the court *shall* award attorney fees to the prevailing party." Because statutes and other drafted documents often use these verbs incorrectly, however, courts must frequently interpret whether they are meant to be mandatory or discretionary.

There are other misuses of the verb "shall." One mistake is to use "shall" to denote the future when in legal drafting the term should be reserved for creating duties. It is not difficult to avoid using "shall" for futurity. Because documents such as contracts and statutes should be written in the present tense, the future tense is rarely needed. When you do need the future tense, use "will." Thus it is inappropriate to say "'Plagiarism' *shall* mean using the words or ideas of another without acknowledgment" because the term "plagiarism" means that *now*: it will not gain that meaning in the future.

Such a definition is also faulty because you cannot give orders or directions to a word or thing—the attempt to do so is known as a "false imperative." "Plagiarism" does not have a duty to do anything. In contrast, it is appropriate to say "Landlords *shall* maintain the common areas," because you can issue directions to people about their behavior.

---

[19] There are at least two good discussions of the misuses of words of authority. *See* Joseph Kimble, *The Many Misuses of Shall*, 3 Scribes J. Leg. Writing 61 (1992); Bryan A. Garner, *A Dictionary of Modern Legal Usage* 939-42 (2d ed. Oxford U. Press 1995).

Another problem with "shall" is that it is sometimes unclear upon whom a duty is imposed. It is inappropriate to say "Tenants' guests *shall* not destroy the premises" because it is the tenants, not the guests, who have the duty to comply with this mandate. You cannot give orders to people who are not parties to a contract or other legal instrument. Some passive voice sentences imposing duties are also problematic, as in "Elevators *shall be inspected* annually," because it is unclear who has the duty—the elevator company, the landlord, or the city? When it is implicitly clear who has the duty, however, some drafters find the passive tolerable, as in "Grades *shall be submitted* before or on the fourteenth day after the examination date." It is clear this duty falls upon teachers. Most drafters would agree that active voice is even better, however, as in "Teachers *shall submit* grades before or on the fourteenth day after the exam date."

"Shall" presents one other problem of interpretation, namely whether the duty the term imposes is so absolute that its violation renders the proceedings invalid, as in "The director *shall* grant a driver a hearing on his license revocation within 20 days of the receipt of the written request." It is unclear whether this provision is mandatory or directory. If the hearing is not held within the specified time period, is the revocation nullified?

To avoid this problem, careful drafters use "must" for conditions precedent, that is, for situations in which one action is conditioned upon the completion of another, as in "Before you can file for a tax reassessment, you *must* submit an appraisal from a licensed real estate broker," or "vehicle owners *must* have their cars inspected before applying for a new registration sticker." You can use "must" even when the condition is implied instead of explicit, as in "Amendments to the Honor Code *must* be ratified by two-thirds of the Judicial Council." In other words, unless there is this kind of ratification, the amendment is not valid. Moreover, "must" is correct because the council is not obliged to ratify. Thus, "must" is often used when one action is conditioned upon another, but the party is not compelled to act or not act. Those who adhere to this usage need to be careful not to misuse "must" and thus unintentionally condition one action upon the completion or existence of another.

Not all respect this usage, however. Thus courts sometimes need to determine whether "must" establishes a mandatory condition precedent or is instead simply directory. For example, the Supreme Court has held that where a defendant in a Section 1983 case[20] uses a qualified immunity defense, a court "*must* first determine whether the plaintiff has alleged the deprivation of an actual constitutional right at all...."[21] Several federal courts of appeals interpret that language as mandatory; a court is required to decide first whether the plaintiff has stated a cause of action before it decides the immunity issue.[22] Other courts of appeals, however, treat that language as not always requiring a court to decide the constitutional issue before it decides whether the defendant is immune from suit.[23]

Given the current, fluid state of usage, it may be too risky to rely solely on words of authority to establish meaning. You may want to make conditions explicit: "Failure to submit grades by the fourteenth day after the exam date means a deduction from your paycheck for each late day." You may also want to define words of authority, for example: "*Shall* means 'has a duty, violation of which will not invalidate the proceeding, although sanctions may ensue on the party who violated the mandate.'" The most important advice is to strive for consistency and uniformity of use.

The following chart outlines a sensible, consistent, and rational way to use words of authority, but as we have noted, this better usage is not yet the common usage. Nonetheless, whenever you can, it is important to work for the consistent use of words of authority.

---

[20] 42 U.S.C. §1983 (2000) allows a person to seek damages from government officials who violate the person's constitutional rights.

[21] *Wilson v Layne*, 526 U.S. 603, 609 (1999), quoting *Conn v. Gabbert*, 526 U.S. 286, 290 (1999).

[22] *See, e.g., Sutton v. Rasheed*, 323 F.3d 236 (3d Cir. 2003); *Jones v. Shields*, 207 F.3d 491, 494 (2000).

[23] *See, e.g., Kalka v. Hawk*, 215 F.3d 90, 94–95 (D.C. Cir. 2000); *Horne v. Coughlin*, 191 F.3d 244, 246 (2d Cir. 1999).

## WORDS OF AUTHORITY

**Shall = Imposes a Duty on the Subject of the Sentence.** (Shall may also be used in passive sentences if the party who has the duty is obvious.)

**Shall Not = Duty Not to Act**

**May = Gives Discretion**

**May Not = Negation of Discretion**

**Must = Creates Condition Precedent** (one condition must be fulfilled before something else can be done—the condition may be implied)

**Is Not Required To**

**Will = Signals Agreement (in Contracts) & Future Tense**

**Will Not = Negates Agreement**

**Is Entitled to = Creates a Right**

**Is Not Entitled to = Negates Right**

—————————— *Exercise 11.1* ——————————

A. *Diagnose sources of confusions in the following sentences, looking for syntactic ambiguity, semantic ambiguity, and vagueness. Then rewrite as necessary.*

1. Owners of residences and commercial properties may be entitled to a tax rebate.
2. Requests for reimbursement for bills from the prior policy year must be made by September 21st.
3. Extra accessories, equipment, or parts detached from the motorized land vehicles are not covered.
4. The office closes between August 10th and August 24th.
5. We do not cover loss resulting directly or indirectly from minor water damage.

6. After the agency supervisor appoints a caseworker, he shall resume normal operations.
7. Statutory classes of people subject to CERCLA liability:
   (1) present owners and operators of a hazardous waste facility, or
   (2) past owners or operators of such a facility
8. Any medically necessary laboratory test is covered in accordance with the terms and conditions of this certificate.
9. The thief was sentenced to nine months in the violin case.
10. No one shall park his vehicle near a loading ramp.
11. Bills up to $20 accepted for tokens.
12. While preparing food, plastic gloves must be worn.
13. Plaintiff is not entitled to consortium damages which are speculative.
14. If the loss covered in this section makes the premises uninhabitable, we cover any essential increase in living expenses incurred by you.
15. The statute imposes a mandatory consecutive two-year prison term on individuals connected to aggravated identity theft if the offender "knowingly transfers, possesses or uses, without lawful authority, a means of identification of another person."
16. The court concluded that the agent's conduct should not be sanctioned.
17. The company plans skirt requirements.
18. The agreement will continue in force for a period of five years from the date it is made, and thereafter for successive five years, unless and until terminated by one year prior notice in writing by either party.

*B. Diagnose problems with words of authority and correct.*

1. A waiver or change of any provision of this policy shall be in writing to be valid.
2. Business expenses will be covered in accordance with the employee handbook.
3. Floor area: Every dwelling shall have at least one room which shall have not less than 120 square feet of floor area. Other habitable rooms, except kitchens, shall have an area not less than 70 square feet. Where two or more persons occupy a room used for sleeping purposes, the required floor area shall be increased at the rate of 50 square feet for each occupant in excess of two.

4. The insured shall give us written proof of a claim to recover.
5. The order following a final pretrial conference shall be modified only to prevent manifest injustice.
6. Service agreements shall begin on the activation date.
7. Either party must cancel this agreement upon 15 days prior written notice to the other.
8. If the serial plate is removed, this contract shall be null and void.
9. A *nolo contendere* plea must be accepted by the court only after due consideration of the views of the parties and the interest of the public in the effective administration of justice.
10. This court shall not enjoin the defendant's conduct without more evidence of abuse.
11. If any county's voting returns are not received by the Department of State by 5:00 p.m. of the seventh day following an election, all missing counties shall be ignored and the results shown by those returns that were filed shall be certified.
12. The landlord shall not abuse the right of access to the tenant's apartment or use it to harass the tenant. Except where access shall be authorized by subsections (f) and (g) above, the landlord shall give notice to the tenant, and such notice shall be provided to each unit, of landlord's intent to enter in no less than two days.
13. The State Board of Equalization shall have the general direction and control of the county assessors in the performance of their duties and shall direct the same.

---

## 2. Definitions

Definitions are an excellent way to avoid semantic ambiguity and unintended vagueness in statutes and regulations and are used increasingly in contracts and wills also. Indeed, the clarity and efficacy of many kinds of legal documents improve with the judicious use of definitions. A skilled legal writer knows *when* to draft definitions, *which* terms to define, *how* to define them simply and sensibly, and *where* to put definitions.

### a. When to Write Definitions

Although definitions should appear before the substantive text that they illuminate, they should not be written before that text. Until you begin writing a first draft of your document, you may not know for certain which terms will need defining; drafters who write their definitions first often define terms that, in the end, they never use. Therefore, you should write a preliminary draft of your document, noting words that need definition, and then write your definitions. When the definitions are done, go back and revise your substantive text so that it includes those defined terms. Be sure that you always use the same word for the same thing: you do not want to define a term and then inadvertently use a synonym.

### b. Which Terms to Define

There are two kinds of definitions: *lexical* definitions, which are the ordinary, dictionary definitions of a word, and *stipulative* definitions, which are definitions that are peculiar to the particular instrument itself and that either limit or expand the dictionary definition or create a term for the special purposes of the drafter.

It is almost never necessary to provide a lexical definition: words are assumed to have their ordinary meaning unless defined otherwise. Thus, if a word is in the dictionary with one clear meaning, you should not as a rule define it. Nonetheless, it is sometimes helpful to supply the lexical definition of an obscure term of art, especially in a consumer document. In addition, it is often necessary to specify which definition is intended for a word with multiple meanings. Otherwise, you define terms only when you wish to add or subtract from the dictionary meaning, to provide the meaning of an esoteric term, or to clarify the contours of a vague term. It will rarely be necessary to define "dog" or "automobile," for instance, but the term "domestic animal" (does that include pet boa constrictors?) or "motor vehicle" (are motorized wheelchairs included?) will most likely generate litigation unless they are defined. The IRS needlessly defined "calendar year" to mean "period of time beginning Jan. 1 and ending Dec. 31." Few would have thought "calendar year" meant anything else. On the other hand, you might need a definition for "fiscal year" or for "year" because "year" may refer to calendar year, fiscal year, or academic year. Use common sense: ask yourself whether the definition is really needed, and then define terms only when clarity requires it.

You can also lighten the prose of your document by using your definition section to create terms that refer to special classes or categories. If you are writing a law school catalogue, you might provide the following definition:

> *Upper Class Writing Requirement* means a document of at least twenty pages, written in at least two drafts, and requiring original research and analysis.

Then you would be able to write concise course descriptions like "This course fulfills the *Upper Class Writing Requirement*," instead of the following wordy and repetitive sentence:

> You can fulfill in this class the requirement that you write a document of at least twenty pages, written in at least two drafts, and requiring original research and analysis before you graduate.

Before you define your term, be absolutely certain that the term you are defining is the right one for your purposes. If you have chosen an inappropriate word, no amount of defining can rescue it. While you can in theory define "up" to include "down," definitions that deprive words of their ordinary meaning often lead straight to disaster. You cannot prevent readers from giving words their ordinary meanings, and deviations invite confusion, non-compliance, or ridicule. A municipal ordinance regulating traffic in parks may stipulate that *"Motor Vehicle* includes bicycle," but most readers of a sign saying "No motor vehicles in the park" will not conclude they must leave their bikes at home.

## c. How to Define

There are three main ways to define a term and stipulate its meaning.[24] First, to clarify the meaning of a lexical term, you can define a term by finding a synonym for it: "*Narcotic drug* means opiates." Second, you can define a term by placing it in a class or subclass: "A *divorce decree* means a legal instrument that finalizes a couple's agreement to dissolve a marriage." Third, you can

---

[24] Dickerson, *supra* n. 1, at 99.

define a term by stipulating some or all of the things to which a term refers: "*Motor vehicle* means motorbike, automobile, truck, van, SUV, or jeep."

Lawyers find stipulative definitions especially useful. Three helpful types of stipulative definitions are those that limit, those that expand, and those that coin a term.[25] *Limiting definitions* retain the lexical meaning of the term, but limit that meaning in one of two ways. First, you can limit the number of particulars to which the term applies. For example:

> *Accident* means the collision between plaintiff's automobile and defendant's truck on January 15, 2003.

This type of limiting definition helps drafters to avoid unnecessary and sentence-clogging repetition. If you are retaining the lexical definition but restricting its reference, "means" is the proper verb to use, and the present tense is the proper verb form.

The second type of limiting definition expressly excludes some particulars from the ordinary dictionary meaning, and is characterized by the verb "does not include." For example:

> *Motor Vehicle* does not include motorized wheelchairs.

*Expanding definitions* change the lexical definition by adding something not usually included. Expanding definitions use the verb "includes." For example:

> *Carpet* includes straw mattings.

Because "carpets" are usually made of fabric, the inclusion of "straw mattings" expands the common meaning. Be careful not to strain your limiting and expanding definitions. Definitions that exclude a thing normally included (*Physician* does not include psychiatrist), or that include a thing normally excluded (*Tuition* includes room and board), deprive a word of its ordinary meaning and will probably be misinterpreted or ridiculed. A few years

---

[25] We are indebted to Barbara Child for these descriptions of stipulative definitions, although she uses different terms. *See* Barbara Child, *Drafting Legal Documents: Principles and Practices* 357–365 (2[d] ed. West Pub. 1992).

ago, a New England senator added a definition of Great Lakes to a bill that re-authorized funds for anti-pollution projects along the ocean coasts and Great Lakes. The definition said *"Great Lakes includes Lake Champlain."* The bill was signed by the President, but the sentence was later removed from the statute.

In addition to limiting or enlarging a lexical definition, it is at times helpful to coin new terms for use within your document. *Coining definitions* tend to offer either analytic or denotative descriptions of the word being created. The "Upper Class Writing Requirement" definition is an example of a useful, economical, analytic definition: *"Upper Class Writing Requirement* means a document of at least twenty pages, written in at least two drafts, and requiring original research and analysis." There are also *coining definitions* that are restrictive: *"Recreation Area* means the playground, ball field, tennis courts, swimming pool, concession stands, picnic tables, and lawns."

Sometimes, you have "nesting" definitions; in other words, you may need to define a term used in another of your definitions.

> *Upper Class Writing Requirement* means a document of at least twenty pages, written in at least two drafts, and requiring original research and *original analysis.*
>
> *Original analysis* means arguments, thoughts, and ideas that cannot be attributed to another.

As noted earlier, you should always use the present tense in writing definitions. In other words, do not say "shall mean," but "means." You neither want to use a false imperative, nor do you want to suggest that your definitions have not yet come into effect. In addition, remember that the best definitions use just these three verb forms.

| <u>Use...</u> | <u>To...</u> |
| --- | --- |
| means, is | • limit lexical meaning: "State" means New York. |
| | • coin a term: "Upper Class Writing Requirement" means.... |

|  | • give the lexical meaning: "Carpet" means fabric floor covering. |
| does not include | • limit the lexical meaning or exclude meaning: "Motor Vehicle" does not include motorized wheelchairs. |
| includes | • add to or expand the lexical meaning: "Bicycle" includes moped. |
|  | Do not use *includes* to add examples of lexical meanings: Not, "Carpet" includes oriental rugs—rather, "Carpet" includes straw mattings. Use *includes* to add to the dictionary definition. |

There are two final considerations in drafting definitions. First, always take into account the larger context. For example, if you are drafting a statute, be aware that the legislature may have defined the terms you use in a statutory interpretation act. You are free to accept or reject these earlier definitions, but if you reject them, do so explicitly.

Second, never legislate in definitions. They are not the place for substantive provisions—for destroying rights, creating duties, or making disclaimers—because no one would think to look for them there, and they may not be enforceable if they are there. Although some consumer documents like insurance policies, warranties, or leases put substance into definitions, the motive for doing so is suspect, as in the following provision from an automobile insurance policy.

> "Hit-and-run automobile" means a motor vehicle which causes bodily injury to an Insured arising out of physical contact of such automobile with the Insured or with an automobile which the Insured is occupying at the time of the accident, provided:
>
> (a) there cannot be ascertained the identity of either the operator or owner of such "hit-and-run automobile";
> (b) the Insured or someone on his behalf shall have reported the accident within 24 hours to a police, peace or

judicial officer or to the Department of Motor Vehicles in the state where the accident occurred, and shall have filed with Protective within 30 days after the accident a statement under oath that the Insured or his legal representative has a cause or causes of action arising out of such accident for damages against a person whose identity is unascertainable, and setting forth the facts in support thereof; and

(c) at Protective's request, the Insured or his legal representative makes available for inspection the automobile which the Insured was occupying, if so, at the time of the accident.

Here, the definition of "hit-and-run automobile" is one that limits the insured's recovery unless the insured has reported the incident to the police within twenty-four hours, made a sworn statement within thirty days, and made her car available for inspection. These stipulations are not intrinsic to the common sense definition of "hit-and-run automobile," and should appear in the body of the policy under a heading like "Reporting an Accident" or "Limitations on Recovery" or "Filing a Claim."

## d. Where to Put Definitions

Definitions that are used throughout a document should be collected in a section at the beginning of a document and arranged in alphabetical order. It is helpful to put defined terms in italics, quotation marks, capital letters, or bold every time they appear in your document so as to alert the reader that those words have a meaning specific to that instrument and that the definitions section should be consulted. Definitions that are used in a single section only are usually placed at the beginning of that section so as to eliminate the need to refer back to the definitions section.

─────────────── *Exercise 11.2* ───────────────

*Read the following definitions. Are they lexical or stipulative? If the latter, what kind of stipulative definitions are they? Are they successful? Are verbs used correctly? Propose rewrites where necessary.*

1. "Medicare" means Title XVIII of the Social Security Act.
2. "Medically Necessary" shall mean services or supplies required to identify or treat your illness and which are consistent with the symptoms or diagnosis and treatment of your condition and appropriate with regard to standards of good medical practice.
3. "Gender": The use of any gender in this Certificate is deemed to include the other gender, and when appropriate, the use of the singular is deemed to include the plural.
4. "Hospital" means an institution rendering inpatient and outpatient services for the medical care of the sick or injured.
5. "Nudity" means the showing of human private parts with less than a fully opaque covering.
6. "Enterprise integration" means the electronic linkage of manufacturers, assemblers, suppliers, and customers to enable the electronic exchange of product, manufacturing, and other business data among all partners in a product supply chain.
7. "Certificate" or "This Certificate" or "Supplemental Certificate" means the Certificate of Coverage and Member Handbook issued to you by Home Insurance, Inc., as it may be from time to time amended.
8. "Member Handbook" includes attached riders.
9. "Rehabilitation Facility" does not include extended care facilities.
10. "Faculty Member" includes law review and moot court students supervising the work of new members.
11. "Substance Abuse Services" include nursing, medical counseling, and therapeutic treatment.
12. "Contract Year" means that twelve-month period commencing on the effective date of the Agreement or any anniversary thereafter, during which the Agreement is in effect.
13. "Medical Emergencies" include severe chest pains, shortness of breath, multiple or severe injuries, loss of consciousness, sudden disorientation, severe bleeding, acute pain, poisoning, convulsions.
14. "Urgent Care Centers" do not include hospitals.
15. "Automotive vehicle" shall mean land-based, engine-powered automobiles, buses, defense vehicles, farm equipment, and motorcycles.
16. "Rare disease" means any disease that affects less than 200,000 persons in the United States a year.

17. "Animals" shall mean dogs and cats. No animals (which do not include domestic fish or birds), livestock, reptiles, or poultry shall be kept in any unit.

18. "Prescription Drugs" are (1) FDA approved legend drugs that can only be legally dispensed when ordered by a Physician, (2) compounded medications of which at least one ingredient is a prescription drug, or (3) insulin on prescription. Prescription drugs shall not include drugs, medication, injections, or intravenous therapies (1) provided at a hospital, (2) provided in connection with any Home Care benefit under the HMO Group Certificate or (3) administered by a Physician or Physician-supervised health professional.

---

## 3. Tabulation

One simple way to avoid syntactic ambiguity and the litigation it generates is the use of "tabulated" sentence structure. By showing the relationship between the elements of a sentence graphically, tabulation clarifies meaning. Remember, for example, our discussion in Section B(4) about the ambiguous scope of the modifier in "Places of public accommodation are wholesale or retail stores and establishments dealing with goods and services of any kind." It is unclear whether "dealing with goods and services of any kind" modifies establishments alone, or whether it also modifies stores, and unclear whether "wholesale or retail" modifies establishments as well as stores. Tabulation can make the drafter's intent clear. One intended meaning could be

Places of public accommodation are

1. wholesale and retail stores, or
2. establishments dealing with goods and services of any kind.

Because the layout attaches the modifiers to discrete items in the enumeration, the definition expressly restricts its reach to those "wholesale or retail stores" and "establishments that deal with goods and services." It also does not impose the "wholesale or retail" requirement on establishments or the "goods and services" restriction on stores. Alternatively, the provision could be tabulated as follows.

> Places of public accommodation are wholesale and retail
>
> 1. stores, or
> 2. establishments
>
> dealing with goods and services of any kind.

Because the adjectives "wholesale" and "retail" are included in the introduction, they modify both nouns. By bringing the modifier "dealing" out to the margin, the drafter expressly imposes the requirement on both stores and establishments.

Tabulated sentence structure serves other useful purposes. You may want to enumerate lists within a sentence to make the sentence easier to read. Tabulation also promotes clarity by emphasizing the exceptions and conditions in a sentence like "The executive board may transfer funds from the organization's account to the conference host only if the host's request for funds is made in writing, the host makes a showing of necessity, and the board approves the additional funds by a two-thirds vote." Tabulation makes the conditions clear.

> The executive board may transfer funds from the organization's account to the conference host only if
>
> 1. the host's request for funds is made in writing,
> 2. the host makes a showing of necessity, and
> 3. the board approves the additional funds by a two-thirds vote.

Tabulation also clarifies the alternative ("or") or cumulative ("and") nature of parallel items.

1. Alternative Items

> I authorize my executor to pay on behalf of any of my minor children to that child's
> a. other parent,
> b. guardian, *or*
> c. other legal representative.

## 2. Cumulative Items

> I appoint my wife, in her discretion, to execute and deliver
>
> a. all good and sufficient deeds,
> b. bills of sale, *and*
> c. instruments of transfer.

To punctuate a tabulated sentence, it is preferable to use semi-colons to separate elements only when any element is internally punctuated with commas.

> The scheduling order may include
>
> 1. time limits;
> 2. dates for pretrial, trial, and post-trial conferences; and
> 3. page limits for briefs.

Where there is no internal punctuation, use commas instead.

> The scheduling order may include
>
> 1. time limits,
> 2. dates for conferences, and
> 3. page limits for briefs.

It is incorrect to use colons between a verb and a complement or object unless the material to follow is tabulated.

> Wrong:   In May, he wrote: three memos, two letters, and two briefs.
>
> Right:    In May he wrote three memos, two letters, and two briefs.

Even when a sentence is tabulated, the preferred usage is to omit the colon when the tabulated elements are the complements of the introductory statement. Thus, it is unnecessary to use the colon in the following sentence.

> The scheduling order may include:
>
> 1. time limits,
> 2. dates for conferences, and
> 3. page limits for briefs.

Many drafters recommend meeting the following criteria in a tabulated sentence,[26] although you should always check for special local rules or conventions governing tabulation, especially when you are inserting a provision or amendment into a pre-existing document and need stylistic consistency.[27]

   a. The tabulation must constitute a complete sentence.
   b. The indented items must be parallel in construction.
   c. The indented items must begin with lower case letters rather than capitals in order to emphasize that they are within a sentence rather than self-contained entities.
   d. At the end of each item except the last one, there must be a comma or a semi-colon. When the items are short and when there is no punctuation within any single item, careful drafters prefer commas to semi-colons.
   e. After the next to the last item, it is essential to put either "and" or "or" to indicate whether the items are cumulative or alternative.
   f. Introductory words and concluding words should read like a grammatical sentence when read with each of the enumerated items.

A sentence like the following violates these criteria.

This warranty does not apply to units that have been subject to

1. Misuse,
2. Neglect,
3. Improper installation, or
4. That have been repaired by unauthorized personnel.

The enumeration here exhibits faulty parallelism because item number 4 is not grammatically parallel to the first three items. Moreover, if the introductory words are read with the fourth item

---

[26] *See* Dickerson, *supra* n.1, at 85; Child, *supra* n. 25, at 352.

[27] For example, after some lead-in language, some legislatures use an em dash to introduce a list, and then separate the tabulated items with commas and semicolons, while others follow lead-in language with a colon, capitalize the first word in each tabulated item, and end each item with a period. *See* Lawrence E. Filson, *The Legislative Drafter's Desk Reference* 235 (Congressional Quarterly, Inc. 1992).

alone, the sentence says: "This warranty does not apply to units that have been subject to that have been repaired by unauthorized personnel." Here is a corrected version.

This warranty does not apply to units that have been subject to

1. misuse,
2. neglect,
3. improper installation, or
4. repair by unauthorized personnel.

Like the sentence immediately above, some sentences are so short that tabulation is not needed. In fact, over-tabulation is distracting and impedes rather than improves the flow of your text. When tabulation promotes clarity and improves the flow of your text, however, pay attention to your numbering system. The most common subdivision system alternates between letters and numbers, and, as to letters, between upper and lower case, as shown below. No matter what system you use, be consistent.

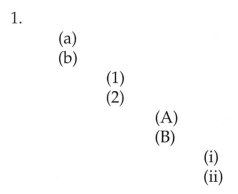

    1.
        (a)
        (b)
            (1)
            (2)
                (A)
                (B)
                    (i)
                    (ii)

Tabulation can also be used in conjunction with other typographic techniques to clarify entire documents. It is particularly valuable for demystifying documents destined to be read by lay persons.

## 4. Lists

In a tabulated sentence, the enumerated items are a grammatical part of the sentence itself. If you leave out the enumerations, the sentence is incomplete, as in "The warranty does not apply to units that have been subject to . . . ." In a list, the introduction is often a complete sentence and the enumerated or bulleted items function like "fill in the blank" examples of that thought.

Warranty service does not include repair of failures caused by any of the following:

- Attachments
- Modifications
- Accidents or misuse

OR

By the beginning of the calendar year, the following departments must all reduce their budgets by 5%.

1. The Development Office.
2. The Human Resources Office.
3. Building Maintenance.

Lists are capitalized and punctuated differently from tabulated sentences. In a list, the introductory sentence may end with either a period or a colon. Each item in the list usually begins with a capital letter and ends with no punctuation or with a period. Finally, lists use neither "and" nor "or" to clarify their cumulative or alternative nature. As in a tabulated sentence, however, the items in a list should be parallel, indented, and introduced by either a number, letter, bullet, or other symbol.

To verify your identity, you must bring one of the following documents.

a. Birth Certificate
b. Passport
c. Driver's license

There is one other kind of list that is always unpunctuated because it is just a heading followed by specifics, as in the following example.

## Acceptable Forms of Identification

Driver's License
Passport
Official New York State Identification Card

───────────────────── *Exercise 11.3* ─────────────────────

*A. Use tabulated sentence structure to clarify the following provision. Break the provision into two if that seems sensible.*

Covered services are subject to Medical Management Department Review in order to determine whether the proposed service, service currently being provided, or service that was provided is a covered service, although if a request for treatment is denied, or coverage for a current service or course of treatment is terminated, or coverage for a service received is denied because the Medical Management Department has made the determination that the service is not Medically Necessary, you may appeal that adverse determination.

*B. Correct the tabulation in the following sentence.*

We will provide the covered service required and then take into account any other coverages, including but not limited to:

   1. any group insurance, prepaid health plans, or other insured or uninsured arrangement of group coverage; and
   2. any automobile insurance contract, pursuant to any federal or state law, which mandates indemnification for medical services to persons suffering bodily injury from motor vehicle accidents,

but only if,

   3. covered services are eligible for payment under the provisions of such automobile policy; and
   4. the automobile policy does not under its rules determine its benefits after the benefits of any group health insurance.

**C.** - *Rewrite in list form and in tabulated sentence form.*
   - *Eliminate legalese*
   - *Put in headings if needed.*
   - *Clarify any contextual ambiguity.*

### Revocation by Divorce

If, after executing a will, the testator shall be divorced or his marriage shall be annulled, the divorce or annulment shall revoke any disposition or appointment of property made by the will to the former spouse, any provision conferring a general or special power of appointment on the former spouse, and any nomination of the former spouse, as executor, trustee, conservator or guardian, unless the will shall expressly provide otherwise. Property prevented from passing to a former spouse because of a revocation by divorce shall pass as if a former spouse had failed to survive the decedent, and other provisions conferring a power or office on the former spouse shall be interpreted as if the spouse had failed to survive the decedent.

────────────────── *Exercise 11.4* ──────────────────

*The following provision is part of a statute forbidding discriminatory housing practices. Tabulate to make the exemption and conditions clearer.*

(b) Exemptions
Nothing in section 3604 of this title (other than subsection (c)) shall apply to—
   (1) any single-family house sold or rented by an owner: *Provided,* That such private individual owner does not own more than three such single-family houses at any one time: *Provided further,* That in the case of the sale of any such single-family house by a private individual owner not residing in such house at the time of such sale or who was not the most recent resident of such house prior to such sale, the exemption granted by this subsection shall apply only with respect to one such sale within any twenty-four month period: *Provided further,* That such bona fide private individual owner does not own any interest in, nor is there owned or reserved on his behalf, under any express or voluntary agreement, title to or any right to all or a portion of the proceeds from the sale or rental of, more than three such single-family houses at any one time: *Provided further,* That

after December 31, 1969, the sale or rental of any such single-family house shall be excepted from the application of this subchapter only if such house is sold or rented (A) without the use in any manner of the sales or rental facilities or the sales or rental services of any real estate broker, agent, or salesman, or of such facilities or services of any person in the business of selling or renting dwellings, or of any employee or agent of any such broker, agent, salesman, or person and (B) without the publication, posting or mailing, after notice, of any advertisement or written notice in violation of section 3604(c) of this title; but nothing in this proviso shall prohibit the use of attorneys, escrow agents, abstractors, title companies, and other such professional assistance as necessary to perfect or transfer the title, or

(2) rooms or units in dwellings containing living quarters occupied or intended to be occupied by no more than four families living independently of each other, if the owner actually maintains and occupies one of such living quarters as his residence.

--------------------- *Exercise 11.5* ---------------------

*Using the techniques described in this chapter, critique and then revise the state statute below. At a minimum, it needs to be divided into subsections with headings and tabulated. The purpose of the statute is to provide accelerated resolution of "SLAPP" lawsuits—the acronym for "strategic litigation against public participation." Anti-SLAPP legislation is the subject of Casefile 4 in Appendix A. Consult the casefile for help understanding the statute. Do not revise the statute for substance; rather, revise for clarity and precision only, in order to better effectuate the apparent intent of the legislature.*

In any case in which a party asserts that the civil claims, counterclaims, or cross claims against said party are based on said party's exercise of its right of petition under the constitution of the United States or of the commonwealth, said party may bring a special motion to dismiss. The court shall advance any such special motion so that it may be heard and determined as expeditiously as possible. The court shall grant such special motion, unless the party against whom such special motion is made shows that: (1) the moving party's exercise of its right to petition was devoid of any reasonable factual support or any arguable basis in law and (2) the moving party's acts caused actual injury to the responding party. In making its determination, the court shall consider the pleadings and supporting and opposing affidavits stating the facts upon which the liability or defense is based.

The attorney general, on his behalf or on behalf of any government agency or subdivision to which the moving party's acts were directed, may intervene to defend or otherwise support the moving party on such special motion.

All discovery proceedings shall be stayed upon the filing of the special motion under this section; provided, however, that the court, on motion and after a hearing and for good cause shown, may order that specified discovery be conducted. The stay of discovery shall remain in effect until notice of entry of the order ruling on the special motion. Said special motion to dismiss may be filed within sixty days of the service of the complaint or, in the court's discretion, at any later time upon terms it deems proper. If the court grants such special motion to dismiss, the court shall award the moving party costs and reasonable attorney's fees, including those incurred for the special motion and any related discovery matters. Nothing in this section shall affect or preclude the right of the moving party to any remedy otherwise authorized by law.

As used in this section, the words "a party's exercise of its right of petition" shall mean any written or oral statement made before or submitted to a legislative, executive, or judicial body, or any other governmental proceeding; any written or oral statement made in connection with an issue under consideration or review by a legislative, executive, or judicial body, or any other governmental proceeding; any statement reasonably likely to encourage consideration or review of an issue by a legislative, executive, or judicial body or any other governmental proceeding; any statement reasonably likely to enlist public participation in an effort to effect such consideration; or any other statement falling within constitutional protection of the right to petition government.

---

### *Exercise 11.6*

*A. Rewrite the following planned community restrictions, using the techniques discussed in this chapter and in Chapter 1 on* Conceptualization *and*

*Chapter 5 on* Clarity. *These regulations need better sentence structure and greater coherence. Provide headings and subheadings where needed.*

1. No building, fence, walls or other structure shall be erected, placed, and altered on any building lot in this subdivision until the building plans, specifications and plot plan showing the location of such structures have been approved as to their harmony with existing structures herein and as to the building with respect to topography and ground elevations by the Architectural and Environmental Control Committee.

2. A. The Association shall have the right at all times to enter upon any lot or parcel of said property that is vacant and unplanted or un-tenanted, by the owner thereof, after reasonable notice to the owner thereof, and at the expense of the Association to plant or replant, trim, cut back, remove, replace, cultivate and/or maintain hedges, trees, shrubs, plants or lawns.

B. The Association shall have the right at all times, and the owners thereof by accepting a deed or contract thereto, and any tenant or les-see of said owners, by accepting possession thereof, expressly grant to the Association such right and waive any and all objection to the exer-cise thereof, to enter upon any lot or parcel of said property, whether vacant or occupied, after the reasonable notice to the owner thereof and to that party or parties in possession thereof, and at the expense of the Association to plant or replant, trim, cut back, remove, replace, cultivate and/or maintain hedges, trees, shrubs, plants or lawns and clean, paint, repair, replace and generally maintain the exterior of the residential building and improvements thereon and any other things in connection thereto necessary or desirable in the judgment of the As-sociation to keep said lot or parcel of said property and the residential building and improvements thereon in neat and good order to conform with the general attractive character of the area.

C. Any and all expenses which may be incurred by the Association in the performance of the acts specified in Sections A and B above, shall be a charge against the owner of the lot or parcel of said property upon which such acts were performed in the form of an assessment as pro-vided elsewhere herein and in the By-Laws of the SENIOR ESTATES COUNTRY CLUB."

3. Article I: No structure shall be altered, placed, or permitted to remain on any 'residential lot' other than one detached single family

dwelling, a private garage, a guest house, and outbuildings for pets as hereinafter described.

Article II: No outbuilding shall be erected, altered, placed or permitted to remain nearer than eight (8) feet to either side line of a lot unless no portion of said building extends nearer to the street line than sixty-five (65) feet.

Article III: No trailer, basement, tent, shack, garage, barn or other outbuilding erected on a building site covered by these covenants shall at any time be used for human habitation temporarily or permanently, nor shall any structure of a temporary character be used for human habitation.

Article IV: No structure of a temporary character, mobile home, trailer, camper, any motorhome, tent, garage, or any outbuilding may be used on any block as a residence either permanent or temporary.

*B. May a homeowner build a woodworking shop on his lot in the subdivision whose restrictions appear above in Part A of this exercise? Does Section 3 Article (III) conflict with Section 3 Article (I)? How would you rewrite these articles for the Association if its members intended not to allow buildings such as woodworking shops?*

*C. May a lot owner place a double-wide mobile home on the lot in the community whose restrictions appear in Part A of this exercise, if he removes its axles and tongues and fastens it to a foundation? Can a lot owner place a manufactured home on the lot if it is constructed off site and transported to the site? Rewrite Section 3 Article IV to reflect the Association's intent not to allow either type of home.*

# Chapter 12

# *BASIC SKILLS: DOCUMENT DESIGN*

## A. IN GENERAL

Document design is about readability. It uses graphic presentation to make substance more understandable and more memorable—and not just with visual aids like graphs and diagrams, but with fonts, white space, headings, and alignment. In fact, psychologists have found that typographical features directly affect reading comprehension and speed. For example, certain fonts and sizes increase reading speed, others decrease it; hierarchical headings and white space between issues or provisions "chunk" information and help recall, while right margin justification decreases speed and concentration because it leads to odd and distracting spacing between letters and words.[1] Thus document design is pragmatic, not just aesthetic: it helps readers to grasp and retain points more easily, thus furthering the reader's confidence in the substance of the document. Unfortunately, good design principles are not always consistent with statutory requirements. Court documents must be formatted according to court rules, consumer documents according to consumer law. But where common sense is allowed to prevail, lawyers should heed the advice of professionals and reap the benefits of good layout and typographic design.

---

[1] Ruth Anne Robbins, *Painting with Print: Incorporating Concepts of Typographic and Layout Design into the Text of Legal Writing Documents*, 2 J. Ass'n Legal Writing Directors, 108, 113-26 (2004). *See also*, Linda L. Morkin, *The Gestalt of Brief-writing: Visual Rhetoric in the Appellate Brief*, 49 No. 9 DRI 27 (2007); Gerald Lebovits, *Document Design: Pretty in Print*, 81-APR N.Y. St. B. J. 64 (2009); Raymond P. Ward, *Good Writing, Good Reading: Advice on Typography*, 47 DRI 60 (2005); Bryan Garner, *The Redbook: A Manual on Legal Style* (2nd ed. Thomson West 2006).

## B. TYPEFACE

### 1. Fonts

For longer documents, most experts recommend using a serif rather than a sans-serif font and using a font with a varied, proportional width rather than a fixed, monospaced width. A serif is a small line, often called a wing or foot, that is attached to the bottom of some letters, especially noticeable with letters like "n" or "m." Because the serif leads the eye to the next letter, a serif font is thought to be easier to read, particularly in longer documents. **Times New Roman** and **Garamond** are widely used serif fonts. A sans-serif font—like **Arial**—does not have these lines and their absence decreases reading speed. Nonetheless, a sans-serif font is a fine contrast for headings and is easy to read on PowerPoint slides and overheads.

To avoid unnecessary distractions, document designers also recommend limiting the number of typefaces used in each document. The headings can be in a different font from the text, but you should avoid using a different font for each subheading. Instead, you can show the hierarchical structure by using boldface or italics.

### a. Proportional versus Monospaced Fonts

In a monospaced font like Courier, each letter is the same width—an 'I' takes the same space as an 'M.' In a proportional font, the width of a letter depends on its shape. The difference can be seen below.

```
Might: Courier
```
Might: Times New Roman

Studies show that monospaced fonts take nearly 5% longer to read because each word occupies more horizontal space and fewer words can be taken in at a glance.[2] Thus proportional fonts are preferable.

---

[2] Robbins, *supra* n. 1, at 121.

## *b. Font Size*

Small font sizes (10 point or less) discourage careful reading because they strain the eyes. Thus, a 10-12 point font is ideal for text and a 14 point font is good for major headings. Anything larger than 14 point heading "screams" at the reader, disrupting the flow.

## 2. All-Caps, Boldface, Italics, and Underline

Although some courts require major point headings in briefs to be in capital letters, all-cap sentences are hard to read because word recognition depends in part on the word's shape. A word's shape comes from its "ascenders"—letters that go above the mid-line, like "f" and "h"—and its "descenders" such as "g." Because the words in all-cap sentences are one height, word recognition is slower, as illustrated below.

THE ADMINISTRATIVE LAW JUDGE IMPROPERLY APPLIED THE PUNITIVE DAMAGE STANDARD WHEN SHE AWARDED TREBLE COMPENSATORY DAMAGES IN A SEX DISCRIMI-NATION CASE BROUGHT BY A FORMER PROBATIONARY GROUNDSKEEPER FOR A UNIVERSITY.

The administrative law judge improperly applied the punitive damage standard when she awarded treble compensatory dam-ages in a sex discrimination case brought by a former probationary groundskeeper for a university.

Although the legibility of short point headings is not greatly af-fected by an all-cap style, avoid all-caps for longer headings like the one above—unless court rules require caps. Because they impede word recognition, caps are especially inappropriate for imparting emphasis.

Underlining blurs the serif lines and descending letters and thus slows reading speed. For this reason graphic designers dis-courage using it as a means of emphasis. Instead, they suggest using italics for short phrases and boldface in all other situations. Studies show that boldface does not seem to slow reading down at all.[3] Nonetheless, when writing for lawyers and judges, avoid

---

[3] Robbins, *supra* n. 1, at 118-119.

excessive emphasis. Expert legal readers are careful readers who rarely need emphasis to get the point. In fact, they may even resent it.

Of course, different typefaces may be used to differentiate hierarchical headings.

## C. SPACING

### 1. White Space

White space is that part of a page that has no text. It includes not only line-spacing, but also margins and the space around headings, block quotes, lists, tabulations, charts, and footnotes. Ideally, 50% of each page should be white space since it breaks the text into manageable portions and gives the reader a breather between courses.

Because of the importance of white space to comprehension and retention, a word count is a better method of controlling length than a page limit because it gives a writer more flexibility in designing a document. To increase white space, writers can

- use 1 ¼" margins,
- shorten paragraphs,
- use headings and subheadings,
- indent a full tab for each paragraph,
- use lists and tabulated sentences, and
- add extra space between paragraphs and around lists, charts, block quotations, and headings.[4]

Be careful, however, not to leave so much space that the reader loses the impetus of the argument or suspects that you are stretching a thin argument.

### 2. Alignment

Left aligned text is best for legal documents. First, the ragged edge on the right margin creates extra white space. Second, the uneven edge helps the reader to find the next line down. You should avoid right margin justification, where the margins line up

---

[4] *See* Lebovits, *supra* n. 1, at 54; Morkan, *supra* n. 1.

evenly on both sides, because this format creates uneven spacing between letters and words.

## 3. Hierarchical Structure

Research has shown that readers need to break information into "chunks" in order to absorb and recall it. Without "chunking," a reader suffers from overload and stops processing.[5] Lawyers may organize their chunks by issue and subissue, by sequence, by categories of provisions (like custody or visitation), but whatever the hierarchy or scheme, document design can highlight the chunks—the structure—and thereby aid recall. A writer's use of headings and spacing are two tools central to "chunking."

### a. Using Headings

Headings reveal the superstructure of a document and provide an outline. You can make the headings more memorable if you use a consistent, but contrasting, combination of typeface, font size, font style, numbering, and indentation. For example, initial headings can be larger than text and bolded; in contrast, subheads can be the same size as the text, but can be differentiated with the use of boldface, italics, or underlining. You can use progressive indents on the left to display the hierarchy of the parts. This is especially helpful in rule-making documents like contracts or statutes, as in the outline below.

EMPLOYMENT CONTRACT

1.  **Scope of Employment**
2.  **Compensation**
    a.  *Salary:*
    b.  *Benefits:*
        i.   health insurance
        ii.  disability insurance
        iii. pension
        iv.  vacation
    c.  *Expenses*
3.  **Termination**

---

[5] Robbins, *supra* n. 1, at 125.

## *b. Spacing of Headings*

To indicate clear chunks of information, you should leave extra white space between one chunk and the next. However, you should keep each heading close to its related text in order to create a visual unit. Too much space between the heading and text makes the relation between the heading and text less apparent. Thus, you should leave more space between "chunks" than between heading and text.

## D. CONSUMER DOCUMENTS

Nowhere is design more important than in consumer documents. The general reading public is largely unfamiliar with and daunted by the writing in traditional legal documents—whether jury instructions, leases, consumer contracts, or insurance policies. This situation leads to confusion and unnecessary litigation. As a result, many states now have plain language statutes requiring readable documents that adhere to many of the recommendations made here and in Chapter 5 on *Clarity*, Chapter 11 on *Precision*, and section (F)(2) of Chapter 14 on *Contracts*.

At the heart of the plain language movement is a commitment to use words with everyday, common meanings. Many plain language statutes impose limits on the length of words and sentences and dictate the size of the typeface. They encourage the use of concrete nouns as subjects, graphs, lists, white space, and active voice. Plain language proponents advise using first and second person pronouns to place the consumer in the document: "To use this software, you must agree to our terms, which are listed below." They regard organization as key, dividing information into sections with clear captions and often using chronology to structure a document. They recommend question and answer formats as particularly helpful for lay readers.[6]

A comparison of the following two warranties illustrates the effectiveness of these techniques. The formatting of the first is

---

[6] For more on consumer documents, see Joseph Kimble, *Plain English: A Charter for Clear Writing,* 9 Thomas M. Cooley L. Rev. 1 (1992); Wayne Schiess, *The Art of Consumer Drafting,* 11 Scribes J. Legal Writing 1 (2007). Another important resource is the journal *Clarity,* which is devoted to plain language drafting.

guaranteed to lose its audience, while the formatting of the second helps to retain it.

## LIMITED WARRANTY

If any part supplied by Company fails because of defect in workmanship or material within 12 months from date of original purchase, Company will repair the product at no charge, provided air conditioner is reasonably accessible for service. If the sealed refrigeration system (defined as compressor, condenser coil, reversing valve, check valve, capillary, filter drier and all interconnecting tubing) supplied by Company fails because of a defect in workmanship or material within 60 months from date of original purchase, Company will pay labor costs and parts necessary to repair the sealed refrigeration system, provided the owner pays the cost of diagnosis, removal and transportation to and from the service agency and the cost of reinstallation. This warranty is applicable only to units retained within the 50 states of the U.S.A. and the District of Columbia. This warranty is not applicable to air filters, fuses, products on which the model and serial numbers have been removed, products which have defects or damage which results from improper installation or misuse. Service will be provided by the company's service organizations in your area. They are listed in the Yellow Pages. This warranty is given in lieu of all other warranties. Any implied warranties of fitness and/or merchantability is limited to the duration of this express warranty. To receive warranty services, owner must provide proof of purchase.

## LIMITED WARRANTY

**Who is covered?**
This warranty covers the original owner.

**What is covered?**
The warranty covers any part of the air conditioner that fails because of a defect in workmanship or material.

**What is not covered?**
This warranty does not apply to any unit that is not within the 50 states of the U.S.A. and the District of Columbia.

The warranty also does not apply to

- Air filters
- Products on which the model number and serial numbers have been removed
- Products with defects or damage that results from improper installation or misuse

**What will Company do and for how long?**
*Within 12 months of original purchase,* the company will repair *at no charge* any part of the air conditioner that fails because of a defect in workmanship or material.

*After month 12 and through month 60,* the company will pay for parts and will pay a labor allowance to repair the sealed refrigeration system if it fails because of a defect in workmanship or material. The sealed refrigeration system is defined as

- compressor
- condenser coil
- reversing valve
- check valve
- capillary
- filter drier
- all interconnecting tubing

**What must you do to obtain service?**

- You must present proof of purchase.
- You must pay the cost of diagnosis, removal, and transportation to and from the service agency and the cost of reinstallation if the sealed refrigeration system fails after 12 months.

**How to get warranty service?**
Look in the Yellow Pages for the company's service organizations in your area.

**Are there limitations on the warranty?**
This warranty is given in lieu of all other warranties. Any implied warranties of fitness and/or merchantability is limited to the duration of this express warranty.

A document is much more readable, and thus more effective, if you pay attention to its appearance, being careful to suit its design to its audience and purpose. At a minimum, your work must look professional. It must be carefully proofread—free of typos, misspellings, and grammar and citation errors. But a document free of error is just the beginning. Truly professional work should have a thoughtful design, one that helps to secure and keep the reader's attention and that promotes retention.

---

### *Exercise 12.1*

*Redraft the following lien law using the following document design techniques.*

- *Appropriate Font Sizes*
- *Headings*
- *Tabulation*
- *White Space*
- *Logical Organization and Conceptualization*
- *Precise, Concise, Consistent Diction*

### § 184. Lien of bailee of motor vehicles, motor cycles, motor boats or aircraft.

A person keeping a garage, hangar or place for the storage, maintenance, keeping or repair of motor vehicles or of motor cycles as defined by the vehicle and traffic law, or of motor boats as defined by article seven of the navigation law, or of aircraft as defined by article fourteen of the general business law, and who in connection therewith stores, maintains, keeps or repairs any motor vehicle, motor cycle, motor boat, or aircraft or furnishes gasoline or other supplies therefor at the request or with the consent of the owner, whether or not such motor vehicle, motor cycle, motor boat or aircraft is subject to a security interest, has a lien upon such motor vehicle, motor cycle, motor boat or aircraft for the sum due for such storing, maintaining, keeping, or repairing of such motor vehicle, motor cycle, motor boat or aircraft or for furnishing gasoline or other supplies therefor and may detain such motor vehicle, motor cycle, motor boat or aircraft at any time it may be lawfully in his possession until such sum is paid, except that if the lienor, subsequent to thirty days from the secural of such lien, allows the motor vehicle, motor cycle, motor boat or aircraft out of his actual possession the lien provided for in this section shall thereupon become void as against all security interests, whether or not perfected, in such motor vehicles, motor cycle, motor boat or aircraft and executed prior to the accrual of such lien, notwithstanding possession of such motor vehicle, motor cycle, motor boat or aircraft is thereafter acquired by such lienor.

# Chapter 13

# *RULE-MAKING: LEGISLATION AND REGULATION*

## A. IN GENERAL

The documents discussed in this chapter do not easily lend themselves to a definition or to a generic term, much though we recognize them when we see them. Legislation is used here in the very broad sense of law enacted by vote, and regulation in the equally broad sense of administrative rules. Each has both public and private incarnations. Thus, at the intersection of the enacted/administrative and public/private distinctions are many rule-making documents that overlap and diverge in complicated and criss-crossing networks:

- statutes, ordinances and administrative rules are public instruments, while articles of incorporation, articles of partnership, and by-laws are private;
- statutes, ordinances, and some by-laws are enacted documents (even though some are public and some are private), while administrative rules and executive orders may be public, but are not enacted.

What then do these documents have in common?

The major commonality of public enacted law, public administrative regulation, and private rule-making is their similarity of function. The function of most rules is to confer a right, privilege, or power; abridge a right, privilege, or power; or oblige a person to act or not to act.[1] In addition, rules "often prescribe the conditions under which they forbid, authorize, or require behavior and/or the consequences that result if one follows, or fails to

---

[1] Reed Dickerson, *The Fundamentals of Drafting* 213–14 (Little, Brown & Co. 1986).

follow the law."[2] These functions then are the tie among all the documents mentioned above.

Admittedly other legal documents have similar objectives. Contracts regulate conduct, but they tend to do so for a special situation or occasion, for only those individuals or small groups of individuals who are parties to the contract, and for a specific period of time. Wills and conveyances may occasionally regulate conduct, but their purpose is primarily dispositive.[3] In contrast, legislation and regulations are almost entirely about regulating conduct and have continuing force as well as broad scope and application.

That said, even legislation and regulations may differ in scope. Public legislation, which includes federal and state statutes as well as local ordinances, may consider a broad range of issues and is subject only to constitutional limitations, existing law, and political reality. In contrast, a public administrative agency's rule-making authority is delegated by and limited to its enabling legislation. Thus an agency's regulations have limited scope, even if the legislation gives the agency substantial discretion as to how to effect its intent in that matter. In contrast, drafters of private regulations may have greater freedom to determine rights, duties, and procedures—though they too must comport with law in the area and their rules may have a narrower reach.

### 1. Lawyers as Drafters

Most law students would acknowledge that, as practitioners, they may need to draw up contracts, prepare wills, or draft leases, but they rarely contemplate a future of regulatory or legislative drafting. And yet the opportunities for rule-making are multiple. First, some lawyers become professional drafters. Employed by a legislative body or executive agency, their sole job is drafting legislation, amendments, or regulations. Second, lawyers who serve as counsel to public interest groups, trade or business associations, corporations, or government agencies might draft a bill that is of special interest to the client for introduction by an elected representative in Congress, a state legislature, or local

---

[2] Jack Stark, *The Art of the Statute* 9 (Fred B. Rothman & Co. 1996).

[3] Dickerson, *supra* n. 1, at 5.

council. Third, lawyers may be asked to draft regulations for the self-governance of a private institution. Fourth, some lawyers serve as elected legislators or as staff to a legislator. Thus, whether as professional drafters or as occasional drafters, lawyers engage in law-making more frequently than law students realize.

## 2. Policy and the Drafter

Drafters have a peculiar relation to substantive policy. They do not make policy in that they are not responsible for the substantive decisions that go into drafting. That is the responsibility and the role of the client or sponsor. But drafters are nonetheless required to effectuate that policy responsibly, even when they disagree with it.[4] That mandate is obviously difficult when the drafter disagrees with the substance of a rule, but it can also be difficult when the drafter agrees with it. Because the proponent of regulations or legislation often has no more than a rudimentary idea of how to effectuate its substance, the drafter cannot simply memorialize the sponsor's intent, even if he or she wants to. Although subject to the sponsor's approval, policy often becomes formulated in the performance of drafting—in understanding the problem; in probing alternative ways of solving the problem; in exploring the consequences of each solution; in examining ways of implementation; and in deciding upon provisions, their arrangement, and their wording.

Drafters need to be aware of the many points at which drafting and policymaking intersect in order to be able to navigate the ethical minefield of rule-making. Were they to consult and defer to clients or elected officials on every decision, the rule-making process would grind to a halt. On the other hand, were they to take initial instructions on policy and proceed without further consultation, the policymaker's role would be usurped. A balance

---

[4] This moral quagmire is faced most frequently by professional drafters of public legislation who must work on bills sponsored by legislators of all political persuasions. They would lose credibility and probably their employment if their drafts did not carry out their sponsors' purposes. *See* Victoria F. Nourse & Jane S. Schacter, *The Politics of Legislative Drafting: A Congressional Case Study*, 77 N.Y.U. L. Rev. 575, 587 (2002). Although the same obligation is imposed when the client is private, there is a greater chance the drafter will be in sympathy with a private client's objectives. The attorney for a public interest group or business client, for example, is likely to share the client's goals and is more likely to have been engaged to advise upon policy matters.

is needed. Thus one mark of a skilled and professional drafter is the ability to make policy choices that flow logically from the client's initial directions. Another mark is knowing when a decision is so consequential that the drafter must explain choices, alternatives, and implications to the sponsor or client, and take instruction upon them.

### 3. Audience

Besides the obligation to implement the sponsor's substantive policy, the drafter must communicate that policy to the appropriate audience. In his germinal work on drafting, Reed Dickerson observed that rules addressed to government officials or to highly specialized segments of the population may need to be written differently from rules addressed to the general public. Thus, agency officials or a specialized group like the pharmaceutical industry, for example, may be familiar with specialized terms and agency or industry conventions, and this familiarity may guide the drafter in determining what must be included and what can be safely omitted because of tacit assumptions of which even courts take judicial notice.[5]

Dickerson includes in this category legislation like the Internal Revenue code, which applies to the public at large, but that is rarely read by the public. Since the IRS and certified public accountants read, explain, and apply the code, it is written for them rather than for the public at large.[6] Dickerson contrasts this drafting situation to regulations that apply to, and are read by, lay persons. University regulations governing student conduct, for example, ought to have the very qualities that are unnecessary in the tax code.

Although Dickerson is undoubtably right that context plays a role in the substance, language, and shape of legislation, contemporary drafters in the United States have become more sensitive to drafting in plain language. In June of 1998, President Clinton issued an Executive Memorandum directing executive depart-

---

[5] Dickerson, *supra* n. 1, at 22.

[6] *See id.* at 20.

ments and agencies to write in plain language.[7] By January of 1999, all proposed and final rule-making documents published in the *Federal Register* were to be in plain language.[8] The President further directed that by January of 2002, all letters, forms, notices and instructions were to be written in plain language.[9] Although subsequent administrations have not had a formal plain language initiative, the movement has taken root in numerous agencies.[10] Thus, while writers traditionally adapt style to particular audiences, there is a trend in drafting—not yet universal—to write for only one audience, namely, the general public.

## B. COMPONENTS

Since legislation and regulation come in so many shapes and sizes, their components are difficult to generalize. Nonetheless, the most frequent components of statutes and of corporate articles and bylaws, described in the next two sections below, give a good idea of what rule-making documents usually contain.

### 1. Statutes

The nature of a law determines the provisions that are needed and how they are to be arranged. Nonetheless, complex statutes have the following sections, some of which may also be found in private regulations.

Long Title
Enacting Clause
Short Title
Statement of Purpose, Policy, or Findings

---

[7] President Clinton's Memorandum explains, "plain language documents have logical organization, easy-to-read design features, and use common, everyday words, except for necessary technical terms; "you" and other pronouns; active voice; and short sentences." Presidential Memorandum on Plain Language, 63 Fed. Reg. 31885 (June 1, 1998). Other advocates of plain language emphasize the accessibility of the question/answer format. *See* Steven L. Schooner, *Communicating Governance: Will Plain English Drafting Improve Regulation?* 70 Geo. Wash. L. Rev. 163 (2002).

[8] Clinton, *supra* n. 7.

[9] *Id.*

[10] *See* www.plainlanguage.gov.

Definitions
Substantive Provisions
Administrative Sections
Miscellaneous Clauses
    Effective Dates
    Savings Clause
    Severability Clause

*a. Long Title*

The "Long Title" describes the gist of the statute. It is the first line after the heading "A Bill" or "An Act" and opens with the words "to" or "relating to."

> ### An Act
>
> To conserve and protect state revenues through efficient and prudent use of state funds in state procurement contracts, and for other purposes.

The "to" phrase often announces whether the bill is amending or repealing legislation.

> ### A Bill
> ### To repeal...
>
> ### An Act
> ### To amend....

Titles should always describe the main idea of the law. In addition, some state constitutions set requirements for information that goes into the title, often asking for explicit references to every purpose. These requirements do not exist on the federal level, where miscellaneous or minor items are frequently handled by appending "and for other purposes" to the end of the title. Nonetheless it is generally a good idea to write long titles in federal statutes so as to avoid under-inclusiveness. In addition, it is advisable to write or rewrite the long title after the bill is finished in order to ensure the title accurately reflects the content of the bill.

## b. Enacting Clause

To become law, a bill must have an enacting clause, that is, a clause that tells the public which legislative body passed this bill into law. Often, the wording of an enacting clause is prescribed by state constitution and must be followed exactly. On federal bills, the clause begins

> *Be it enacted by the Senate and House of Representatives of the United States of America in Congress assembled,*

and then leads into the short title.

## c. Short Title

Because long titles are unwieldy, most statutes have short titles that make referral easier. Thus the long title given above might be shortened to the "State Procurement Act." In addition to making referral easier, some drafters see the short title as a persuasive occasion. By describing the bill attractively—as "Tax Reform Act" or "Child Protection Act"—they may persuade other legislators to pass it.

The short title usually appears immediately after the enacting clause.

## d. Statement of Purpose, Policy, or Findings

Sponsors like statements of findings and purposes because they continue the public relations campaign in the document itself. Professional drafters are rightly more cautious. Purpose statements that precede the enacting clause (preambles) are not part of the statute proper and are therefore without legal effect, unless the court construing the statute is willing to go outside the four corners of the document. Policy statements that follow the enacting clause may have some legal effect, especially to clarify the scope of a regulation in a new subject area or to provide guidance to administrators in regulatory documents. You should be careful, however, not to use the purpose statement as a substitute for clear and accurate provisions in the rule itself.

The preambles of older statutes often begin with a series of "whereas clauses."

> Whereas it is the policy of the state to conserve and protect state revenue through the efficient and prudent use of state funds in procurement contracts; and
>
> Whereas the operation of an efficient procurement information system is an effective tool in the economic development of the state: Now Therefore Be It
>
> *Resolved*, that the state create a central information source....

Modern purpose clauses are written in paragraph form.

> The legislature hereby finds and declares that is it the policy of the state to conserve and protect state revenue through the efficient and prudent use of state funds in procurement contracts. It further finds that the operation of an efficient procurement information system is an effective tool in the economic development of the state. To promote this policy, it is in the best interest of the state to create a central information source that will alert businesses to new opportunities to participate in state procurement activities. To accomplish these public purposes, public notice of state procurement contracts shall be given by regular publication of compilation of the state's needs for goods and services.

### e. Definitions

Definitions are discussed extensively in Section (C)(2) of Chapter 11, *Precision*, but a few key concepts need to be summarized here. You do not need to define terms used in their ordinary dictionary sense. However, you should define terms that have more than one meaning or are unfamiliar. One of the virtues of definitions is that they promote internal consistency by ensuring those terms have the same meaning throughout the document. In addition, it is helpful to create terms for complicated concepts in order to have a simple, concise way of referring to a notion.

> "Procurement contract" means any written agreement entered into by an agency for the acquisition of goods or services of any kind in the actual or estimated amount of five thousand dollars or more. The term does not include an agreement for employment in the civil service.

A definition like this spares the drafter from spelling out what is meant by "procurement contract" every time that term is used. It also permits other provisions to be stated simply and concisely. For example,

> The commissioner shall publish on a weekly basis notices of "procurement contract" opportunities.

Definitions used throughout a bill are placed in their own section, generally early in the bill. They are usually arranged in alphabetical order. A definition used only in one section of a bill is usually placed at the beginning of that section.

Finally, the verb "means" is used to establish the meaning of the term: "procurement contract means...." Use "includes" to enlarge the ordinary lexical definition so that the term applies to things not normally included. Use "does not include" to narrow the lexical definition.

### f. Substantive Provisions

The substantive provisions of a law are those that articulate its principal objectives. These are the provisions that set out the rights, duties, powers, or privileges of a person or entity and the exceptions to those provisions.

Start with the general rule or rules, and put each major point into a separate section. Thus an academic honor code could have separate sections on plagiarism, unauthorized use of materials, and unauthorized collaboration. Or it could be written as one provision, "Academic Dishonesty," and have subdivisions for types of dishonesty. Decide which organization works best for your purposes, and then use headings to clarify the parts.

If possible, place exceptions in the same section as the general rule so that they read as a unit and do not require cross-referencing. In fact, simple exceptions are often written into the general rule itself. Thus a drafter can exempt senior citizens from a requirement by inserting into the general rule the words "individuals under 65 years of age are required to...." If there are many exceptions, however, they are sometimes placed in a section of their own immediately following the general rule section.

Remember to use words of authority carefully: the better practice is to use "shall" when requiring action, "must" when creating a condition precedent, and "may" when permitting an action. Their difference is crucial and misuse often causes litigation. For more on words of authority, see Section (C)(1) of Chapter 11, *Precision.*

### g. Administrative Sections

Some legislation is self-executing in that it is effective as soon as it is signed into law. Moreover, there are often standing government entities ready to enforce it. A criminal statute does not need administrative provisions, for example, because the task has already been allocated to law enforcement agencies.

Other legislation identifies or creates a committee or an agency to administer and enforce a rule. If so, the legislation may outline the agency or committee's organization, personnel, powers, and procedures, or it may leave the details to that body. Generally, drafters advise including at least some administrative provisions to ensure the act is implemented in accordance with the sponsor's desires. Many worthy and well written substantive provisions are undermined by hastily conceived or deficient administrative procedures. One example of this is the Sarbanes-Oxley Act, which created the Public Company Accounting Oversight Board to audit the auditors of public companies. One commentator on the Act reported "the law establishing the board was full of compromises. Just how thorough those inspections will be, or even who will do them, is up to the board."[11]

You should also think about which sanctions best achieve the objective of the policy. Sometimes the end is best achieved by thinking of rewards. Sometimes penalties are more appropriate. One state senator reminds us that legislators or agencies

---

[11] Floyd Norris, *Will Audit Reform Die Before It Begins*, Col.2 The New York Times, C1 (December 27, 2002).

can choose from a "small arsenal" of devices: licenses, permits, charters, civil or criminal sanctions.

> To force motorists to purchase no-fault auto insurance, legislators have imposed criminal penalties on the uninsured, required vehicle owners to submit proof of insurance or a policy number when licensing a motor vehicle, excluded from benefits those who fail to insure, exposed the uninsured to liability for negligence, and authorized revocation of motor vehicle and driver licenses of uninsured motorists.[12]

### h. Miscellaneous Clauses

Most statutes have an "effective date provision" that specifies when the act becomes effective. This may be at the time of enactment or there may be a period in which to give those to whom the act applies notice of its provisions. In addition to having effective date clauses, some acts have "sunset" provisions that suspend the operation of the act either because the measure was intended as temporary or because the legislative body wants to review it.

Other typical legislative provisions are a savings clause, that is, a clause indicating that the statute applies prospectively and does not affect the rights individuals had under the prior law, and a severability clause. The latter clause declares that if any part of the statute is found invalid, the rest of it remains in effect. Because courts uniformly construe laws this way, severability clauses are not actually necessary.

You will need to review the entire range of miscellaneous clauses to determine which are needed in your legislation.

### i. Amendments

New legislation may also require provisions needed to fit the legislation into the existing code. For example, you may need to add provisions that amend or repeal other clauses. This can be done in a variety of ways. Within the text itself, you can eliminate, insert, or change language by direct reference (i.e., "section 0 of the Act is amended by striking x"). You can rewrite the provision,

---

[12] Jack Davies, *Legislative Law and Process* 145 (West Pub. Co. 1986).

omitting the deleted language and inserting the new, or you can put a line through the language you are omitting and add new language in boldface or italics. It is the custom of some legislative bodies to have a section repealing the provision that is being amended.

## 2. Corporate Articles and Bylaws

Articles of Incorporation (also called a Corporate Charter, Articles of Association, or Certificate of Incorporation) are written when an organization decides to incorporate.[13] To incorporate, the organization needs to file them with the appropriate state agency. Most organizations also adopt a code of bylaws at the organizational meeting.

The articles "constitute an enforceable agreement between the state and the corporation, the corporation and its shareholders [or members], and among [the members] or shareholders themselves."[14] State statutes control the content of the articles; if any provision of the articles conflicts with the statutes, therefore, the statutes prevail. On the other hand, the articles override any bylaw that conflicts with them.

Articles of Incorporation usually include three types of provisions:

> (1) mandatory provisions required of all corporations (e.g., name, registered agent, location, etc.); (2) provisions changing the default rule provided by statute, changes which often must be in the articles to be effective (e.g., cumulative voting, preemptive rights); (3) additional provisions the participants may desire to include in the articles as to governance, financing or other matters.[15]

---

[13] Organizations often incorporate in order to have powers distinct from individual incorporators—such as the ability to enter into contract or to pay taxes. A corporate organization can also limit the personal liability of its directors. Kim A. Zeitlin & Susan A. Dorn, *The Nonprofit Board's Guide to Bylaws: Creating a Framework for Effective Governance* 3 (National Center for Nonprofit Boards 1996) (on file with authors).

[14] Marvin Hyman, *Corporation Forms* §2.1 (Westgroup 2001).

[15] F. Hodge O'Neal & Robert B. Thompson, *O'Neal's Close Corporation* §3.02, p.4 (3d ed., Westgroup 2002).

Once the governing body drafts and approves them, the articles are filed in public offices and become available for public inspection. Their repeal or amendment is subject to procedures provided in the articles themselves and in the state's corporate code.[16] Even then, they are usually difficult to change, requiring a vote of directors and shareholders or members,[17] and a new filing. Given this burdensome procedure, the articles usually contain only those provisions needed to establish corporate status and to comply with statutory requirements, as well as those provisions expected to be fairly permanent or intended to protect minority shareholders.[18]

Because bylaws are not public documents, and thus more easily repealed or amended, they are used to regulate the day-to-day activities of the corporation. They contain many of the rules and regulations governing the organization's structure and functions.[19] Even then, there is another layer of written authority, namely, board resolutions. Resolutions are made when more procedural detail is needed than is provided in the bylaws. Resolutions provide a means to handle details that need to be adjusted with some frequency.[20]

Bylaws have three important functions. First, they determine how an organization is structured. For example, most bylaws specify whether an organization has stockholders (in a for-profit corporation) or members (in a not-for-profit corporation). They set out the duties of the stockholders or members to the corporation and among themselves and the powers and duties of the directors

---

[16] *See* Hyman, *supra* n. 14, at § 3.1; Henry M. Robert III, et al., *Robert's Rules of Order* 11 (10th ed. Persus Publishing 2000).

[17] O'Neal et al., *supra* n.15, at § 3.01.

[18] *Id*. at §3.06.

[19] Robert et al., *supra* n. 16, at 11.

[20] For example, one resolution might be "nominations for the board of directors must be submitted to the chairperson of the nominating committee on or before February 1. The nominating committee will consider all submissions and conduct interviews if desired." Because the date might change or criteria might be added or deleted, a board resolution is the best way to handle the details. In New York, there is no statute specifying when resolutions are necessary or desirable, but some states explicitly permit board action as an alternative to a by-law provision, for example, fixing a record date: "the by-laws may provide for the fixing [of a record date to determine shareholders entitled to vote] or, in the absence of such provision, the board may fix...." NYBCL 604.

and officers.[21] They identify standing board committees.[22] In non-profit corporations, an important function of bylaws (if this matter is not covered in the articles) is to specify how directors and officers are elected.

Second, bylaws—along with state law—determine the rights of the participants in the structure. They specify the degree to which stockholders or members control or relinquish detailed management of the organization to a board of directors.[23] They set out the rights of stockholders or members and define the rights of directors and officers. They include items like the rights of members to be notified of meetings, the rights of board members or officers whom others want to remove from office, and the rights of board members to indemnification.

Third, bylaws determine many procedures by which rights can be exercised. For example, bylaws may specify whether board meetings can be held by telephone or elections conducted by mail.[24]

Choices like these are consequential. For example, when bylaws require a large board of directors, the board may find it hard to operate efficiently. On the other hand, if the bylaws require a small board, the directors may be overtaxed.

State law establishes rules to which bylaws must conform; in fact, some state statutes provide a basic skeleton, allowing members to make certain choices within that structure. For example, state law may require the bylaws to specify the manner of election or appointment of directors, the time and place of annual meetings, or the number needed for a quorum. Many unincorporated associations comply with these rules in anticipation of future incorporation.[25]

The articles and bylaws of organizations may vary considerably since they establish an organization's basic structure and manner of operation and must be drafted to meet the legal requirements

---

[21] *See* Hyman, *supra* n.14, at § 3.1

[22] *Id.*

[23] *See* Robert et al., *supra* n. 16, at 549.

[24] *See* Zeitlin et al., *supra* n. 13, at 2.

[25] Barbara A. Schatz & Wendy P. Seligson, *Bylaws: A Guide for New York Not for Profit Organizations and their Lawyers* (Booklet of Council of New York Law Associates, ©Bank Street College of Education 1971) (on file with authors).

of the state and the individual needs of the organization. Some of the more common provisions included, however, described below.[26]

### a. General Provisions

**Name.** This article gives the full, exact, and properly punctuated name of the organization.

**Purpose.** The purpose of the organization is often stated in a single sentence, with its various activities set off in tabulated subsections. Some organizations, however, omit this article, preferring to state their objectives in a preamble before the first article.

**Powers.** Corporations can only act within the provisions of their articles. Thus they must specify the powers, purposes and limitations that they want and are permitted by law. Sections within this article might include provisions on the right to sue, to have a corporate seal, to purchase real and personal property, to enter into contract, to conduct its business, etc.

**Place of Business.** This article gives the location of the organization's office.

**Amendment.** This article prescribes the procedure for amendment, including the manner of giving notice of amendment, quorum requirements, and the vote necessary for adoption of an amendment.

### b. Other Provisions

**Members.** This article might cover eligibility requirements for membership or shareholders (if any), categories of membership (individual, student, group), and information on dues and deadlines (if there are dues). If not in a separate article, there may also be sections on notice required for membership meetings, quorum requirements, meeting procedures (prescribing the adoption of

---

[26] For model articles and bylaws, see, for example, Marvin Hyman, *Corporate Forms*, § 3.1 (Westgroup 2001); Henry M. Robert III, et al, *Robert's Rules of Order* (10th ed., Persus Publishing, 2000); F. Hodge O'Neal & Robert B. Thompson, *O'Neal's Close Corporation* (3rd ed., Westgroup 2002); Kurt F. Pantzer & Richard E. Deer, *The Drafting of Corporate Charters and Bylaws* (American Law Institute 1968).

a manual on parliamentary procedure that then governs the organization), removal, or voting procedures.

**Board of Directors.** This article establishes a board entrusted with the organization's administrative authority. The article specifies the number of directors, requisite qualifications, terms of office, selection and removal, frequency of meetings, and powers.

**Officers.** This article specifies the officers the organization requires; requisite qualifications; rank; and manner of nomination, election or appointment, rotation, and removal. The officers' duties are often included in this article, although—if they are extensive—officers' duties may constitute a separate article.

**Meetings.** This article includes sections on shareholder or member meetings, and on Directors' meetings. It or the bylaws may set out a schedule of regular meetings, authorization for calling special meetings, notice and locations of meetings, and information on voting eligibility and quorum requirements.

**Committees.** This article establishes committees that the organization knows will be required. Sections should provide each committee with a name, composition, selection process, term of office, and description of duties. The articles can also establish a procedure for the appointment of special committees.

**Fiscal Matters.** This article may cover indemnification, duties of the treasurer, audit committee and audits, liability insurance, etc.

## C. WRITING PROCESS

In this section we first describe the drafting process generally, and then describe three specific contexts that inform that general process—the legislative context (whether federal or state), the federal regulatory context, and the private regulatory context.

### 1. General Considerations

#### a. Understanding and Implementing Purpose

Drafting begins long before pen is put to paper. It begins when you first meet with your sponsor or client and attempt to understand the problem that party wants to solve and the resolution he or she is proposing. Seldom will the party have more than a rough idea of what the document should include. Thus you need to ask probing questions.

Grasping the problem is your first task. You need to be clear about the factual situation that creates the dilemma by asking the following types of questions.

- Who or what is affected by the problem?
- How are they affected?
- When are they affected?
- Why are they affected?
- Who or what is affected by the current remedy, if any?
- What problems are untouched or created by the current remedy?

If these questions cannot be answered, you or your client should investigate further since a document might not achieve its intended purpose if the dimensions of the problem are too broadly or narrowly understood.

When the problem is understood, the drafter should ensure that the sponsor considers first whether there are viable and timesaving alternatives to a new rule. Indeed, one lawyer recommends that every drafting project begin by asking whether there is any way to avoid drafting the rule.[27] Is there already sufficient law for an agency, board, or committee to address the problem through administrative regulation? Could the problem be solved through an appropriation of funds or an executive order? Consider also whether the power to fix the problem rests with the legislative body approached. Does federal law preempt the field? Does a state constitution prohibit the law?

If there are no viable alternatives to a new rule and no restrictions prohibiting it, the drafter should help the sponsor to explore various solutions. It is often helpful to start by determining if there are existing or analogous rules in other countries, states, counties, or organizations that deal with the problem. If there are, research their effectiveness and decide if their difficulties, if any, are surmountable. If existing solutions are inadequate, however, try listing all the solutions you can think of—from the least to the

---

[27] David A. Marcello, *The Ethics and Politics of Legislative Drafting*, 70 Tulane L. Rev. 2440, 2443 (1996).

most radical. Then try creating hypotheticals to explore the effects, beneficial or detrimental, that each solution would generate.

Professional drafters are aware that every rule designed to promote a basic policy creates subsidiary policy questions, each of which has its own ramifications. They consider it a major challenge to keep all the pieces together so that those pieces combine to promote the policy, and do so without conflicting with other internal provisions or external rules and without unintended effects. Basic policy issues may be fairly obvious: central to a law intended to prevent fraud and abuse in a major federal program, for example, are the definitions of those terms. But even at this stage, drafters sometimes find it difficult to maintain focus on the problem, a situation that has unexpected and often far-reaching consequences. For example, one commentator criticized the "Racketeer Influenced and Corrupt Organizations Act" (RICO)[28] for loss of focus.[29] RICO was intended to fight drug dealing, prostitution, extortion, and a host of other offenses by racketeers across state lines. When the drafter and sponsor defined "racketeer" as anyone who engages in any two of those crimes, however, RICO gradually came to be used as a means of prosecuting illegal activity unrelated to organized crime. Thus, the bill turned out broader in scope than intended.[30]

Even when the scope is clear, the drafter may lose focus when a host of subsidiary issues arise as he or she determines how a provision is to work in practice. This may be less of a problem if the rule is self-regulatory (for example, an honor code), or if much is being left to future administrative determination, although fear of administrative discretion may require some standards and procedures to be spelled out.

For example, one choice that must be made is whether to fashion a solution that permits, requires, or forbids certain conduct, since implementation and sanctions might vary with each approach. Thus a municipal ordinance intended to promote fireworks safety can do so by requiring handlers to obtain a license or permit, or by forbidding the launch of fireworks within one hundred feet of

---

[28] 18 U.S.C. §1961 et seq. (2002).

[29] Lawrence E. Filson, *The Legislative Drafter's Desk Reference* 47–48 (Congressional Quarterly Inc. 1992).

[30] *Id.*

a street, building, or spectator, or by permitting their launch if appropriate fire fighting equipment is at hand. If safety is promoted by license or permit, the legislature must assign some municipal authority the task of issuing them. The bureaucratic costs can be offset by licensing or permit fees. If safety is promoted by imposing conditions on conduct, no initial bureaucratic mechanism is needed, but violations must be processed and met with civil or criminal sanctions. Civil sanctions like fines generate revenue, do not carry the stigma of criminal penalty, but also have less deterrent effect. Criminal sanctions drain state revenue, are not self-enforcing, and have harsh consequences for the defendant. The options need to be thought through. The drafter and client or sponsor must determine which is the most effective, efficient, and thrifty way of achieving their goal.

If the rule is not self-regulatory, some person, committee, or agency must be given the task of enforcement. The decision can be politically significant and require the drafter and sponsor to speculate about how the regulatory approach of one department might differ from that of another. Might one agency be likely to motivate landlords to comply with rules on housing conditions by providing incentives for capital improvements, while another agency might be likely to deter violations by imposing penalties (fines for substandard conditions)? Which is more effective? If a committee is to enforce a rule, its membership is consequential and requires careful thought. For example, may non-resident property owners serve on a town zoning appeals board? Should students be on a committee that hears charges of academic dishonesty? What are the pros and cons?

Thus understanding purpose and staying focused on that purpose is of the essence as you work through a draft. Otherwise, you endanger the appropriate scope of the rule and its consistency.

### b. Researching the Legal Framework

Drafting rules in an unregulated area and working in an intricately integrated system of rules are equally but differently challenging for the drafter.

New regulation or legislation is challenging because of the burdens it places on foresight. Determining the best approach to a problem and foreseeing its ramifications are arduous and creative endeavors, more arduous in this situation than the research task, given that your initial explorations will have shown you that there are no existing rules governing your problem. Nonetheless, even in this situation, you will want to see how other jurisdictions or organizations have dealt with the problem since they may have rules and policies that can be a source of inspiration and accumulated knowledge. You will also want to determine what impact your rules might have on related areas.

Most proposed rulemaking is not freestanding, however. It adds, amends, or must comport with current rules and thus must fit within an existing scheme. To fit within the system, drafters must determine how their changes necessitate other changes within the code. There are both substantive and mechanical changes.

Substantive changes require decisions about where to place an amendment, whether the amendment requires repeal of a provision, or whether the amendment requires new additional sections. If the amendment adds a duty, for example, is there an existing penalty for failing to perform it or must one be added?

Mechanical changes include renumbering provisions as one is added or dropped and then adding or changing cross-references. Do not think mechanical changes are without substantive impact. One state legislature decided to give the mentally disabled the same free fare on public transportation as the physically disabled. The drafter put it in one relevant part of the state transportation law, but not in another. As a result the mentally disabled got a discount on commuter trains, but not on city buses. Fortunately this kind of error can frequently be avoided. Most state codes have indices that will help drafters to identify relevant statutes that will be affected or that need to be changed, as well as a table of statutory cross-references.

In addition to researching the conceptual and mechanical changes that need to be made to the particular statute being amended, drafters need to research related statutes because even if there is no conflict, statutes are interpreted *in pari materia*, in light of related statutes. Thus work on inheritance law for adopted children should be done in the context of the family law sections on adoption. Existing common law must also be researched. Private regulations should comply with legal precedents, while drafters of new legislation should know if they are changing precedent.

## c. Finding a Structure

Experienced drafters often begin their search for structure by examining boilerplate, and similar or analogous statutes[31] or regulations. Many rules, as well as provisions within them, fall into categories. You should take advantage of this. Laws creating study commissions, for example, are structured in the same way, differing only in the area to be studied and membership. Laws establishing new programs are often similar, for example, loan programs and grant programs. Bylaws of non-profit organizations are often similar. Thus there are usable models everywhere. In addition, many provisions appear frequently and can simply be inserted into your documents.[32] These models help drafters identify the elements needed for completeness and provide versions of their arrangements and language. But as helpful as these models are, they—like boilerplate and forms—can be counter-productive if they are not thoughtfully critiqued, modified, and adapted.

Even without models, you should be able to find outlines to help you get started. The order of a statute's standard clauses or an organization's standard articles, as described above in Section B of this chapter, provides a starting point. The real organizational challenges are in developing and sequencing substantive and procedural provisions appropriate to the subject matter of your legislation or regulation. This process is described at length in Section (C)(2) of Chapter 1, *Conceptualizing*. The important point to remember here is to begin by dumping onto paper every point you need to make. Then begin to organize your provisions—grouping related points, dividing points into provisions and sub-provisions, adding and subtracting, ordering and re-ordering—until you achieve a logical outline.

## d. Writing a First Draft

Once you have a tentative structure, the provisions must be worded. Many of the issues involved in wording provisions are discussed in Chapter 11, *Precision*—finding the appropriate level of generality, avoiding ambiguity, using words of authority

---

[31] Filson, *supra* n. 29, at 102–05; Stark, *supra* n. 2, at 39.

[32] Stark, *supra* n. 2, at 39.

responsibly, and so on. So our discussion here will be brief, focusing on only a few points.

First, legislation and public regulation are commands from a sovereign and usually have sanctions attached. Thus it is important for people to know what they may or may not do, and this mandate means there is less room in public rule-making documents for vague language than in private documents like contracts, though even the language of public legislation is often negotiated and may end up deliberately general or vague.

Second, although statutes use both general and specific language, choice is often subject-related. Civil rights law tends to be general because it is meant to be applied on a flexible case-by-case basis and it expresses fundamental values, which are often stated generally. In contrast, tax statutes are usually specific because the government wants tight control over economic behavior in order to protect its revenue.[33] Thus drafters should become familiar with the cases applying statutory construction in the subject area to help determine the appropriate level of generality.

Third, while clarity and readability are important in legislation and regulation, accurate expression is more important. A drafter's first duty is to convey "the intended meaning with the greatest possible precision, not to convey a meaning clearly."[34] Thus ease of comprehension should not come at the expense of accuracy.

### e. Revising

Like most written documents, rules should be revised in stages. Checking for specific problems helps to uncover mistakes that may have been overlooked in the drafting process. Begin with substance—checking in turn for completeness, consistency, and accuracy. Focus on one substantive issue at a time. Is there a procedure and sanction for the violation of every duty? Are words used as they were defined? Are synonyms avoided? Are there loopholes, gaps, measures that undermine the rule's purpose?

Then review structure for clean divisions, clear units and subunits, effective headings, and logical order. Is there needless repetition? Are separate points intertwined?

---

[33] *Id.* at 25.

[34] *Id.* at 2.

Finally, screen for comprehensibility: for syntactic ambiguity caused by sloppy syntax or punctuation, for needed or faulty tabulation and enumeration, for semantic ambiguity, and for mechanical errors in numbering and cross-referencing.

It is especially helpful to seek the editorial advice of an outside reader or readers, especially someone knowledgeable in the field. These readers may be able to discover complications you failed to recognize, but which will help you to complete and polish the document. Professional legislative drafters admit they regularly consult with lobbyists, although they define this group broadly, as "including everyone from the White House to the local church group...."[35] Although drafters are concerned about the "power of interest groups," they regard lobbyists as having the expertise and subject matter knowledge to "see things we might miss... [and] help flesh out potential problems."[36]

## 2. The Legislative Process: State and Federal Statutes

The initial idea for a law may come from a variety of sources—constituents, lobbyists, scholars, bureaucrats, as well as a legislator's own perception of federal, state, or local problems needing legislative solutions.[37] Generally, a problem that is suitable for legislative solution is a problem of broad applicability or importance for which there is widespread demand for a solution, and for which there is a solution that is financially feasible and amenable to effective implementation and sanctions. Even when these conditions are satisfied, the laborious nature of the legislative process means legislators will look first to existing law to see if it can stretch to solve that problem. For example, there may be no need for a law forbidding users of state parks from leaving garbage in the woods when there is an existing provision giving the Department of Parks the right to promulgate regulations.

---

[35] Nourse et al., *supra* n. 4, at 610.

[36] *Id.* at 611.

[37] For example, one staff member of the Senate Judiciary Committee reported working on a constitutional amendment "drafted in consultation with legal scholars, policy experts, and representatives of law enforcement," while another described working on an intellectual property bill that was largely "negotiated between the private parties," and yet a third was revising an employment discrimination bill in light of recent Supreme Court decisions. *Id.* at 584.

Even those ideas that survive this step rarely become law. Most bills that are introduced die in committee. Even if they make it to the floor, it is unlikely they will be enacted. During the 2008 term of the New York State Legislature, for example, 7,771 bills were introduced in the Senate and 10,525 bills were introduced in the Assembly, while only 830 were passed by both houses, of which the governor vetoed 177.[38]

There is both a formal and informal side of the legislative process. The formal process is established by the rules of the legislative body. These rules dictate the framework for the introduction, consideration, and amendment of a bill as well as its form and style. The formal process takes place within an informal political context, however. To build a majority, the proponent of a bill must make tactical decisions about everything from which legislative instrument to use to which terminology to use.

### a. The Formal Process

To introduce a bill, a legislator must file the bill with the appropriate officer. A reference committee or house leader appointed to the task then assigns the bill to a committee of the legislature for consideration. This committee may hold open or closed hearings for testimony by interested parties on the bill's merits. The committee itself will often hold closed hearings to deliberate and amend the bill before voting to disregard ("pigeon hole"), defeat, or accept it. Upon passage in the committee, the bill is then sent to the entire house for floor action. Here too there will be floor debate and possible amendment. If one chamber passes the bill as submitted or with amendments, it is referred to the second chamber for floor action, unless the bill is brought before a unicameral legislature. If the second chamber passes the bill in a form different from the first chamber, both houses appoint a conference committee to work out an acceptable compromise. Finally, if the compromise bill is approved by both chambers, it then goes to the President, Governor, or other Executive, who may either sign or veto the act. If signed, the act becomes law. If

---

[38] Our thanks to Kathleen Darvil, librarian at Brooklyn Law School, for compiling these figures for us.

vetoed, the act returns to the legislative body to see if the veto can be overridden.

## b. The Informal Process

Most rule-making documents are in some sense political. For example, few partnership agreements or contracts are signed without extensive negotiation and compromise. Yet the legislative process is political to a much greater extent because a bill's passage involves so many more individuals with different interests—the committee members, the committee staff, testifying witnesses, the media, the entire membership of the legislature, lobbyists, the agencies involved, the executive branch, and the general public. Thus negotiation and compromise are just about inevitable once a bill is introduced.[39]

Yet political maneuvering often begins even before the bill is considered by these audiences. For example, a sponsor's choice of legislative instrument is political. Assume a Farm Bureau is lobbying to repeal a state environmental law that prevents the run-off of manure into the state's waterways. It knows that the governor, an environmentalist, is likely to veto such a repeal. The Farm Bureau might then propose drafting a resolution that suspends the law for a year, knowing that this restriction, unlike an environmental law, is unlikely to be reviewed by the Governor.[40]

A sponsor's description of a bill is often politically motivated because the description often determines a bill's committee assignment. Assume, for example, that a public law center wants to propose a bill that allows welfare applicants to litigate agency action in their domicile rather than the agency's domicile. If the Health and Welfare Committee has a history of being influenced by the welfare agency, which is unlikely to approve of such a change, the law center might describe the bill not as a "health and

---

[39] In fact, professional drafters complain about "the dangers of drafting bills on the floor, as this increase[s] the risks of the process becoming... haphazard, and driven by political imperatives." Nourse et al., *supra* n.4, at 592–93. Specific fears include "losing track of whether one provision squared with another," *id.*, "politics driving ambiguity," *id.* at 596, and the inability to do legal research during floor debate, *id* at 599. Many commend the bicameral system because it allows for correction of some of the ensuing mistakes. *Id.* at 593.

[40] This example is discussed in Marcello's article, *supra* n. 27, at 2444–46. In Louisiana, the legislature can suspend a law for a year by concurrent resolution.

welfare" measure, but as a "civil procedure-venue" measure, a description that would send the bill to the more neutral Civil Law and Procedure Committee.[41] Similar tactical reasoning is involved when deciding which agency is the right one to administer an act and what sanction to attach.

These political considerations affect the drafter in fundamental ways. They influence his conceptualization of the bill and the options and alternatives he proposes to the bill's sponsor. Thus a skilled drafter ignores the legislative political process at his peril.

### 3. The Administrative Rule-making Process: Federal Regulations

Although enacted legislation gets more attention, regulations most directly touch individuals and organizations. The federal Administrative Procedure Act [APA] sets out the procedural requirements all federal agencies must follow when issuing a rule, which the APA defines as a statement "designed to implement, interpret, or prescribe law or policy or describing the organization, procedures, or practice."[42]

The APA establishes both a formal and informal rule-making process, but most rules are adopted under the informal process.[43] Informal administrative rule-making usually begins in response to a statutory directive. A group of agency staff members will be assigned the task of transforming a statutory directive into a rule. The group will compile and assess data and develop options. Once this is done, the group will seek suggestions and consensus from other interested agencies and the agency's decision makers. The President's Office of Management and Budget clears rules—that is, ensures there is no duplication and conflict—and edits them for clarity.[44] Moreover, some acts give Congress review of

---

[41] *Id.* at 2452.

[42] 5 U.S.C. § 551(4). States have their own administrative procedure acts, or they may have adopted the Model State Administrative Procedure Act.

[43] Robert J. Martineau, *Drafting Legislation and Rules in Plain English* 45 (West Pub. Co. 1991); Filson, *supra* n. 29, at 142.

[44] Schooner, *supra* n. 7, at 171.

executive agency rule-making.[45] In addition, public participation is required before an agency adopts substantive rules, that is, "rules which implement the statute...[and] have the force and effect of law."[46] The agency must publish the rules and request public comment.[47] Thus the regulation writer toils within a thicket of review. Nonetheless, despite possibly conflicting and contentious input, drafters have greater control over regulations than legislation because regulations do not involve a floor vote and are less subject to amendment at the eleventh hour.

When the drafting group achieves a consensus and the agency's policy makers are satisfied, the agency must publish the final rule. The rule must include a preamble explaining the basis and purpose of the rule. It must also respond to public comment, explaining why it did or did not incorporate the public's suggestions into the regulation. This requirement is one important restraint on administrative discretion. Finally, the rule must be published in the Federal Register at least 30 days before its effective date.[48]

## 4. The Private Regulatory Process: Corporate Rules

When an organization decides to incorporate, it must develop articles of incorporation and bylaws and will most frequently retain counsel to help draft these instruments. Developing articles of incorporation and bylaws requires groundwork.[49] The participants in the organization need to have detailed discussions among themselves and with counsel to determine the substance of the articles and the bylaws. Moreover, because these instruments fall under state law, the drafting lawyer should be a specialist in the field who is able to alert the participants to valid options under the law.

---

[45] *Id.*

[46] The Attorney General's Manual on the APA 30, n. 3 (1947) (1971 reprint).

[47] This participation is not required for interpretative rules, which are statements about the agency's construction of statutes, rules of procedure or practice, or general statements of policy. *See* Martineau, *supra* n. 43, at 47.

[48] 5 U.S.C. 553(b).

[49] Articles of incorporation and bylaws of a corporation are adopted at its first meeting, but the bylaws of an unincorporated entity may be adopted at any time.

The drafter begins by acquiring necessary facts from the client. To ensure adequate fact-gathering, lawyers often rely on questionnaires, checklists, and corporate form books that take the parties through the topics commonly included.[50] Then the drafter needs to assist the client in selecting provisions that are appropriate to that corporation's business and that are within the confines of the law. Finally, unless governing corporate law determines this, the drafter must help the client decide which provisions should be included in the charter and which should be in the bylaws or left to board resolutions.

Many factors are weighed in deciding where provisions should go. For example, bylaws that are adopted or approved by shareholders can include provisions that limit or restrict shareholder interference with the organization's directors, but if the bylaws are adopted by the directors, the bylaws cannot limit or restrict shareholders.[51] If the directors wish to deny customary rights or privileges of shareholders, that denial should be clear and included in the articles.[52] Moreover, since bylaws are not publicly filed or recorded, any provision binding third parties should be done in the articles in order to provide notice to those parties.[53] On the other hand, because article amendments must be publicly filed, and thus their amendment is a more cumbersome procedure than the amendment of bylaws, drafters often prefer to insert structural and procedural rules into the bylaws, where they can be more easily changed.[54]

An organization might begin the drafting process by appointing a committee to work with the drafter. The drafter may take the committee through the issues included in practitioner's manuals, questionnaires, checklists, and forms[55]—issues like who may call

---

[50] *See, e.g.,* Kurt F. Pantzer & Richard E. Deer, *The Drafting of Corporate Charters and Bylaws* (ALI-ABA Joint Committee on Continuing Legal Education, Philadelphia, Pa., 1968) at 19–26; Barbara A. Schatz & Wendy P. Seligman, *Manual on Organization, Financing, and Administration of Day Care Centers in New York City,* (© Bank Street College of Education 1971) (on file with authors).

[51] Pantzer et al., *supra* n. 26, at 30.

[52] *Id.*

[53] *Id.* at 29.

[54] *Id.* at 31.

[55] See, for example, the questions and topics in Barbara A. Schatz & Wendy P. Seligman, *Manual on Organization, Financing, and Administration of Day Care Centers in New*

a special meeting or how directors may be removed. Then the group might procure and study copies of the bylaws of various other organizations similar to the one being formed. After this review, the drafter and the committee must determine how to adapt these forms and samples to its own organization's structure and purpose. For example, the new organization may have a parent body and the subsidiary's bylaws must comport with those of the parent organization. Or the organization may want to eliminate some of the detail in forms if it is contemplating a provision that may need frequent amendment (like the amount of dues). Or it may add detail if the forms omit important areas like nominating procedures. One major area of discussion is how to guide the organization's operations without unduly restricting management's freedom.

After conferences on topics like these, the lawyer or committee appointed to draft the rules will begin working. Once there is a complete first draft, the future directors or oversight committee will meet to give the document a detailed, critical examination. Revision will almost certainly be required. But once a draft is approved, the committee is ready to report to the voting body. This body will in turn review the draft and perhaps propose revisions. The process is repeated until the documents are approved.

*York City* (©Bank Street College of Education 1971) (on file with authors); Kim A. Zeitlin & Susan E. Dorn, *The Nonprofit Board's Guide to Bylaws: Creating a Framework for Effective Governance* (©National Center for Nonprofit Boards 1996) (on file with authors).

## D. SAMPLE STATUTE

The following statute amends a state technology law.

### STATE TECHNOLOGY—"INTERNET SECURITY AND PRIVACY ACT"[56]
Approved March 26, 2002, effective as provided in section 2

AN ACT to amend the state technology law, in relation to enacting the 'internet security and privacy act'[57]

The People of the State of New York, represented in Senate and Assembly, do enact as follows:[58]

§ 1. Article II of the state technology law, as added by chapter 578 of the laws of 2001, is amended to read as follows:

### ARTICLE II
### INTERNET SECURITY AND PRIVACY ACT

§ 201. Short title. This article shall be known and may be cited as the "internet security and privacy policy act."

§ 202. Definitions. As used in this article, the following terms shall have the following meanings:[59]

1. "Collect" shall mean to store information, including via cookie technology, for purposes of retrieval at a later time to initiate communication with or make determinations about the person who is the subject of such information.

2. "Disclose" shall mean to reveal, release, transfer, disseminate or otherwise communicate information orally, in writing or by electronic or other means, other than to the person who is the subject of such information.[60]

---

[56] N.Y. Tech. Law Art. II (McKinney 2003).

[57] This is the statute's long title.

[58] This is the enacting clause.

[59] Note the incorrect use of "shall" in these definitions. It creates a false imperative because you cannot order a word to have a meaning. Moreover, statutes should be written in the present tense. The definitions do follow the traditional alphabetical organization, however.

[60] Is "or by electronic or other means" a helpful distinction because electronic is neither oral nor written, or is it redundant because electronic or "other" communication is covered by "orally or in writing"?

3. "Internet" shall mean a system of linked computer networks, international in scope, that facilitate data transmission and exchange.[61]

4. "Office" shall mean the state office for technology.

5. "Personal information" shall mean any information concerning a natural person which, because of name, number, symbol, mark or other identifier, can be used to identify that natural person.

6. "State agency" shall have the same meaning as the meaning given to "agency" under subdivision one of section ninety-two of the public officers law.[62]

7. "State agency website" shall mean an internet website operated by or for a state agency. Such term shall include those websites operated on behalf of state agencies by other public or private entities, but shall not include any portions of the internet outside the control of the state agency.

8. "User" shall mean any natural person who uses the internet to access a state agency website.

§ 203. Model internet privacy policy.[63]

1. The office shall adopt rules and regulations in conformity with the provisions of this article, and specify a model internet privacy policy for state agencies that maintain state agency websites. Such model privacy policy shall include, but not be limited to, the following elements:[64]

> (a) a statement of any information, including personal information, the state agency website will collect with respect to the user and the use of the information;

> (b) the circumstances under which information, including personal information, collected may be disclosed;

---

[61] Is this a necessary definition or the common meaning of "internet"?

[62] This definition alerts the reader to an already existing and applicable statutory definition.

[63] This is the first substantive provision. Notice that the policy is not set out in a preamble or statement of purpose and findings. Instead the policy emerges through the rules that implement it.

This statute does not indicate terms that have stipulated definitions by putting them in italics, bold, or quotation marks. It would be helpful if it did. On the other hand, the drafters avoid one common pitfall: they do in fact use every term they define.

[64] The drafters use correctly punctuated and reader-friendly tabulation here. Notice, however that (c) and (f) break the parallelism. They could read: "a statement about whether the information collected will be retained...."

(c) whether any information collected will be retained by the state agency, and, if so, the period of time that such information will be retained;

(d) the procedures by which a user may gain access to the collected information pertaining to that user;

(e) the means by which information is collected and whether such collection occurs actively or passively;

(f) whether the collection of information is voluntary or required, and the consequences, if any, of a refusal to provide the required information; and

(g) the steps being taken by the state agency to protect the confidentiality and integrity of the information.

2. Each state agency that maintains a state agency website shall adopt an internet privacy policy which shall, at a minimum, include the information required by the model internet privacy policy. Each state agency shall post its internet privacy policy on its website. Such posting shall include a conspicuous and direct link to such privacy policy.[65]

3. The model internet privacy policy specified by the office shall also be made available at no charge to other public and private entities.

§ 204. Collection and disclosure of personal information. No state agency shall collect personal information concerning a user through a state agency website, or disclose personal information concerning a user to any person, firm, partnership, corporation, limited liability company or other entity, including internal staff who do not need the information in the performance of their official duties pursuant to a state agency purpose meeting the requirements of subdivision one of section two hundred six of this article, unless such user has consented to the collection or disclosure of such personal information.[66] For the purposes of this section, the voluntary disclosure of personal information to a state agency by a user through a state agency website, whether solicited or unsolicited, shall constitute consent to the collection or disclosure of the information by the state agency for the purposes for which the user disclosed it to the state agency, as reasonably ascertainable from the nature and terms of the disclosure.

---

[65] Except for some general rules, implementation of state policy is left to individual state agencies, including sanction if this duty is breached. Would it have been helpful to provide some guidelines on this?

[66] Notice that the exception to the rule is imbedded in the rule itself. Would tabulation improve the readability of this provision?

§ 205. Access to personal information. Except as otherwise provided by law, a state agency shall provide users with access to all personal information pertaining to such user which has been collected through its state agency website. Access to such personal information and the opportunity to request correction or amendment of such personal information shall be provided to users in the manner provided for access to and correction or amendment of personal information under section ninety-five of the public officers law. A state agency shall provide a user access to such personal information via the internet when such access is feasible and only if that access can be provided in a secure manner.[67]

§ 206. Exceptions. Notwithstanding section two hundred four of this article, a state agency may collect or disclose personal information if the collection or disclosure is:[68]

1. necessary to perform the statutory duties of the state agency that collected or is collecting the personal information, or necessary for that agency to operate a program authorized by law, or authorized by state or federal statute or regulation;

2. made pursuant to a court order or by law;

3. for the purpose of validating the identity of the user; or

4. if the information is used solely for statistical purposes and is in a form that cannot be used to identify any particular person.[69]

§ 207 Construction. Nothing in this article shall abridge public access to information available or permitted by any other provision or rule of law, including without limitation article six of the public officers law. Nothing in this article shall authorize the collection or disclosure of information the collection or disclosure of which is prohibited or restricted by any other provision of law, including without limitation article six-A of the public officers law. Nothing in this article shall alter the obligations of state agencies and users pursuant to article six-A of the public officers law.[70]

§ 2. This act shall take effect on the same date as chapter 578 of the laws of 2001 takes effect.[71]

---

[67] Again the statute is silent about procedures and sanctions for breach.

[68] Should this exception follow the relevant substantial provision—§ 204?

[69] This clause does not work with the introductory clause. Moreover, the parallel sentence structure required for correct tabulation falters here. Can you preserve the parallelism and make the point?

[70] This section fits the act into the existing code.

[71] This is the effective date provision—one of the miscellaneous, housekeeping clauses.

# E. SPECIAL CONCERNS: STATUTORY CONSTRUCTION

However carefully drafted, a rule-making document, whether public or private, may eventually be subject to judicial interpretation. Thus it is helpful to be familiar with the techniques courts use so that you comply with their strictures and avoid as far as possible unintended constructions.

Courts look first to the plain meaning of the language. Thus a drafter's first and foremost goal is to use language so accurately and clearly that the intended interpretation is the only one possible. All the skills outlined in the chapters on conceptualization, clarity, and precision must be brought to bear for this to happen.

When the language is ambiguous, courts will go outside the four corners of the document to determine legislative intent or purpose, that is, they consider extrinsic evidence. They might look at the title, preamble, and section headings as guides to meaning. They will track all the legislative documents generated while the bill was making its way through the legislative process—including committee reports, hearing reports, sponsor statements, floor debates, and amendment history. This material is usually copious for acts of the United States Congress and sometimes sparse for state statutes.

Admittedly, some judges are critical of the use to which legislative history is put. Justice Scalia, for example, is vocal in his criticism that legislative history undermines the role of Congress because that history is often written by staffers and lobbyists rather than legislators and because judges often pick the committee reports and floor statements that support their decisions. Despite these criticisms, drafters say legislative history serves an institutional purpose. Reports are used to obtain support, facilitate consensus, and inform the public and agencies about the law. Moreover, given that the price of passage is sometimes "consensual ambiguity" and given time pressures that make it impossible to foresee all contingencies, the legislation itself, despite the sponsor and drafter's best efforts, will never answer all the interpretive questions.[72] As one commentator remarks, clarity is adversely affected by "diverse external inputs, eleventh-

---

[72] *See* Nourse et al., *supra* n. 4, at 618.

hour amendments, constraints associated with drafting around the existing code, or the rigors of the committee or conference structure."[73] Thus, legislative history will inevitably be called upon to resolve issues that were not resolved in the statutory text itself.

When there is no legislative history, or in addition to legislative history, courts also look at other kinds of extrinsic evidence—at related statutes, similar statutes in other jurisdictions, and agency constructions. Extrinsic sources are particularly important when a court needs to determine purpose rather than intent. Intent asks what is meant by a word or a provision. Purpose is relevant when the words or provision is clear, but it is unclear how it should apply to a particular set of facts.[74] Even when language is clear, unforeseen circumstances may trigger an inquiry into purpose in order to determine if the rule applies to the new situation. For example, in *Matter of Erickson*,[75] the court needed to decide if a 1935 Wisconsin statute's exemption of a "mower" from a creditor's judgment applied to a modern haybine, a machine that did not exist when the statute was drafted. To update the statute, which had no legislative history, the court considered "the structure and function of the statute."[76] It concluded that the function or purpose of the statute was to allow farmers to keep minimum equipment so that they could continue to work and farm. Since mowers have become obsolete and farmers use haybines instead, a haybine is necessary to work the land; thus, the court exempted it from a creditor's judgment.[77]

When the extrinsic evidence is not conclusive, courts consider the canons of construction and may use them as background norms. There are some canons particularly relevant to statutes.

- Statutes *in pari materia* (on the same subject) must be construed together.
- A remedial statute will be construed liberally.

---

[73] Schooner, *supra* n.7, at 165.

[74] *See* Martineau, *supra* n. 43, at 25–26.

[75] 815 F.2d 1090 (7th Cir. 1987).

[76] *Id.* at 1094.

[77] *Id.*

- A statute in derogation of the common law will be construed strictly.
- *Expressio unius est exclusio alterius:* the mention of one thing excludes another.
- *Noscitur a socis:* a word takes some of its meaning from the words with which it is used.
- *Ejusdem generis:* a general word is limited by the more specific words with which it is used.
- Words are used in their ordinary meaning unless a technical meaning is suggested by the other words in a statute.
- Every word in a statute must be given effect.
- Words are to be interpreted according to the rules of grammar and punctuation.

Because some of the canons contradict each other, and none of the canons is binding, adherence to their dictates may support the interpretation you intended, but does not guarantee it. Moreover, the canons do not always provide a clear-cut answer. For example, in *Matter of Erikson*, the court relied on the canon that remedial statutes should be liberally construed, but acknowledged that liberal construction "does not help us figure out how far to go."[78] The court therefore had to predict at what point a broad construction would have the negative consequence of drying up credit for the farmers.[79]

Admittedly, it is impossible to predict which rules of statutory construction will be brought to bear when the meaning of a rule is questioned in court. Nonetheless, although total control is probably beyond any drafter's reach, if drafters are aware of the techniques commonly used, they can limit the risk that judicial interpretation will be contrary to the drafter's intent.

─────────────────────── *Exercise 13.1* ───────────────────────

*The following exercise is based on the first draft of our sample statute. In the draft, additions are indicated by bold and deletions by strikeout. Try to*

---

[78] *Id.*

[79] *Id.*

*determine what problems the drafters or legislators saw with the original provisions and whether the amended language resolves those problems.*

(1) **2.** "Disclose" ~~or "disclosure"~~ shall mean to ~~make personal~~ **reveal, release, transfer, disseminate or otherwise communicate** information ~~known, including by sale or rental of such information.~~

(2) **5.** "Personal information" ~~(a)~~ shall mean~~:~~

~~(i) information which identifies a specific user or such user's interactive computer service address; or~~
~~(ii) information collected or submitted via the internet that identifies a user's home or work address, e-mail address, telephone number, credit or debit card information, social security number, birth date, gender, marital status or other personal identifier.~~
~~(b) shall not include any record of aggregate data which does not identify, either directly or indirectly, a user or such user's interactive service address.~~
~~5.~~ **any information concerning a natural person which, because of name, number, symbol, mark or other identifier, can be used to identify that natural person.**

(3) **6.** "State agency" shall ~~mean any state department, board, bureau, division, commission, committee, public authority, public benefit corporation, council, office, or other governmental entity performing a governmental or proprietary function for the state, except the legislature and judiciary. For the purposes of this article, entities that perform state services via contractual agreements shall be included in this definition as related to such services rendered to the public~~ **have the same meaning as the meaning given to "agency" under subdivision one of section ninety-two of the public officers law.**

(4) **8.** "User" shall mean any **natural person who uses** ~~a computer capable of interacting with~~ the internet **to access a state agency website**.

(5) § ~~207~~ **206**. Exceptions. Notwithstanding section two hundred ~~three~~ **four** of this article, a state agency may **collect or** disclose personal information if the **collection or** disclosure is:

1. necessary ~~in the ordinary course of business as defined in applicable state law~~ **to perform the statutory duties of the state agency that collected or is collecting the personal information,**

**or necessary for that agency to operate a program authorized by law, or authorized by state or federal statute or regulation;**

2. made pursuant to a court order or by law;

3. for the purpose of validating the identity of the user; ~~and~~ **or**

4. if the information ~~or data~~ is used solely for statistical purposes ~~in aggregate form~~ **and is in a form that cannot be used to identify any particular person.**

---

*Exercise 13.2*

---

*Rewrite these substantive sections of a Michigan statute. Edit for generality and specificity, ambiguity, organization, wordiness, and readability. This "Good Samaritan" statute protects medical professionals who voluntarily help in an emergency.*[80]

### 691.1502 Hospital or Other Medical Care Facility Personnel

(1) In instances where the actual hospital duty of that person did not require a response to that emergency situation, a physician, dentist, podiatrist, intern, resident, registered nurse, licensed practical nurse, registered physical therapist, clinical laboratory technologist, inhalation therapist, certified registered nurse anesthetist, x-ray technician, or paramedical person, who in good faith responds to a life threatening emergency or responds to a request for emergency assistance in a life threatening emergency within a hospital or other licensed medical care facility, shall not be liable for any civil damages as a result of an act or omission in the rendering of emergency care, except an act or omission amounting to gross negligence or wilful and wanton misconduct.

(2) The exemption from liability under subsection (1) shall not apply to a physician where a physician-patient relationship existed prior to the advent of the emergency nor to a licensed nurse where a nurse-patient relationship existed prior to the advent of the emergency.

(3) Nothing in this act shall diminish a hospital's responsibility to reasonably and adequately staff hospital emergency facilities when the hospital maintains or holds out to the general public that it maintains such emergency room facilities.

---

[80] Our thanks to Joseph Kimble who brought this statute to our attention in his discussion of it in *The Lessons of One Example*, 42 Clarity 59 (1998).

―――――――――――― *Exercise 13.3* ――――――――――――

*Rewrite this Illinois statute using headings and tabulation. Are there any contingencies omitted?*

### 765 ILCS 710/1 [Return of security deposit]

Sec. 1. A lessor of residential real property, containing 5 or more units, who has received a security deposit from a lessee to secure the payment of rent or secure performance under a rental agreement may not withhold any part of that deposit as compensation for property damage unless he has, within 30 days of the date that the lessee vacated the premises, furnished to the lessee, delivered in person or by mail directed to his last known address, an itemized statement of the damage allegedly caused to the premises and the estimated or actual cost for repairing or replacing each item on that statement, attaching the paid receipts, or copies thereof, for the repair or replacement. If the lessor utilizes his or her own labor to repair any damage caused by the lessee, the lessor may include the reasonable cost of his or her labor to repair such damage. If estimated cost is given, the lessor shall furnish the lessee with paid receipts, or copies thereof, within 30 days from the date the statement showing estimated cost was furnished to the lessee, as required by this Section. If no such statement and receipts, or copies thereof, are furnished to the lessee as required by this Section, the lessor shall return the security deposit in full within 45 days of the date that the lessee vacated the premises.

Upon a finding by a circuit court that a lessor has refused to supply the itemized statement required by this Section, or has supplied such statement in bad faith, and has failed or refused to return the amount of the security deposit due within the time limits provided, the lessor shall be liable for an amount equal to twice the amount of the security deposit due, together with court costs and reasonable attorney's fees.

### 765 ILCS 715/1 [Computation of interest]

Sec. 1. A lessor of residential real property, containing 25 or more units in either a single building or a complex of buildings located on contiguous parcels of real property, who receives a security deposit from a lessee to secure the payment of rent or secure performance by the lessee under a rental agreement shall pay interest to the lessee computed from the date of the deposit at a rate of 5% per year on any deposit held by the lessor for more than 6 months.

---------------------------- *Exercise 13.4* ----------------------------

*In* In re Adoption of RMZ, *a biological mother and her same-sex do-mestic partner filed a joint petition for adoption; the partner sought to adopt the mother's child. The father had already legally relinquished the child. The Supreme Court of Atlantis denied the adoption petition, holding that the Adoption Act does not permit a non-spouse to adopt a child where the legal parents have not relinquished their respective parental rights. The legal par-ent in* In re Adoption of RMZ *had attached a consent form to the adoption petition, but omitted the phrase indicating she intended to permanently give up her rights to her child.*

*On behalf of this couple and others similarly situated, the Atlantis Gay Caucus has asked Senator Smith to propose an amendment to the Adoption Act. The caucus convinced Senator Smith that the Act is not in the best interest of children because it denies them the benefits of adoption, which include the legal protection of existing familial bonds; the rights to financial support from two parents; and the right to other available dependent benefits, such as health care insurance, social security benefits, and inheritance from either parent.*

*Read § 2711 and § 2903 and then decide how to amend the Act. Should the language within either of these sections be changed or should an exception be drafted? If an exception is contemplated, should it be narrow in scope to prevent unlimited adoptions by legally unrelated adults? Should the courts be given the discretion to determine the best interests of the child in each individual case? Amend the statute.*

## TITLE 23. DOMESTIC RELATIONS
## PART III. ADOPTION
### § 2711. Consents necessary to adoption

**(a) General rule.**—Except as otherwise provided in this part, consent to an adoption shall be required of the following:

(1) The adoptee, if over 12 years of age.

(2) The spouse of the adopting parent, unless they join in the adoption petition.

(3) The parents or surviving parent of an adoptee who has not reached the age of 18 years.

(4) The guardian of an incapacitated adoptee.

(5) The guardian of the person of an adoptee under the age of 18 years, if any there be, or of the person or persons having the custody of the adoptee, if any such person can be found, whenever the adoptee has no parent whose consent is required.

...

**(d) Contents of consent.—**

(1) The consent of a parent of an adoptee under 18 years of age shall set forth the name, age and marital status of the parent, the relationship of the consenter to the child, the name of the other parent or parents of the child and the following:

I hereby voluntarily and unconditionally consent to the adoption of the above named child.

I understand that by signing this consent I indicate my intent to permanently give up all rights to this child.

I understand such child will be placed for adoption.

I understand I may revoke this consent to permanently give up all rights to this child by placing the revocation in writing and serving it upon the agency or adult to whom the child was relinquished.

I understand I may not revoke this consent after a court has entered a decree confirming this consent or otherwise terminating my parental rights to this child. Even if a decree has not been entered terminating my parental rights I may not revoke this consent after a decree of adoption of this child is entered.

I have read and understand the above and I am signing it as a free and voluntary act.

(2) The consent shall include the date and place of its execution and names and addresses and signatures of at least two persons who witnessed its execution and their relationship to the consenter.

## § 2903. Retention of Parental Status

Whenever a parent consents to the adoption of his child by his spouse, the parent-child relationship between him and his child shall remain whether or not he is one of the petitioners in the adoption proceeding.

----------------------------- *Exercise 13.5* -----------------------------

*You are the attorney for the Pacifica Assisted Reproduction League. The League is interested in legislation to meet the following situation involving social security survivor benefits. The Social Security Act, 42 U.S.C. §402 (d)(1) provides child benefits for a dependent child of a deceased parent who was insured under the Act. One way to determine if a non-marital child is a dependent child is if the domicile state's intestate succession law treats the child as an intestate heir of the deceased insured parent. 42 U.S.C. §402 (d)(3); §416 (h)(2)(A), 20 CFR §404.355 (a)(1); 20 CFR §404.361(a).*

*The League was involved in a case in which a child, Lilly, had been conceived after the father had died, by artificial insemination of the man's widow using the decedent's sperm. The sperm had been frozen and stored in a sperm bank. Lilly is considered a nonmarital child because, her father having died, her mother was no longer married at the time of Lilly's birth. The birth certificate did not name a father.*

*Lilly was born 18 months after the father had died. Thus, she is not a posthumous child. Under state law, a posthumous child is a marital child who was conceived during the father's lifetime, but born within 300 days of the father's death and is deemed the child of the deceased. A posthumous child is entitled to inherit from the deceased father's estate.*

*The statutes governing proof of paternity during the father's lifetime in Pacifica are as follows.*

**Pacifica §—Posthumous Children**

1. Posthumous children are considered as living at the death of their parent.
2. A posthumous child is one who was conceived before the decedent parent's death and born within 300 days thereafter.

**Pacifica §—Proof of Paternity for Nonmarital Children**

Paternity cannot be established after the father's death unless

1. A court order was entered during the father's lifetime declaring paternity, or
2. Paternity is established by clear and convincing evidence that the father has openly held out the child as his own.

*Lilly cannot prove paternity under either of the statutory criteria.*

*The League has asked you to draft amendments or to create new statutes to protect children conceived after the father's death so that they will receive social security survivor benefits and will share in the father's estate as an intestate heir. Besides the child's interests, take account of the need for the state to determine paternity accurately and to ensure efficient and timely closings of estates.*

---
### Exercise 13.6
---

### A. Bylaws Exercise[81]

*You are preparing bylaws for a newly incorporated not-for-profit theater arts group that has been operating for quite some time without bylaws. Ms. Z is the founder of the group and she only has two other people on the board of directors. Many other people are involved in the group as performers, but the board is small. You have met not only with Ms. Z but with another director as well and both of them agree that the bylaws should allow Ms. Z to retain as much on-going power as possible and assure her a continual role in the organization.*

*The state not-for-profit corporation law requires an annual meeting for the election of directors and the only qualification required for directors is that they be at least 18 years of age. There must be three of them. Officers are required to be elected by the board of directors. The law allows for committees to be appointed by the board of directors or set out in the bylaws.*

*What avenues would you explore to maximize Ms. Z's power on an on-going basis? Think about the units of power in a corporation: the board of directors, the officers, and the committees. Then explore whether a continuing role for Ms. Z can be built in each area.*

### B. Bylaws Exercise

*You have been asked by a housing co-op organized as a business corporation to review its bylaws. One provision entitled "Removal of Directors" reads as follows:*

*"The term of any Director who becomes more than two (2) months behind in payment of his or her maintenance charges shall be automatically terminated and a replacement shall be duly elected."*

---

[81] We thank Debra Bechtel, of Brooklyn Law School, for providing these exercises.

*The provision entitled "Vacancies" provides that "Vacancies occurring in the office of any Director, for any reason, including for removal with or without cause, shall be filled by a vote of shareholders representing a majority of Meeting Votes."*

1. *What questions come to mind that you think you can answer by looking at other provisions in the by-laws?*
2. *Are there other co-op agreements/documents you might have to review?*
3. *What practical problems do you see with this removal policy?*
4. *How might you re-draft these provisions?*

─────────── *Assignment 13.1* ───────────

*The following statute permits seniors who move into senior citizen housing to cancel their residential leases. Read and critique it. Are there any ambiguities or undefined terms? Then revise the statute, clarifying or defining where necessary and using headings and tabulation. Finally, write a notice explaining the provisions of the statute to prospective residents of a senior citizen housing complex covered by the statute. This notice should use a question-and-answer format, because readers find information faster when questions are used as headings.*

**Termination of residential lease by senior citizens moving
to a residence of a family member or entering certain
health care facilities, adult care facilities or housing projects.**

**1.** In any lease or rental agreement covering premises occupied for dwelling purposes in which a lessee or tenant has attained the age of sixty-two years or older, or will attain such age during the term of such lease or rental agreement or a husband or wife of such a person residing with him or her, there shall be implied a covenant by the lessor or owner to permit such lessee or tenant: (a) who is certified by a physician as no longer able, for medical reasons, to live independently in such premises and requiring assistance with instrumental activities of daily living or personal activities of daily living, and who will move to a residence of a member of his or her family, or (b) who is notified of his or her opportunity to commence occupancy in an adult care facility (as defined in subdivision twenty-one of section two of the social services law) except for a shelter for adults (as defined in subdivision twenty-three of section two of such law), a residential health care facility (as defined in section two thousand eight hundred one of the public health law), or a housing unit which receives substantial assistance of grants, loans or subsidies from any federal, state or local agency or instrumentality, or any not-for-profit philanthropic organization one of whose primary purposes is providing low or moderate income housing, or in less expensive premises in a housing project or complex erected for the specific purpose of housing senior citizens, to terminate such lease or rental agreement and quit and surrender possession of the leasehold premises, and of the land so leased or occupied; and to release the lessee or tenant from any liability to pay to the lessor or owner, rent or other payments in lieu of rent for the time subsequent to the date of termination of such lease in accordance with subdivision two of this section; and to adjust to the date of surrender any rent or other payments made in advance or which have accrued by the terms of such lease or rental agreement.

**2.** Any lease or rental agreement covered by subdivision one of this section may be terminated by notice in writing delivered to the lessor or owner or to the lessor's or owner's agent by a lessee or tenant. Such termination shall be effective no earlier than thirty days after the date on which the next rental payment subsequent to the date when such notice is delivered is due and payable. Such notice shall be accompanied by a documentation of the physician's certification, accompanied by a notarized statement from a family member stating that the senior citizen is related, and will be moving into their place of residence for a period of not less than six months or admission or pending admission to a facility set forth in subdivision one of this section.

**3.** Any person who shall knowingly seize, hold, or detain the personal effects, clothing, furniture or other property of any person who has lawfully terminated a lease or rental agreement covered by this section or the spouse or dependent of any such person, or in any manner interferes with the removal of such property from the premises covered by such lease or rental agreement, for the purpose of subjecting or attempting to subject any of such property to a purported claim for rent accruing subsequent to the date of termination of such lease or rental agreement, or attempts so to do, shall be guilty of a misdemeanor and shall be punished by imprisonment not to exceed one year or by fine not to exceed one thousand dollars, or by both such fine and imprisonment.

---
### *Assignment 13.2*
---

*Atlantis Law School wants to formalize rules for its law review writing competition and has asked you to draft the regulation. It wants sections governing those students who create the writing competition problem, those who administer the competition, and those who participate in the competition. Other sections—like a statement of purpose or a definitions sections—may be needed.*

*To help you get started, read the writing competition schedule below. This informal schedule has been the sole source of institutional memory in the past, but there may be important omissions that need to be addressed. The schedule is, of course, organized chronologically. You must decide whether this is a sensible organizing principle for the regulation.*

### The Writing Competition Schedule

1. Send out notice in December with the schedule for and information about selection for our journals. Memo should include instructions for students who need to pick up the problem later, including Sabbath Observers. Notices should include schedule of fees.
2. March—send out second notice for writing competition through Legal Writing faculty.
3. April—before exams have begun, post flyers regarding fees and deadlines for writing competition. Also send out an e-mail to all first years. Organize an informational meeting.
4. May—competition packet must be ready for reproduction and contain all the necessary components, from instructions to hypothetical or case for comment to closed-universe readings. The packet should also include information on procedures and sanctions for violations of competition rules.
5. May—Have approximately 200 copies made and charged to journals.
6. May—Secretaries number envelopes and insert one problem into each envelope.
7. May—Journal editors coordinate staff for pick up and drop off—at least 6 people for pick up.
   Establish procedure for tying competition number to person.
   Tell participants to check the number of pages <u>before</u> they leave
8. May—Get list for late submissions. (Establish and agree upon acceptable excuses and proof ahead of time. Also set deadline for excuse requests at least several days before the competition).

9. May—Arrange for late submission pick up.
10. May—Reproduce bench memo and evaluation sheets for scorers and charge to journals.
11. July—send out offers. Include information on membership requirements.

─────────── *Assignment 13.3* ───────────

*Your assignment is to critique, revise, and rewrite the attached draft of a regulation forbidding plagiarism and related forms of academic dishonesty (e.g., discussing take-home exams or using forbidden materials in an exam). Be sure to fill any gaps that you find in the draft—revising the language is not sufficient. For background, read Ralph D. Mawdsley's article,* Plagiarism in Higher Education, *13 Journal of College and University Law, 65 (1986).*

*Your proposed regulation must give students notice of what conduct is forbidden and what conduct is required. It must also include procedures for implementing the regulations and sanctions for violating them. In other words, retain the sections in the draft regulation: a preamble, a definitions section, a prohibitions section, a procedures section, and a sanctions section.*

*Before revising and rewriting it, critique the attached regulation. In particular, pay attention to the following concerns.*

1. *The Three Principles of Organization*
   – *Are the parts mutually exclusive or do they overlap?*
   – *Do the parts form a whole, i.e., are all necessary provisions present or are there gaps?*
   – *Are the parts in a logical order?*
2. *Conceptualization*
   – *Are the headings informative and at the appropriate level of generality?*
   – *Do provisions within the sections contradict each other or are they consistent?*
   – *Are terms consistently used?*
   – *Are the definitions and provisions sensible?*
3. *Word-and Sentence-Level Problems*
   – *Are words of authority correctly used?*
   – *Are the right words defined and are definitions appropriately formulated?*
   – *Are there problems with tense?*

– *Are words used that are ambiguous or vague?*
– *Is there redundancy or wordiness?*
– *Is there syntactic (sentence structure) ambiguity?*
– *Is there faulty parallelism?*
– *Are sections and provisions correctly and consistently numbered?*
– *Is tabulated sentence structure helpfully and correctly used?*
– *Are there punctuation errors?*

## Article 8. Plagiarism

### Sec. 1. Preamble

The purpose of this section is to provide a clear guideline to students by defining, prohibiting and providing sanctions for plagiarism and related forms of academic dishonesty when producing works of scholarship. The goal to be achieved by this guideline is to promote originality in the works of students as well as to encourage thorough research, thereby preserving the integrity and the reputation of this institution.

### Sec. 2. Definitions

(a)  A student includes a person
    1.  currently enrolled in the institution, or
    2.  attending any classes at this institution.
(b)  "The Committee on Academic Affairs" consists of
    1.  the Dean of Academic Affairs, and
    2.  two professors appointed by the Dean of Academic Affairs for a one-year term.
(c)  Plagiarism shall mean the intentional or unintentional failure to provide proper acknowledgment
    1.  for direct quotations
    2.  language, facts or ideas that have been paraphrased or summarized
(d)  Academic Dishonesty means
    1.  using material not authorized by the instructor during an examination,
    2.  or in preparing an assignment,
    3.  participating in discussions prohibited by the instructor during an examination or in preparing an assignment, or
    4.  assisting another student to commit any of the above offenses.

## Sec. 3. Prohibited Conduct

(1) Any form of academic dishonesty by a student is prohibited. A form of academic dishonesty is plagiarism. Examples of plagiarism are:
    (a) attributing a quoted passage to a source that does not contain that quoted passage;
    (b) attributing material to a source that does not support the passage for which it is cited;
    (c) the word for word copying of another's work, regardless of length, without quotation marks; and
    (d) paraphrasing important concepts without acknowledging the source.

(2) Examples of cheating are:
    (a) viewing any material that was expressly forbidden to be used, and
    (b) sharing or listening to any information that was expressly forbidden to be disclosed in an in-class exam or take-home exam.

(3) Members of the Law School Community shall file good faith reports of alleged acts of dishonesty.

## Sec. 4. Procedure

1. Reporting allegations of academic dishonesty
    (a) A student or professor who wishes to make an allegation of academic dishonesty must make a complaint to the Office of the Dean.
    (b) Upon receiving a complaint, the Office of the Dean must then:
        i. forward one copy of the complaint to the Committee on Academic Dishonesty.
        ii. personally serve one copy of the complaint upon the student, and
        iii. retain one copy for record keeping purposes.

2. Notice
Prior to conducting a hearing, the Committee on Academic Dishonesty may
    (a) provide written notice to the accused student that it has received a formal registered complaint naming the accused student, and

       (b) provide written notice to the accused student thirty days prior to holding a hearing on the matter.

3.   Hearing

       (a) Hearings must be conducted no later than 60 days after the Office of the Dean has received a formal registered complaint.

       (b) Hearings may only be conducted in the presence of

          i.   the entire Committee on Academic Dishonesty, and

          ii.  the accused-student.

4.   Duties of the law school

       (a) The law school must appoint a member of the faculty as prosecuting counsel.

       (b) Prior to the hearing, the law school's counsel must provide the accused student with a witness list.

       (c) At the hearing the law school's counsel must

          i.   make an opening statement, and

          ii.  present testimonial or documentary evidence in support of the allegation(s) of Academic Dishonesty.

5.   Rights of the Accused Student

       (a) The accused student may represent himself at the hearing, or retain counsel for such purposes.

       (b) At the hearing the accused student or their counsel may

          i.   make an opening statement,

          ii.  challenge the admissibility of evidence,

          iii. cross-examination of any witness called to testify by counsel for the law school,

          iv. present testimonial or documentary evidence,

          v.  make a closing statement.

6.   Post-Hearing Deliberations

       (a) During deliberations the Committee on Academic Dishonesty may only consider evidence previously admitted at the hearing.

       (b) The Committee on Academic Dishonesty shall issue a formal finding.

## Section 4: Appeals

1.   A student who wishes to appeal must file a notice of appeal with the Office of the Dean within 10 days.

2.   The filing of a notice of appeal shall temporarily suspend the enforcement of the sanction imposed on the accused student.

3.   Appeals must be heard by the Board of Appeals within seven days of the filing of a notice of appeal.
4.   In order to affirm, the Board of Appeals must
   (a) unanimously agree that the accused student violated Sec. 3 beyond a reasonable doubt, and
   (b) set forth in writing the evidence that persuaded the Board to affirm the formal finding.

## Sec. 7  Sanctions

Any student found guilty of academic dishonesty or plagiarism may be sanctioned by

a. receiving a failing grade for the course,
b. being dismissed from the course,
c. being suspended from the Law School,
d. being dismissed from the Law School, and
e. notification to Bar authorities of the student's violation of the rules imposed by this section.

## Sec. 8  Exceptions to Prohibited Conduct

1.  Exceptions may be made when:

a. Professors authorize collaboration between students.

# Chapter 14

# *RULE-MAKING: CONTRACTS*

## A. IN GENERAL

A lawyer's most common form of private-law drafting is probably the drafting of contracts. A lawyer drafts contracts for many purposes, such as for the sale of goods, leases of real estate and equipment, partnership agreements, and employment agreements. Like statutes and other forms of enacted law, contracts regulate future conduct and should be drafted to stand the test of time. Also like enacted law, contracts are often the product of collaboration and negotiations undertaken to hammer out language that all parties will accept. It is here that the parties must decide how specific the language should be (an employment contract for one year at a salary of $65,000 per year) or how vague (employee will use her best efforts to promote employer's products). A lawyer must also balance the negotiation impulses of her client, who may be eager to close the deal, and the demands of the other party and her lawyer, which may be unacceptable to the client. Throughout, the lawyer must seek to implement the client's intent, to seek the most favorable terms for the client, and to facilitate the completion of the particular transaction.

An attorney who drafts a contract can draw on forms from many sources. The client may have contracts that were previously used for a similar transaction, and the lawyer's firm most likely has developed form contracts and contracts that were previously used for other clients. Indeed, you may be instructed to use a contract drafted for a previous transaction as the basis for your drafting. Moreover, many sources of contracts exist online and in form books published by bar associations, publishing companies, and continuing legal education committees.

Inexperienced attorneys especially should be careful about using these forms, even forms from your client's previous contracts. For the contract previously written for your client, the client may have been a buyer or an employer, but you represent the client now as a seller or an employee. Or that contract may have been negotiated with very specific and unique goals in mind that are inconsistent with your client's present needs.

These forms, moreover, may be written in legalese, such as "the party of the first part," or may include terms that are unenforceable in your jurisdiction, or may be so one-sided that the other party will never agree to them.[1] Thus, use the forms only as guides to the matters that the particular type of contract should include and to its format. But rewrite to avoid legalese, to insert your client's specific contract terms, to omit inappropriate boilerplate, and of course, to change the names.

## B. COMPONENTS

### 1. Heading and Introductory Paragraph

The heading, sometimes called the caption, is at the top of the first page. It identifies the type of contract, for example, calling it a "Contract of Sale" or "Lease." The heading should not include details of the document, however. So a landlord's form should be headed "Landlord's Notice to Resume Possession," rather than the longer "Landlord's Notice Terminating Residential Tenancy and Seeking Possession."

The introductory paragraph identifies the parties to the contract, using their correct legal names, and the nature of their agreement. If one party is a business organization, make sure that it is accurately named, for example, by the name under which it is incorporated. Many lawyers then provide a short form name to identify each party, sometimes identifying them by their legal position such as Landlord and Tenant or Mortgagor and Mortgagee. The parties should then be identified by those designations throughout the document. The opening paragraph

---

[1] For a discussion of form contracts and why attorneys rarely change them, see Claire A. Hill, *Why Contracts are Written in "Legalese,"* 77 Chi-Kent L. Rev. 59 (2001).

often includes the date of the agreement, although a date here is not legally necessary.

An introductory paragraph with a date may look like this:

> This contract of sale made this 30th day of May 2002 is entered into by Stanley R. Jackson, of Chicago, Illinois, hereafter "Seller," and Deborah Stevens, of Lake Bluff, Illinois, hereafter "Buyer."

Contracts often include in the introductory paragraph a statement of mutual agreement in order to establish consideration, as illustrated in the paragraph below, which is undated and identifies the parties by shorthand reference to their names.

> Stanley R. Jackson ("Jackson") of Chicago, Illinois, and Deborah Stevens ("Stevens") of Lake Bluff, Illinois, enter this agreement for the sale of three paintings and mutually agree to the following terms. [or agree as follows]

Some drafters, however, do not insert the language establishing consideration until after the next traditional component, the recitals. Because consideration is a contractual requirement, the important point here is that the contract must recite within its four corners that consideration was paid or must contain mutual promises.

## 2. Recitals

The recitals traditionally form the next component of the contract. Recitals explain the background of the contract. They tell what the contract is about and why the parties are entering into it. They tell "the story of the deal."[2] Recitals can also provide other background facts and understandings, for example, to explain why the contract includes particular terms, such as a time-is-of-the-essence term. Recitals often supply facts that a court will rely on if the parties go to litigation. Recitals should not be promissory, however, and the parties should not make representations in this part of the contract. Legally enforceable promises should appear

---

[2] Sidney G. Saltz, *Drafting Made Easy*, 15 Probate & Property 32 (May/June 2001).

only in the body of the contract. As one text warns, "The more particular the recitals, the more dangerous they are. Particular recitals have been held . . . conclusive evidence of the facts they state."[3]

By tradition each recital starts with the word "Whereas." These traditional "whereas" statements are often not complete sentences. More modern recitals omit the word "whereas," and are written as complete sentences. A traditionally written recital in an employment agreement may look like this:

> Whereas the employer desires the employee's employment with the employer, and the employee wishes to accept such employment, upon the terms and conditions set forth in this agreement.

This recital could also have been written without the term "Whereas," as are the recitals in this licensing agreement.

> Broadcom is a developer of digital signaling technology. Intel is a developer of hardware and software technologies. Intel desires to license Broadcom's technology for use in jointly developing with Broadcom an XXX silicon chip.

The language confirming consideration for the contract may appear after the recitals. A rather verbose, but traditional, statement of consideration is

> Now, therefore, in consideration of the respective representations and agreements hereinafter contained, and other good and valuable consideration, the receipt and sufficiency of which are hereby acknowledged, the Employer and Employee, intending to be legally bound, agree as follows:

This paragraph could be written simply as "The parties mutually agree to the following terms."

---

[3] Barbara Child, *Drafting Legal Documents: Principles and Practices* 125 (West Pub. 2d ed. 1992).

## 3. Definitions

The definitions section is an important component of a contract, although it should not be included if there are no words that need defining. In some contracts, the definition section runs for several pages. Some definition sections, however, include terms that need not be defined, such as terms that have a common lexical meaning and are clear in the context of the contract. For example, a contract may not need to define "calendar year" when it refers only to the period beginning January 1st and ending December 31st, or define "salary" when it refers simply to the amount that a party will be paid for services.

Another caveat is that a definition should not be a substantive term of the agreement. Definitions are not enforceable terms. The enforceable terms should appear only in the body of the agreement; that is, in the terms of the contract. So, for example, a definition in a sales contract should not define "place of delivery" as "place of delivery means buyer's warehouse at 300 Water Street, Lake City, goods to be delivered no later than the second day of every month in the year 2002." Instead the terms of the delivery should be in the body of the contract. Definitions are discussed more fully in Chapter 11, *Precision*, Section C(2).

In long contracts, it may help the reader if, in the body of the agreement, you underline or italicize the words that appear in the Definitions.

## 4. The Terms/Body of Contract

The parties set forth the terms, that is, their enforceable promises, in the body of the contract. Many attorneys use a checklist of essential terms, such as escrow agreements and remedies for breach, to ensure that they include all the necessary terms in the contract. The most important things here are to include all the terms that make up the contract, to express them in a way that accurately reflects the parties' intent, and to organize them into a coherent structure. Organizing requires that you group and divide the terms into categories, introduce each with a heading and with subheadings where needed, and organize the categories in a logical sequence. See below, Section D(3)(b) and Chapter 1, *Conceptualizing*, Section C(2).

## 5. Housekeeping Provisions

The housekeeping provisions of the contract contain the more administrative types of terms to which the parties have agreed. Although the term "housekeeping" may imply that these provisions are less important than the other terms, these provisions are often crucial ones. They are often "what if" provisions, providing a response to the question, "What if something goes wrong?"[4] Typical housekeeping provisions include:

- choice of law (identifying which state's or country's law will control enforcement of the agreement);
- choice of forum (identifying forum for any litigation);
- modification (specifying how the agreement may be changed);
- merger (specifying that the contract is the final agreement of the parties and that it supercedes prior agreements);
- force majeure (excusing performance of contractual duties if extraordinary, unanticipated circumstances arise);
- severability (declaring that if a part of the contract is declared unenforceable, the remainder remains in effect);
- assignment and delegation (permitting or prohibiting a party from assigning or delegating its duties);
- notices (providing address for notices that the contract requires).

Liquidated damages provisions sometimes are placed with housekeeping provisions. Some lawyers consider these terms so important, however, that they include them with the substantive terms or put them under a separate heading in the contract.

## 6. Signatures

The parties sign the contract and date it at the end of the document. If one of the parties is a business entity, be sure that the person who signs is someone who is authorized to do so.

---

[4] *See* Scott J. Burnham, *Drafting Contracts: A Guide to the Practical Application of the Principles of Contract Law* 190 (Michie Co. 2d ed. 1993).

Some contracts that will be recorded must be notarized, for example, a contract for sale of realty. The notary certificate and signatures come below the parties' signatures.

─────────────── *Exercise 14.1* ───────────────

*Rewrite, to eliminate legalese, the following recitals in an agreement between husband and wife.*

Whereas certain domestic difficulties have arisen between the parties; and whereas by deed bearing even date herewith and about to be recorded said Alexandra Michalski has conveyed to said George Michalski a one-half interest in and to certain properties described in the Attachment hereto, to the end that the same may be held by them as tenants in common; and whereas said parties desire to make certain agreements in respect to the premises as hereinafter stated:

In consideration of the premises it is hereby agreed as follows . . . .

─────────────── *Exercise 14.2* ───────────────

*Rewrite this agreement between Isabel Yeats (first party) and Helen Adams (second party). Assume that Walter Beck was used as a straw man to convey the property in joint tenancy to Ms. Yeats and Ms. Adams. Reorganize to separate out the recitals and the terms, and rewrite to eliminate legalese.*

Whereas the First Party has this day and date vested title in the parties hereto as joint tenants in the Marshall County, Illinois, farm owned by the First Party, all evidenced by certain deeds executed by the First Party and Martin A. Yeats, her husband, and Walter Beck, all of the within date;

Now therefore, in consideration of having vested title of said real estate as aforesaid, The Second Party herein, in consideration thereof, agrees with the First Party that said First Party shall have all the rentals from said real estate and the possession thereof during the term of her natural life, with power and authority to insure the buildings thereon, make repairs and do such other things thereon as she could or would do were she the sole and exclusive owner thereof. This Agreement shall not, however, in any manner affect the joint tenancy of said real estate nor the legal incidents accompanying same.

Dated this 31st day of May, 1939.

## C. SAMPLE CONTRACT

### Premarital Agreement[5]

This agreement is made between the future husband Michael Jones of 100 Lake Street, Lake City, Ill. and the future wife Faith Green of 200 Prairie Ave., Lake City, Ill. Jones and Green are also designated as "the parties," or individually as "the party."

### Background[6]

The parties are soon to enter into marriage with each other.

Both Jones and Green have had previous marriages. Each party's marriage ended by the death of the party's spouse. Each party has two adult children from that prior marriage.

The parties agree that this contract does not apply to any children that may be born to them or adopted by them during their marriage.

Each party owns property individually, and has fully disclosed the nature and extent of that property to the other. Both parties have attached to this agreement a complete schedule of their respective property and its fair market value. The parties agree that they currently own property of approximately equal value.

The parties understand that their coming marriage will entitle each to certain legally-defined rights and claims to the property of the other. By this agreement, the parties intend to relinquish all those rights and claims.

The parties wish, by this agreement, to fix their interests in the property of the other in lieu of any other claims they may have at the termination of their marriage by legal separation or by divorce or the death of either party.

Both parties had independent legal advice before entering this agreement.

### Definitions[7]

1. "Property" means an interest, present or future, legal or equitable, vested or contingent, in real or personal property, including income and earnings.[8]

---

[5] Another common name for this agreement is an antenuptial agreement or contract.

[6] The contract does not use the "whereas" form for these recitals. Are all these recitals necessary?

[7] These definitions are not in alphabetical order. There are only a handful of definitions and the drafter wanted to define "property," "after-acquired property," and "prior-acquired property" consecutively.

[8] This is the definition of property in the state's premarital agreement act.

2. "Prior-acquired property" means property acquired before the parties' marriage to each other.

3. "After-acquired property" means property acquired after the parties' marriage to each other.

4. "Marital dissolution" means the ending of the parties' marriage by legal separation or divorce or by death of one of the parties.

5. "Legally-defined property rights" means homestead, dower, curtesy, election against the will, spousal allowance, and other property rights that arise by reason of their marriage.

In consideration of the mutual promises and the parties' coming marriage, the parties agree to the following provisions.

## A. Parties to Retain Separate Property

1. Michael Jones will retain[9] sole ownership and control of all his property, both prior-acquired and after-acquired, as his sole and absolute property, and during his lifetime he may dispose of his property by sale, gift or other means as he wishes. By his last will, he may dispose of his property as if he had remained unmarried.

2. Faith Green will retain sole ownership and control of all her property, both prior-acquired and after-acquired, as her sole and absolute property. During her lifetime, she may dispose of her property by sale, gift, or otherwise as she wishes. By her last will, she may dispose of her property as if she had remained unmarried.

## B. Waiver of Rights

3. Each party waives and releases all legally-defined property rights in the property of the other party in the event of marital dissolution.

## C. Spousal Rights and Responsibilities

4. The parties agree to share the financial responsibility during their marriage to provide mutual support in a manner consistent with their reasonable and customary[10] standard of living, including but not limited to food, clothing, shelter, health care, transportation, and vacation. This agreement does not affect the parties' legal obligation of support.

5. Neither party is liable for any liabilities incurred by the other, except for those expenses in section 4, whether incurred before or after their

---

[9] This contract follows the practice of using the verb "will" to denote agreement. *See* "Words of Authority" in Chapter 11, *Precision.*

[10] Is this vague term appropriate? Do the parties need the more specific list that follows?

marriage. The parties will satisfy their individual debts exclusively from their solely-owned property.

6. The parties agree that each will bequeath $100,000 in their last will to the other party if they remain married.

7. The parties agree to purchase a condominium in Lake City, Ill. as their primary residence and to take title as tenants in common.[11]

8. The parties agree to each purchase a life insurance policy of the amount of $300,000, which they will keep current, and to name the other as primary beneficiary for as long as they remain married.

9. The parties will take all steps necessary and execute all instruments necessary, which they will deliver to the other party, to put into effect the provisions of this agreement.

## D. Acknowledgments

10. The parties acknowledge that each has entered into this agreement with full knowledge of the extent and value of the other's property, and that Schedules A and B accurately disclose that property.

11. The parties acknowledge that each has been advised of the rights in the property of the other to which each would have been entitled by law except for this agreement.

12. The parties acknowledge that each has received independent legal advice from an attorney of their own choosing.

## E. Interpretation and Modification

13. This agreement is to be interpreted under the laws of the State of Illinois.

14. This agreement may be modified only by a written modification signed by both parties.

Signed _____

_____

---

[11] The consequences will be that the beneficiaries of the first to die of husband and wife will own the condo with the surviving spouse. Their attorney must be sure to explain that outcome.

## D. WRITING PROCESS

### 1. Gathering Information

The first obligation of the attorney is to determine the goals that his client wishes to achieve and the terms by which the client wishes to achieve them—whether it is to purchase goods over a period of time under a long-term supply agreement or to receive a favorable severance package if her job is terminated. Thus, the drafting attorney must gather the facts, including all relevant documents, to know the client's needs.

The attorney's job, however, requires more than transcribing the information the client provides. The attorney needs to think through the structure of this deal with the client, to fill in gaps that the client may not have considered, to find out about particular problems that the contract should address, and to suggest terms necessary to protect the client's interest.

The attorney must engage in "due diligence," that is, investigate the facts and the law. She must know the law governing contracts generally and the laws governing the particular type of contract involved. For example, a contract for the sale of goods may disclaim warranties, an area of law governed by the state's Uniform Commercial Code provisions. Similarly, a shareholder's agreement must comply with a state's business corporations act. An employment contract may include a non-competition agreement, the terms of which typically must be "reasonable," as interpreted under state law. A real estate contract should include the seller's warranty of marketable title, which also will be interpreted under state law.

Some legal constraints require specialized knowledge by the attorney. For example, suppose you are hired to write covenants and restrictions for a planned residential community. The governing board wants to include a restriction on the number of satellite dishes any homeowner may install. You should know that Federal Communications Commission regulations limit the restrictions that building regulations can place on installation and maintenance of satellite services. Or, if you are drafting an appliance store's form sales contract with an arbitration clause, you should know that the Supreme Court has said that an arbitration agreement can be invalid if the arbitration's high costs preclude the buyer from vindicating federal statutory rights.[12]

## 2. Negotiating the Agreement

Representative negotiation is an essential aspect of lawyering. Lawyers negotiate when they represent a client in a deal, divorce, or collective bargaining session. Litigators negotiate when plea bargaining. In fact, negotiation is so central to litigation that the work has been described as a "litogotiation."[13] Given its prevalence, every law student should have some familiarity with negotiation. This section introduces its basic considerations.

### a. Approaches to Negotiation

While the goal of negotiation is singular—to reach an agreement on a conflict or deal—the approaches to it are dual: there is the adversarial, winner-take-all approach and the cooperative, problem-solving approach, and combinations of the two. Because the first years of law school focus so much on "zealous advocacy," many law students assume aggressive, zero-sum bargaining is the way to go. Yet an increasing number of legal professionals are adopting a cooperative approach to negotiation in certain circumstances because they think agreement will more likely be achieved if both parties' interests have been accommodated. Each approach, discussed in more detail in the following paragraphs, affects the way the negotiator defines goals and structures the negotiation, and thus, students should be familiar with both.

### i. Adversarial Negotiation

Underlying an adversarial negotiation is the assumption that the parties are bargaining over a finite resource. Like a pie, that resource can be sliced into pieces of different sizes, but it cannot

---

[12] *Green Tree Financial Corp.-Alabama v. Randolph*, 531 U.S. 79, 90 (2000).

[13] Marc Galanter & M. Cahill, *Most Cases Settle: Judicial Promotion and Regulation of Settlements*, 46 Stan. L. Rev. 1335, 1342 (1994).

be enlarged.[14] As a result, an adversarial negotiation begins with each party asking for a large piece of the pie, and unless one party holds the line and the other caves in, each gradually makes limited, reciprocal concessions until they arrive at an agreement. The process is described as linear[15] because the solution falls on a line between the parties' fixed initial positions and their bottom line—the point at which they will walk away from the table because the alternative to a negotiated agreement is better than the terms of that agreement.

That alternative is called the BATNA, the Best Alternative to a Negotiated Agreement.[16] For example, if a seller wants to get a minimum of $240,000 for a house and a potential buyer offers only $200,000, the seller might prefer to rent the house until the housing market improves. That alternative is the seller's BATNA. If, however, the best alternative to an agreement is worse than a bad agreement, the party may have to rethink acceptable terms. For example, if the seller tried and failed to find a tenant before putting the house on the market, a lower purchase price may be preferable to continuing to pay the mortgage. Thus, the better the BATNA, the less the party is willing to compromise. In our hypothetical, if the seller's walk away point is $200,000 and the buyer's is $230,000, then negotiators consider the "bargaining range" to be between $200,000 and $230,000, or the negotiation fails. Thus, before any negotiation, the representative should elicit the client's bottom line. Central to the negotiation as it proceeds is the representative's attempt to determine the other side's bottom line.

In conflict negotiation—where litigation is the probable alternative to a negotiated agreement—bargaining is conducted in the "shadow of the law."[17] In other words, the parties' demands and concessions are influenced by the law and judicial remedies.[18]

---

[14] *See* Alex J. Hurder, *The Lawyer's Dilemma: To Be or Not to Be a Problem-Solving Negotiatior*, 14 Clinical L. Rev. 253, 262 (2007).

[15] *See* Carrie Menkel-Meadow, *Toward Another View of Legal Negotiation: The Structure of Problem Solving*, 31 UCLA L. Rev. 754, 767 (1984).

[16] Roger Fisher & William Ury, *Getting to Yes: Negotiating Agreement Without Giving In* 99 (Houghton Mifflin Co. 2d ed. 1991).

[17] Robert H. Mnookin & Lewis Kornhauser, *Bargaining in the Shadow of the Law: the Case of Divorce*, 88 Yale L.J. 950,950 (1979).

[18] *See* Hurder, *supra* n. 14, at 259; *see also* Menkel-Meadow, *supra* n. 15, at 789.

In a transactional negotiation, negotiation is first and foremost about the business terms that form a new or different contractual relationship, but even these terms might be influenced by the law and common business practices. [19] For example, some states impose disclosure rules for negotiating the sale of a residential property. In addition to prohibiting affirmative misstatements, sellers must disclose known material facts that buyer does not know and has not asked about.‑

Negotiations conducted in the shadow of the law or common practice have appeal because the precedents provide objective limits and standards for settlement. [20] On the other hand, some lawyers—problem-solving negotiators in particular—do not want to be limited to remedies created by the industry or the court because the parties themselves might be able to create alternatives that better fit their situation.[21]

The adversarial negotiation process not only affects the originality of solution, but also the process by which the parties reach their solution. Adversarial negotiators seek to protect their positions by maximizing their gains. They do this by opening with high demands and by maintaining a high level of demands while making only infrequent, insignificant concessions. Some withhold information that might help the other party's position and stretch the facts to support their positions. Of course, this aggressive approach sometimes needs to be modified, especially when the parties are repeat players and have a long-term relationship. In this situation in particular, effective negotiators need to listen to the other parties and try to figure out their irreducible demands and their breaking points. They try to determine what they can realistically secure and they de-escalate their demands if necessary.

## ii. Problem-Solving Negotiation

The problem-solving negotiator seeks common ground and focuses on the needs and objectives of both parties in order to find an objectively fair solution. Rather than planning demands and concessions, cooperative negotiators plan solutions. They

---

[19] Menkel-Meadow, *supra* n. 15, at 792.

[20] Hurder, *supra* n. 14, at 263.

[21] *Id.* at 259.

begin by trying to establish an atmosphere of trust in which the participants feel comfortable about identifying their long-term and short-term monetary, social, ethical, and legal needs.[22] Once these interests have been identified, negotiators try to focus on these interests, rather than on positions,[23] in order to brainstorm a variety of ways of satisfying them. Since problem-solvers understand that what benefits one party may not cost the other party dearly, they look at both direct solutions and trade-offs.[24] Instead of engaging in a zero-sum battle for the largest piece of a finite pie, they put multiple resolutions and variations on the table on the theory that an array of solutions creates both greater opportunities for favorable outcomes and fewer breakdowns in bargaining. The problem-solver begins by exchanging information and generating solutions before moving on to discuss the relative merits of the solutions.

Thus, in a cooperative negotiation, an entrepreneur might want to rent a commercial property, but is concerned about the low initial profits and start-up costs of a new business. Her representative may put three proposals on the table: a lower than normal fixed rent, a lower rate than the standard five percent of gross revenue rent, or a sliding percentage rate lease based on profits. The entrepreneur might be willing to accept the sliding scale lease because it gives her some initial breathing room. The lessor might be amenable to such a scheme if the property has gone unrented for months and the initial short fall could yield to a higher long-term rent.

The different goals of adversarial and cooperative negotiation— zero sum versus mutual benefit—mean negotiators take a different attitude towards sharing information. Although both types of negotiators share and withhold information as the situation requires, the problem-solver is more inclined to share information that could aid a resolution because the parties fashion solutions out of the interests of all the parties.

---

[22] Menkel-Meadow, *supra* n. 15, at 803.

[23] *See* Fisher and Ury, *supra* n. 16.

[24] *See* Menkel-Meadow, *supra* n. 15, at 795.

## iii. Dealing with Conflicting Approaches

From a description of adversarial and cooperative models of negotiation, it may seem as if they are mutually exclusive. In reality, even if an individual leans towards one style of negotiation, most lawyers move back and forth between approaches at different stages in the negotiation. Nonetheless, commentators note that cooperative bargainers may be vulnerable when confronted with adversarial negotiators because the cooperative bargainer tends to disclose information and "make concessions in an effort to induce reciprocal behavior."[25] Thus, problem-solvers who notice the other party is adopting an adversarial style of negotiation must address the difference. They could, for example, switch their tactics and adopt the other side's approach. Or they could decide to begin with full disclosure on low risk issues in an effort to get the other side to change approach before the stakes grow higher.[26] Alternatively, they might make concessions, but protect themselves by conditioning them on cooperation in other areas.[27]

### b. Planning a Negotiation

The first step in negotiation is to explore the client's aspirations and priorities. Once the client's interests are understood, the lawyer should give the client his assessment of the strength of the client's position in order to help the client form realistic expectations.[28] Sometimes "goal setting itself can be a negotiation, for often the client's assessment of the transaction ... is in tension with the lawyer's assessment."[29] In this situation, the two must engage in a dialogue, but ultimately, the client must decide its goals and bottom line. The client must also be clear about what is up for trade, for example whether the client will lower its price, provide more services, or push back a closing date. Finally, the

---

[25] *See* Nancy L. Schultz and Louis J. Sirico, *Legal Writing and Other Lawyering Skills* 209-210 (LexisNexis 4 ed. 2004).

[26] *See* Anthony G. Amsterdam, Peggy Cooper Davis, Aderson Bellegarde Francois, *Lawyering by The Book* 257 (2008).

[27] *See* Schultz and Sirico, *supra* n. 25, at 210.

[28] Amsterdam et al., *supra* n. 26, at 246.

[29] *Id.*

lawyer and client must figure out the relative advantages to each negotiation approach and settle on the best style for them.

If an adversarial perspective is taken, the client should share its bottom line with its lawyer. The lawyer in consultation with the client should determine a starting position as well. The lawyer may also plan the types and order of concessions he is prepared to make knowing, however, that unforeseen arguments, developments, and facts will emerge and they must remain flexible. If a problem-solving approach is taken, the lawyer and client must determine what proposals they are interested in making and what proposals the other side might make. They should discuss the merits of each. The lawyer must also learn whether there are issues or circumstances that the client thinks might justify a shift in strategies during the negotiation.

Thus armed, the lawyer can prepare for the four stages of negotiation. The first phase in a negotiation is the beginning orientation, where issues like the length of the negotiation and the agenda are settled.

The second phase varies depending upon approach. Adversarial negotiation would begin with initial proposals and supporting arguments, whereas a problem-solving negotiation might begin the second phase as information exchange. Here, the parties may realize there are areas of agreement as well as areas of conflict. Where the parties agree, the issues may be quickly resolved. Other issues remain at initial stages. In a cooperative process, the parties hold off on making arguments about these thorny issues and instead generate multiple solutions. Only after this brainstorming is done do they move into phase three, debating the merits of each issue. But regardless of whether the information exchange precedes or succeeds the opening bid, the information exchange helps to narrow and define the real disputes, a process that may reveal the strengths and weaknesses of each party's positions. During this phase, each party may need to adjust their expectations about what they can obtain. As the bargaining proceeds, the parties must make and track trade-offs and concessions.

Phase four is the pivotal stage when the parties will reach an agreement or the negotiations will break down. If the parties reach an agreement, the lawyers should review the terms to make sure both parties have the same understanding of the agreement. The last step is to memorialize the agreement. Often one party offers to write a letter summarizing the agreement, and it is always advantageous to volunteer to undertake this because the drafter gets to frame the terms. Sometimes this letter is detailed, while at other times the agreement is described in broad strokes, with details to be worked out later. If the recipient of the letter has a different understanding from that of the writer, the parties will negotiate further. In any event, the activities that occur at the end of the negotiation not only confirm the agreement, but help to reestablish the parties' working relationship, which may have become somewhat frayed through the bargaining process. When the parties have an ongoing relationship, this stage is especially important.

If the parties appear deadlocked, they must decide whether they are willing to make any concessions or willing to generate new alternatives. They also need to be flexible and come up with some creative solutions that satisfy as many of the parties' stated interests as possible, or generate new alternatives. If they cannot, the negotiation has failed. It is worth remembering, however, that even when the negotiation fails, the breakdown may not be final. Some apparent deadlocks are ploys designed to pressure the opponent or to gain time to consult with client or colleagues. Sometimes the meetings may have become so heated, a postponement is necessary so the parties can regroup and compose themselves. The lawyer and client will need to decide whether it is worth making another approach in the future.

### c. Negotiation Ethics

During negotiations, many lawyers overstate their clients' positions. They bluff; they give partial answers to questions; they use "puffery"; they become aggressive; they believe that the purpose of the negotiation is to deceive the other party. Thus, negotiations involve a good deal of what may be considered unethical conduct. The ABA Model Rules of Professional Conduct speak only briefly to transactions with parties other than clients or the court. Rule 4.1, "Truthfulness in Statements to Others," says that a lawyer, in the course of representing a client, "shall not knowingly make a false statement of material fact or law,"[30] and shall not "fail to disclose a material fact to a third person

---

[30] MRPC R.4.1(a)(2009).

when disclosure is necessary to avoid assisting a . . . fraudulent act by a client."[31] In 1983, the ABA did not adopt a draft rule that required attorneys to "be fair in dealing with other participants" in negotiation. Thus, the Rule prohibits only fraud during negotiations. But since negotiations, unlike litigation, are conducted privately and without court stenographers, there is little policing of the attorneys' conduct. Moreover, for a false statement to be fraudulent, it must be knowingly made or, under some court decisions, recklessly made, and the false statement must be a statement of a material fact. Statements of opinion or "puffery" are not actionable. So, even if attorneys are negotiating the sale of a commercial building and the seller's attorney says, "This is the best block in the downtown area for retail," that statement is not actionable even if the block did not have as many shoppers as some other downtown streets. The statement is puffery. But if a seller's attorney misrepresents facts ("The roof does not leak"), then she will have violated R.4.1(a).

For certain types of transactions, however, disclosure rules, often by statute, impose constraints, such as for the purchase or sale of securities, or the sale of contaminated property. As noted earlier, in some states, the disclosure rules for negotiating the sale of a residential property (rather than commercial property) are stricter than R.4.1(a). In addition to prohibiting affirmative misstatements, a seller must disclose known material facts that the potential buyer does not know and has not asked about. The remedies against the seller for these transgressions of nondisclosure are rescission of the purchase contract or damages (if the property has already changed hands), but are not yet ethical violations by the lawyer. Even in these states, must an attorney disclose that a fraternity has just bought the property down the street or that there is a dispute over the identity of the artist who painted a painting the sale of which is being negotiated? The comment to Rule 4.1 states that a lawyer "generally has no affirmative duty to inform an opposing party of relevant facts." An ABA Formal Opinion said that a lawyer has no duty to inform the other party in a negotiation that the statute of limitations had run on a claim of the attorney's client.[32] However, some attorneys

---

[31] MRPC R.4.1(b)(2009).

[32] ABA Committee on Ethics and Professional Responsibility, Formal Op. 94-387 (2006).

have been disciplined for their implicit misrepresentation when they failed to make material truthful statements, such as that their clients had died.[33]

Another reason that it is difficult to draft clear standards of ethical behavior for negotiating is that negotiation occurs in many different contexts, for example, between employer and union over a labor contract, between husband and wife negotiating financial and child custody issues in a divorce, between prosecutor and criminal defendants in plea bargains.

In the absence of clear rules and professional norms, it is hard to balance advocacy and professional aspiration. Certainly material misrepresentations—if discovered—will likely damage the lawyer's credibility during the negotiation. It could also harm the client by having a negative impact on the client's relationship with the contractual partner. Finally, the lawyer's reputation in the larger community could suffer. The most effective enforcement of ethical negotiations is the attorneys' reputations. Thus there are practical as well as aspirational reasons to exercise moral judgment while bargaining, and novices must think through these issues.[34]

## 3. Conceptualizing

### a. Anticipating Future Problems

As you create your draft, think through the substantive and administrative features of this deal to ensure that you have covered all the bases and have created a coherent structure. Check for future problems that may befall your client—the "what if's" of what could go wrong—and draft for foreseeable problems and risks. An important aspect of many contracts is the allocation of risk—for example, in sales contracts by warranties and disclaimers. Because as we explained above, contracts will be negotiated with other parties and their attorneys who will be looking out for their own clients' interests, it is important for the drafter to anticipate pitfalls for her own client and protect against them. The conditions that affect the contractual relationship may change

---

[33] ABA Committee, *supra* n. 32, Formal Opinion 06-439 (2006).

[34] For further information, read Fisher & Ury, *supra* n. 16, a seminal work.

enough to affect your client's interests—sometimes dramatically. For example, suppose your client is being hired by a corporation that imposes confidentiality and non-competition terms on its employees. Your client wants to ensure that these terms do not overly restrict her use of certain information, such as customer lists, personnel information, and technical data, in the event her employment is terminated. You may try to place limits on the employer's restrictions, for example, by excluding information that the client learned through sources other than her employer.

Other examples of drafting for "What if's" include the following.

- You are drafting a partnership agreement and will need contingency planning, such as for division of profits or continuation of the partnership name, in the event that one or more partners leave the partnership or new partners join the partnership.
- You are drafting an agreement merging two companies. The agreement should be clear about whether one company will assume the other's liabilities, and if so, which one(s).
- You are drafting a contract for the sale of residential real estate. The contract is contingent on the buyer's obtaining a mortgage not to exceed a named interest rate. The contract should protect the seller against unreasonable delay and other possible setbacks to her buyer securing a mortgage. If you represent the buyer, you would protect against encumbrances on the seller's title and certain defects, such as termites, in the house.
- You are drafting a property settlement and child support agreement for a divorcing client. The agreement should be clear whether the non-custodial parent must pay the child's tuition and living costs for her higher education and whether that obligation includes costs of graduate school.

By identifying situations like these early in the process, and using flexible contractual language and terms allowing modification, you will protect your client's ability to respond to future changes or circumstances.

## b. Organizing

One of the most important tasks for the drafter of contracts is to impose a coherent organization on the contract terms by categorizing the terms topically, including the correct terms under each topic, and arranging your categories in a proper sequence. Some experienced drafters, because they know which categories of information are required, devise a form for different types of contracts so that they can fill in the terms under each category. They then create new categories, where they are needed, to suit a particular client's deal. Other attorneys first collect the information they need and then sort out the terms.

When organizing the terms of an agreement, under either system, your overall aim is to permit the parties to locate easily the terms that they need. To reach this goal, the attorney needs categories that are internally consistent and mutually exclusive, are introduced with headings that achieve the correct level of generality, accurately reflect the terms included under them, and are arranged in a logical sequence. Examples of logical sequences, depending on the type of contract involved, would be the most commonly consulted terms first, or the terms in the chronological order in which they will be carried out, or the more general terms first and then those that are more specific.

Read the following property settlement in a divorce and note how it is incorrectly categorized.

A. Real Property: The marital home at 1 Lake Drive, Lakeview City to Wife. The vacation home at 1 Mountain Drive, Palisades County to Husband, including its furnishings.

B(1) Household furnishings: All household furnishings, subject to the exceptions in Section B(2) below, to Wife, including all furniture, kitchen appliances, china, silver flatware, jewelry subject to the exceptions in B(2), and hollowware, and stocks evidenced by certificates filed in Wife's desk drawer.

(2) Exceptions: All Husband's collectibles including stamp and coin collections to Husband, all paintings hanging in the living room and bedrooms of the marital home on the date of this agreement, except the two Marin watercolors

> hanging over the living room fireplace to Husband; all items given to Husband and Wife by Husband's parents, including money deposited in three certificates of deposit with Second National Bank, Lakeview City; all Husband's jewelry consisting of gold watch and cuff links; all other stocks, all to Husband.

In this agreement, the headings are under-inclusive and over-inclusive. Section A includes personal property (household furnishings) as well as real property. Section B(1) includes intangible personal property (stock certificates) and tangible personal property that is not household furnishings (jewelry). Section B(2) also includes intangible personal property (bank CDs) and includes the two paintings that go to the wife. The agreement is also not clear whether the husband takes the household furnishings in the vacation home (Part A) or whether "all household furnishings" to the wife in B(1) includes furnishings in the vacation home.

This settlement could be reorganized, using the following headings and subheadings.

> A. Real Property
>    1. Residence to wife
>    2. Vacation home to husband
> B. Personal Property
>    1. Tangible property [listing property to each]
>    2. Intangible property [listing property to each]

These headings and subheadings could also be organized by husband and wife instead of by the type of property.

> A. Property to Wife
>    1. Real property: marital residence at 1 Lake Drive, Lakeview City
>    2. Tangible personal property
>       a. household furnishings . . .
>       b. jewelry
>       c. two Marin watercolors . . .
>    3. Intangible personal property
>       [listing property]

B.  Property to Husband
1.  Real property: vacation home at 1 Mountain Drive, Palisades County.
2.  Tangible personal property
    a.  household furnishings of 1 Mountain Drive
    b.  paintings in . . .
    c.  jewelry of husband
    d.  husband's collectibles
    e.  property from husband's parents
3.  Intangible personal property
    a.  certificates of deposit [listing]
    b.  stock certificates [listing]

Note that well organized, readable documents often make considerable use of enumeration and tabulation. Long, involved paragraphs strain a reader's understanding.

## 4. Writing the First Draft

After ascertaining the relevant facts from your client, mastering the relevant body of law, negotiating with the other party, advising your client about additional or different terms, and conceptualizing, you should write a preliminary draft that knits this all together. After going over the draft with your client, you can then offer this draft to the other party. The choice of who writes the first draft can be important, and may require some doing on your part. For certain types of contracts, custom often dictates the party that writes the draft. For example, the landlord drafts the lease; the financial institution drafts the loan agreements; the purchaser drafts the corporate acquisition agreement.[35] For other agreements, however, volunteer to draft the first agreement, because preparing the first draft is often advantageous to the preparing party. Explain to your client that your time will be well worth the fee involved. If, however, you are the recipient of the other party's draft, study it thoroughly and cautiously and prepare a list of suggested and required changes. If the list is

---

[35] James C. Freund, *Lawyering, A Realistic Approach to Legal Practice* 191 (Law J. Seminars Press 1979).

long, write a memorandum of your changes and deliver it to the drafting attorney before your meeting.[36]

This stage requires skill as a negotiator, and the language skills discussed in Chapter 11 on *Precision*. For example, the attorneys may decide to employ a vague term or terms when the parties cannot agree to terms that are more specific. Then the attorneys' challenge is to find terms that are vague enough for the parties to agree, but not so vague that they are unenforceable or likely to be interpreted adversely against their clients by a court if the terms are litigated.

Contracts enforceable in a state that has enacted a plain language law obviously must comply with the language requirements of that law. These statutes usually apply to consumer and insurance contracts, and are explained in Section F(2) below.

---

### *Exercise 14.3*

**A.** *Your new client is the owner of a large apartment building. He wants you to draft a form lease for him. Before you interview him, develop your own form for the interview. List the categories and subcategories of terms that you foresee the lease requiring.*

**B.** *Evaluate and rewrite the following terms in the lease of The Landmark Cooperative Apartments, a large cooperative apartment complex, correcting their classifications, headings, and sequence.*

Janitor's Duties: The janitorial personnel is made up of three men. The Head Janitor lives on premises in Apt. E-5. They are helpful and courteous. Call them when you need assistance.

If you will be moving furniture or other heavy articles in or out of the building, advise the Head Janitor so that he can protect the elevators from damage.

Any major move in or out of the buildings requires a deposit of $200, payable prior to the move, to the building management. Fees will be refunded within one month, minus the cost of any damage.

Noise Levels: Construction of the building and composition of the floors are such that unless floors are carpeted, including pads, noise

---

[36] *Id.* at 193.

will travel to lower apartments. All floors, except kitchen and bath-room, must be carpeted to within six inches of the walls.

Do not talk loudly on balconies, stair wells, lobbies, or in hallways in order not to disturb others.

Radio, TV, Stereo, etc.: Do not play musical instruments, TV, radio, stereo before 8:00 A.M. or after 11:00 P.M. Regulate the volume even during permitted hours.

Do not use typewriters or computers after 11:00 P.M.

Fire Laws: Fire laws preclude storage of property in open areas of the basement. All bicycles, strollers, scooters, etc. must be identified by name and secured to the bicycle racks provided in the basement.

All large furniture must be stored in the basement Trunk Rooms.

All other storage items must go in your personal locker in the basement.

Stairwells: Fire laws require that nothing be stored in stairwells or in any way that will hinder stairwell traffic. We will remove any items.

Delivery of Rent: All rent checks should be made out to Landmark Apartments and delivered to the Office in Building B.

Rent is due by the 15th of each month. Any rent received after the 15th of the month will be charged a late fee of $25.

Tenants whose accounts are more than two months in arrears will be charged a fee of $100. They will be moved to the bottom of the list for parking upgrades, and their account will be referred to the building's attorney for collection.

―――――――――――――― *Exercise 14.4* ――――――――――――――

*John Lee, your client, is president of New Textile Co. and has asked you to draw up an employment agreement. He has been negotiating with Steven Sands to employ Sands as a sales manager.*

*This is the information he has given you about their negotiations so far.*

I have offered Sands a salary of $100,000 a year. I told him that he can start right after the new year, probably the first Monday of the year. He is to be a sales manager, so he manages and directs the sales department and has to do everything that a sales manager customarily does. But if he becomes disabled, he's terminated, the last day of active employment. Naturally if he dies, our contract is over. Of course he gets a company-paid life insurance policy, the face amount is three times his annual salary, and gets the company's long-term and short-term disability policy.

Let's see, put in that as sales manager, he hires and fires sales personnel and clerical and secretarial also, supervises them, manages the department, etc.

If he dies or becomes disabled, I can terminate him on short notice, make it five days, make that written notice, and can get rid of him if he breaches the agreement or for cause, neglects his duties, violates company policy, or he's dishonest. Also if he breaches confidentiality. He can't disclose any confidential information. He can't take confidential information from the office without my permission. He can't work for anyone else. I expect him to work full time here and devote full time and energies to his job here. He can't take customer lists.

Also make sure there is a non-competition agreement for after he leaves, and either party can terminate his employment without cause with sixty days' notice. The noncompetition—he can't compete—directly or indirectly—with my business in any region of the country where I sell. Right now, that's Illinois, Wisconsin, Iowa, and Minnesota. Let's make that for one year after he leaves. He can't solicit my employees for any competing business.

And another reason to fire him for cause, if he has any criminal violations or other improper conduct.

Besides his salary, I told him I give a percentage of the company's annual net profits; I decide the amount, but not less than 2%, and also an annual bonus; I decide this amount also. He gets annual vacation time of three weeks, but no carryover year to year, and longer after he's been here three years. And sick leave twelve days a year, plus paid traditional holidays. We also have a Blue Cross/Blue Shield health insurance plan; it's a co-pay. We pay his business travel, hotel, transportation, business calls, tips.

And, a new one for me, I told him we would reimburse for student loan payments not over $75k, but the first $50k goes towards satisfaction of his bonus.

Put in the typical housekeeping provisions, and an arbitration clause, at either party's request, we split the expenses and it's binding as much as law allows.

*Draft the terms of this contract, organizing by dividing the terms into categories with headings and putting them in a logical sequence. Make a list of any questions you have for Mr. Lee and any suggestions to change these terms.*

*List any terms that you should define in the contract.*

*Write a cover letter to Mr. Lee explaining your draft of the contract.*

---

## 5. Revising

Contracts usually are written in successive drafts. One party submits a draft and the other responds. Thus, after you have written your draft, submit it first to your client and then to the other party and his attorney. After you receive the other party's comments, be prepared to engage in more rounds of negotiation and drafting. This process continues until both, or all, parties are satisfied with its terms and believe that their interests have been protected.

During this process, continue to revise the contract. Reread it with an eye toward its clarity and coherence. Check for ambiguities, for omitted terms, for proper definitions. Edit out irrelevant boilerplate provisions. Tabulate or enumerate to improve readability.

Also edit for appropriate use of words of authority. Because "shall" and other words of authority are often used carelessly, when you revise your contract you need to pay special attention to them. These terms are especially important in drafting contracts, for the very nature of a contract is to impose obligations. Remember that the better usage is to use "shall" to impose a duty on the subject of the sentence. Yet too often, agreements are written that confusingly use "shall" to mean future tense when the contract should be written in the present tense, or to impose an obligation on a subject that cannot perform that obligation because the subject is an inanimate object or is not party to the contract. To write, "The corporation's fiscal year shall run from July 1st to June 30th" imposes a duty that the fiscal year cannot fulfill. Instead, the sentence should read simply, "The corporation's fiscal year runs from July 1st to June 30th." For future tense, use "will," as in "This option will expire on June 1st." However, the drafter could have written this sentence in present tense, "This option expires on June 1st."

Some drafters prefer to use "will" instead of "shall" in contracts because "will" indicates that the parties have agreed to the terms; "shall" gives an order. However, this use of "will" may cause confusion if the drafter uses "will" for future tense,[37] such as in "The parties will negotiate in good faith." See Chapter 11, Section C for a discussion of words of authority.

One skilled attorney has written that "[n]egotiated agreements rarely resemble models of draftsmanship or generate intellectual pride; more typically, a complex contract ends up as a hodge-podge document, with substitutions and additions cropping up in unlikely places, detracting from the careful organization embodied in the initial draft."[38] Take the time, if possible, for that one more edit that will prevent your contract from being a hodge-podge document.

---

### *Exercise 14.5*

*Evaluate the use of words of authority in these excerpts from a Stock Purchase Agreement. Rewrite sentences where necessary.*

#### Stock Purchase Agreement

This agreement is dated as of May 31, 2002, and is between Bernice Rose of 1507 North Avenue, Lake City, Atlantis 50622 ("Seller"), and Richard Kartugian of 2605 West Street, Lake City, Atlantis 50645 ("Buyer").

#### Recitals

. . .

---

[37] *See* Joseph Kimble, *The Many Misuses of Shall*, 3 Scribes J. Leg. Writing 61, 69 (1992).

[38] Freund, *supra* n. 35, at 193.

## Agreement

1. <u>Purchase Price</u>. The Purchase price for Seller's shares shall be $150,000 plus the Additional Amount set forth in Paragraph 2. The Purchase Price shall be paid in three (3) equal installments as follows:

| | |
|---|---|
| At the Closing | $50,000 |
| July 1, 2003 | $50,000 |
| July 1, 2004 | $50,000 |

2. <u>Additional Amount</u>. On July 1, 2004, Buyer shall pay Seller an Additional Amount that will be equal to 2 % of the gross sales of the Corporation during the period July 1, 2003 to June 30, 2004 in excess of $300,000. Seller must determine gross sales in accordance with generally accepted accounting principles consistently applied.

3. <u>Closing</u>. The Closing shall take place on July 1, 2002 at 10:00 AM at the office of the Corporation. At the Closing, Buyer must deliver to Seller a certified or cashier check in the amount of $50,000, and Seller shall deliver to Buyer a certificate of stock for 333 shares, which shall represent one-third (1/3) of the issued and outstanding capital stock in the Corporation, duly assigned to Buyer.

4. <u>Buyer's Due Diligence</u>. Between the date of this agreement and the Closing, Seller is to give Buyer free access to the books and records of the Corporation. Buyer shall keep confidential and shall not use for his own individual gain any information regarding the Corporation that has been, or shall hereafter be, made available to him by Seller.

—————————————— *Exercise 14.6* ——————————————

*Rewrite these clauses in a commercial lease. Tabulate or enumerate to improve their readability.*

a. TENANT'S DUTY OF CARE AND MAINTENANCE. Tenant shall, after taking possession of said premises and until the termination of this lease and the actual removal from the premises, at its own expense, care for and maintain said premises in a reasonably safe and serviceable condition, except for structural parts of the building. Tenant will furnish its own interior and exterior decorating. Tenant will not permit or allow said premises to be damaged or depreciated in value by any act or negligence of the Tenant, its agent or employees, ordinary wear and tear excepted. Without limiting the generality of the foregoing, Tenant will make necessary repairs to the sewer, the plumbing, the water pipes and electrical wiring, and all other component parts of the building and land, and Tenant agrees to keep faucets closed as to prevent waste of water and flooding of premises; to promptly take care of any leakage or stoppage in any of the water, gas or water pipes. The Tenant agrees to maintain adequate heat to prevent freezing of pipes, if and only if the other terms of this lease fix responsibility for heating upon the Tenant. Tenant at its own expense may install floor covering and will maintain such floor covering in good condition. Tenant will be responsible for the plate glass in the windows of the leased premises and for maintaining the parking area, driveways and sidewalks on and abutting the leased premises, if the leased premises include the ground floor, and if the other terms of this lease include premises so described. Tenant shall make no structural alterations or improvements without the written approval of the Landlord, of the plans and specifications therefore.

b. Only Tenant shall have the right to terminate this lease without cause or Landlord default. Landlord shall have the right to terminate this lease only in the event of Tenant default in performance of its obligations contained in this lease. In accordance with terms of this paragraph, Landlord and Tenant shall each give the other six (6) months notice of its intention to terminate the lease. The 6-month notice shall run from the day the notice is sent, Certified Mail—Return Receipt Requested, and the monthly rental and other expenses shall be paid in full during said 6-month period. It is further agreed that 6-month notice of termination provided to Tenant cannot be given until eighteen (18) months of the initial 24-month lease term have expired. Any other 6-month notice of termination shall expire six (6) months after receipt, and Tenant shall pay all amounts provided for in the lease until the expiration of the 6-month period.

---

## E. NONCONTRACTUAL AND CONTRACTUAL LETTERS

One frequent cause of litigation is whether a document is in fact intended as a binding agreement. Negotiating parties may use a letter format, that is a letter of intent, as a step in their negotiations, or as a binding agreement itself. These letters are frequently used in business transactions to allow the parties to negotiate their deal in stages, yet the parties may later disagree as to the binding nature of the document.

The following discussion classifies three types of letters.[39] The first, a letter that is not intended to bind the parties; the second, a letter that is intended as a binding agreement; the third, a letter intended to bind the parties to limited terms and to negotiate as to other terms. Lawyers who draft any of these must be sure to make clear their clients' intent as to their obligations under the document.

## 1. Letters of Intent

A letter of intent is often a preliminary step to forming a contract, but is not itself a contract. Instead, the letter sets out preliminary terms for the parties to discuss and negotiate. It may be a binding agreement to agree or negotiate in good faith if the parties intend that interpretation. In order to ensure that any terms in the letter are not binding, however, the caption should not contain words of contract, but should be captioned a Letter of Intent or, as the authors of one article suggest, a "tentative proposal," "status letter," "term sheet," or "list of proposal points,"[40] and should say clearly that it is not intended to be enforceable as a contract.

A letter should also say clearly whether it is intended as the writer's offer, which if signed by the recipient, would bind the parties to its terms. For example, a letter that began "This letter offer will serve to set forth the parameters for an offer from X Corp. to purchase 78 acres of land from Y," would not itself be an offer because its language indicates that X Corp. intended an offer at a later date.[41]

If the parties do agree on the terms in the letter and they memorialize that agreement by some accepted formality, and if a

---

[39] Other classifications and permutations exist. *See, e.g.,* Gregory G. Gosfield, *The Structure and Use of Letters of Intent*, 38 Real Prop., Prob., and Trust J. 99 (2003); *Teachers Ins. and Annuity Ass'n v. Tribune Co.*, 670 F. Supp. 491 (S.D.N.Y. 1987).

[40] Thomas C. Homburger & James R. Schueller, *Letters of Intent—A Trap for the Unwary*, 37 Real Prop., Prob. and Trust J. 509, 526 (2002).

[41] *See Ocean A. Dev. Corp. v. Aurora Christian Schs.*, 322 F.3d 983 (7th Cir. 2003).

court can extract essential terms from the letter that effectively constitute a contract, then the terms may be enforceable.

A letter of intent also often includes a statement that it is confidential and intended only for the recipient, his attorney, and any other parties essential to the deal, such as a bank's loan department.

A letter of intent may look like this.

Dear Ms. Hoyt:

This letter is a letter of intent only and not a contract of sale, and is not intended to be legally binding on any party or impose any duty to negotiate in good faith. The letter sets out the terms discussed thus far, but not yet agreed upon, for the sale of Lakeview Towers, a professional building located at 300 Lakeview Terrace, Lake City, Atl., by Hiram Jackson to Medico-Legal Partnership. Those terms are enclosed as Attachment A [not provided with this example].

The terms still to be discussed are enclosed as Attachment B [not provided with this example].

No terms are binding until a contract is signed by both parties.

This letter is confidential and to be shown to the parties only, their attorneys, accountants, and their respective loan officers at Second National Bank.[42]

A more formal letter of intent for commercial real estate may, in part, look like this.[43]

Re: Parcel of property, constituting ___ acres, located at ___ in Lake County, Atl.

The undersigned, Mammon Realty (MR), a Maryland corporation, submits this letter of intent (LOI) to Smithco (Seller) so as to confirm its interest in proceeding with Seller toward the negotiation

---

[42] More detailed confidentiality clauses may include duration, identify type of information that is confidential, purposes for which the parties may use the information, etc. *See* Gosfield, *supra* n. 39, at 158–59.

[43] Our thanks to Howard Nagelberg of Barack Ferrazzano Kirschbaum Perlman & Nagelberg LLC, Chicago, IL for supplying the letter on which this sample is based.

and execution of a binding purchase agreement for the property described above on the following basis:

[then, describing terms that were discussed but not finalized regarding, for example, price, earnest money, due diligence, warranties, inspections, closing date, and surveys and ending]

<u>Legal Effect</u>: As indicated above, this LOI is not intended to serve as a binding agreement of purchase and sale, or to otherwise obligate Seller to sell or MR to purchase the Property. This LOI is instead intended only to confirm the mutual interest of Seller and MR in proceeding with further negotiations toward attempting to enter into a definitive and binding Purchase Agreement, and neither party is obligated to sell or purchase the Property or to negotiate exclusively with the other party unless and until such definitive and binding Purchase Agreement is in fact finalized and bilaterally executed.

## 2. Letters of Agreement

Unlike a letter of intent, what we will call a letter of agreement is one that is intended to bind the signatories to the terms in the letter. It is a fully enforceable agreement.[44] The parties may use this form of binding agreement if their agreement does not involve lengthy terms, as a means of formalizing an informal negotiating process, or, if the parties are under time pressure, to save time. The letter of agreement does not include the components of the more typical contract explained above in Part B. Instead, the drafter should explain the purpose of the letter (to commit their agreement to writing), list all of the terms of the agreement, which should be sufficient to implement an enforceable contract, and request that if the other party agrees to the terms, the other party sign a copy and return it to the sender. Thus, each contracting party has a copy signed by both. The parties may intend to execute a more formal contract, but that step is not necessary.

The following is an example of a letter of agreement.

---

[44] *See Teachers Ins., supra* n. 39, 670 F. Supp. at 498.

**The Printmaker, Inc.**
**715 North Avenue**
**Suite 300**
**Lakeview, Atl. 00011**

July 15, 20___

Robert Belister, President
Belister Computer Graphics, Inc.
16 West Street
Lakeview, Atl. 00607

Dear Bob:

You asked me to draft a written record of the agreement between our respective companies on pre-press and printing work for Midwest Publishing Co. These are the terms of our agreement.

1. BCG will scan materials provided by Printmaker, produce page proofs and provide other pre-press and printing services as requested.

2. BCG will cooperate with us in making presentations to Midwest Publishing Co.

3. BCG will bill us for services provided on a job-by-job basis at the rates set forth on the discounted price list that you have furnished to us and which is attached to this agreement. Printmaker will pay your invoices within ten days after the receipt of payment from Midwest Publishing Co. Printmaker will be responsible for billing and collecting payments from Midwest Publishing Co.

4. Both Printmaker and BCG will keep confidential the terms of the arrangements with Midwest Publishing Co.

5. BCG will make available for our use at your Damen Street facility an area sufficiently large to accommodate two computer work stations and two Printmaker representatives on a regular, daily basis.

6. BCG will be responsible for paying and supervising its own employees and Printmaker will likewise be responsible for its employees.

7. BCG will not provide pre-press or printing services to Midwest Publishing Co. during the terms of this arrangement and for a period of two years thereafter, except through Printmaker.

8. This agreement will remain in effect through December 31, 20__, by which time we will decide jointly whether the agreement should be modified, extended or terminated.

If I have accurately memorialized our negotiations, please sign a copy of this letter signifying your agreement and intent to be bound and return it to me for our file. We will then send the first materials to be scanned.

Sincerely,

Adrian Foster
President[45]

Agreed:
Belister Computer Graphics, Inc.

By _____
Robert Belister, President

## 3. Letters of Understanding

In between a letter of intent and a contractual letter agreement is what we will call a letter of understanding.[46] In this type of letter, the parties document and sign their agreement to certain agreed terms and, understanding that the agreement is incomplete, they bind themselves to continue working towards a final agreement. The purpose of this letter is to allow the parties to begin acting on the contract in reliance on the agreed terms.[47]

The letter may begin by the writer acknowledging that the parties are working diligently to complete their agreement and to draft a final contract. Until that time, the parties each wish to implement the terms to which they have already agreed. The parties thus agree that each will perform the listed steps, such as, the seller will ship 200 posters to the buyer by a specified date.

---

[45] Again we are indebted to Tom Morsch for the letter on which this sample is based.

[46] This type of agreement has also been called a binding preliminary commitment. *Teachers Ins., supra* n. 39, 670 F. Supp. at 498.

[47] Some attorneys advise their clients against this type of agreement, and do not use them in connection with certain types of agreements. They use them only if the performance of the contract can be halted without significant repercussions to any of the parties.

The writer should then explicitly limit the parties' liabilities and indemnifications to that agreed performance. The final paragraph should then supply a specific date by which the agreement will expire if the parties have not executed a final agreement by that time, and state that the terms of the final agreement, when executed, will supplant the terms in the letter.

The following paragraphs combine the parties' intent not to be bound with a statement of the provisions to which they will be bound.[48]

> This letter is intended only to express the interest of the parties to purchase and sell the property. Except as set forth below, neither buyer nor seller is legally obligated to purchase or sell the property unless and until the contract is executed and delivered by the parties. The parties acknowledge that this nonbinding letter of interest does not address all essential terms of the contract and that such essential terms will be the subject of further negotiation.
>
> Notwithstanding the foregoing, the following provisions are intended by the parties to be a legally binding agreement and are made in consideration of one another: Seller acknowledges that buyer has incurred and will incur substantial expense in performing its preliminary underwriting and investigations concerning the property. In consideration of this acknowledgment, seller agrees not to solicit, entertain or accept any formal or informal offers to purchase the property, or any part thereof, until the first to occur of (a) mutual written revocation of this letter by both buyer and seller; or (b) written disapproval of the purchase of the property by buyer during the inspection period.

## F. SPECIAL CONCERNS

### 1. Ambiguity and Rules of Construction

Ambiguous terms are one of the main causes of contract litigation. Like other legal documents, contracts are interpreted to

---

[48] Our thanks again to Howard Nagelberg for the letter from which this sample was taken.

implement the parties' intent. Where the language is unambiguous, the parties' intent will be determined from the language as written (by its plain meaning without extrinsic evidence, or by the meaning as defined in the contract). In contract law, admission of evidence extrinsic to the contract is controlled by the parol evidence rule and its exceptions. Under the parol evidence rule, courts will use extrinsic evidence to interpret ambiguous wording in order to determine the parties' intent. The traditional rule, however, is that parol evidence is inadmissible if it will contradict the written terms of the contract. Where the court cannot determine intent, ambiguous language will be interpreted against the drafter.[49] Thus, it is especially important for the drafter to avoid ambiguity. See Chapter 11, Section C for advice on how to avoid ambiguity, for example, by using tabulation.

The canons of construction apply to interpretation of contracts. Two of the more commonly used canons are 1) *ejusdem generis* (of the same genus or class), which is used to interpret a catch-all phrase that follows a specific enumeration of items and requires an interpretation similar to the specified terms, and 2) *expressio unius, exclusio alterius* (expression of one thing excludes another), usually just known as *expressio unius*, which is used to limit a list of specific items to include only what is mentioned. Under *expressio unius*, if a contract term provides that an employer will reimburse an employee's travel expenses of hotels, meals, transportation, and business calls, the employee will not be reimbursed for personal calls home to his family. However, suppose the list of reimbursable expenses ended with the phrase, "and other travel expenses." Given that language, a court might refer to *ejusdem generis* to determine whether the employee could include in his expenses his calls home and the entrance fee for use of the hotel health club on the theory that they are similar in nature to the listed reimbursable expenses.

Courts also use other principles of contract interpretation to interpret disputed language. For example, the Uniform Commercial Code recognizes course of dealing and usage of the trade or

---

[49] Some courts, however, do not apply this rule of interpretation if both parties are commercially sophisticated and represented by counsel, *see, e.g., Beanstalk Group, Inc. v. AM Gen. Corp.*, 283 F.3d 856 (7th Cir. 2002), or if the parties actively negotiated the agreement, *see, e.g., Herring v. Teradyne, Inc.*, 256 F. Supp.2d 1118, 1126 (S.D. Calif. 2002).

of the locality as factors that can explain or supply terms of an agreement. Thus, courts would recognize the custom in certain agricultural counties that leases of farm lands begin on March 1st, unless the parties agree otherwise.

Under another principle, a court will not interpret language in a way that renders a contract term meaningless. In one case a court was required to interpret the term "administrative discharge" in an employment agreement ("employee forfeits his bonus if employee is terminated before the time bonuses are paid unless termination resulted from administrative discharge"). The employer argued that under the employee's definition of the term as "a supervisor's decision to terminate a person's employment," all terminations would be administrative discharges. The employer argued that this definition was incorrect because it rendered the word "administrative" meaningless. However, the court held that the employee's interpretation did not render the term meaningless because the employee could have been terminated in other ways, for example, by a constructive discharge.

Another interpretive rule requires that a contract be read as a whole to determine the parties' intent, that is, sentences and terms of the contract should not be read in isolation. An example involves litigation over whether language in an employment contract obligated the employer to pay into an employee's employer-funded pension plan for the years that the employer had paid into that employee's union fund during the time that the employee had been a union member. The employer argued that it was obligated to pay into the pension plan only for the more limited time dating from the time the employee had assumed his managerial job and had terminated his union membership. Language in one section of the contract, read in isolation, could have been interpreted to require the employer to pay for the longer period of employment. However, the court, reading the contract as a whole, rejected that interpretation because it would have conflicted with other contractual language that clearly relieved the employer from double contributions towards an employee's pension.

Finally, when contract provisions are inconsistent, specific terms control over general terms. So, for example, if one section of a lease provides generally for a landlord to make repairs, but another section relieves the landlord from the responsibility to repair appliances broken by the tenant, the terms of the more specific section for appliances would prevail if the tenant broke an appliance like a dishwasher.

## 2. Plain Language Statutes

Several states have enacted what are called plain language statutes that apply to consumer and insurance contracts. Moreover, some state bar associations have created plain language committees to foster clear writing in legal documents generally.[50] The plain language statutes codify drafting rules in order to improve the readability of consumer contracts and to save time and money lost in litigation because of poorly drafted contracts. The New York Plain Language Law is probably the best known.[51] It requires that residential leases, and leases and sales of personal property used "for personal, family or household purposes" where the agreements do not involve "amounts in excess of fifty thousand dollars," be "written in a clear and coherent manner using words with common and everyday meanings." The statute also requires that a contract be "appropriately divided and captioned by its various sections."[52]

Other statutes impose readability formulas that impose specific limits on sentence and word length, the latter by limiting the number of syllables permitted in a word. These statutes may also specify the size of type in which contracts, or specified parts of contracts, must be printed; require a table of contents or index for long contracts; and specify size of margins. The New York Insurance Code imposes these additional requirements on insurance contracts and requires that those contracts be approved by the superintendent of insurance.[53]

If you are drafting a contract to satisfy a readability formula, consider using active voice (passive voice sentences are longer than sentences written in active voice), editing out unneeded

---

[50] Joseph Kimble, *Plain English: A Charter for Clear Writing* 9 Thomas M. Cooley L. Rev. 1, 2 (1992). Our thanks to Joe Kimble for supplying information about the Plain English movement.

[51] N.Y. Gen. Oblig. L. §5-702(a) (McKinney 2001).

[52] *Id.*

[53] N.Y. Ins. L. §3102(c) (McKinney 2006).

words such as modifiers, and shortening your sentences. Also consider using tabulation, because each item in the tabulated list is considered a separate sentence.[54]

——————————————— *Exercise 14.7* ———————————————

*Rewrite the following provisions to correct ambiguities, wordiness, poor use of words of authority, and other confusing language.*

**A.** *From a contract for sale of a home:*

If said condition report [from a prior inspection of the house] reveals any structural, mechanical, and electrical defects for which the cost of correcting shall exceed $1,000.00, the Seller shall have the following options, to wit: (1) effecting the necessary correction of said defects, (2) negotiating the cost of correcting said defects, (c) a declaration that said agreement is null and void, and buyer's deposit shall be refunded.

**B.** *From Articles of Incorporation:*

During the period of five years commencing with the date of incorporation the Directors shall have authority to allot and/or otherwise dispose of any shares of the Company up to the total amount which shall remain unissued to such persons and for such consideration and upon such terms and conditions as they may determine.

**C.** *From a lease:*

If any sums payable as rent to the landlord under this lease shall not be paid to the landlord by the time of the due date, which is the first of each month, the same shall be payable with 5% interest before the 5th of the month.

**D.** *From a deed:*

Title to the land shall remain in the said Railway Co. its successors and assigns as provided in Exhibit 'A', as long as the same shall be used for the purposes enumerated therein, and that in case it should be abandoned for such uses according to the terms of said Exhibit 'A',

———————————

[54] Burnham, *supra* n.4, at 203. See also Chapter 12, Document Design.

then and in that event the title to said land shall revert to the City of Falls City, the donor of said land under the terms aforesaid.

### E. *From a lease:*

The landlord shall not abuse the right of access to the tenant's apartment or use it to harass the tenant. Except where access shall be authorized by subsections (f) and (g) above, the landlord shall give notice to the tenant, and such notice shall be provided to each unit, of landlord's intent to enter in no less than two days.

### F. *From a creditor's security agreement:*

"Creditor's (Van Supply Co.) security interest shall be in all inventory, including but not limited to agricultural chemicals, fertilizers, and fertilizer materials sold to debtor by Van Supply Co. whether now owned or debtor shall hereafter acquire."

Does the creditor's security interest extend to all the debtor's inventory or only to inventory sold to the debtor by Van Supply Co.?

### G. *From a stock purchase contract between parties, neither of which was domiciled in Illinois, but each of which was subject to personal jurisdiction in Illinois and Missouri, is the forum selection clause mandatory or permissive? The clause provides:*

"This agreement shall be governed by and construed and enforced in accord with the laws of the State of Illinois [this is the choice of law clause], and the parties consent to jurisdiction in the state courts of Illinois [this is the forum selection clause]."

The plaintiff files as a diversity action in federal court in Illinois.

—————————— *Assignment 14.1* ——————————

*Your client is Joe Rodriguez. For the past thirty years, Joe's uncle Alex owned a small apartment building at 100 Windy Lane that has ten apartments in a neighborhood near a university. When Joe's uncle died, Joe inherited the apartment building and decided to manage the building himself. Joe recently read the standard lease agreement that his uncle used, and he found that it is outdated. Joe asked you to draft a new standard lease agreement form that he can use when renting out his apartments.*

*Joe realizes that law constrains the terms that he can put into a lease, but, to the extent possible, he would like you to fulfill the following preferences.*

- Joe would like to have tenants commit to at least one year, but he is otherwise indifferent to the type of tenancy the lease creates and would like to be flexible.
- Joe's uncle has typically attracted young professionals that do not have pets and tend to be quiet tenants. Joe would like to continue this trend, and therefore requests that the lease agreement includes provisions prohibiting undergraduate students from occupancy and restricting pets and noise.
- Joe is very particular about the tenants he chooses, and therefore he wants to restrict the ability of tenants to sublet or assign their apartments without Joe's consent.
- Joe has heard from his uncle about the problem of holdover tenants, and so he would like the lease to state that incoming tenants, rather than Joe, are responsible for dealing with holdover tenants.
- Although Joe will ensure that apartments are habitable when new tenants arrive, in order to avoid any liability, he would like the lease agreement to waive the tenants' right to bring suit for his breach of the covenant of habitability, such that the tenants take their apartments "as is."
- Joe would like to include a forfeiture clause, so that he can terminate the lease upon the breach of any of the tenant's covenants, like payment of rent.
- Joe wants to require 30 days' notice that tenants are vacating their apartments, and he also would like to waive his duty of mitigation to tenants that terminate their leases.

*Please draft Joe's lease agreement to comply with state and local law. In addition to the terms that Joe mentions above, be sure to include other pertinent information, such as identification of the parties and premises, a provision for rent, a provision for security deposits, and provisions for the various duties and rights of the parties. Provide your own terms where needed.*

*Additionally, Joe would like an explanation of the lease agreement. Therefore, please write to Joe to provide an explanation of the following: the extent to which the law constrained the way you drafted the provision; the extent to which you diverged from Joe's preferences and why; other relevant decisions you made in drafting the provision, particularly discussing any material provisions that Joe can change if he would like.*

--- *Assignment 14.2* ---

*This assignment asks you to negotiate and draft a separation agreement for Alan and Aliza Roth. The Roths have three minor children, all living at home. They have agreed to divorce and need to decide custody and visitation, as well as distribution of their property. They live in the mythical state of Pacifica.*

*Your professor will either ask you to choose a negotiating partner or will assign partners. One partner will represent Aliza Roth and the other will represent Alan Roth. Once you know whether you are representing Alan or Aliza, your professor will give you a confidential summary of facts gathered at an initial interview with your client. You will then negotiate and draft the agreement using only these facts and the materials that follow.*

*Before beginning negotiations, read the materials and prepare a tentative outline of the agreement you would like to reach for your client. Then begin negotiations, continuing until you have reached agreement on all terms. Finally, draft the separation agreement together.*

*Your agreement should begin with an introductory clause, recitals, and a separation clause. Samples are provided in this assignment—they are substantively correct, but need to be adapted for our facts and revised for clarity, precision, and legalese.*

*The rest of your agreement will consist of the provisions listed below in alphabetical order. When you draft your agreement, put them in more appropriate and useful order—grouping related provisions and considering importance and chronology as you organize.*

*Attorney's Fees*
*Applicable Law*
*Arbitration*
*Child Support*
*College Education Expenses*
*Custody*
*Division of Debt*
*Income Taxes*
*Life Insurance*
*Maintenance*
*Medical Insurance for Children*
*Medical Insurance for the Wife*

*Property Division*
*Modification*
*Notices*
*Partial Invalidity: Severability*
*Property Settlement*
*Remedies for Breach*
*Visitation Rights*
*Visitation Schedule*
*Signatures*

*Finally, your agreement must comport with the relevant portions of the Pacifica Domestic Relations Law, provided here.*

## SAMPLE INTRODUCTION, RECITALS, AND SEPARATION CLAUSE

This Settlement Agreement for the dissolution of the marriage of John Doe and Susan Doe, is entered into as of April 5, _____, by John Doe ("Husband") and Susan Doe ("Wife").

WHEREAS, the parties were married in Chicago, Illinois on January 2, _____, and have 3 minor children, Amy, born on January 26, _____, Beth, born on February 17, _____, and Will, born on March 17, _____.

WHEREAS, as a result of disputes and serious differences that have caused the marriage of the parties to breakdown irretrievably, the parties separated on October 26, 20__, and are now living apart. They intend to continue to remain permanently apart.

WHEREAS, the parties want to settle by agreement their affairs, including custody and support of their minor children, spousal support and maintenance, the division of their joint and separate property, and any other claims and demands each might have against the other by reason of marriage.

WHEREAS, each party has fully disclosed the extent of their estate, income, and financial prospects and has been fully informed concerning the extent of the estate, income, and financial prospects of the other, as appears in the sworn financial statements attached as Exhibits to this agreement. Each party has been represented in the preparation of this agreement by independent counsel. Each has been fully advised of his or her rights by such counsel. Each party considers the terms of this agreement to be fair and reasonable.

WHEREAS, the parties agree to dissolve the marriage in an action pending in court that bears docket number 12345678.

NOW THEREFORE, in consideration of the promises and the mutual promise herein contained, the parties hereby agree as follows:

### 1. Separation

Each party shall live separately from the other for the remainder of his or her life at any place or places that he or she may choose. Neither party shall annoy, harass, molest, threaten, injure, or interfere with the other party in any manner whatsoever, or seek to induce the other to cohabit or reside with him or her by any legal or other proceedings or by any manner whatsoever. Each party shall have the right to engage in any employment, business, profession, or any other activity without interference from the other party, in any manner he or she considers advisable for his or her sole use and benefit.

## RELEVANT STATUTORY PROVISIONS

### Pac. Dom. Rel. § 236(A). In General

. . . .

3.   Agreement of the parties. An agreement by the parties, made before or during the marriage, shall be valid and enforceable in a matrimonial action if such agreement is in writing, subscribed by the parties, and acknowledged or proven in the manner required to entitle a deed to be recorded. Such an agreement may include (1) a contract to make a testamentary provision of any kind, or a waiver of any right to elect against the provisions of a will; (2) provision for the ownership, division or distribution of separate and marital property; (3) provision for the amount and duration of maintenance or other terms and conditions of the marriage relationship, provided that such terms were fair and reasonable at the time of the making of the agreement and are not unconscionable at the time of entry of final judgment; (4) provision for the custody, visitation, care, education and maintenance of any child of the parties, subject to the provisions of section two hundred forty and two hundred and forty-one of this chapter, and (5) provision for alternative dispute resolution.

. . . .

# Pac. Dom. Rel. § 236(D). Equitable Distribution of Marital Property

. . . .

4.   The term "marital property" shall mean all property acquired by either or both spouses during the marriage and before the execution of a separation agreement or the commencement of a matrimonial action, regardless of the form in which title is held, except as otherwise provided in an agreement pursuant to subdivision three of Subpart (A) above.

5.   Disposition of property in certain matrimonial actions.

a.   Except where the parties have provided in an agreement for the disposition of their property pursuant to subdivision three of Subpart (A) above, the court, in an action wherein all or part of the relief granted is divorce, or the dissolution, annulment or declaration of the nullity of a marriage, and in proceedings to obtain a distribution of marital property following a foreign judgment of divorce, shall determine the respective rights of the parties in their separate or marital property, and shall provide for the disposition thereof in the final judgment.

b.   Separate property shall remain such.

c.   Marital property shall be distributed equitably between the parties, considering the circumstances of the case and of the respective parties.

d.   In determining an equitable disposition of property under paragraph c, the court shall consider:

(1)   the income and property of each party at the time of marriage, and at the time of the commencement of the action;

(2)   the duration of the marriage and the age and health of both parties;

(3)   the loss of inheritance and pension rights upon dissolution of the marriage as of the date of dissolution;

(4)   any award of maintenance;

(5)   any equitable claim to, interest in, or direct or indirect contribution made to the acquisition of such marital property by the party not having title, including joint efforts or expenditures and contributions and services as a spouse, parent, wage earner and homemaker, and to the career or career potential of the other party;

(6)   the liquid or non-liquid character of all marital property;

(7)   the probable future financial circumstances of each party;

(8)   the tax consequences to each party;

(9)   any other factor which the court shall expressly find to be just and proper.

## Pac. Dom. Rel. § 236(E). Distributive Award

. . . .

6.   The term "distributive award" shall mean payments provided for in a valid agreement between the parties or awarded by the court, in lieu of or to supplement, facilitate or effectuate the division or distribution of property where authorized in a matrimonial action, and payable either in a lump sum or over a period of time in fixed amounts. Distributive awards shall not include payments which are treated as ordinary income to the recipient under the provisions of the United States Internal Revenue Code.

## Pac. Dom. Rel. § 236(F). Maintenance

a.   The term "maintenance" shall mean payments provided for in a valid agreement between the parties or awarded by the court ... to be paid at fixed intervals for a definite or indefinite period of time, but an award of maintenance shall terminate upon the death of either party or upon the recipient's valid or invalid marriage unless the parties explicitly provide by agreement that maintenance will continue after the death of payor spouse.

. . . .

6.   Maintenance.

a.   Except where the parties have entered into an agreement pursuant to subdivision three of this part providing for maintenance, in any matrimonial action the court may order temporary maintenance or maintenance in such amount as justice requires . . . .

## Pac. Dom. Rel. § 240. Child Support

. . . .

(b)   For purposes of this part, the following definitions shall be used:

. . . .

(1)  "Basic child support obligation" shall mean the sum derived by adding the amounts determined by the application of subparagraphs two and three of paragraph (c) of this subdivision except as increased pursuant to subparagraphs four, five, six and seven of such paragraph.

(2)  "Child support" shall mean a sum to be paid pursuant to court order or decree by either or both parents or pursuant to a valid agreement between the parties for care, maintenance and education of any unemancipated child under the age of twenty-one years.

(3)  "Child support percentage" shall mean:

(i)  seventeen percent of the combined parental income for one child;

(ii)  twenty-five percent of the combined parental income for two children;

(iii)  twenty-nine percent of the combined parental income for three children;

(iv)  thirty-one percent of the combined parental income for four children; and

(v)  no less than thirty-five percent of the combined parental income for five or more children.

(4)  "Combined parental income" shall mean the sum of the income of both parents.

(5)  "Income" shall mean, but shall not be limited to, the sum of the amounts determined by the application of clause (i) of this subparagraph reduced by the amount determined by the application of clause (ii) of this subparagraph:

(i)  gross (total) income as should have been or should be reported in the most recent federal income tax return.

(ii)  alimony or maintenance actually paid or to be paid to a spouse that is a party to the instant action.

. . .

(c)  The amount of the basic child support obligation shall be determined in accordance with the provision of this paragraph:

(1)  The court shall determine the combined parental income.

(2)  The court shall multiply the combined parental income by the appropriate child support percentage and such amount shall be prorated in the same proportion as each parent's income is to the combined parental income.

(h)   A validly executed agreement or stipulation voluntarily entered into between the parties after the effective date of this subdivision presented to the court for incorporation in an order or judgment shall include a provision stating that the parties have been advised of the provisions of this subdivision, and that the basic child support obligation provided for therein would presumptively result in the correct amount of child support to be awarded. In the event that such agreement or stipulation deviates from the basic child support obligation, the agreement or stipulation must specify the amount that such basic child support obligation would have been and the reason or reasons that such agreement or stipulation does not provide for payment of that amount. Nothing contained in this subdivision shall be construed to alter the rights of the parties to voluntarily enter into validly executed agreements or stipulations which deviate from the basic child support obligation provided such agreements or stipulations comply with the provisions of this paragraph.

### Pac. Dom. Rel. § 241. Visitation

. . . .

(2)  Parents Who Reside 100 Miles or Less Apart

(a)   The term "custodial parent" shall mean a parent to whom custody of a child or children is granted by a valid agreement between the parties or by an order or decree of a court. In the event of joint custody, "custodial parent" shall mean a parent with residential custody.

(b)   If the non-custodial parent resides 100 miles or less from the primary residence of the child, the non-custodial parent shall have the right to possession of the child as follows:

(1)   on weekends beginning at 6 p.m. on the first, third, and fifth Friday of each month and ending at 6 p.m. on the following Sunday or, at the custodial parent's election made before or at the time of the rendition of the original or modification order, and as specified in the original or modification order, beginning at the time the child's school is regularly dismissed and ending at 6 p.m. on the following Sunday; and

(2)   on Wednesdays of each week during the regular school term beginning at 6 p.m. and ending at 8 p.m., or, at the custodial parent's election made before or at the time of the rendition of the original or modification order, beginning at the time the child's school is regularly dismissed and ending at the time the child's

school resumes, unless the court finds that visitation under this subdivision is not in the best interest of the child.

(c)   The following provisions govern visitation of the child for vacations and holidays and supersede conflicting weekend or Wednesday periods of possession. The custodial parent and the non-custodial parent shall have rights of custody of the child as follows:

(1)   the custodial parent shall have possession in even-numbered years, beginning at 6 p.m. on the day the child is dismissed from school for the school's spring and winter vacation and ending at 6 p.m. on the day before school resumes after that vacation, and the non-custodial parent shall have possession for the same period in odd-numbered years;

(2)   if a custodial parent:

(A)   gives the non-custodial parent written notice by April 1 of each year specifying an extended period or periods of summer possession, the custodial parent shall have possession of the child for 30 days beginning not earlier than the day after the child's school is dismissed for the summer vacation and ending not later than seven days before school resumes at the end of the summer vacation, to be exercised in not more than two separate periods of at least seven consecutive days each; or

(B)   does not give the non-custodial parent written notice by April 1 of each year specifying an extended period or periods of summer possession, the custodial parent shall have possession of the child for 30 consecutive days beginning at 6 p.m. on July 1 and ending at 6 p.m. on July 31;

(3)   if the non-custodial parent gives the custodial parent written notice by April 15 of each year, the non-custodial parent shall have possession of the child on any one weekend beginning Friday at 6 p.m. and ending at 6 p.m. on the following Sunday during one period of possession by the custodial parent under Subdivision (2), provided that the non-custodial parent picks up the child from the custodial parent and returns the child to the same place; and

(4)   if the non-custodial parent gives the custodial parent written notice by April 15 of each year or gives the custodial parent 14 days' written notice on or after April 16 of each year, the non-custodial parent may designate one weekend beginning not

earlier than the day after the child's school is dismissed for the summer vacation and ending not later than seven days before school resumes at the end of the summer vacation, during which an otherwise scheduled weekend period of possession by the custodial parent will not take place, provided that the weekend designated does not interfere with the custodial parent's period or periods of extended summer possession or with Father's Day if the custodial parent is the father of the child.

(d)   If a weekend period of possession of the custodial parent coincides with a school holiday during the regular school term or with a federal, state, or local holiday during the summer months in which school is not in session, the weekend possession shall end at 6 p.m. on a Monday holiday or school holiday or shall begin at 6 p.m. Thursday for a Friday holiday or school holiday, as applicable.

(e)   A validly executed agreement or stipulation voluntarily entered into between the parties after the effective date of this subdivision presented to the court for incorporation in an order or judgment shall include a provision stating that the parties have been advised on the provisions of this subdivision. In the event that such agreement or stipulation deviates from the visitation provisions in this section, the agreement or stipulation must specify that such agreement or stipulation deviates from these provisions. Nothing contained in this subdivision shall be construed to alter the rights of the parties to voluntarily enter into validly executed agreements or stipulations which deviate from the visitation provisions, provided such agreements or stipulations comply with the provisions of this paragraph.

## Pac. Dom. Rel. § 242. Alternative Dispute Resolution

### (A)  Arbitration Procedures.

On written agreement of the parties, the court may refer a suit for dissolution of a marriage to arbitration. The agreement must state whether the arbitration is binding or nonbinding.

### (B)  Mediation Procedures.

On the written agreement of the parties or on the court's own motion, the court may refer a suit for dissolution of a marriage to mediation.

## —————— *Assignment 14.3* ——————

A. *Before becoming your client, Mr. Jonathan Johns purchased an undeveloped landlocked parcel of land. He now wants you to negotiate an easement* with the neighboring land owner, Ms. Eloise Burns, allowing him a right of way across Burns' property to the state road.

What facts do you need to get from Mr. Johns about what he wants to achieve with the easement? Which "what if's" do you want him to consider?

Write up a draft of the easement to present to Ms. Burns.

**B.** Jonathan Johns, who is an artist, holds a valid copyright on five botanical drawings. He is contemplating a commercial venture creating derivatives of these drawings, such as posters and note cards. Your client is the Lakeview Art Center, a small art center in the village of Lakeview, a suburb of a large city. The Center's gift shop is expanding its stock and is interested in creating its own line of items, such as note cards, to sell in the gift shop. The manager Ms. Eloise Burns thinks that Mr. Johns' drawings will sell well, and wants you to negotiate a licensing agreement for the shop to create a line of merchandise, suitable for a small museum gift shop, featuring reproductions of Mr. Johns' drawings.

What other facts do you need to get from Ms. Burns about her plans?

Write up a draft of a license agreement to present to Mr. Johns and his attorney.

**C.** Jonathan Johns wants to retain you as his attorney. Write a retention contract for this purpose for either the Part A or B issue. See William C. Becker, The Client Retention Agreement—The Engagement Letter, 23 *Akron L. Rev.* 323 (1990), which may be useful.

# Chapter 15

# *RULE-MAKING: WILLS*

---

## A. IN GENERAL

### 1. Purpose

A will is a document in which a person leaves instructions about how her property is to be distributed at her death and how that distribution is to be administered. People who make valid wills are known as testators.[1] If a person does not leave a will or the will is not valid, in whole or in part, we say that person dies intestate or partially intestate. In that case, that person's property is distributed according to state intestacy statutes, as is any property not included in the will. A will can be a very simple or a very complex document, and it may be written by the testator herself or by an attorney, or by any other person competent to do so. However, those testators who have accumulated enough wealth so that their estate is subject to estate taxes often use attorneys to draft sophisticated estate plans. They use lifetime and testamentary trusts and other estate planning tools in addition to more complex wills in order to minimize taxes.[2] Lawyers who draft those estate planning documents must be very familiar with federal and state estate, inheritance, and gift tax codes. In this chapter we will discuss only the basic simple will and not those more complex documents that require trusts and tax planning.

---

[1] In older cases, a male was called a testator and a female was called a testatrix. Some lawyers may still use the different suffix to show gender.

[2] One sample will, described as a simple will for an uncomplicated estate, included a trust and some provisions to minimize estate taxes, and ran to 25 pages. ABA Comm. on Est. Plan. and Drafting, *A Sample Simple Will*, 27 The Practical Lawyer 21 (Mar. 1, 1981).

## 2. Audience

A will has a succession of audiences. The first audience for the drafter to consider is the testator. The drafter should accommodate the testator in two ways. First, the drafter should produce a will that is not only substantively correct and complete, but one that is also understandable to the testator-client and preferably one with which the testator feels comfortable, especially because the testator communicates through the will to beneficiaries and administrators. This goal may certainly be achieved for the more simple wills that do not involve intricate estate planning. Yet to most testators, their will as drafted may as well be in a foreign language. Even though the will is the testator's document, signed by the testator as her own, most testators recognize little of their own voice in the document. Second, the drafter should produce a will that accurately conveys the testator's wishes.

In addition to the testator, the testator's family and other beneficiaries are an important audience. The family will most likely read the will either before or after the testator's death. The testator may even want to communicate with her family and friends by means of her will after her death. For example, the testator may request or require beneficiaries to use their gifts in particular ways, or may explain why certain family members were disinherited. The tone of the will can influence the beneficiaries' attitude towards the testator and can be important in preserving family harmony. For example, rather than simply disinheriting or virtually disinheriting one child in favor of another, the will could say, "Although I love my children equally, my daughter X is now independently wealthy, and has only one dependent. I leave her my personal effects. My son Y is in greater need, and I leave the rest to him." On the other hand, your client may prefer to explain these gifts to her children privately and omit the explanations from the will. A will becomes a public document and your client may not want to include private information in a document of public record.

Another audience for wills is the administrator, an individual or a corporate institution that is named as the executor. If the testator's will includes a trust or trusts, the trustee is also an audience for the will. Individual executors and trustees may be laymen who are unfamiliar with legal jargon in general and wills jargon in particular. If the will is a complicated one, the administrators will of course need a lawyer to advise them, but a simple will should be written as clearly as possible so the executor and trustee can administer the will and distribute the testator's property.

In addition to the executor and trustee, a later audience to consider for a will is the probate judge. The judge must enter the will for probate and approve its administration. If the will is not well drafted, or its language is ambiguous, the administrator may bring a suit for the court to interpret the will. Moreover, disappointed heirs may contest the will. The drafter's challenge is to prepare a will that is legally correct and comprehensible to its several potential audiences.

## B. COMPONENTS

The format of a will varies depending on the drafter's custom, the simplicity or complexity of the will, and the simplicity or complexity of trusts, if any are included in the will. However, all wills should include an introduction that identifies the document as a will and that identifies the testator; dispositive provisions that identify the testator's property and the beneficiaries of that property; and administrative provisions that identify the executor, the guardian of the testator's children, if the testator's children are minors or otherwise require a guardian, and the trustee, if the will includes testamentary trusts. Wills often also enumerate the administrators' powers, and the terms by which they are to distribute the testator's property. Finally, wills must be signed by the testator and witnesses. If the will is a handwritten will in a jurisdiction that recognizes holographic wills, no witnesses are necessary. It is good practice for a witnessed will also to include a self-proving affidavit (see Section B(4) below).

## 1. Introduction

Typically, a will begins with introductory information identifying the testator and the document. The older term for this introduction is the exordium. Now, this part may be called the preamble,[3] the introduction, or even the overture.[4] In this

---

[3] *See, e.g.,* Leonard Levin, *A Student's Guide to Will Drafting* 29 (M. Bender 1987).

[4] Thomas L. Shaffer, Carol Ann Mooney & Amy Jo Boettcher, *The Planning and Drafting of Wills and Trusts* 174 (Foundation Press 4th ed. 2000).

introductory part, the testator also typically revokes all her previous wills and codicils (documents that amend wills).

A sample introduction in plain English looks like this:

> ## Will of Faith Jones
>
> I, Faith Jones, of Cook County, Illinois, declare this to be my Will and revoke all my prior wills and codicils.[5]

The more traditional opening of a will—still seen in many wills—often looks like this:

> In the name of God, amen. I, Faith Jones residing in Cook County, Illinois, being of sound and disposing mind hereby declare, make, and publish this as my last will and testament, hereby revoking all prior wills and codicils by me heretobefore made.

Other than the testator's name and domicile none of the language in the second example is needed for the will to be legally valid. The will is valid without the revocation clause, but the clause avoids confusion if the testator has an earlier will. A will is a personal document, however, and if your client wishes a more personal introduction—for example, one that expresses her religious faith— then by all means allow her to have it. You need not include an old fashioned religious opening out of tradition alone, however, and you need not include excess words such as "hereby declare, make, and publish," which have no added legal effect.

It is good practice to follow the introductory paragraph with one that straightforwardly identifies the testator's family by their individual names. Some drafters instead identify family members with definitions. For example, they may say, "'My children' means my daughter Jacqueline Jones, my son Ben Jones, and any other children born to my husband and me or adopted by us."

Other drafters use both a paragraph that identifies family and a definition section. So, for example, to identify the testator's spouse and children in a separate paragraph, the will could say

---

[5] The introduction should identify the testator by her formal name, but often also includes the name by which the testator is more generally known.

> I am married to Gabriel Jones whom I hereafter refer to as "my husband." We have two children, a daughter Jacqueline Jones Rivers and a son Ben Jones. References to "my children" are to Jacqueline and Ben. I now have four grandchildren [naming the grandchildren].

A separate definition section may then define other terms in the will, for example, defining the terms "descendants" and "issue" to include the testator's children and all their lineal descending generations, including children by adoption and non-marital children.

There are several legal advantages to providing this information. It identifies the testator's immediate family for purposes of administering the estate, it establishes that the testator knows her family (one of the factors of testamentary capacity), and it allows the testator to refer throughout the will to "husband," "children," "grandchildren," or "descendants." In addition, it names the testator's children and grandchildren for purposes of complying with some states' "pretermitted heir" statutes,[6] and it reminds the attorney to ascertain whether the testator wants to include future adopted or nonmarital children as beneficiaries.

If the will includes class gifts other than to issue and descendants, it should also define those classes. Another important distinction to define is that between a distribution per stirpes and per capita.

---

*Exercise 15.1*

---

*A. Write definitions for per stirpes and per capita distributions that follow the law of your state.*

*B. Write definitions for tangible and intangible personal property.*

---

[6] Pretermitted heir statutes require a testator to name or provide for the testator's children, or to otherwise show that she intended to omit a child. Omitted children receive an intestate share of the testator's estate. Some statutes impose that requirement for both children and grandchildren. Other statutes apply only to children born after the testator executed her will. The purpose of these statutes is to prevent unintended disinheritance.

## 2. Dispositions of the Testator's Property

Many attorneys follow the introduction and definitions with the property dispositions. Gifts of the testator's real property have been traditionally known as devises; gifts of personal property have been traditionally known as bequests. Thus many will forms use the language "I give, devise, and bequeath." The distinction is now unnecessary and a modern will is perfectly valid if the testator says only "I give . . . ." However, unless your client is giving all her property to one person, you should separate out different types of gifts into categories of real property, tangible personal property, and intangible personal property. You should also separate gifts into specific gifts, more general gifts, and a residuary gift (all property not otherwise already disposed of). It is traditional first to devise the testator's real property. If the testator and her spouse own real property as joint tenants with right of survivorship or as tenants by the entireties, or if the testator holds property as a joint tenant with right of survivorship with anyone else, that property goes by the terms of the deed and should not be included as a gift in the will. If the testator is giving all her real property to the person who will be the residuary beneficiary, such as her spouse, then you need not include a specific gift of real property.

A simple disposition of real property may look like this:

> Article 2: If my husband Gabriel Jones survives me by thirty days, I give him my vacation home in Geneva, Atlantis, with all rights associated with the property,[7] and any insurance on the property. If my husband does not survive me by thirty days, my executor is to sell my vacation home and add the proceeds to the residue to be distributed under the terms in Article Six.

Specific gifts of tangible personal property may be written as follows:

---

[7] An example is an easement over neighboring property, although a gift in a will is not necessary for the easement to continue.

Article 3: I give to my sister Deborah Wilson the brass candle sticks and the diamond ring that were our mother's. If my sister does not survive me by thirty days, then I given these items to her eldest living daughter.

Article 4: I give $500 to my neighbor Diane Katz if she survives me.[8]

Article 5: I give $1000 to the Legal Aid Society of Lake City, Atlantis.

The dispositive provisions usually end with a residuary clause. The residue usually comprises the largest share of a person's estate and thus the residuary beneficiary or beneficiaries are usually those who are the most important to the testator.

Article 6: I give all the rest and residue of my estate, real and personal, including the property subject to the testamentary power of appointment given me under the will of my brother Nathaniel Lunt dated August 31, 2001, to my husband if he survives me by thirty days. If my husband does not survive me by thirty days, then I give my residuary estate to the Symphony Society of America.

## 3. Administrative Provisions

The testator should name fiduciaries, that is, those who will administer her estate as her executor, and her trustees, if the will includes any trusts. If the testator has a minor child or children, or children who otherwise require a guardian, she should name a guardian of those children. It is good practice to also name substitute fiduciaries. Some drafters place these provisions before the dispositive paragraphs because of their importance. The will often directs the executor to pay various expenses, debts, and taxes, although the executor is required to pay them anyway. This part of the will for administrative provisions may also specify how the executor is to make these payments, that is, from which

---

[8] If the neighbor does not survive the testator, in most states this gift lapses.

source the payments are to come. The will may also enumerate the fiduciaries' powers. If it does not, the fiduciaries will have the powers provided by state law. The testator may also wish to waive the bond requirement for one or more of the fiduciaries, especially if they are personally known to her.

## 4. Signatures

In all jurisdictions, the testator must sign the will;[9] a number of jurisdictions require the testator to sign the will at the end. Moreover, unless the will is one that is handwritten in a jurisdiction that allows holographic wills, the will also must be signed by witnesses. Although the required signatures alone are sufficient, will forms usually include a sentence before the testator's signature traditionally known as the testimonium, which begins, "In testimony whereof I hereby set my hand . . ." or sometimes "In witness whereof . . ." The testator signs below that sentence.

The witnesses then sign immediately after the testator signs, and they sign below the testator's signature. Although not a requirement, it is good practice for the witnesses to sign an attestation clause, which is a paragraph in which the witnesses attest to the enumerated steps required in that jurisdiction, and indeed in other jurisdictions, to execute a will. The drafter should include an attestation clause because in many jurisdictions an attestation clause provides prima facie evidence of proper execution.

It is also good practice to add a self-proving affidavit to the end of the will. In the affidavit, the testator and the witnesses swear before a notary public that they have fulfilled the specific requirements for execution of the will in that jurisdiction. The testator, witnesses, and notary then sign the affidavit. In many jurisdictions, the affidavit is conclusive on the issue of proper execution. In other jurisdictions, the self-proved affidavit raises a rebuttable presumption of proper execution.

Note that the testator and witnesses will be signing twice, once at the end of the will itself and once in the notarized affidavit,[10] a step that sometimes leads to mistakes in execution if they sign

---

[9] A will may be signed by someone acting for the testator at the testator's request.

[10] This type of affidavit is signed after the will execution has taken place.

only once in the affidavit.[11] It is also possible in some states to use an affidavit form that combines will execution and affidavit so that the testator and witnesses sign only once.

--- *Exercise 15.2* ---

To: Associate

Re: Smith Estate

As you know, our client Joan Smith, an Illinois resident, died a few weeks ago. We will be administering her estate. She left a will, which she executed in 1990. She also executed an addition to her will in 1995 to include some property that hadn't been included in the will, and which she wanted to leave to some nieces. For some reason, this addition (the codicil) wasn't done correctly and, we just learned, isn't valid. That property will go by intestacy.

She also left property as trust property in a small inter vivos trust, and also held some real property in joint tenancy with right of survivorship. The trust beneficiary is her husband, Ted. The beneficiary of her will is her husband also, except for a few other specific gifts to others. He is also her intestate heir. The Smiths had no children.

Ted Smith is the executor and wants to know what property there is and whether it comes by will or by intestacy or by the trust, or otherwise, and to whom it will be given.

Here's a list of the property. Write to Ted Smith and answer his questions. Organize your answer by appropriate categories. Do not just list the property as it appears here.

1. House in Columbus Ohio as joint tenant with sister Jamie Adams with right of survivorship.
2. Jewelry received from Ted Smith, by will to Ted Smith.
3. 1000 shares of stock of IBM in trust.
4. 1000 shares of stock of AT&T in trust.
5. 100 shares of stock of Liz Corp. by will to friend Susan Johns.
6. Vacation home in Wisconsin in joint tenancy with Ted Smith.
7. 3 savings accounts in Bank One by will to Ted Smith.

---

[11] *See, e.g., Will of Ranney*, 589 A.2d 1339 (N.J. 1991).

8. 2 certificates of deposit in NBD Bank by intestacy.
9. Diamond necklace inherited from mother to niece Amy Lee by will.
10. Silver tableware by will to Ted Smith.
11. Trust savings account in NBD bank.
12. 1000 shares of stock of Bank One by will to Ted Smith.
13. Residence in Chicago as tenants by the entireties with Ted Smith.
14. Pearl jewelry inherited from mother to niece Allison Lee by will.
15. Two bond funds by intestacy.
16. Fidelity stockfund by will to sister Jamie Adams.

## 5. Codicils

Codicils are amendments or additions to wills. A codicil can also partially revoke a will. A codicil must be executed with the same formality (or lack of formality if the jurisdiction recognizes holographic wills) as a will. When you draft a codicil you should be careful to identify the will to which it is a codicil, and to identify the articles or paragraphs of the will that you are amending or revoking. If you are adding provisions to the will, label them as additions.

A codicil may begin like this:

> ### Codicil to the Will of Faith Jones
>
> I, Faith Jones of Cook County, Illinois, make this codicil to amend my will of January 1, 2000.
>
> 1. I revoke Article 4 of my will and substitute the following Article 4.
>
> Article 4: I give to my neighbor Diane Katz the four botanical prints by the artist Korling Berg now hanging in my dining room.
>
> 2. I revoke Article 5 of my will and substitute the following Article 5.
>
> Article 5: I give $2000 to the Legal Aid Society of Chicago, Illinois.

A codicil usually ends by the testator ratifying her will in all other respects. Some testators amass several codicils to their wills, labeled, for example, "Third Codicil to the will of Faith Jones." A better practice is to revoke the earlier codicils and incorporate all the changes into one new cumulative codicil.

## C. SAMPLE WILL

Will of Faith Jones[12]

I, Faith Jones, County of Cook, State of Illinois, declare this to be my will. I revoke all wills and codicils previously made.[13]

1. Identifications:

a. I am married to Gabriel Jones. All references to "my husband" are to Gabriel Jones.

b. I have two children, Jacqueline Jones Rivers and Ben Jones. All references to "my daughter" are to Jacqueline Jones Rivers. All references to "my son" are to Ben Jones. All references to "my children" are to my daughter, my son, and to any other children born to or adopted by me. I intentionally do not provide for or include my stepson Craig Jones,[14] who has never accepted me as a parent.

c. I have three grandchildren, Jerome and Kathryn Rivers and Samuel Jones. Samuel Jones was adopted by my son. All references to my grandchildren or to my children's issue or descendants include these three and all other children born to my children or adopted by one of my children while the adopted child was a minor.

2. Payment of Debts: I direct that my executor, named below in paragraph 9, pay out of my estate my funeral expenses, just debts, and expenses of administration as soon as practicable.[15]

3. Gifts of Realty: I give my remainder interest in the home of my mother, Gertrude Joseph, at River Road, Harbor City, Michigan to my husband,[16] if he survives me by thirty days.

---

[12] This is a sample will for an estate that is not subject to estate tax.

[13] This introductory paragraph, traditionally called the exordium, identifies the testator and revokes existing testamentary documents.

[14] The testator may have included this sentence to avoid the state's pretermitted heir statute; however, the explicit disinheritance is not necessary because a step child is not the testator's child or issue. On the other hand, the testator may have intended a final explanation or a final insult, but it is better practice to omit insults, especially from a will.

[15] This is a boilerplate provision.

[16] The testator and her husband may own their own home as tenants by the entireties or joint tenants with right of survivorship. If so, the testator cannot devise her interest and their residence would not be included in the will. If not, the testator will devise her residence, if any, in paragraph 3.

4. Pecuniary Gifts:

a. I give $10,000 to each of my children and grandchildren who survive me by thirty days.

b. I give $10,000 to X College for its general fund.[17]

5. Gifts of Tangible Personal Property:

a. I give the pearl jewelry that I inherited from my maternal grandmother (consisting of necklace, earrings, and pin) and the diamond ring I inherited from my paternal grandmother to my daughter with the wish that she will leave them to her daughter.[18] If my daughter does not survive me, then I give these items to the eldest female issue of either of my children. If no child of mine has female issue, then I give these items to my sister Deborah Wilson.

b. I leave my albums of wild flower photographs to my neighbor Diane Katz.[19]

6. Gifts of Intangible Personal Property: I give all my shares of Massive Corp. to my cousin Laurel Joseph.[20] If I no longer own this stock at the time of my death, or if the company is no longer identified by this name, then I leave to Laurel Joseph whatever proceeds are traceable to this property.

7. Residuary:[21] All the rest and residue of my property real and personal, wherever situated, including that property over which I hold a general power of appointment from the will of my brother Stanley Lunt, dated June 10, 1999, I give to my husband. If my husband does not survive me by thirty days, I give the residue to my children in shares of approximately equal value. If my children cannot agree on a division of property, then my sister Deborah Wilson's decisions will be binding

---

[17] If there is a question whether the testator's estate can fund these cash gifts—and if the testator intends to give cash also to her husband by way of the residuary clause—then the testator may want to cap the gifts to a certain percent of her estate.

[18] The drafter should be sure that the jewelry is clearly identified by this description. The last part of this sentence is "precatory." That is, the testator expresses her hopes but the terms are not legally binding.

[19] In almost all jurisdictions, this gift will lapse and become part of the residuary estate if the neighbor does not survive the testator. If the testator wishes to name an alternate beneficiary if Ms. Katz does not survive her, she should do so.

[20] If the testator sells her shares or if Massive Corp. merges with another company under a different name, the cousin will not receive this gift. Thus, the testator includes the next sentence.

[21] This is the traditional residuary clause, disposing of the rest of the testator's property.

on my children. I will leave a memorandum of my wishes for distribution of my personal effects between my children.[22] If either child does not survive me by thirty days I give his or her share to his or her issue per stirpes. If no issue of mine survive me, I give the residue to my sister, Deborah Wilson. If my sister does not survive me by thirty days, then I give the residue to her issue per stirpes. By per stirpes, I mean

_____.[23]

8. Trust for Minors: If any person who takes under this will is under the age of twenty-one years at the time property would be distributed to him or her, I name my executor or executors named in paragraph 9 of this will as trustee(s), to retain the property in trust, to invest and reinvest the property as permitted under the laws of the state of Illinois and to distribute from the income, as the trustee deems necessary, for the education and support of the beneficiary until the beneficiary reaches the age of twenty-one. At that time the trustee shall transfer to and pay over the principal and accumulated income to the beneficiary. In making payments for the beneficiary's education and support, the trustee need not take into account the beneficiary's other sources of income and support.

9. Executor:

a. I name my husband as executor of this my last will, and I direct that he not be required to give bond or other security. If my husband does not survive me, or if he does not wish to serve, or does not qualify to serve, I name my children as co-executors. I direct that neither of my children be required to give bond or other security.

b. I give my executor full powers to administer my estate under the law of the state of Illinois.[24]

10. No contest clause: Anyone who contests this will forfeits all gifts under this will.[25]

_____

[22] This memorandum will not be enforceable as part of the testator's will, except in those jurisdictions in which legislation gives binding effect to a signed memorandum written after the will was executed.

[23] Here the drafter defines the term to follow the testator's preference. If the term appeared in other clauses, the drafter would include the definition in Paragraph 1.

[24] Many wills include specific powers of executors and trustees. These are often part of the attorney's boilerplate.

[25] This no contest clause may have been intended to prevent a contest by the testator's stepson. If so, the clause is ineffective because the testator did not include the stepson in her will. The clause is effective only against a person who is a beneficiary of an amount sufficient to discourage challenge.

I sign this document, which consists of ___ pages, as my last will, dated August 7, 2006.[26]

_____
Signature

The above instrument consisting of ___ pages was declared by the testator Faith Jones to be her will and signed by the testator in our presence, and we in the presence of the testator and of each other sign below as witnesses. We declare that at the time the testator executed this instrument, the testator was of sound mind.[27]

_____    _____
Witness                                             Address

_____    _____
Witness                                             Address

_____

[26] This clause is traditionally known as the Testimonium. It traditionally begins with "In testimony whereof . . . " but that introduction is not required.

[27] This paragraph, the attestation clause, is not required (the witnesses' signatures are) but should be included. It provides prima facie evidence of proper will execution. The paragraph should specify all the formalities for will execution in that state. For example, this clause should add that the testator asked the witnesses to sign the document, if that is required in that state. Many clauses recite formalities required in any state.

## D. WRITING PROCESS

### 1. Gathering Information

Gathering information is crucial for properly drafting a will and serving your client. Wills are creatures of state statutes and the attorney must be familiar with the statutory requirements for executing a will in that jurisdiction, as well as with statutory provisions governing the substantive law of wills and the interpretations of those statutes. Just as crucial as the attorney's legal research is the step of gathering information from the client. This step requires tact and circumspection. Although attorney-drawn wills may in the end seem cold and bloodless, wills deal with intensely personal matters. After all, in answering your questions, your client must contemplate her own death. Your client also must review her personal life, her family situation, and the nature and extent of her accumulated property. Gathering the information requires you to be a careful and patient listener if you are to find out what your client wants. You need to get all the facts accurately about the people to whom your client wants to give her property and the property that she wants to give. You also need to explore with your client her wishes in regard to changes in her family and property that occur over the years. Although you should advise your client and explain the available choices and their consequences, you should not inject your own choices or influence your client to accept them.

Then you must put the law and facts together. Suppose that your client is unmarried and has no children and tells you that she wants to give her property to her five nieces and nephews. Before you describe the gift as one to "my heirs at law," you must ascertain that the nieces and nephews are her heirs at law.[28] In one well known case,[29] the testator's gift went to her aunt and not to her nieces and nephews because the aunt was her heir. The court will not correct an error of that kind.

If your client is married, be sure to collect full information about her nuclear family members. For example, if she is estranged from

---

[28] The example arises from the fact that the technical meaning of "heir" is the person who inherits the decedent's intestate property.

[29] *Mahoney v. Grainger*, 186 N.E. 86 (Mass. 1933).

her husband and wants to disinherit him, you need to know the state's law on elective shares—that is, the share that most non-community property states provide a surviving spouse from the decedent spouse's estate—and whether that law allows her to avoid her husband taking a share of her estate. If you practice in a community property state, you must determine which property is community property that will be divided half to your client's estate and half to her spouse.[30] If your client has a child or children that she wants to disinherit, you must explain the state's preter-mitted heir statute,[31] and draft the will to avoid that statute.

It is also crucial to elicit detailed financial information about your client's assets, liabilities, and existing financial planning, such as retirement plans, insurance policies, and existing trusts. Ask your client to bring all relevant documents to the interview, including divorce settlements. As part of your planning, you should determine from your client exactly what property she holds and how she holds it. For example, if your client holds her real estate or personal property such as stocks as a joint tenant with right of survivorship, that property will not be distributed under the terms of her will but will go to the surviving joint tenant. Your client may want to take that fact into account when she decides to whom to give the property that she holds in her own name. If your client runs a family corporation, you need full information about how she wants to pass on that corporation, and whether any agreements such as buy-out agreements are already in place.

As you interview your client, you should begin planning to account for the particular needs of the client's family and financial situation, including needs that experience teaches arise from the passage of time.

## 2. Conceptualizing: Anticipating Contingencies

The passing of time brings changes to family, friends, and property. An especially important part of gathering information and planning is to ascertain how your client wants to provide for

---

[30] Estate planning for community property requires full understanding of that property system.

[31] *See supra* n.6.

future changes to her property and in the lives of her beneficiaries. Wills must be far-seeing; they are often written and executed many years before the client dies or becomes incompetent to write another will. Longer life expectancies have increased this time frame.

State statutes provide default rules in addition to the intestacy rules that control who takes which property when changes have occurred to persons and property. Your client may not want the consequences of those default rules. For example, if one of the intended beneficiaries dies before the testator does, a statute known as an anti-lapse statute may replace that beneficiary with the deceased beneficiary's issue if the issue survive the testator. Your client may want only her named beneficiary to take the property and will want you to draft the gift so that the anti-lapse statute does not apply. Or your client may now live in a home that she plans to give to her oldest daughter. Years later, however, the client may decide to sell the house and buy a condominium unit. If so, does the client want the daughter to get the condominium? Or to get the proceeds of the sale of the house? The daughter will not receive an alternative gift unless it is included in the will. It is important to gather this type of information when you interview your client so that default rules do not produce unwanted results.

Another change may be that the testator's estate may shrink by the time of her death. If the testator has given specific monetary gifts in her will, these gifts may deplete her estate below the amount the testator wants to give the residuary beneficiary, who the testator usually intends to be the principal beneficiary. You can avoid that result by careful drafting, for example, by limiting specific monetary gifts to a percentage of the client's estate.

Part of your interviewing may require you to raise possibilities that are emotionally difficult for your client to consider. One important example is how your client wishes to divide her property among grandchildren if your client's children all predecease her. This type of information can be difficult, but necessary, for the attorney to elicit.

Another question that may be difficult for you to raise and for your client to consider is whether family disharmony may prompt a will contest after the client dies. If so, your client should consider a "no-contest" clause. This type of clause, not enforceable in every state, provides that if a beneficiary contests the will, she will lose her gift under the will. These clauses, however, will not deter a contest by a person who does not receive a gift under the will, or receives only a minor one.

Because there are so many personal and financial bases to cover, many attorneys have developed detailed questionnaires for client interviews in order to anticipate and record information needed to draft a will. These forms also help the attorneys avoid repeated calls to the client to get information they neglected to get during the interview.

────────────────── *Exercise 15.3* ──────────────────

*A. Develop a questionnaire to interview a client. Which categories of information would you include?*

*B. Use the questionnaire to interview a student in the class.*

## 3. Drafting and Reviewing

Once you have gathered the basic information you need from your client, have thought through and planned for future contingencies, and have organized and drafted the will, as explained in Section B, you need to go back and review the will before showing it to your client. Check that you have used as much plain language and simple sentence structure as possible; that you have included all the definitions that you need, and that you have used all the words that you defined; that the dispositive provisions are consistent; that your internal references to other articles are correct; that the will is clearly written and unambiguous; and that you have followed your client's instructions completely and accurately.

## D. SPECIAL CONCERNS

## 1. Form Wills and Legalese

Most law firms have form wills on hand or subscribe to one of several online drafting systems. If not, many form books and continuing legal education books have form wills from which you can borrow. In fact, clients can buy form wills at stationery stores or find them online. However, you must be cautious about using forms, never employing them without taking account of particular circumstances. A good form should illustrate the customary format and alert you to the kinds of provisions that often are included in wills. However, as we explained in Chapter 1, you must customize the form to your client. To take an obvious example, a form will probably includes paragraphs for major gifts to the testator's spouse and children. If your client isn't married and has no children, then omit these provisions and include your client's individual choices instead.

Form wills are notorious for their legalese, wordiness, and archaic language, none of which is necessary to prepare a valid will. Wills are often the target for criticisms and jokes about lawyers' legalese, which often use examples from will forms. If you use one, think critically about its language as you go through it, rewriting where necessary. Nevertheless, use the correct technical terms where the law requires them. For example, most courts interpret the term "heir" in its technical legal meaning if a lawyer used the term.

As we mentioned in Section B, you may find that some clients prefer some old-fashioned phrases and redundancies that are characteristic of boilerplate will forms, perhaps because some of the language has a ritualistic resonance. These preferences may arise from the fact that your client is confronting her mortality. So long as the traditional language is unlikely to cause confusion—and litigation—be guided by your client's preference for particular phrasing. But bear in mind that most clients prefer a document that they can understand.

──────────────── *Assignment 15.1* ────────────────

*Evaluate for legalese and verbosity the following testimonium, attestation clause, and affidavit similar to those in form wills. Rewrite into simpler language where needed. Draft the attestation clause and affidavit to reflect the requirements to execute a will in your state.*

**A.** Testimonium

In Testimony Whereof, I have hereunto set my hand and my seal this _____ day of _____ 20__.

**B.** Attestation clause

The foregoing instrument, consisting of _____ typewritten pages, including this page, was signed, published and declared by the above named testator to be his last will, in the presence of us; we, in his presence, at his request, and in the presence of each other, have hereunto subscribed our names as witnesses; and we declare that at the time of the execution of this instrument the testator, according to our best knowledge and belief, was of sound mind and disposing memory and under no constraint.

Dated at _____, ___, this __ day of ____, ____.

[Signature lines.]

**C.** Acknowledgment and Affidavit

The State of _____

County of _____

We, _____, _____, and _____, the testator and the witnesses, respectively, whose names are signed to the attached or foregoing instrument, being first duly sworn, do hereby declare to the undersigned authority that the testator signed and executed the instrument as the testator's will and that [he] [she] had signed willingly (or willingly directed another to sign for [him] [her]), and that [he] [she] executed it as [his] [her] free and voluntary act for the purposes therein expressed, and that each of the witnesses, in the presence and hearing of the testator, signed the will as witness and that to the best of [his] [her] knowledge the testator was at that time eighteen years of age or older, of sound mind, and under no constraint or undue influence.

_____
Testator

_____
Witness

_____
Witness

## 2. Rules of Interpretation and Construction

Even a carefully drawn will may not be completely clear to the executor or may be subject to challenge by a will contest. The will may contain a mistake, it may be ambiguous, or it may omit needed information. The court will first try to interpret the will by determining what that testator intended by its language. If the court determines that the will's language has a plain meaning (subject to only one interpretation), then it will enforce that language, even if it is not what the testator intended. As noted earlier, one court held that a testator's aunt took the testator's estate because the testator's attorney drafted the gift to her "heirs." Under the state's intestacy statute, the aunt was the testator's heir at law, even though the testator intended the gifts for her nieces and nephews.[32]

If language in a will is ambiguous, the court will admit extrinsic evidence to clear up the ambiguity. However, a number of jurisdictions still follow the traditional rule and do not admit extrinsic evidence if the ambiguity is "patent," that is, the ambiguity appears on the face of the will. An example is a will provision "I give 80 acres of my 200 acre tract in Lake County to my niece Alison, and the rest of the tract jointly to my nieces Amanda, Jamie, and Foster." Which 80 acres does Alison get? Under the traditional rule, the court is limited to the words of the will itself to resolve the ambiguity. The court deciding this case could not resolve this ambiguity, and the gift failed.[33]

A "latent" ambiguity is one that does not appear on the face of the will. An example of a latent ambiguity is a will that gives a gift to "my nephew Jonathan," but the testator has two nephews named Jonathan (known as an equivocation). The court will admit extrinsic evidence to determine which nephew the testator intended.

If the court cannot determine from the will itself or from extrinsic evidence what a testator specifically intended, it will use

---

[32] *See supra* n.29.

[33] In this case to save the gift, the will could have been interpreted to give Alison a right of selection, or to create concurrent estates in fractional shares. *See* Jesse Dukeminier & Stanley M. Johanson, *Wills, Trusts, and Estates* 425 (6th ed., Aspen 2000).

rules of construction to ascribe a meaning to the testator's words. Some commonly used rules of construction are the following:

- A court interprets will language to avoid intestacy as to certain property because the law presumes that a testator did not intend to die intestate;
- A court gives technical terms their technical meanings, especially if an attorney drafted the will (so that the term "issue" would mean all a person's descending generations, not just the generation of children);
- Where the testator has left more than one will (because her latest will did not revoke prior wills), a court will construe the wills together as much as possible so as not to imply revocation.

A rule still applied in many states involving payment of estate taxes is the "burden on the residue" rule, a rule requiring that taxes be paid from the residue unless the testator directs otherwise.

It is important to note that these rules can differ dramatically from state to state. Some states recognize exceptions to the plain meaning rule and admit extrinsic evidence to correct certain types of mistakes, for example, mistakes by the attorney who drafted the will. In some states, a court will fill gaps in the will, either by inferring the testator's intent or by admitting extrinsic evidence. Assume that a will gives "a life estate to my mother, but if she does not survive me, then to my brother Gabriel." If the testator's mother does survive the testator, does the remainder after her life estate go by intestacy? Or did the testator intend Gabriel to take the remainder? A court, especially using the presumption that the testator did not intend to die intestate as to his property, might read the whole scheme of the will and conclude that the testator intended to name Gabriel as the remainderman. And, of course, the various rules of construction included in your property or future interests course, such as time of vesting and whether a property interest is a fee simple or a more limited estate, are important in interpreting gifts in wills. The most important point is that if rules of interpretation and construction do not accord with your client's wishes, draft carefully to avoid them.

--------------------------------- *Exercise 15.4* ---------------------------------

*Evaluate and rewrite this residuary clause.*

All the rest, residue and remainder of my estate, both real and personal and wheresoever situate, including any property over which I may have the power of disposition by will or otherwise, I give, devise and bequeath to my Trustees, hereinafter named, IN TRUST, NEVERTHELESS, to invest and reinvest the same, collect the income therefrom, and to pay to or apply to the use of my daughter, EUGENIA M. HEALEY, and her issue or some or any of them, during the lifetime of my said daughter, so much of the income and/or principal, in such amount or amounts and at such time or times, as my Trustees in their absolute discretion shall see fit to pay or apply, and to accumulate and reinvest any income not so paid or applied, and upon the death of my said daughter, I direct my Trustees to pay, transfer and set over the then trust fund, including any accumulated income, or upon my death if my said daughter shall predecease me, I direct the Executors to distribute my residuary estate, to the issue then living of my daughter, EUGENIA M. HEALEY, and of my sons, JAMES BRUCE MAGNOR, JR., and ROBERT MAGNOR, per stirpes.

--------------------------------- *Exercise 15.5* ---------------------------------

*Identify the ambiguity or other drafting error in these clauses and rewrite them (supply your own meaning).*

**1.** *I give $1000 to my nephew John Jones if he is more than 21 years old at the time of my death.*

**2.** *I direct my executor to select worthy educational and religious charities.*

**3.** *My farm in Stevens Township to Mary Jones and to the children of Thomas Jones.*

**4.** *I give my savings accounts in Fiduciary Bank to my brother John and my sister Linda in equal shares, and if either does not survive me then to the survivor.*

**5.** *On the settlor's death, the trustee shall transfer the remaining trust assets to the settlor's son John Smith if he shall then be living.*

**6.** *From a text:*
*Under the Statute of Wills, the testator must sign the will in the presence of the two witnesses together at the foot of the will.*

**7.** *From the codicil to a will:*

*a) to the Unitarian Service Committee of Boston, I give $5,000;*

*b) to the Wisconsin Council of the Blind, and*

*c) to the Children's Village of the U.S.A., and*

*d) to Presbyterian Manor of Kansas, and to each of above, I give all the rest and residue of my estate.*

**8.** *From a text:*

*Whether a declaration by a court that an accumulation provision is void in whole or in part should necessitate an additional decree that the entire convey-ance is void, and that interests unconnected with the accumulation clause do not take effect, depends on the view of the court as to what settlor would have desired if he could have foreseen that his direction for accumulation would be declared illegal.*

**9.** *Duties of Executor*

*My executor shall have the right to name the charitable beneficiary in the trust created in Article 7 and shall have the right to change the terms of the gift created thereunder by written instrument executed by the executor and delivered to the trustee within four weeks of assuming office.*

**10.** *Reservations Affecting the Trust*

*Donor reserves the right to amend this agreement from time to time in any and all respects; to revoke the trust hereby created, in whole or in part; and to change the identity or number (or both) of the trustee or trustees hereunder, by written instrument executed by Donor and delivered to any trustee during Donor's lifetime; provided, however, that the duties and responsibilities of the Trustee shall not be substantially increased by any such amendment without its written consent.*

--- ***Exercise 15.6*** ---

*Adam Jones has brought you a will that he just drafted himself. Adam is leaving on a business trip to Europe very soon. He had asked a local lawyer to draft a simple will for him to execute before he left, but the lawyer has not done so yet. Adam is not a lawyer. He is married and has a one-year-old child, Erin Jones. He also has a 19-year-old child from a previous marriage, Sam, whom he wants to disinherit. You are his friend and a law student.*

*Evaluate his efforts for him. He relied in part on a form he bought in a stationery store. Explaining that you are not licensed yet to practice law, suggest changes to the will.*

## Last Will and Testament

State of Pacifica
County of Lincoln

Know all men by these presents, that I, Adam X. Jones, of the County of Lincoln, State of Pacifica, being in good health, of sound and disposing mind and memory, and above the age of eighteen years, do make and publish this my last will and testament, hereby revoking all wills by me at any time heretofore made.

First: I direct that all my debts and funeral expenses be fully paid as soon after my death as practicable by the person I nominate as executor in paragraph fourth.

Second: I give, devise, and bequeath all my property, real and personal wheresoever located, to my beloved wife Eva, to have and to hold as her property absolutely. Whatever is left at her death, I would like her to give as we have discussed.

Third: I give my gold cuff links and watch to my brother Paul.

Fourth: I give my stamp and coin collections to my cousins Able, Baker, and Charley.

Fifth: If any one contests this will, any gifts to that person are revoked.

Sixth: I hereby appoint my said wife Eva the independent executrix of this, my last will and testament, and direct and provide that no bond shall be required of her. I specifically authorize my said executrix to sell and dispose of any of the property belonging to my estate without obtaining court order to do so.

Seventh: I give $1,000 (ten thousand dollars) to my parents in gratitude for their patience in raising me.

This I make and publish as my last will and testament, hereunto signing and subscribing my name this ＿＿ day of ＿＿ 20＿. In the presence of ＿＿＿＿ and ＿＿＿＿ who attest the same at my request.

＿＿＿＿＿＿＿＿＿＿＿＿＿＿＿＿
Testator

Witnesses:

＿＿＿＿＿＿＿＿＿＿＿＿＿＿＿＿

＿＿＿＿＿＿＿＿＿＿＿＿＿＿＿＿

———————————————— *Assignment 15.2* ————————————————

*Your clients are Jack and Susan Lowry. They have asked you to write their wills. The Lowrys are in their late 30's; they have no children. Their parents have died. They each have one sibling, a brother. Each has a close relationship with the respective sibling. Ms. Lowry inherited valuable personal property from her parents when they died in an auto accident. Most of that property consists of family heirlooms from her maternal grandmother, Mary Mayers. This property is very important to her as her link with her deceased ancestors. This property includes diamond jewelry that is now in a safety deposit box at First Bank, Chicago, Illinois; pearl and other gemstone jewelry; antique desk, Windsor chair, and grandfather clock; and an investment account #0123 with Roberto and Brothers, investment advisors.*

*Jack Lowry is a one-quarter owner of a large farm in neighboring Rapid County, held in common with his brother and two uncles, and he holds a one-half interest in a real estate note and mortgage on land sold to Ed Michie by Jack's parents.*

*Together the Lowrys own their residence as joint tenants with right of survivorship. Some of the furnishings were inherited from each set of parents, but the couple has purchased two large oriental rugs and several paintings and etchings.*

*The Lowrys each wish to give their property to the other spouse and each wishes his or her brother to then receive the property from that side of the family.*

*Draft wills for each of the Lowrys, filling in names where necessary. Do not include powers of the administrators or tax apportionment clauses.*

*Remember that each will should account for the situation in which the testator survives the other spouse.*

## E. LIVING WILLS AND HEALTH CARE PROXIES

### 1. Living Wills

Disposition of property is not the only kind of end-of-life decision that your client may choose to memorialize in writing. Developments in modern medical technology have provided an increasing number of circumstances in which patients have choices about whether to receive end-of-life care and, if so, what kinds. An advance directive, more commonly known as a living will, is a written instrument that allows a presently competent person to exert control over when and whether he will want to be provided certain types of care in case he becomes incompetent to make those choices.

End-of-life decision-making is largely governed by state law and is usually directed by statute. Each state now has legislation addressing end-of-life decision making and living wills. In drafting such instruments, lawyers should always consult with the relevant statute to meet its requirements. Most state statutes include a form to follow for the living will, and in two states, this form must be followed precisely in order for the document to be valid.[34] Still, if a living will is valid in the state where it is executed, it will usually be treated as valid in any state, even if it does not meet that particular state's drafting requirements.

The states are fairly uniform in that generally any person at least 18 years old and legally competent may execute an advance directive that specifies his wishes for end-of-life decision-making. All states require that the document be in writing, signed, and dated. Most states require either one or two witnesses, with limitations on who those witnesses can be.

The key thing to remember in drafting an advance directive is specificity: Because the signer is attempting to make decisions in advance for circumstances that have not yet arisen, the drafter should cover as many contingencies as possible. A living will should specify the circumstances under which it is to take effect (i.e. when the signer is in a coma, when the signer is in a persistent vegetative state, or when the patient is terminally ill). The document should specify which treatments are to be administered or refused, including mechanical ventilation, artificial nutrition and hydration, medication, blood transfusions, surgery, kidney dialysis, cardiopulmonary resuscitation, organ donation, diagnostic tests, comfort care, and any other tests, treatments, or procedures about which the signer is concerned. However, though the living will should be as specific as possible, not every possibility can be anticipated. To accommodate unanticipated situations, a living will should indicate that any given examples or lists are intended to be illustrative and not exclusive.

---

[34] N.C. Gen. Stat. § 90-321(d1); Wis. Stat. Ann. § 154.03.

Just as the attorney who drafts a client's will must make the client aware of the changes that may occur over time to the client's will beneficiaries and his property, the attorney who drafts a client's living will when the client is in good health should counsel her client that, over the years, he may change his mind about withdrawing life-support too quickly. As he becomes more elderly, but not ready to let go of life, the client may wish to extend acceptable care and put off its termination.

Once a living will is drafted and executed, its signer should provide copies to his primary care physician and treating physician so that the instrument becomes a part of his medical records. If the signer lives in a nursing home or other facility, that institution should also receive a copy. It is also a good idea to provide copies to anyone else who may have an interest in the signer's end-of-life care, such as family members and even those who might oppose the signer's wishes. If the signer locks away his living will in a safe deposit box where no one may think to look for it at the appropriate time, then the living will does the signer no good.

## 2. Health Care Proxies

In addition to or in place of a living will, your client may wish to designate a health care agent (also called a proxy decision maker) to make medical decisions for him should he become unconscious and/or incompetent. A document designating a health care agent augments or replaces a living will by authorizing another party to make any decisions a patient himself would make if he were conscious and competent.

Probably the most important consideration in creating a health care proxy is the choice of agent. Many people choose to appoint their adult child, their spouse, or a sibling. Unless a person (e.g. the client's physician or the administrator of a health-care facility where your client resides) is prohibited from being your client's agent by virtue of their relationship, your client may designate almost anyone she chooses. She may also designate an alternate agent, in the event that the original designee is unavailable or unwilling to make these decisions. However, to avoid overriding the purpose of appointing a health care agent in the first place, the document should be drafted so that only one person at a time has the power to make decisions for your client.

Any designated agent/proxy needs to be clearly identified in the document with name, address, and telephone number, and should know he is being designated. To this end, some states require a signed acknowledgment by the designated agent, signifying his awareness and acceptance of the associated duties. Anyone appointed health care agent should not also be a witness to the document.

A document designating a health care agent should, like a living will, become part of your client's medical records. Again, a document of this type lying in a safe deposit box will be of no use. These documents should also be reviewed periodically to maintain currency. Many life events may affect the eligibility or desirability of the designated agent. For instance, in most states, if your client has designated her husband as her agent, their divorce will nullify his authorization to make medical decisions for her. Similarly, if the designated agent dies, moves, or becomes otherwise unwilling to make decisions for your client, the document will need to be redrafted.

### 3. Sample Health Care Directive[35]

**Advance Health-Care Directive**

OF

_____

*Explanation*

You have the right to give instructions about your own health care. You also have the right to name someone else to make health-care decisions for you. This form lets you do either or both of these things. It also lets you express your wishes regarding the designation of your primary physician. If you use this form, you may complete or modify all or any part of it. You are free to use a different form.

Part 1 of this form is a power of attorney for health care. Part 1 lets you name another individual as agent to make health-care decisions for you if you become incapable of making your own decisions or if you want someone else to make those decisions for you now even

---

[35] This is the statutory directive of the state of Mississippi.

though you are still capable. You may name an alternate agent to act for you if your first choice is not willing, able or reasonably available to make decisions for you. Unless related to you, your agent may not be an owner, operator, or employee of a residential long-term health-care institution at which you are receiving care.

Unless the form you sign limits the authority of your agent, your agent may make all health-care decisions for you. This form has a place for you to limit the authority of your agent. You need not limit the authority of your agent if you wish to rely on your agent for all health-care decisions that may have to be made. If you choose not to limit the authority of your agent, your agent will have the right to:

(a) Consent or refuse consent to any care, treatment, service, or procedure to maintain, diagnose, or otherwise affect a physical or mental condition;

(b) Select or discharge health-care providers and institutions;

(c) Approve or disapprove diagnostic tests, surgical procedures, programs of medication, and orders not to resuscitate; and

(d) Direct the provision, withholding, or withdrawal of artificial nutrition and hydration and all other forms of health care.

Part 2 of this form lets you give specific instructions about any aspect of your health care. Choices are provided for you to express your wishes regarding the provision, withholding, or withdrawal of treatment to keep you alive, including the provision of artificial nutrition and hydration, as well as the provision of pain relief. Space is provided for you to add to the choices you have made or for you to write out any additional wishes.

Part 3 of this form lets you designate a physician to have primary responsibility for your health care.

After completing this form, sign and date the form at the end and have the form witnessed by one of the two alternative methods listed below. Give a copy of the signed and completed form to your physician, to any other health-care providers you may have, to any health-care institution at which you are receiving care, and to any health-care agents you have named. You should talk to the person you have named as agent to make sure that he or she understands your wishes and is willing to take the responsibility.

You have the right to revoke this advance health-care directive or replace this form at any time.

*PART 1*

## POWER OF ATTORNEY FOR HEALTH CARE

(1) DESIGNATION OF AGENT: I designate the following individual as my agent to make health-care decisions for me:

Agent's Name:
Address:
Telephone 1:
Telephone 2:

OPTIONAL: If I revoke my agent's authority or if my agent is not willing, able, or reasonably available to make a health-care decision for me, I designate as my first alternate agent:

First Alternate's Name:
Address:
Telephone 1:
Telephone 2:

OPTIONAL: If I revoke the authority of my agent and first alternate agent or if neither is willing, able, or reasonably available to make a health-care decision for me, I designate as my second alternate agent:

Second Alternate's Name:
Address:
Telephone 1:
Telephone 2:

(2) AGENT'S AUTHORITY: My agent is authorized to make all health-care decisions for me, including decisions to provide, withhold, or withdraw artificial nutrition and hydration, and all other forms of health care to keep me alive, except as I state here:

(3) WHEN AGENT'S AUTHORITY BECOMES EFFECTIVE: My agent's authority becomes effective when my primary physician determines that I am unable to make my own health-care decisions unless I mark the following box. If I mark this box [  ], my agent's authority to make health-care decisions for me takes effect immediately.

(4) AGENT'S OBLIGATION: My agent shall make health-care decisions for me in accordance with this power of attorney for health care, any instructions I give in Part 2 of this form, and my other wishes to the extent known to my agent. To the extent my wishes are unknown,

my agent shall make health-care decisions for me in accordance with what my agent determines to be in my best interest. In determining my best interest, my agent shall consider my personal values to the extent known to my agent.

(5) NOMINATION OF GUARDIAN: If a guardian of my person needs to be appointed for me by a court, I nominate the agent designated in this form. If that agent is not willing, able, or reasonably available to act as guardian, I nominate the alternate agents whom I have named, in the order designated.

## PART 2

## INSTRUCTIONS FOR HEALTH CARE

If you are satisfied to allow your agent to determine what is best for you in making end-of-life decisions, you need not fill out this part of the form. If you do fill out this part of the form, you may strike any wording you do not want.

(6) END-OF-LIFE DECISIONS: I direct that my health-care providers and others involved in my care provide, withhold or withdraw treatment in accordance with the choice I have marked below:

[ ] (a) Choice Not To Prolong Life

I do not want my life to be prolonged if (i) I have an incurable and irreversible condition that will result in my death within a relatively short time, (ii) I become unconscious and, to a reasonable degree of medical certainty, I will not regain consciousness, or (iii) the likely risks and burdens of treatment would outweigh the expected benefits, or

[ ] (b) Choice To Prolong Life

I want my life to be prolonged as long as possible within the limits of generally accepted health-care standards.

(7) ARTIFICIAL NUTRITION AND HYDRATION: Artificial nutrition and hydration must be provided, withheld or withdrawn in accordance with the choice I have made in paragraph (6) unless I mark the following box. If I mark this box [ ], artificial nutrition and hydration must be provided regardless of my condition and regardless of the choice I have made in paragraph (6).

(8) RELIEF FROM PAIN: Except as I state in the following space, I direct that treatment for alleviation of pain or discomfort be provided at all times, even if it hastens my death:

(9) OTHER WISHES: (If you do not agree with any of the optional choices above and wish to write your own, or if you wish to add to the instructions you have given above, you may do so here.) I direct that:

*PART 3*

**PRIMARY PHYSICIAN**

(OPTIONAL)
(10) I designate the following physician as my primary physician:

Physician's Name:
Address:
Telephone 1:
Telephone 2:

OPTIONAL: If the physician I have designated above is not willing, able, or reasonably available to act as my primary physician, I designate the following physician as my primary physician:

Physician's Name:
Address:
Telephone 1:
Telephone 2:

(11) EFFECT OF COPY: A copy of this form has the same effect as the original.
(12) SIGNATURES: Sign and date the form here:

DATED this the _____ day of _____, 200_.

_____

Name:
Address:
Telephone 1:
Telephone 2:

(13) WITNESSES: This power of attorney will not be valid for making health-care decisions unless it is either (a) signed by two (2) qualified adult witnesses who are personally known to you and who are present when you sign or acknowledge your signature; or (b) acknowledged before a notary public in the state.

## *Witnesses*

I declare under penalty of perjury pursuant to Section . . . that the principal is personally known to me, that the principal signed or acknowledged this power of attorney in my presence, that the principal appears to be of sound mind and under no duress, fraud or undue influence, that I am not the person appointed as agent by this document, and that I am not a health-care provider, nor an employee of a health-care provider or facility. I am not related to the principal by blood, marriage or adoption, and to the best of my knowledge, I am not entitled to any part of the estate of the principal upon the death of the principal under a will now existing or by operation of law.

_____          _____
WITNESS (sign and date)          ADDRESS

Name:
Address:
Telephone 1:
Telephone 2:

_____          _____
WITNESS (sign and date)          ADDRESS

Name:
Address:
Telephone 1:
Telephone 2:

STATE OF _____

COUNTY OF _____

On this _____ day of _____, in the year _____, before me, _____ (insert name of notary public) appeared _____, personally known to me (or proved to me on the basis of satisfactory evidence) to be the person whose name is subscribed to this instrument, and acknowledged that he or she executed it. I declare under the penalty of perjury that the person whose name is subscribed to this instrument appears to be of sound mind and under no duress, fraud or undue influence.

DATED this the _____ day of _____, 200__.

_____
NOTARY PUBLIC

My Commission Expires:

*Appendices*

# Appendix A

# *CASEFILES*

---

## CASEFILE # 1

### *Williams v. Grace Church*

Nancy Williams has come to your office seeking legal advice. A summary of her interview, a copy of her employment contract, and relevant excerpts from the Minnesota Human Rights Act follow.

---

### Interview

In February of last year, Nancy Williams, a 30 year-old woman with Master's degrees in social work and divinity, was hired as Director of Youth Social Services by Grace Church, a large and prominent inter-denominational Protestant church in Minneapolis. She was hired by the Board of Parish Life, which is composed of the members of the Board of Deacons and the Board of Trustees, who are elected by the congregation. The Board of Parish Life ("BPL") is responsible for all personnel decisions. Ms. Williams and the BPL signed an initial two-year employment contract.

Ms. Williams moved to Minneapolis from New York City, and took up her work enthusiastically, and apparently with great success. Her innovative programming dramatically increased attendance at the Church's sports and tutoring programs, and her counseling services for truants and other troubled young people—she combined traditional psychology with spiritual counseling—were the subject of several positive articles in the Minneapolis press. Ms. Williams was well-liked at the Church by both clergy and congregation. In addition to Ms. Williams, the professional staff consisted of an Administrative Minister, a Social Justice Associate, a Pastoral Services Minister, a Music Director, and a Senior Minister, the Rev. Michael Bryant, whose responsibilities included preaching and supervising the rest of the professional staff.

Soon after Ms. Williams' arrival, it became apparent that the Rev. Bryant, married and 65 years old, was very much attracted to her. Shortly, he began to make sexual advances that were unwelcome to Ms. Williams, whose fiancé had remained in the East temporarily. The Rev. Bryant, who referred to himself jokingly as "the tactile preacher," frequently came up behind Ms. Williams and ran his fingers through her hair and down her back, letting his hand come to rest on the small of her back, from which position she invariably removed it. On many occasions, he put his hands on Ms. Williams' waist and pulled her tight against his body, admonishing her for being "an uptight Wasp" when she struggled out of his embrace. On several occasions he put his hand on her thigh when they sat next to each other.

The Rev. Bryant also invited Ms. Williams to spend weekends with him at a wilderness lodge that the Church maintained as a retreat center. He constantly referred to the two of them as "lovers," and insisted on Ms. Williams' companionship outside the workplace.

When her constant admonishing of the Rev. Bryant had no effect, Ms. Williams complained to the Personnel Sub-Committee of BPL, and when that body failed to investigate or take any action, she complained to the BPL itself. The BPL declined to take any action other than advising Ms. Williams to "exercise some Christian compassion and forbearance" toward the Rev. Bryant, and not expect him "to be a women's libber at his age." The most sympathetic members urged her to "try and put up with it until he retires." They told her that they had spoken to him a few times about his "old fashioned" ideas about women staff members, but they had given up, concluding he was a hopeless old "lady killer" but he didn't mean any harm.

When the Rev. Bryant's advances continued, Ms. Williams told the BPL that she was going to file sex discrimination charges against him and against the BPL with the Minnesota Department of Human Rights. On November 10, of last year, shortly after this conversation, the BPL summarily fired her at a board meeting. The reason stated for her discharge was that she "had inappropriate relationships" with teenagers in her youth groups. Ms. Williams denied this untrue allegation, but to no avail.

Ms. Williams was devastated by the BPL's action. On Thanksgiving Day she took an overdose of Valium, but was fortunately rescued when her fiancé asked her best friend to look in on her. She spent several weeks in the psychiatric facility at Lakeland-University Hospital, and is currently undergoing intensive outpatient treatment for "severe reactive depression." Her psychiatrist believes that she will probably recover completely in time and that she will be able to return to her career.

The Rev. Bryant retired this year on January 1. Thus far, the incident has received no publicity outside of the church. Ms. Williams believes that she has thus far kept her suicide attempt secret—only her best friend, fiancé, and doctors know about it.

---

## EMPLOYMENT CONTRACT

The Board of Parish Life of Grace Church, 300 Celtic Avenue, Minneapolis, Minnesota, 94114, ["Employer"] and Nancy Williams, 74 Fifth Street, Minneapolis, Minnesota, 94112, ["Employee"] enter this contract for the employment of Employee by Employer as Director of Youth Social Services. The parties mutually agree as follows.

### 1. Definition

"Employment year" means a period of 12 successive months, beginning on the date of this contract or any annual anniversary date.

### 2. Background

Employer is a large inter-denominational Protestant Church in Minneapolis. Employee has Master's degrees in social work and divinity from Harvard University and was employed as Youth Minister at St. Ann's Church in New York City, New York.

## 3. Scope of Employment

Employee's responsibilities as Director of Youth Social Services include supervision of the Church's sports, tutoring, and counseling services.

## 4. Duration of Employment

Employee will begin her employment on March 1, 20__. It will expire at the close of the business day on the last business day of the second employment year unless this contract has been terminated earlier under paragraph 6 of this contract or unless Employer and Employee agree earlier on terms of renewal.

## 5. Compensation

Employer will pay Employee an annual salary of $65,000 in equal bi-weekly installments.

## 6. Termination

### a. By Employer

Employer may terminate this contract before the end of Employee's second employment year for cause after 30 days' written notice to Employee. Examples of cause are moral turpitude, dishonesty, illegal conduct, or neglect of duty.

### b. By Employee

Employee may terminate this contract before the end of Employee's second year, regardless of cause, after 30 days' written notice to the Board of Parish Life.

## 7. Modification

This contract may be modified only by dated written agreement which is signed by Employer's authorized agent and Employee.

## 8. Governing Law

This contact is governed by Minnesota law.

GRACE CHURCH

By:

| | |
|---|---|
| _____ | _____ |
| Mr. John Bishop | Ms. Nancy Williams |
| Chair, Board of Parish Life | |
| Employer | Employee |
| Date: _____ | Date: _____ |

## STATUTE

**Minn. Stat. §363.03 Unfair Discriminatory practices**

**Subdivision 1. Employment.** Except when based on a bona fide occupational qualification, it is an unfair employment practice:

\* \* \*

(2) For an employer, because of race, color, creed, religion, national origin, sex, marital status, status with regard to public assistance, membership or activity in a local commission, disability, sexual orientation, or age,

> (a) to refuse to hire or to maintain a system of employment which unreasonably excludes a person seeking employment; or

> (b) to discharge an employee; or

> (c) to discriminate against a person with respect to hiring, tenure, compensation, terms, upgrading, conditions, facilities, or privileges of employment.

**Subd. 7. Reprisals.** It is an unfair discriminatory practice for any individual who participated in the alleged discrimination as a perpetrator, employer, labor organization, employment agency, public accommodation, public service, educational institution, or owner, lessor, lessee, sublessee, assignee or managing agent of any real property, or any real estate broker, real estate salesperson, or employee or agent thereof to intentionally engage in any reprisal against any person because that person:

(1) Opposed a practice forbidden under this chapter or has filed a charge, testified, assisted, or participated in any manner in an investigation, proceeding, or hearing under this chapter; or

(2) Associated with a person or group of persons who are disabled or who are of different race, color, creed, religion, sexual orientation, or national origin.

A reprisal includes, but is not limited to, any form of intimidation, retaliation, or harassment. It is a reprisal for an employer to do any of the following with respect to an individual because that individual has engaged in the activities listed in clause (1) or (2): refuse to hire the individual; depart from any customary employment practice; transfer or assign the individual to a lesser position in terms of wages, hours, job classification, job security, or other employment status; or inform another employer that the individual has engaged in the activities listed in clause (1) or (2).

*   *   *

### Sec. 363.01 Definitions

*   *   *

**Subd. 14. Discriminate.** The term "discriminate" includes segregate or separate and, for purposes of discrimination based on sex, it includes sexual harassment.

*   *   *

**Subd. 41. Sexual harassment.** "Sexual harassment" includes unwelcome sexual advances, requests for sexual favors, sexually motivated physical contact or other verbal or physical conduct or communication of a sexual nature when:

(1) submission to that conduct or communication is made a term or condition, either explicitly or implicitly, of obtaining employment, public accommodations or public services, education, or housing;

(2) submission to or rejection of that conduct or communication by an individual is used as a factor in decisions affecting that individual's employment, public accommodations or public services, education, or housing; or

(3) that conduct or communication has the purpose or effect of substantially interfering with an individual's employment, public accommodations or public services, education, or housing, or creating an intimidating, hostile, or offensive employment, public accommodations, public services, educational, or housing environment.

## Sec. 363.071 Hearings

\* \* \*

**Subd. 2. Determination of discriminatory practice.** The administrative law judge shall make findings of fact and conclusions of law, and if the administrative law judge finds that the respondent has engaged in an unfair discriminatory practice, the administrative law judge shall issue an order directing the respondent to cease and desist from the unfair discriminatory practice found to exist and to take such affirmative action as in the judgment of the administrative law judge will effectuate the purposes of this chapter. The order shall be a final decision of the department. The administrative law judge shall order any respondent found to be in violation of any provision of section 363.03 to pay a civil penalty to the state. This penalty is in addition to compensatory and punitive damages to be paid to an aggrieved party. The administrative law judge shall determine the amount of the civil penalty to be paid, taking into account the seriousness and extent of the violation, the public harm occasioned by the violation, whether the violation was intentional, and the financial resources of the respondent. Any penalties imposed under this provision shall be paid into the general fund of the state. In all cases where the administrative law judge finds that the respondent has engaged in an unfair discriminatory practice the administrative law judge shall order the respondent to pay an aggrieved party, who has suffered discrimination, compensatory damages in an amount up to three times the actual damages sustained. In all cases, the administrative law judge may also order the respondent to pay an aggrieved party, who has suffered discrimination, damages for mental anguish or suffering and reasonable attorney's fees, in addition to punitive damages in an amount not more than $8,500.... In addition to the aforesaid remedies, in a case involving discrimination in

(a) employment, the administrative law judge may order the hiring, reinstatement or upgrading of an aggrieved party, who has suffered discrimination, with or without back pay...or any other relief the administrative law judge deems just and equitable.

## CASEFILE # 2

### *Johnson v. Wagner*

In September of this year, Charles and Emily Johnson brought an action in wrongful birth in Superior Court in Newark against Joshua Wagner, M.D. As guardian *ad litem* of their daughter, Dora Johnson, Ms. Johnson also brought an action for wrongful life. After the complaint was filed, the defendant did not answer its allegations on the wrongful birth action, but rather, moved for dismissal of the complaint on the ground that the action was barred by the statute of limitations. The judge has held a hearing on the motion and decided in favor of defendant Wagner. Relevant excerpts from the hearing testimony are as follows.

---

### Testimony of Emily Johnson (Excerpt)

\* \* \*

Q. Had you seen Dr. Wagner before your pregnancy with Dora four years ago?

A. Oh, yes. For years. He delivered my first two children, John and Tracy.

Q. And what happened in January four years ago?

A. Well, when I thought I was pregnant, I went to see Dr. Wagner. He confirmed this and suggested that since I was 37 years old, it would be wise to have an amniocentesis to be sure the baby was all right.

Q. Were those his words?

A. Not exactly. He told us—my husband was there too—that the test "would eliminate the possibility of any genetic defects."

Q. And did you have the test?

A. Yes, I did.

Q. And what were you told about the results?

A. Doctor Wagner told me "everything was completely normal."

Q. And what would you have done if he had told you that the tests indicated the presence of Turner Syndrome?

A. I would not have had Dora. I would have had an abortion.

Q. When did you next have occasion to discuss the test results?

A. In the hospital, after Dora was born with Turner syndrome.

Q. Did you ever question Dr. Wagner about the test?

A. Yes. As soon as he came to see me I asked him what happened and he told me that the test just did not show Turner Syndrome.

Q. Did he tell you anything else?

A. No, but he said that if I wanted him to answer any more questions, he would, but I was just too upset to think.

Q. And when if ever, did you find out more about the test for Turner Syndrome?

A. When Dora was four years old, in July of this year, I went to a support group for parents of Turner children. I found out that the test is 100 percent accurate when it is properly performed.

Q. Did you continue to see Doctor Wagner after the birth of your daughter?

A. I saw him a few times after the birth, and then I stopped when we moved to Pittsburgh.

## Testimony of Bartholomew Ives

* * *

Q. Now, in your capacity as Genetic Counselor at the Hospital did you have occasion to work with Doctor Wagner four years ago?

A. Yes, frequently. I would do the initial genetic screening interview with the prospective parents. After the lab test results were in, I would review them with Doctor Wagner. But he always gave the parents the results.

Q. And what did you do when you determined that the laboratory tests on the amniotic fluid in the Johnson case had not been properly performed?

A. I told Doctor Wagner. He agreed with me that the lab had done very sloppy work and that he was going to complain to the director.

Q. Did you make any professional judgment as to what the results of such careless lab work could be?

A. Yes, I did.

Q. And that was?

A. The kind of mistakes the technician made could compromise the 100 percent reliability and create a margin of error.

Q. And did you express this concern to Doctor Wagner?

A. Yes.

Q. And what, if any, was his response?

A. He agreed with me, said the lab should "get its act together."

Q. Did this conversation take place before or after Doctor Wagner saw the Johnsons about their results?

A. It was before that visit.

\*  \*  \*

Q. What is Turner Syndrome, Dr. Ives?

A. Turner Syndrome is a genetic defect that results from a female being born with a single X chromosome rather than two X chromosomes. Turner Syndrome babies suffer from congenital heart disease, a condition that results in shortened life expectancy. They also have short, "webbed" necks, cystic hygroma, which is a tumor of the lymphatic system, narrow palates, shield chests, widely spaced and poorly formed nipples, and ovarian abnormalities that often result in sterility and other chromosomal abnormalities.

**Testimony of Maureen Donovan—Registered Nurse (Excerpt)**

\*  \*  \*

Q. And did you have a conversation with Mrs. Johnson in her room at Woodrow Wilson Hospital when she delivered Dora four years ago?

A. I did, yes, poor lady.

Q. And what was the subject of that conversation?

A. She was wanting to know how her girl could be born with Turner Syndrome when the test was negative.

Q. And what, if anything, did you tell her?

A. I made a terrible mistake. I told Mrs. Johnson that the amino can't rule out Turner syndrome completely, only 90 percent.

Q. And did you believe that to be the truth?

A. I did, so help me.

Q. Do you still believe it?

A. No. The test is 100 percent if it is properly done.

Q. And when did you learn this?

A. After you came to talk to me about the case, a few months back it was.

---

SUPERIOR COURT OF THE STATE OF NEW JERSEY

------------------------------------------------------X

CHARLES & EMILY JOHNSON, :

                   Plaintiffs, :

                             : CASE NO. 12345/92

        v.                      : OPINION

                             :

JOSHUA WAGNER, M.D. :

                Defendant. :

------------------------------------------------------X

## SIMMONS, J.

Plaintiffs Charles and Emily Johnson filed a wrongful birth suit against Dr. Joshua Wagner some four years after their daughter was born with a severe birth defect. The defendant moved for dismissal on the ground that the Johnsons' claim was barred by the two year-statute of limitations. In an affidavit and memorandum in opposition to the defendant's motion, plaintiffs contended that the so-called "discovery rule" prevented the running of the statute of limitations because plaintiffs reasonably were unaware until last year that they were injured due to the fault of another and that, once aware, they timely filed suit. They also contended the fraudulent concealment exception to the statute of limitations tolled the statute. A hearing was held to determine when plaintiffs were aware, or should have become aware, of the essential facts, and whether defendant concealed or misrepresented the wrongful conduct leading to the plaintiffs' injuries. The defendant's motion to dismiss was accordingly deemed a motion for summary judgment.

The discovery rule exception to the statute of limitations is a rule of equity, and we must therefore weigh the fairness of it in light of the impact on both parties. *[Citations omitted.]* We conclude that fairness here does not require the defendant to defend against the plaintiffs' claim. We hold that plaintiffs' suit is time barred, because the facts adduced at the hearing, even considered, as they must be here, in the light most favorable to the plaintiffs, simply do not suffice to delay accrual of either of the plaintiffs' claims and to exempt them from the bar of the statute of limitations. *[Citations omitted.]*

The fraudulent concealment exception is equally inapplicable to the facts at bar.

Simply put, the plaintiffs slept on their rights.

Much though we sympathize with the plaintiffs and their genetically damaged child, whose fate is not a happy one, we are forced to conclude that the defendant is entitled to judgment in his favor as a matter of law and accordingly, we grant defendant's motion for summary judgment and dismiss the complaint.

SO ORDERED

# CASEFILE # 3

## *People v. Burke*

Timothy Burke, an advocate for medical marijuana, has been indicted in state court in Valhalla County, New York, on charges of possessing a large amount of marijuana with intent to distribute. His attorney moved to suppress the evidence (the marijuana) that was found in the defendant's apartment by Detective Malcolm Jones. Last week, the judge held a hearing on the motion, at which Jones was the only witness. Also included in the record of this case is the information that Burke is a 38 year-old social worker with Bachelor of Arts and Master of Social Work degrees.

The motion to suppress and the relevant portions of the hearing testimony follow.

---

Supreme Court of the State of New York

\---------------------------------------------------------

| | |
|---|---|
| The PEOPLE of the State of NEW YORK | Ind. No. 973-05 |
| | NOTICE OF |
| -against- | MOTION |
| | TO SUPPRESS |
| Timothy Burke, Defendant. | TANGIBLE |
| | EVIDENCE |

\---------------------------------------------------------

PLEASE TAKE NOTICE that upon the annexed affirmation of the under-signed, Thomas Kinsella, and upon all the papers and proceedings in this case, the undersigned will move this court on January 15, 20__, at the Courthouse, 1 Civic Oval, Center City, Room 600, at 9:30 a.m. or as soon thereafter as counsel can be heard, for an order pursuant to Section 710.20 of the Criminal Procedure Law suppressing tangible evidence on the ground that its warrantless seizure violated the Fourth Amendment to the United States Constitution, and in the alternative, for a hearing on this motion, as well as such other relief as this court may deem just.

Dated: December 26, 20__.

_____

Attorney for Defendant
Kinsella, Zorn, & Faulkner, LLP 250 Main St.
Center City, NY
Tel: (333)953-6391

To: Lisa Johnson
District Attorney
Valhalla County
15 Civic Oval
Center City, NY
Tel: (333)593-1089

CLERK
Supreme Court
1 Civic Oval
Room 700
Center City, NY

---

Supreme Court of the State of New York

--------------------------------------------------------

| The PEOPLE of the State of NEW YORK | Ind. No. 973-05 |
| | AFFIRMATION |
| -against- | IN SUPPORT OF |
| | MOTION |
| | TO SUPPRESS |
| Timothy Burke, Defendant. | TANGIBLE |
| | EVIDENCE |

--------------------------------------------------------

STATE OF NEW YORK        )
COUNTY OF VALHALLA     )

Thomas Kinsella affirms under penalty of perjury, as follows.

1. I am an attorney duly licensed to practice in the State of New York, and I am representing the defendant in this case; the defendant was indicted by the Grand Jury of Valhalla County on November 10, 20__, for the crime of criminal possession of marijuana in the_____ degree.

2. I have discussed this case with the defendant on numerous occasions and am familiar with the facts; I make this affidavit on behalf of the defendant and in support of the defendant's motion for an order suppressing from use by the prosecution tangible evidence in the form of a quantity of marijuana seized as the result of a search of defendant's apartment on the ground that defendant's consent to the warrantless search was obtained by the government through

coercion and thus violates the Fourth Amendment to the United States Constitution.

3. On information and belief, the District Attorney of the County of Valhalla intends to use the marijuana seized in evidence against the defendant at trial.

4. On information and belief, on August 15th, 20__, Detective Malcolm Jones of the Center City Police Department gained entry to defendant's apartment at 35 West 89th Street in Center City by asking defendant whether he could use the apartment to observe suspected terrorist activity.

5. On information and belief, once inside the apartment, the detective told defendant that defendant was suspected by other tenants in the building of being a drug dealer.

6. On information and belief, the detective refused to leave the apartment or to allow defendant to leave until defendant gave the detective permission to search the apartment for drugs.

7. On information and belief, at no time was defendant informed by the detective that he had a right to refuse permission for a warrantless search.

8. On information and belief, defendant eventually consented to a search, whereupon the detective seized the marijuana and arrested the defendant.

9. On information and belief, defendant's consent to the search was not given voluntarily.

WHEREFORE, affiant asks this Court to suppress the tangible evidence on the ground that it was seized as the result of defendant's involuntary consent to the warrantless search of his home and thus in violation of the Fourth Amendment's proscription of unreasonable searches and seizures. In the alternative, affiant asks this Court to grant a hearing on the voluntariness of defendant's consent, and requests such other relief as this Court deems just.

Dated: December 26, 20__.

_____

Thomas Kinsella
Attorney for Defendant
Kinsella, Zorn, & Faulkner, LLP 250 Main St.
Center City, NY
Tel: (333)953-6391

Supreme Court of the State of New York

-----------------------------------------------------------

The PEOPLE of the State of NEW YORK          Ind. No. 973-05

            -against-                        HEARING
                                             TESTIMONY
                                             OF MALCOLM
Timothy Burke, Defendant.                    JONES

-----------------------------------------------------------

\* \* \* \*

Q. Detective Jones, what information led you to defendant's apartment on August 15th?

A. Well, I live in the building and someone else gave me some information that he believed the defendant was distributing marijuana from his apartment, the defendant's apartment, and so I thought I would look into it if I could.

Q. And would you tell us what transpired when you went to defendant's apartment?

A. The first thing I noticed when he let me into the apartment was a big old movie poster with the title "Reefer Madness." This made me more suspicious, so I asked the defendant about the poster.

Q. How did he respond?

A. He indicated that he didn't intend to get into a discussion.

Q. What transpired then?

A. I told him flat out that people in the building were saying that he was distributing pot.

Q. And how did the defendant react?

A. He just shrugged his shoulders and said something to the effect that people say all kinds of stuff, but that doesn't make it true. Then he indicated that I should go, because he had to go out.

Q. And what, if anything, transpired next?

A. I indicated that if defendant wasn't involved, the best thing would be to let me take a quick look around and then there'd be no more rumors.

Q. And what, if anything, was defendant's response?

A. He indicated at that time that he would not agree to let me look around his apartment.

Q. What happened subsequently, if anything?

A. I repeated my request two, three more times, maybe four to be sure he understood. Finally, he just said, "O.K. Go look around."

Q. And what did you do then?

A. I asked the defendant to take me on a tour of the premises. On the kitchen counter I observed a pile of baggies full of green vegetable matter, which I ascertained from my expertise to be marijuana.

Q. And then?

A. I placed the defendant under arrest.

Q. Just two more questions, detective. What, if any use, did you make of your gun during this incident?

A. None whatsoever.

Q. And what, if any, physical contact did you have with the defendant?

A. None whatsoever, until I handcuffed him after his arrest.

\* \* \* \*

## Cross Examination

\* \* \* \*

Q. Detective Jones, is it true that you gained access to defendant's apartment on August 15th by telling him you needed to use his window as an observation post because there was an individual across the street who was suspected of being connected to a terrorist group?

A. I might have said that.

Q. Might have, or did?

A. O.K., yes.

Q. And the story you told him about needing to use his apartment was in fact a lie, isn't that so?

A. It was an investigative strategy, yes.

Q. And isn't it also true that defendant saw through your strategy and asked you to leave, and you remained?

A. Yes. I wanted to talk further with him.

Q. Isn't it also true that until defendant agreed to the search, you stood with your back to the door?

A. Yes, I was probably standing where I came in.

Q. And is it true that you remained in that position for approximately half an hour, until defendant let you search?

A. I wasn't looking at my watch, counselor. It could have been half an hour.

Q. And would you agree that you are a tall man?

A. Not as tall as some, but yes, counselor, I'm pretty tall.

Q. And you're in pretty good shape?

A. I'm no Schwarzenegger, but yes, I can take care of myself.

Q. Now, did you ever inform defendant that he had a right to refuse to let you conduct a warrantless search?

A. No, I did not tell him in so many words.

Q. Did you tell him in any words?

A. No.

\* \* \* \*

## CASEFILE # 4

### Anti-SLAPP Legislation

Bill Patterson is a member of the Pacifica State Legislature. Patterson has been contacted by constituents who feel strongly that Pacifica should have an "anti-SLAPP suit" statute. SLAPP is an acronym for "strategic lawsuits against public participation."[1] SLAPP suits are civil lawsuits filed against non-governmental individuals and groups, usually for having communicated with a government body, official, or the electorate, on an issue of some public interest or concern. SLAPP suits are filed in response to a wide range of political activities including zoning, land use, taxation, civil liberties, environmental protection, public education, animal rights, and the accountability of professionals and public officials.

SLAPP suits seek to retaliate against political opposition, attempt to prevent future opposition and intimidate political opponents, and are employed as a strategy to win an underlying economic battle, political fight, or both. The SLAPP plaintiff's goal is not necessarily to "win" the lawsuit, but rather to deter public participation in the democratic process by chilling debate on public and political issues. This goal is realized by instituting or threatening multimillion-dollar lawsuits to intimidate citizens into silence. SLAPP suits have a chilling effect on two core democratic freedoms: the First Amendment rights of free speech and "to petition the government for a redress of grievances."[2]

SLAPP suits can be difficult to identify, because they appear to be ordinary lawsuits. Most SLAPPs share three characteristics, however: first, the defendant's activity complained of by the

---

[1] The problem of SLAPP suits was identified and the acronym coined by law professor Penelope Canan and sociologist George W. Pring in 1988 in a landmark article—*Strategic Lawsuits Against Public Participation,* 35 Soc. Problems 506. Canan and Pring's article gave impetus to the anti-SLAPP movement and spawned a large body of scholarly literature. *See, e.g.,* Jerome I. Braun, *Increasing Slapp Protection: Unburdening the Right of Petition in California,* 32 U. C. Davis L. Rev. 965 (1999).

[2] The First Amendment right "to petition the government for a redress of grievances" means that any genuine, "objectively reasonable" attempt to affect government action—no matter how base the petitioner's intent—cannot give rise to liability. *See, e.g., Professional Real Estate Investors, Inc., v. Columbia Pictures Industries, Inc.,* 508 U.S. 49, 57 (1993).

plaintiff implicates the constitutional right of free speech, the right to petition for the redress of grievances, or both; second, the type of legal claim against the defendant is generally a claim for defamation, tortious interference with business or contract, civil conspiracy or abuse of process, constitutional or civil rights violations, or nuisance; and finally, SLAPP filers are typically real estate developers and other corporations, especially those vulnerable to charges of environmental violations: property owners and state or local government agencies.

The defendant in a SLAPP suit (often called the "target") can of course defend against the suit in all the traditional ways—by raising defenses based on state and federal rights of petition and free speech as well as by putting the plaintiff (often called the "filer") to its proof. However, the sheer expense of fighting the suit causes many targets, especially individuals or grass-roots organizations, to settle unmeritorious claims against them. Moreover, even when targets persevere and prevail against filers, no deterrent is created, since the filers' aim is not to win, but to discourage opposition. Even the most dedicated activist may waver at the thought of a long, stressful, expensive battle in trial and appellate courts even when eventual victory appears certain. Thus, a strong argument can be advanced that the SLAPP problem is not adequately addressed by existing protections against unmeritorious lawsuits.

In response to an increasing use of SLAPPs over the past decade, several States have passed "anti-SLAPP" measures of various sorts. They provide varying amounts of protection for defendants (most often individuals or organizations) and, consequently, burden the litigation process for plaintiffs (most often businesses) to a greater or lesser degree. Now a coalition of public interest advocacy groups is lobbying for anti-SLAPP legislation in the state of Pacifica. The have presented legislator Patterson with documentation that includes numerous case histories, including the following.

- Dr. Mary Nelson, archaeology professor at Pacifica State University, had long been interested in an ancient Native American village site called Churinga. But Churinga is on land now owned by the university, and the university wanted to build a parking lot on the site. The university hired a consultant, who reported (as the university wished) that building the lot would cause no significant harm to the site. Dr. Nelson criticized the consultant's report in public comment procedures established under the Pacifica Environmental Quality Act. The consultant sued Dr. Nelson personally for $600,000 "for intentional and negligent interference with contractual relations and prospective economic advantage, libel, slander, and trade libel."

- Adam Richman led community opposition to a large waste-burning plant his local sanitation district wanted to build in Ocean County. He spoke against it at district meetings and before a grand jury, and was a lead plaintiff in a taxpayer's action based on allegedly improper use of public funds for feasibility studies for the proposed plant. The sanitation district cross-complained against Richman personally for $42 million for interference with prospective advantage.
- Jenny Gold is a senior citizen living in a government-subsidized housing complex. She believed the firm managing the project was taking excessive fees and wrote about her concerns in the project newsletter, asking management to open its books. The management firm sued Gold for libel, demanding two million dollars in actual and punitive damages.[3]

The public interest advocacy groups naturally want legislation that provides the greatest possible protection for SLAPP targets. Thus, they favor a broad definition of "public participation," protection against a broad range of causes of action, provision for accelerated resolution, favorable burdens of persuasion and proof, and provisions for award of attorney's fees, costs, and punitive damages against SLAPP filers.

Of course, some of Patterson's constituents oppose anti-SLAPP legislation, arguing first that sufficient recourse exists for victims of frivolous lawsuits and that existing law provides sufficient deterrence against the filing of such claims. Assuming that some

---

[3] The preceding examples are adapted from examples in Braun, *supra* n. 1, at 967–68.

form of anti-SLAPP legislation is inevitable, however, these opponents wish to see a narrow definition of "public participation," application only to a restricted number of causes of action, and procedures and standards that put the least burden on their access to the courts. They argue that, paradoxically, some of the most "target-friendly" state anti-SLAPP statutes unconstitutionally burden the very right those statutes seek to protect—the right of injured "filers" to petition the court for the redress of grievances. Opponents of anti-SLAPP legislation also argue that statutes on the California model violate the right to trial by jury.[4]

As a legislator, Patterson needs to consider the views of all of his constituents, as well as considering the likelihood of acceptance by the rest of the legislature. He is currently evaluating the approaches of other states. Some typical, and widely contrasting, anti-SLAPP statutes follow.

### California

Cal. Civ. Pro. Code § 425.16 (West Supp. 1999).

(a) The Legislature finds and declares that there has been a disturbing increase in lawsuits brought primarily to chill the valid exercise of the constitutional rights of freedom of speech and petition for the redress of grievances. The Legislature finds and declares that it is in the public interest to encourage continued participation in matters of public significance, and that this participation should not be chilled through abuse of the judicial process. To this end, this section shall be construed broadly.

(b)(1) A cause of action against a person arising from any act of that person in furtherance of the person's right of petition or free speech under the United States or California Constitution in connection with a public issue shall be subject to a special motion to strike, unless the court determines that the plaintiff has established that there is a probability that the plaintiff will prevail on the claim. (2) In making its determination, the court shall consider the pleadings, and supporting

---

[4] The New Hampshire Supreme Court held unconstitutional the same anti-SLAPP statute that the California courts have approved. The California court held that the statute did not unconstitutionally deprive plaintiffs/filers of the right to a jury trial by having a judge decide whether there was a "probability" that plaintiffs/filers could prove their allegations against defendants/targets; the New Hampshire court held to the contrary. Compare *Opinion of the Justices (SLAPP Suit Procedure)*, 641 A.2d 1012, 1015 (N.H. 1994) with, e.g., *Wilcox v. Superior Court*, 33 Cal. Rptr. 2d 446 (Ct. App. 1994).

and opposing affidavits stating the facts upon which the liability or defense is based.

(3) If the court determines that the plaintiff has established a probability that he or she will prevail on the claim, neither that determination nor the fact of that determination shall be admissible in evidence at any later stage of the case, and no burden of proof or degree of proof otherwise applicable shall be affected by that determination.

(c) In any action subject to subdivision (b), a prevailing defendant on a special motion to strike shall be entitled to recover his or her attorney's fees and costs. If the court finds that a special motion to strike is frivolous or is solely intended to cause unnecessary delay, the court shall award costs and reasonable attorney's fees to a plaintiff prevailing on the motion, pursuant to Section 128.5.

(d) This section shall not apply to any enforcement action brought in the name of the people of the State of California by the Attorney General, district attorney, or city attorney, acting as a public prosecutor.

(e) As used in this section, "act in furtherance of a person's right of petition or free speech under the United States or California Constitution in connection with a public issue" includes: (1) any written or oral statement or writing made before a legislative, executive, or judicial proceeding, or any other official proceeding authorized by law; (2) any written or oral statement or writing made in connection with an issue under consideration or review by a legislative, executive, or judicial body, or any other official proceeding authorized by law; (3) any written or oral statement or writing made in a place open to the public or a public forum in connection with an issue of public interest; (4) or any other conduct in furtherance of the exercise of the constitutional right of petition or the constitutional right of free speech in connection with a public issue or an issue of public interest.

(f) The special motion may be filed within 60 days of the service of the complaint or, in the court's discretion, at any later time upon terms it deems proper. The motion shall be noticed for hearing not more than 30 days after service unless the docket conditions of the court require a later hearing.

(g) All discovery proceedings in the action shall be stayed upon the filing of a notice of motion made pursuant to this section. The stay of discovery shall remain in effect until notice of entry of the order ruling on the motion. The court, on noticed motion and for good cause shown, may order that specified discovery be conducted notwithstanding this subdivision.

(h) For purposes of this section, "complaint" includes "cross-complaint" and "petition," "plaintiff" includes "cross-complainant" and "petitioner," and "defendant" includes "cross-defendant" and "respondent."

## Georgia

Ga. Code Ann. § 9-11-11.1 (Harrison 1998)

(a) The General Assembly of Georgia finds and declares that it is in the public interest to encourage participation by the citizens of Georgia in matters of public significance through the exercise of their constitutional rights of freedom of speech and the right to petition government for redress of grievances. The General Assembly of Georgia further finds and declares that the valid exercise of the constitutional rights of freedom of speech and the right to petition government for a redress of grievances should not be chilled through abuse of the judicial process.

(b) For any claim asserted against a person or entity arising from an act by that person or entity which could reasonably be construed as an act in furtherance of the right of free speech or the right to petition government for a redress of grievances under the Constitution of the United States or the Constitution of the State of Georgia in connection with an issue of public interest or concern, both the party asserting the claim and the party's attorney of record, if any, shall be required to file, contemporaneously with the pleading containing the claim, a written verification under oath as set forth in Code Section 9-10-113. Such written verification shall certify that the party and his or her attorney of record, if any, have read the claim; that to the best of their knowledge, information, and belief formed after reasonable inquiry it is well grounded in fact and is warranted by existing law or a good faith argument for the extension, modification, or reversal of existing law; that the act forming the basis for the claim is not a privileged communication under paragraph (4) of Code Section 51-5-7; and that the claim is not interposed for any improper purpose such as to suppress a person's or entity's right of free speech or right to petition government, or to harass, or to cause unnecessary delay or needless increase in the cost of litigation. If the claim is not verified as required by this subsection, it shall be stricken unless it is verified within ten days after the omission is called to the attention of the party asserting the claim. If a claim is verified in violation of this Code section, the court, upon motion or upon its own initiative, shall impose upon the persons who signed the verification, a represented party, or both an appropriate sanction which may include dismissal of the claim and an order to pay to the other party or parties the amount of the reasonable expenses incurred because of the filing of the pleading, including a reasonable attorney's fee.

(c) As used in this Code section, "act in furtherance of the right of free speech or the right to petition government for a redress of grievances under the Constitution of the United States or the Constitution of the State of Georgia in connection with an issue of public interest or concern" includes any written or oral statement, writing, or petition made before or to a legislative, executive, or judicial proceeding, or any other official proceeding authorized by law, or any written or oral statement, writing, or petition made in connection with an issue under consideration or review by a legislative, executive, or judicial body, or any other official proceeding authorized by law.

(d) All discovery and any pending hearings or motions in the action shall be stayed upon the filing of a motion to dismiss or a motion to strike made pursuant to subsection (b) of this Code section. The motion shall be heard not more than 30 days after service unless the emergency matters before the court require a later hearing. The court, on noticed motion and for good cause shown, may order that specified discovery or other hearings or motions be conducted notwithstanding this subsection.

(e) Nothing in this Code section shall affect or preclude the right of any party to any recovery otherwise authorized by common law, statute, law, or rule.

(f) Attorney's fees and expenses under this Code section may be requested by motion at any time during the course of the action but not later than 45 days after the final disposition, including but not limited to dismissal by the plaintiff, of the action.

## Massachusetts

Mass. Gen. Laws Ann ch. 231 § 59H (West Supp.1998)

In any case in which a party asserts that the civil claims, counterclaims, or cross claims against said party are based on said party's exercise of its right of petition under the constitution of the United States or of the commonwealth, said party may bring a special motion to dismiss. The court shall advance any such special motion so that it may be heard and determined as expeditiously as possible. The court shall grant such special motion, unless the party against whom such special motion is made shows that: (1) the moving party's exercise of its right to petition was devoid of any reasonable factual support or any arguable basis in law and (2) the moving party's acts caused actual injury to the responding party. In making its determination, the court shall consider the pleadings and supporting and opposing affidavits stating the facts upon which the liability or defense is based.

The attorney general, on his behalf or on behalf of any government agency or subdivision to which the moving party's acts were directed, may intervene to defend or otherwise support the moving party on such special motion.

All discovery proceedings shall be stayed upon the filing of the special motion under this section; provided, however, that the court, on motion and after a hearing and for good cause shown, may order that specified discovery be conducted. The stay of discovery shall remain in effect until notice of entry of the order ruling on the special motion.

Said special motion to dismiss may be filed within sixty days of the service of the complaint or, in the court's discretion, at any later time upon terms it deems proper.

If the court grants such special motion to dismiss, the court shall award the moving party costs and reasonable attorney's fees, including those incurred for the special motion and any related discovery matters. Nothing in this section shall affect or preclude the right of the moving party to any remedy otherwise authorized by law.

As used in this section, the words "a party's exercise of its right of petition" shall mean any written or oral statement made before or submitted to a legislative, executive, or judicial body, or any other governmental proceeding; any written or oral statement made in connection with an issue under consideration or review by a legislative, executive, or judicial body, or any other governmental proceeding; any statement reasonably likely to encourage consideration or review of an issue by a legislative, executive, or judicial body or any other governmental proceeding; any statement reasonably likely to enlist public participation in an effort to effect such consideration; or any other statement falling within constitutional protection of the right to petition government.

### Tennessee

Tenn. Code Ann. §4-21-1002-10004

§1002 Intent and findings

(a) It is the intent of the general assembly to provide protection for individuals who make good faith reports of wrongdoing to appropriate governmental bodies. Information provided by citizens concerning potential misdeeds is vital to effective law enforcement and the efficient operation of government.

(b) The general assembly finds that the threat of a civil action for damages in the form of a strategic lawsuit against political participation (SLAPP), and the possibility of considerable legal costs, can act as a deterrent to citizens who wish to report information to federal, state, or local agencies. SLAPP suits can effectively punish concerned citizens for exercising the constitutional right to speak and petition the government for redress of grievances.

§1003 Immunity; recovery of costs

(a) Any person who in furtherance of such person's right of free speech or petition under the Tennessee or United States Constitution in connection with a public or governmental issue communicates information regarding another person or entity to any agency of the federal, state or local government regarding a matter of concern to that agency shall be immune from civil liability on claims based upon the communication to the agency.

(b) The immunity conferred by this subsection shall not attach if the person communicating such information:

(1) Knew the information to be false; or

(2) Communicated information in reckless disregard of its falsity; or

(3) If such information pertains to a person or entity other than a public figure, whether the communication was made negligently in failing to ascertain the falsity of the information.

(c) A person prevailing upon the defense of immunity provided for in this section shall be entitled to recover costs and reasonable attorneys' fees incurred in establishing the defense.

§ 1004. Intervention; governmental agency; attorney general

(a) In order to protect the free flow of information from citizens to their government, an agency receiving a complaint or information under the provisions of § 4-21-1003 may intervene and defend against any suit precipitated by the communication to the agency. In the event that a local government agency does not intervene in and defend against a suit arising from any communication protected under this part, the office of the attorney general and reporter may intervene in and defend against the suit.

(b) An agency prevailing upon the defense of immunity provided for in § 4-21-1003 shall be entitled to recover costs and reasonable attorneys' fees incurred in establishing the defense. If the agency fails to establish such defense, the party bringing such action shall be entitled to recover from the agency costs and reasonable attorneys' fees incurred in proving the defense inapplicable or invalid.

## Delaware

Del. Code Ann. Tit. 10 § 8136-8138 §8136 Actions involving public petition and participation.

(a) For purposes of this section, the following terms shall have the meaning ascribed herein: (1) An "action involving public petition and participation" is an action, claim, cross-claim or counterclaim for damages that is brought by a public applicant or permittee, and is materially related to any efforts of the defendant to report on, rule on, challenge or oppose such application or permission.

(2) "Public applicant or permittee" shall mean any person who has applied for or obtained a permit, zoning change, lease, license, certificate or other entitlement for use or permission to act from any government body, or any person with an interest, connection or affiliation with such person that is materially related to such application or permission.

(3) "Communication" shall mean any statement, claim or allegation in a proceeding, decision, protest, writing, argument, contention or other expression.

(4) "Government body" shall mean the State and any county, city, town, village or any other political subdivision of the State; any public improvement or special district, public authority, commission, agency or public benefit corporation; any other separate corporate instrumentality or unit of State or local government; or the federal government.

(b) In an action involving public petition and participation, damages may only be recovered if the plaintiff, in addition to all other necessary elements, shall have established by clear and convincing evidence that any communication which gives rise to the action was made with knowledge of its falsity or with reckless disregard of whether it was false, where the truth or falsity of such communication is material to the cause of action at issue.

(c) Nothing in this section shall be construed to limit any constitutional, statutory or common-law protection of defendants to actions involving public petition and participation.

§ 8137 Standards for motion to dismiss and summary judgment in certain cases involving public petition and participation.

(a) A motion to dismiss in which the moving party has demonstrated that the action, claim, cross-claim or counterclaim subject to the motion is an action involving public petition and participation as defined in § 8136(a)(1) of this title shall be granted unless the party responding to the motion demonstrates that the cause of action has a substantial basis in law or is supported by a substantial argument for an extension, modification or reversal of existing law. The court shall grant preference in the hearing of such motion.

(b) A motion for summary judgment in which the moving party has demonstrated that the action, claim, cross-claim or counterclaim subject to the action is an action involving public petition and participation as defined in § 8136(a)(1) of this title shall be granted unless the party responding to the motion demonstrates that the cause of action has a substantial basis in fact and law or is supported by a substantial argument for an extension, modification or reversal of existing law. The court shall grant preference in the hearing of such motion.

§ 8138 Recovery of damages in actions involving public petition and participation.

(a) A defendant in an action involving public petition and participation, as defined in § 8136(a)(1) of this title, may maintain an action, claim, cross-claim or counter-claim to recover damages, including costs and attorney's fees, from any person who commenced or continued such action; provided that: (1) Costs, attorney's fees and other compensatory damages may be recovered upon a demonstration that the action involving public petition and participation was commenced or continued without a substantial basis in fact and law and could not be supported by a substantial argument for the extension, modification or reversal of existing law; and (2) Punitive damages may only be recovered upon an additional demonstration that the action involving public petition and participation was commenced or continued for the purpose of harassing, intimidating, punishing or otherwise maliciously inhibiting the free exercise of speech, petition or association rights.

(b) The right to bring an action under this section can be waived only if it is waived specifically.

(c) Nothing in this section shall affect or preclude the right of any party to any recovery otherwise authorized by law.

## CASEFILE #5

### Dorothy Pierce

Our clients are John and Lynn Pierce and their daughter Dorothy. The Pierces are residents of Topeka, Kansas. Mr. Pierce is the chief financial officer for a brick laying and construction business. Ms. Pierce is a products liability defense attorney. Dorothy is a full-time student in the ninth grade.

Dorothy has been described as a typical young teenage girl. She is fourteen. Dorothy plays tennis on the school's junior varsity tennis team during the fall term and is a member of the swim team during the winter term. Dorothy is not employed, although she worked part-time last summer in the mail room of her father's firm. That job was Dorothy's first employment except baby-sitting and pet-sitting.

For her birthday last April, Dorothy received a new ten-speed bicycle which she liked very much. That summer, Dorothy rode her bicycle back and forth to tennis lessons. Unfortunately, on July 1, 20__, it rained during Dorothy's tennis lesson, and her bicycle became wet. Coming out of a blind alley on her way home, Dorothy applied pressure to her brake, which slipped because of the dampness, and she was hit by a small foreign car driven by Mr. Mercury Williams. Although both Dorothy and Mr. Williams had been going slowly, the collision knocked Dorothy off her bicycle onto the hard pavement. Dorothy's leg was broken in two places.

Mr. Williams put the bicycle into his trunk and took Dorothy to the local hospital emergency room, at which time the nurses at the desk continually but unsuccessfully attempted to contact her parents. Dorothy's father was out of town on business and her mother was in court. No doctor saw Dorothy during that time. After two hours, Dr. Lucien Marcus, the staff surgeon finally saw Dorothy and explained to her that they could not contact her parents and therefore could not get her parents' consent to treat Dorothy. Dorothy consented to treatment herself and Dr. Marcus set and cast her leg.

There was no negligence on the doctor's part, but Dorothy's leg did not mend well. Dorothy had been an excellent tennis player. Her coaches had expected her to play on the varsity team.

Her prospects for competing satisfactorily in the rigorous junior tournaments were essentially dashed.

Mr. Pierce is terribly dissatisfied with this situation. Mr. Pierce insists the procedure performed on Dorothy was "illegal" because neither he nor his wife consented. He wants to know if has a case.

One of your firm's senior partners, Marie Del Oeste, wants you to prepare a memorandum of [ ] pages on the relevant issues. Ms. Del Oeste has provided you with transcripts of interviews she conducted with the Pierces.

---

### CLIENT INTERVIEW WITH DOROTHY PIERCE

DEL OESTE: First, Dorothy, I'd like to know how old you are.

DOROTHY: I'm 14.

DEL OESTE: So tell me what how you broke your leg.

DOROTHY: I rode my bike to tennis lessons, but they were cancelled because it was raining. On my way home, I was coming out of an alley. I couldn't see any cars coming until it was too late. I used my brakes, but they slipped because it was wet. That's when Mr. Williams' car hit me. I was knocked off my bike and onto the ground. I knew right away something was wrong with my leg.

DEL OESTE: How did you get to the hospital?

DOROTHY: Mr. Williams drove me. He put my bike in his trunk and drove to Doctor's Hospital Emergency Room.

DEL OESTE: Once you were there, did anyone at the hospital ask you how the could contact your parents?

DOROTHY: Yes. First, I gave them my mother's work phone number at her law firm. When they told me they couldn't get a hold of my mother there, they asked for my father's number. I told them my father was out of town on business. But then I gave them my dad's work number, in case they knew where he could be reached. I also told the nurse our home phone number. But she said she just got the answering machine.

DEL OESTE: How long did you wait in the Emergency Room before Dr. Marcus saw you?

DOROTHY: I was there for about two hours. My leg was really hurting and getting more swollen and I couldn't concentrate.

DEL OESTE: What did Dr. Marcus do?

DOROTHY: After they x-rayed my leg, he told me it was broken in two places. He said they hadn't been able to reach my parents, so they could not get my parents' consent to treat me. Dr. Marcus then explained that he wanted to set and cast my leg. I told him to 'Go ahead and do what you have to do.'

DEL OESTE: Then what happened?

DOROTHY: Dr. Marcus then set and cast my leg.

DEL OESTE: Why didn't you wait for your parents?

DOROTHY: I was in so much pain and just wanted my leg fixed. I didn't know where my parents were or why the hospital couldn't get in touch with them. The whole thing was so upsetting, I just wanted it over.

## CLIENT INTERVIEW WITH JOHN PIERCE

DEL OESTE: When did you find out about Dorothy's accident?

MR. PIERCE: I checked my office voice mail and there was a message from my wife.

DEL OESTE: So the hospital never got in touch with you?

MR. PIERCE: No, they didn't.

DEL OESTE: Would you have consented to the treatment had you been contacted?

MR. PIERCE: Not by Dr. Marcus. If my wife or I had been contacted, we would have brought Dorothy to our orthopedic surgeon.

## CLIENT INTERVIEW WITH LYNN PIERCE

DEL OESTE: How did you find out about Dorothy's accident?

MS. PIERCE: I was at court, and during a break, I called our house to check if Dorothy had returned from tennis practice. When Dorothy didn't pick up the phone, I checked the answering machine messages. There was a message from the hospital. I called the Emergency Room and found out Dorothy's leg was broken and the doctor had treated her.

DEL OESTE: Would you have consented to the treatment if someone from the hospital had talked to you directly?

MS. PIERCE: No. I would have called our orthopedic surgeon and would have had him look at Dorothy's leg.

## CASEFILE #6

### *A.M. v. S.M. & D.C.*

Adam Massey has timely filed a complaint against his ex-wife, Stephanie, and Daniel Costello in a New Jersey court specialized in family matters, located in the mythical county of Seagrove. Stephanie Massey has made a timely motion to dismiss the complaint.

---

SUPERIOR COURT OF NEW JERSEY
CHANCERY DIVISION
FAMILY PART, SEAGROVE COUNTY

Adam Massey,                 :
Plaintiff,                  :

                        :

            v.               :      COMPLAINT
                        :      Civil Action No. 12-3-456
Stephanie Massey & Daniel Costello,   :
Defendants.               :

Plaintiff Adam Massey, residing at 310 Central Avenue, Mayville, Seagrove County, New Jersey, by way of Complaint says the following through his attorney, Melissa Frank.

### COMMON ALLEGATIONS

1. Plaintiff Adam Massey ("Adam") and defendants Stephanie Massey ("Stephanie") and Daniel Costello ("Costello") were at all times mentioned residents of Seagrove County, New Jersey.

2. Adam and Stephanie were married on June 1, 19__. They were divorced sixteen years later, on December 1, 20__.

3. For about a year early in the marriage, between approximately October, 19__ and December, 19__, unknown to Adam, Stephanie was involved in an extra-marital affair with Costello, a friend of both spouses.

4. On June 24, 19__, Stephanie gave birth to Lee Massey ("Lee"). Although strongly suspecting that Costello was the child's father, Stephanie allowed Adam to believe Lee was his biological child. She did, however, confide her suspicions to defendant Costello.

5. In March of 19__, when Lee was almost three, her left eye began to hurt her and redden. On April 13 of that same year, Adam and Stephanie brought her to a local hospital for diagnosis and treatment, and a few days later, Lee was diagnosed with retinoblastoma, a tumor of the eye.

6. Retinoblastoma is a hereditary condition caused by an abnormal gene, the Rb gene. The gene may be carried by either parent and transmitted to their offspring. The first sign of the condition is often a white pupil that does not reflect the light (leucocoria). The affected eye often looks white in photographs taken with a flash. Afflicted children often squint and, when the tumor is large, have a painful red eye. Although 90% of children with retinoblastoma are cured, children with the disease are at an increased risk for a wide spectrum of other tumors.

7. Adam and Stephanie immediately sought consultations at several renowned medical facilities, including St. Jude's Children's Hospital. Because the tumor was large, the physicians at St. Jude's ruled out cryotherapy, laser therapy, and thermotherapy as possible treatments. The eye was removed surgically (enucleation) and an artificial eye was fitted.

8. When Costello learned Lee was diagnosed with retinoblastoma, he told Stephanie that one of his first cousins had suffered from this tumor. This strengthened their suspicions that Costello was Lee's biological father.

9. Fearing that genetic testing would reveal neither parent as a carrier of the disease and thus reveal that Adam was not the child's biological father, Stephanie prevailed upon Adam not to seek genetic testing and counseling. She argued that the carrier would feel guilty. The couple agreed not to seek testing until and unless they contemplated having another child.

10. In 19__, when Lee was five-years old, Costello became engaged to be married. Because he suspected Lee to be his biological daughter, he sought genetic testing and learned that he was indeed a carrier of the Rb gene.

11. As soon as he knew, Costello revealed the results of his test to Stephanie, at which point, both became convinced that Lee was his biological child, but neither told Adam, who continued to believe Lee was his, Adam's, biological child.

12. In June of 20__, when Lee was eight, she began to complain of swelling in her leg. She often awoke at night in pain. She developed an

unexplained limp. One day that month, while running in the playground, she fell and broke her tibia. An MRI done in the emergency room and a subsequent biopsy revealed osteoscarcoma, a bone cancer. The cancer had spread from the bone into nearby nerves and blood vessels. She was treated with chemotherapy, followed by surgery (her leg was ampu-tated beneath the knee), and then given more chemotherapy. Towards the end of her chemotherapy treatments, Lee began eight months of physical therapy and rehabilitation, painfully learning how to walk, first with crutches and then with a prosthetic leg.

13. In order to home-school and care for Lee while she was adjusting to her new disabilities, both Adam and Stephanie altered their work schedules so that each worked part time. Adam reduced his hours at the architectural firm of Rossant & Rossant and Stephanie hers at a Newark law firm.

14. The emotional, financial, and physical burden of caring for Lee took an increasing toll on Adam's physical and mental health. He sought out-patient psychiatric treatment, and in addition to psychotherapy, he was treated with several psychotropic drugs, including Bupropion for depression and Atavan for anxiety.

15. Despite costly, constant, often excruciating, treatment, Lee's con-dition slowly deteriorated. In January of 20__, when Lee was eleven, Adam and Stephanie learned that the chemotherapy had damaged Lee's heart. She died of heart failure on March 17, 20__, at the age of 13.

16. From the time of Lee's diagnosis until her death, Adam had endured constant emotional pain, distress, anxiety, and grief as he watched the child suffer and weaken.

17. On the day of Lee's funeral, March 20, 20__, grief-stricken and remorseful, Stephanie confessed to Adam that Costello may have been Lee's father. Adam confronted Costello and demanded Costello undergo DNA testing to determine whether he was indeed the child's biological father.

18. The results of the DNA testing indicated that it was 99.99% certain Costello was Lee's biological father. Adam thus learned that Costello, a man he had considered to be his friend, had fathered Lee and that for most of the child's tragic life, Stephanie and Costello had strongly suspected Adam was not the child's biological father, but nonetheless let him take up the emotional and financial burdens of parenting a terminally ill child.

19. As a result of Stephanie's confession and Costello's DNA testing, Adam suffered a nervous collapse and was hospitalized for several weeks, suffering post-traumatic stress disorder, depression, disphoria, and suicidal ideation.

20. At no time during her life or thereafter did Costello contribute financially to the support of Lee Massey.

### FIRST CAUSE OF ACTION
### INTENTIONAL INFLICTION OF EXTREME EMOTIONAL DISTRESS
### (Both Defendants)

21. The allegations in paragraphs 1 to 19 are realleged.

22. Defendants engaged in the conduct toward plaintiff detailed in paragraphs 1 to 19 with intent to cause him severe distress, or with reckless disregard that such distress would occur.

23. Defendants' conduct toward plaintiff detailed in paragraphs 1 to 19 was so extreme in degree as to go beyond all possible bounds of decency and be regarded as atrocious and utterly intolerable in a civilized society.

24. Defendants' conduct toward plaintiff as detailed in paragraphs 1 to 19 was the proximate cause of plaintiff's distress.

25. The distress suffered by plaintiff as the result of defendants' conduct detailed in paragraphs 1 to 19 was severe. He suffered a nervous collapse and great mental and emotional pain and anguish.

### SECOND CAUSE OF ACTION
### FRAUD
### (Stephanie Massey)

26. The allegations in paragraphs 1 to 19 are realleged.

27. For all of the child's life, defendant Massey represented to plaintiff that Lee Massey was his biological daughter.

28. Defendant Massey made this representation with no reasonable ground to believe it was true. For the last eight years of the child's life, she had good reason to believe that plaintiff was not the biological father of her child, which indeed he was not.

29. Defendant Massey made this representation in order to induce plaintiff to incur the responsibilities of parenthood with respect to the child.

30. Relying on defendant Massey's representations, plaintiff took on all the emotional and financial responsibilities of parenthood.

31. After the child's death, plaintiff learned that defendant's representations were false.

### THIRD CAUSE OF ACTION
### UNJUST ENRICHMENT
(Daniel Costello)

32. The allegations in paragraphs 1 to 20 are realleged.

33. Believing defendant Costello's child to be plaintiff's biological child, plaintiff supported the child financially until her death.

34. To the extent of these expenditures, defendant Costello, the child's biological father, has been unjustly enriched at plaintiff's expense.

### FOURTH CAUSE OF ACTION
### REIMBURSEMENT OF CHILD SUPPORT
(Daniel Costello)

35. Defendant Costello was the biological father of Lee Massey. On May 20, 20__, two months after Lee's death, defendant signed a voluntary acknowledgment of paternity, attached hereto as Exhibit A.

36. As Lee's biological father, defendant Costello had a duty under the Parentage Act, N.J.S.A. 9:17-59, to support the child from birth until majority.

37. Defendant did not provide any financial support for the child.

38. Plaintiff furnished financial support for Lee for thirteen years, from her birth on June 24, 19__, until her death on March 17, 20__.

39. Under the Parentage Act, Costello is required to reimburse plaintiff for expenses related to Lee's support.

40. As a direct and proximate result of defendants' wrongful acts and the injuries sustained by plaintiff, plaintiff has been damaged in an amount to be proved at trial.

41. As a further direct and proximate result of the acts of defendants, plaintiff lost earnings in the amount of approximately $200,000.

Therefore, plaintiff requests judgment against defendants for:

1. Damages in an amount to be proved at trial;

2. Loss of earnings in the amount of approximately $200.000;

3. Plaintiff's costs of suit; and

4. Any other and further relief as the court deems proper in this case.

## DESIGNATION OF TRIAL COUNSEL

Pursuant to Rule 4:25-4, Melissa Frank is designated as trial counsel for the plaintiff, in the above matter.

## CERTIFICATION OF NO OTHER ACTIONS

Pursuant to Rule 4:5-1(b)(2), it is stated that the matter in controversy is not the subject of any other action pending in any other court or of a pending arbitration proceeding to the best of our knowledge or belief. Also, to the best of our belief, no other action or arbitration proceeding is contemplated. Further, other than the parties set forth in this pleading, we know of no other parties that should be joined in the above action. In addition, we recognize the continuing obligation of each party to file and serve on all parties and the Court an amended certification if there is a change in the facts stated in this original certification.

## JURY DEMAND

The plaintiff, Adam Massey, demands trial by a jury on all of the triable issues of this complaint, pursuant to Rules 1:8-2(b) and 4:35-1(a).

Dated: January 12, 20__
[Signature]
Melissa Frank
Attorney for Plaintiff
800 Shore Drive
Atlantis City
New Jersey 08212
609 999-3456

SUPERIOR COURT OF NEW JERSEY
CHANCERY DIVISION
FAMILY PART, SEAGROVE COUNTY

| | | |
|---|---|---|
| Adam Massey, | : | |
| Plaintiff, | : | |
| | : | MOTION TO DISMISS |
| | : | FOR FAILURE |
| v. | : | TO STATE A CLAIM |
| | : | |
| | : | Civil Action No. |
| | : | 12-3-456789-1 |
| Stephanie Massey & Daniel Costello, | : | |
| Defendants. | : | |

To: Melissa Frank, Attorney for Adam Massey, 800 Shore Drive, Atlantis City, New Jersey 08212.

Please take notice that on February 17, 20___ at 9:30 a.m., or as soon after that as counsel can be heard, in Room 300 of the Superior Court, Chancery Division, Seagrove County, New Jersey, defendant Stephanie Massey, by her attorney, Stephen Greenberg, will move the court to dismiss the above-entitled action for failure to state a claim on which relief can be granted, on the ground that suit on all claims alleged against defendant is barred as a matter of public policy by N.J.S.A. 2A:23-1 ("The Heart Balm Act") and on the further ground that the claim of intentional infliction of emotional distress fails to allege conduct that is "extreme and outrageous," as more clearly appears from the memorandum of Stephen Greenberg, attached hereto.

Dated : February 2, 20___

_____

Stephen Greenberg
55 Elm Street
Atlantis City
New Jersey 08212
609-884-09118

# Appendix B

# *INCLUSIVE LANGUAGE*

The new Model Code of Judicial Conduct (1990) uses gender neutral language throughout. Rule 8 in *The Judicial Opinion Writing Manual: A Product of the Appellate Judges Conference* tells judges to avoid gender-based language and gives some suggestions on how to do so.[1] Gender neutrality is required in the New York State courts.[2] More than thirty states have gender-based task forces. These developments suggest that attorneys who use gender-biased language do so at their peril: "No attorney who wants to persuade can afford to offend or distract readers with gender-biased language."[3]

The use of gender-neutral language may not yet be instinctive, but it is not too difficult a habit to acquire. The following guidelines will help.

## 1. Use Gender-Neutral Terms

- *Delete Sexist Titles*

| *Not* | *But* |
|---|---|
| Fellow Colleagues | Colleagues |
| Madam Justice | Justice |
| Miss or Mrs. (unless requested) | Ms. |

---

[1] Judicial Administration Division, 47–48 (West 1991).

[2] *N.Y.S. Judicial Committee on Women in the Courts: Gender-Neutral Language in the Courts* (2d ed. OCA 1997).

[3] Gerald Lebovits, *He said–She said: Gender-Neutral Language*, 74-Feb N.Y.S. Bar Journal 64 (2002).

- *Avoid the Prefix Man-*

| Not | But |
|-----|-----|
| mankind | humanity |

- *Avoid the Suffix -man*

| Not | But |
|-----|-----|
| workman's compensation | worker's compensation |
| workmanship | skill |

- *Avoid the Suffixes -ette, -ess, -trix*

| Not | But |
|-----|-----|
| usherette | usher |
| stewardess | flight attendant |
| executrix | executor |

## 2. Revise Names of Occupations

| Not | But |
|-----|-----|
| newsman | reporter |
| foreman | supervisor |
| fireman | fire fighter |
| coeds | students |

## 3. Treat Females and Males in a Parallel Manner

| Not | But |
|-----|-----|
| man and wife | man and woman |
| | husband and wife |
| | spouses |
| Alfred Einstein and Madame Curie | Mr. Einstein and Madame Curie |
| | Albert Einstein and Marie Curie |

## 4. Alternate the Order of Gender

| Not | But |
|-----|-----|
| men and women | women and men |

## 5. Eliminate the Generic Use of Male Pronouns

This is perhaps the most challenging aspect of gender-neutral writing. Fortunately, there are a number of techniques to assist you.

*Avoid*

A lawyer must submit *his* brief in a timely manner.

- **Use Plurals**

Lawyers must submit *their* briefs in a timely manner.

- **Omit Pronouns**

Lawyers must submit briefs in a timely manner.

- **Use A, An, The, Any**

A lawyer must submit *a* brief in a timely manner.

- **Use Who**

A lawyer *who* submits a brief must do so in a timely manner.

- **Use One, We, You, Ones, Our, Your**

As lawyers, *we* must submit *our* briefs in a timely manner.

- **Use Passive Voice**

The brief must be submitted in a timely manner.

- **Repeat a Noun**

If the lawyer submits a brief, the lawyer should do so in a timely manner.

- **Use 'He or She' or Alternate 'She' and 'He,' but Do Not Always Link Elite Jobs to Men and Menial Jobs to Women.**

> *Not*
> A *doctor* always respects *his* patient's privacy and a *nurse* *her* patient's needs.
>
> *But*
> A *doctor* always respects *her* patient's privacy and a *nurse* *his* patient's needs.

# INDEX

*(References are to pages)*